SEBASTIÃO SALGADO

AMAZÔNIA

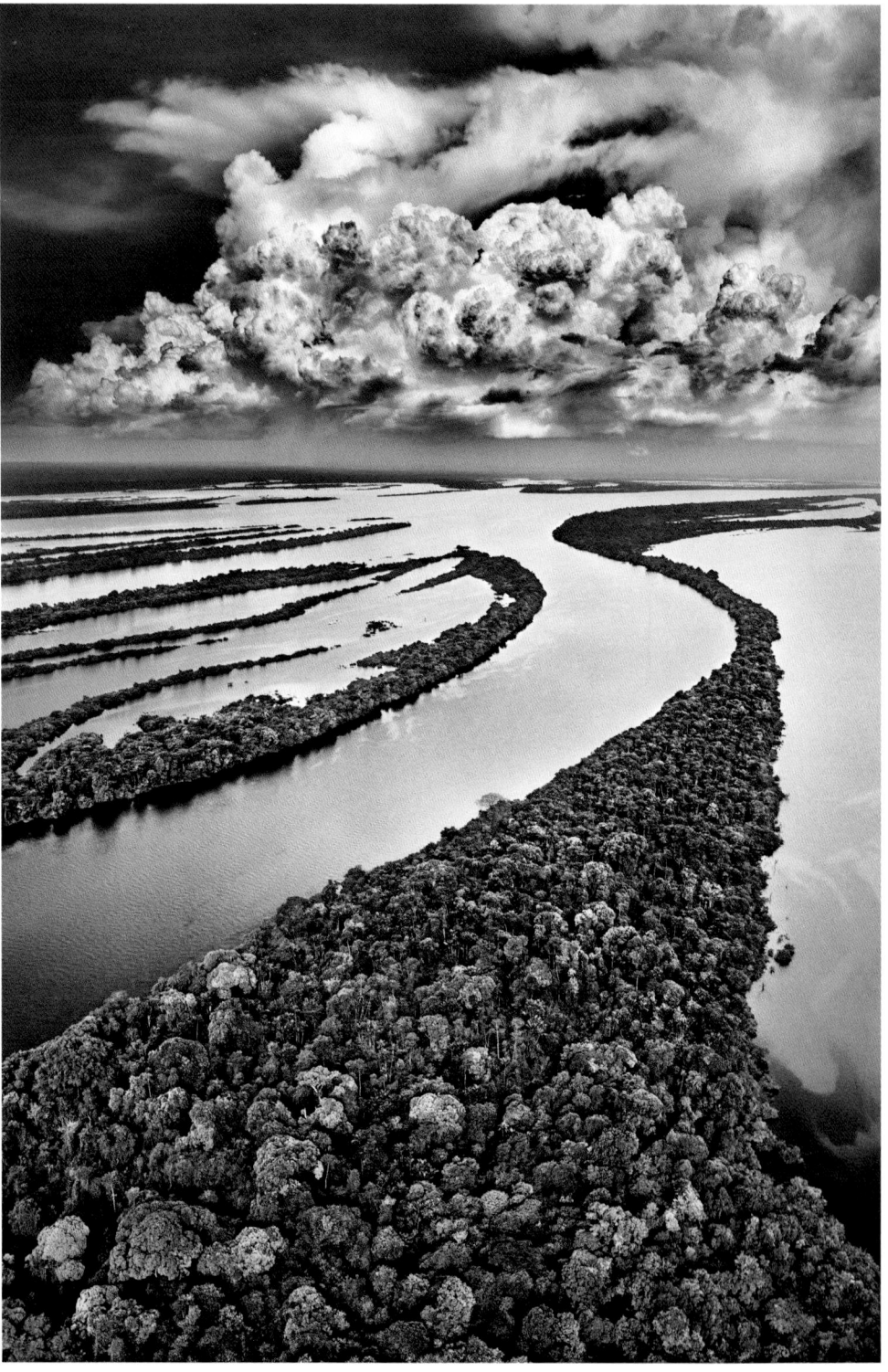

SEBASTIÃO SALGADO

AMAZÔNIA

Editing, Concept & Design
LÉLIA WANICK SALGADO

TASCHEN

This book is dedicated to the Indigenous peoples of Brazil's Amazon region. It is a celebration of the survival of their cultures, customs, and languages.

It is also a tribute to their role as the guardians of the beauty, natural resources, and biodiversity of the planet's largest rainforest in the face of unrelenting assault by the outside world.

We are eternally grateful to them for allowing us to share their lives.

Sebastião Salgado and Lélia Wanick Salgado

Page 2 Because the water levels can vary by some 20 meters (65 feet) from one season to another, Anavilhanas National Park is ever changing, as canals, sandbanks, and lakes appear in the dry season and some small islands vanish when the waters rise. Many of the larger islands, however, are freestanding stretches of rainforest. Anavilhanas National Park, state of Amazonas, 2009.

Opposite Tetxo Asháninka and his daughter. Kampa do Rio Amônea Indigenous Territory, state of Acre, 2016.

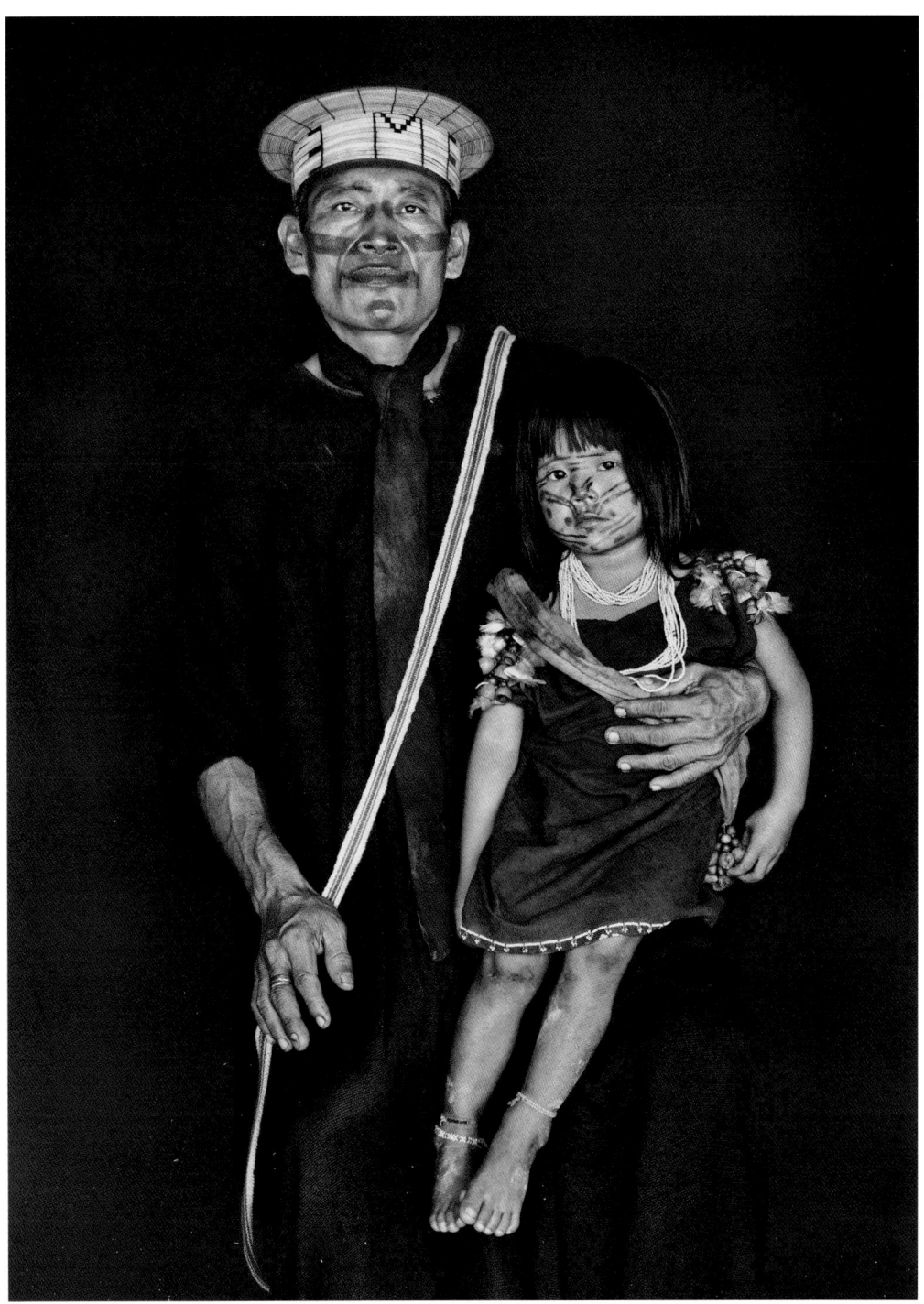

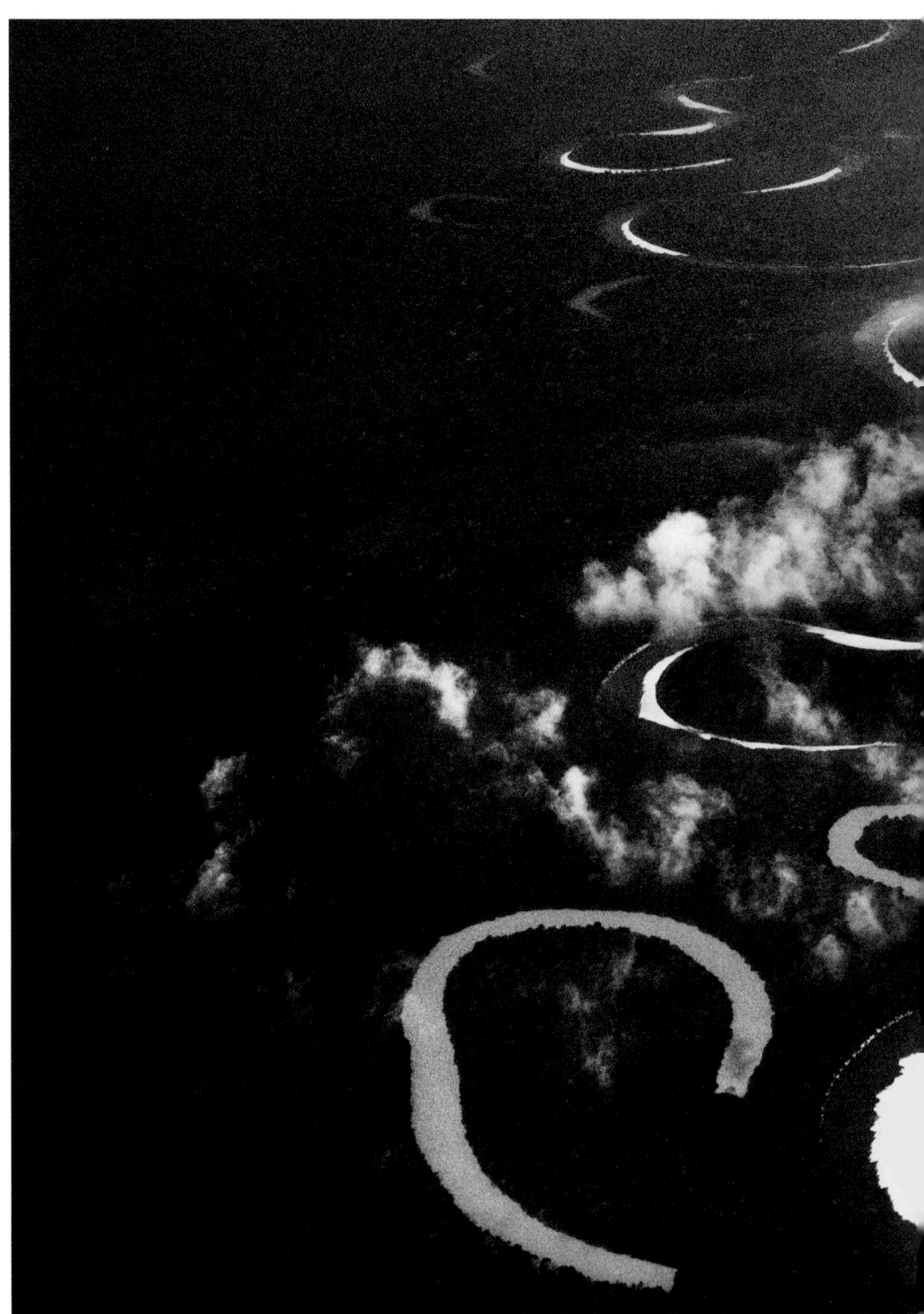

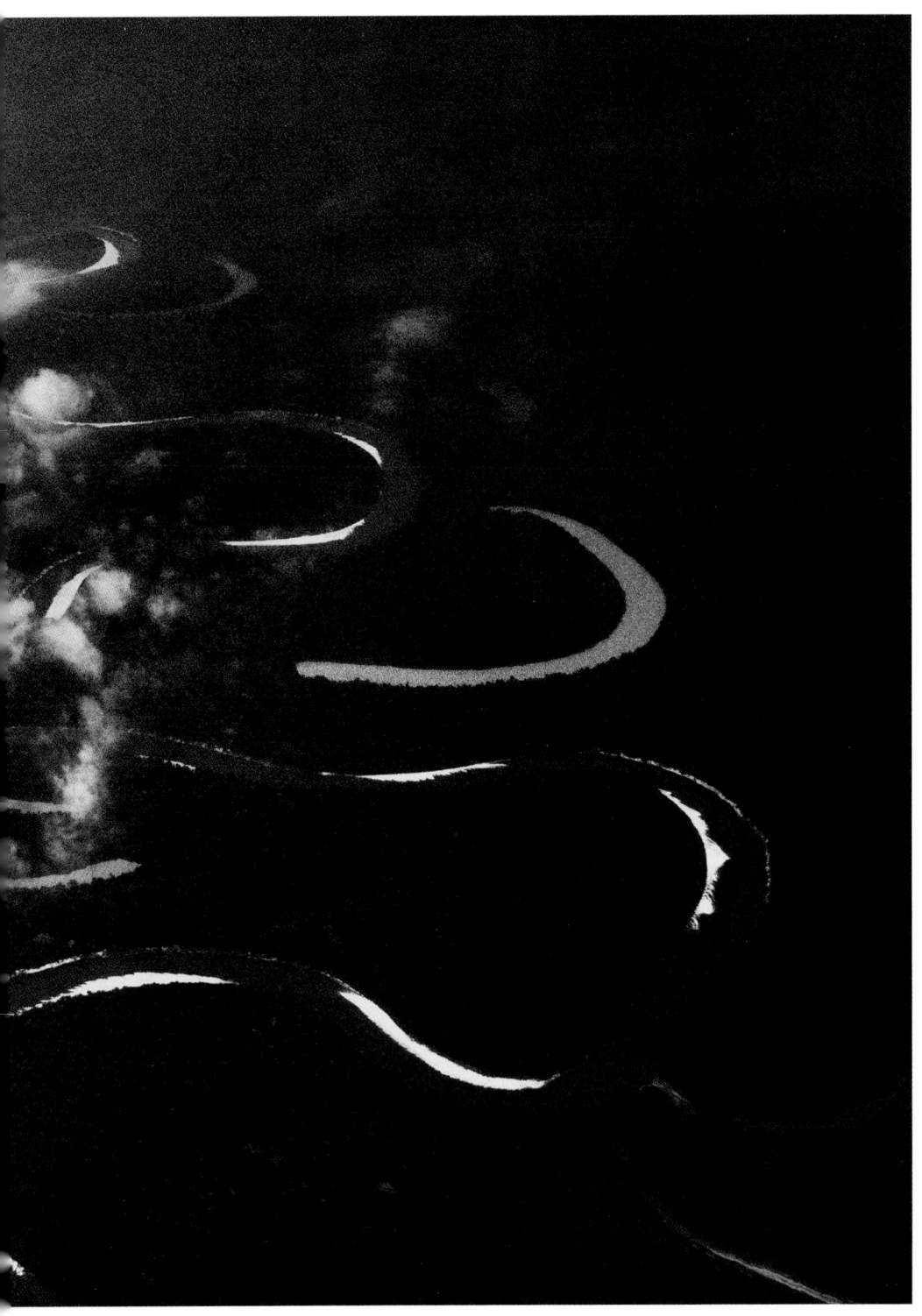

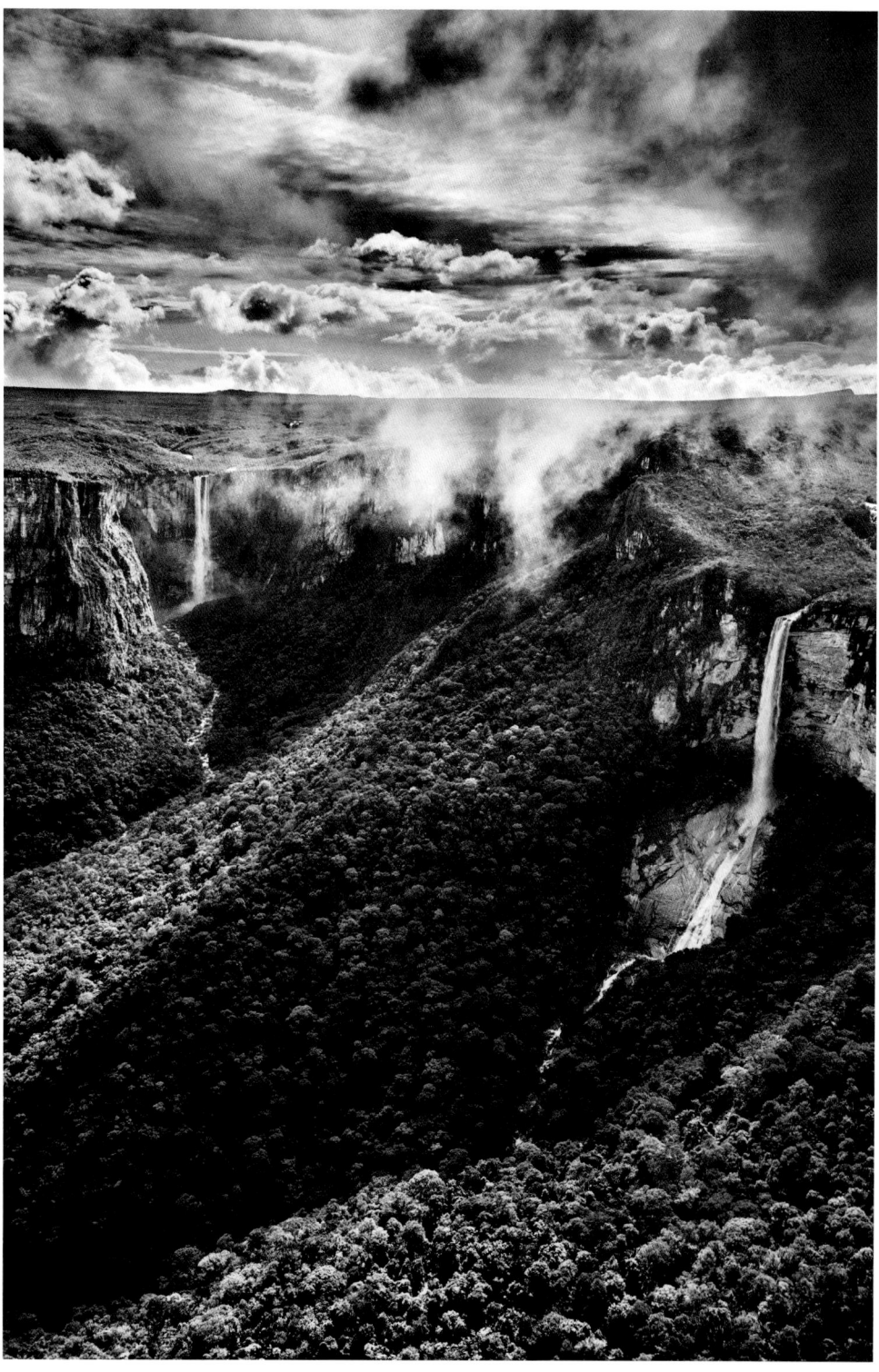

AERIAL VIEWS

It is only possible to grasp the true dimension of the Amazon forest from space, occupying as it does one-third of the South American continent, an area larger than the entire European Union. Not marked are the land borders of the nine countries that share this ecosystem, although by far the largest part of the territory—over 60 percent—lies inside Brazil. At the heart of this extravaganza of nature is the Amazon River which, fed by some 1,100 tributaries, including 17 over 1,500 kilometers (930 miles) long, disgorges 20 percent of the world's fresh water when it finally enters the Atlantic Ocean.

Viewed from a plane or a helicopter, the rainforest suddenly becomes real, a vast green carpet decorated with the twisting and curling lines of slow-moving rivers. In the wet season, this neat tapestry is disrupted as rivers overflow their banks, in places flooding 100 kilometers (60 miles) into the forest, in others creating lakes and lagoons, only to return to their previous paths—or to carve new ones—once the waters recede. So flat is this landscape that at Tabatinga on Brazil's western frontier with Colombia, the Amazon River is only 73 meters (240 feet) above sea level—and it still has 4,660 kilometers (2,900 miles) to go.

Yet on the horizon, an unexpected sight may appear. At least 60 percent of the basin is indeed flat, but some areas present a landscape of successive small hills, while others feature entire mountain ranges. Then there are clouds, clouds almost hugging the trees, clouds rising thousands of meters in ever-changing shapes and colors before turning dark and menacing and releasing the water that gives life to the aptly named rainforest, the world's largest.

The rainforest also plays a crucial role in slowing climate change, notably as what is known as a "carbon sink." Put simply, every year its trees absorb around two billion tons of carbon dioxide, equivalent to five percent of total emission of greenhouse gases driving global warming. At the same time, the forest not only produces an important portion of the oxygen we breathe, but it also determines how much rain is delivered to other regions of South America and beyond.

Yet this cycle of nature, which has survived millions of years, is now in peril. Notably on the peripheries of the jungle, where roads have drawn migrant farmers, loggers, and miners, deforestation is accelerating. For the most part, this is taking place on publicly owned land, while only a small part of the forest in indigenous territories and national parks has been razed. Nonetheless, with at least 17.25 percent of the biomass already cut down, the fear is that deforestation may soon reach "a point of no return" where the biome cannot recover, turning large areas of forest into tropical savannas.

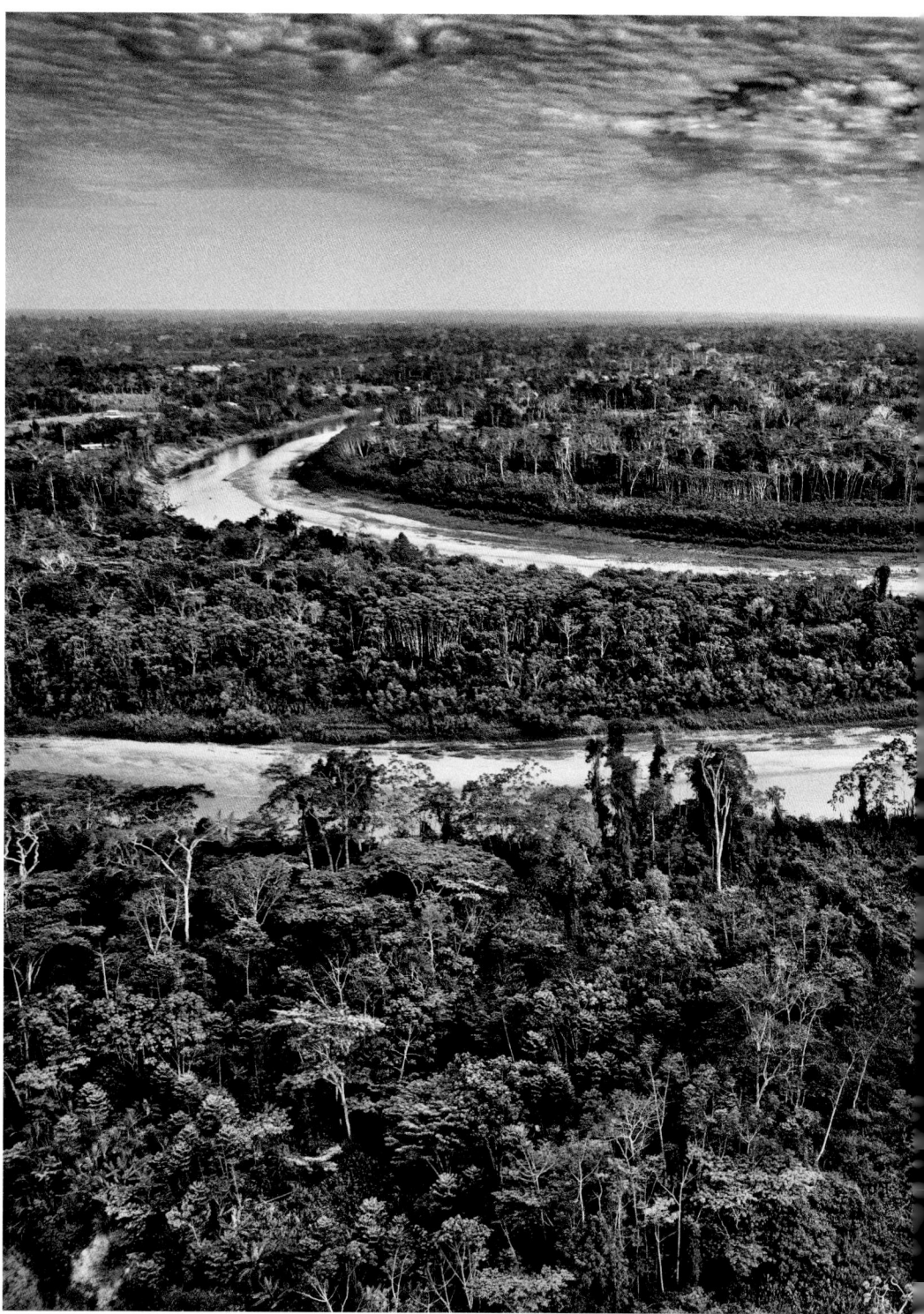

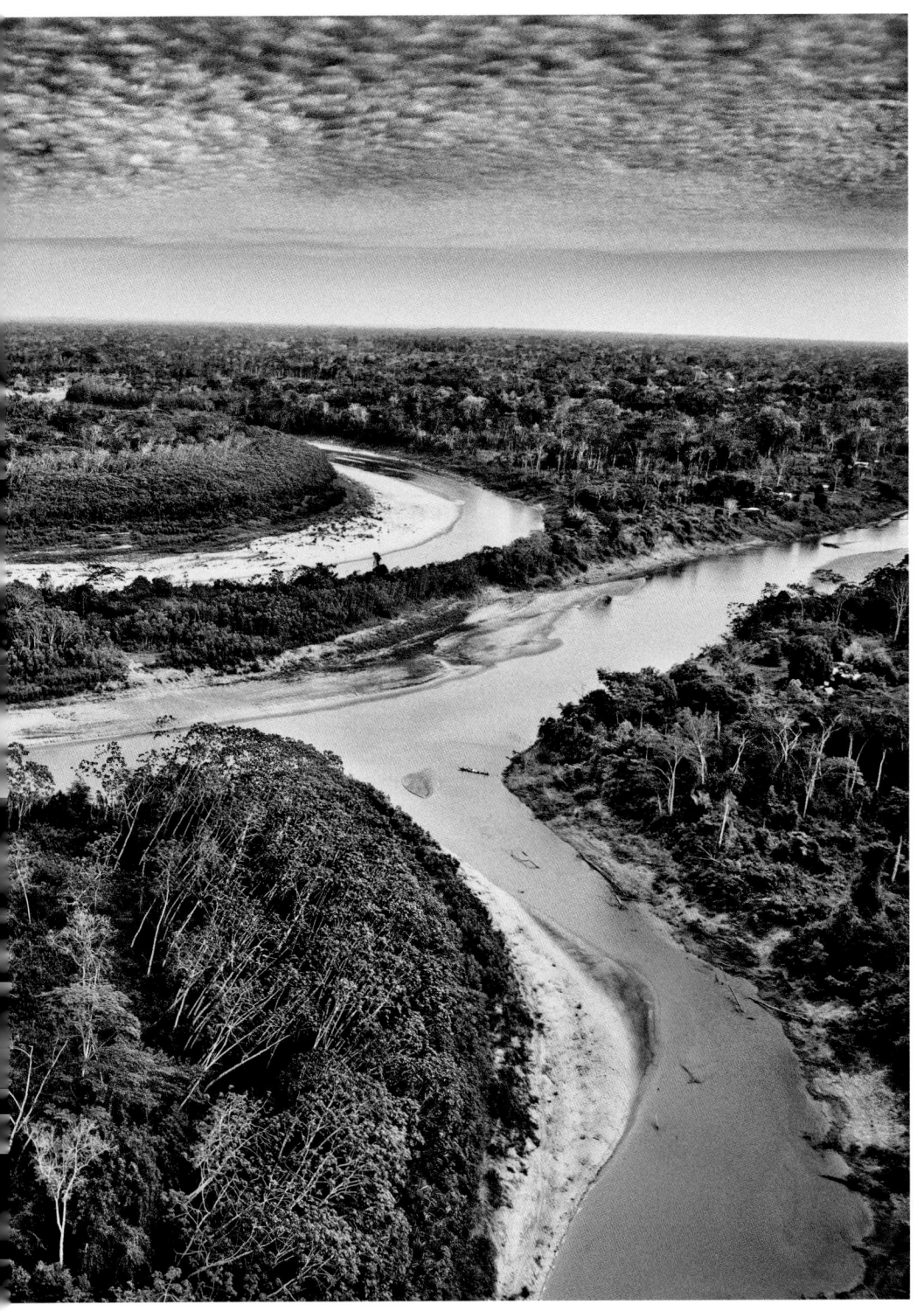

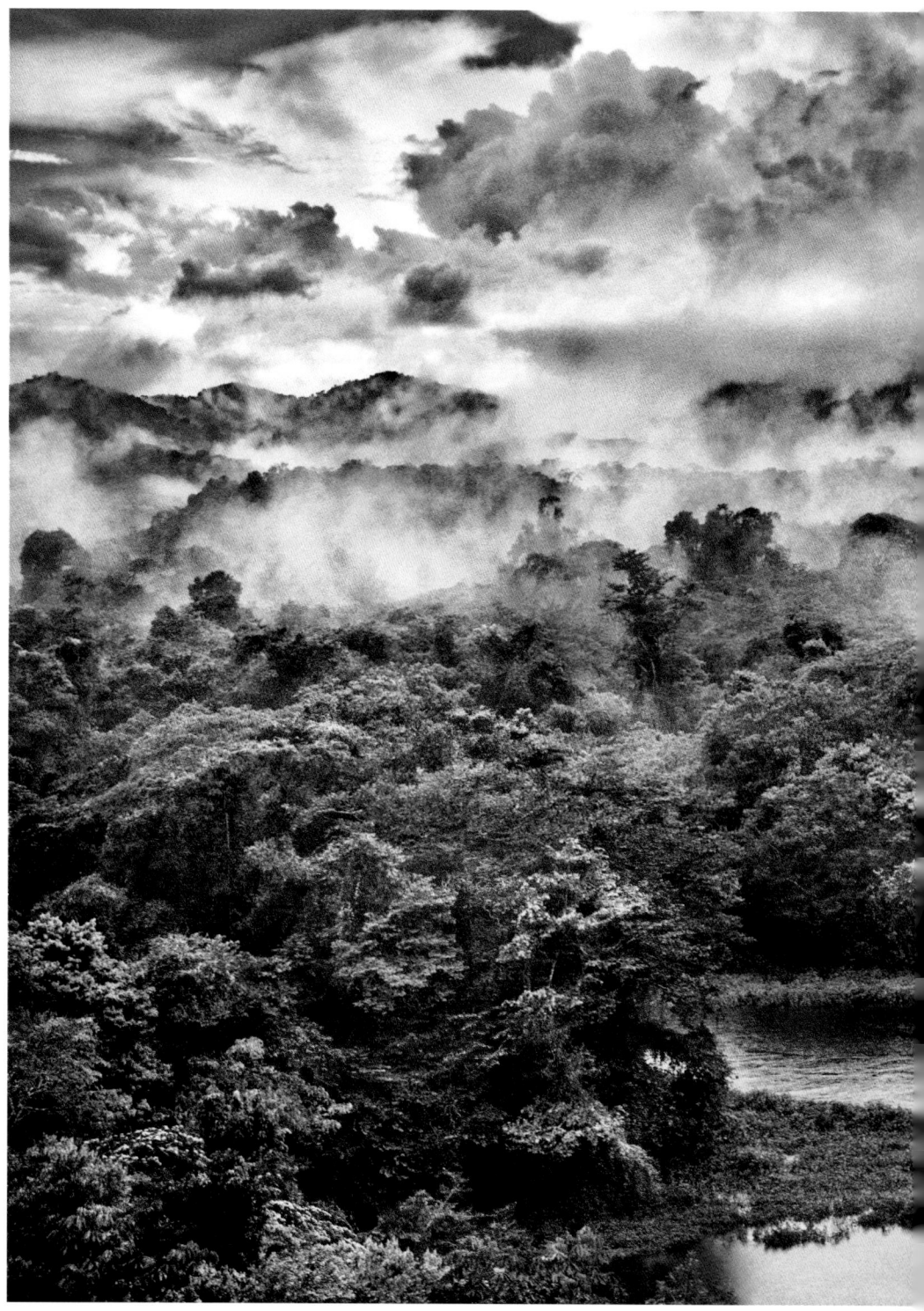

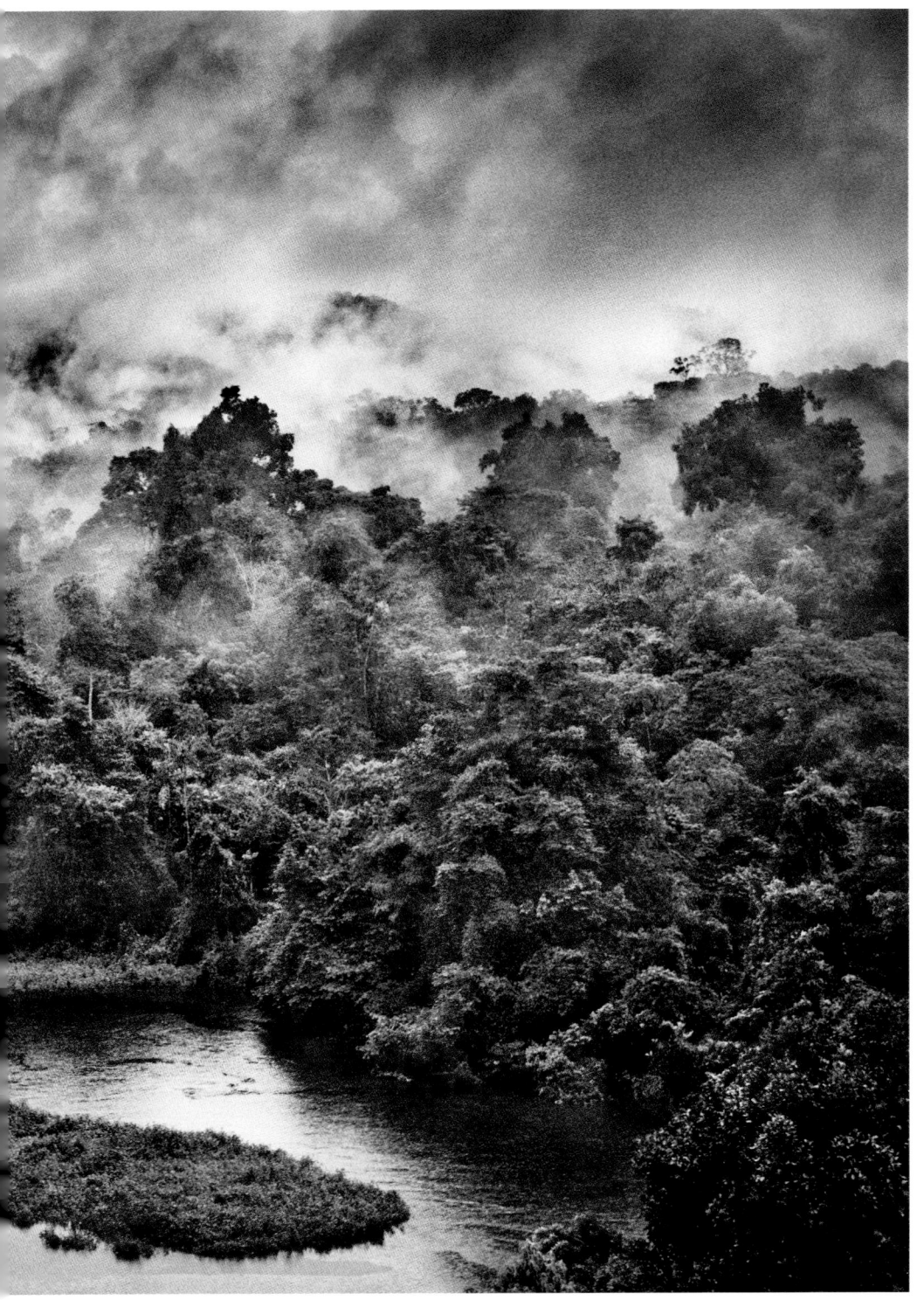

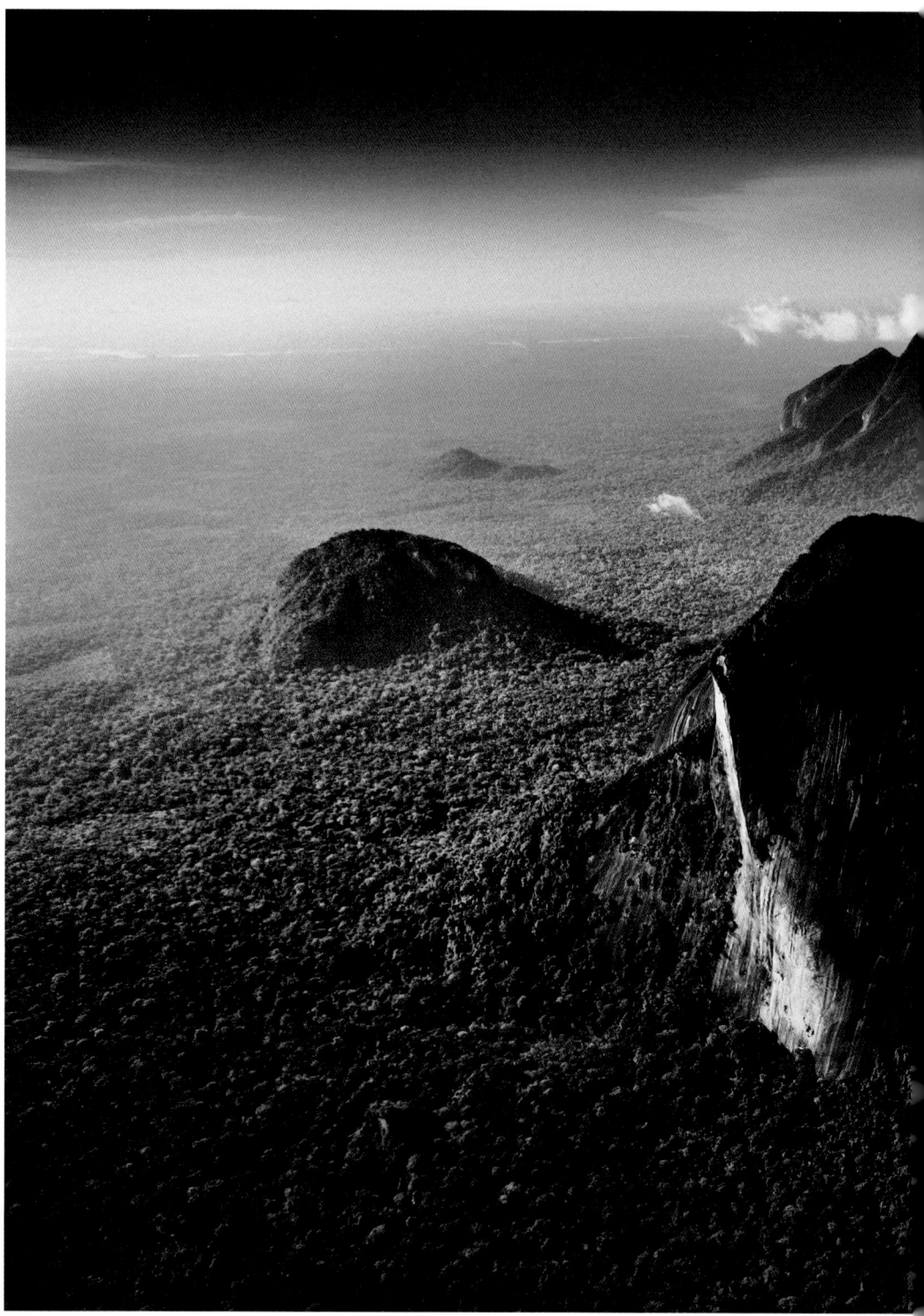

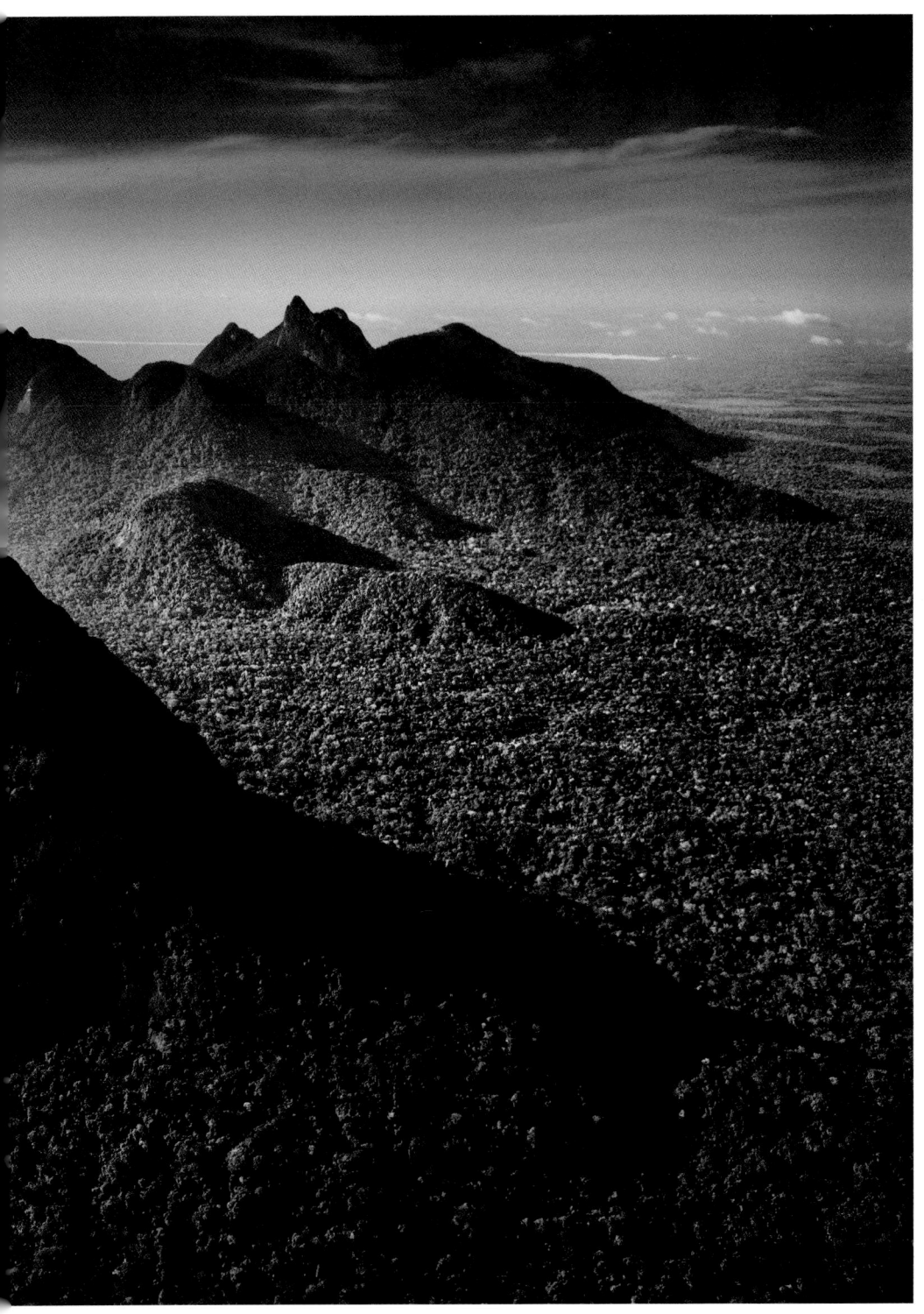

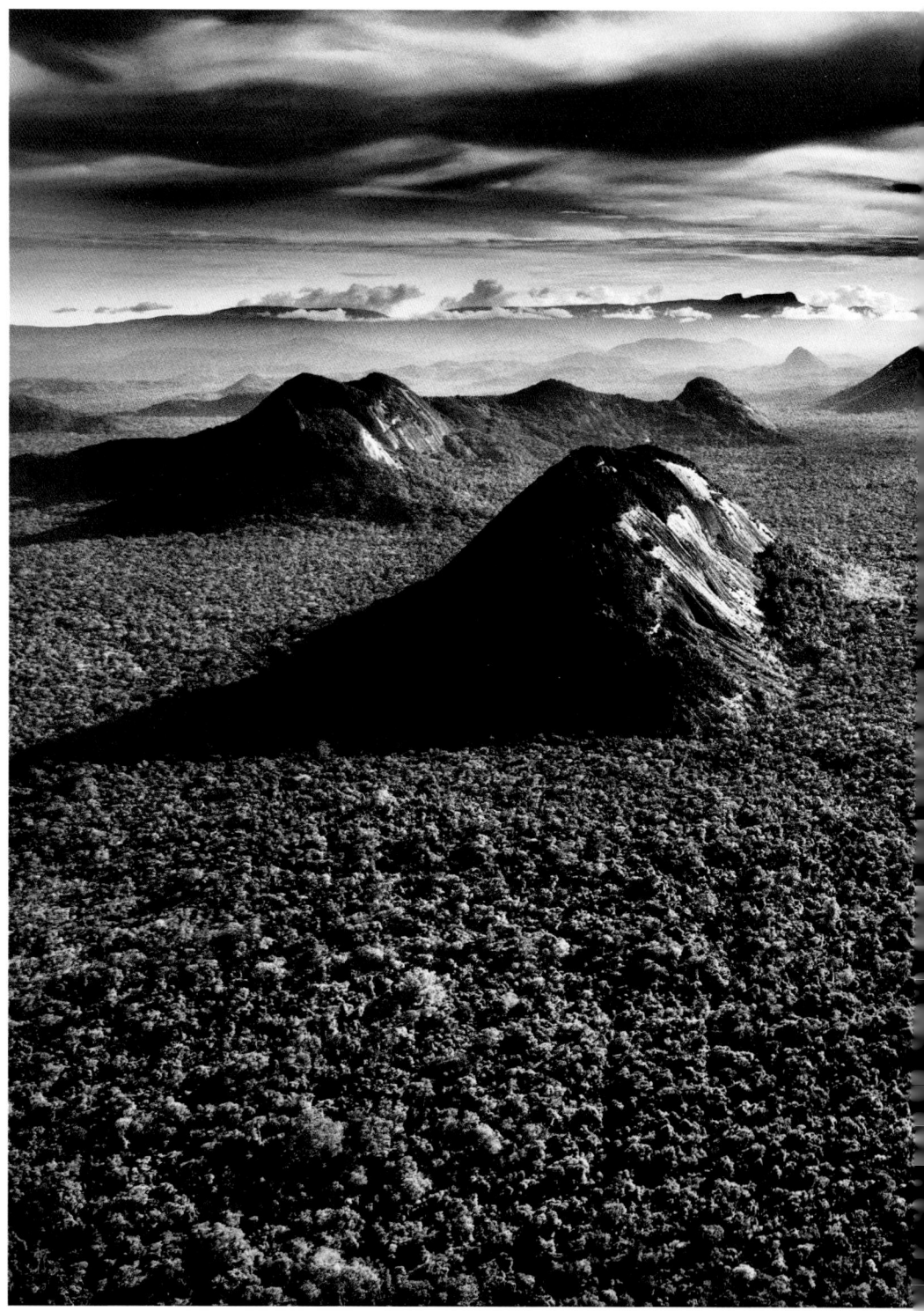

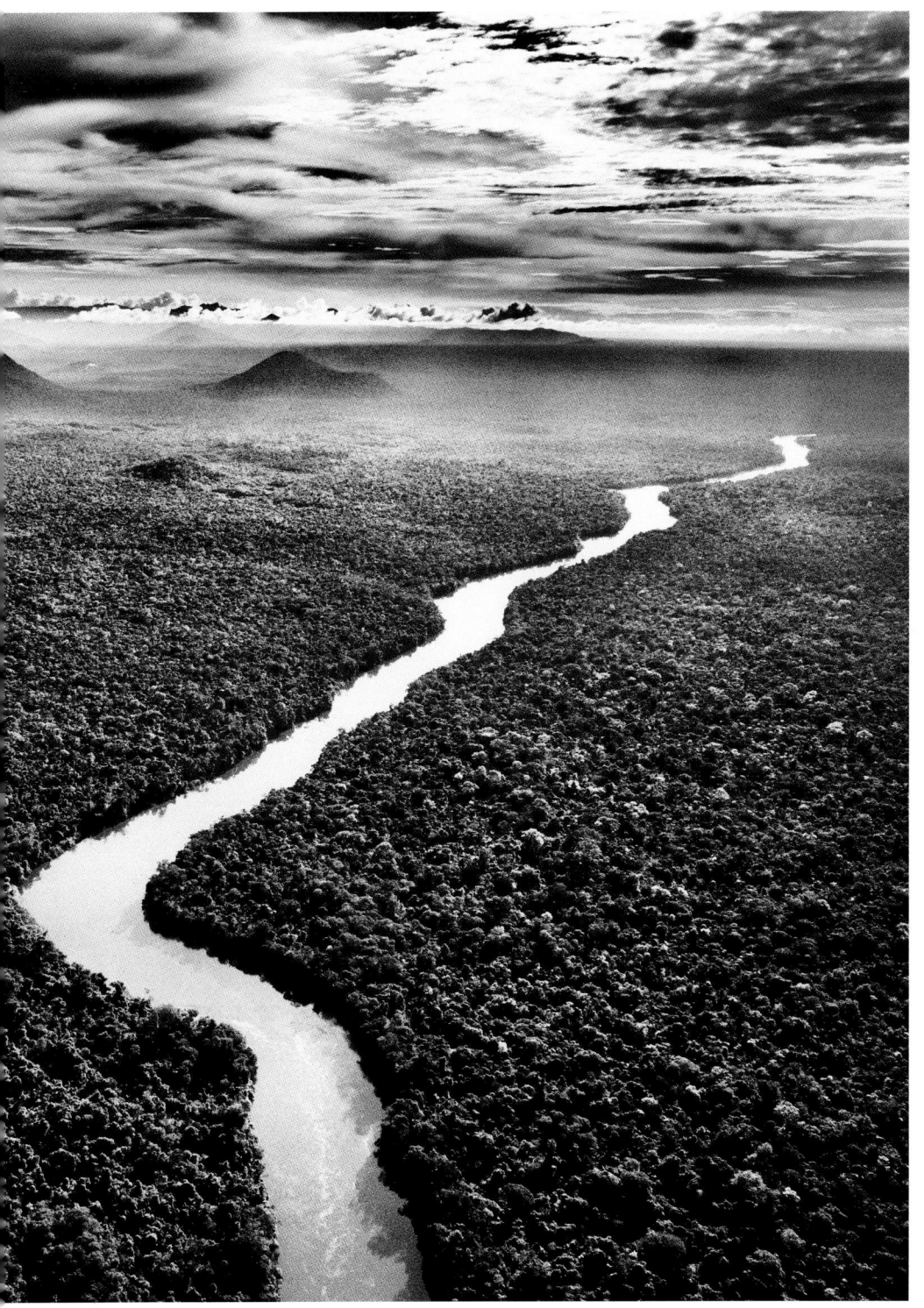

Pages 6/7 Aerial view of the Jutaí River. Because of the extremely flat terrain, it winds through the forest in snakelike curves. State of Amazonas, 2017.

Page 8 Aracá State Park. El Dorado Falls (background) and Desabamento Falls (foreground). *Tepuis* are geological mesa formations with sandstone and quartzite soil, and with water plunging down their sides in waterfalls. State of Amazonas, 2019.

Pages 10/11 A stretch of the Juruá River, near the municipality of Marechal Thaumaturgo, which forms a circle as if it were an island. With a length of about 3,000 kilometers (1,860 miles), it originates in Peru, flows into the Solimões River, and serves as a waterway for dozens of communities. State of Acre, 2016.

Pages 12/13 The sky darkens with tropical rain over the Auaris River in the Parima Forest Reserve, near the Yanomami Indigenous Territory. The rising steam that shrouds the treetops is the result of rain that fell in the preceding hours and reveals the constant movement of water. State of Roraima, 2018.

Pages 14/15 The Curicuriari mountain range is called the "Sleeping Beauty Mountains" among the inhabitants of São Gabriel da Cachoeira, who can see it on the horizon. Located in the Middle Rio Negro region, south of São Gabriel da Cachoeira, this elevated grouping looks like an island surrounded on all sides by forest. State of Amazonas, 2009.

Pages 16/17 The Demini River is a tributary of the Rio Negro and flows through the Yanomami Indigenous Territory, bordering the elevations of Serra do Aracá Park. State of Amazonas, 2019.

Opposite In the background, Mount Roraima, exactly where the triple borders of Brazil, Guyana, and Venezuela meet. Its elevation is 2,810 meters (9,220 feet). Macuxi Indigenous Territory Raposa–Serra do Sol, state of Roraima, 2018.

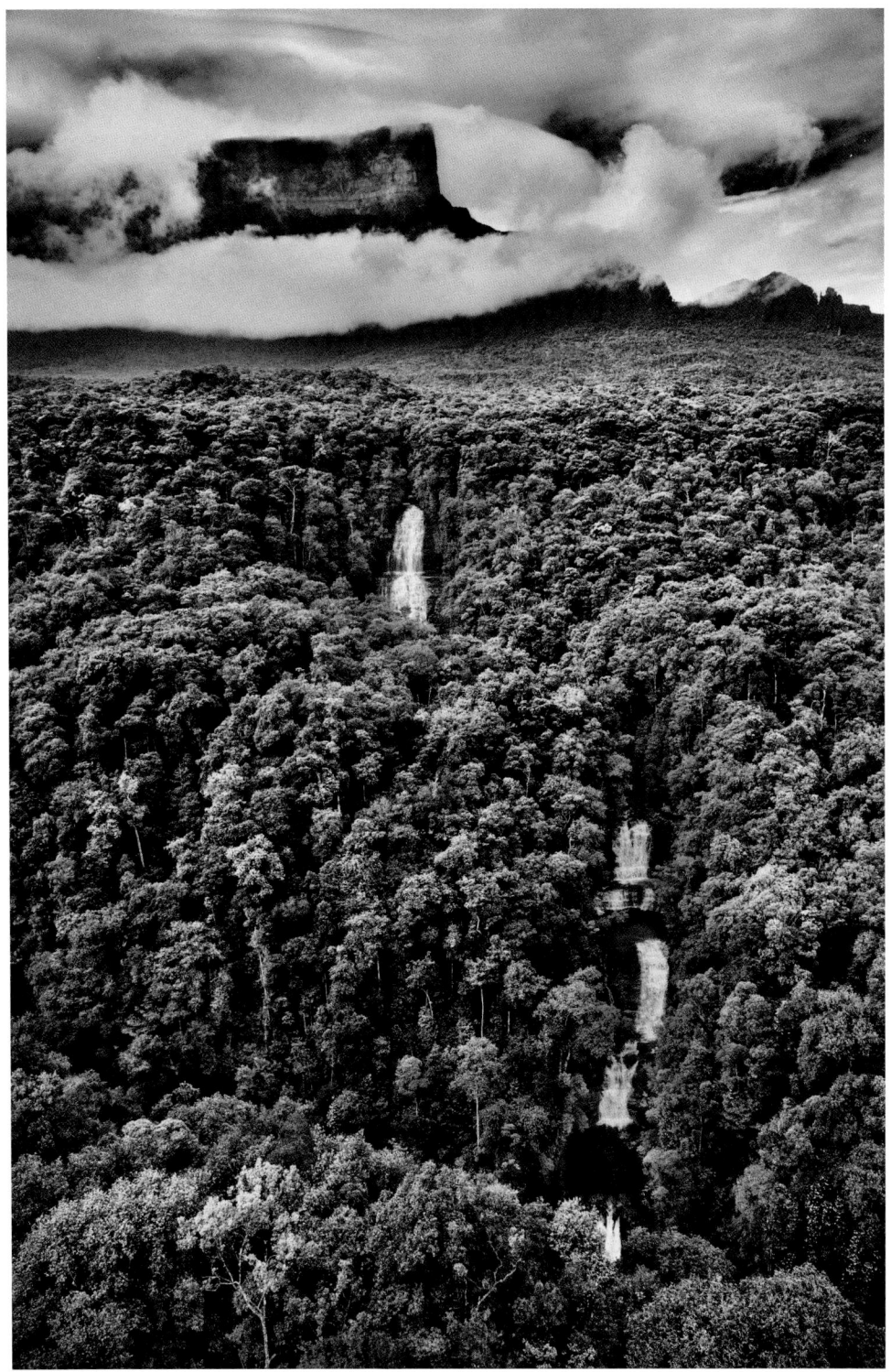

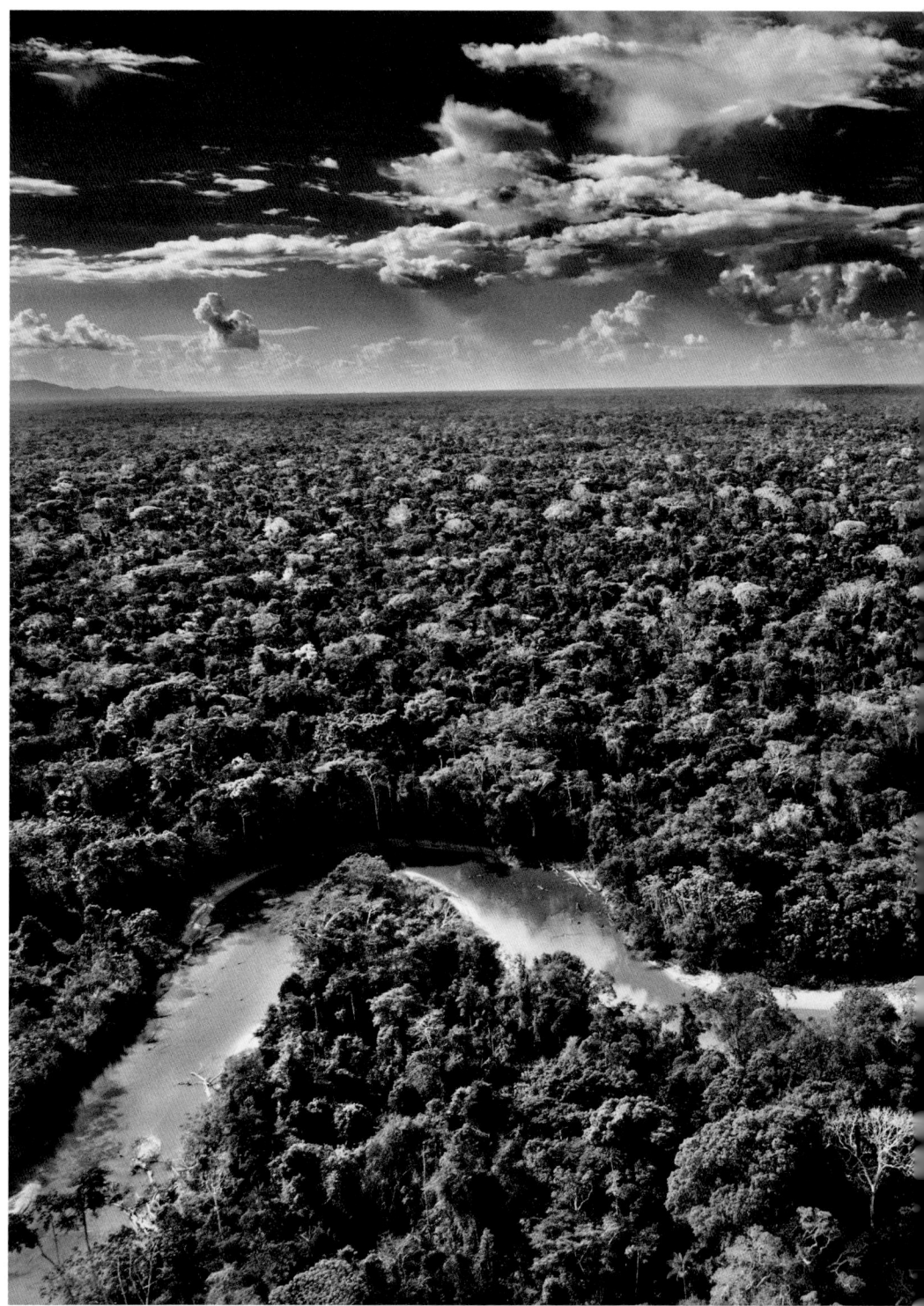

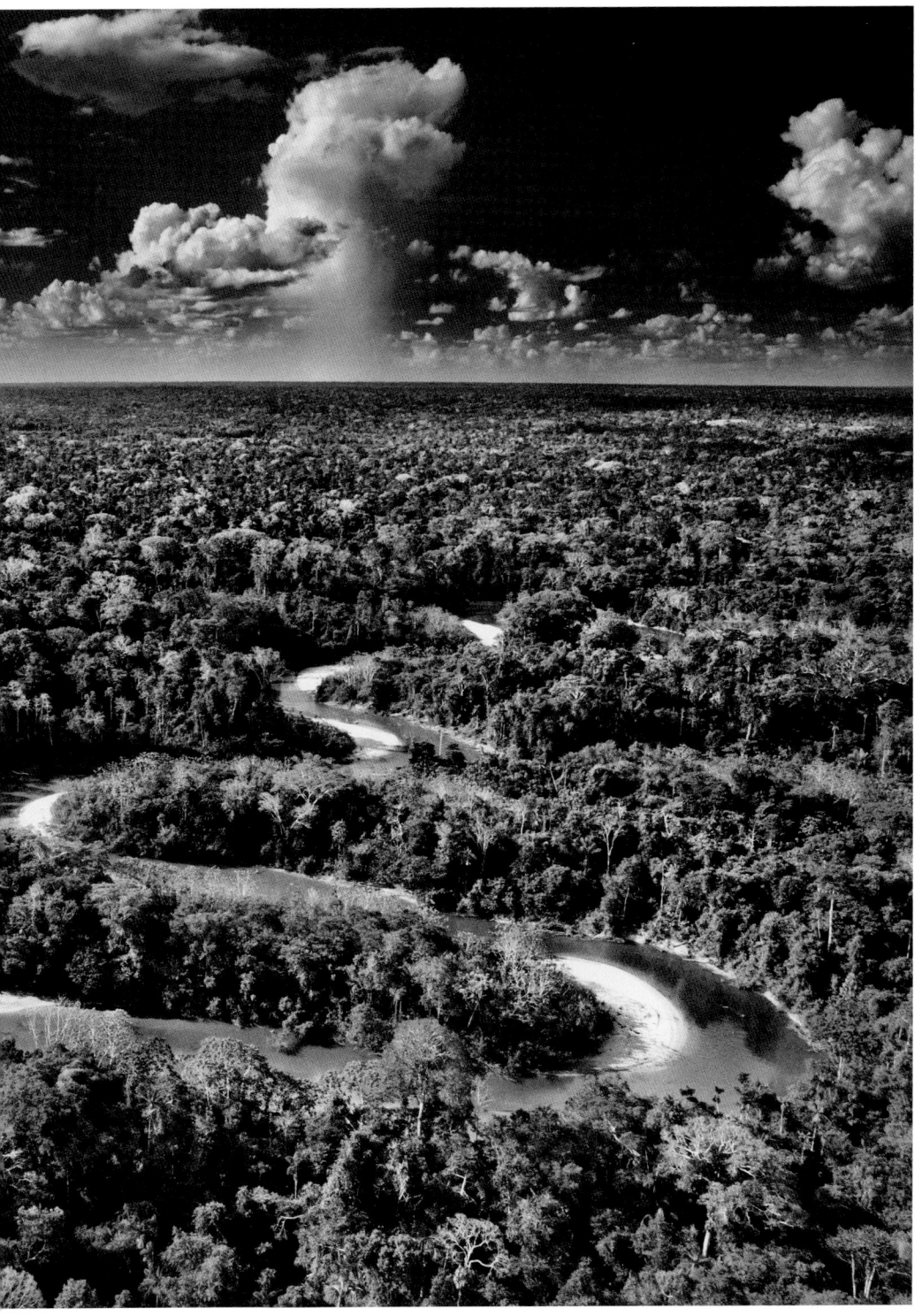

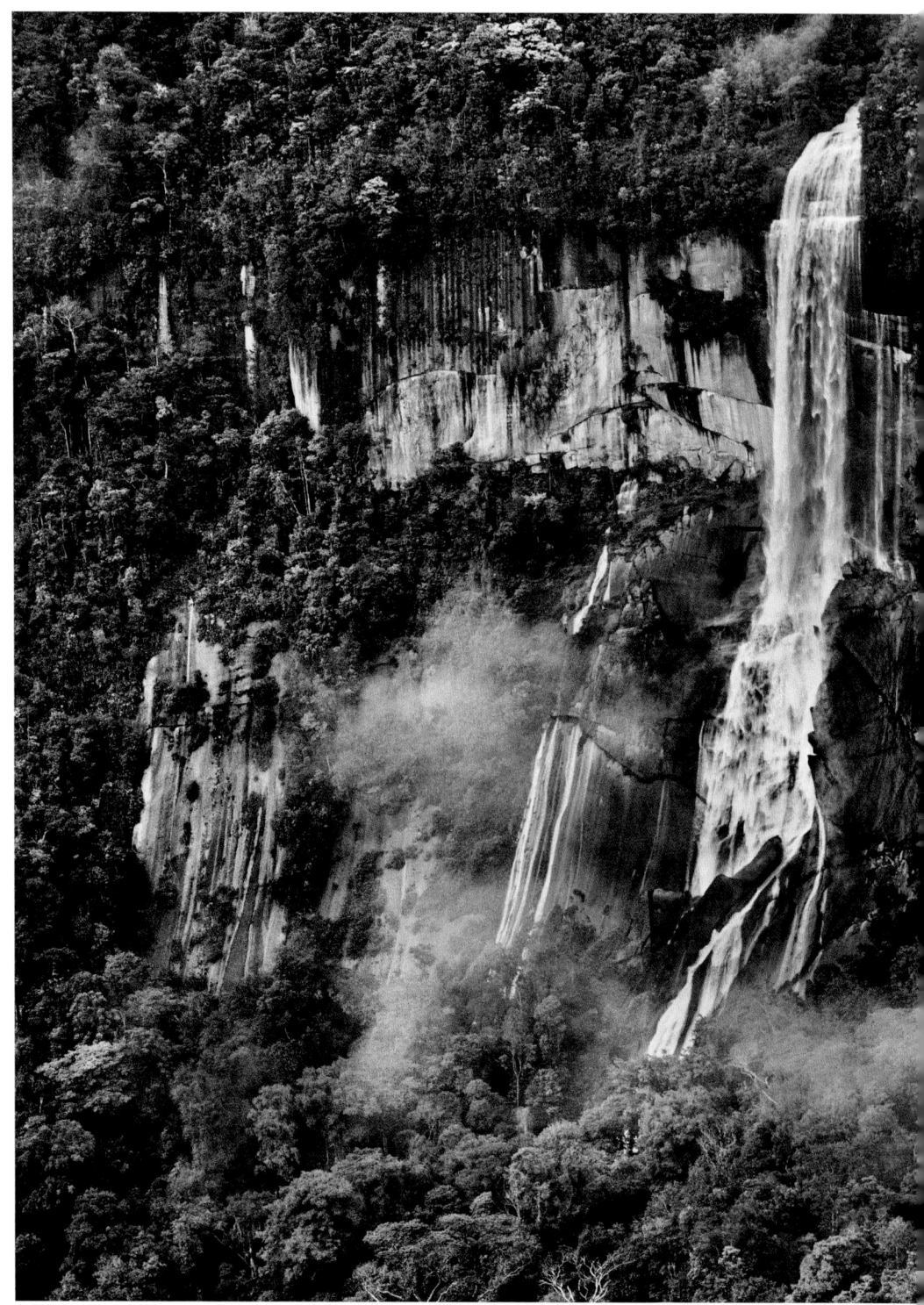

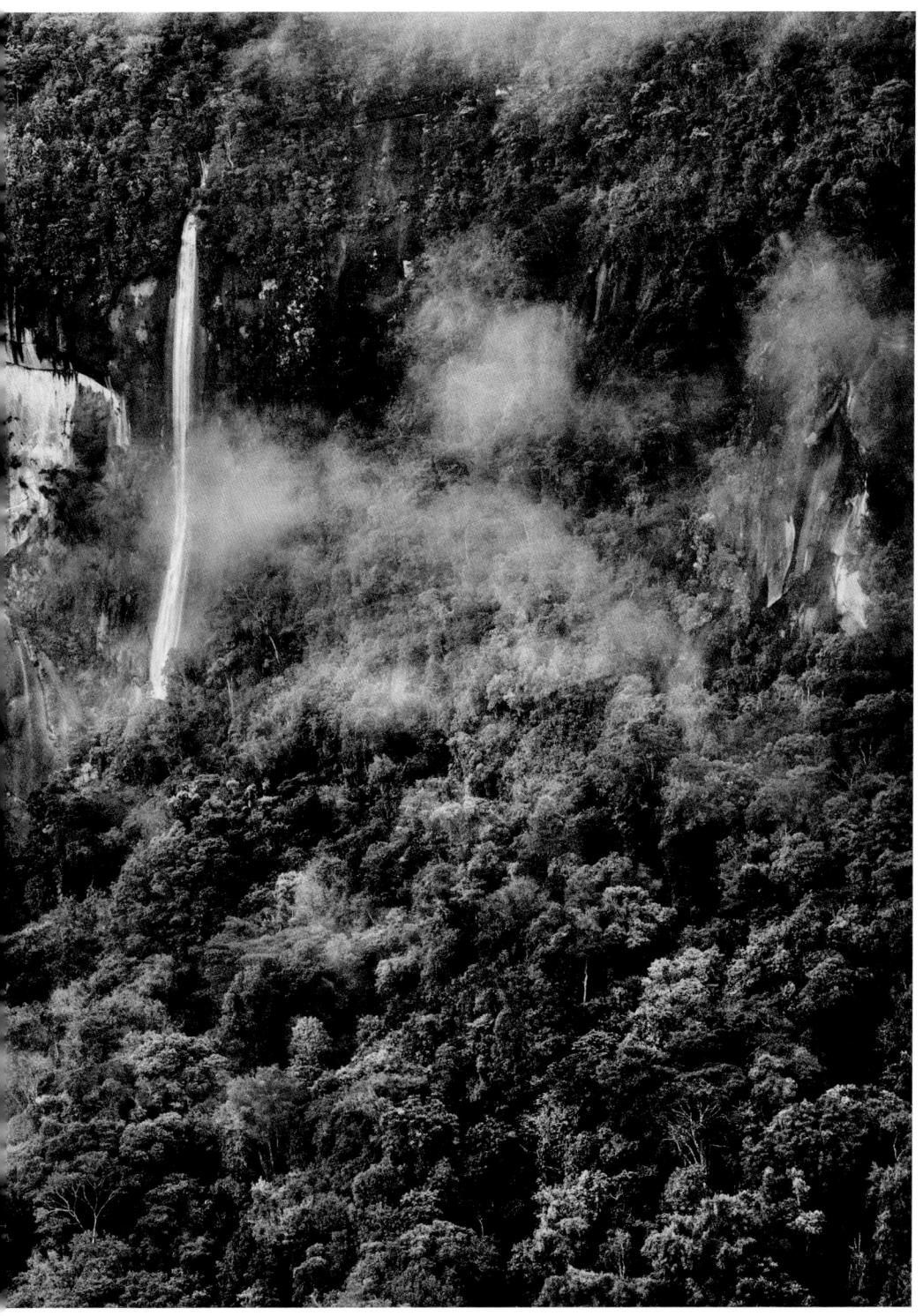

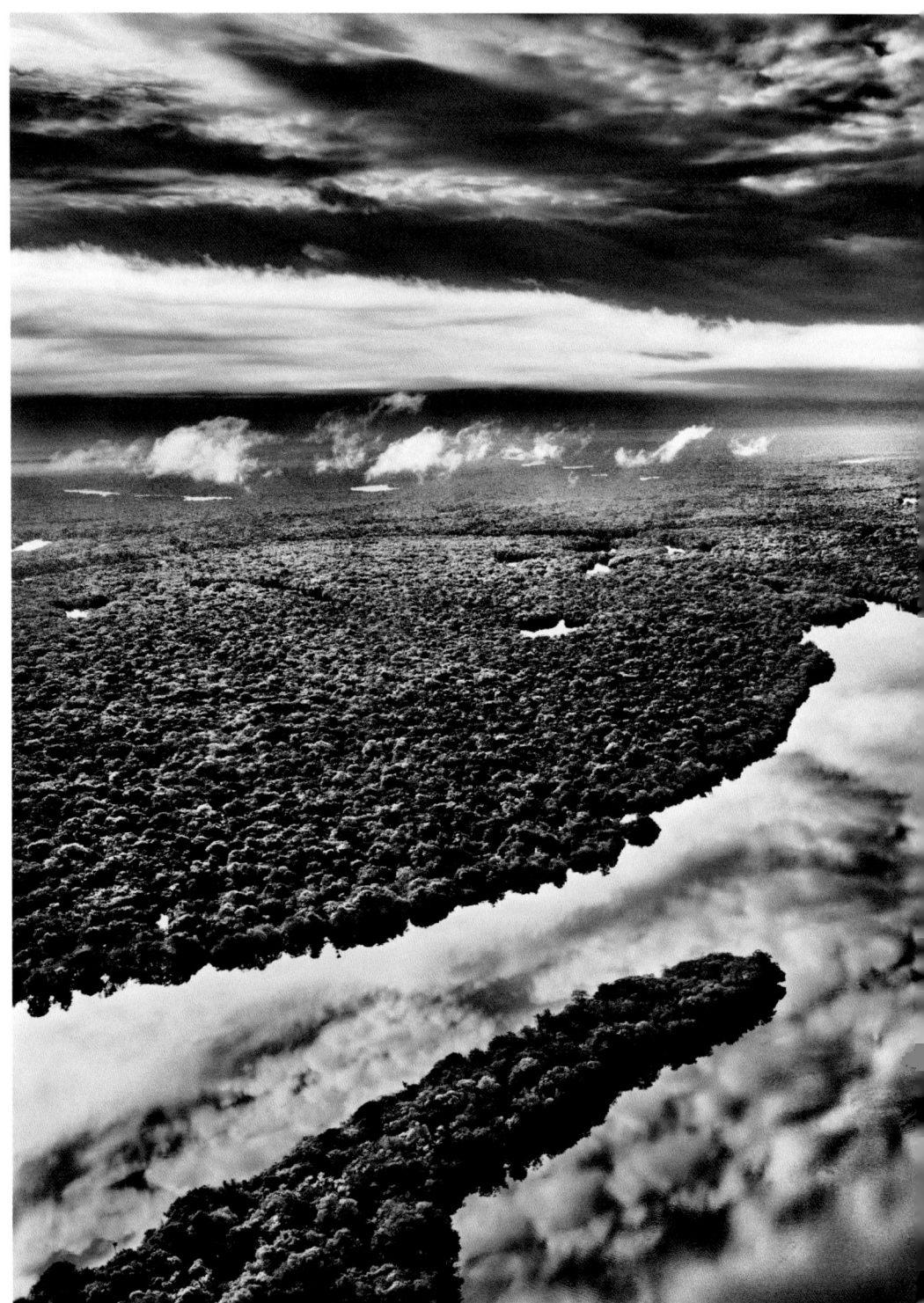

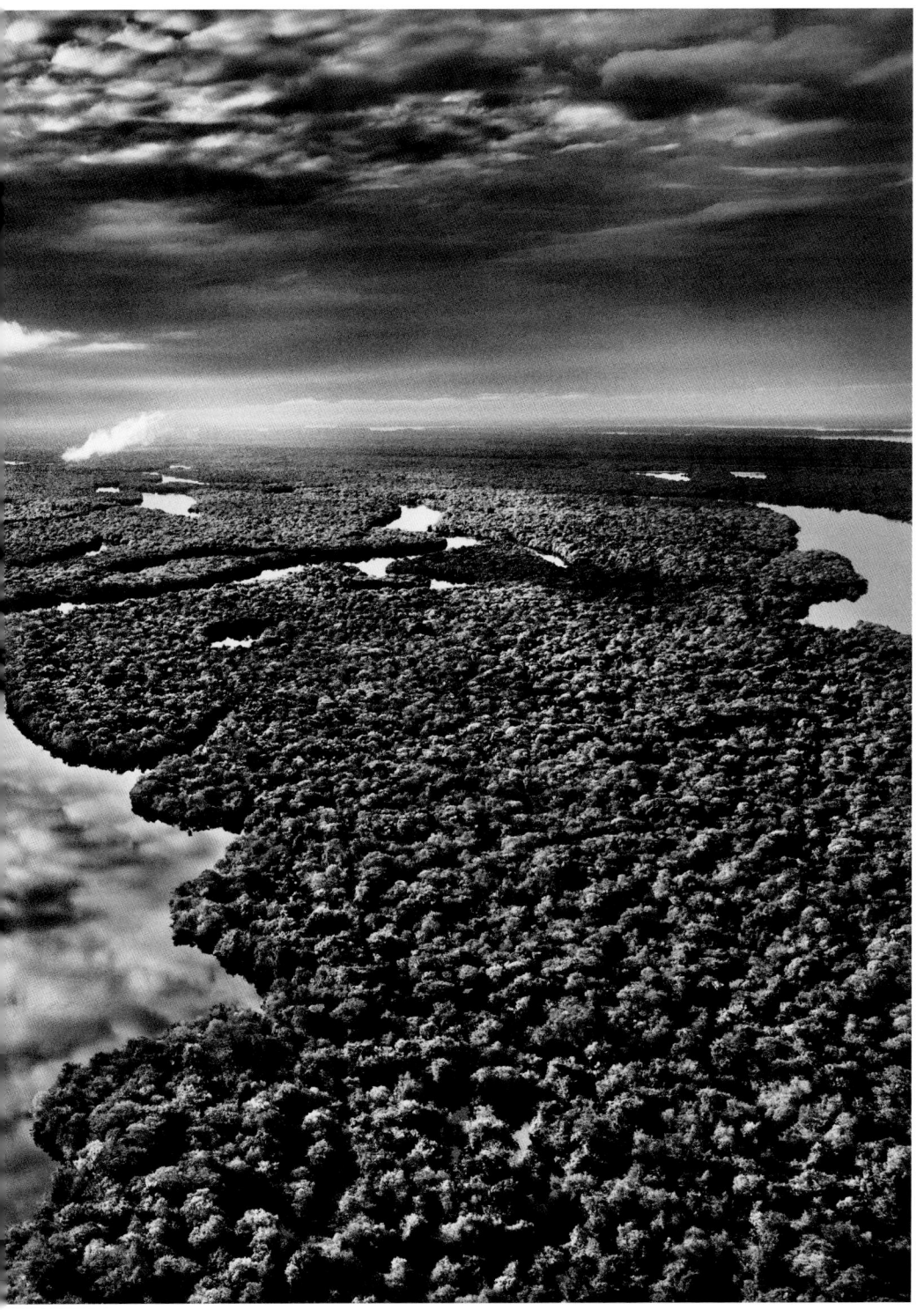

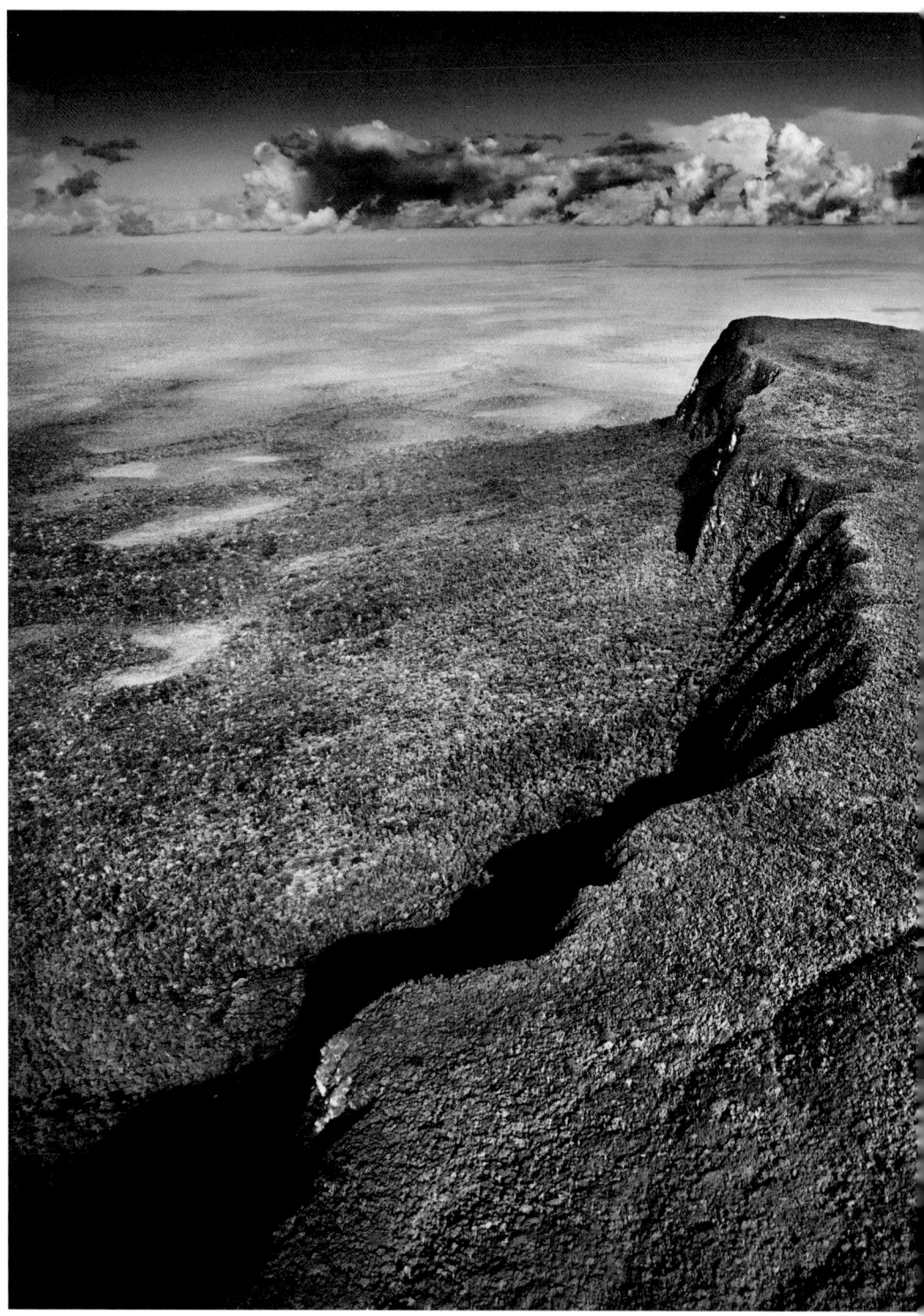

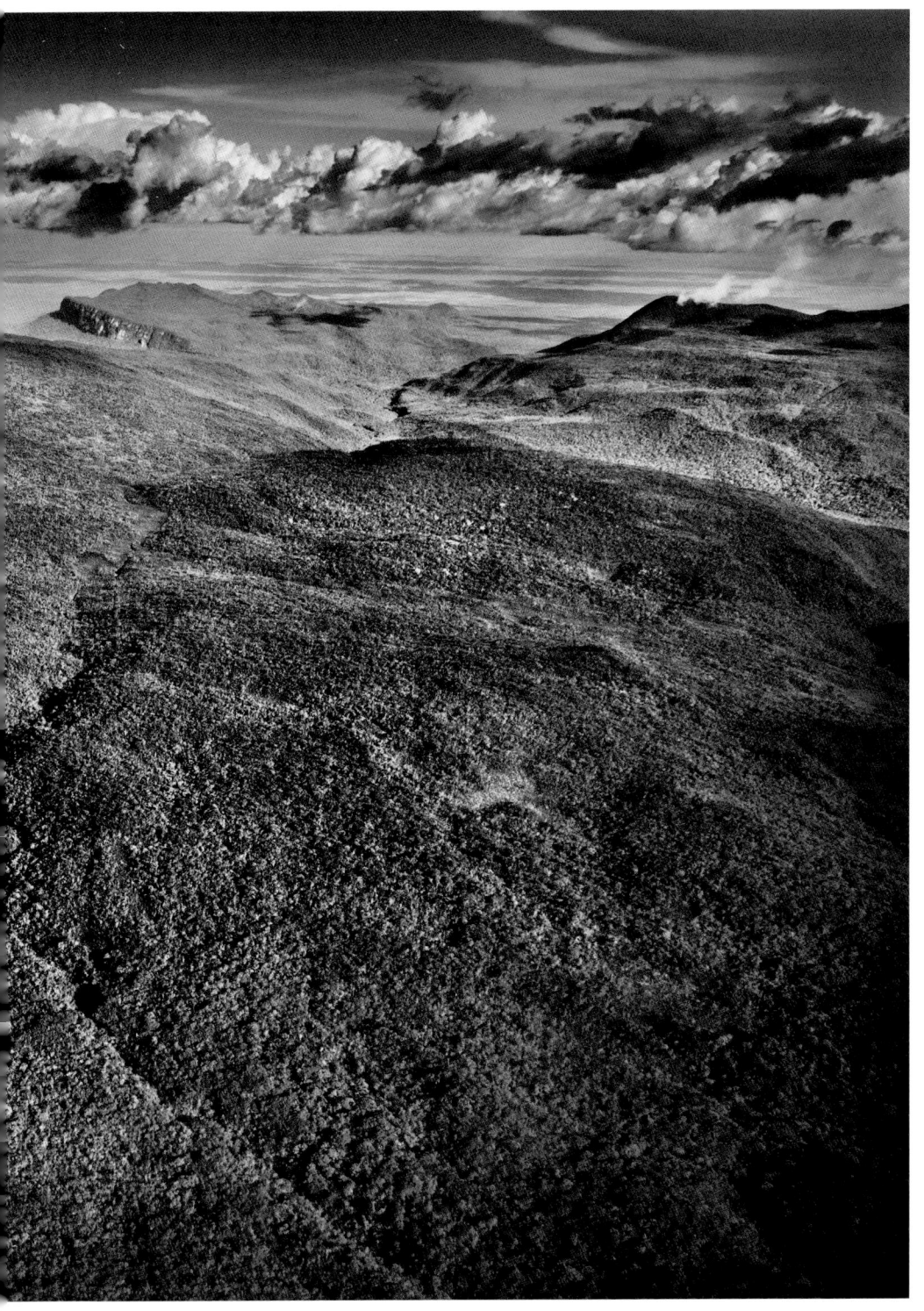

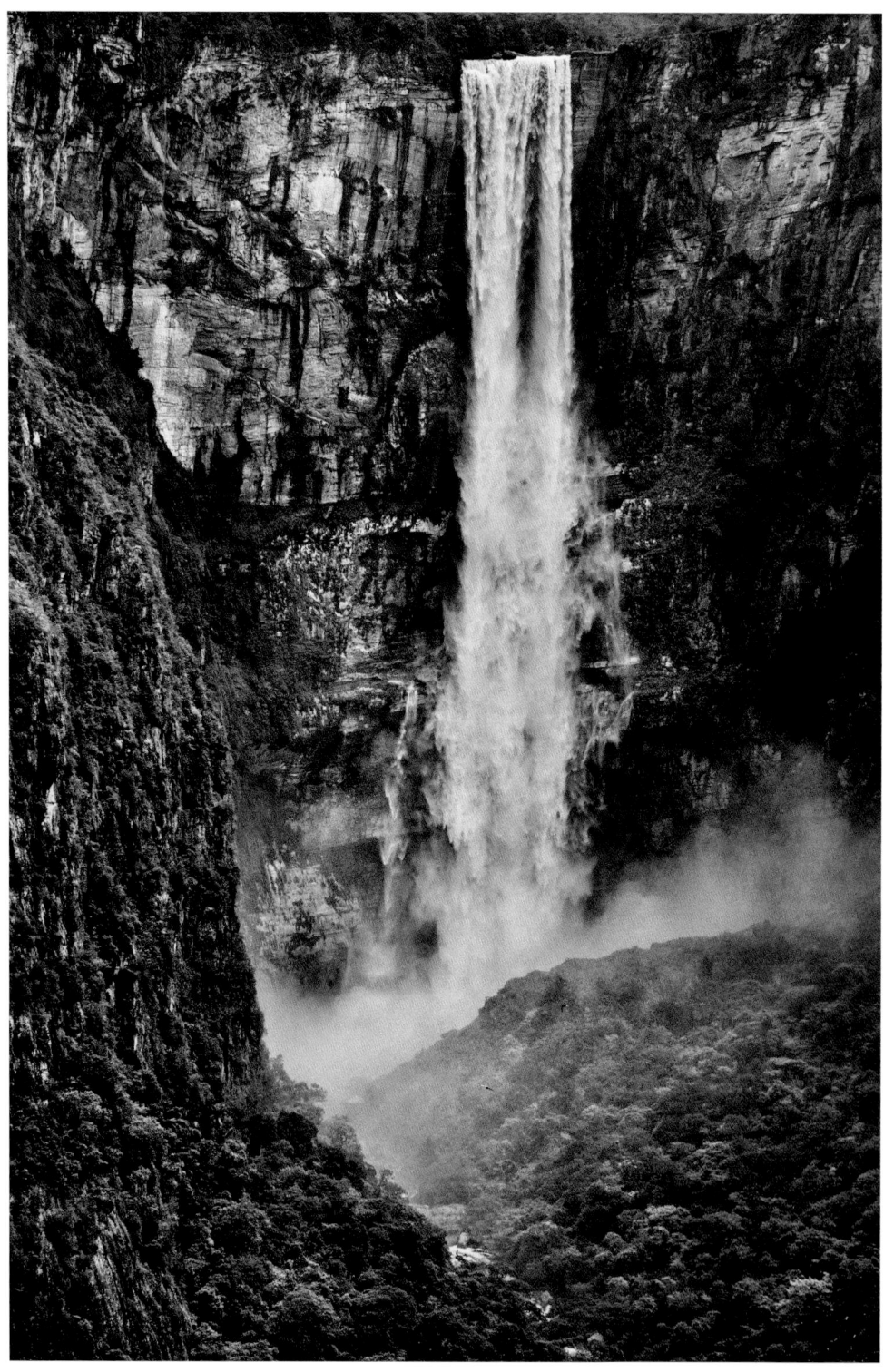

Pages 20/21 The Gregório River has a length of 350 kilometers (215 miles). It flows through the states of Acre and Amazonas, across a vast plain of "new lands" that change the river's course frequently as the riverbanks give way to the force of floodwaters. Yawanawá Indigenous Territory, state of Acre, 2016.

Pages 22/23 The rugged terrain of the Parima Mountains produces huge waterfalls such as the Parima River Falls. The water drops down the steep wall of a tepui, or mesa, a geological formation typical of the region. Yanomami Indigenous Territory. Parima Forest Reserve, on the border with Venezuela. State of Roraima, 2018.

Pages 24/25 Dense clouds herald heavy rain over the Anavilhanas Archipelago, a chain of river islands in the Rio Negro. North of the city of Barcelos, state of Amazonas, 2009.

Pages 26/27 Aracá mountain range. Aracá State Park, state of Amazonas, 2019.

Opposite Aracá State Park. El Dorado Falls, state of Amazonas, 2019.

Pages 30/31 The municipality of São Gabriel da Cachoeira is located in the far north of Brazil, in a region called Cabeça do Cachorro (Dog's Head) because of the shape of the region's borders. In that part of the country, the plains yield suddenly to rugged mountains, the highest in Brazil. Cauaburi River, Yanomami Indigenous Territory, state of Amazonas, 2018.

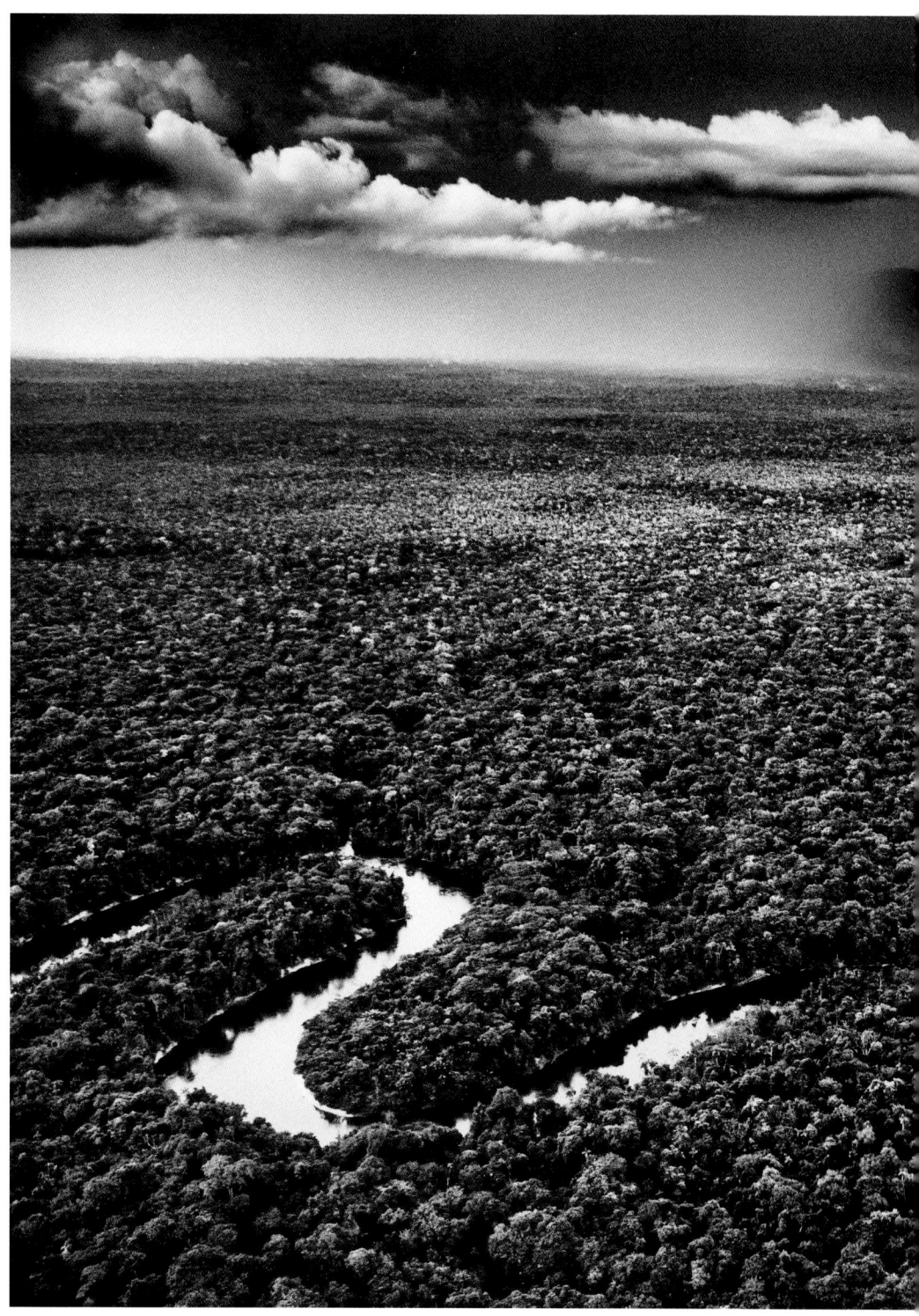

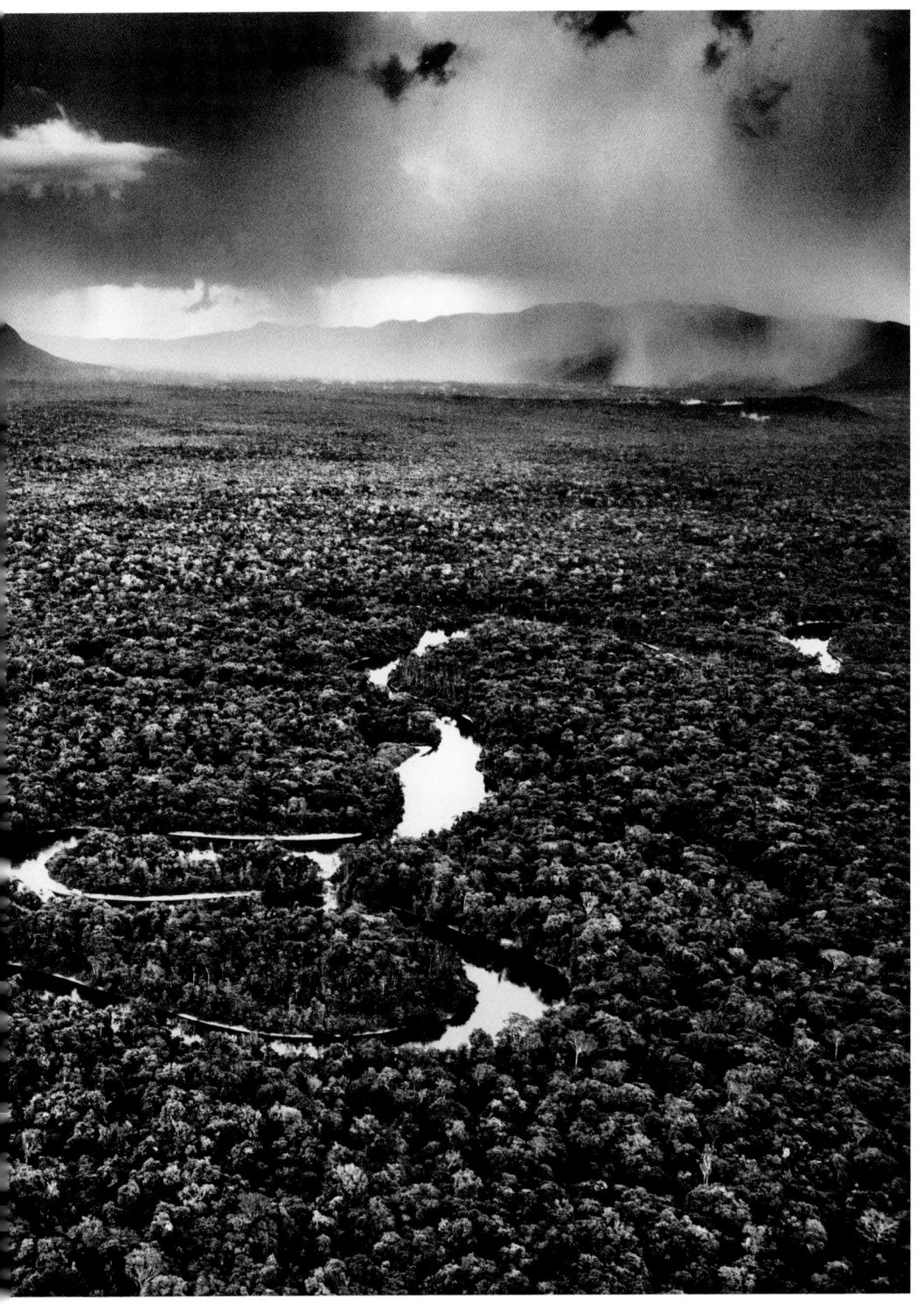

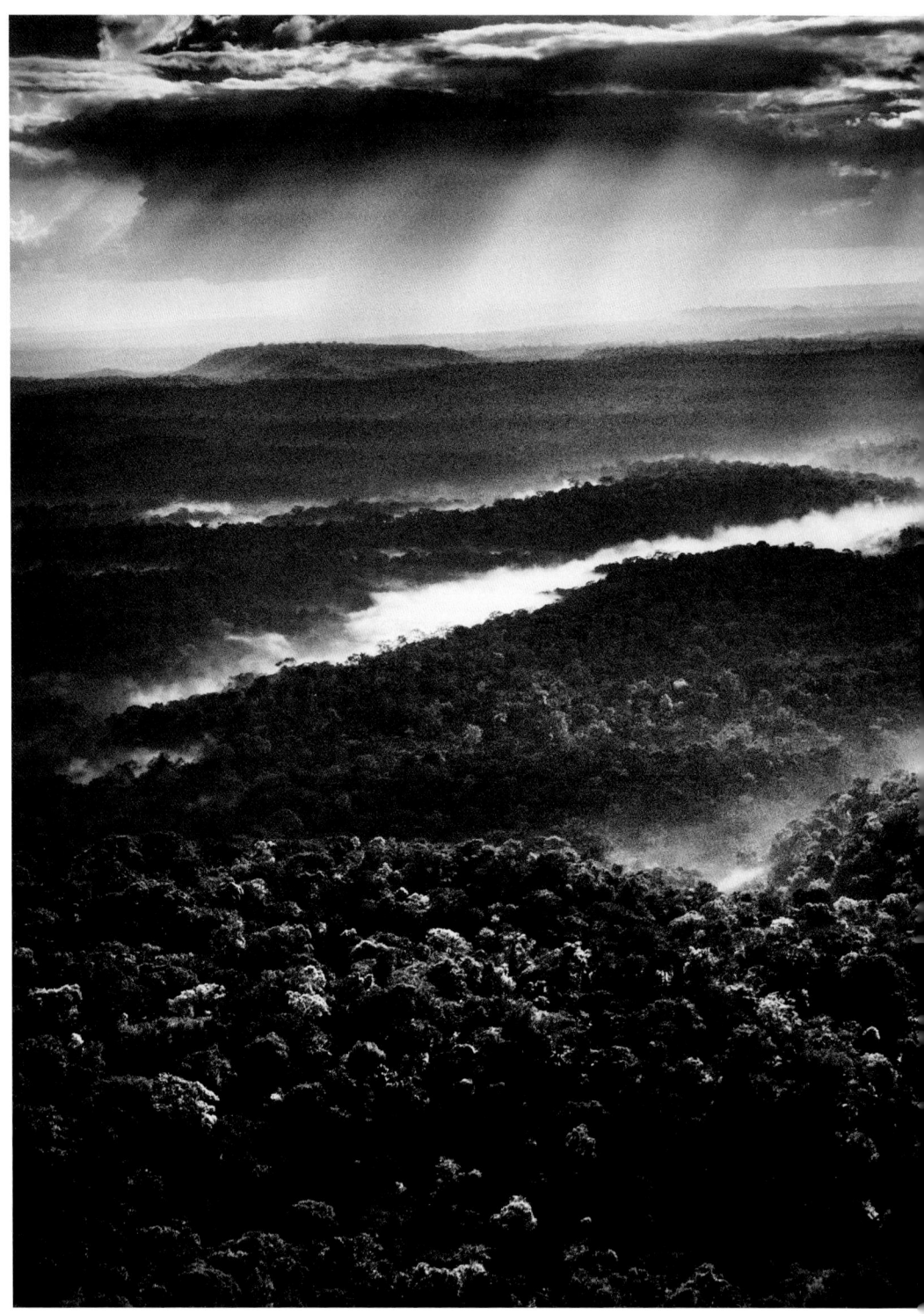

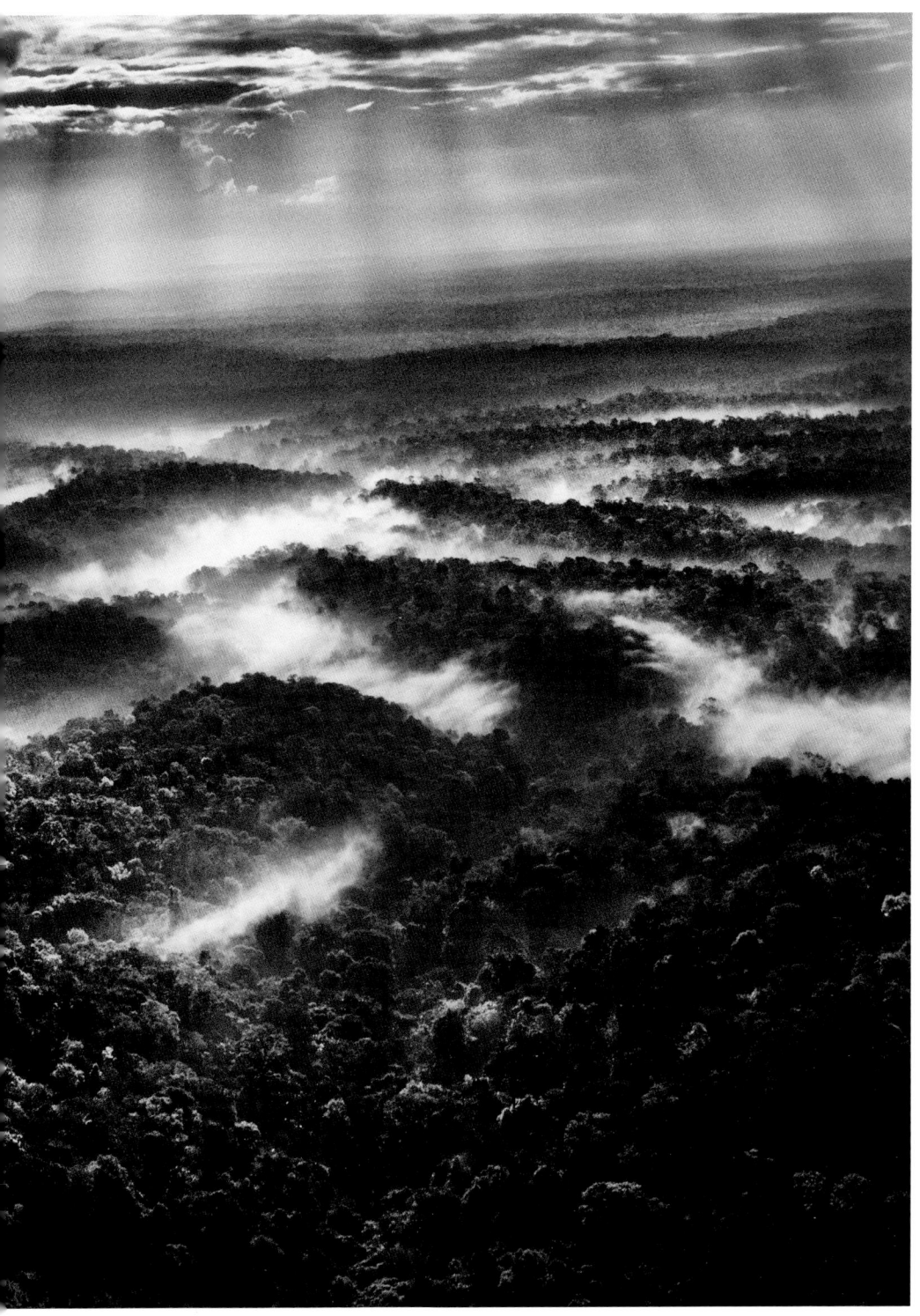

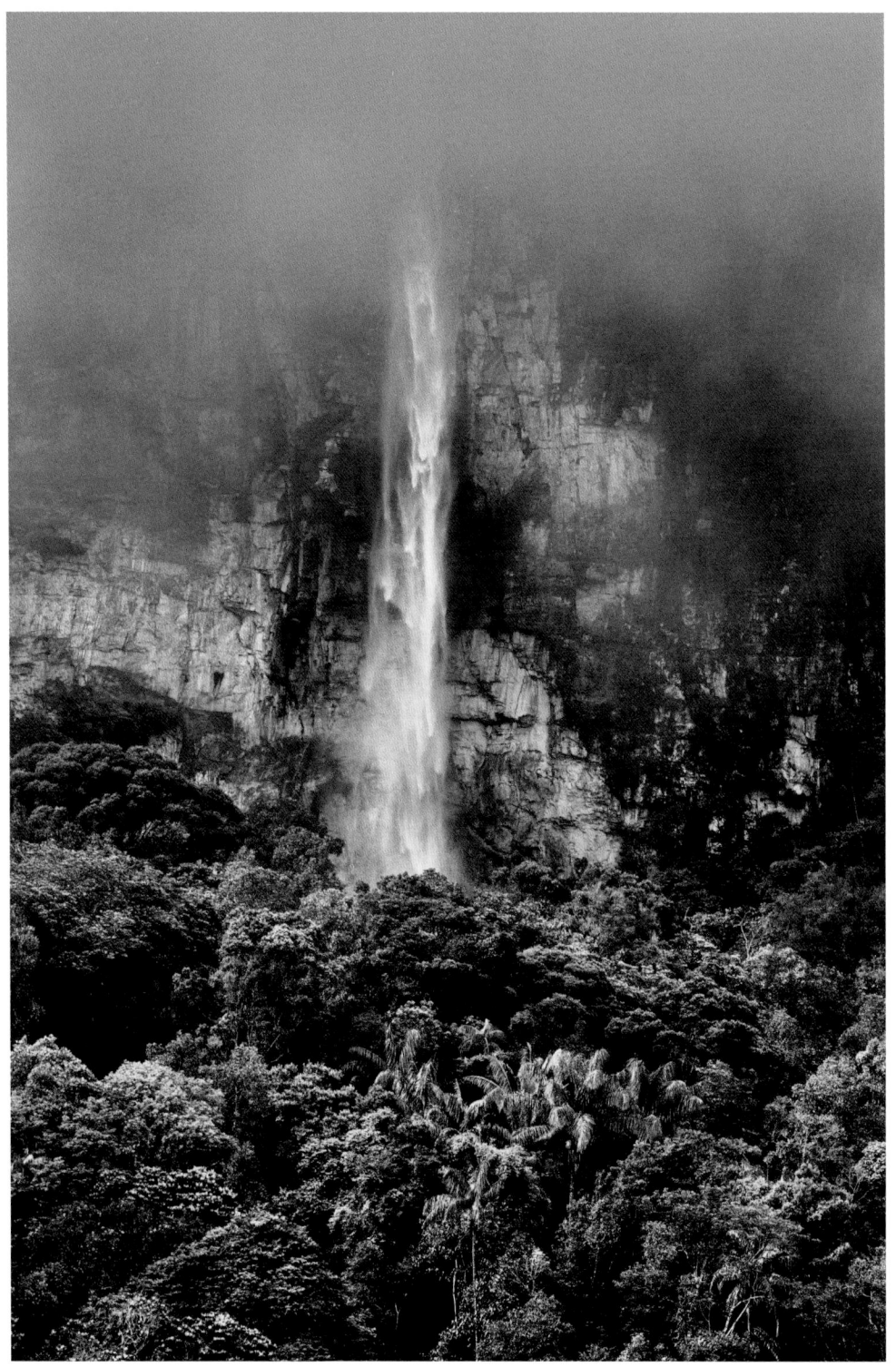

Pages 32/33 In the flood season, heavy clouds signal imminent rain, while intense evaporation forms microclouds that will return to the clouds, renewing the water cycle. Awá-Guajá Indigenous Territory, state of Maranhão, 2013.

Opposite Aracá mountain range. Aracá State Park, state of Amazonas, 2019.

Pages 36/37 Municipality of São Gabriel da Cachoeira. Cauaburi River, Yanomami Indigenous Territory, Maturacá region, state of Amazonas, 2018.

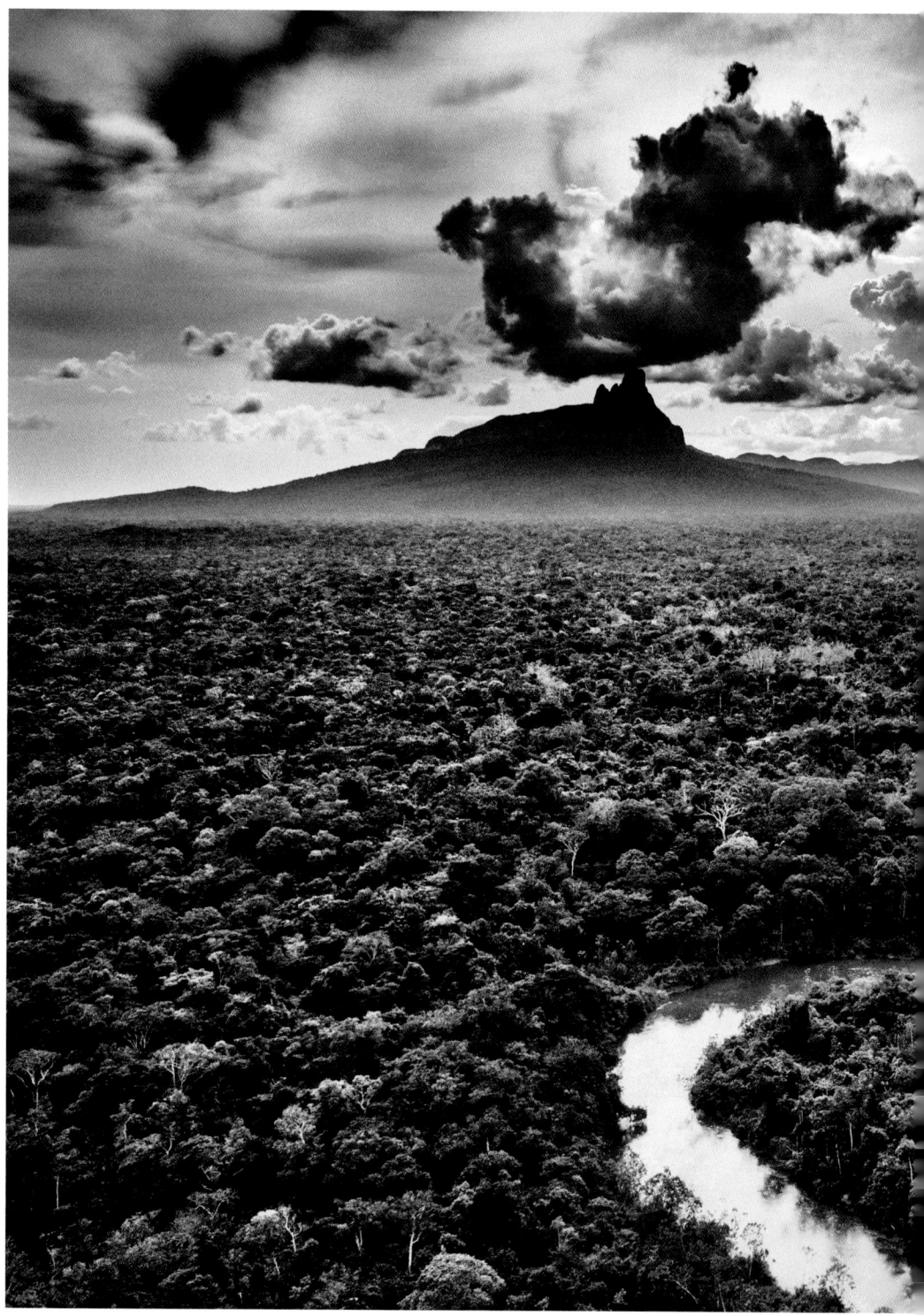

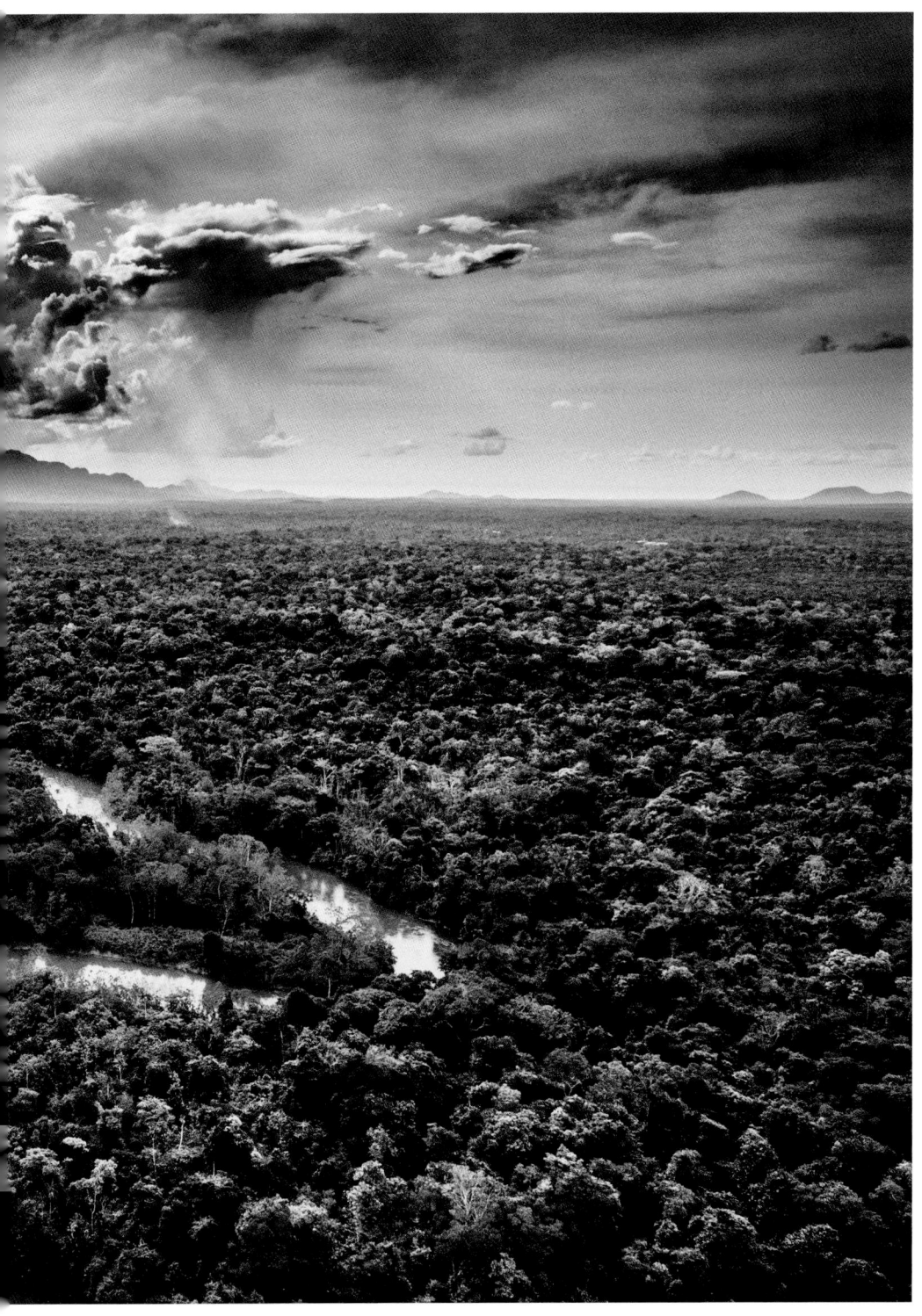

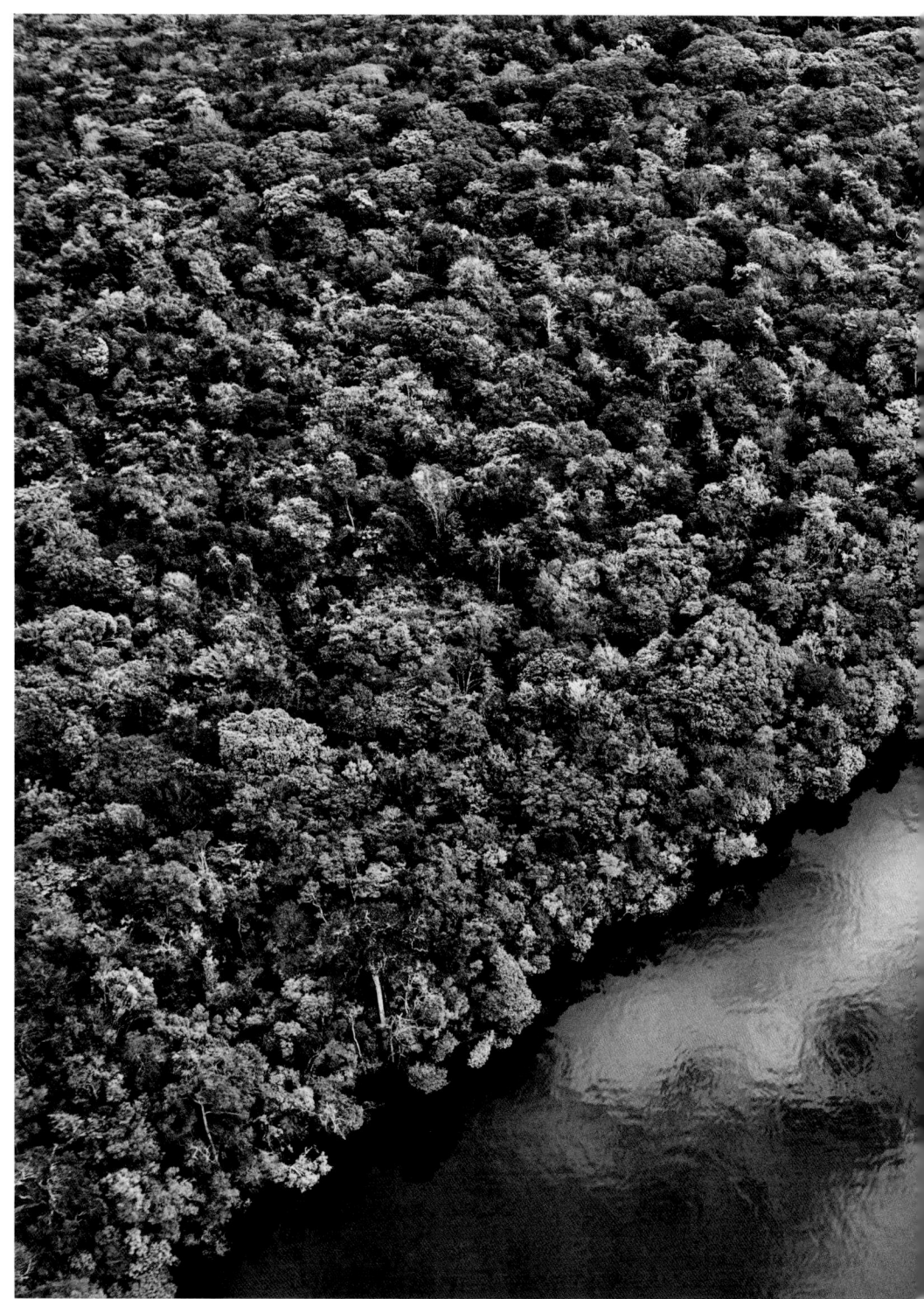

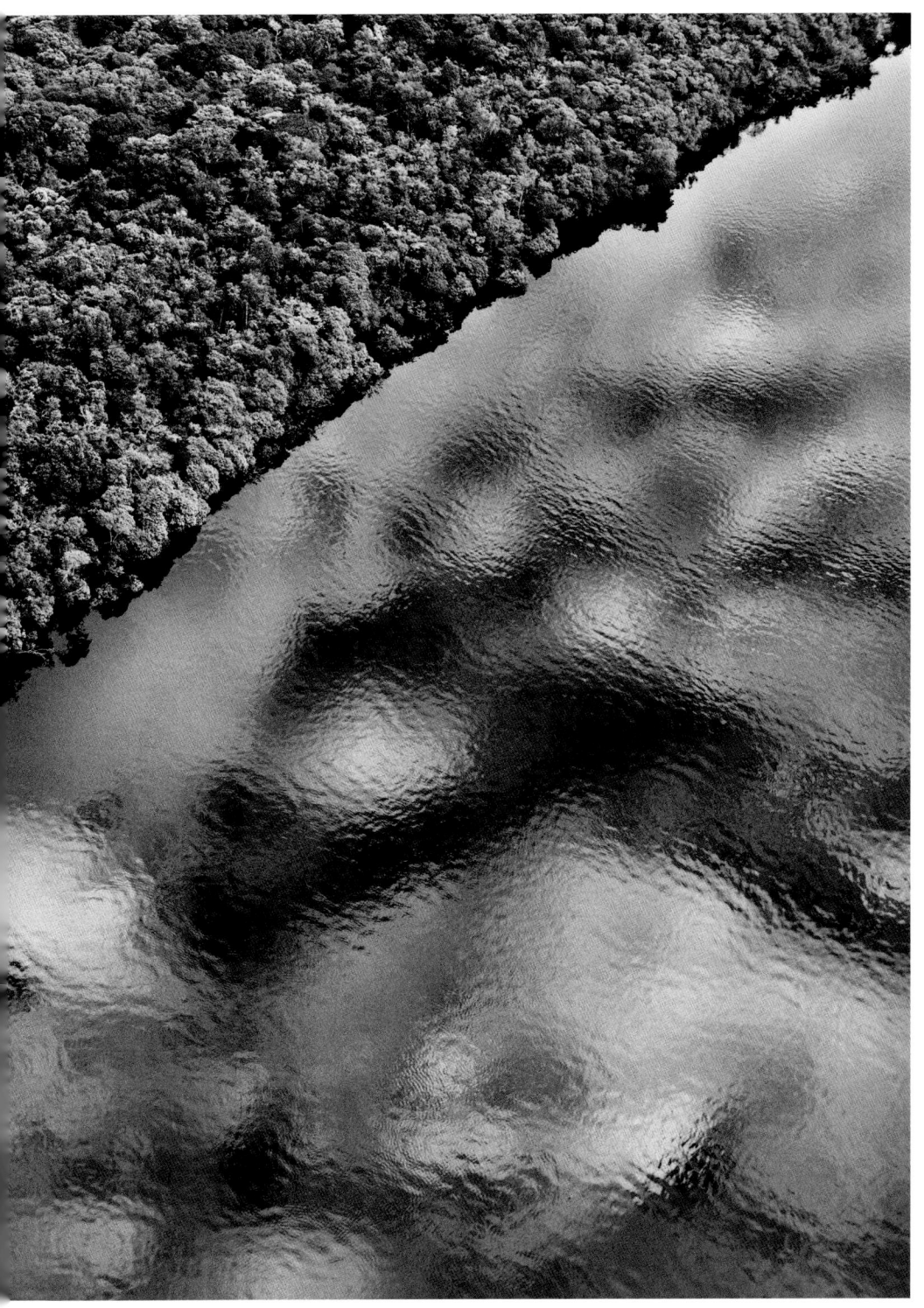

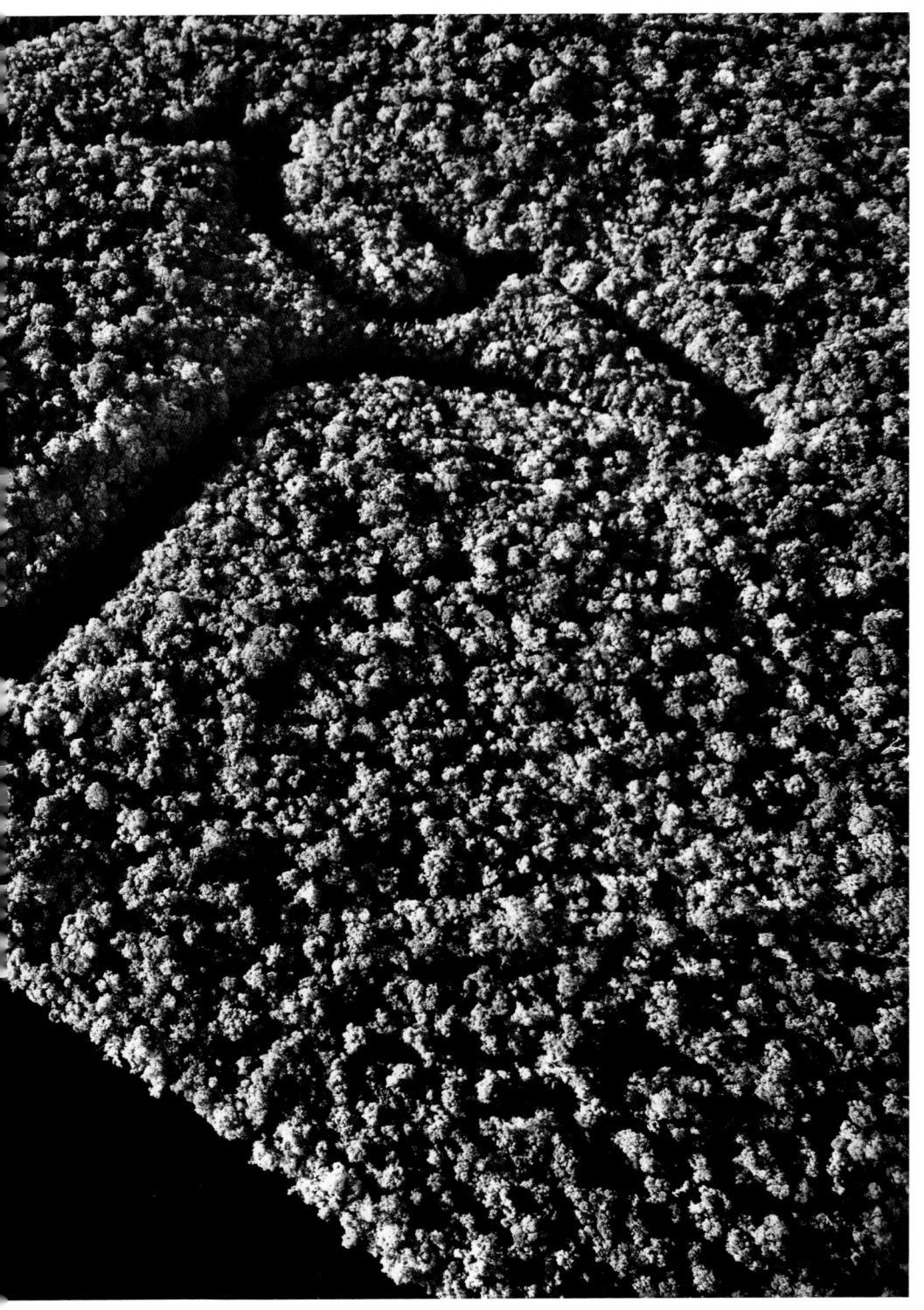

Pages 38/39 and 40/41 The Rio Negro, the world's largest blackwater river, will merge with the muddy Solimões River in the Manaus region, where they form what Brazilians consider the starting point of the Amazon River. Most of the source rivers originate in the Northern Hemisphere. Some of those tributaries originate in Venezuela and Colombia, where the waters come from the northern Andes. State of Amazonas, 2009.

Opposite The Cauaburi River shines in the sun in the Pico da Neblina National Park area of northern Amazonas. The park overlaps with the Yanomami Indigenous Territory, state of Amazonas, 2018.

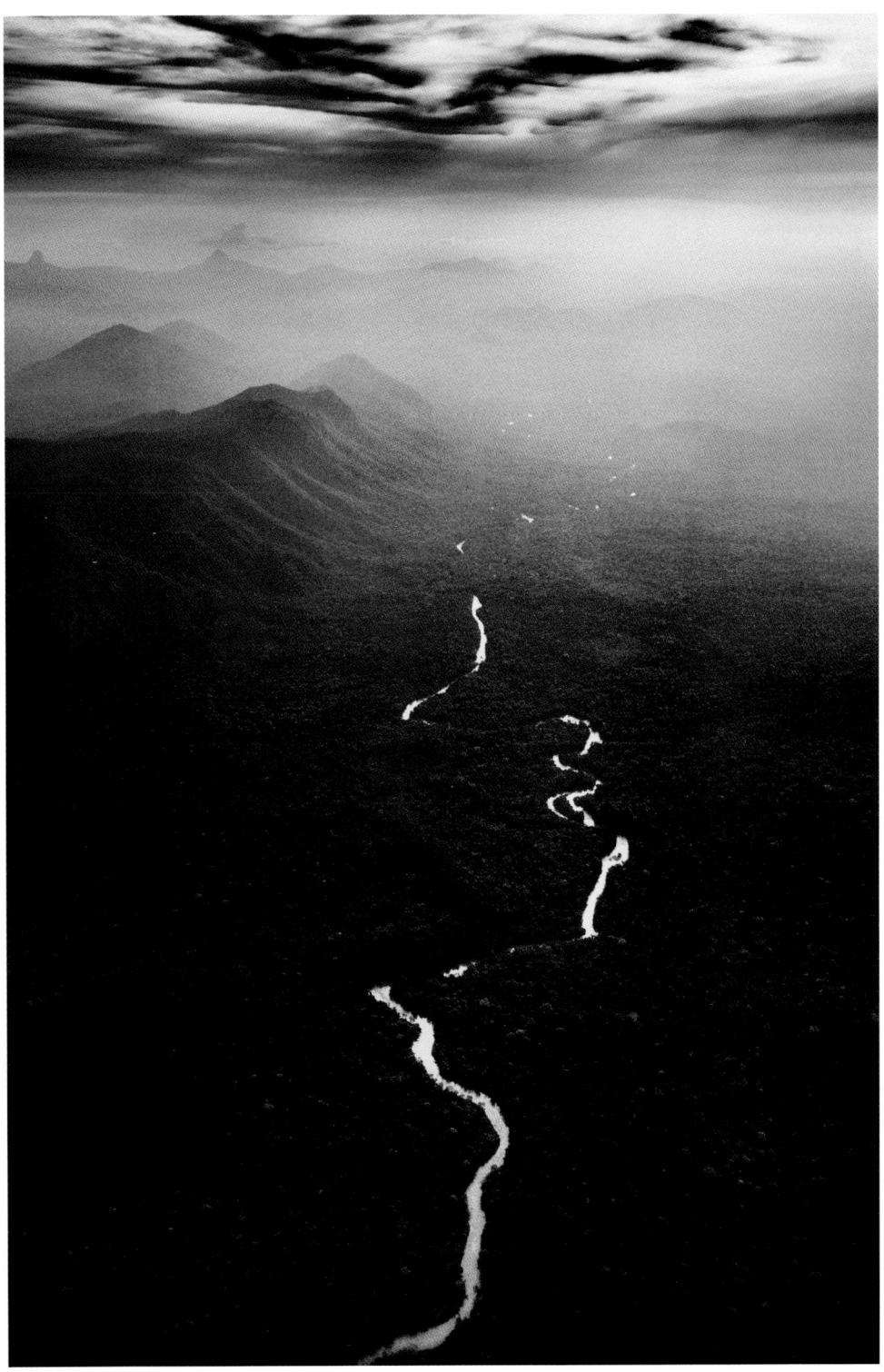

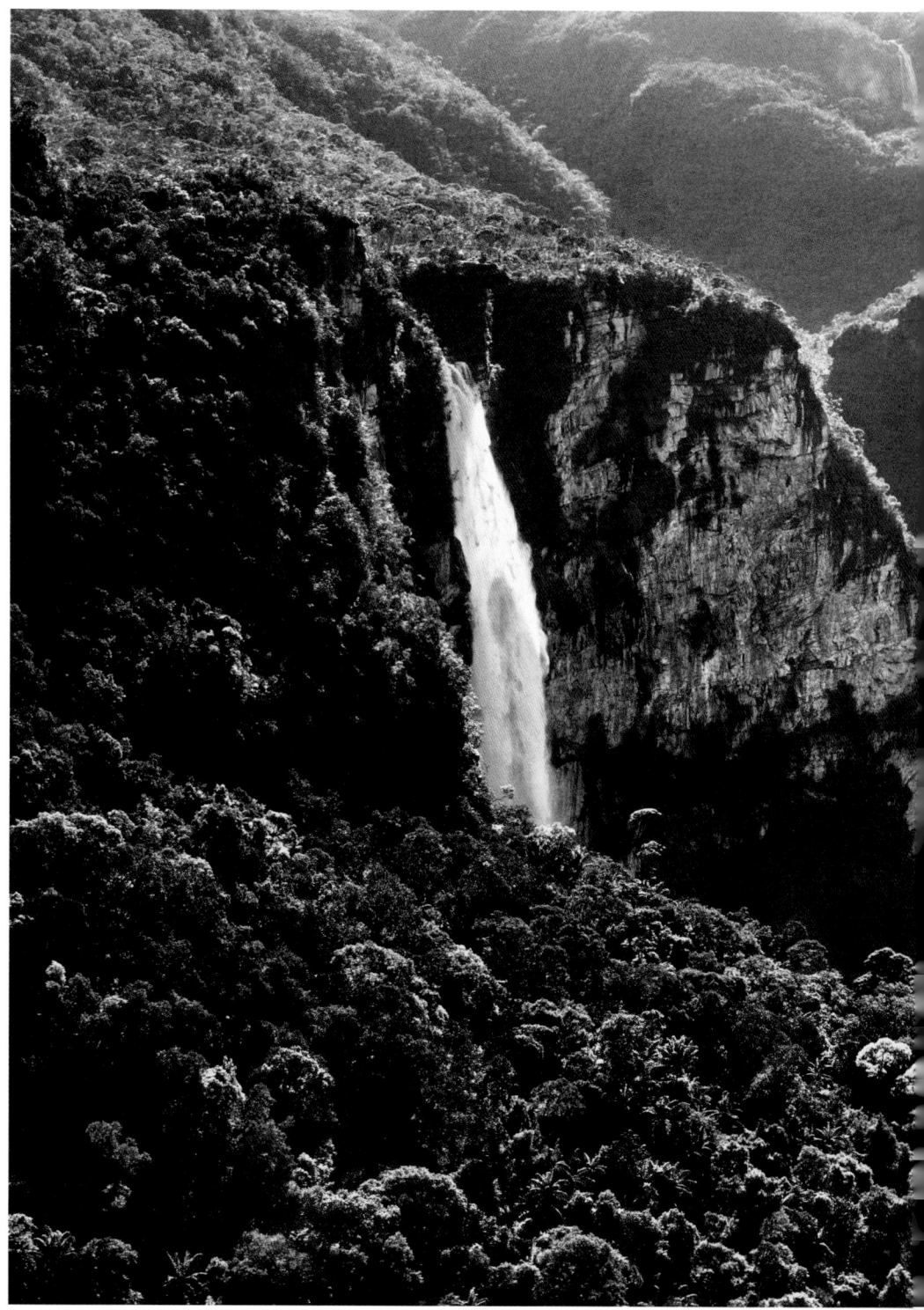

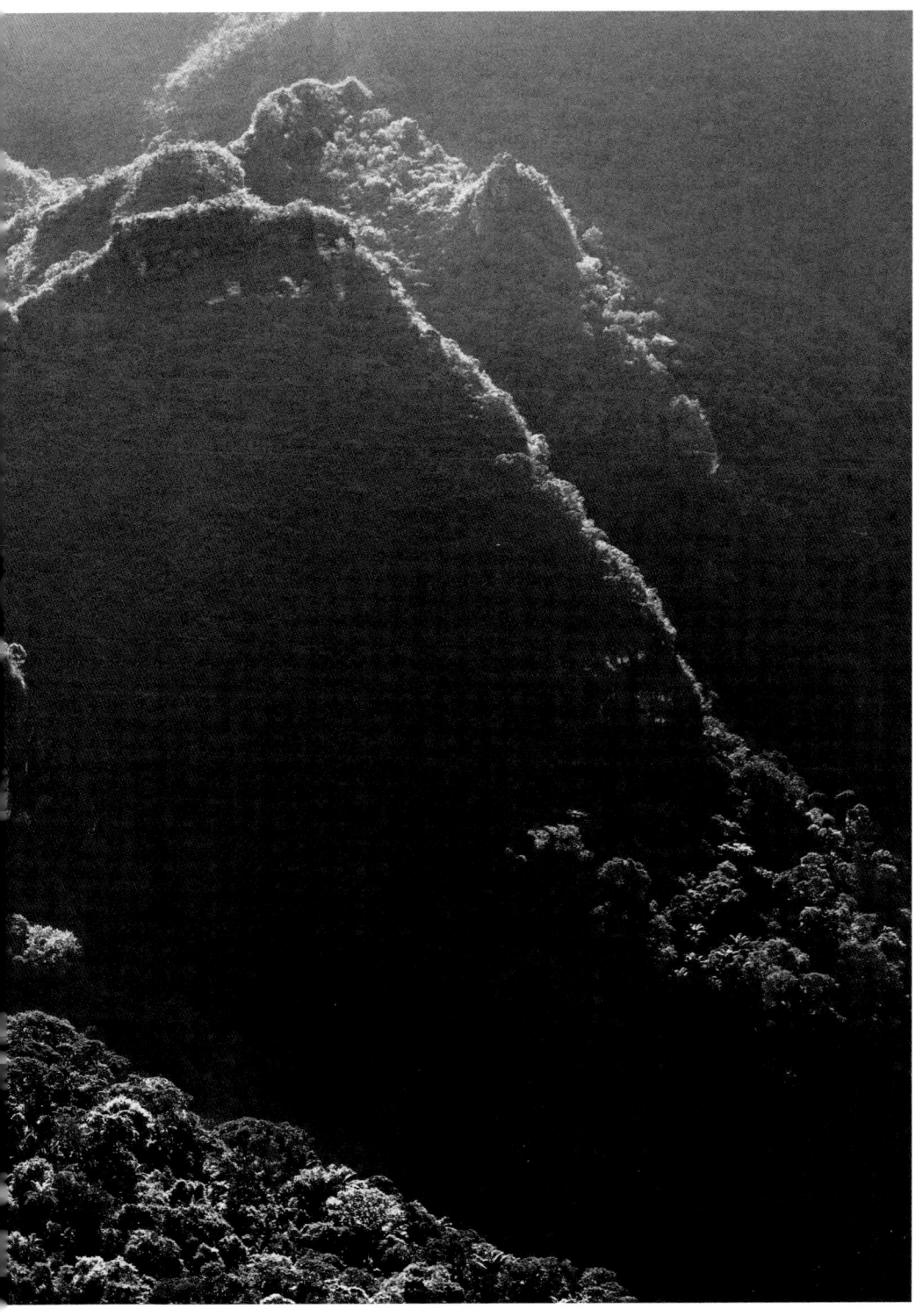

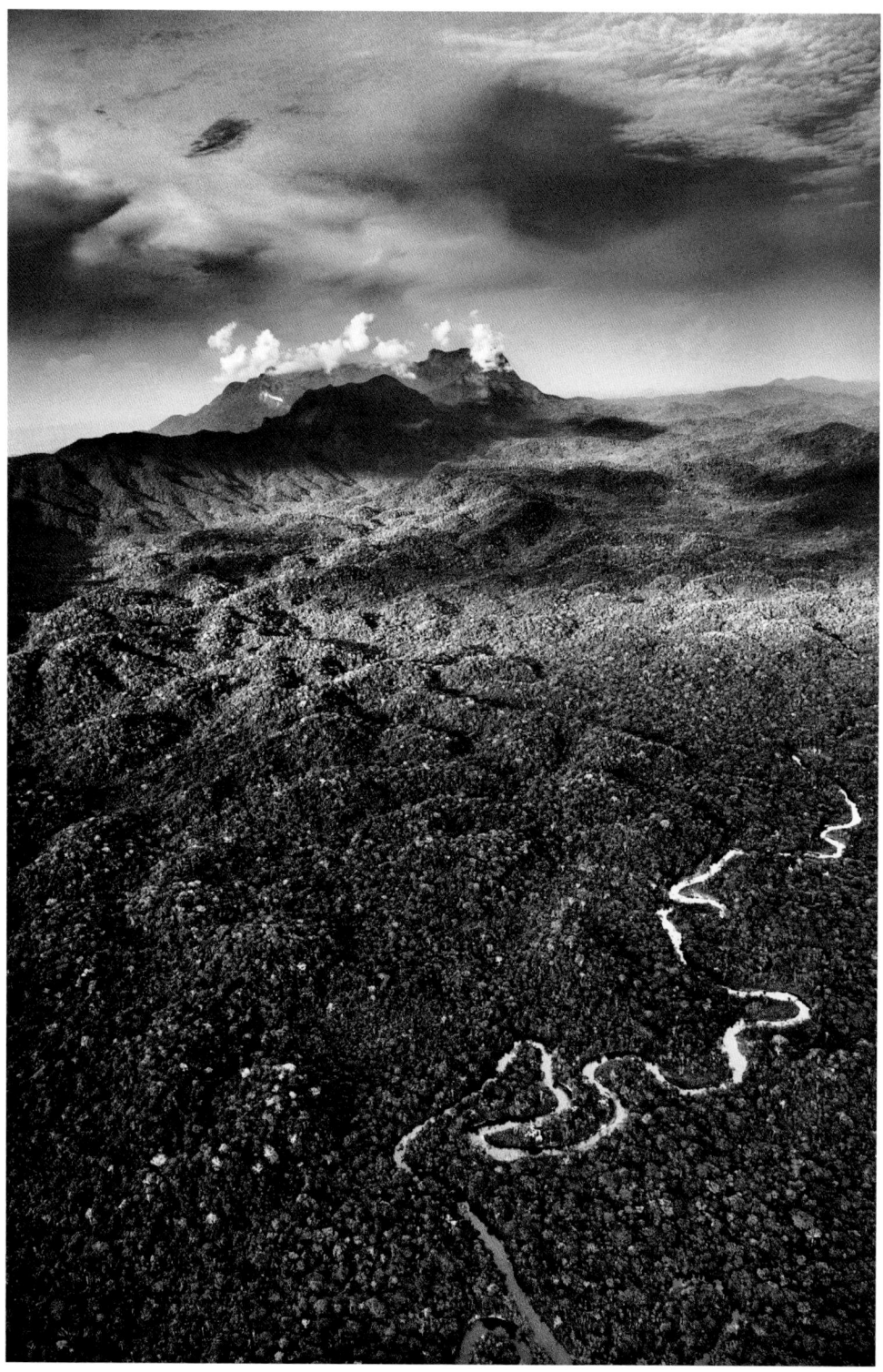

Pages 44/45 Aracá State Park. Desabamento Falls, state of Amazonas, 2019.

Opposite The Maiá River in Pico da Neblina National Park, in the São Gabriel da Cachoeira area. Yanomami Indigenous Territory, state of Amazonas, 2018.

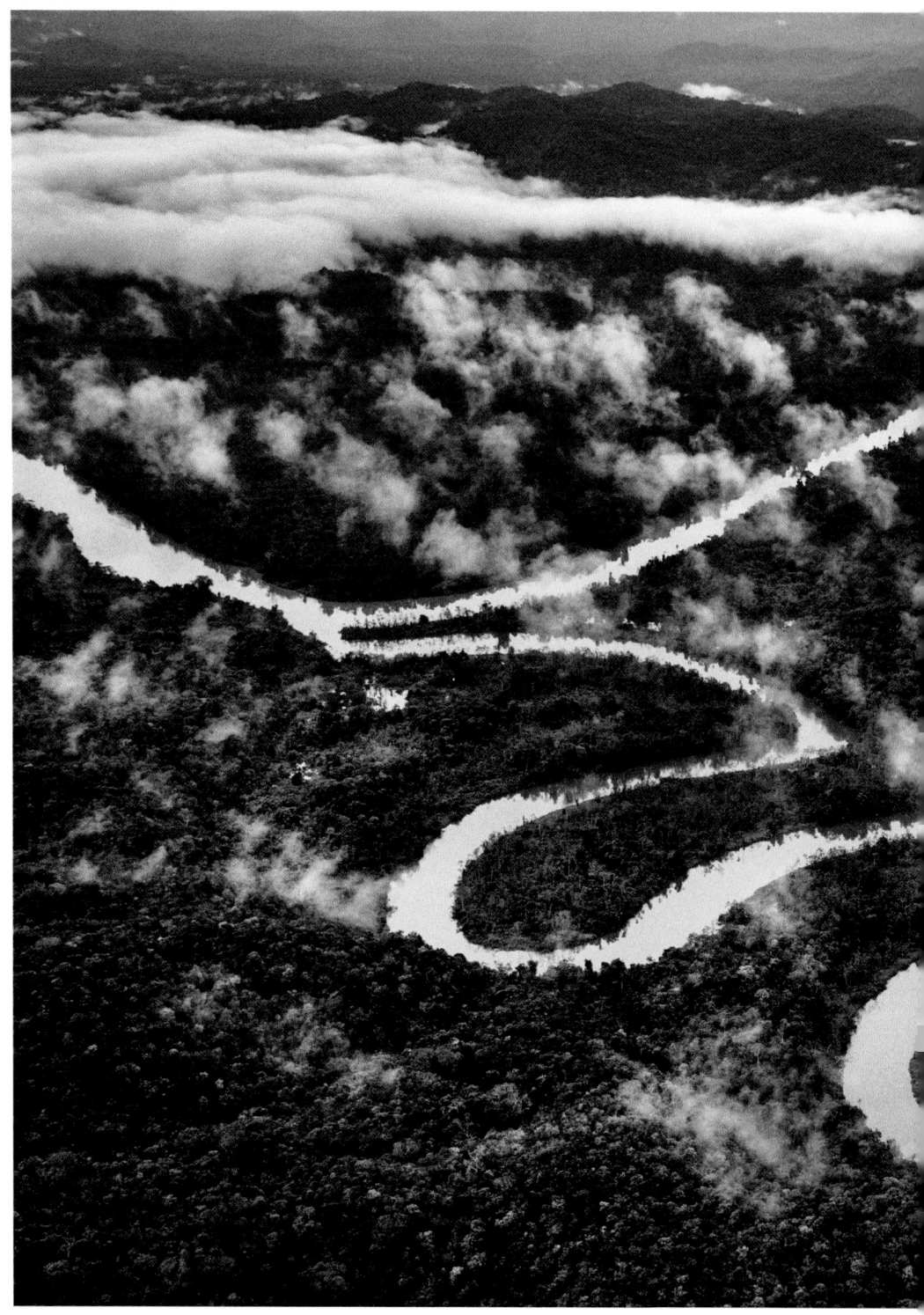

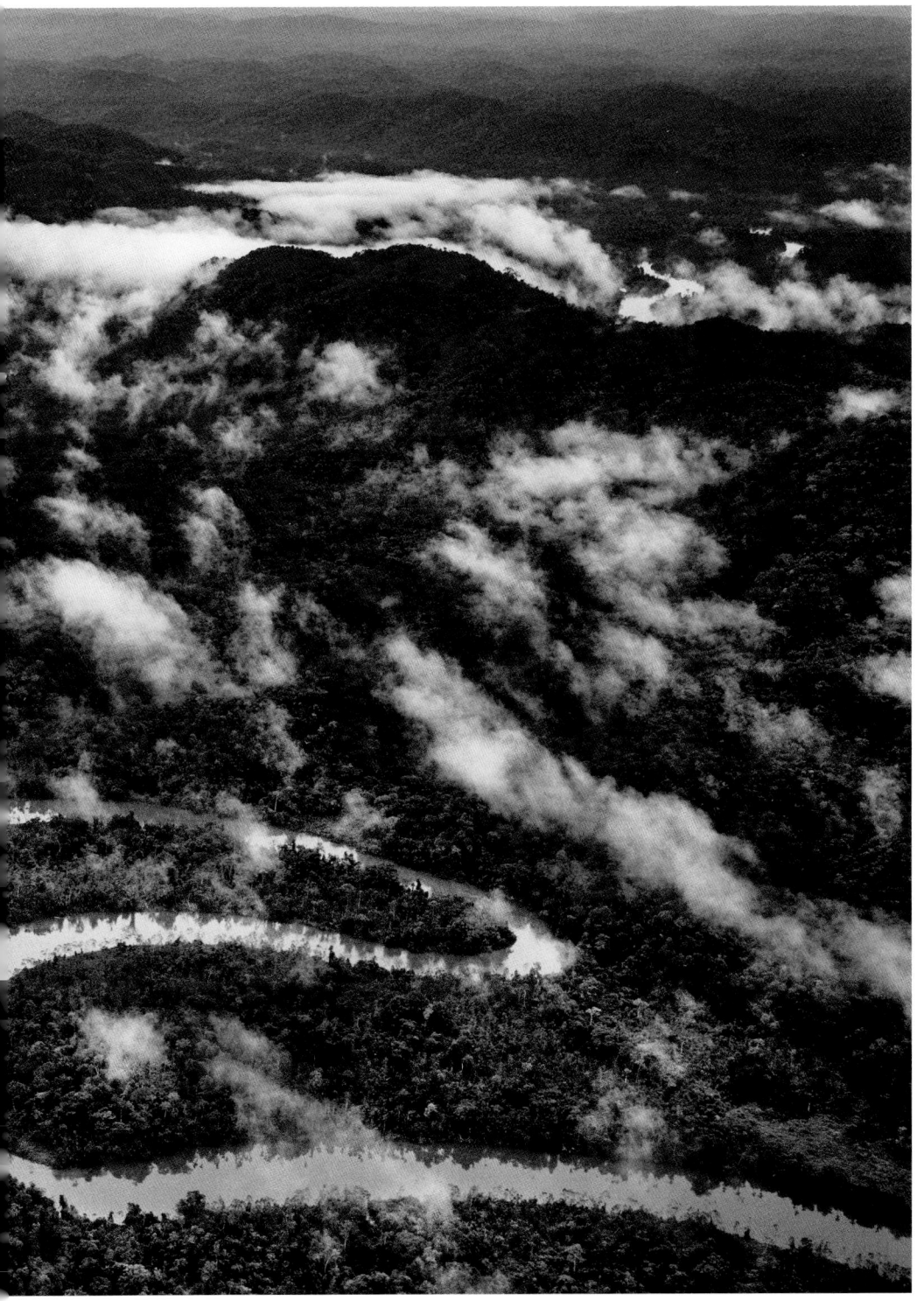

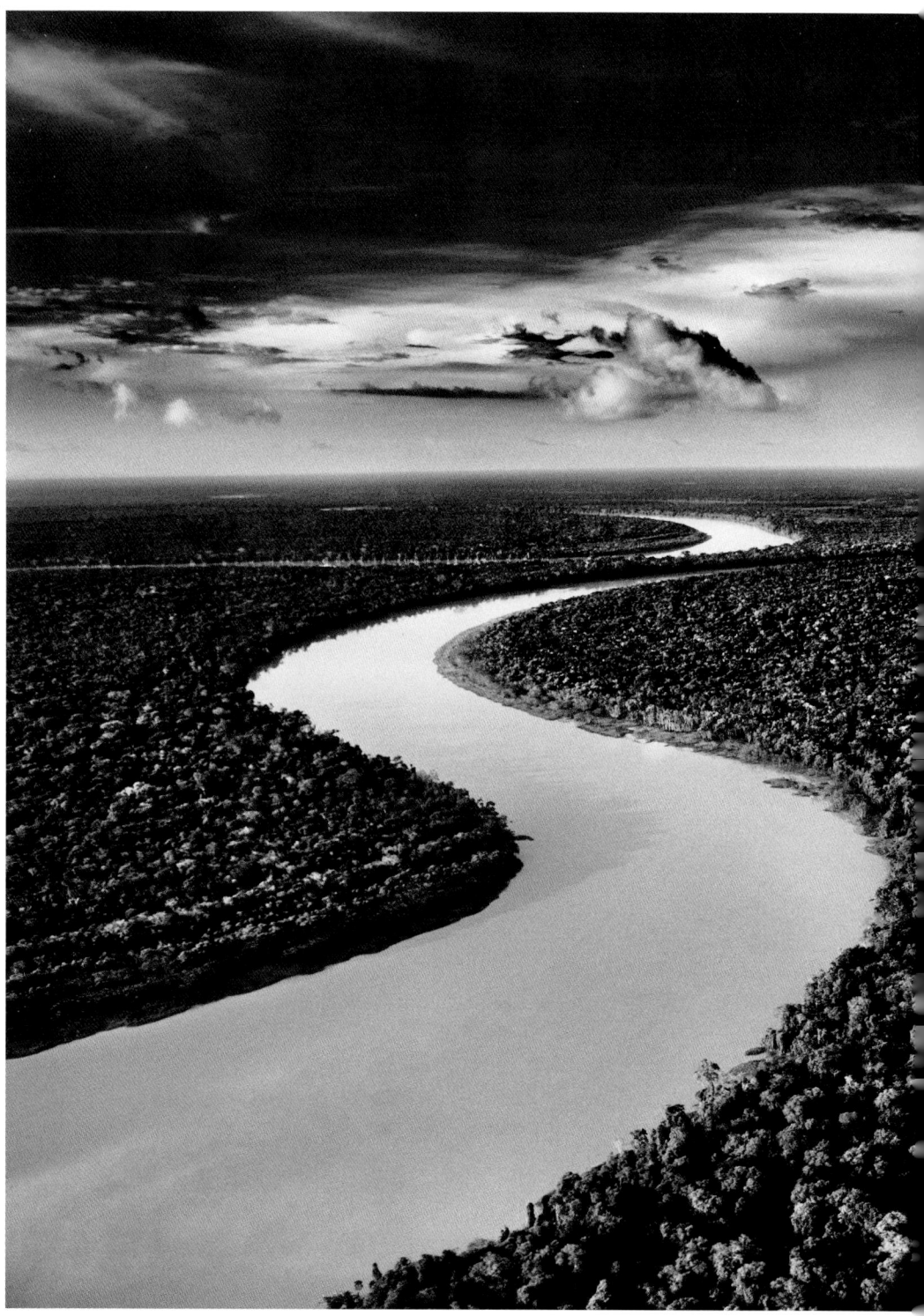

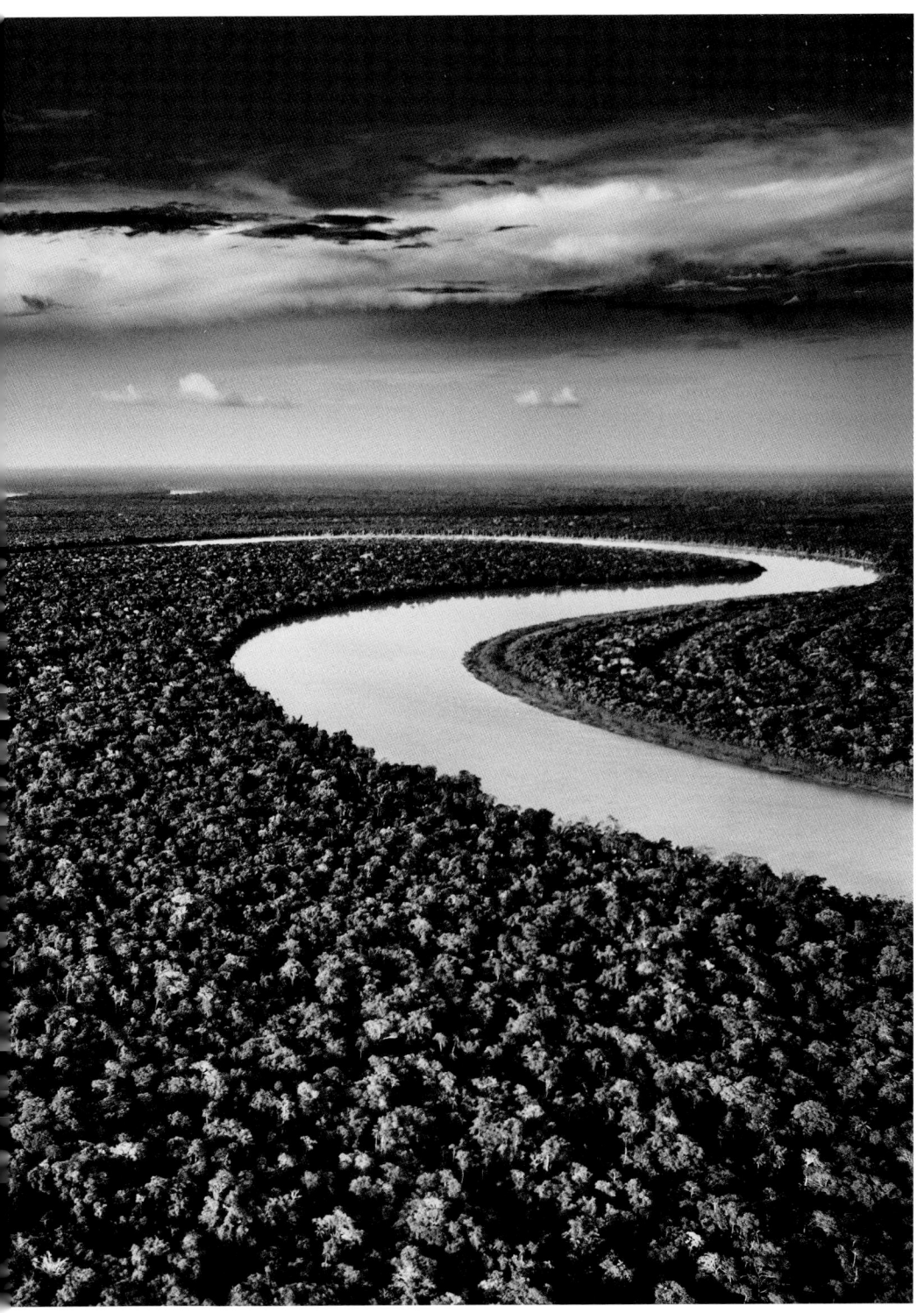

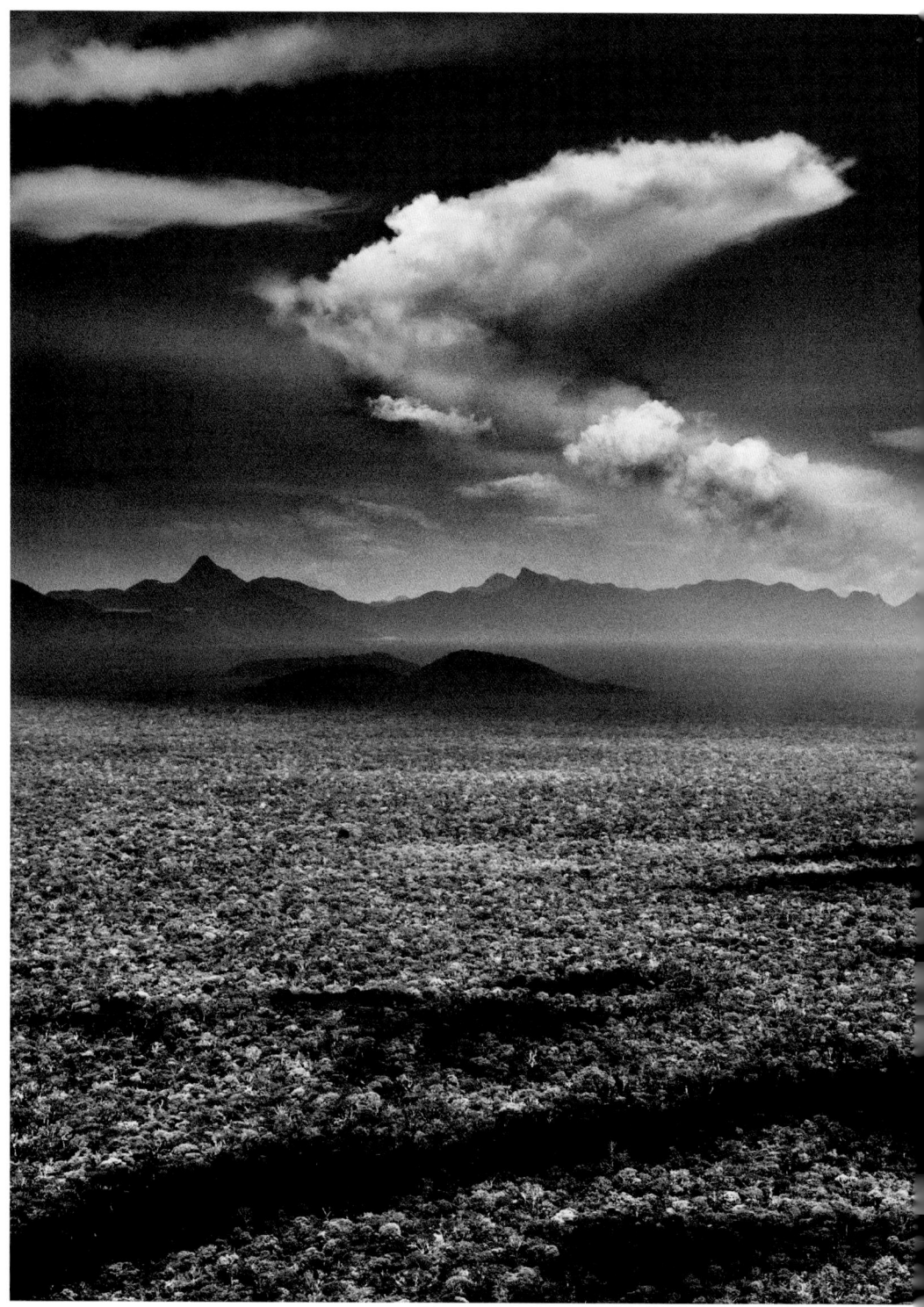

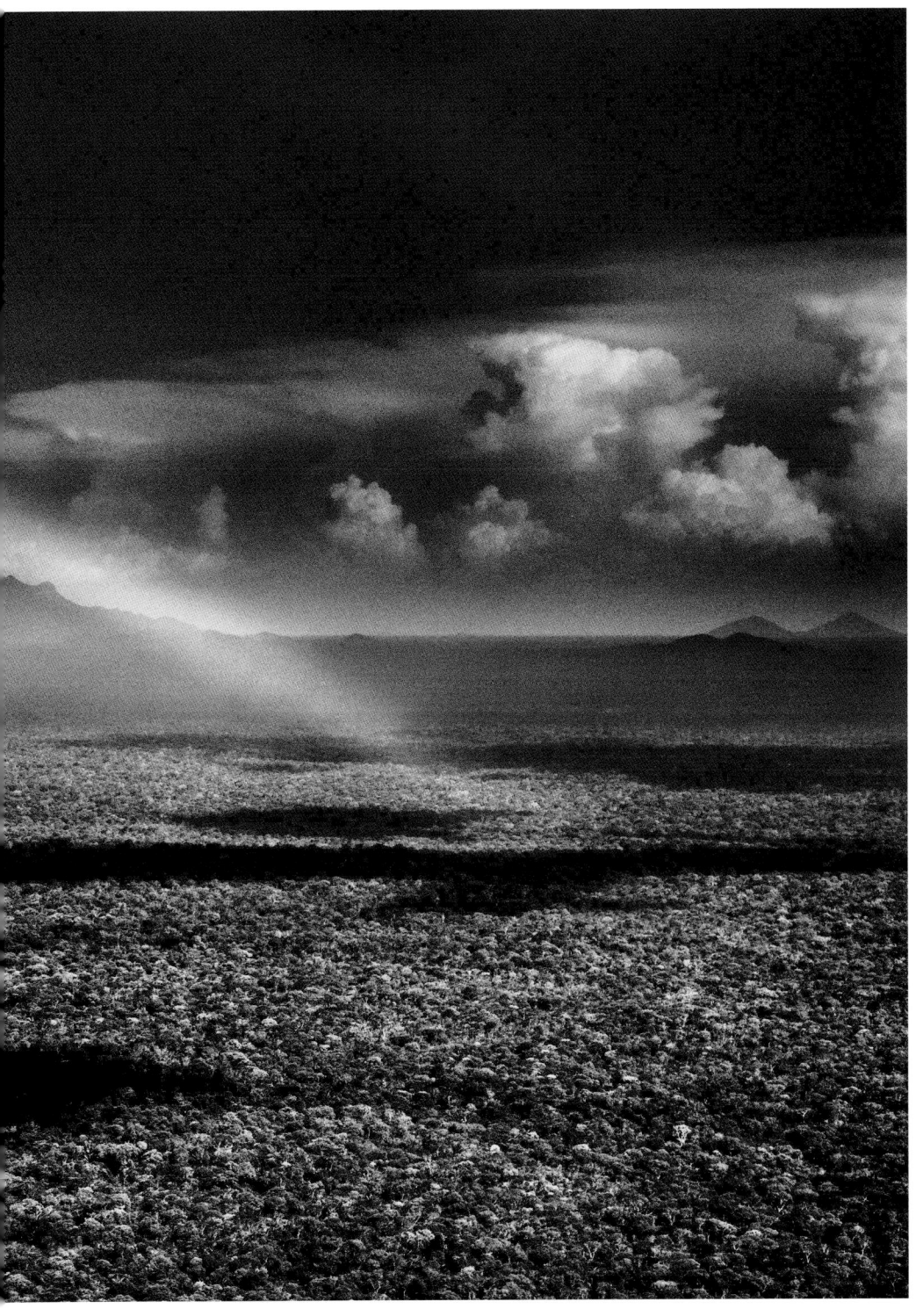

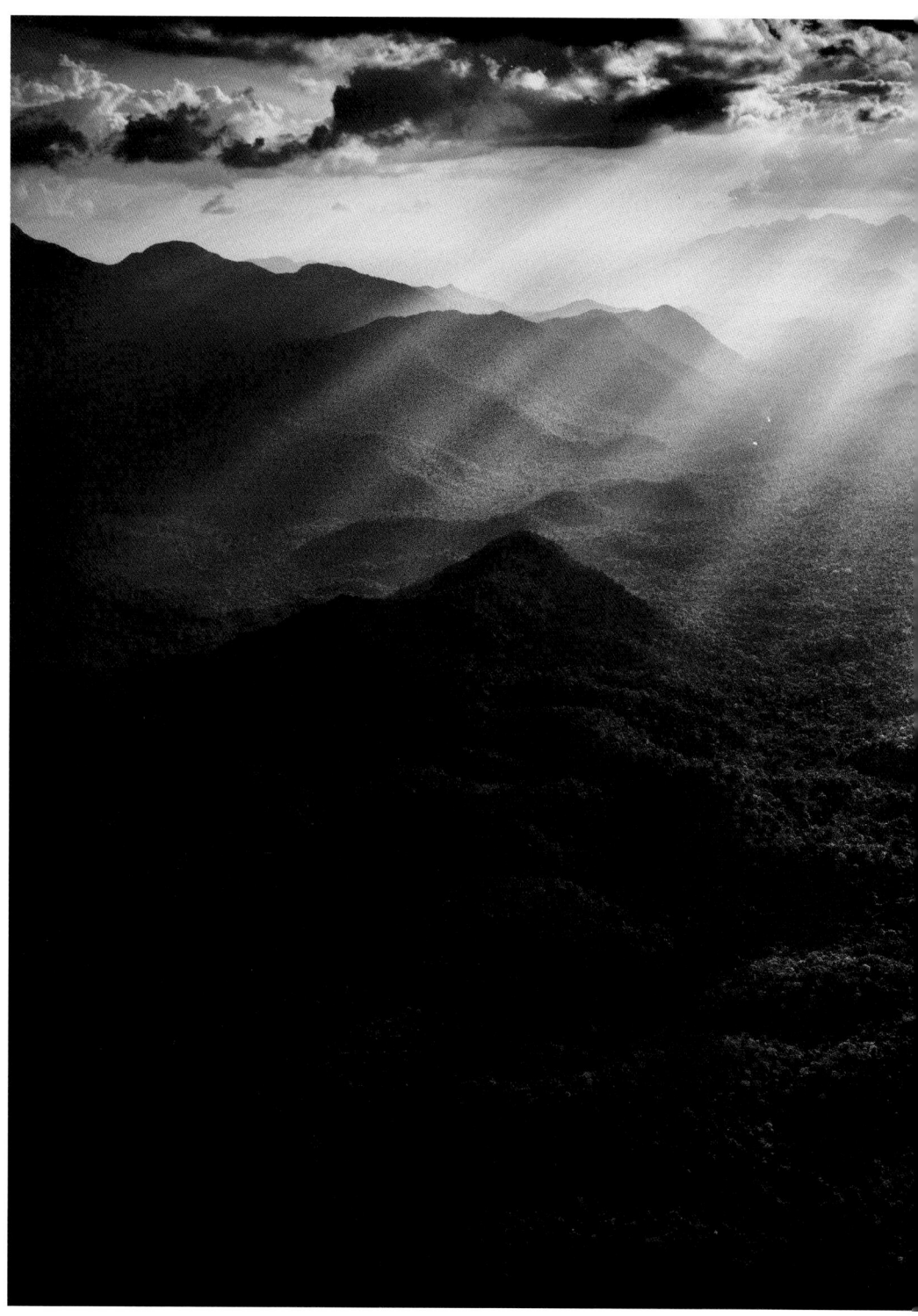

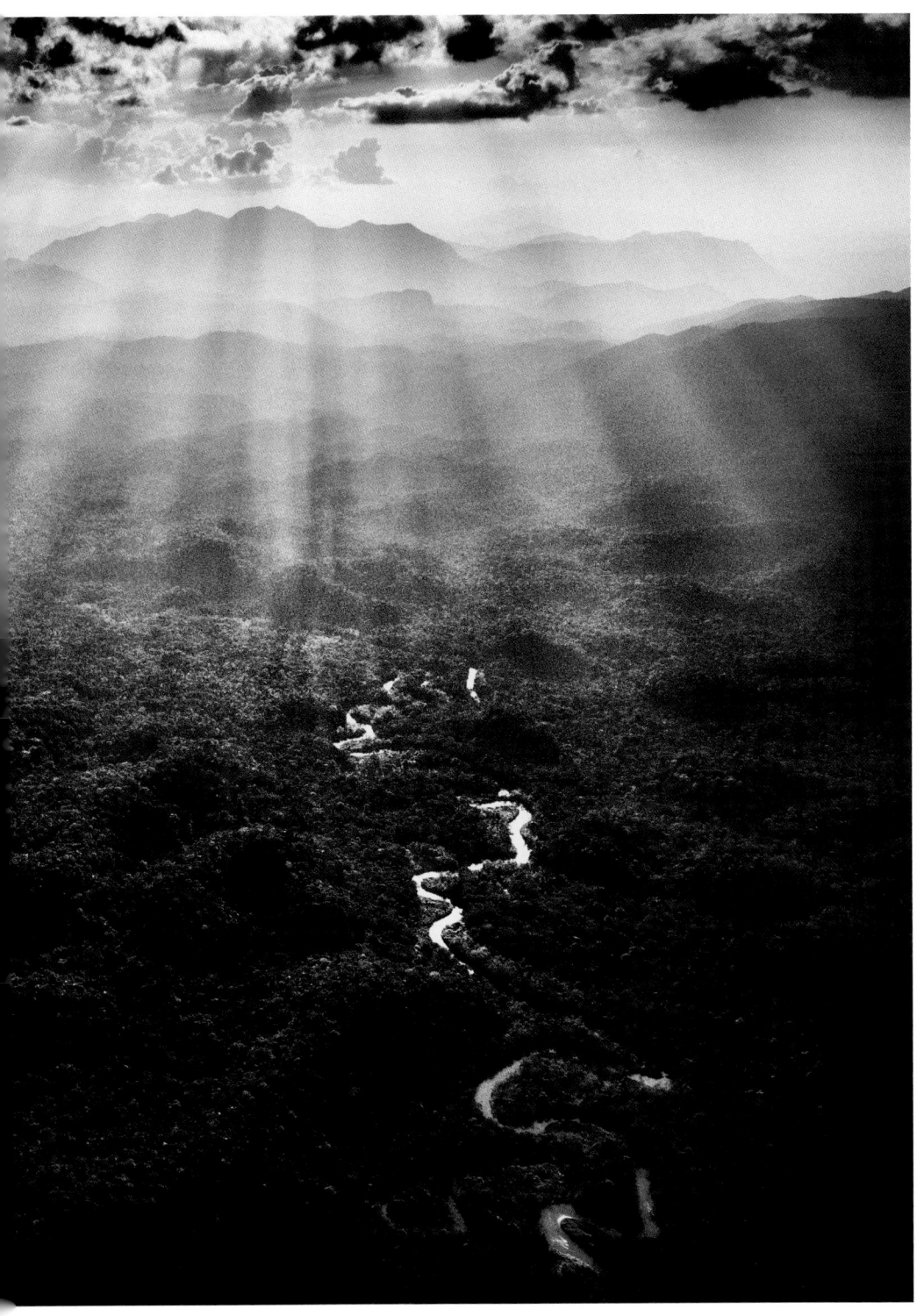

Pages 48/49 The Auaris River starts in the highlands of the Parima mountain range, on the border between Brazil and Venezuela. It snakes down through the Parima Forest Reserve until it flows into the Uraricoera, one of the rivers that form the Rio Branco. Yanomami Indigenous Territory, state of Roraima, 2018.

Pages 50/51 With a length of about 2,400 kilometers (1,500 miles), the Juruá River is one of the Amazon River's longest tributaries. It begins in the mountains of the Ucayali region of Peru before entering the Brazilian state of Acre, and is navigable for 1,800 kilometers (1,120 miles) before joining up with the Solimões River. However, as soon as it enters the flat lowlands known as the Amazon depression, west of Manaus, it becomes restless, swerving left and right to travel a single kilometer. Even with favorable currents, it requires immense patience from any navigator. State of Amazonas, 2009.

Pages 52/53 Balaio region, north of the city of São Gabriel da Cachoeira. Yanomami Indigenous Territory, state of Amazonas, 2018.

Pages 54/55 Imeri mountain range. São Gabriel da Cachoeira area. Yanomami Indigenous Territory, state of Amazonas, 2018.

Opposite Serra Urutanin Falls, Parima Forest Reserve. Yanomami Indigenous Territory, state of Roraima, 2018.

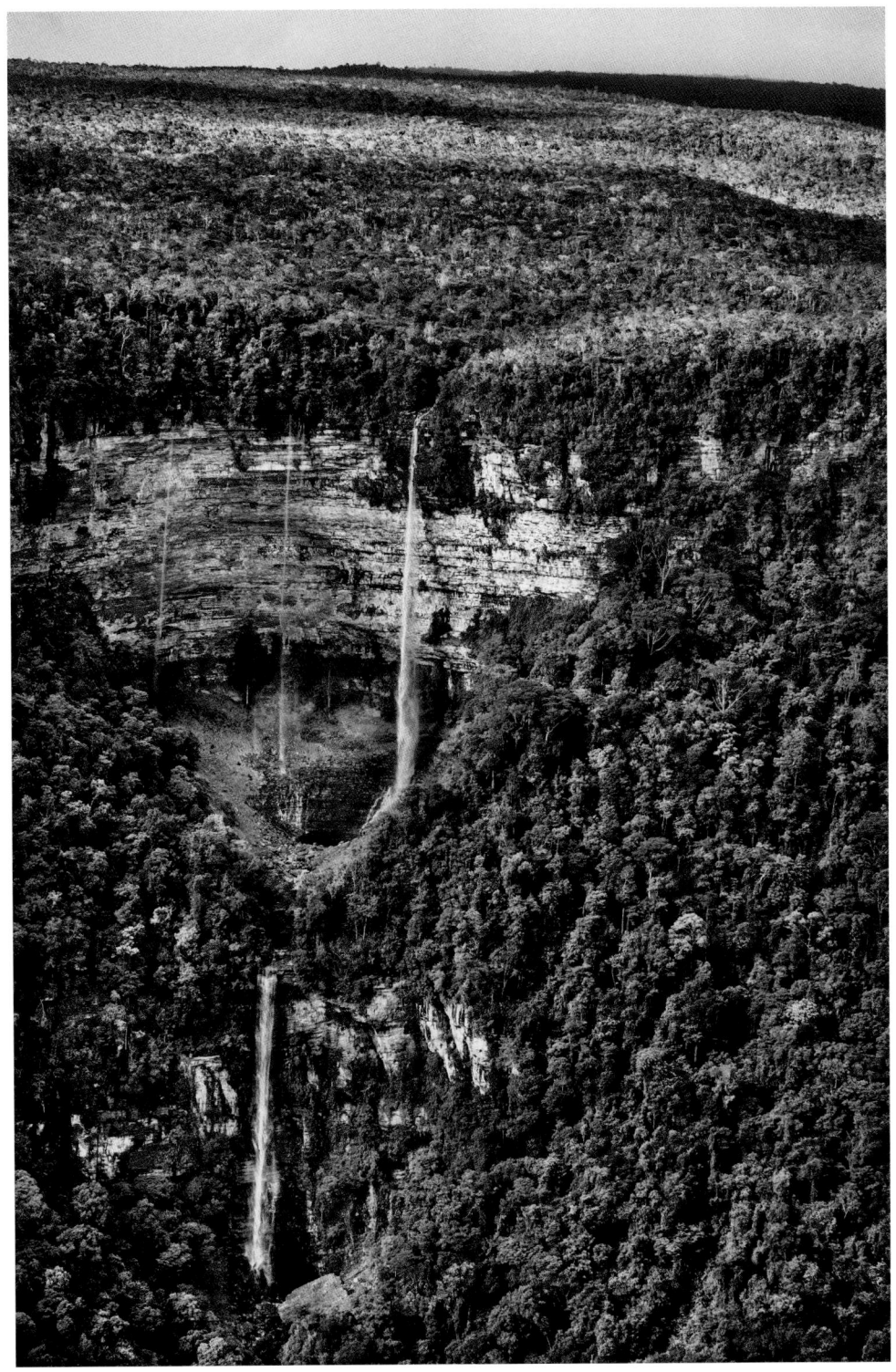

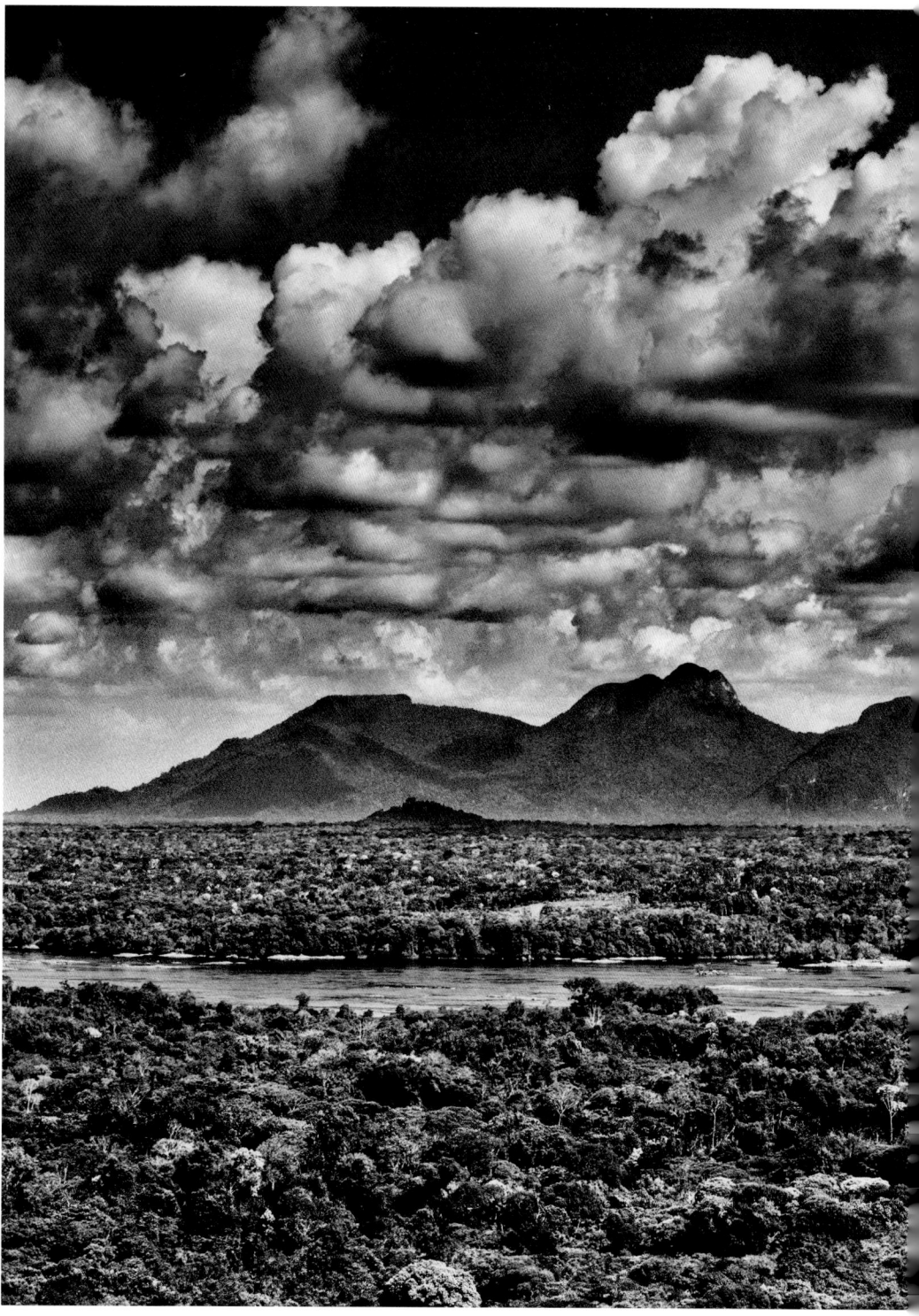

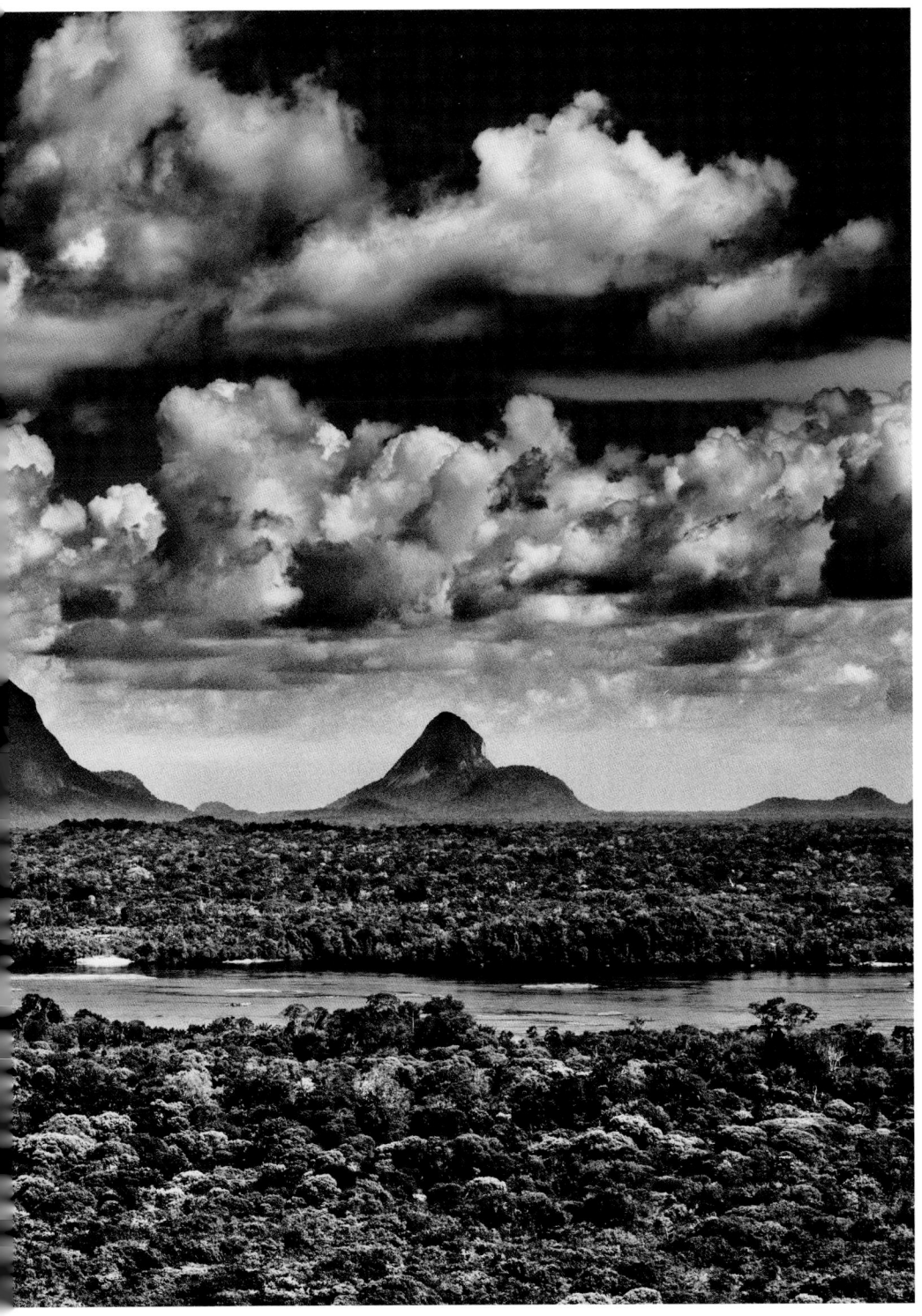

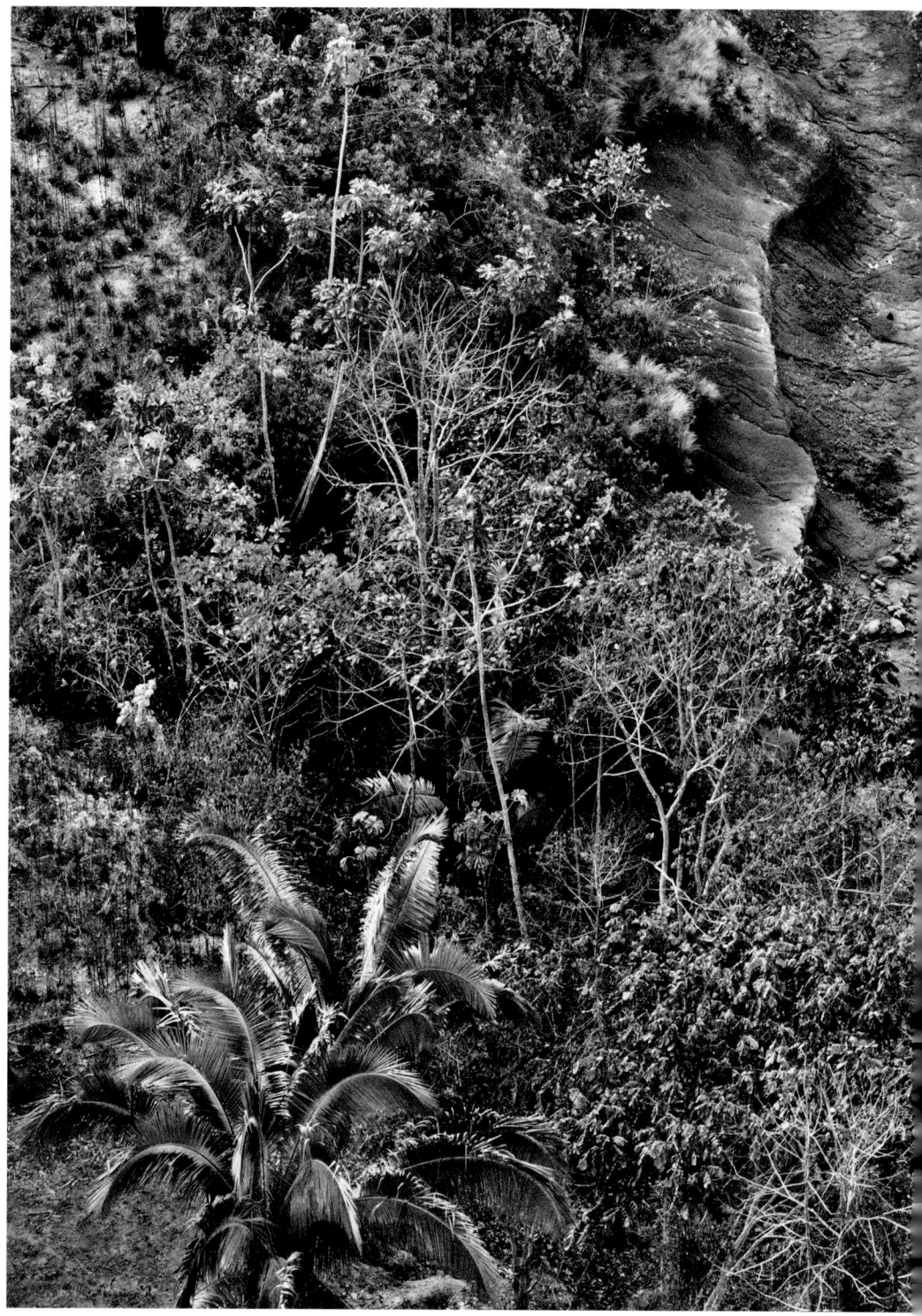

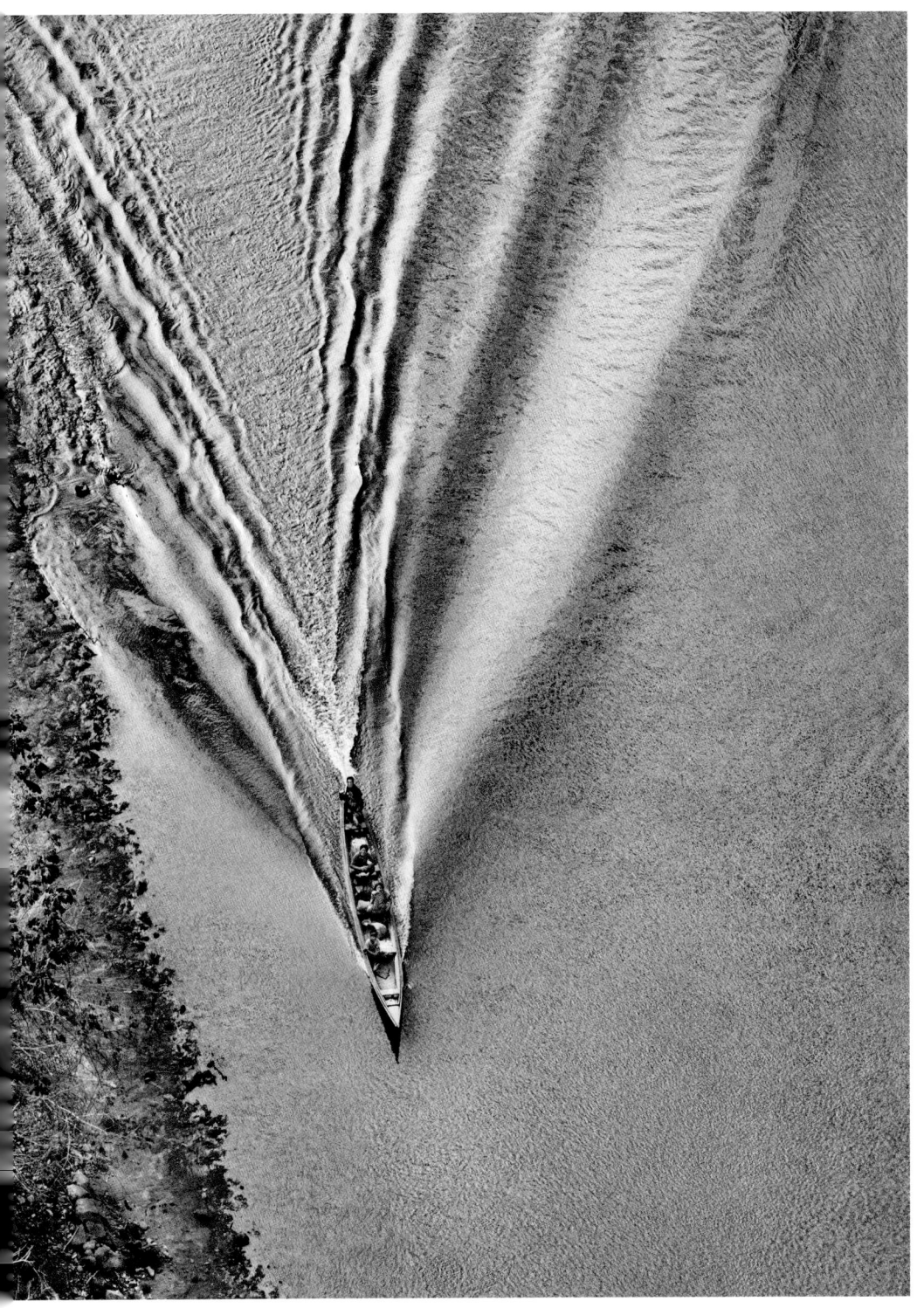

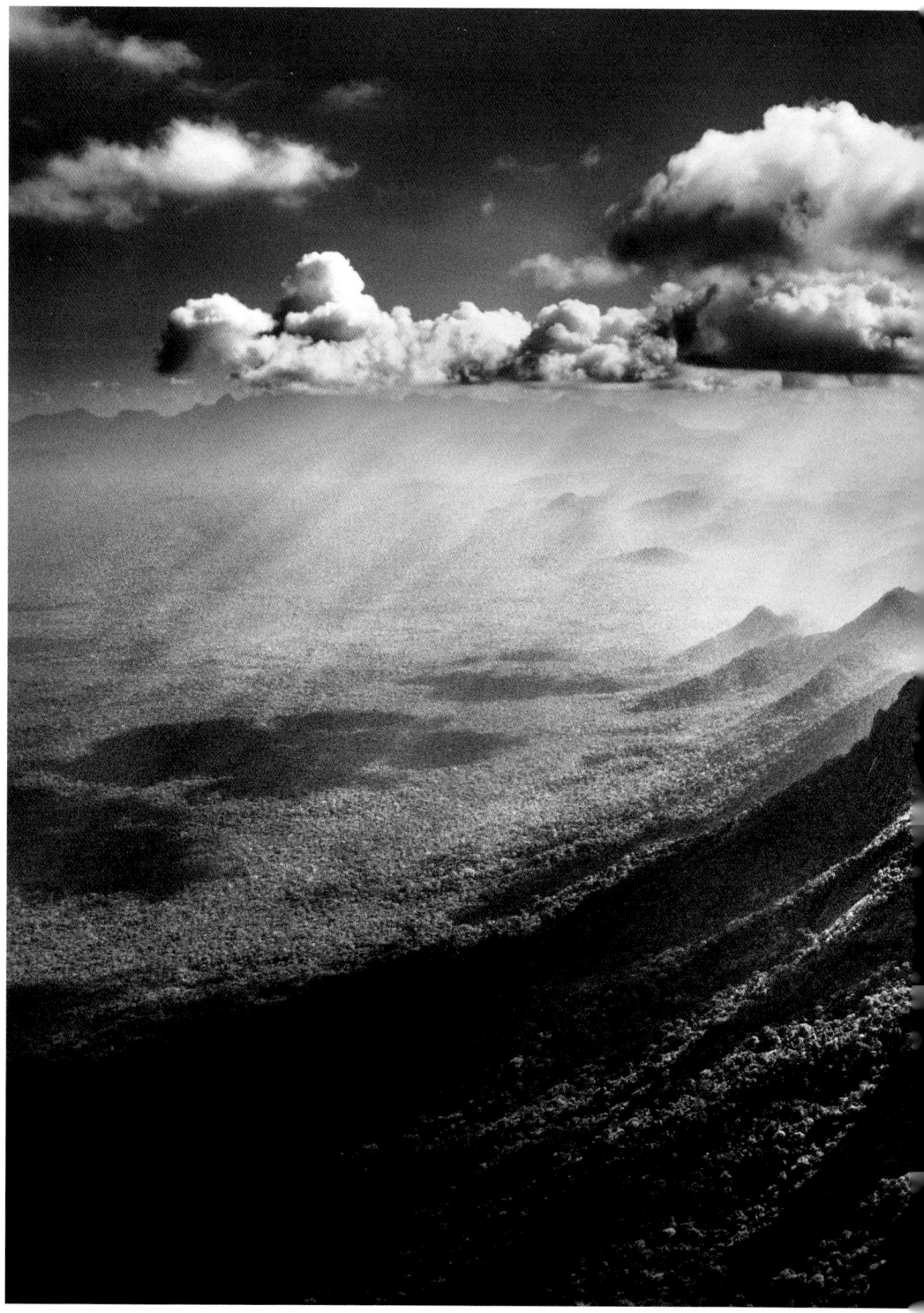

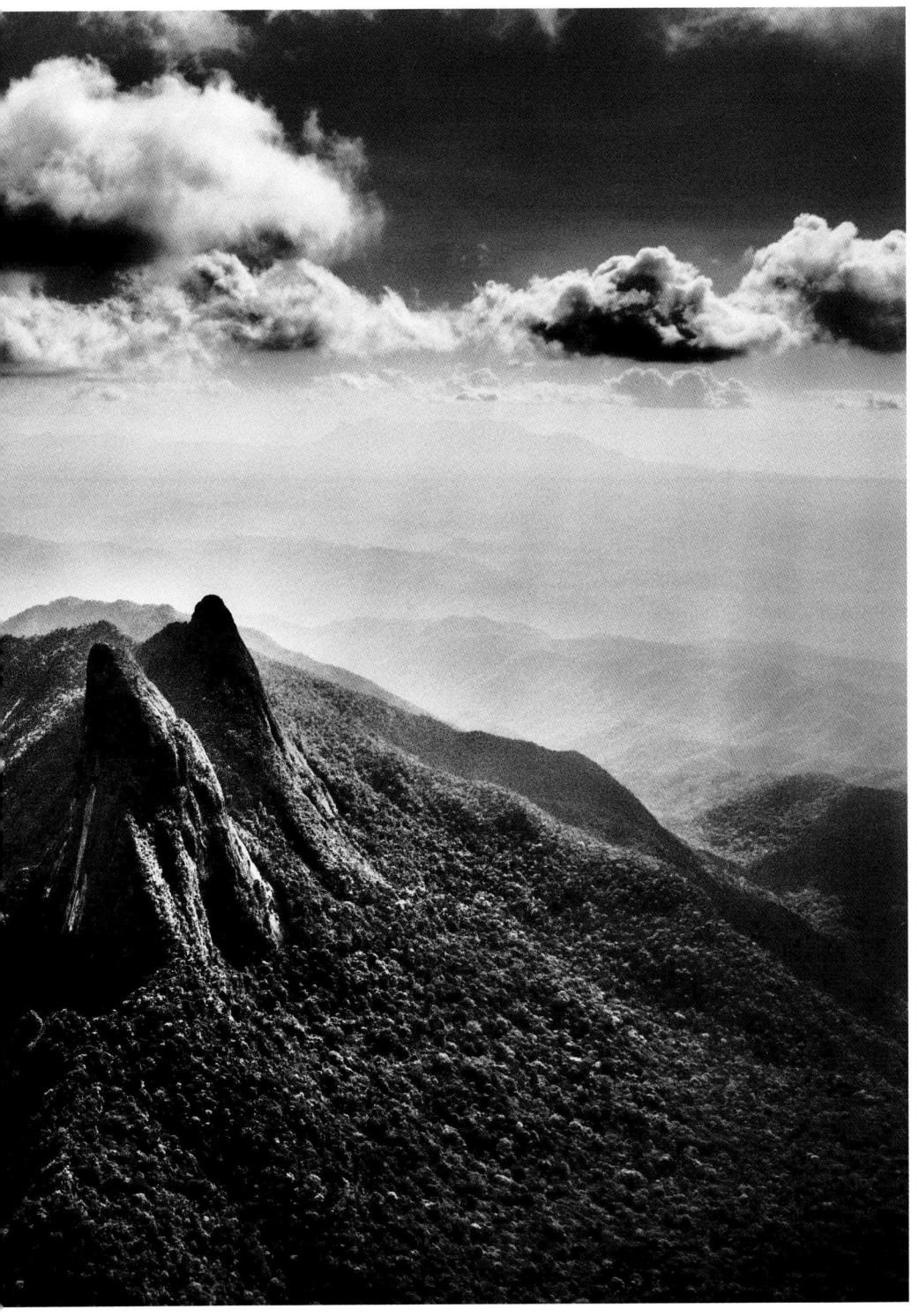

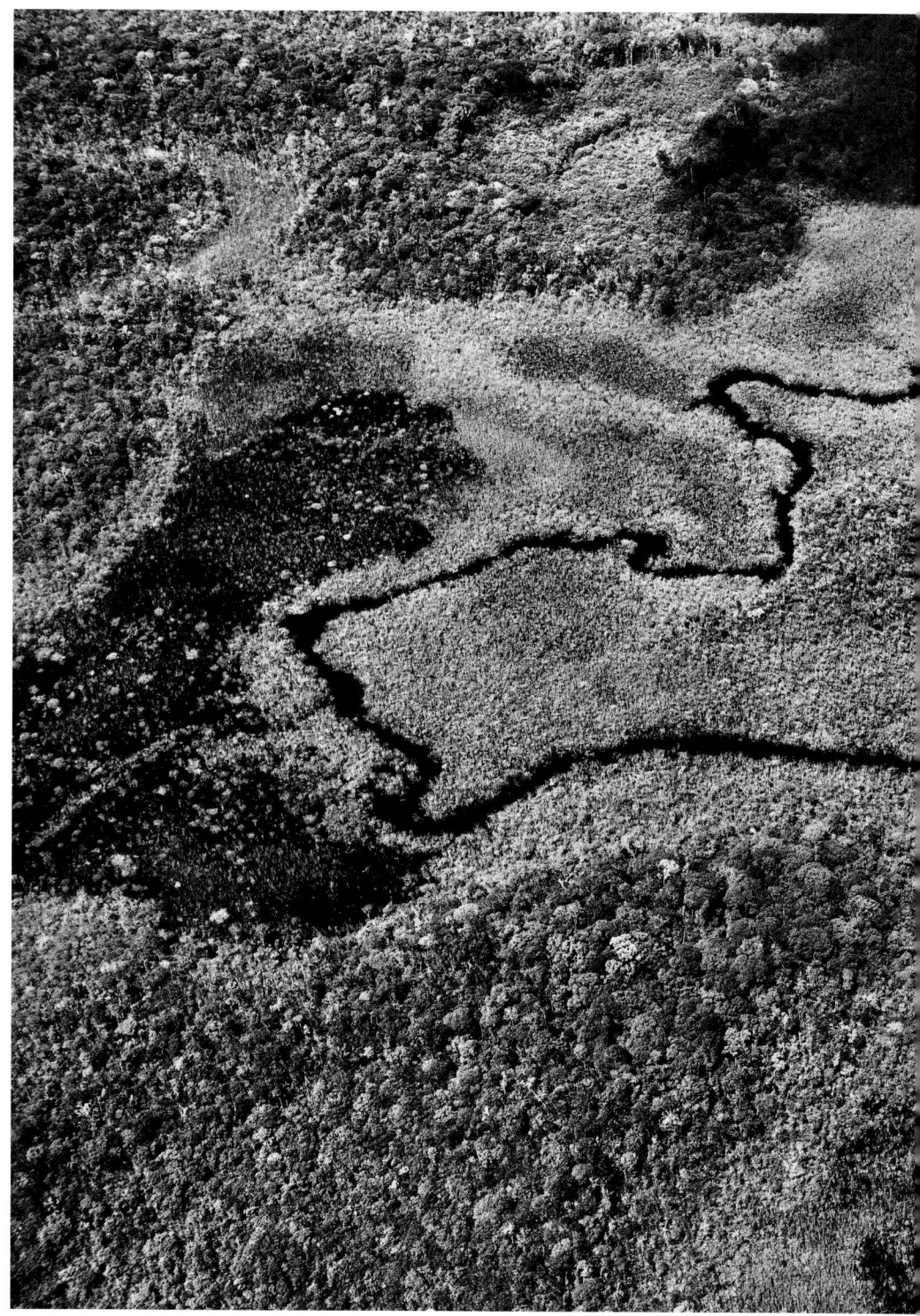

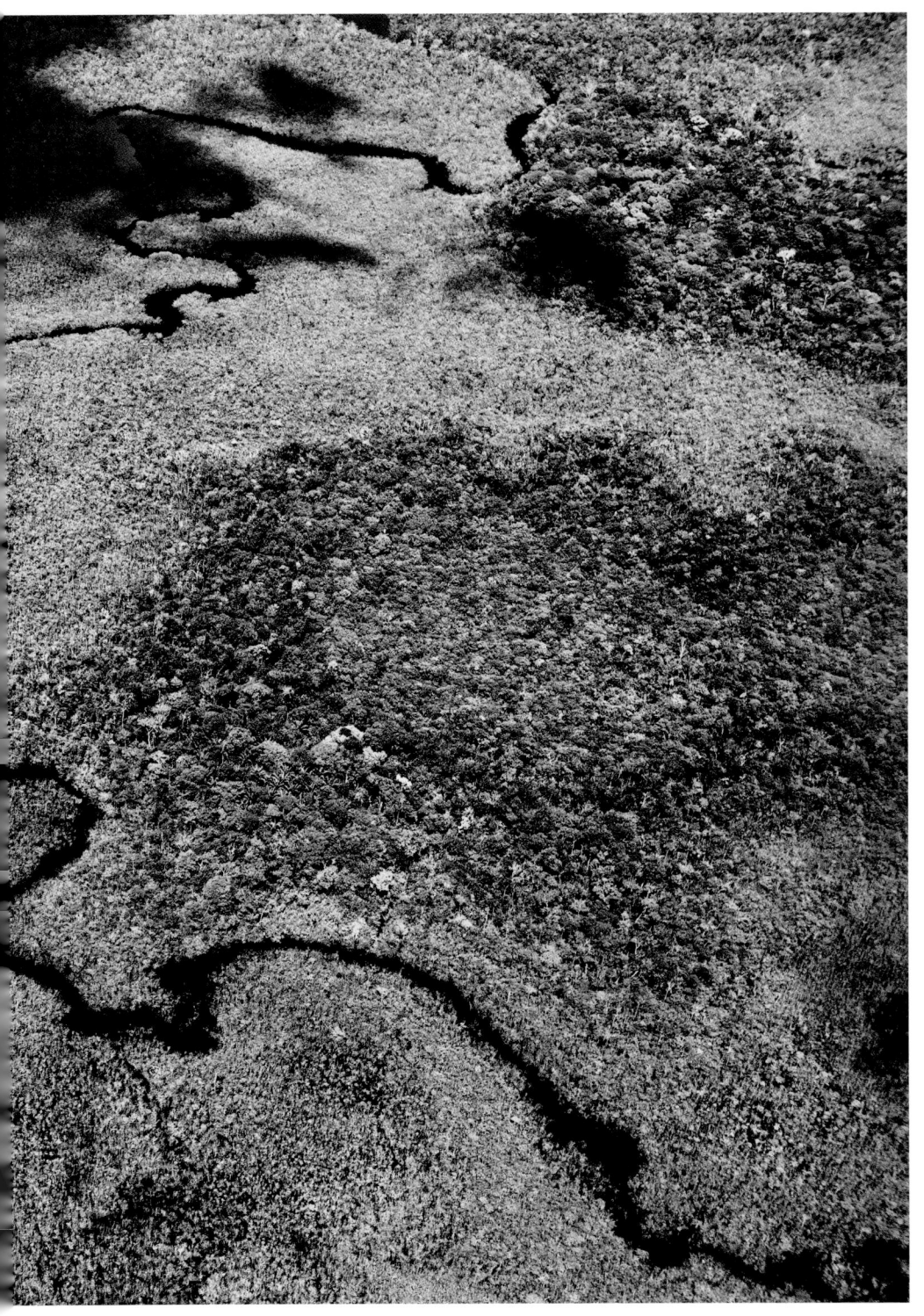

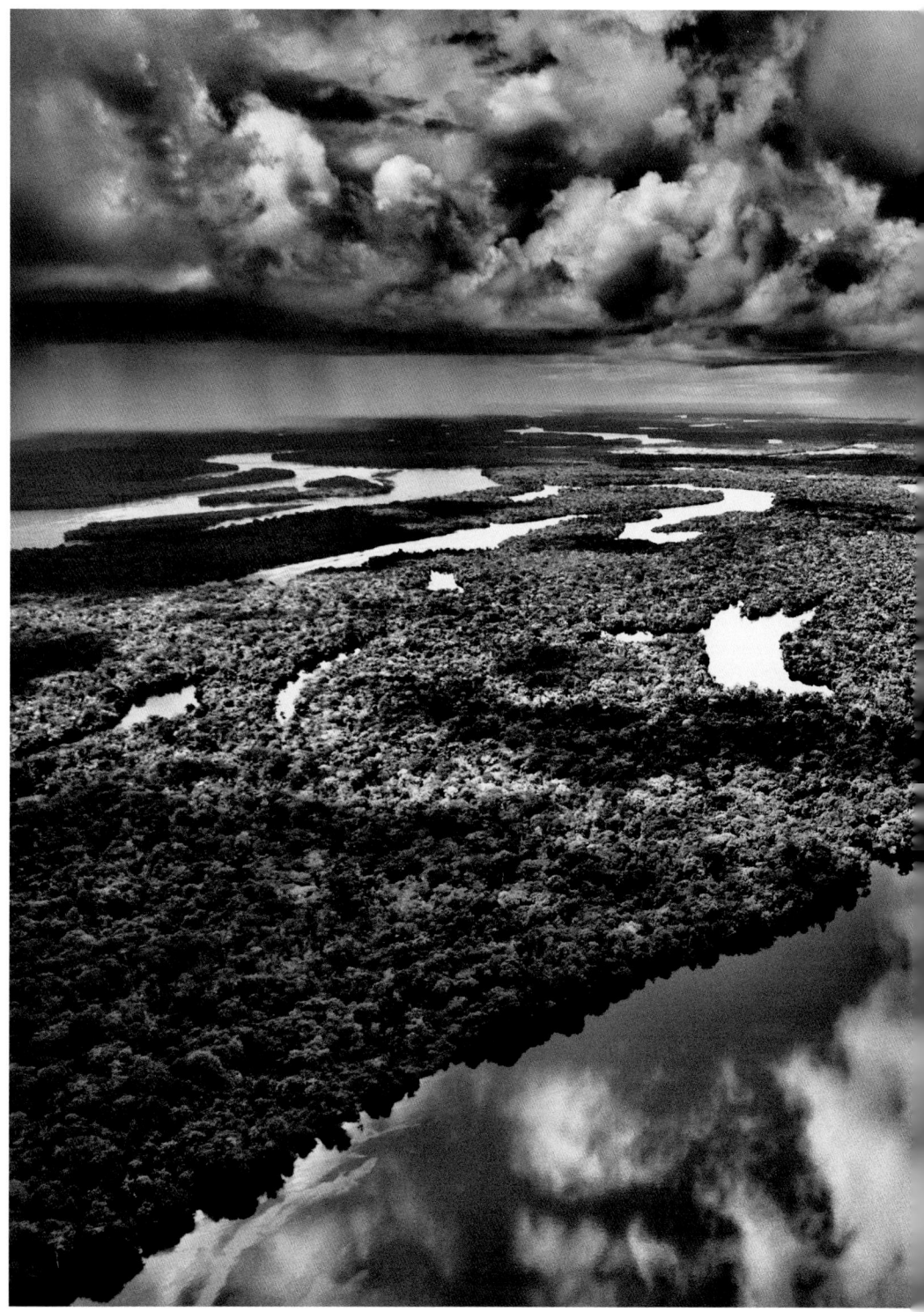

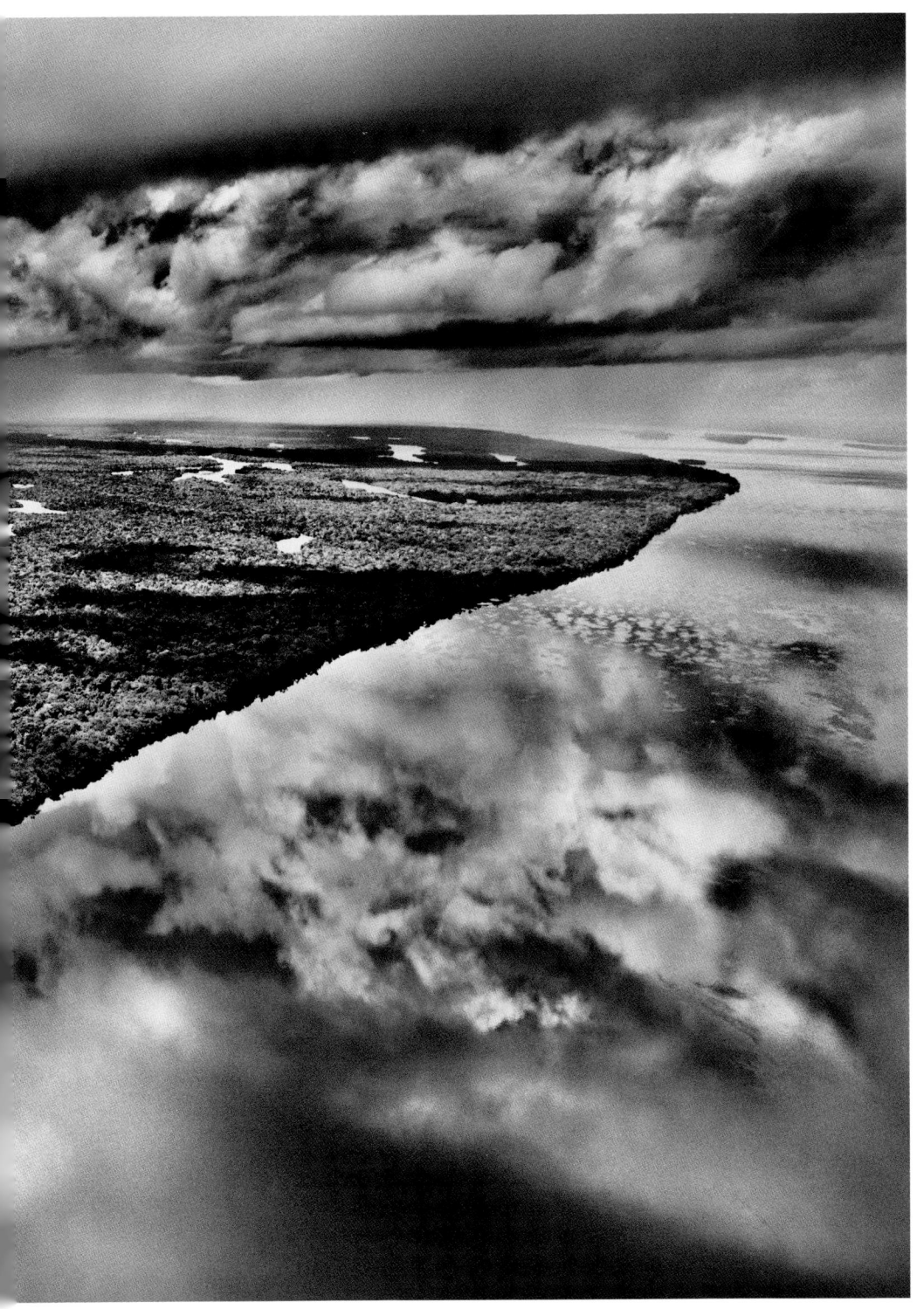

Pages 58/59 The Rio Negro in the foreground and a view of the "Sleeping Beauty Mountains" (as the Curicuriari mountain range is called locally), south of São Gabriel da Cachoeira, state of Amazonas, 2009.

Pages 60/61 Gregório River, state of Acre, 2016.

Pages 62/63 The Guimarães Rosa Peak, elevation 2,105 meters (about 6,900 feet), is part of the Imeri mountain range. The range formed about 65 million years ago when part of the Earth's crust rose in the region to form peaks or inselbergs (mountains that look like islands sprouting up from the forest). Yanomami Indigenous Territory, state of Amazonas, 2018.

Pages 64/65 Wetland along the Cuyuní River: vegetation masks a flooded area that the explorer/traveler Alexander von Humboldt described as a "gulf." Right bank of the Rio Negro, Barcelos region, state of Amazonas, 2009.

Pages 66/67 The Rio Negro is the world's largest blackwater river. Its sources are found in Venezuela and to the west in Colombia, where its water springs from the northern Andes. State of Amazonas, 2019.

Opposite The "Meeting of Waters" is the name given to the place where the black water of the Rio Negro meets the denser muddy water of the Solimões River. Here they merge and together they form the Amazon River, for the Brazilians. Because of the different density and temperature of the two flows, their waters run side by side for several kilometers as they mix together gradually. Manaus, state of Amazonas, 2019.

Pages 70/71 The Arauató *paraná* is connected to the Amazon River by a canal, creating an image of two parallel rivers. In Portuguese, *paranás* are lake-like bodies of water connected to major rivers by canals called *furos* (punctures). During floods, the two often merge as if the river were widening. The Arauató connects to the Amazon in the Itacoatiara area. State of Amazonas, 2009.

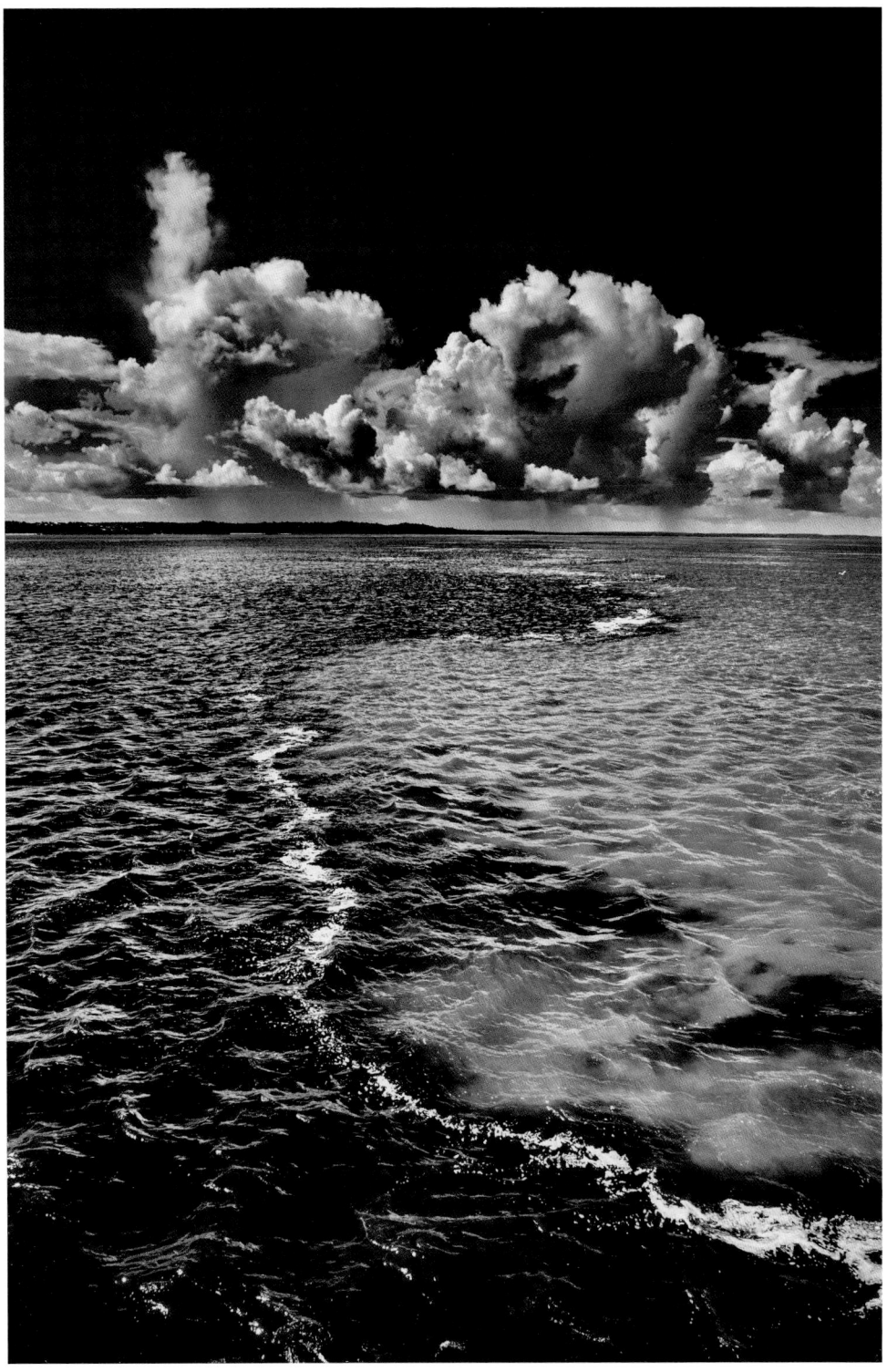

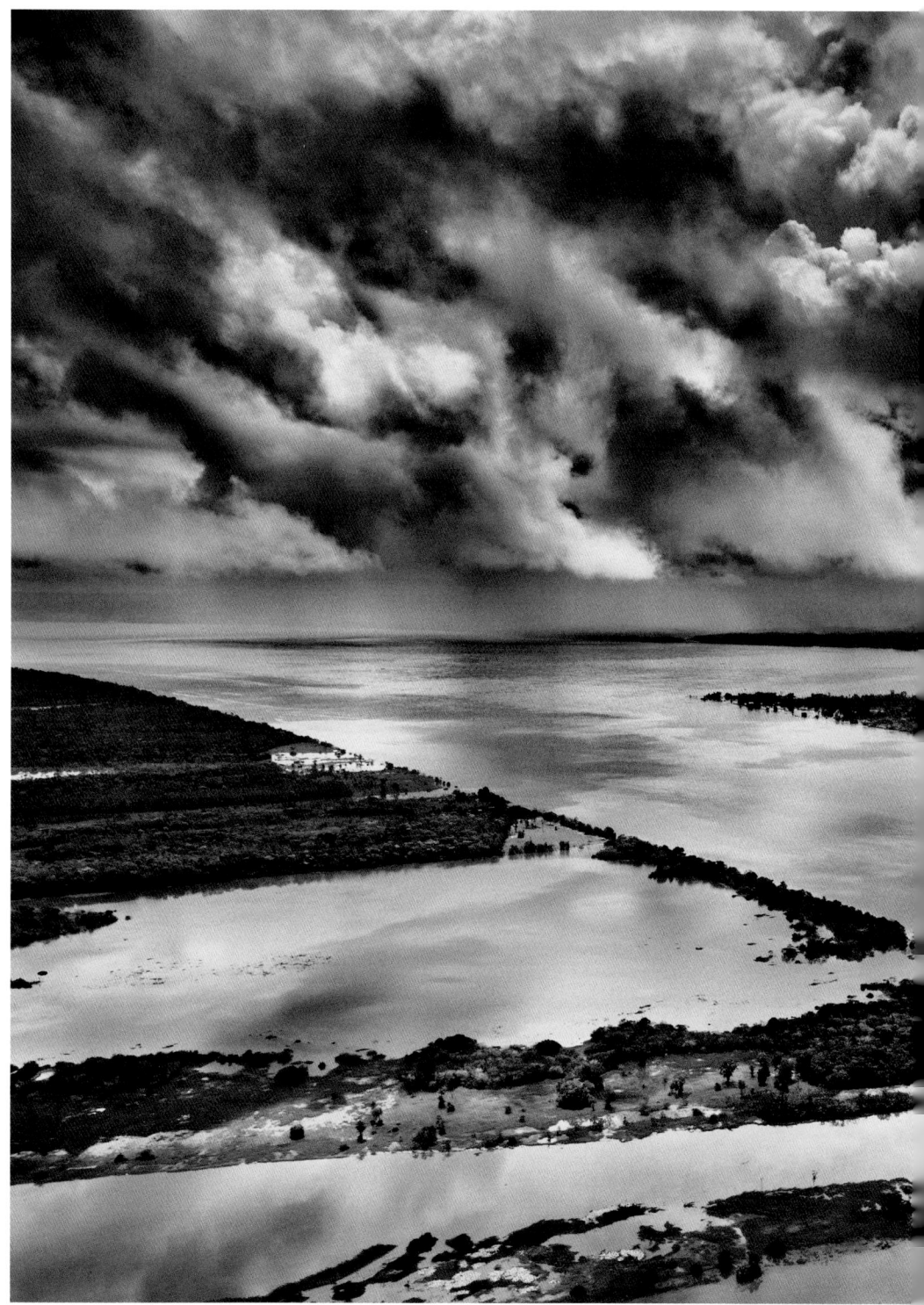

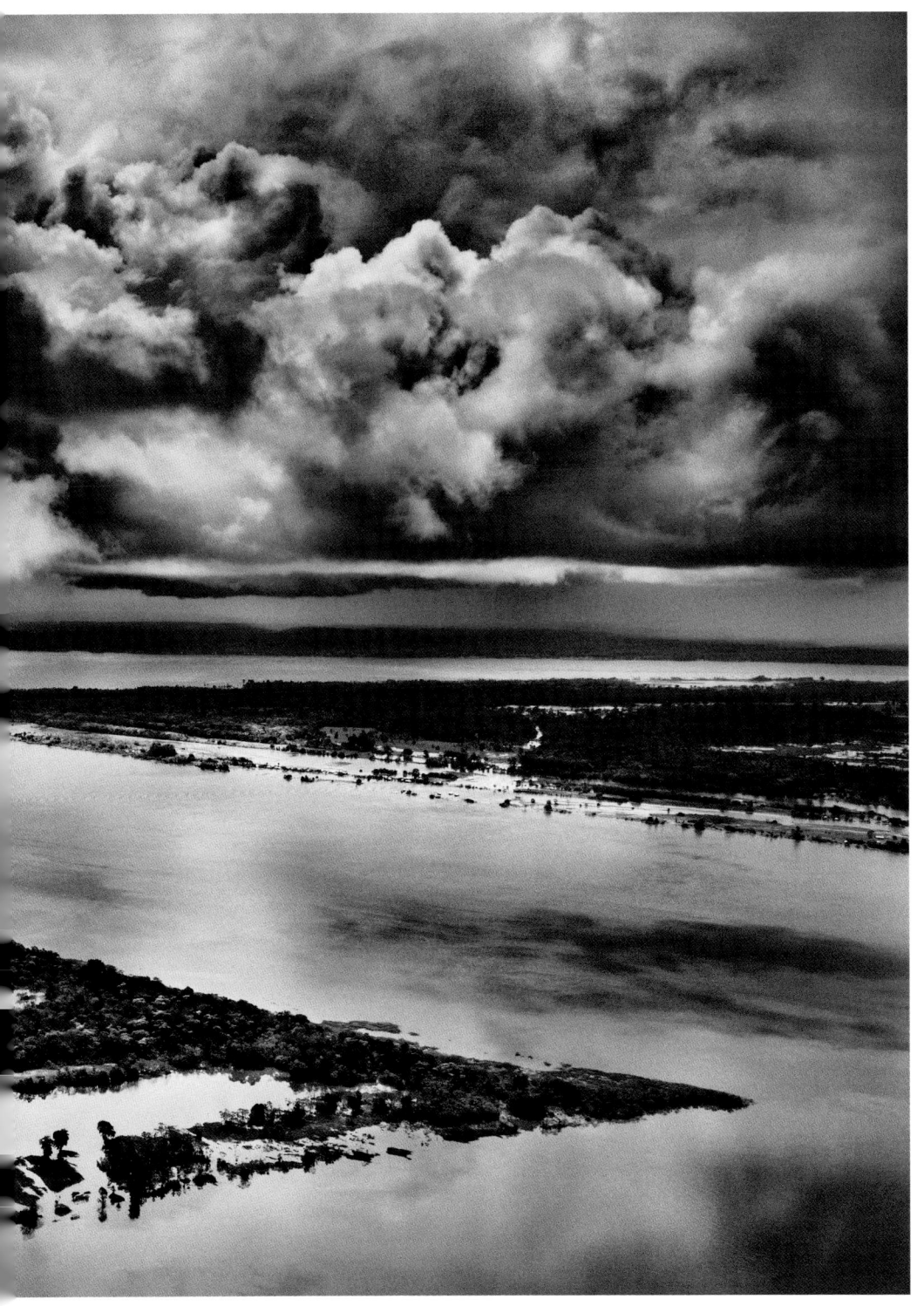

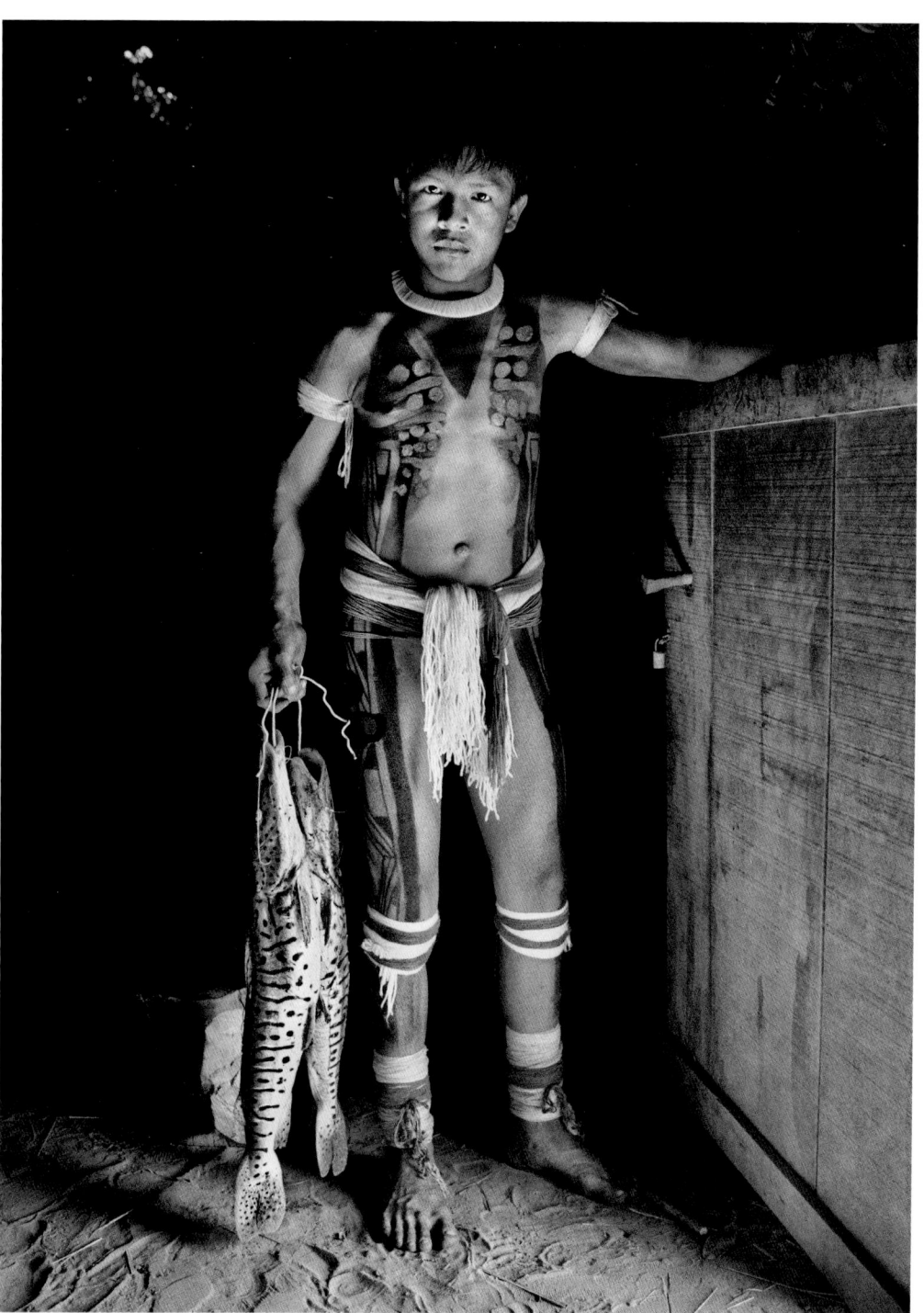

XINGU INDIGENOUS TERRITORY

Brazil's most famous indigenous territory, known throughout the world from pictures of its festivals and its influence on Brazilian literature in the second half of the 20th century, Xingu Park was the first large indigenous reserve established to protect multiple ethnic groups. That decision, made in 1961 during the brief presidency of Jânio Quadros, came in response to a national campaign in the Brazilian mass media led by the Villas-Bôas brothers—Claudio, Leonardo, and Orlando—the best-known *sertanistas* in Brazilian history.

Located in what is now the state of Mato Grosso, the Xingu Indigenous Territory (its official name) is home to a population of 6,000, representing 16 ethnic groups, and speaking the languages of five language families. Located between the Amazon biome and the Cerrado savanna, it shares characteristics of both biomes, with similar fauna and luxuriant forest but a regime of rain and drought far more marked than in the Amazon rainforest to the north.

When the park was established, the peoples of the Upper Xingu were facing a series of epidemics and a population crisis. Every group suffered from falling population. The most severe case was the Yawalapiti, who in the 1960s consisted of just a few individuals. A joint effort involving other ethnic groups led to interethnic marriages and a recovery of the population, which in turn rescued a vanishing culture. Today, only a fraction of the Yawalapiti speak the language.

The villages consist of communal houses arranged in an oval perimeter, around a dirt plaza. In the center of the plaza is the "Men's House," where they keep the sacred flutes that women are forbidden to see. Therefore, the flutes are played only in this smaller house or at night, when the women are gathered elsewhere. The plaza is the site of public events: celebrations, funerals, leaders' speeches, and ceremonial fights.

The community houses are shaped like half an oval. They are thatched, with a roof of about 10 meters (almost 35 feet) high, and just two entrances: one facing the central plaza and the other on the opposite side.

The system of coexistence among different indigenous groups began to coalesce around 1,500 years ago, as shown by the oldest archeological traces, the ruins of walled urban complexes comprising four different towns, in a geometric design that repeats in the evidence left by 25 of these towns. These urban communities formed when the first Arawak peoples arrived in the region (ancestors of the current Waurá, from Central America and northern South America), probably soon followed by Carib groups (originally from coastal South America and from the Caribbean), such as the Kuikuro and Kalapalo. These two peoples already had regimes of complementary coexistence in areas north of South America and probably replicated the partnership once they migrated to the Xingu.

Groups from these peoples created their own form of exchange and coexistence that other peoples joined over the centuries, until the Europeans arrived in the Americas. In that era, in the 16th century, epidemics of smallpox, measles, and influenza devastated perhaps 80 percent of the population of the Americas, racing even faster than the conquistadors. The Xingu was not exempt: the ruins show a sudden abandonment of the big cities around the start of the 17th century. The survivors reorganized themselves into smaller villages but preserved the systems of integration and economic complementarity.

From the 16th century to the end of the 19th century, the indigenous peoples suffered attacks and epidemics from the *bandeirantes* (explorers of European origin searching for mineral wealth and slave labor). In 1884, when the pioneering expedition of German ethnologist Karl von den Steinen recorded the first population data about the tribes of the Upper Xingu, they numbered about 3,000 people. Successive invasions by prospectors and loggers, epidemics of unfamiliar diseases, and attacks between indigenous groups drastically reduced the population over the course of the 20th century.

Despite the founding of the national park, with the permanent presence of Indian Protection Service agents starting in 1961, the population reached its low point in 1965: 540 indigenous people. Throughout the region, indigenous groups were facing an extinction-level crisis.

The park administrator appointed by successive Brazilian administrations, Orlando Villas-Bôas, adopted the practice in the 1960s and 1970s of encouraging the endangered peoples of the region to relocate into the demarcated zone. That is what happened with the Kaiabi, Ikpeng, Panará (or Krenhakarore), and Tapayuna. Some, like the Panará and the Tapayuna, returned to their areas of origin after reestablishing population balance; others ended up becoming Xinguans.

The cultural integration system, with social division of production of goods, leads each group to be identified as the most sophisticated creator of objects desired by all, such as the Waurá's ceramics, the Kamayurá's bows and arrows, the Kuikuro's snail shell necklaces, and the Aweti's and Mehinako's salts. These products are traded in the exchange rituals known as *moitarás*, which take place at the end of major festivals.

These large celebrations are the most visible affirmation of the harmonious relations among the inhabitants of the Upper Xingu. Kuarup, Javari, and Yamurikumã rituals prompt large gatherings of residents from various different communities for shared rituals in which even the different mythologies of these peoples combine and intertwine.

Kuarup culminates the tributes to those who have died recently. According to the origin myth of the Kamayurá, a demiurge, Mavutsinin, created the first men from tree trunks. When some of them died, he resurrected them using other trunks, always asking the men not to watch the ritual. Feeling betrayed when someone peeked, the creator had it decreed that from that moment on there would be no more rebirths, only memorial celebrations.

About a year after people's deaths, trunks dressed and adorned as representatives of those who have gone will be honored as though they were the people themselves and will then be thrown into the nearest pond. During the day of celebrations, warriors from the different villages will face each other in the fight called *huka-huka*, as representatives of their ethnic groups, in a sort of Olympic contest. Once the winners have been honored, the teenage girls come out of isolation and are introduced in a procession, led by two warriors playing long flutes. After a year confined in the darkness of their homes, they have long hair and absolutely white skin.

The Javari celebration honors great spear throwers with a darts championship. Anthropologist Carmen Junqueira says that Javari affirms the identity of each people, whereas in Kuarup, "the indigenous people identify as 'Upper Xinguans' more than with their specific cultures."

The festival called Yamurikumã affirms women's power: on that day, the men leave the center of the villages and the women symbolically take over and create an exclusively female society, in which men are transformed into pigs.

The peoples of the Upper Xingu eat a diet consisting largely of fish, which they eat with *beiju* cakes and porridges made from "wild" cassava. The cassava is grown on family farms: the men plant and the women harvest. They fish in several ways, but the fish is then always dried on a rack over embers, to preserve it so it can be eaten over the course of several days. They eat large amounts of fish in the dry season, when water levels drop and it is easier to fish. In the rainy season, they usually round out their diet with crops such as corn, papaya, pumpkin, watermelon, and foods they can gather such as berries, honey, *pequi*, genipap, *mangaba*, ants, and turtle eggs. At that time of year when fish are scarce, people may eat some hunted birds and small animals.

Page 72 "Samuraia" Tapiÿrÿ, a young Kamayurá warrior, holding two fish, both spotted sorubim (*Pseudoplatystoma corruscans*). In the Upper Xingu, indigenous peoples' diets consist largely of dishes made with cassava and with fish protein. Xingu Indigenous Territory, state of Mato Grosso, 2005.

Pages 76/77 At daybreak, Waurá fishers travel by canoe to collect the "waiting net" that caught fish overnight. During major festivals, communities expecting visits from other villages prepare copious extra food to welcome and feed guests during their stay, and so they will have food to take with them on the journey home. Xingu Indigenous Territory, state of Mato Grosso, 2005.

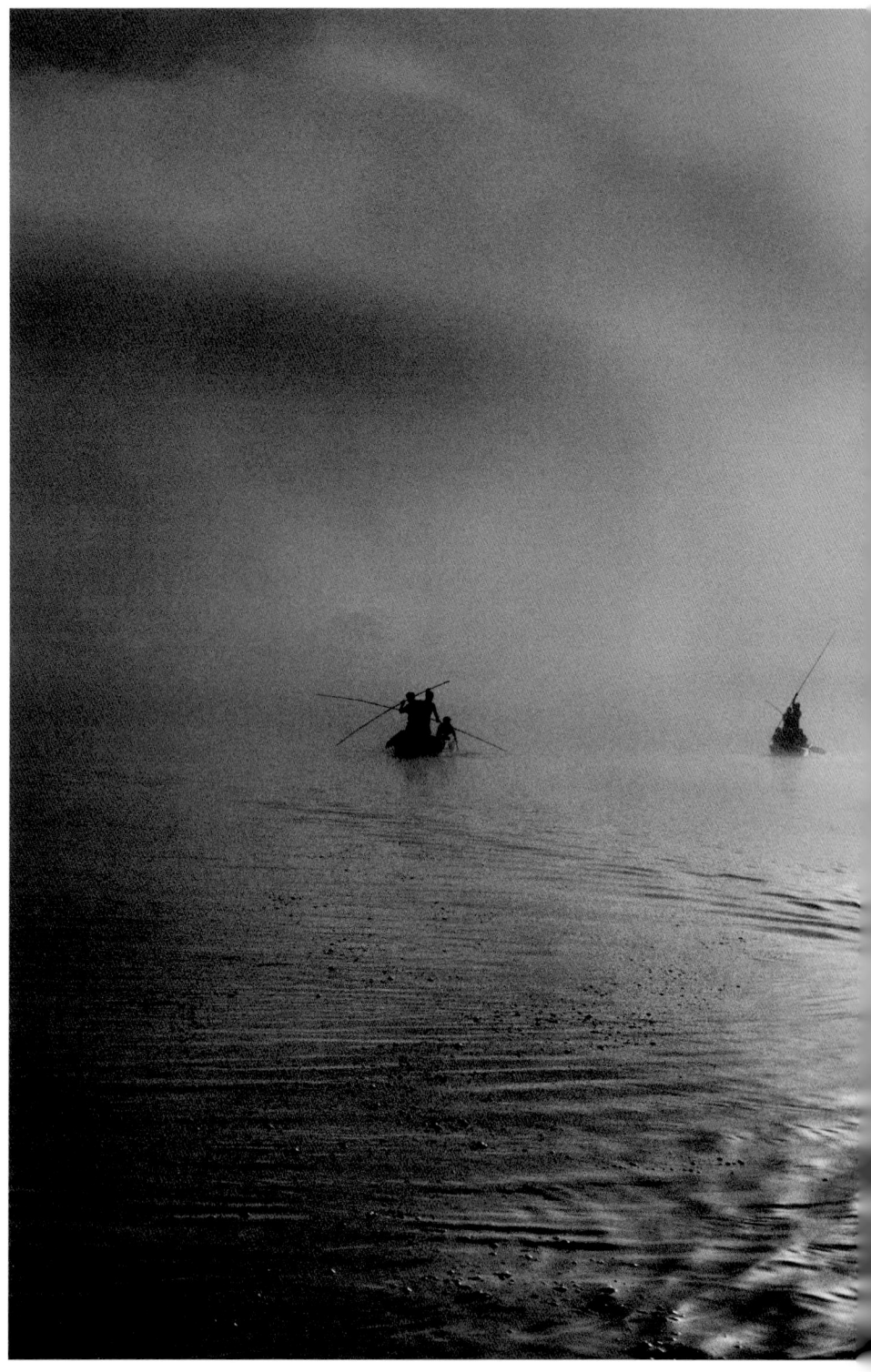

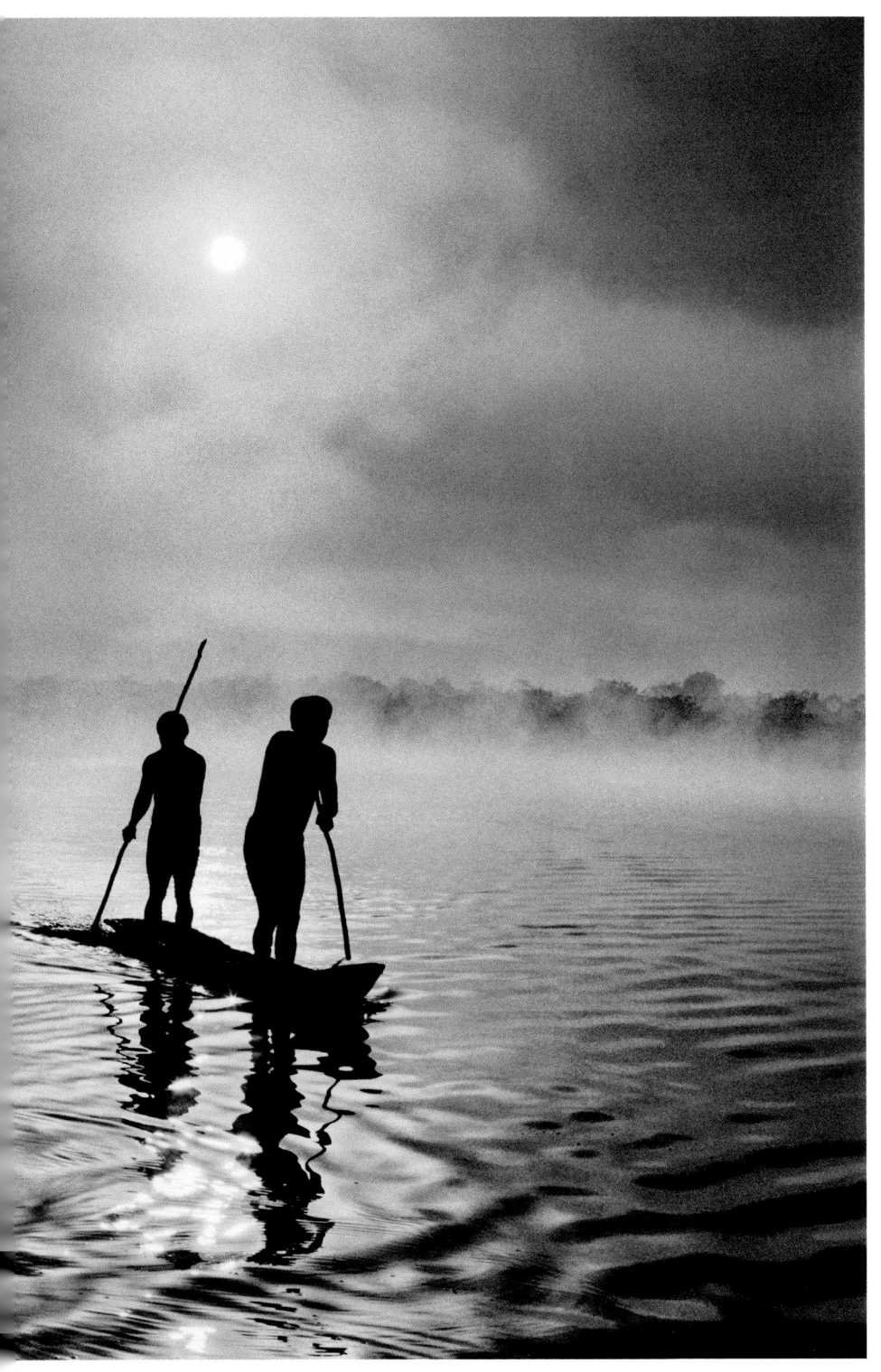

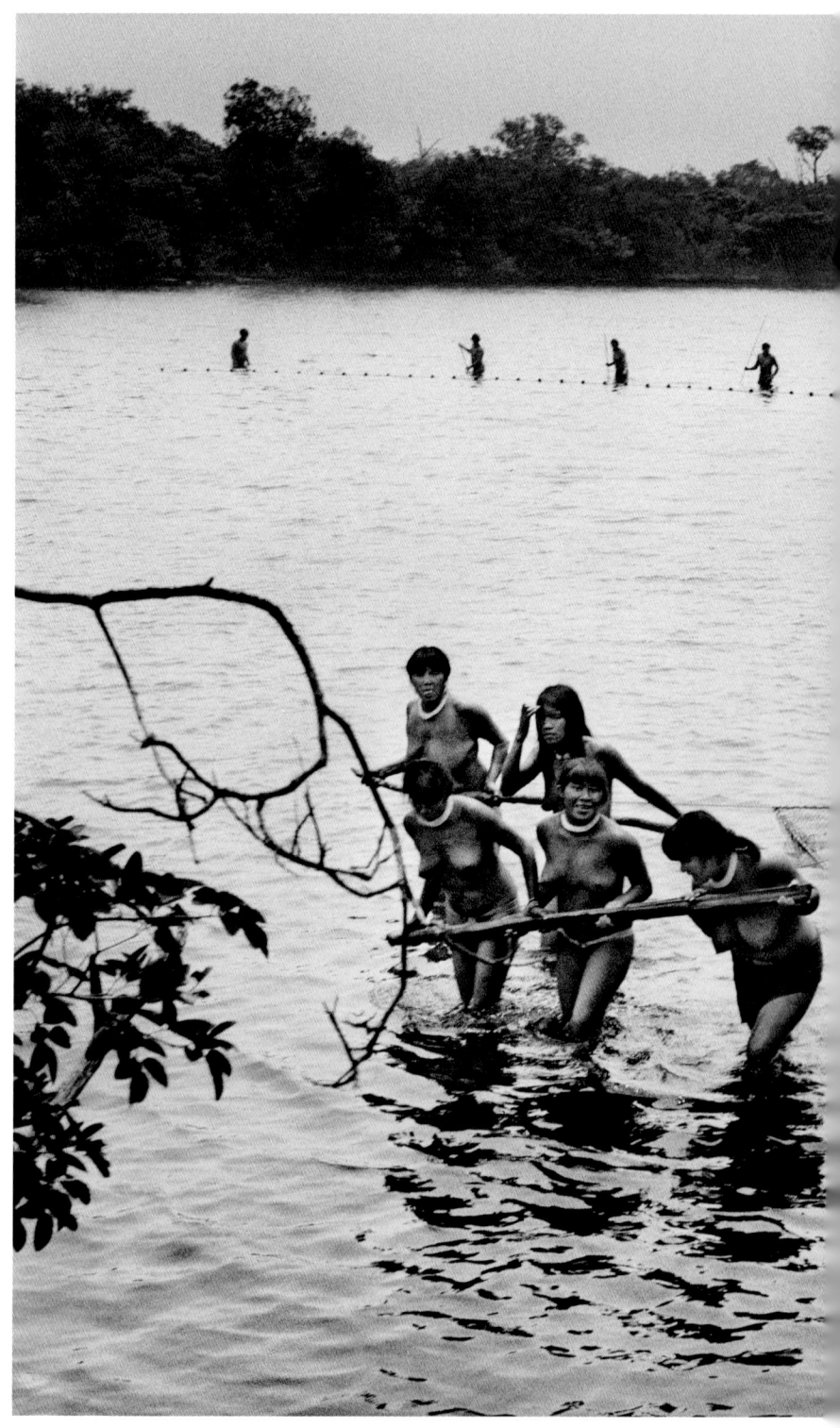

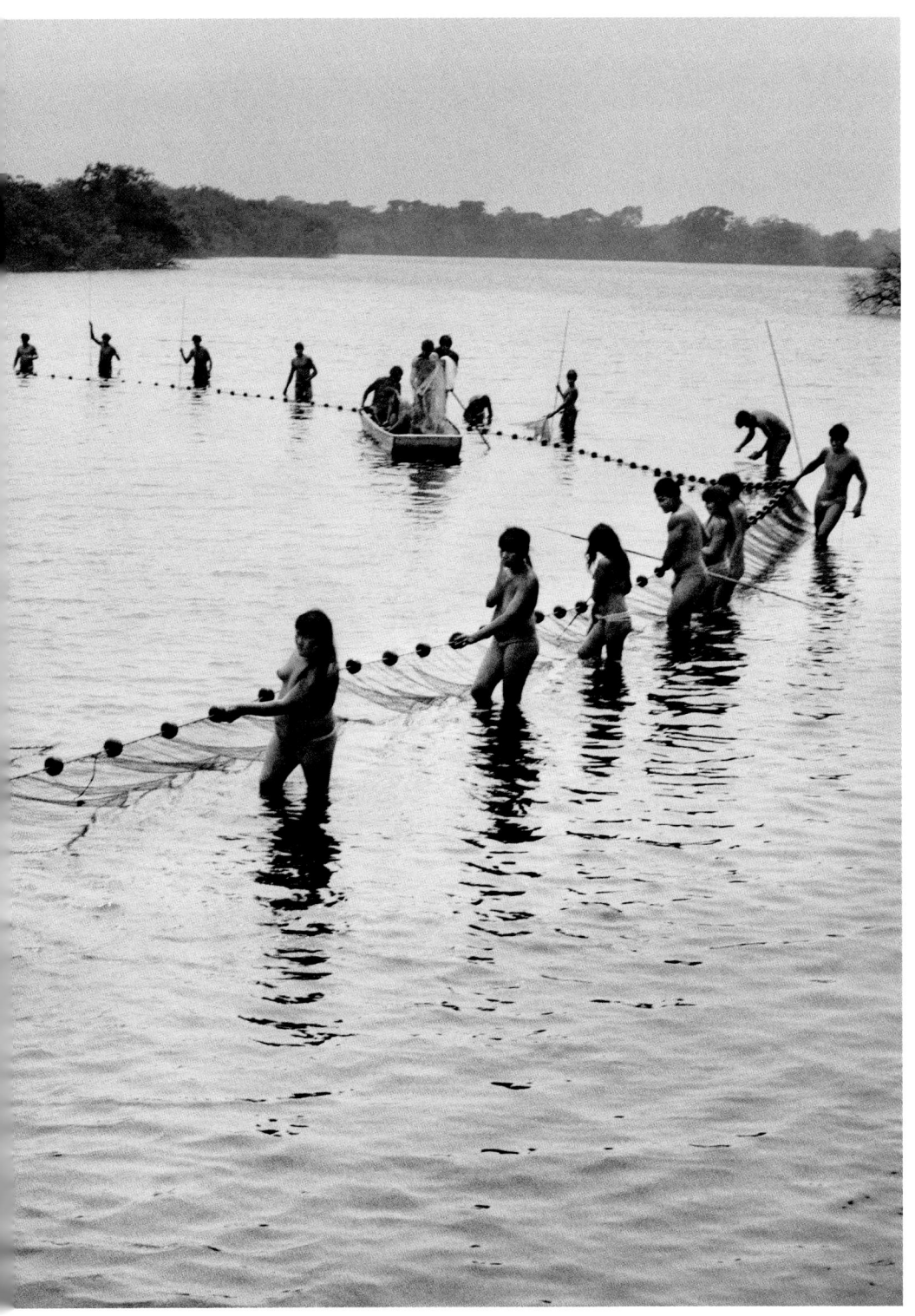

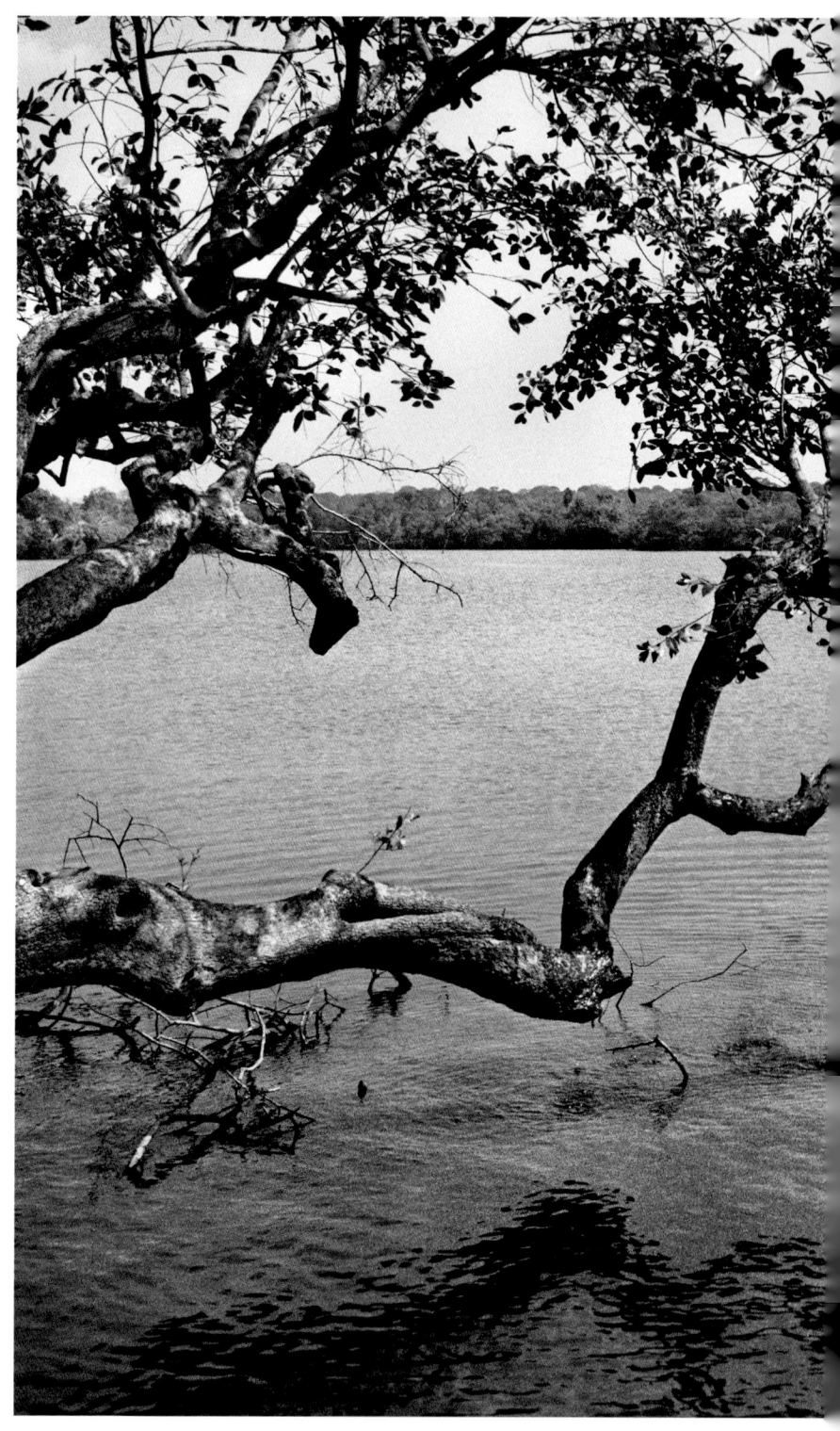

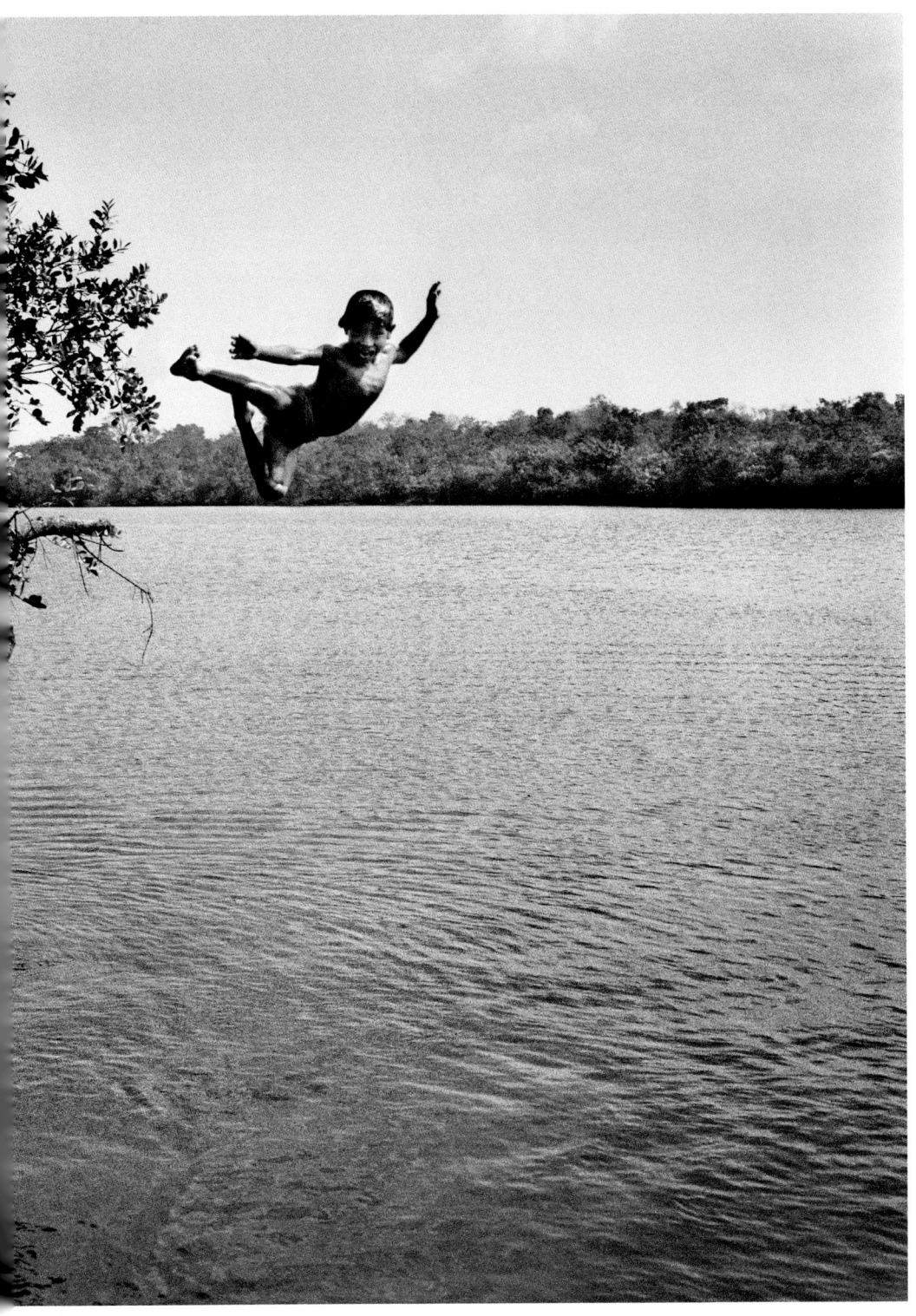

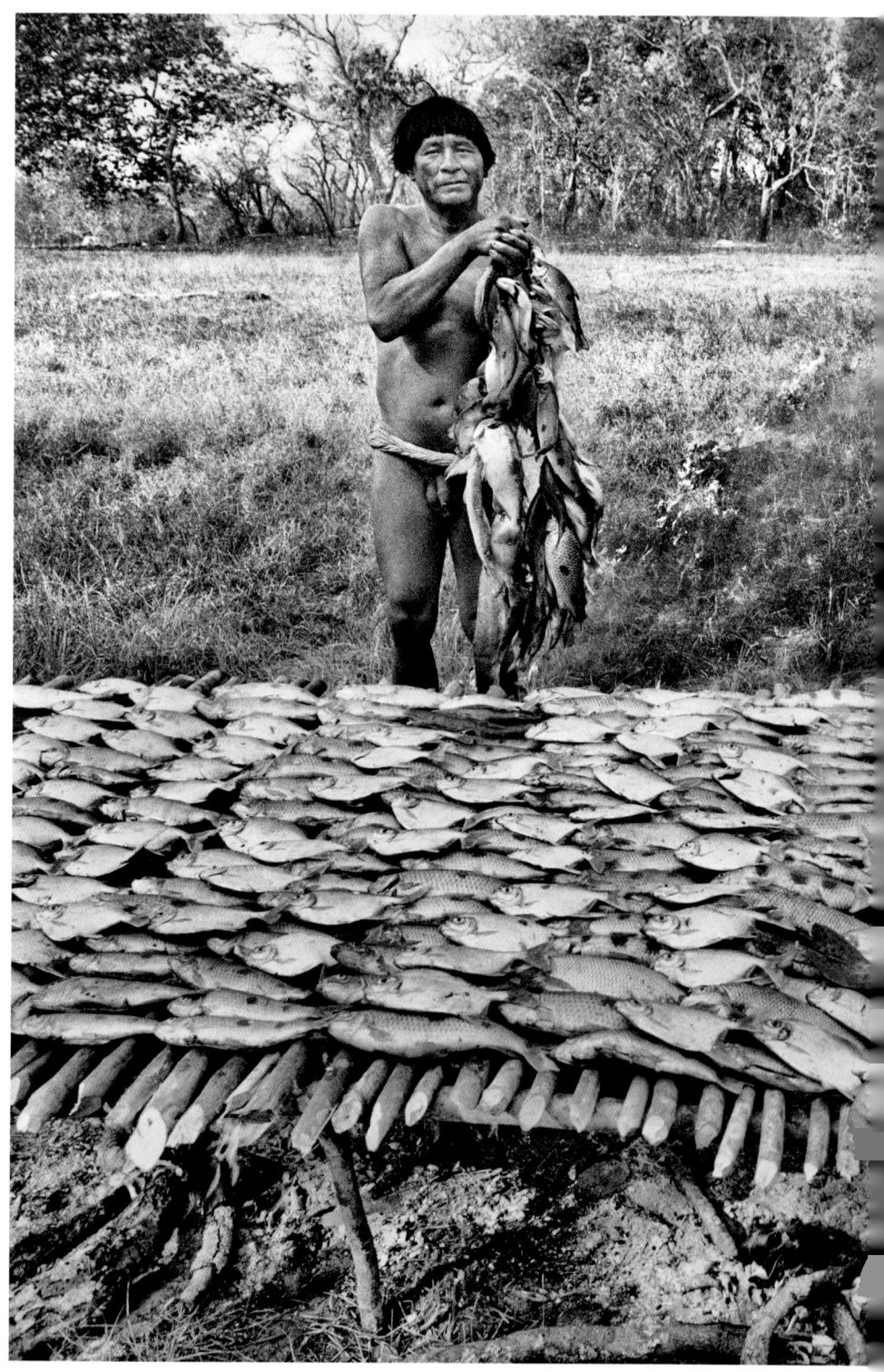

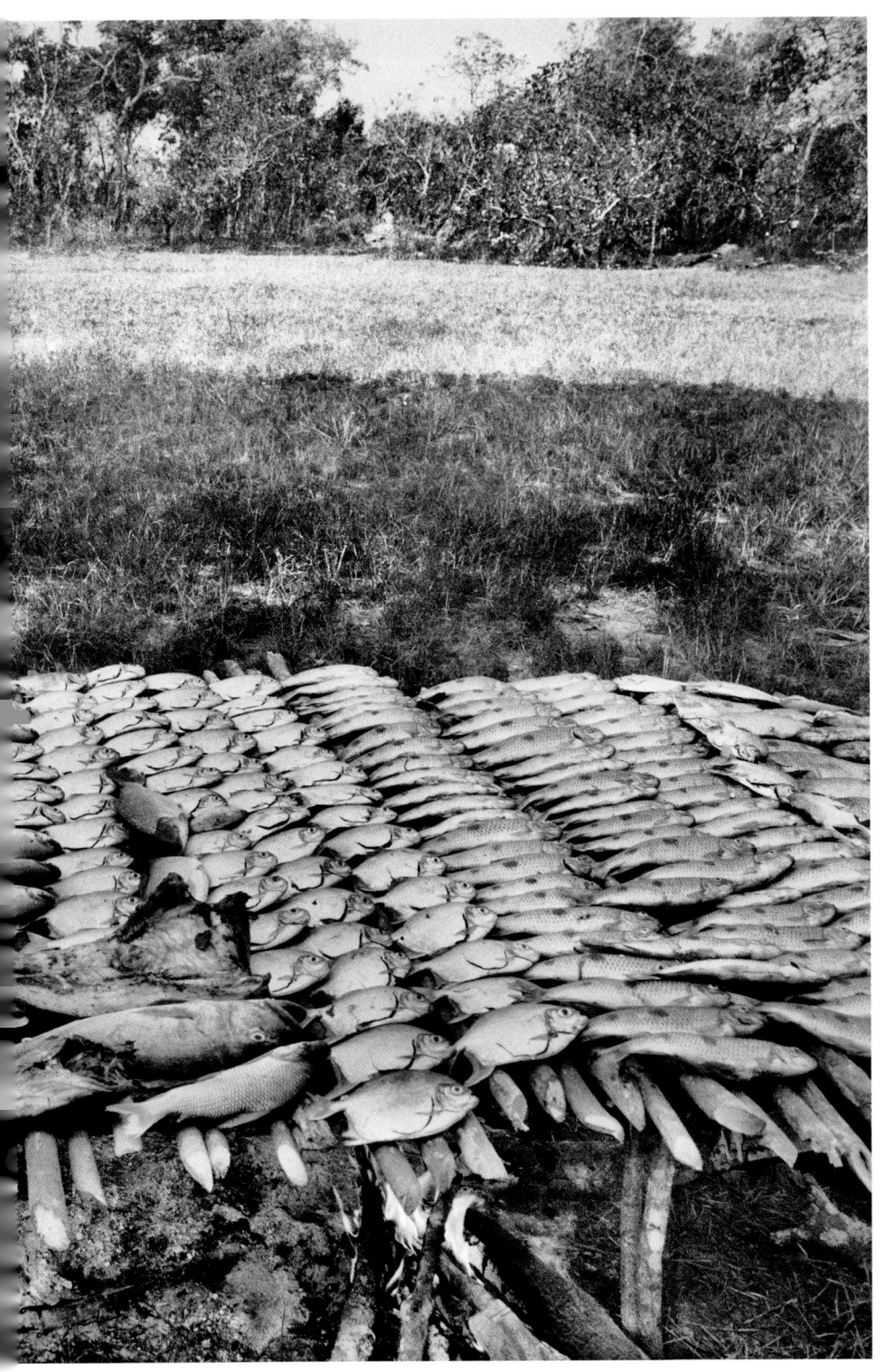

Pages 78/79 Kamayurá fishers pull a net in the Ipavu lake as the community prepares for the women's celebration of Yamurikumã. Xingu Indigenous Territory, state of Mato Grosso, 2005.

Pages 80/81 A Kamayurá boy leaps into the Tuatuari River on a fishing trip. Xingu Indigenous Territory, state of Mato Grosso, 2005.

Pages 82/83 Pirakumã Kamayurá bringing more fish to cook during preparations for the women's festival, Yamurikumã. They are cooked using the most common technique among the indigenous peoples of the Amazon: they are dried on a rack over coals at a temperature too low to roast them but high enough to preserve them for days or weeks. Xingu Indigenous Territory, state of Mato Grosso, 2005.

Opposite During the Kuarup festival, two Kuikuro warriors lead two adolescent girls who just ended a year of seclusion after their first menstruation. The girls are then presented ritually to the communities present, in a sort of parade. Kuikuro village, Xingu Indigenous Territory, state of Mato Grosso, 2005.

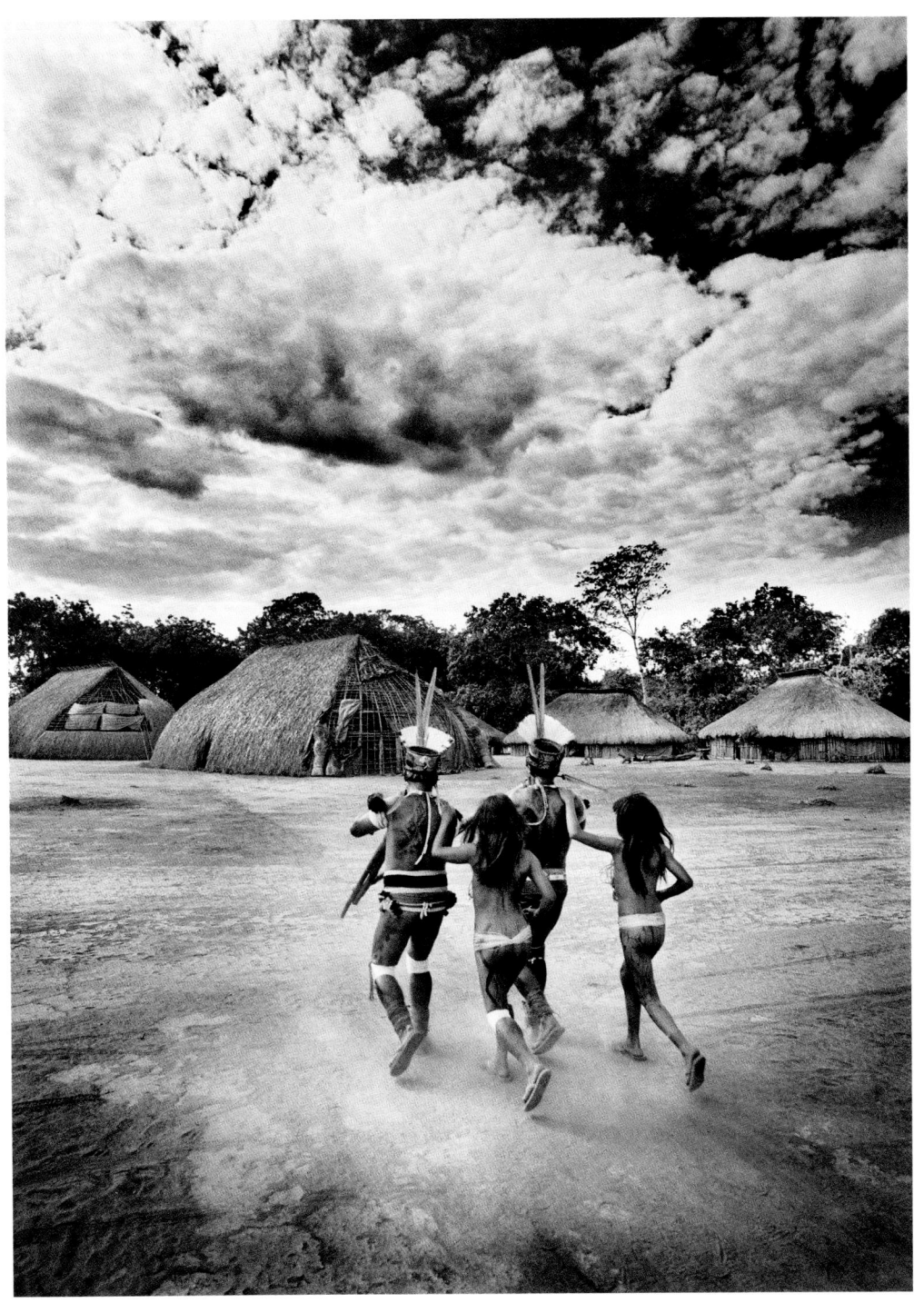

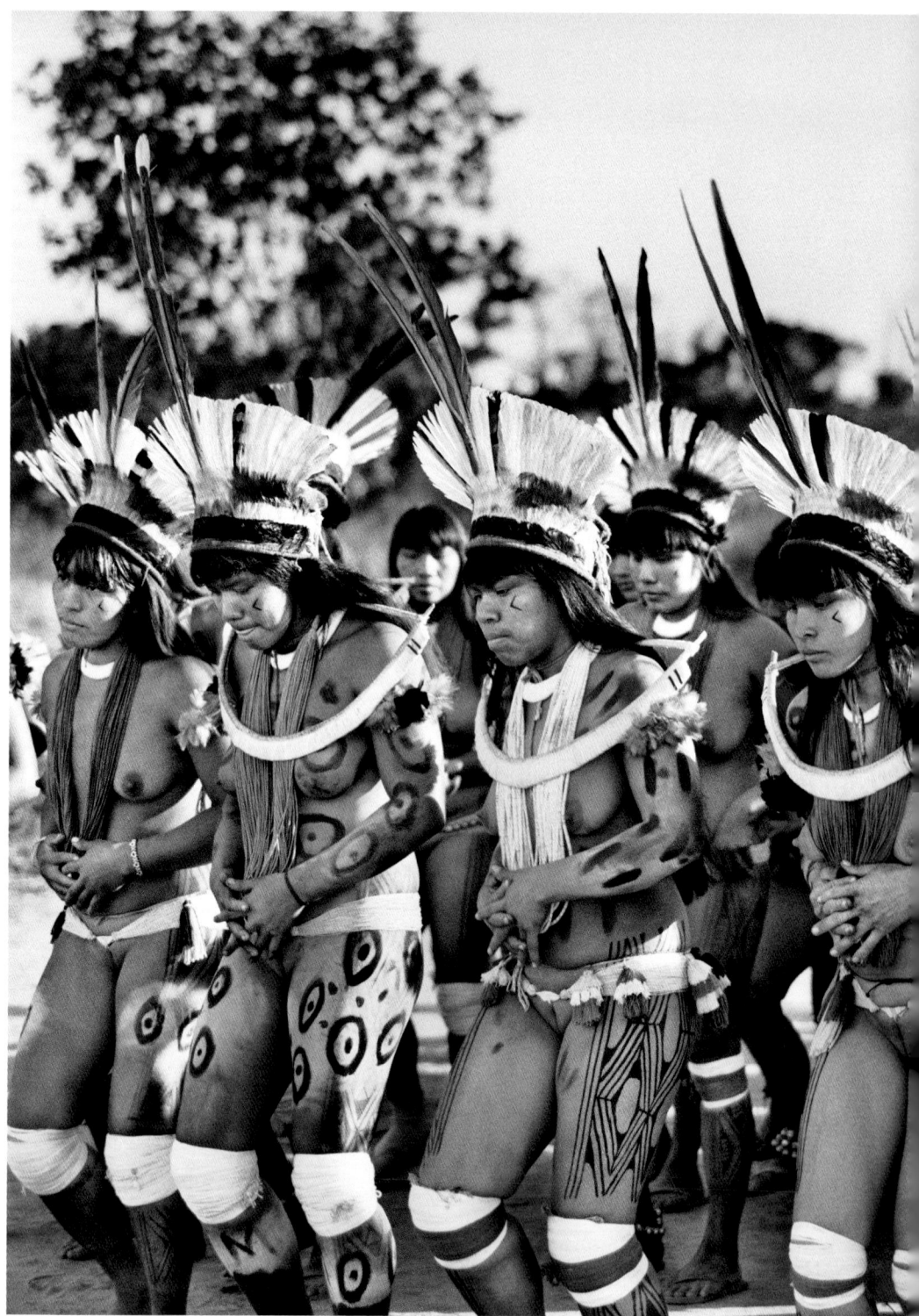

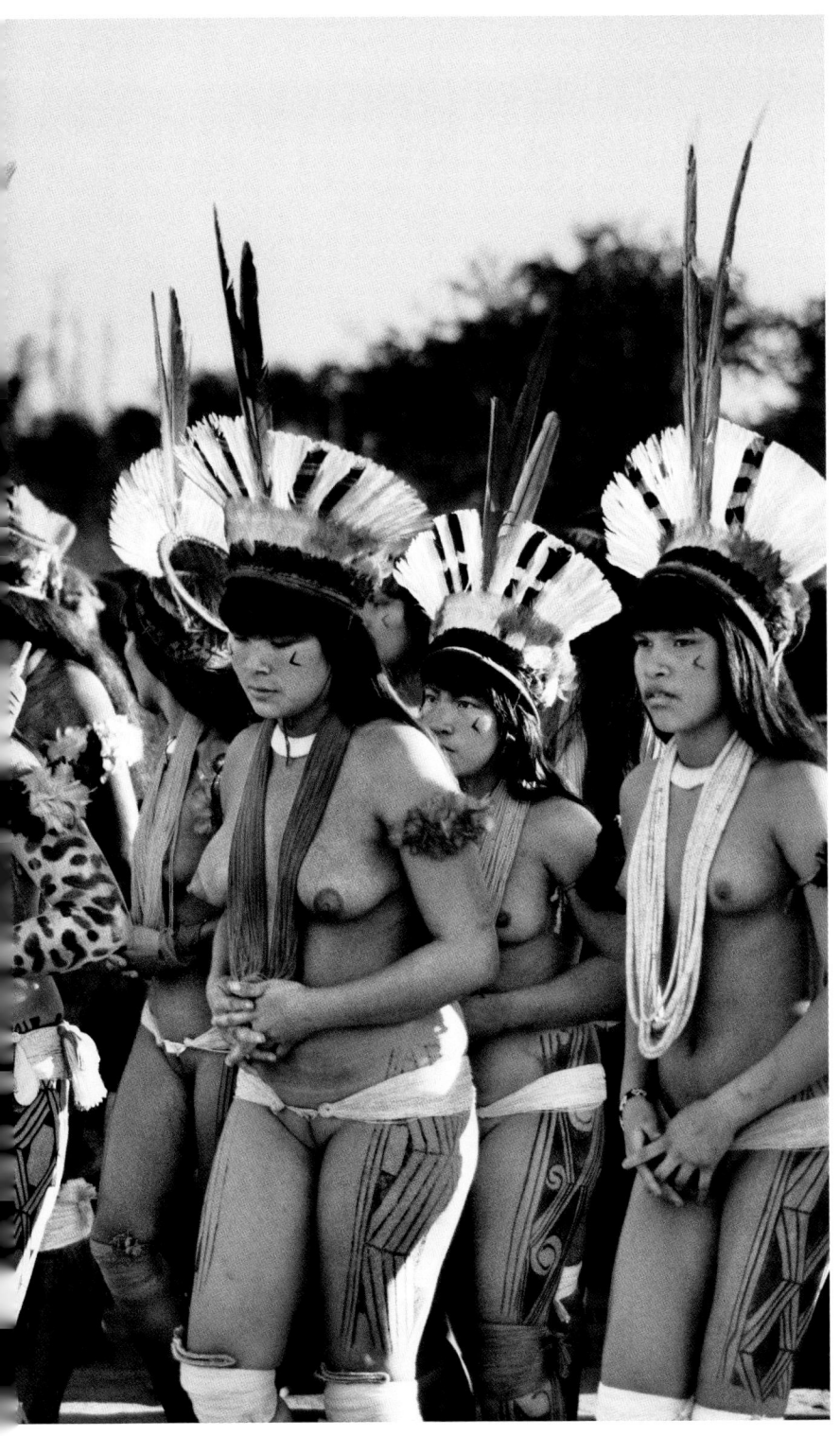

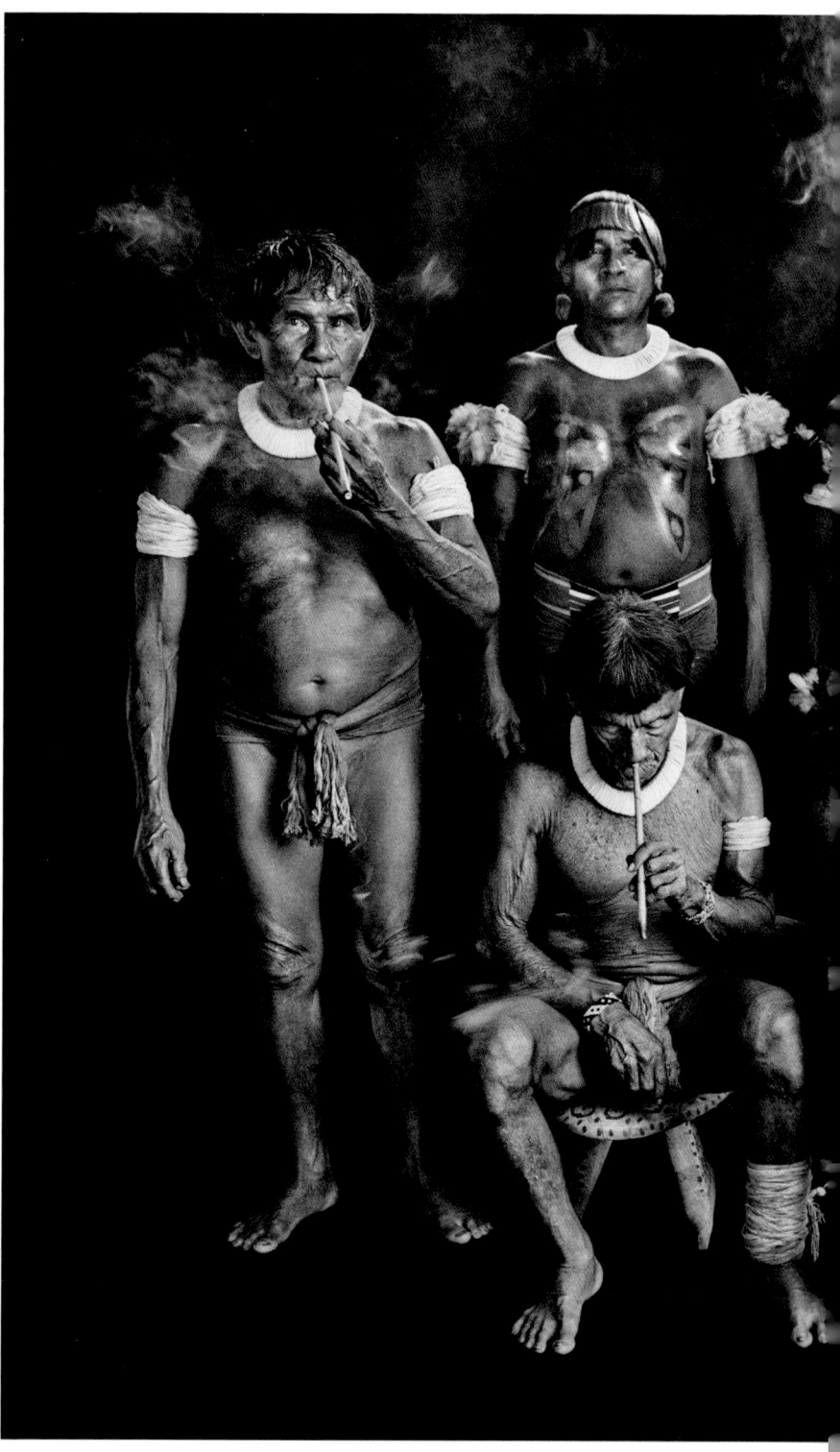

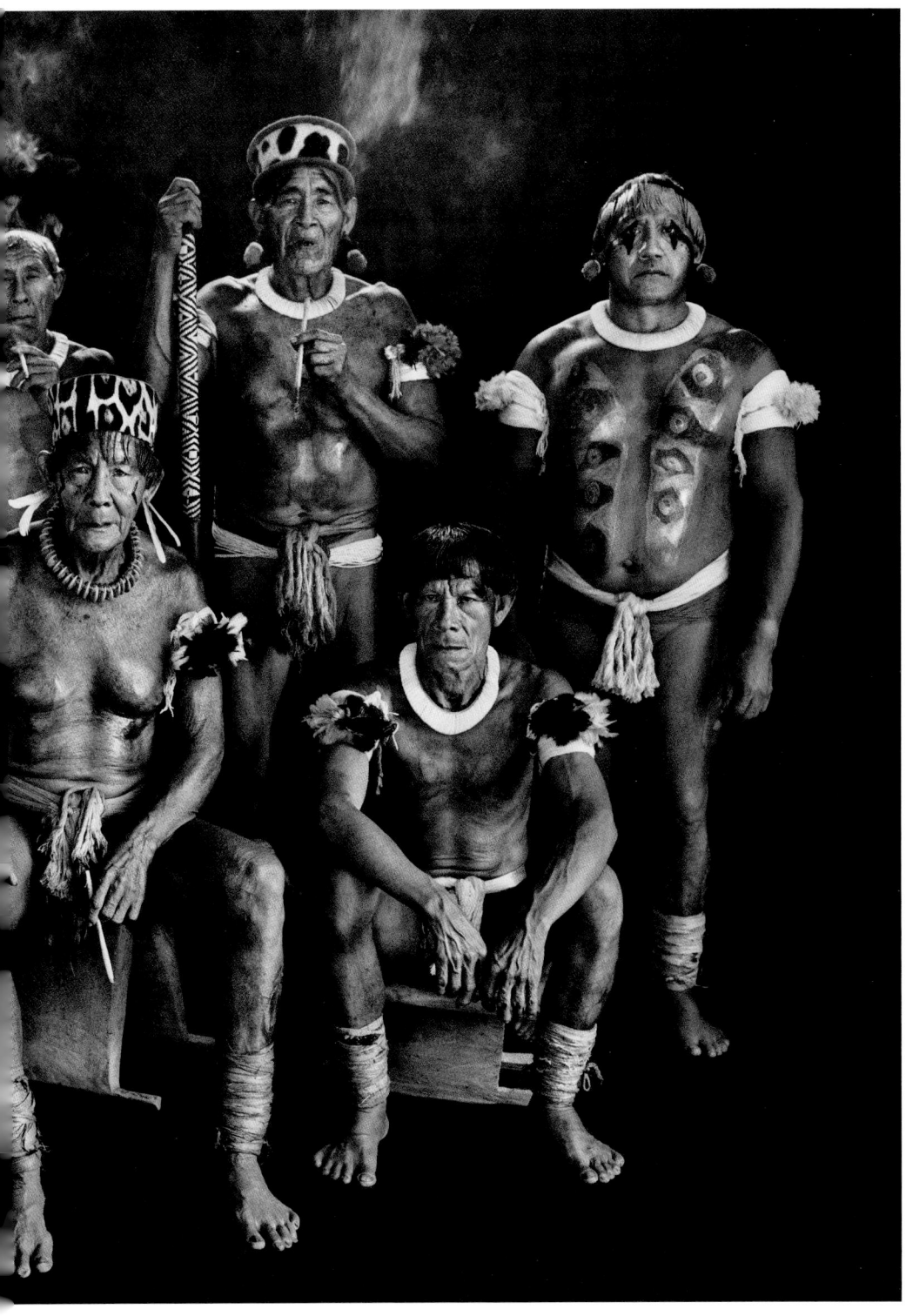

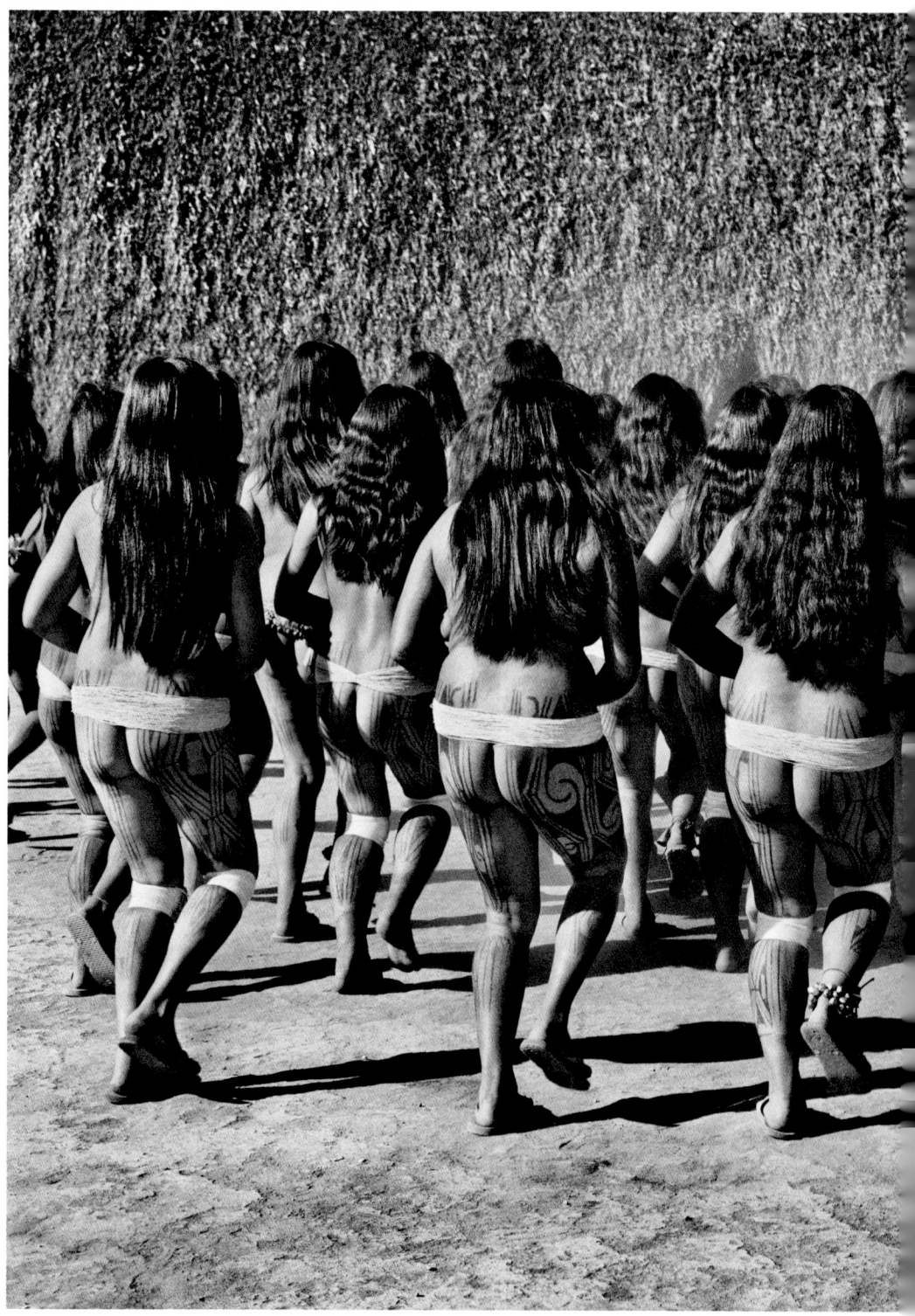

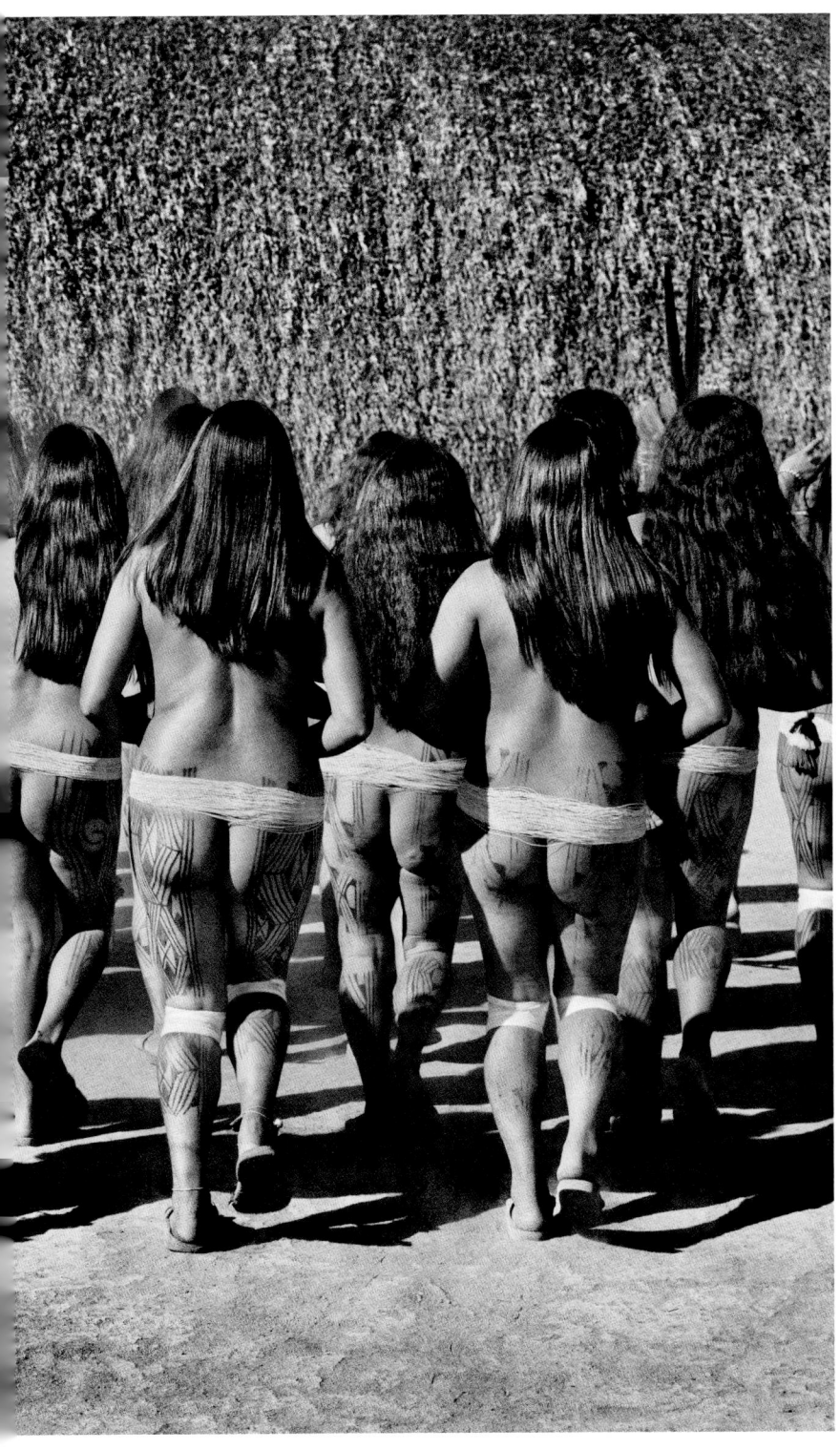

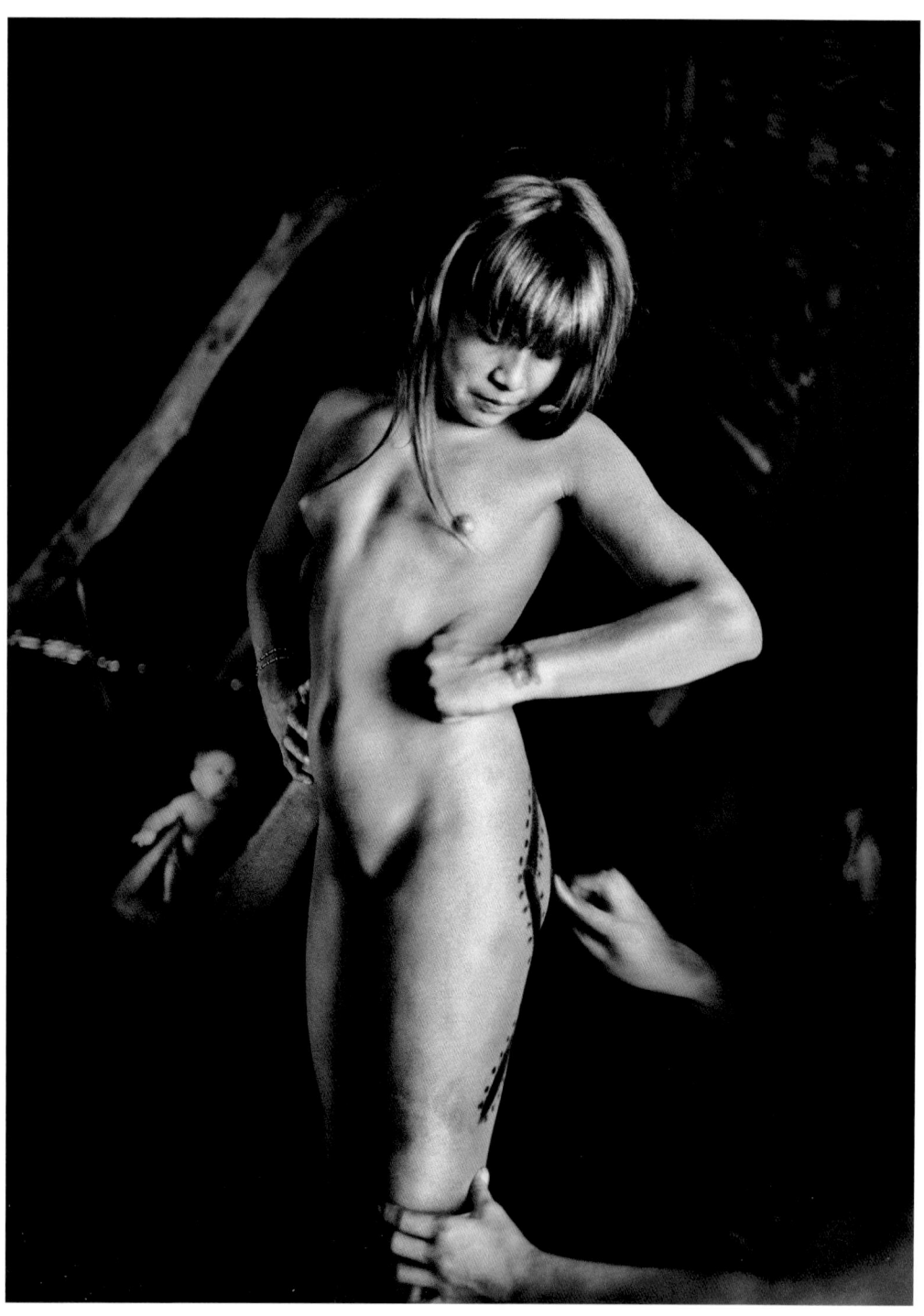

Pages 86/87 Yawalapiti women dance at the women's festival, Yamurikumã, Kamayurá village. Xingu Indigenous Territory, state of Mato Grosso, 2005.

Pages 88/89 Kamayurá *pajés* (shamans). Standing, back row (left to right): Pirakumã, Kanari, Kanutari, Kalalawá and Pataku. Seated: Akutsapÿ, Takumã, and Makari. In the Kamayurá cultural tradition, only *pajés* smoke tobacco, which they plant themselves. Xingu Indigenous Territory, state of Mato Grosso, 2005.

Pages 90/91 Kuikuro women dance at the Yamurikumá celebration, Kamayurá village. Xingu Indigenous Territory, state of Mato Grosso, 2005.

Opposite Rosana Kaitsalô Kamayurá is painted during preparations for the women's celebration, Yamurikumã. Xingu Indigenous Territory, state of Mato Grosso, 2005.

Pages 94/95 The family, prepared for the women's festival, Yamurikumã: the *pajé* Mapulu, standing with her son Takumalu in her arms; seated, her husband, "Raul" Awirinapu, along with their daughter Kailu. Kamayurá village, Xingu Indigenous Territory, state of Mato Grosso, 2005.

Pages 96/97 Chief Afukaká, main leader of the Kuikuro ethnic group. Xingu Indigenous Territory, state of Mato Grosso, 2005.

Pages 98/99 Katiwá and Kukulu Kamayurá. Xingu Indigenous Territory, state of Mato Grosso, 2005.

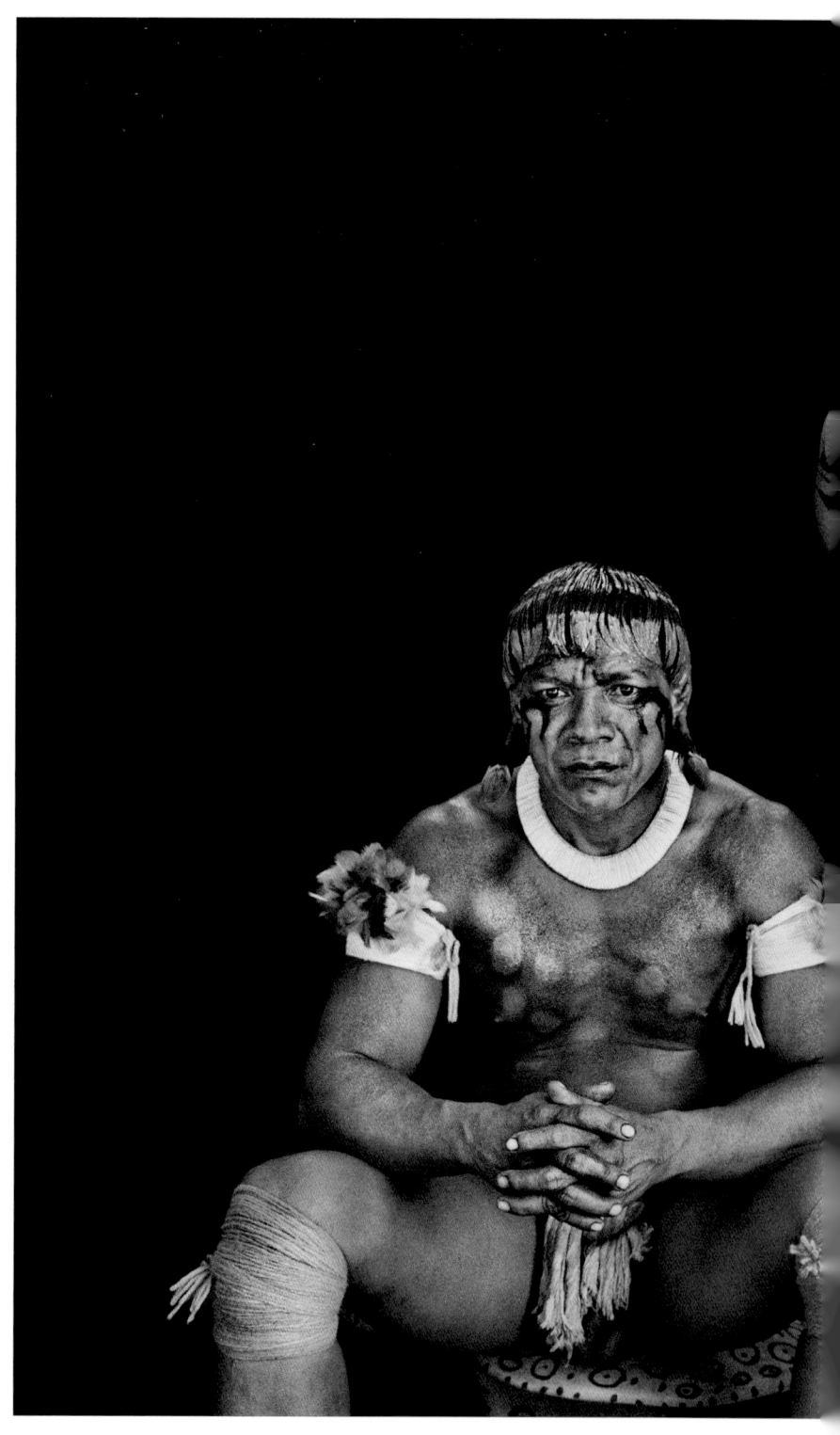

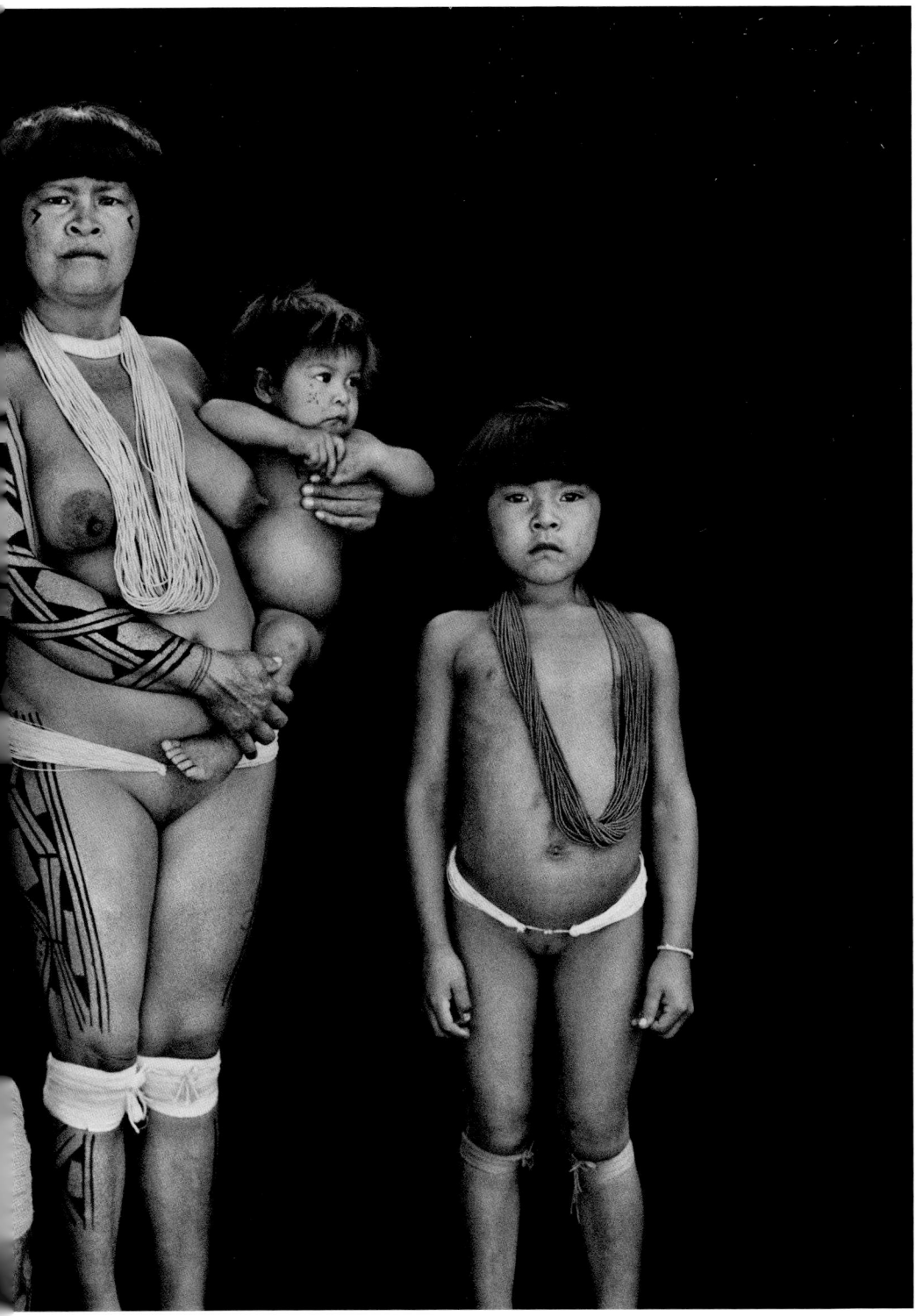

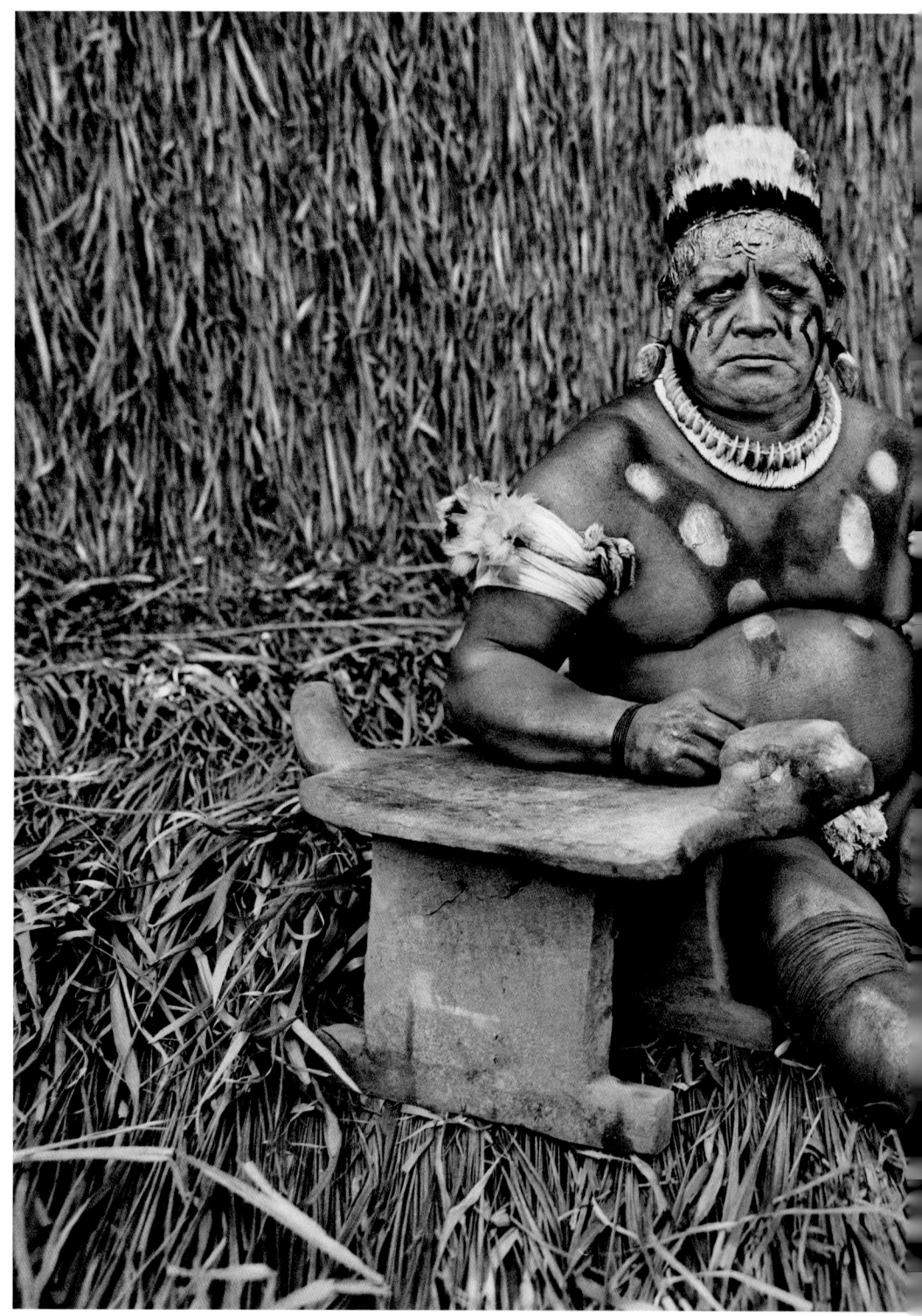

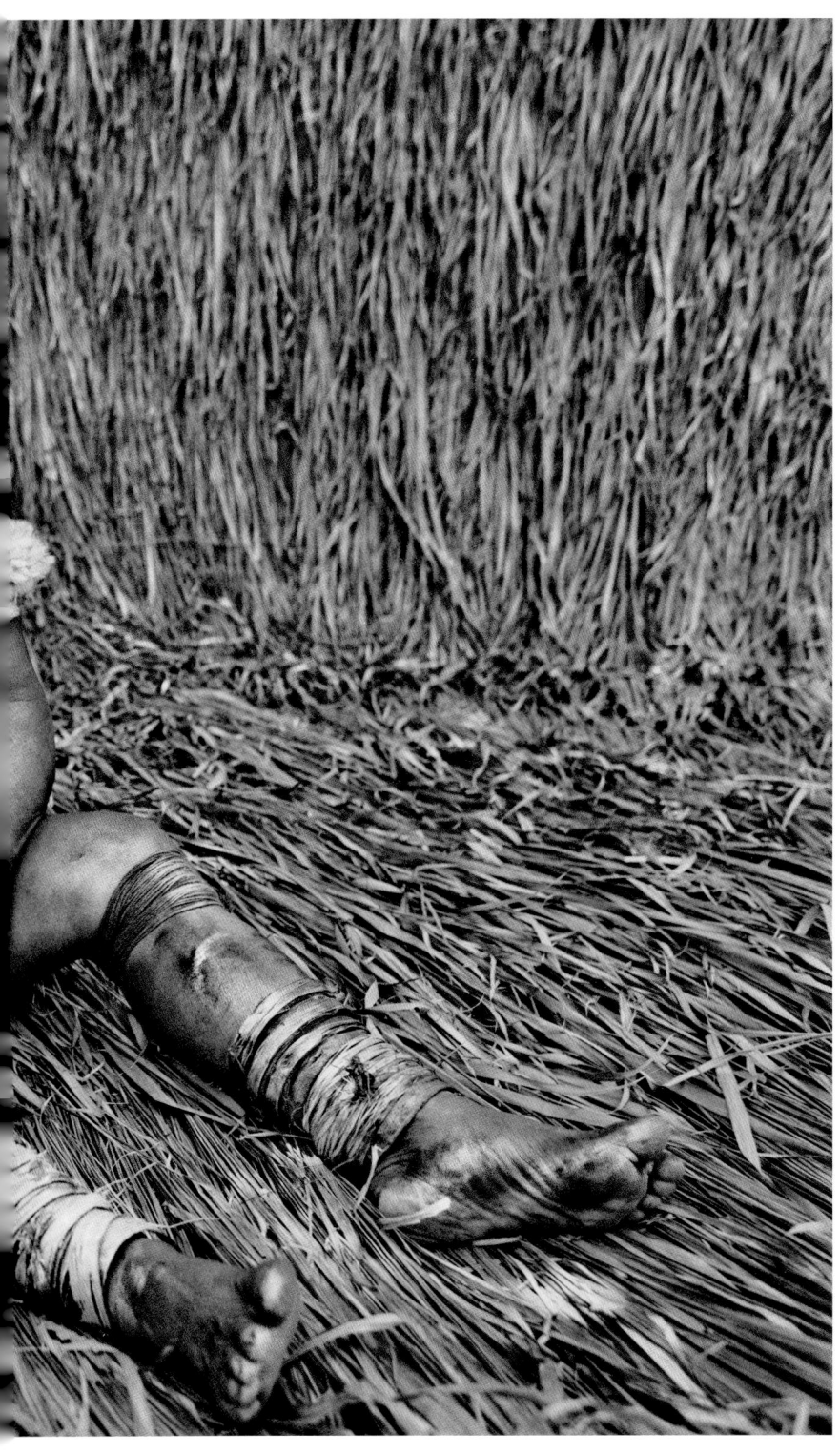

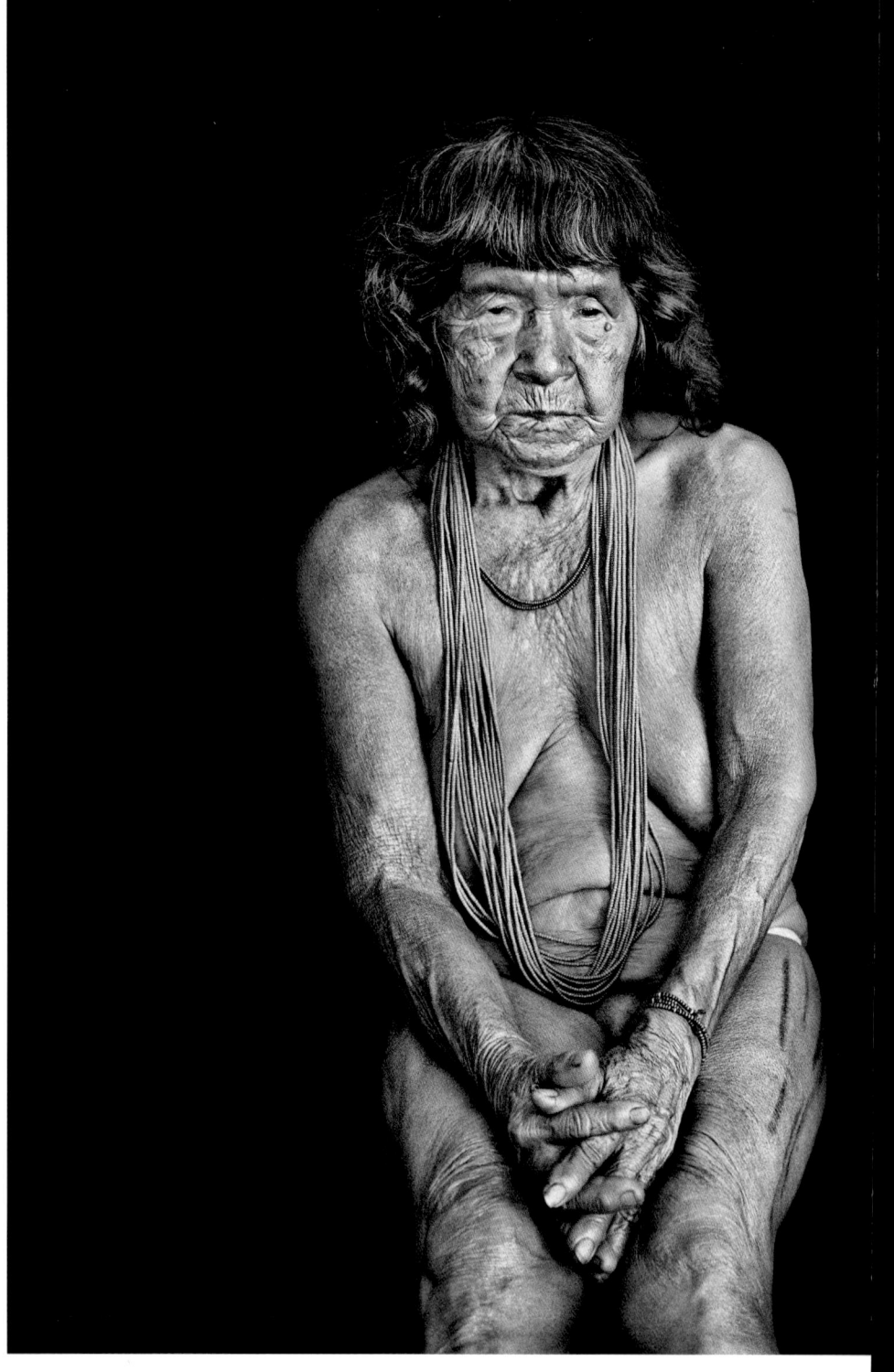

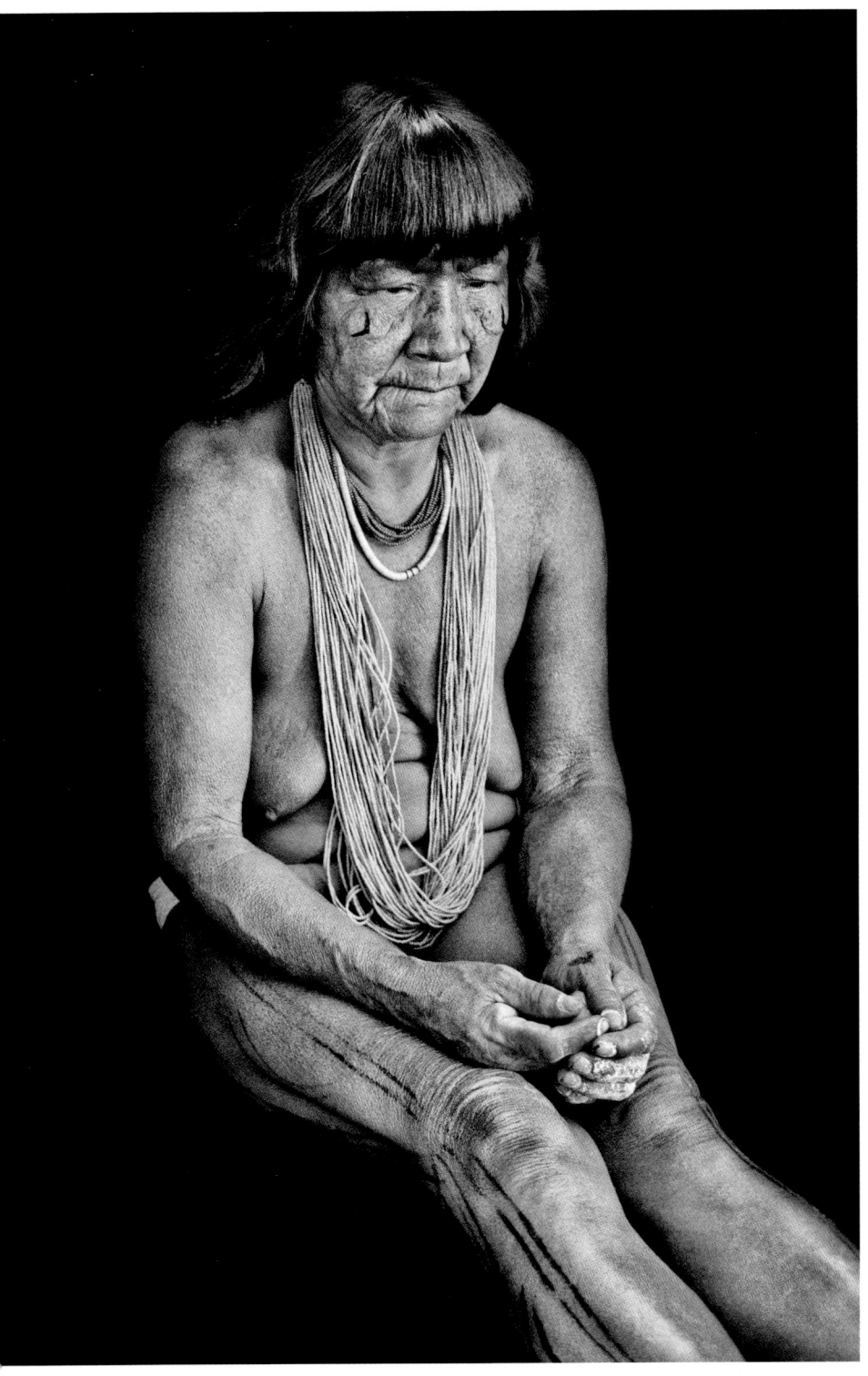

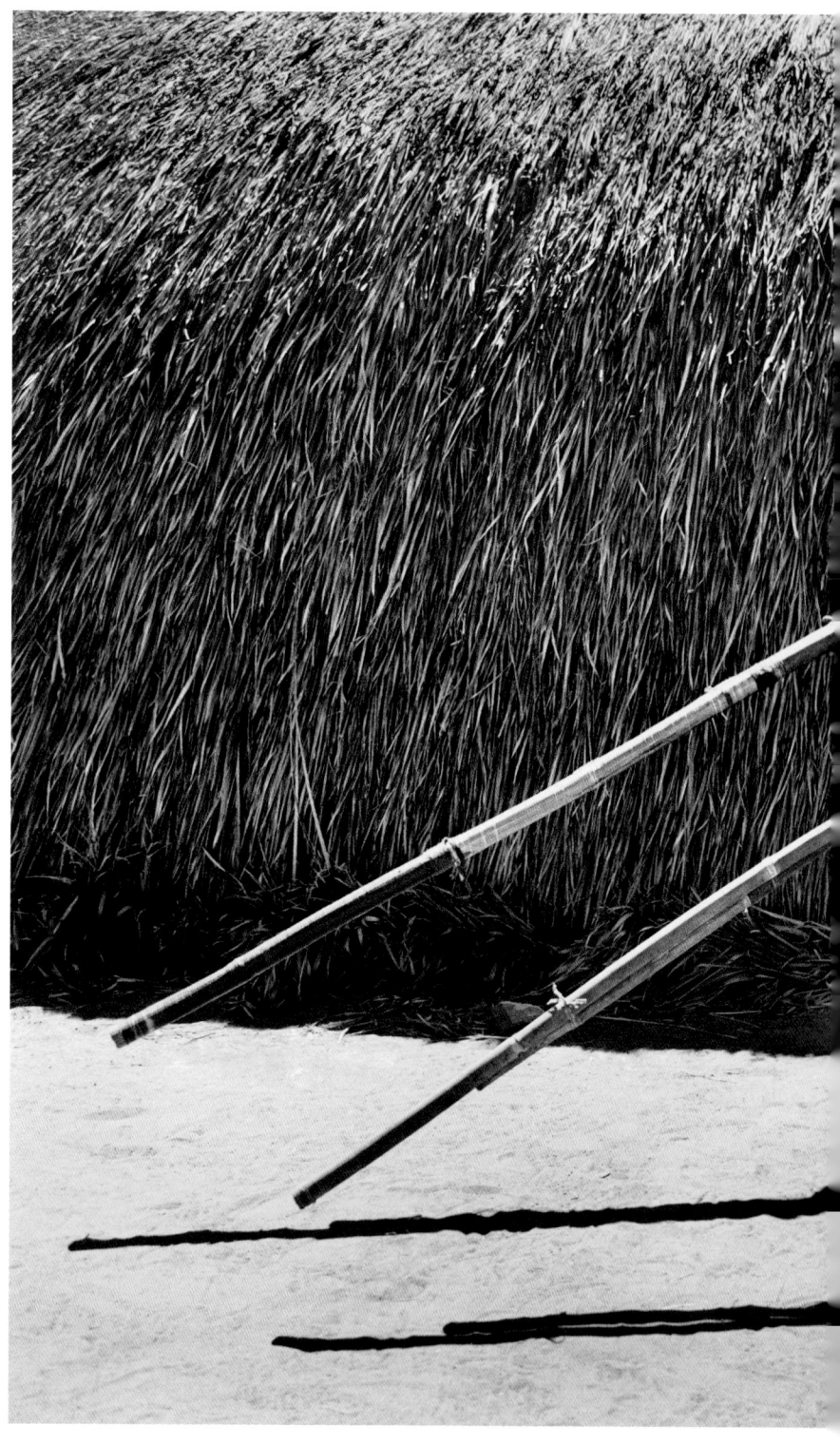

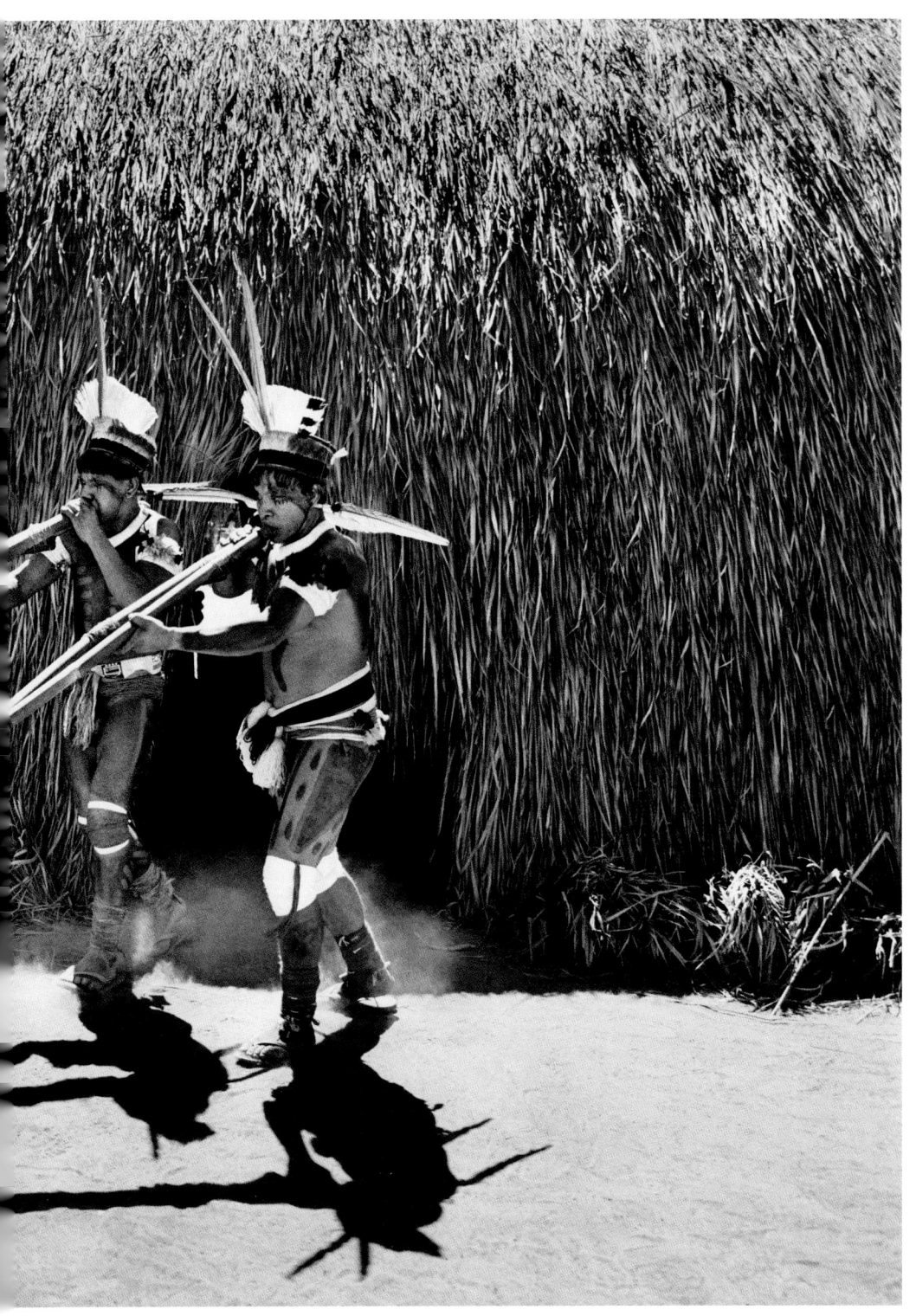

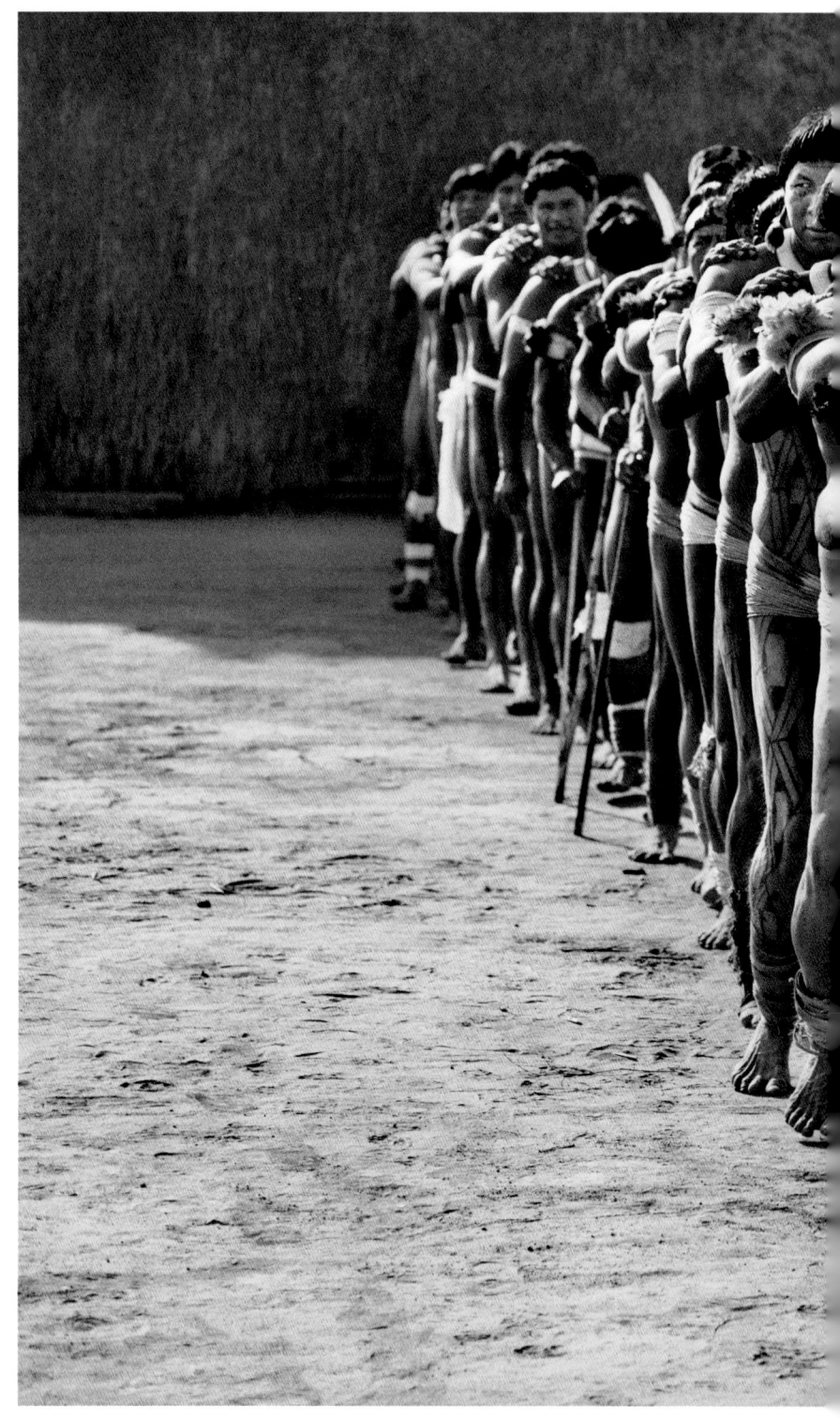

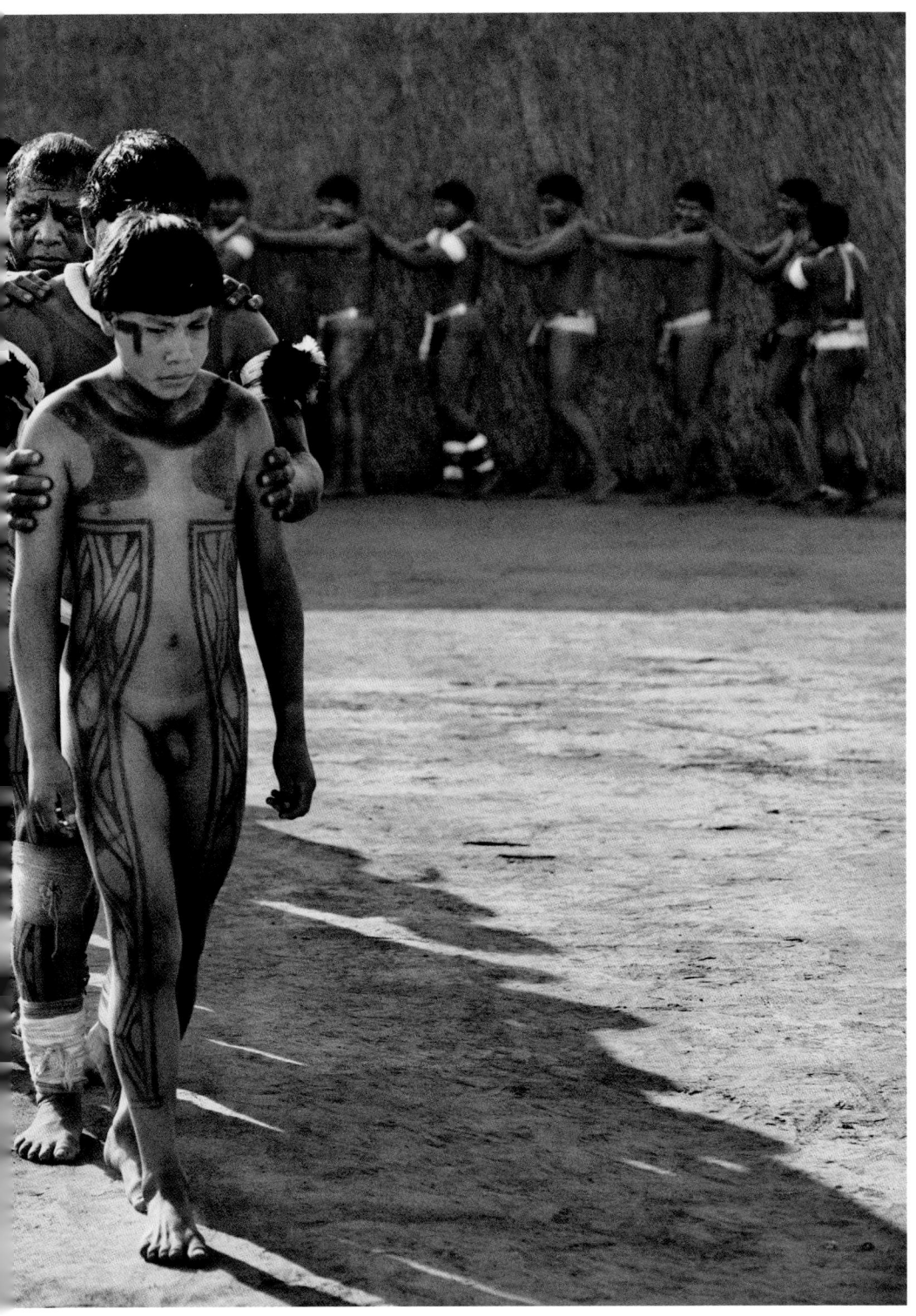

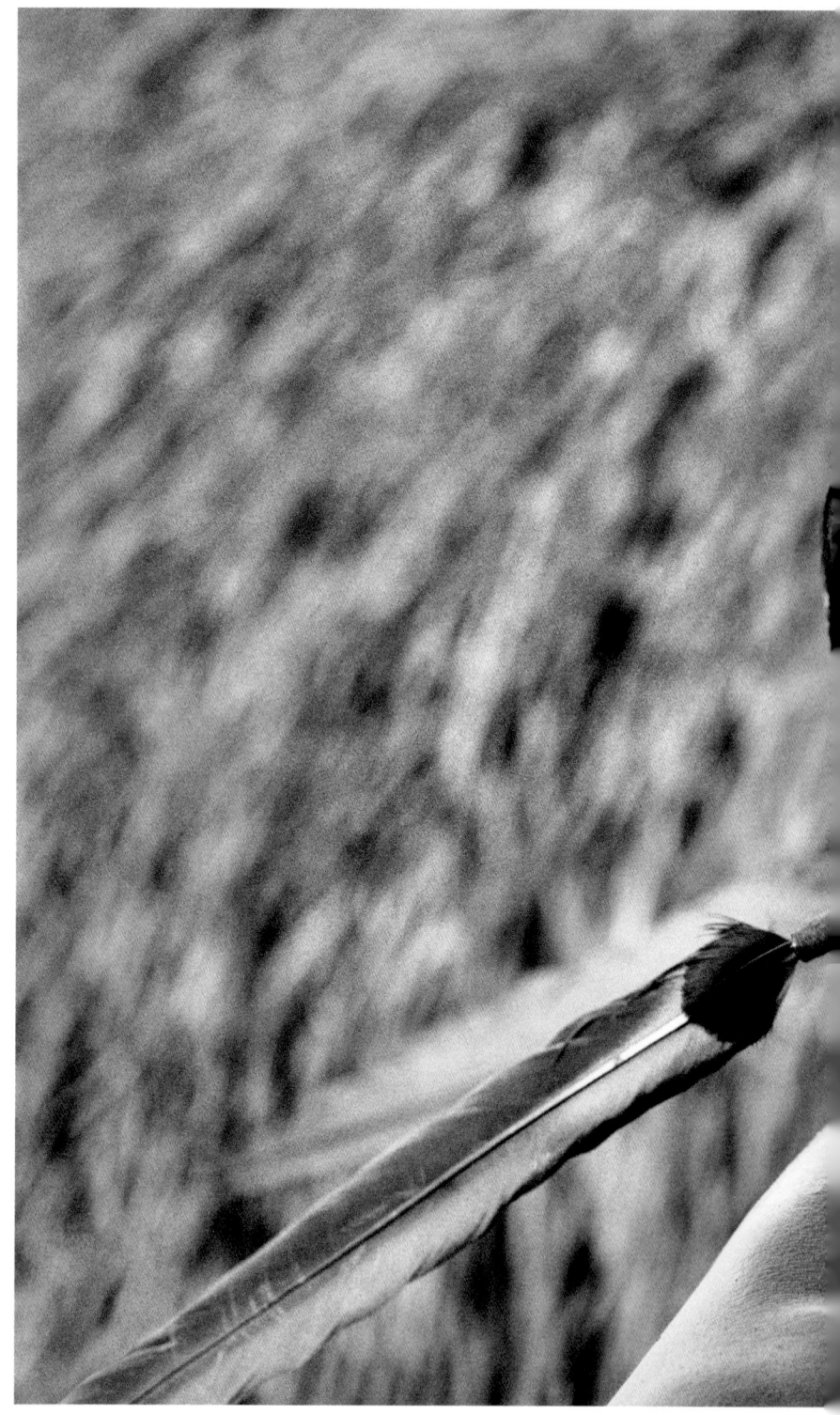

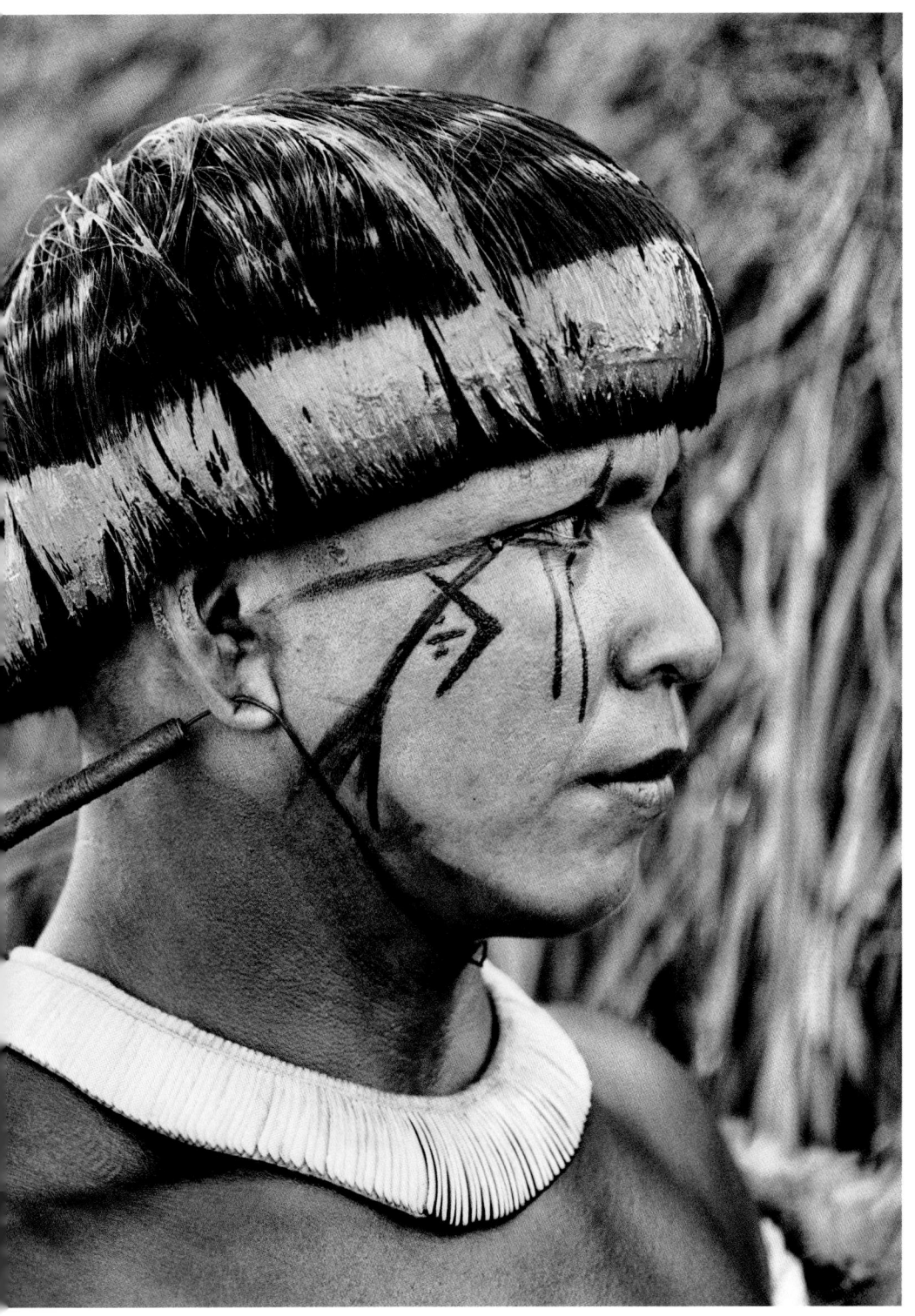

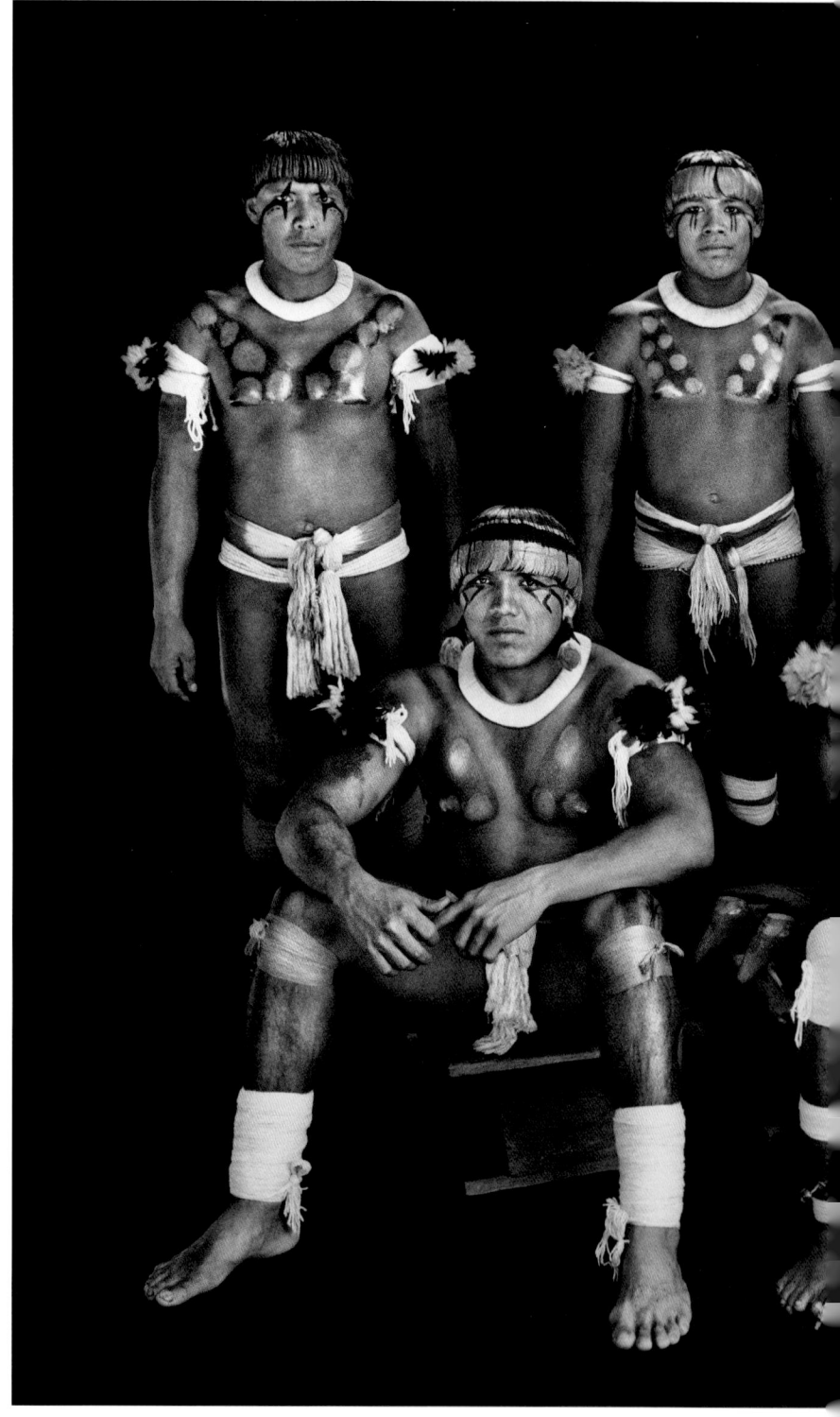

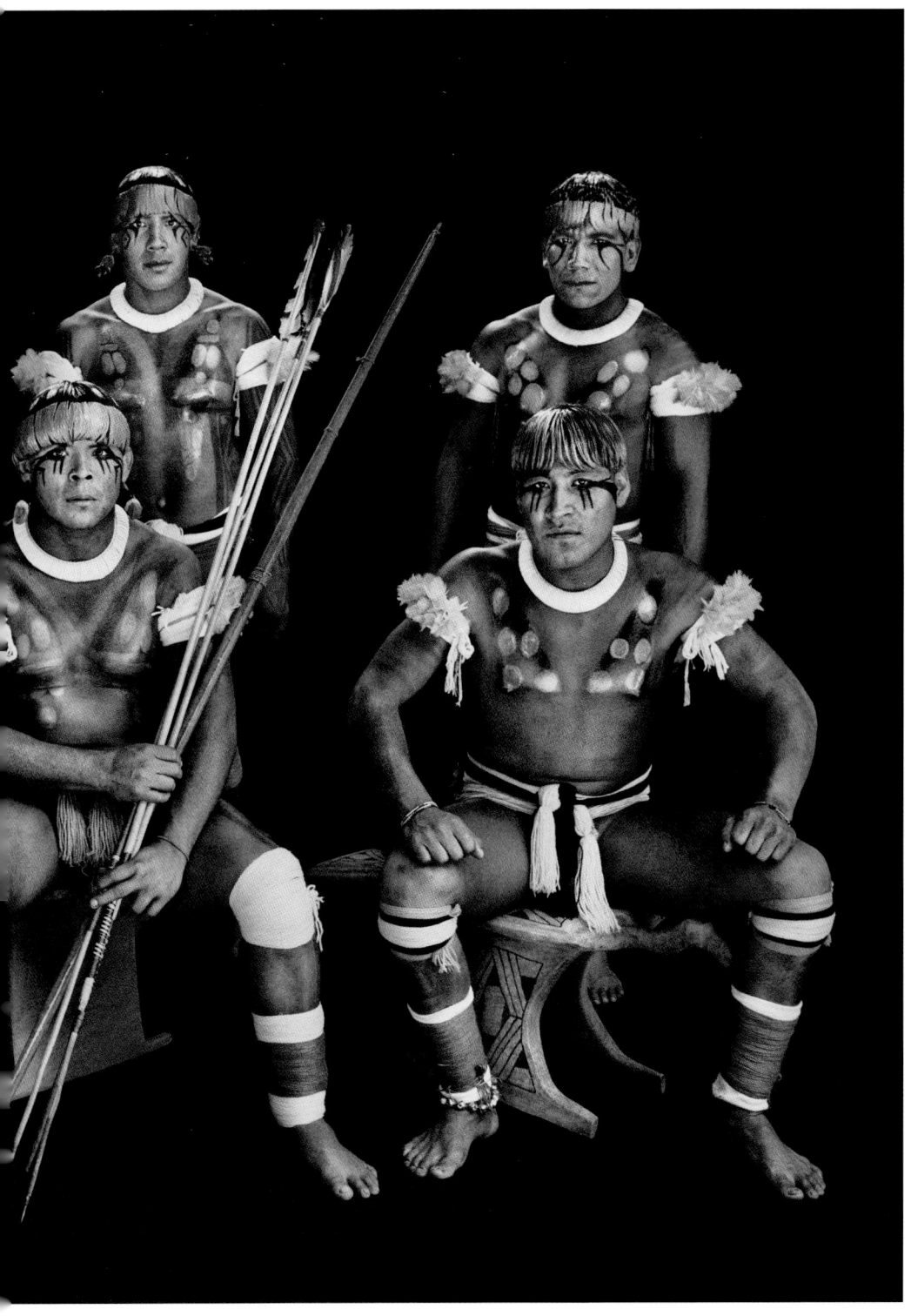

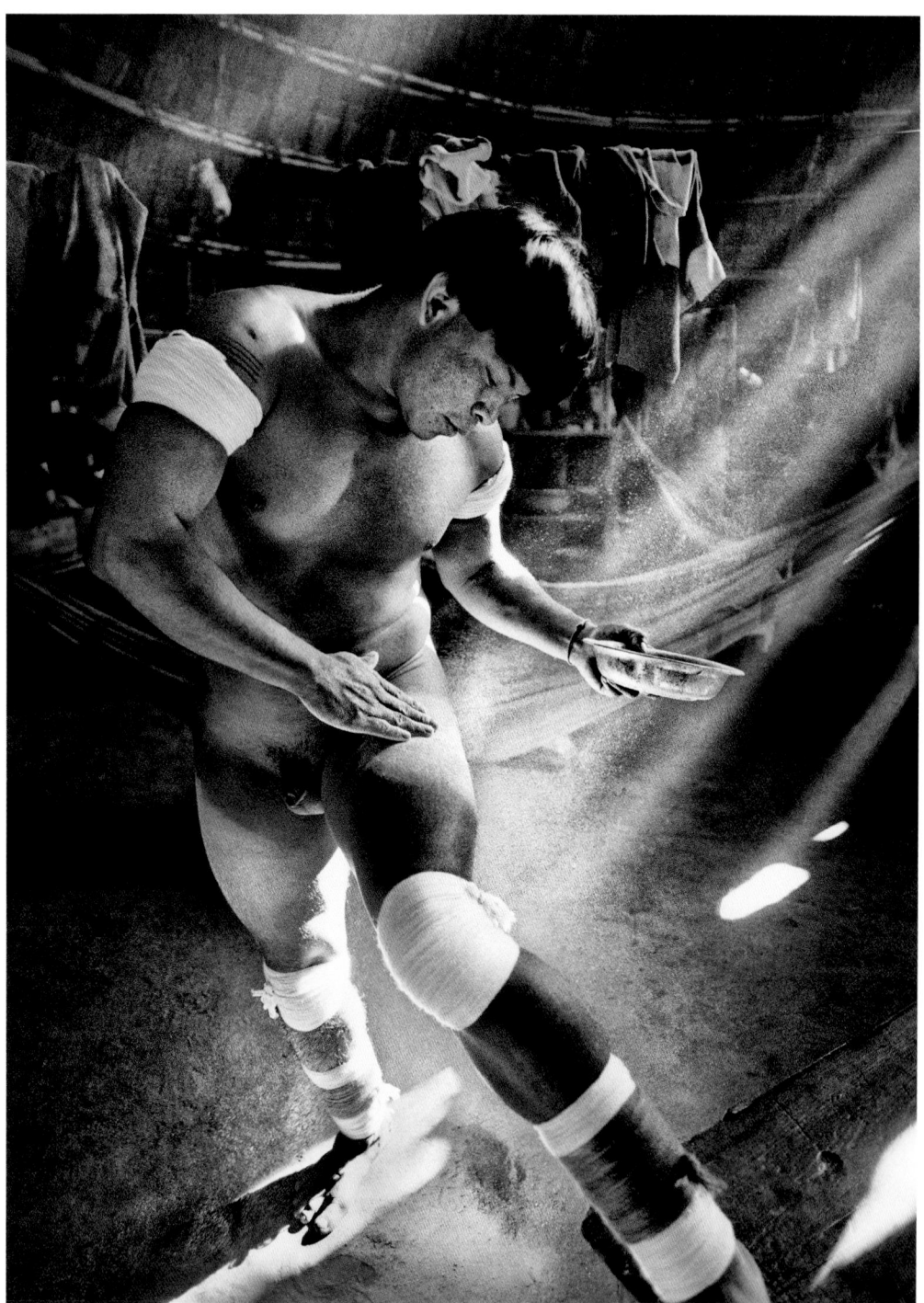

Pages 100/101 In the Waurá village during the festival of Kuarup, two men playing flutes go to escort adolescent girls who are ending their yearlong seclusion. They lead them in a kind of parade through the central plaza, seen by visitors from all the communities present. From that moment, the girls are eligible to marry. Xingu Indigenous Territory, state of Mato Grosso, 2005.

Pages 102/103 A young Kuikuro walks through the village to a ceremony in which his ears will be pierced as part of his initiation into adulthood. Xingu Indigenous Territory, state of Mato Grosso, 2005.

Pages 104/105 Yaukuma, a young Waurá warrior painted for Kuarup, with his hair impregnated with urucum. Around his neck, the distinctive necklace of snail shells collected in the region; in his ear, the feather earring worn at festivals. Xingu Indigenous Territory, state of Mato Grosso, 2005.

Pages 106/107 Kamayurá warriors. Standing in back (left to right): Tsaukumã, "Rafael," Makaulaka, and Ayawá. Seated: Ka'awã, Mayaru, and Tsimô. Kamuyurá village, Xingu Indigenous Territory, state of Mato Grosso, 2005.

Opposite Preparing to attend Yamurikumã, the women's festival, Mayaru Kamayurá paints his body already bound with white bands that emphasize his muscles. Xingu Indigenous Territory, state of Mato Grosso, 2005.

Pages 110/111 Kuarup in the Waurá village: warriors face off in the *huka-huka* fight. At the festival, groups from this village face off with each of the visiting groups, one after another. The fight is won when a warrior touches the back of his opponent's leg or, better yet, successfully knocks him over. Xingu Indigenous Territory, state of Mato Grosso, 2005.

Pages 112/113 Chief Kotok, leader of the Kamayurá, died in 2024. Xingu Indigenous Territory, state of Mato Grosso, 2005.

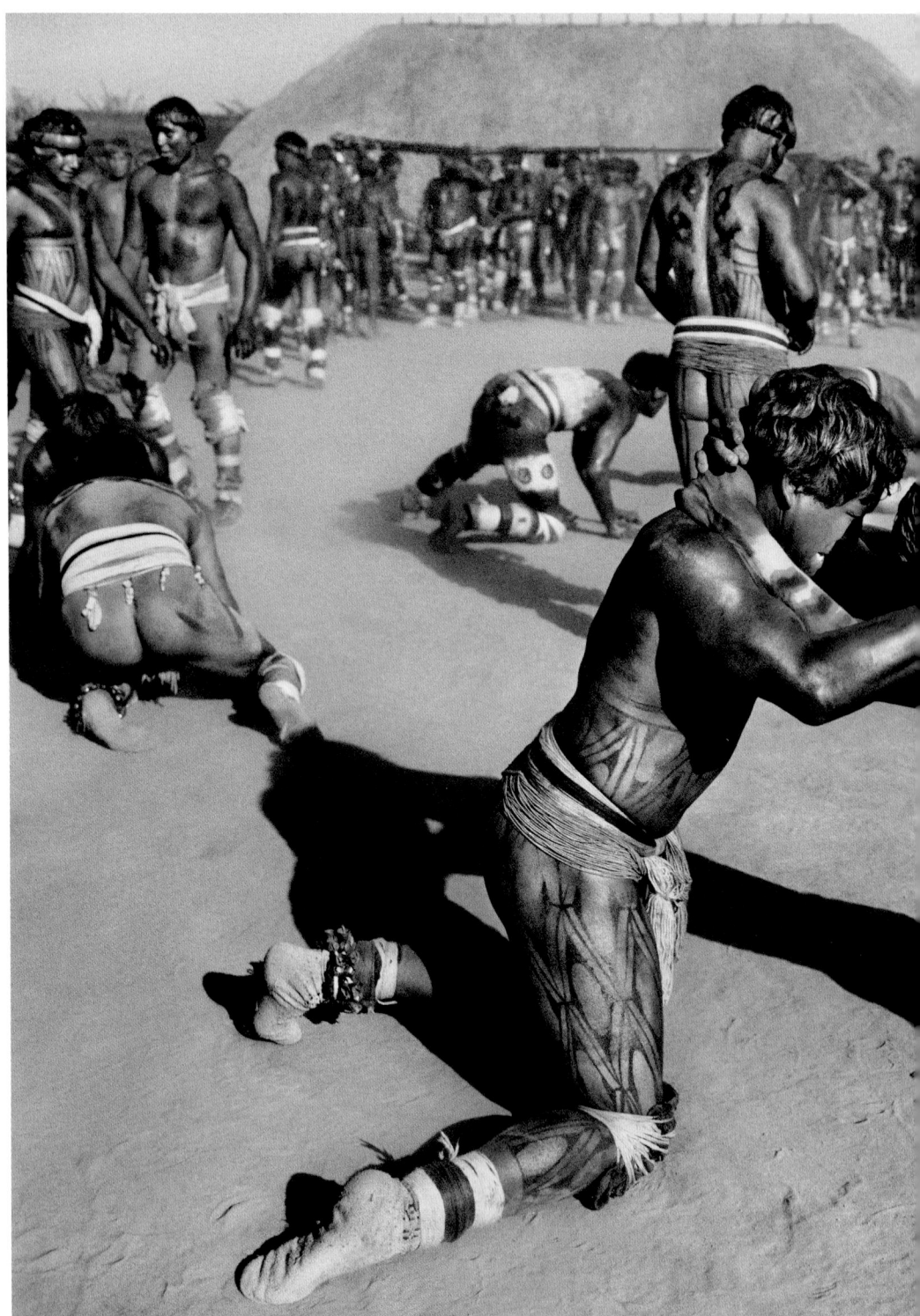

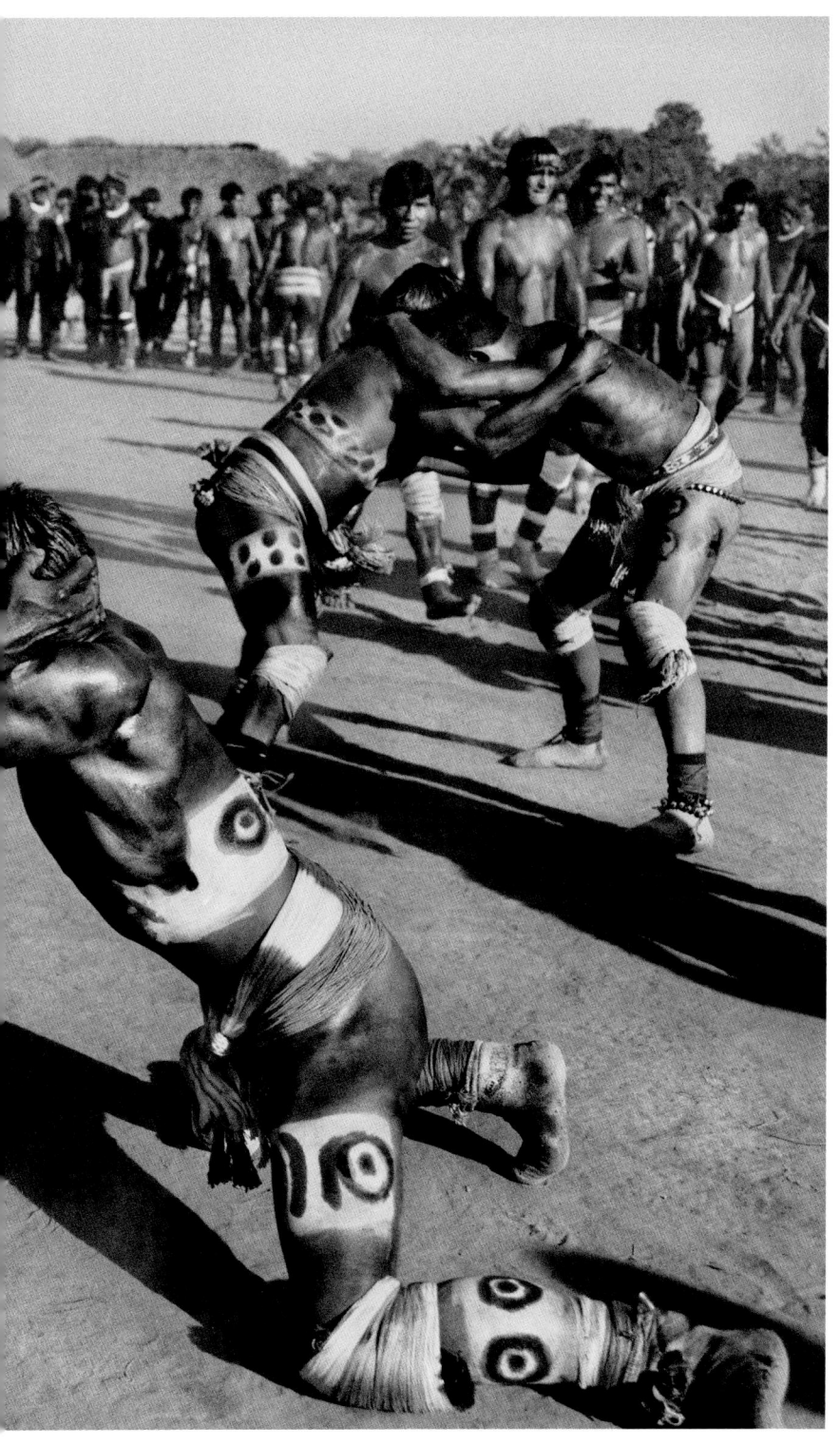

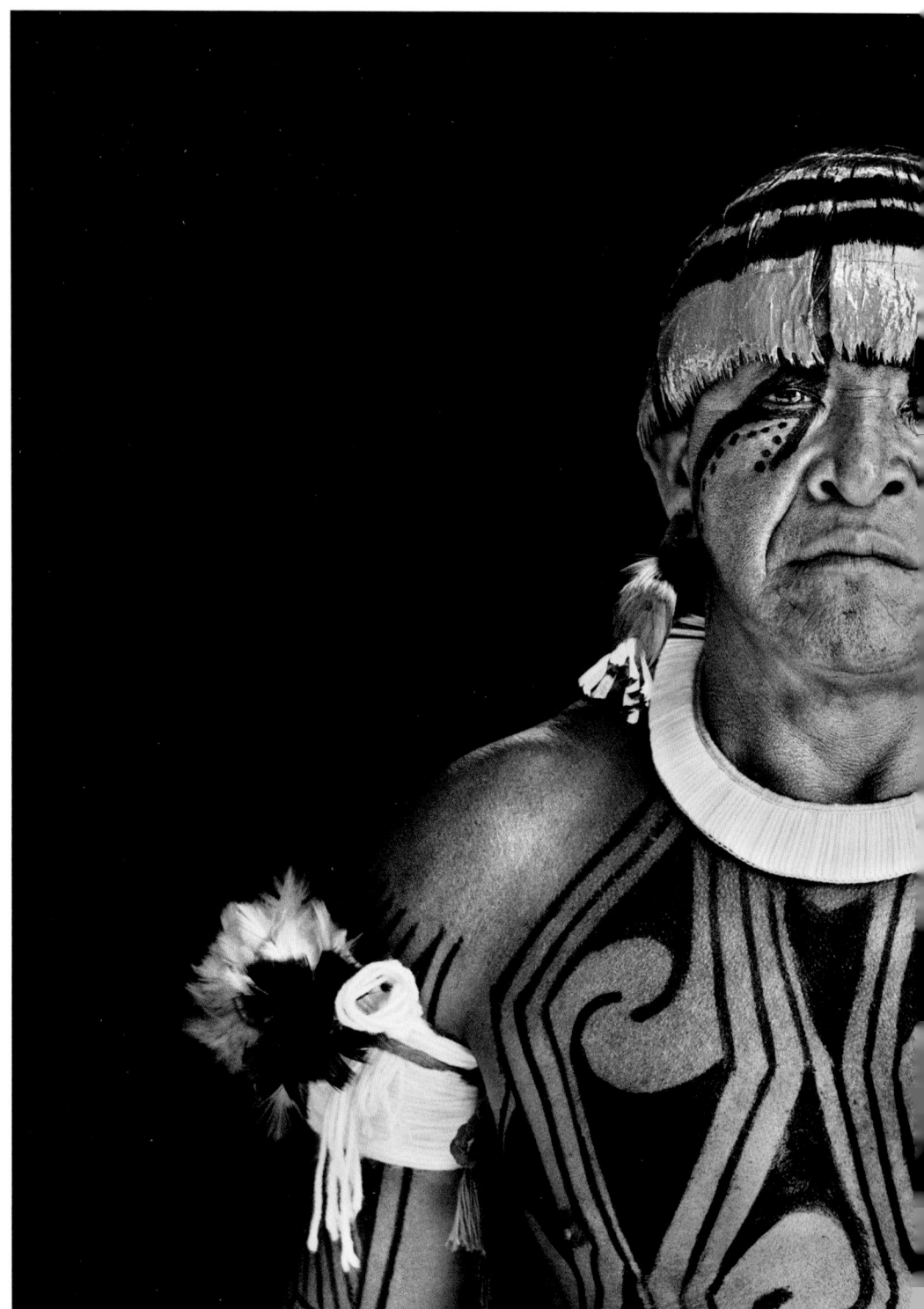

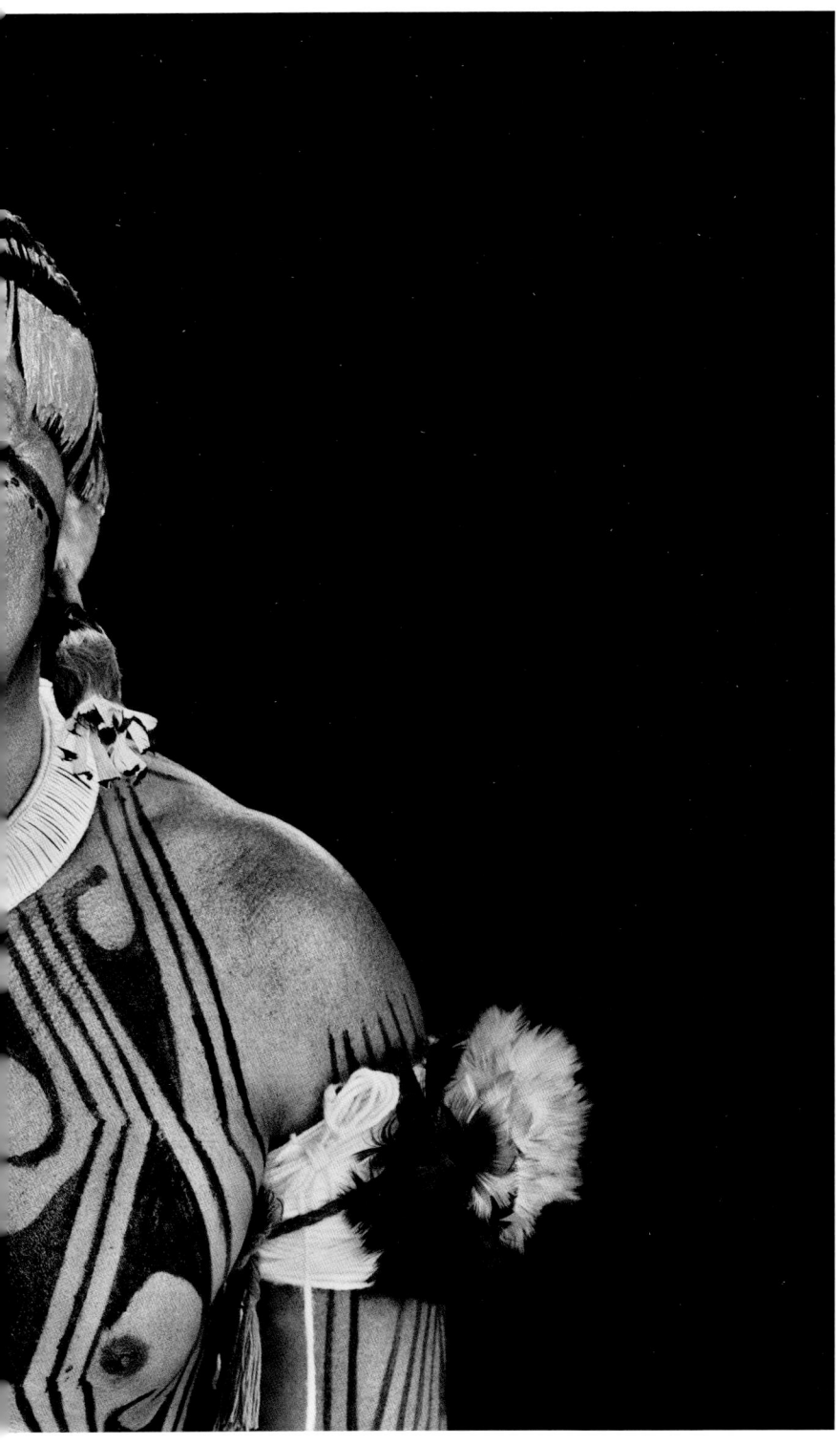

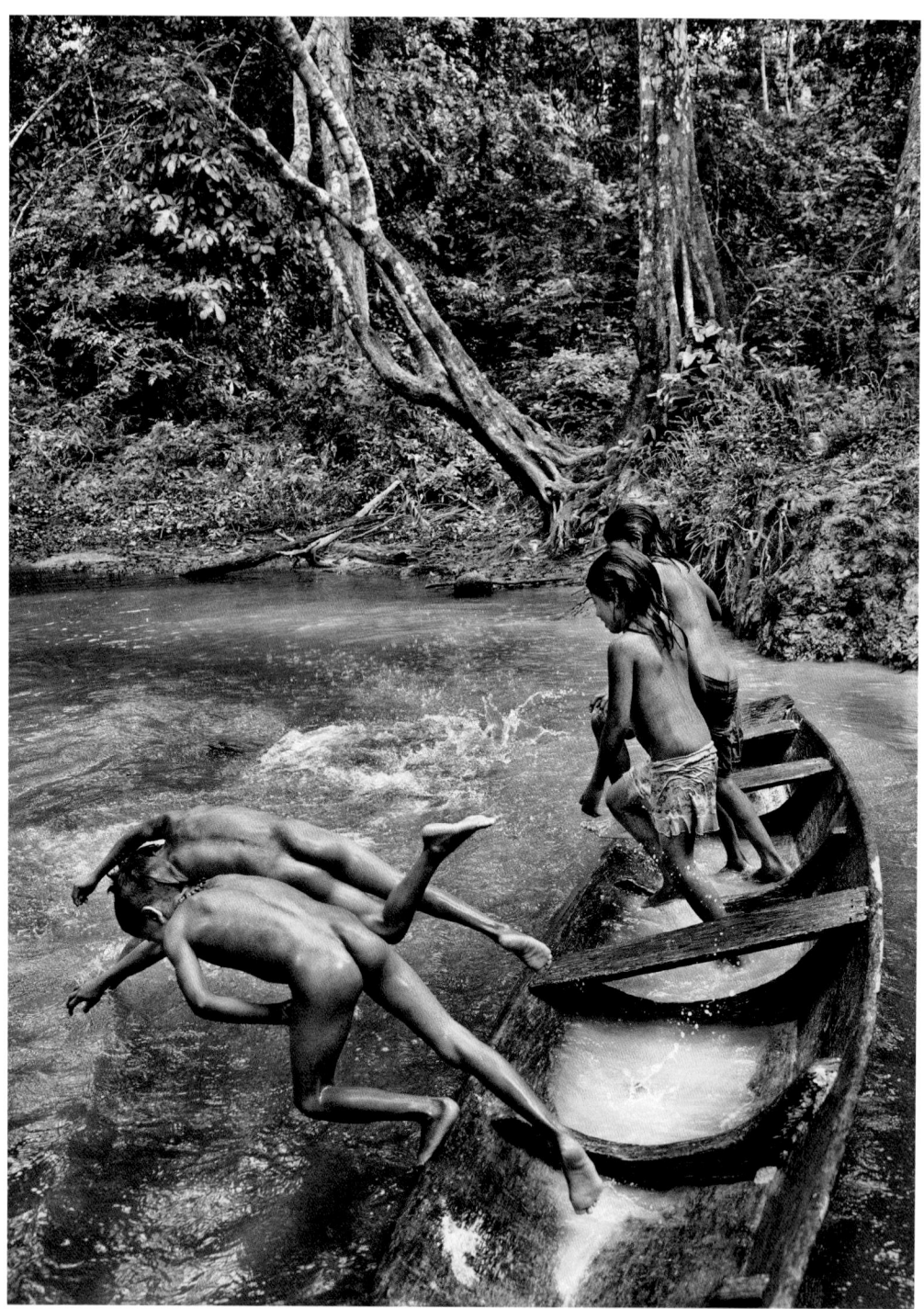

AWÁ-GUAJÁ

The Awá-Guajá are a low-contact (nearly "isolated") indigenous people, even though they live in the state of Maranhão, a state that in recent decades has undergone intensive illegal logging. The name combines their official identification, Guajá, with their name for themselves, Awá. Ethnolinguistic studies indicate that they inhabited territory in what is now the state of Pará, to the west, when they were part of the same Tupi–Guarani language group as the indigenous Guajajara and Tenetehara. In the early 19th century, they split off and migrated east, towards Maranhão. Today, they live in two indigenous territories (Upper Turiaçu and Carú), which they share with other ethnic groups that have greater outside contact: the Ka'apor, Timbira, and Guajajara.

The devastation of their lands began after vast deposits of iron ore were discovered in the area in the 1970s and the Brazilian government built a railroad and a highway system that cut through Awá land, to transport iron ore from the Carajás Mountains to the coast. Thousands of illegal invaders occupied the area and many Awá families were brutally massacred.

Today, the Awá remain in still-surviving remains of the forest, living as one of the last hunter-gatherer peoples in Brazil. They rely on the woods for food and survival. They hunt animals such as monkeys, armadillos, peccaries, and nasuas, and collect fruit and honey. Their houses are built using forest materials. Illegal logging on their land is making it harder and harder for Awá hunters to find prey in the forest, and they often refrain from hunting, fearing violent attacks by the loggers who are "closing in" on their communities, operating just 3 kilometers (2 miles) away. Families are going hungry.

Some 50 years after the first invasion by illegal loggers, Awá-Guajá territory continues to shrink, and indigenous defense organizations make accusations of genocide and extinction. That is why a campaign by the English nongovernmental organization Survival International describes the Awá-Guajá as "Earth's most threatened tribe."

There are now about 450 of them, of whom around one hundred live in isolation (divided into three different groups).

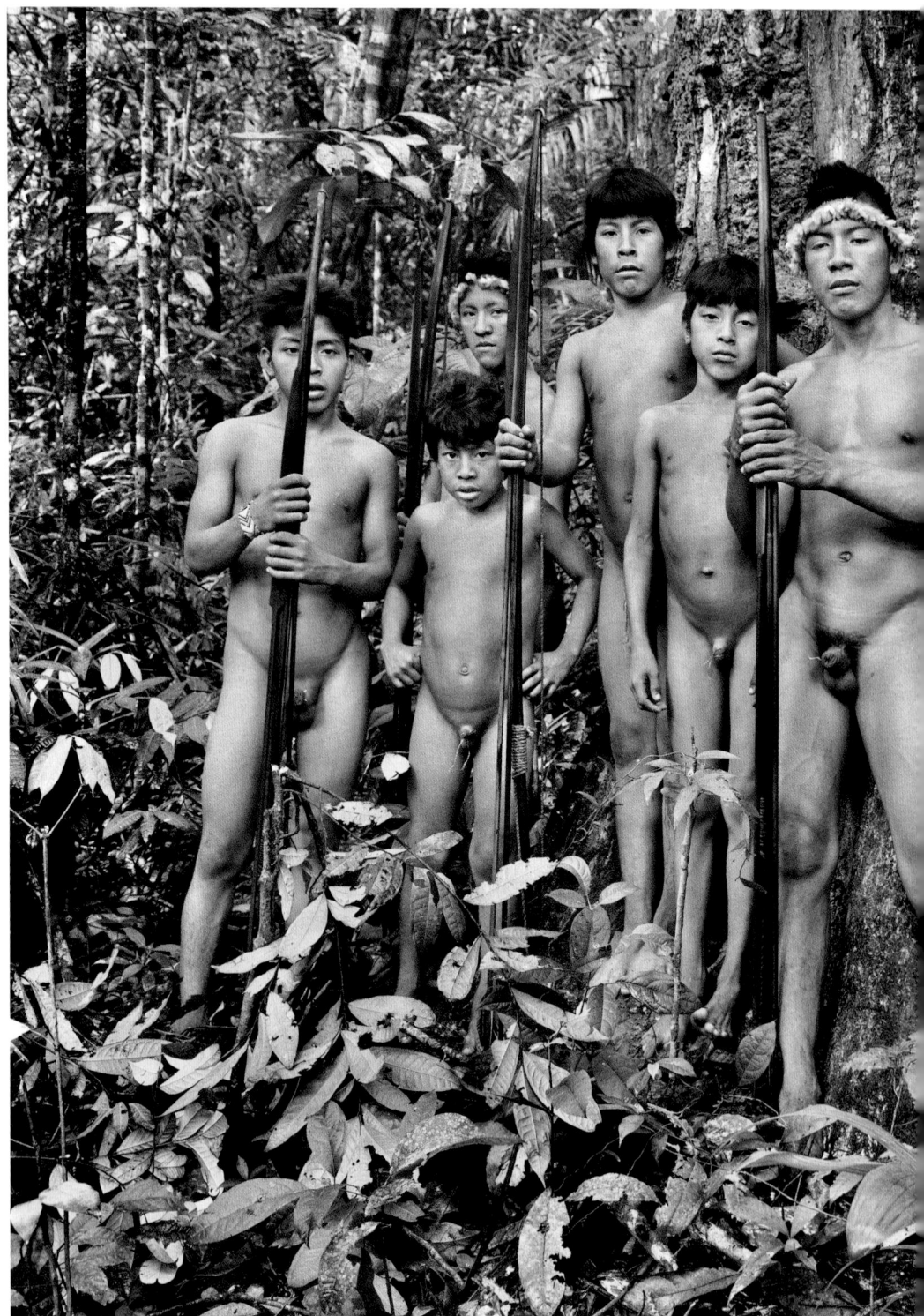

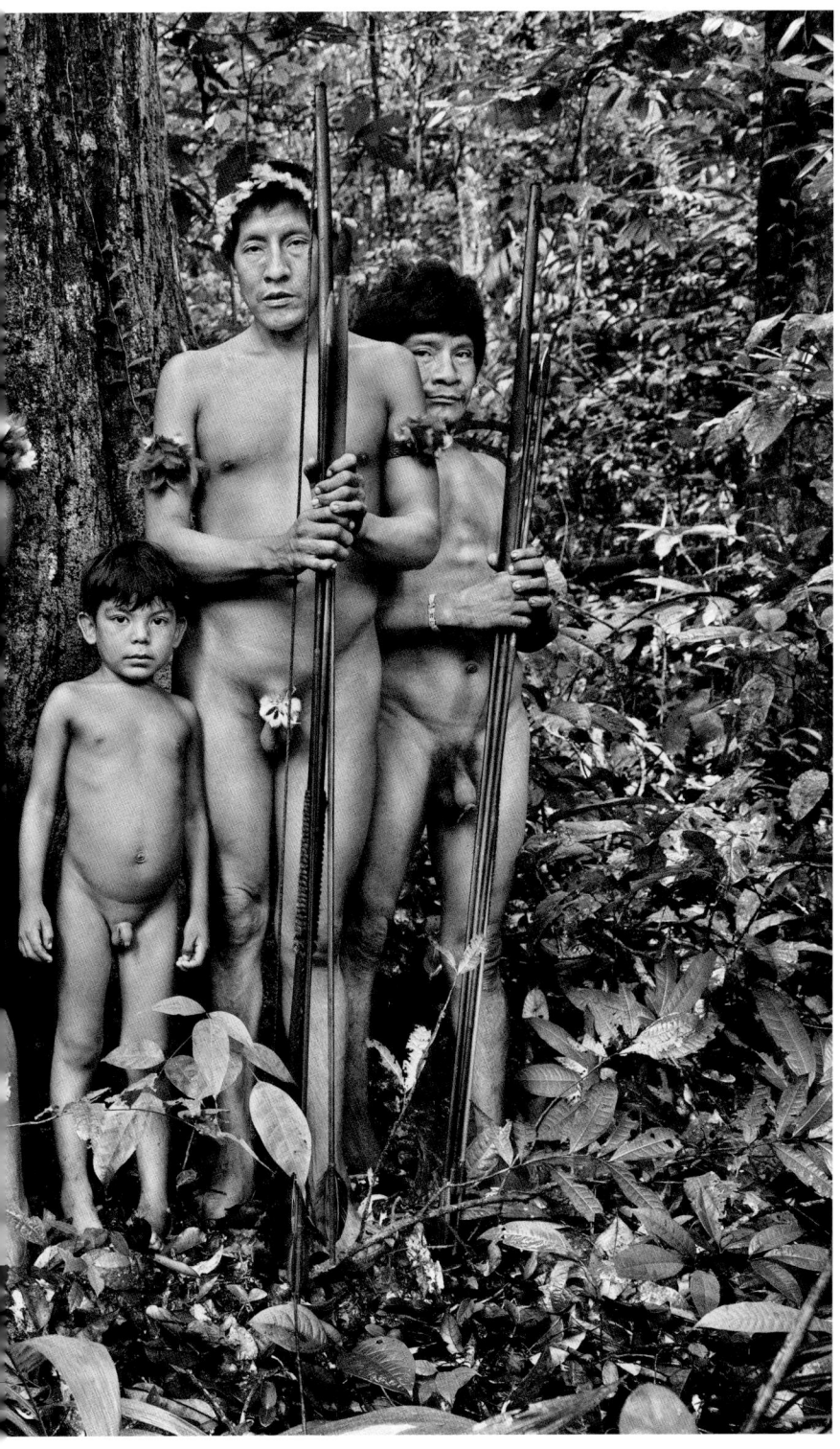

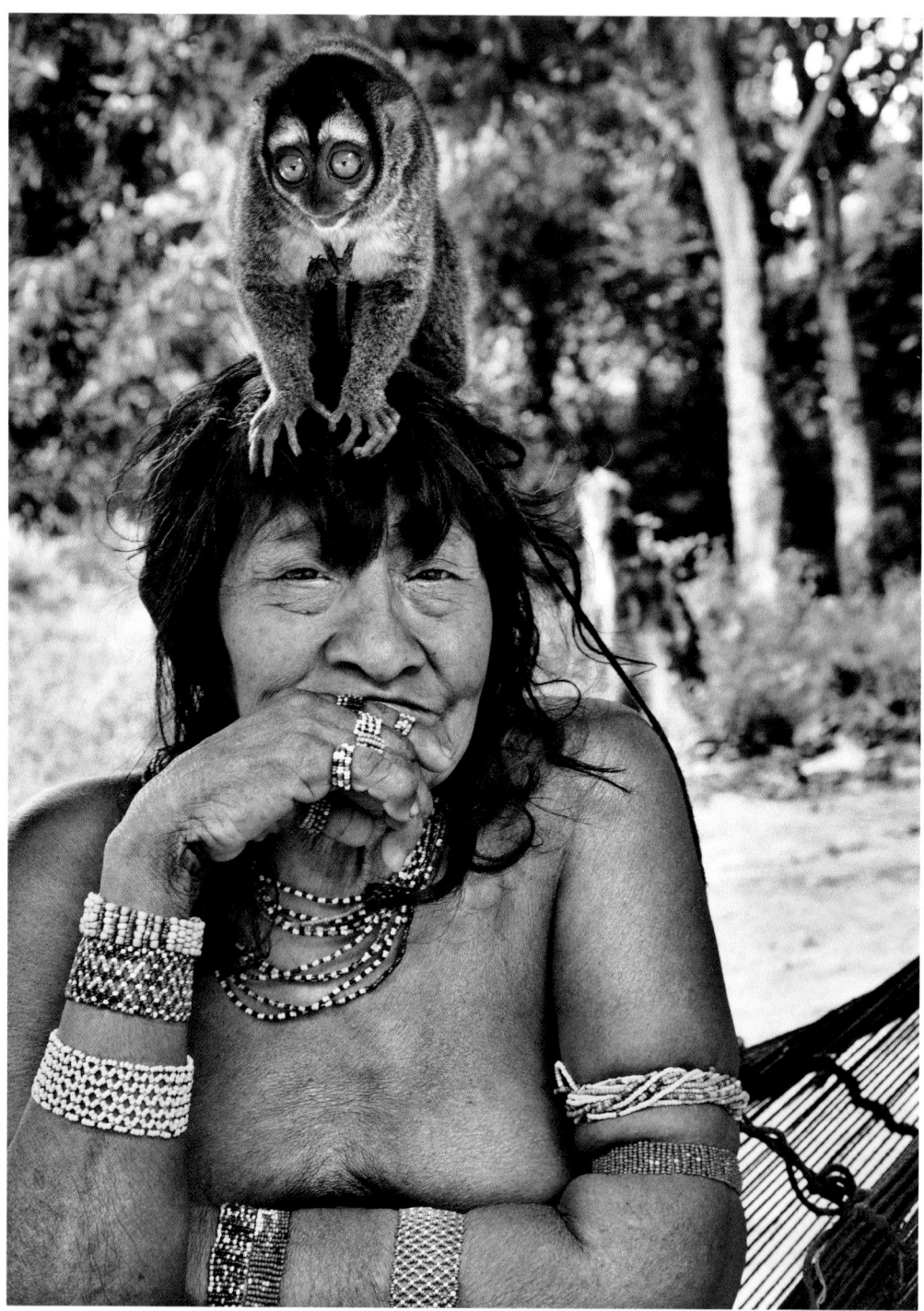

Page 114 Children playing in the Carú River near the village of Juriti. Awá-Guajá Indigenous Territory, state of Maranhão, 2013.

Pages 116/117 Right to left: Typaramatxia Awá, Pira-y-ma-a Awá, Maiakatan Awá, Yui Awá, Yhara Awá, Kiripy-tan Awá, Makoray Awá, Tikakoa Awá, and Takuary Awá travel through the forest searching the ground for signs of invaders and loggers violating their territory. Awá-Guajá Indigenous Territory, state of Maranhão, 2013.

Opposite Amapyranawin Awá in the village of Juriti with a tamarin monkey (*Saguinus niger*). The indigenous peoples of the Amazon commonly raise the young of animals they have hunted as if they were family members. This custom is even stronger among those of Tupi-Guarani origin, the culture that gave Portuguese the word *xerimbabo*, meaning "farm animal." Awá-Guajá Indigenous Territory, state of Maranhão, 2013.

Pages 120/121 Amerytxia Awá, the oldest person in the village of Juriti. She made a personal decision to live alone in the forest, far from the village itself. However, she visits the village often. Its residents also visit her to bring food, and the children play around her house. Awá-Guajá Indigenous Territory, state of Maranhão, 2013.

Pages 122/123 Typaramatxia Awá (foreground) and Kiripy-tan (background) on a hunt. Typaramatxia carries a monkey, a bearded saki (*Chiropotes satanas*) that he has just hunted with a bow and arrow. Monkey meat is one of the most desired types of meat among many indigenous cultures of the Amazon. These monkeys live in the treetops. To get at them, Awá hunters must climb the trees and keep their balance as they walk out on branches more than 30 meters (100 feet) above the ground. They call to their prey, imitating their cries, and shake the small branches. Either they hit their target with the first arrow or the animal gets away. Sometimes, a second hunter climbs a nearby tree as backup. Awá-Guajá Indigenous Territory, state of Maranhão, 2013.

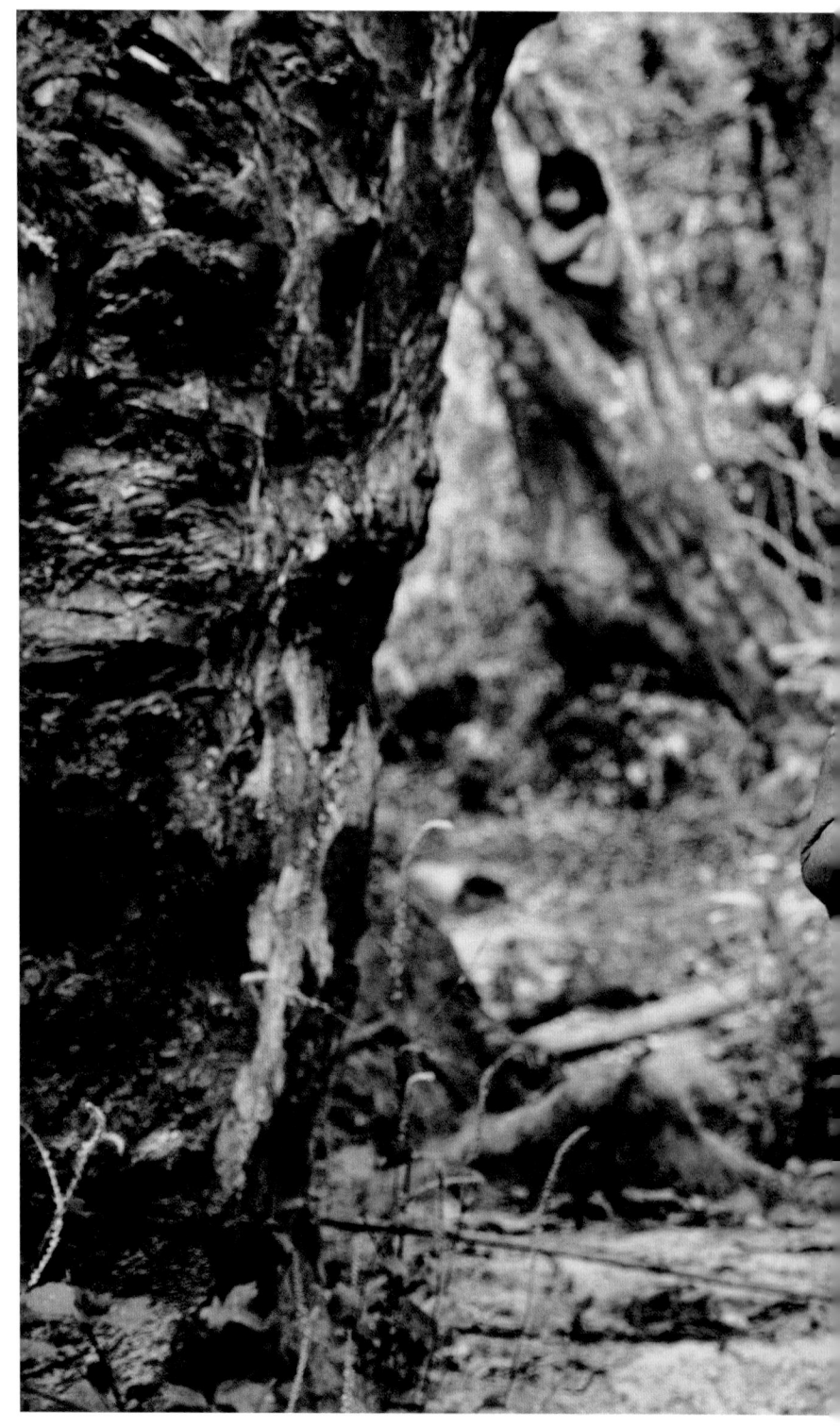

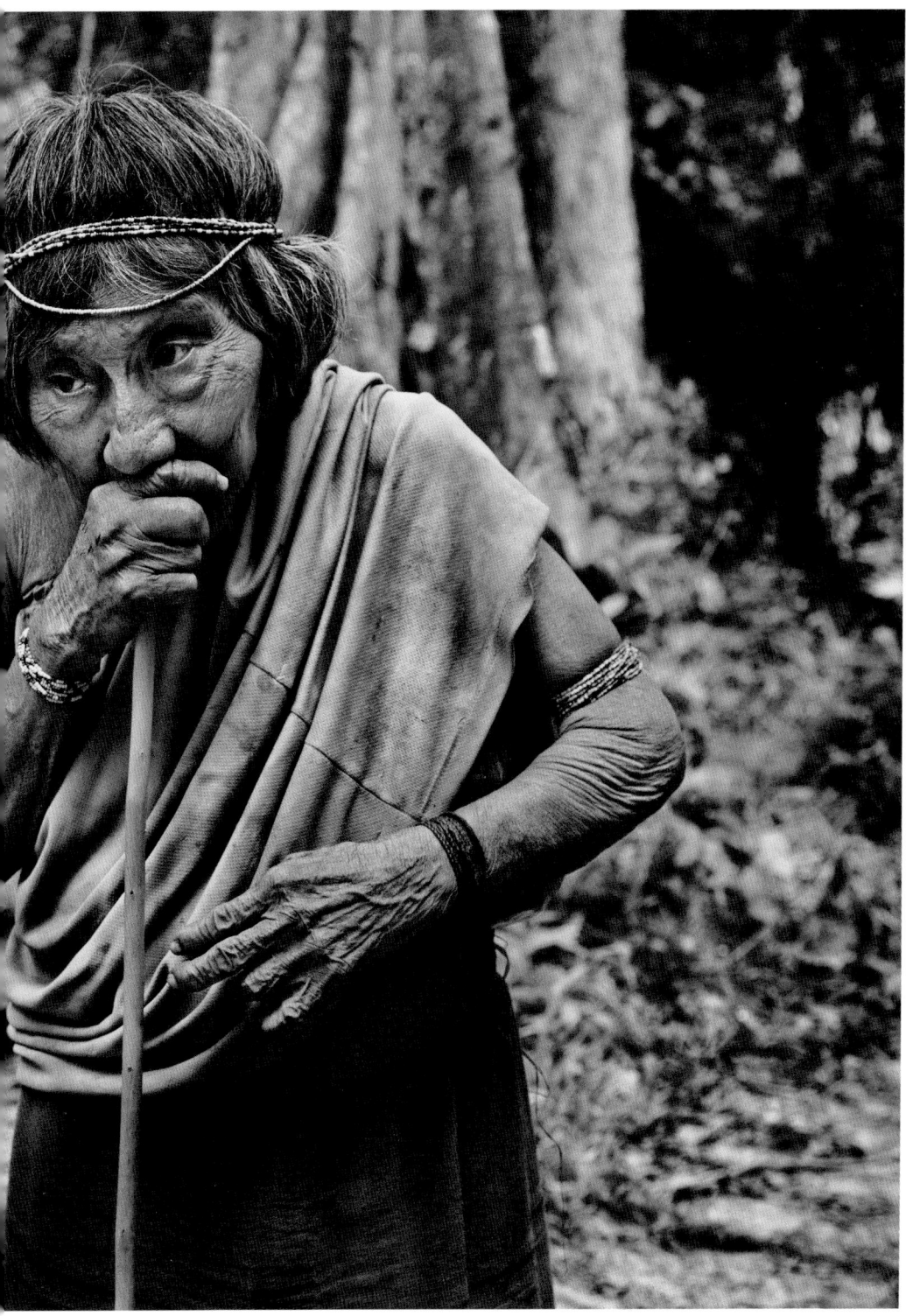

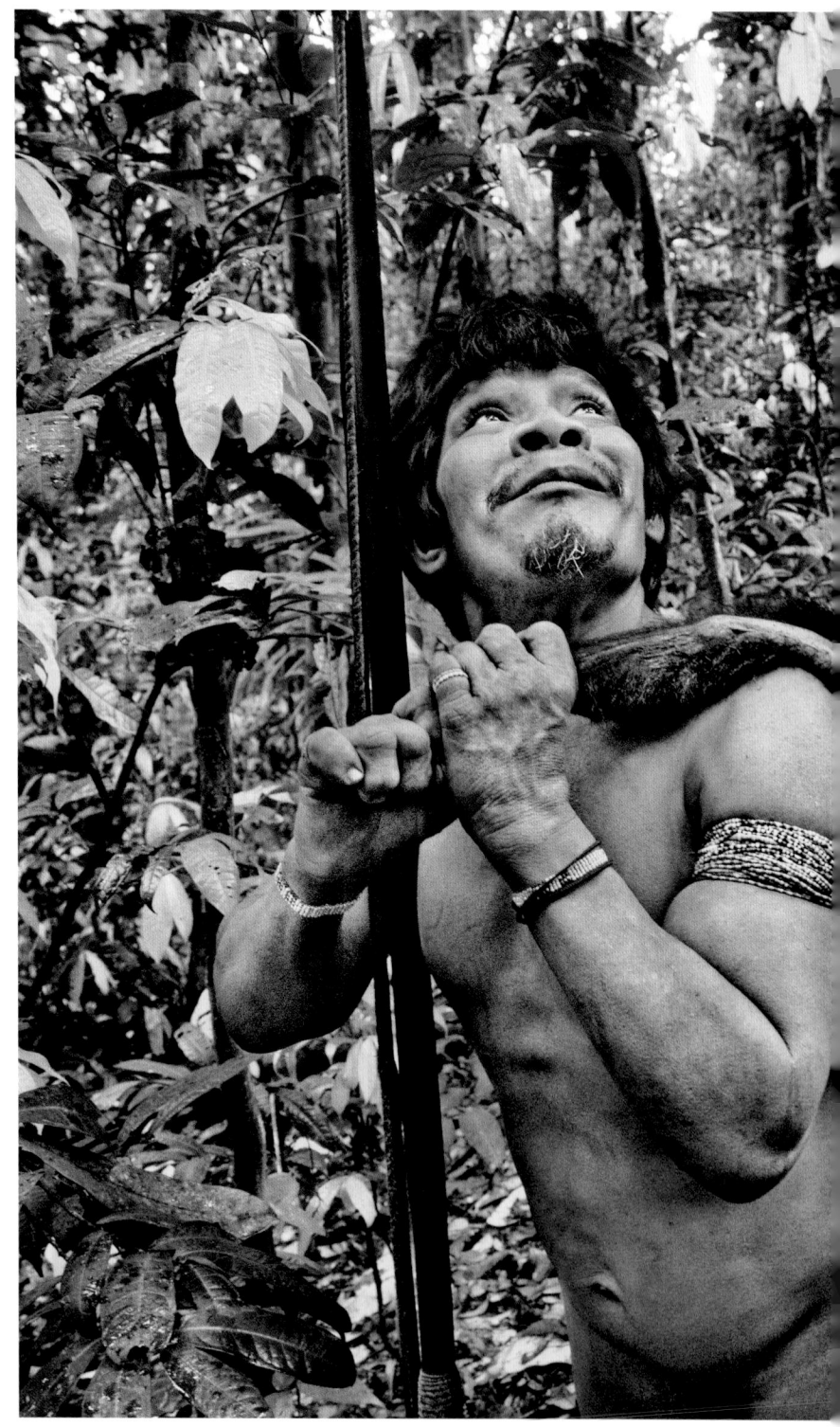

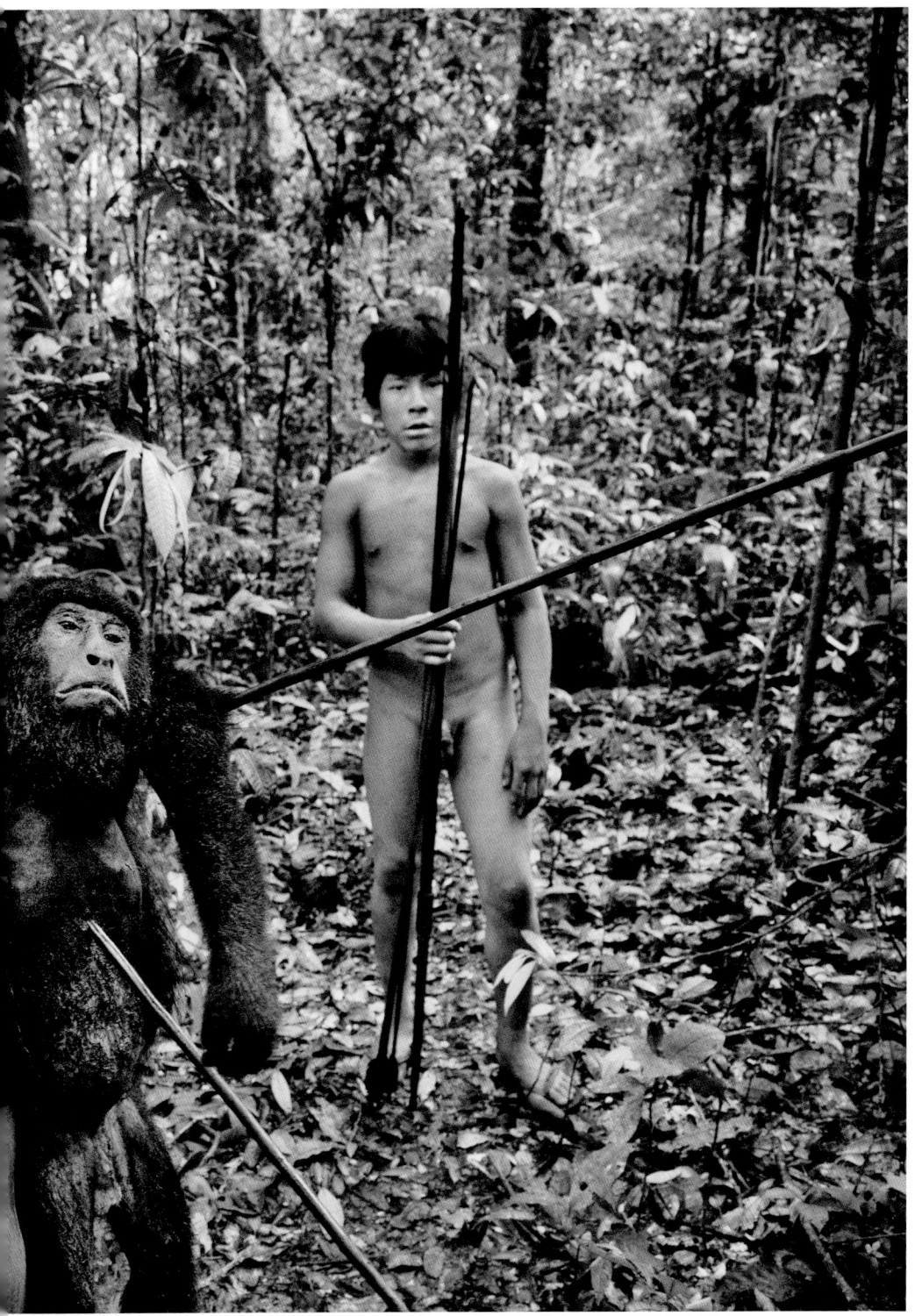

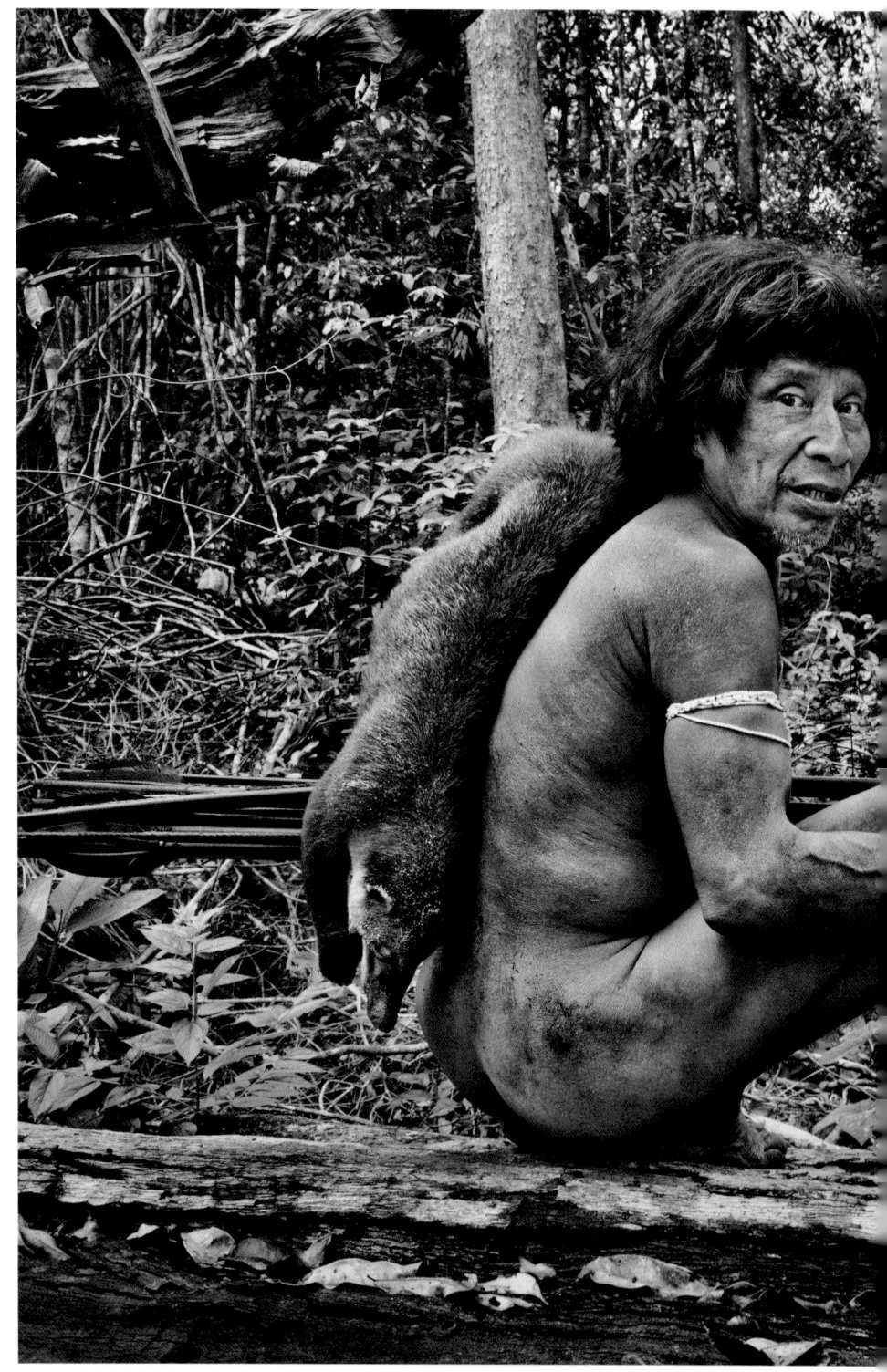

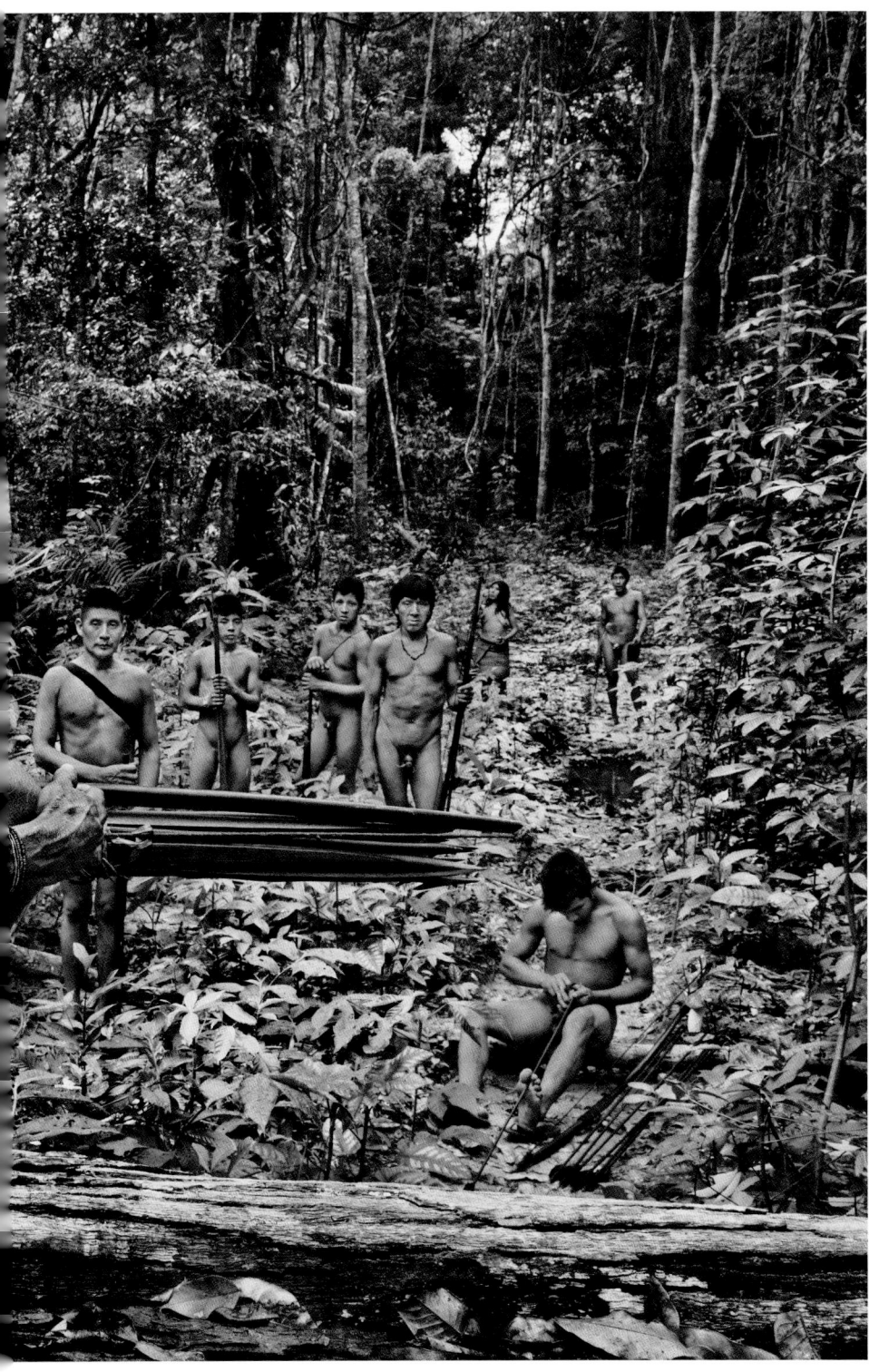

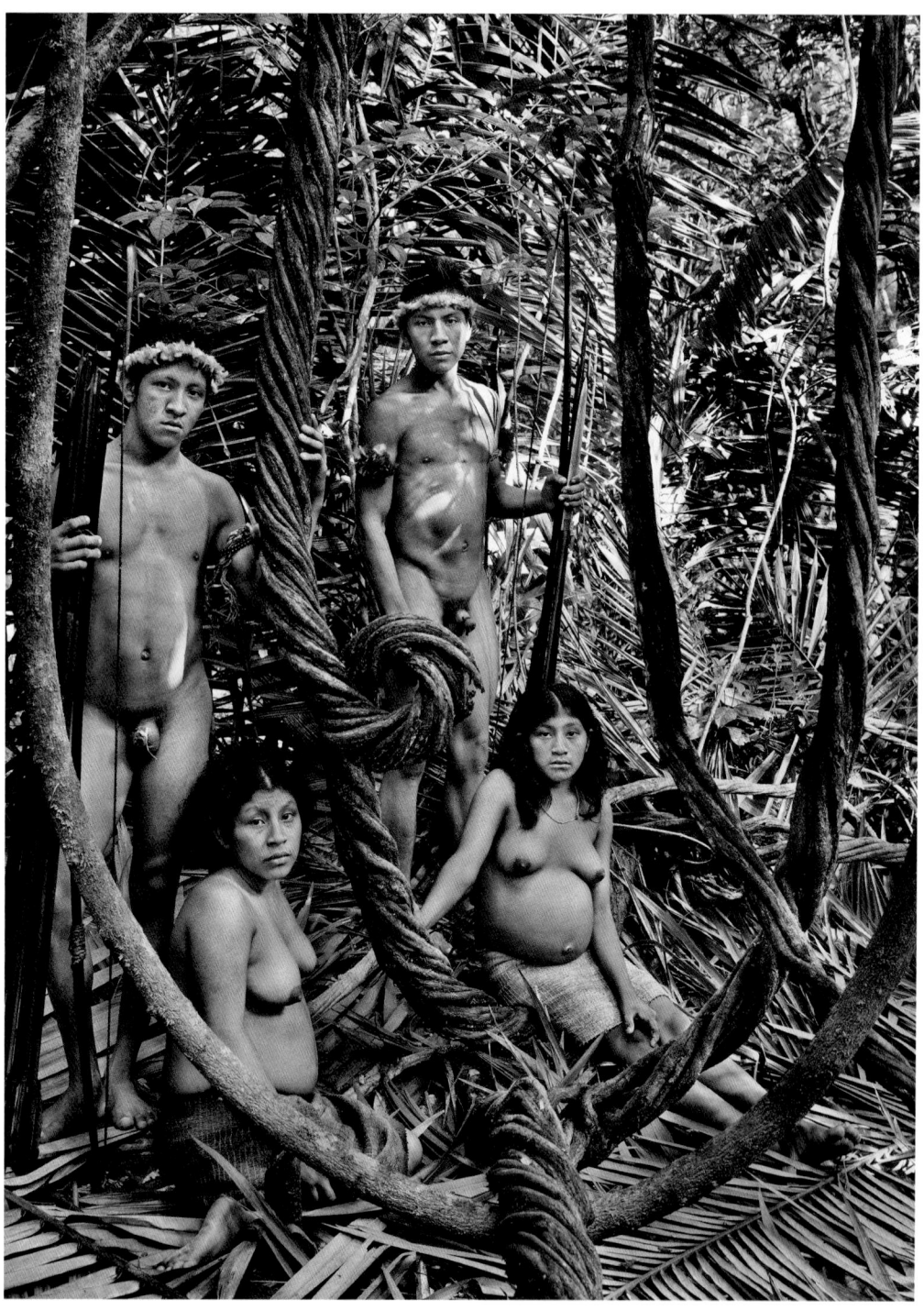

126

Pages 124/125 Mituruhum has killed a coati (*Nasua nasua*). On the hunting expedition, members of the Awá-Guajá community find tread marks from the tractors of illegal loggers who invade the forest on Awá lands, cut down trees, and steal the wood for export. To cut down one tree that produces precious wood, they cut a road into the forest so their trucks can access and transport the wood. In the process, illegal loggers destroy hundreds of other trees and open a path for future invaders and other intruders. Awá-Guajá Indigenous Territory, state of Maranhão, 2013.

Opposite Left to right: Tikakoa Awá and his wife, Pananiwia Awá, and Yui Awá with his wife, Tikapion Awá, in a hunting encampment. Awá-Guajá Indigenous Territory, state of Maranhão, 2013.

FLYING RIVERS

One of the most extraordinary—and perhaps least known—features of the Amazon rainforest is a phenomenon known colloquially as "flying rivers." It may seem like a contradiction to talk of a "river" that cannot be seen, yet these "flying rivers" carry more water than the Amazon River itself, supplying it to much of South America and beyond. Scientists have estimated that, while 17 billion tons of water enter the Atlantic from the Amazon River each day, over a similar period 20 billion tons of water rise into the atmosphere from the jungle and leave the rainforest, earning it the nickname "Green Ocean."

How does this work? In a process often compared with natural geysers or with using a straw to drink, a tree sucks groundwater through its roots to feed its growth. The moisture that eventually reaches its leaves evaporates as vapor. Then, most crucially, by making contact with bio-aerosols emitted by the forest, such as pollen, or perhaps dust blown over from the Sahara or other miniscule particles, the vapor forms raindrops that replenish the groundwater. Thus a natural circle is completed.

What is remarkable, though, is the scale on which this takes place. A large tree can suck water from as much as 60 meters below the ground and produce as many as 1,000 liters (265 gallons) of water per day. And since this is repeated by between 400 and 600 billion trees, it is easy to see how the Amazon forest generates an important proportion of the water that it later receives. In fact, even the water that reaches the mainland through evaporation of seawater is itself quickly recycled by the jungle in a process known as evapotranspiration.

This initial stage is visible most mornings when low-lying puffs of clouds appear across the horizon. Then, as the day advances, these rise and form larger clouds, in some cases joining middle- and high-level clouds at an altitude of 2,000 to 4,000 meters (6,500 to 13,000 feet), before disgorging their rain or becoming "flying rivers" which gain even greater strength as they move west across the Amazon. When blocked by the towering Andes, they then turn towards the south and southeast of the continent. Thus, what may appear to be seasonal cloud formations are in fact "rivers" serving as conveyor belts to provide water for cities, industries, hydroelectric power plants, and farms thousands of kilometers away in southern Brazil, Paraguay, Uruguay, and Argentina. Thus, a poor wet season in the Amazon translates easily into a drought in a wide stretch of the continent.

But if the "flying rivers" are vital to the economic welfare of tens of millions of people, mainly in Brazil, they also impact weather patterns across the globe and are themselves vulnerable to the effects of deforestation and global warming. And in both cases, what happens in the Amazon is a key variable. Scientists believe that, as a result of accelerated deforestation and climate change, the ground-level temperature of the basin has already risen by 1.5 °C (2.7 °F) and is set to rise a further 2 °C (3.6 °F) if current trends are maintained. Similarly, they fear a drop of annual rainfall of between 10 and 20 percent as a result of global warming.

Pages 130/131 The Uraricoera River flows through the forest in the Parima Forest Reserve area. Yanomami Indigenous Territory, state of Roraima, 2018.

Pages 132/133 Strong winds from the Atlantic reach the continent and blow across the Amazon rainforest and over the Mount Roraima area, in the far north of Brazil. The wind concentrates the clouds, already heavy with recent evaporation, and makes visible the "flying river" that will carry moisture thousands of kilometers. Macuxi Indigenous Territory Raposa–Serra do Sol, state of Roraima, 2018.

Pages 134/135 A dark cloud announces imminent rains on the Jaú River, Jaú National Park, state of Amazonas, 2019.

Pages 136/137 In front of the Mariuá Archipelago in the Middle Rio Negro, clouds are reflected in the black water of the Rio Negro. State of Amazonas, 2019.

Pages 138/139 Evaporation in the forest by the Auaris River, in the Parima Forest Reserve. Yanomami Indigenous Territory, state of Roraima, 2018.

Pages 140/141 River landscape, estuary of the Jaú River. Jaú National Park, state of Amazonas, 2019.

Pages 142/143 Jaú River, Jaú National Park. View of an *igapó*, a type of forest frequently flooded by black water from rivers and a cumulonimbus cloud formation. State of Amazonas, 2019.

Pages 144/145 The *paraná* connecting the Rio Negro with the Cuyuní River. In Portuguese, *paranás* are lake-like bodies of water connected to major rivers by canals called *furos* (punctures). During floods, the two often merge as if the river were widening. State of Amazonas, 2019.

Pages 146/147 Rain in the Parima Forest Reserve area, in the Aracacá region, Yanomami Indigenous Territory, state of Roraima, 2018.

Pages 148/149 Rain clouds above the Marié-Mirim mountain range, Yanomami Indigenous Territory. Municipality of São Gabriel da Cachoeira, state of Amazonas, 2018.

Pages 150/151 An inselberg ("island mountain") in the Parima Forest Reserve. Yanomami Indigenous Territory, state of Roraima, 2018.

Pages 152/153 View of an *igapó*, a seasonally flooded blackwater forest, in the Mariuá Archipelago, Middle Rio Negro, state of Amazonas, 2019.

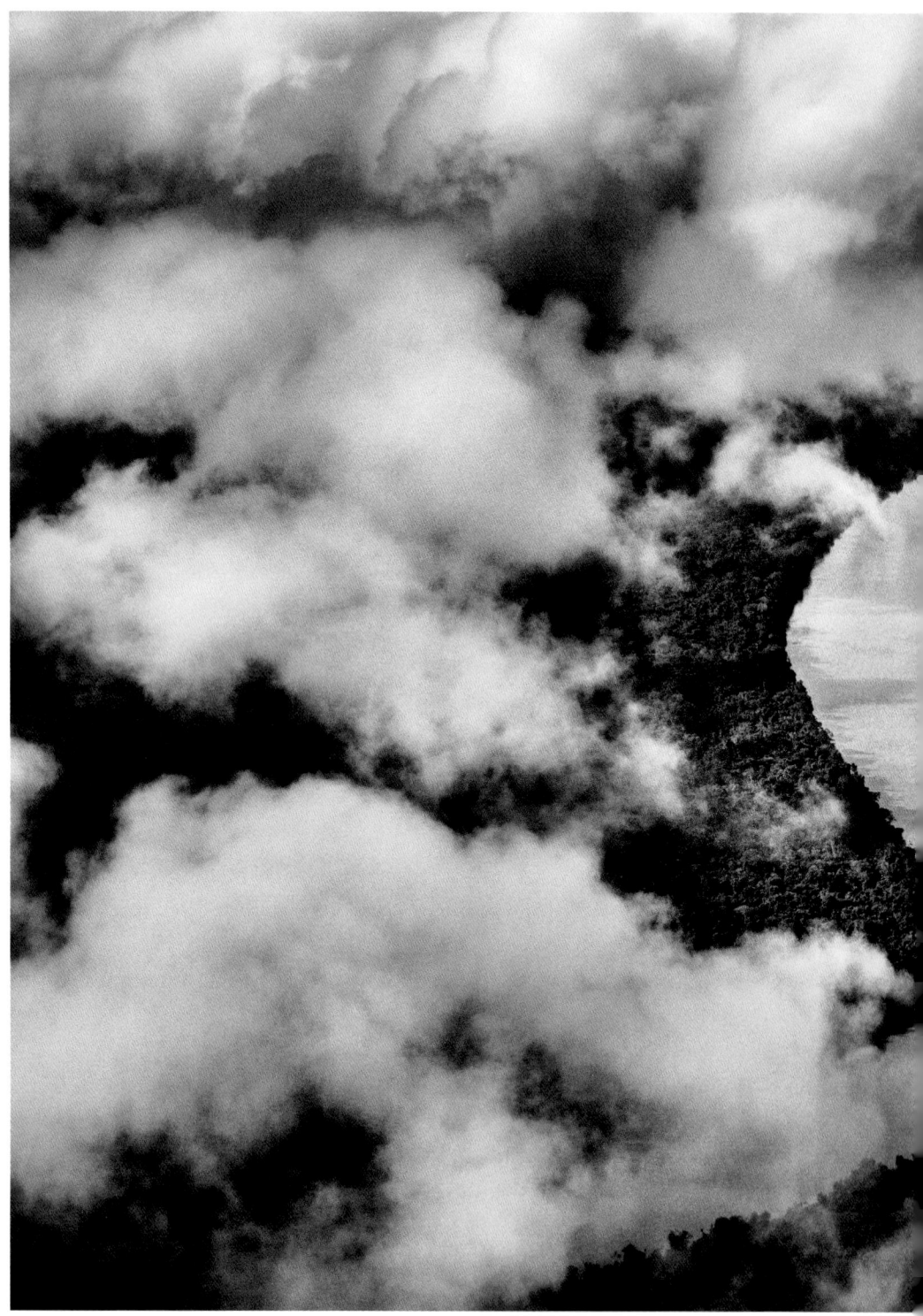

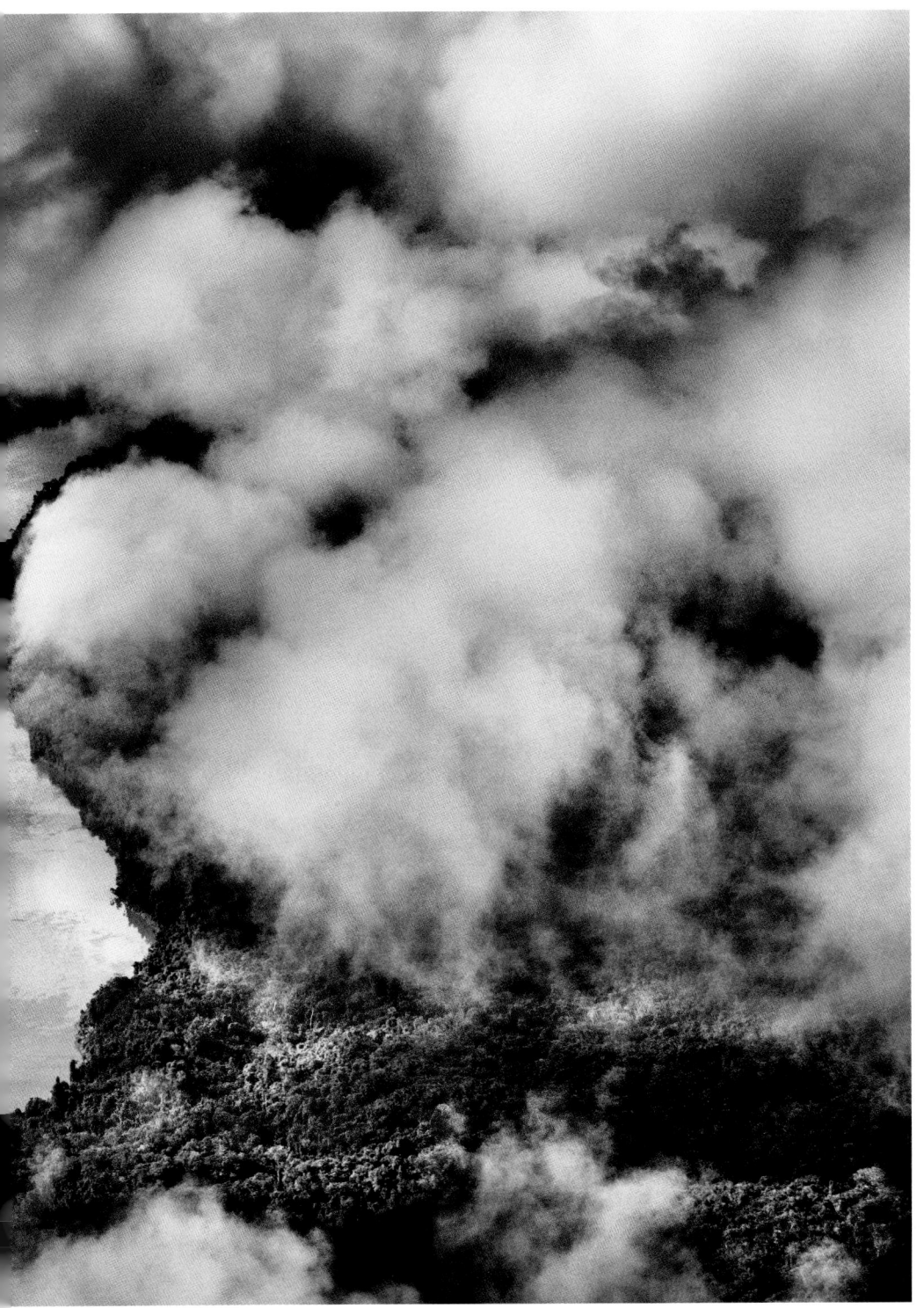

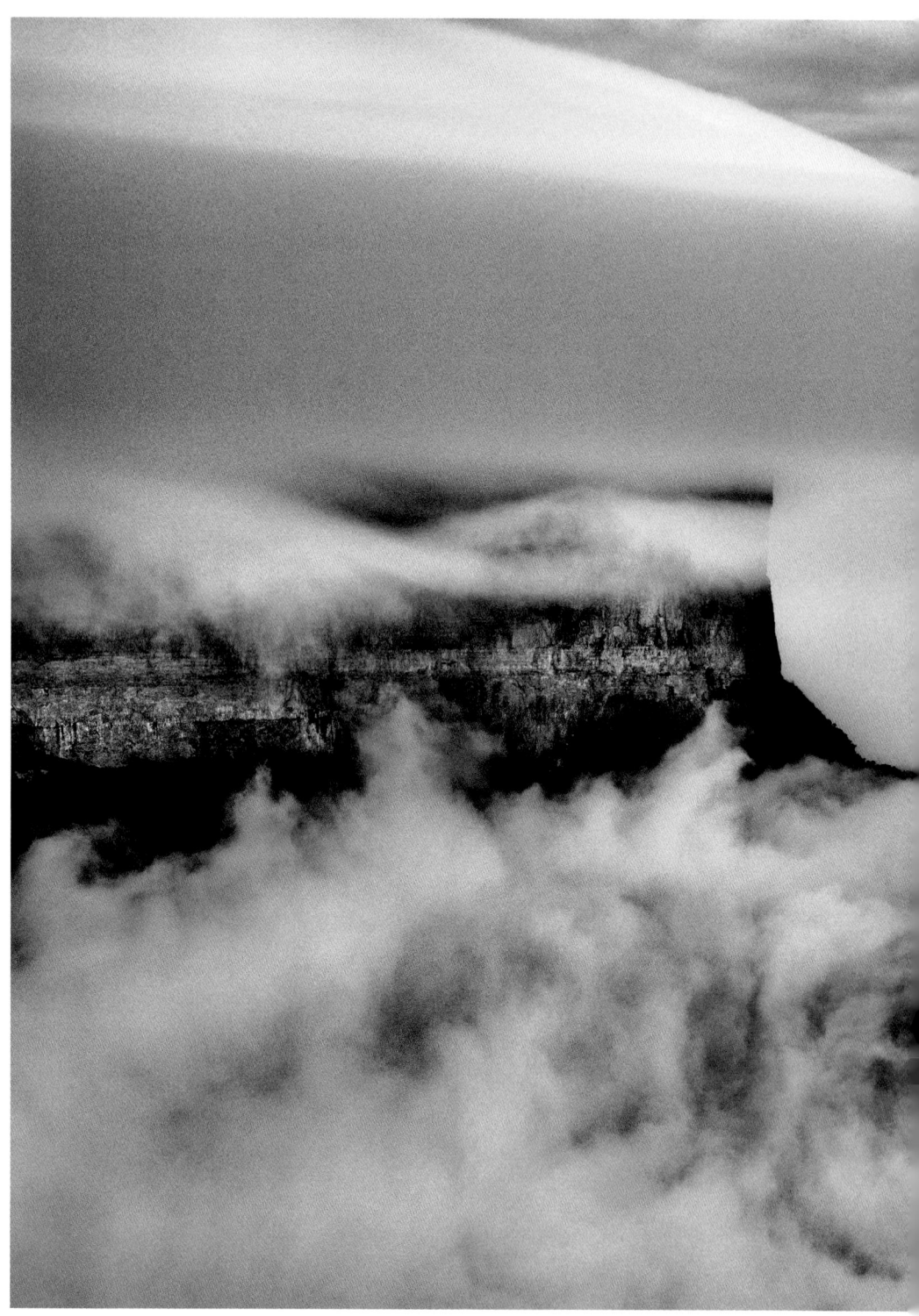

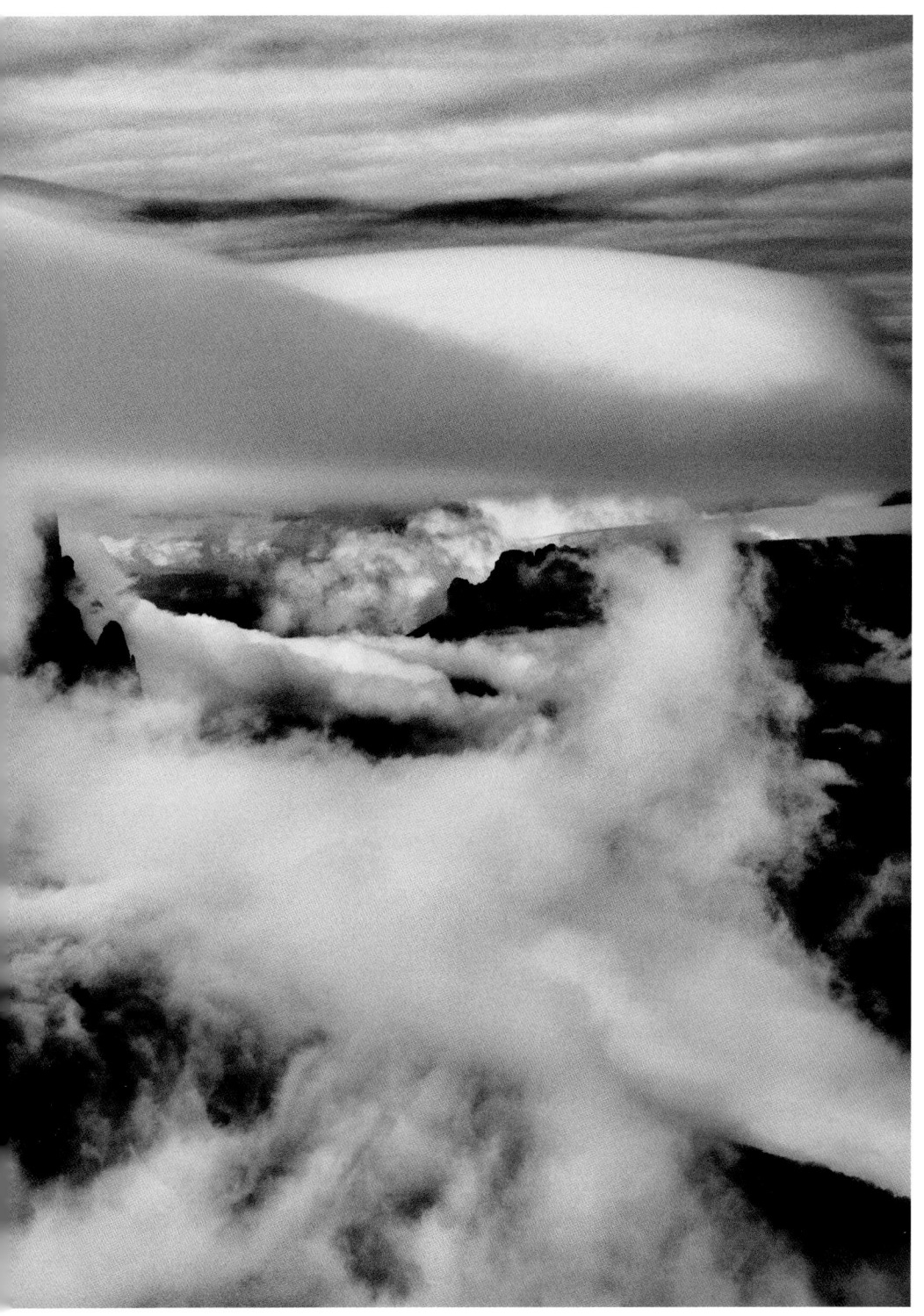

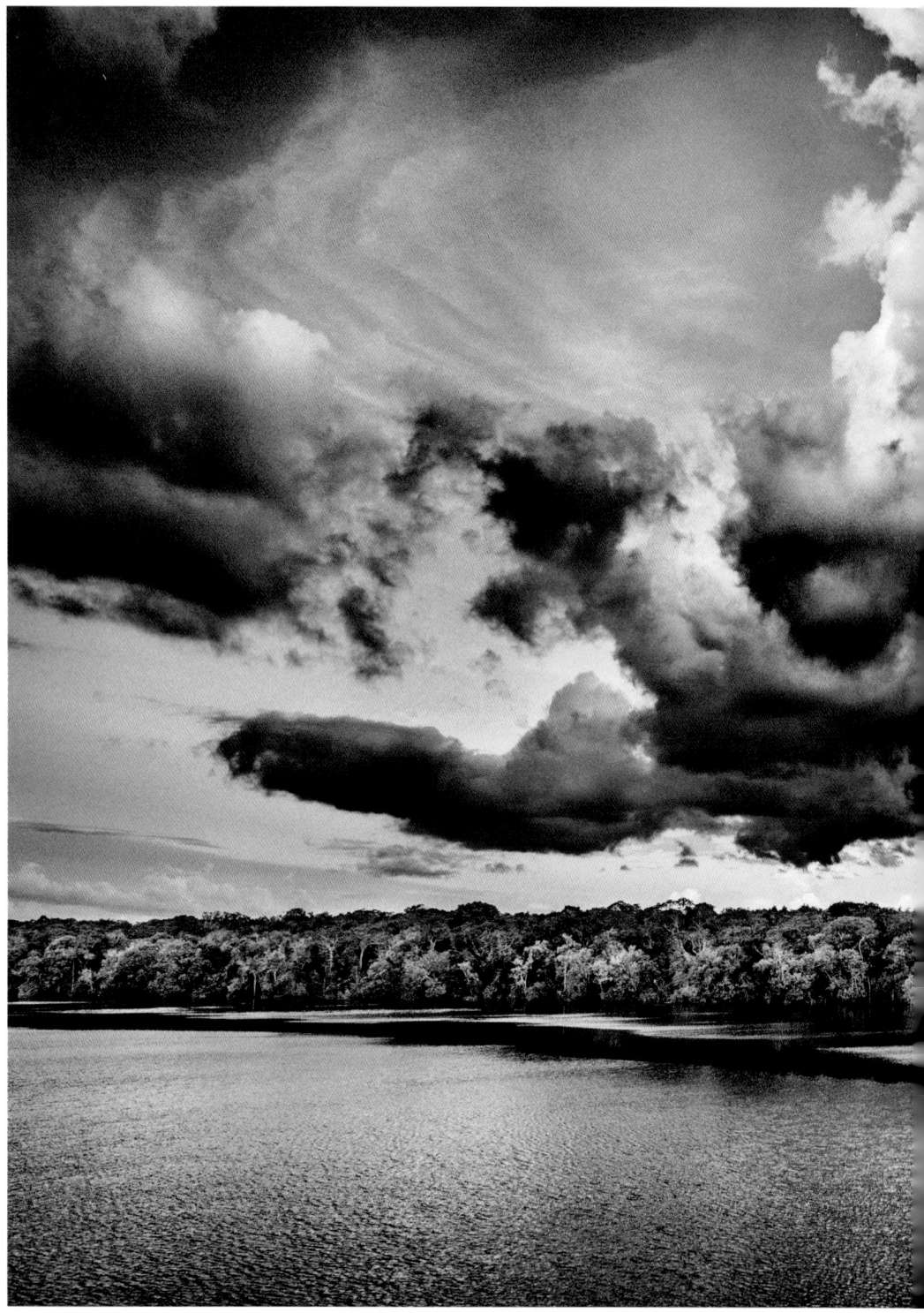

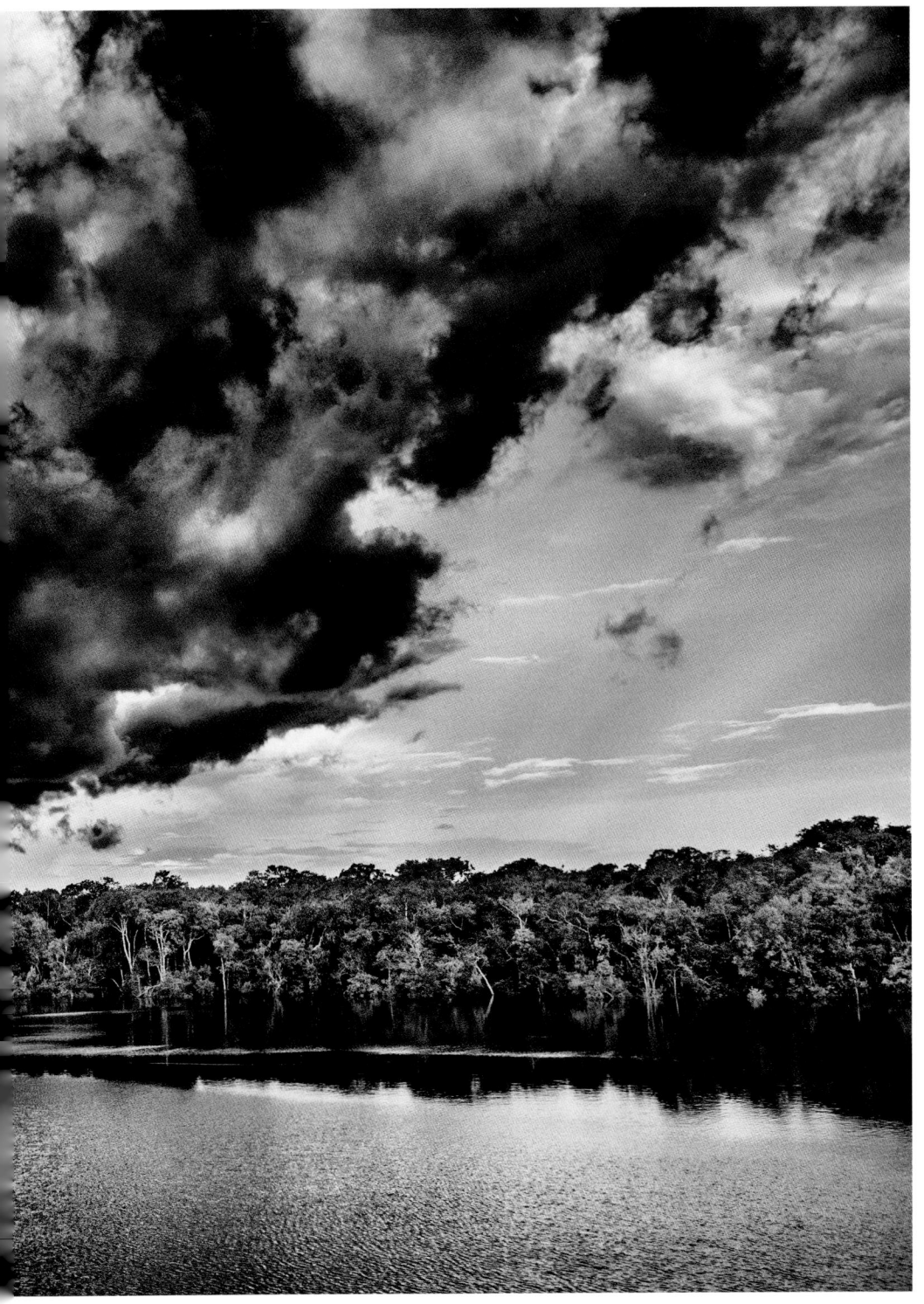

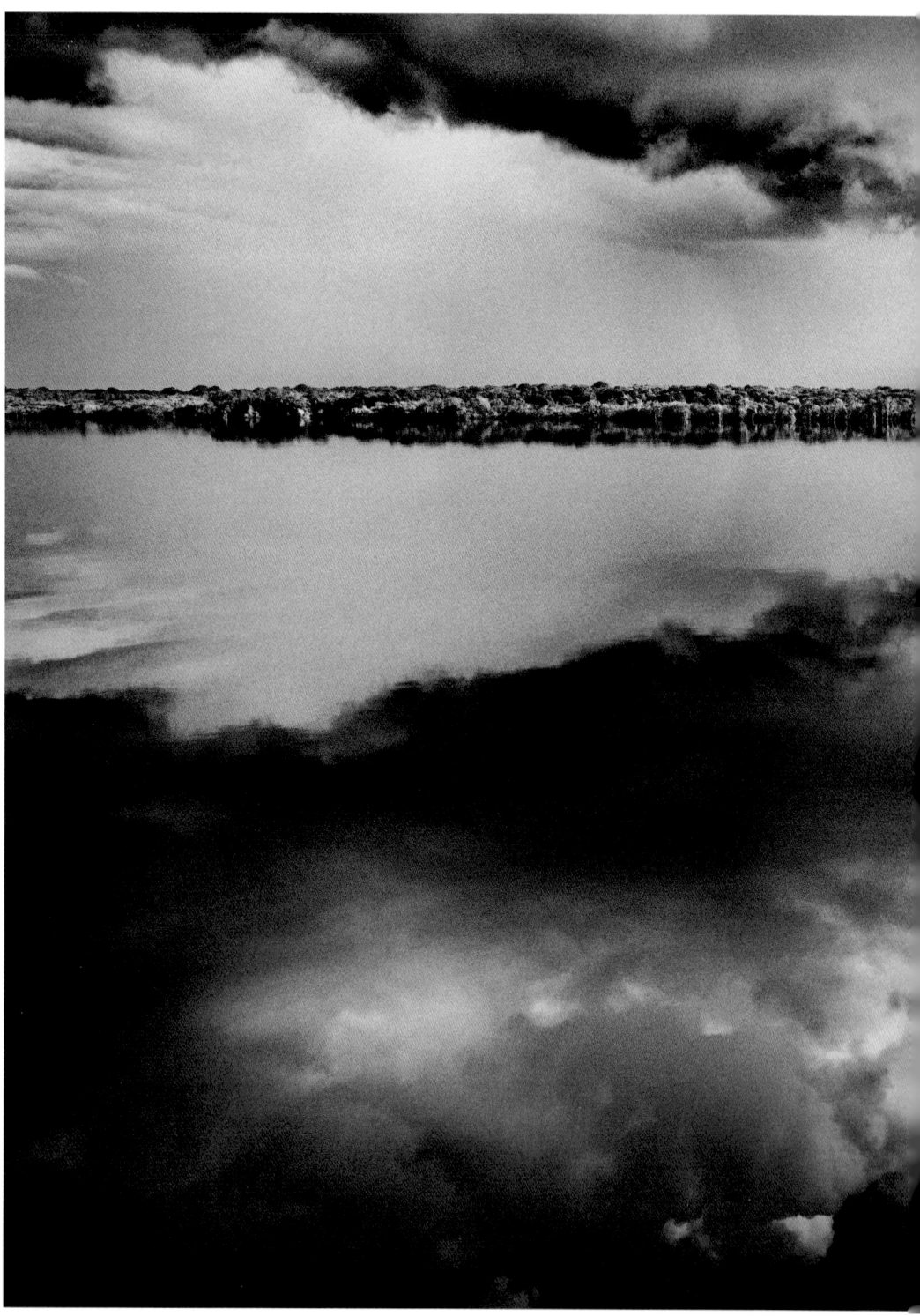

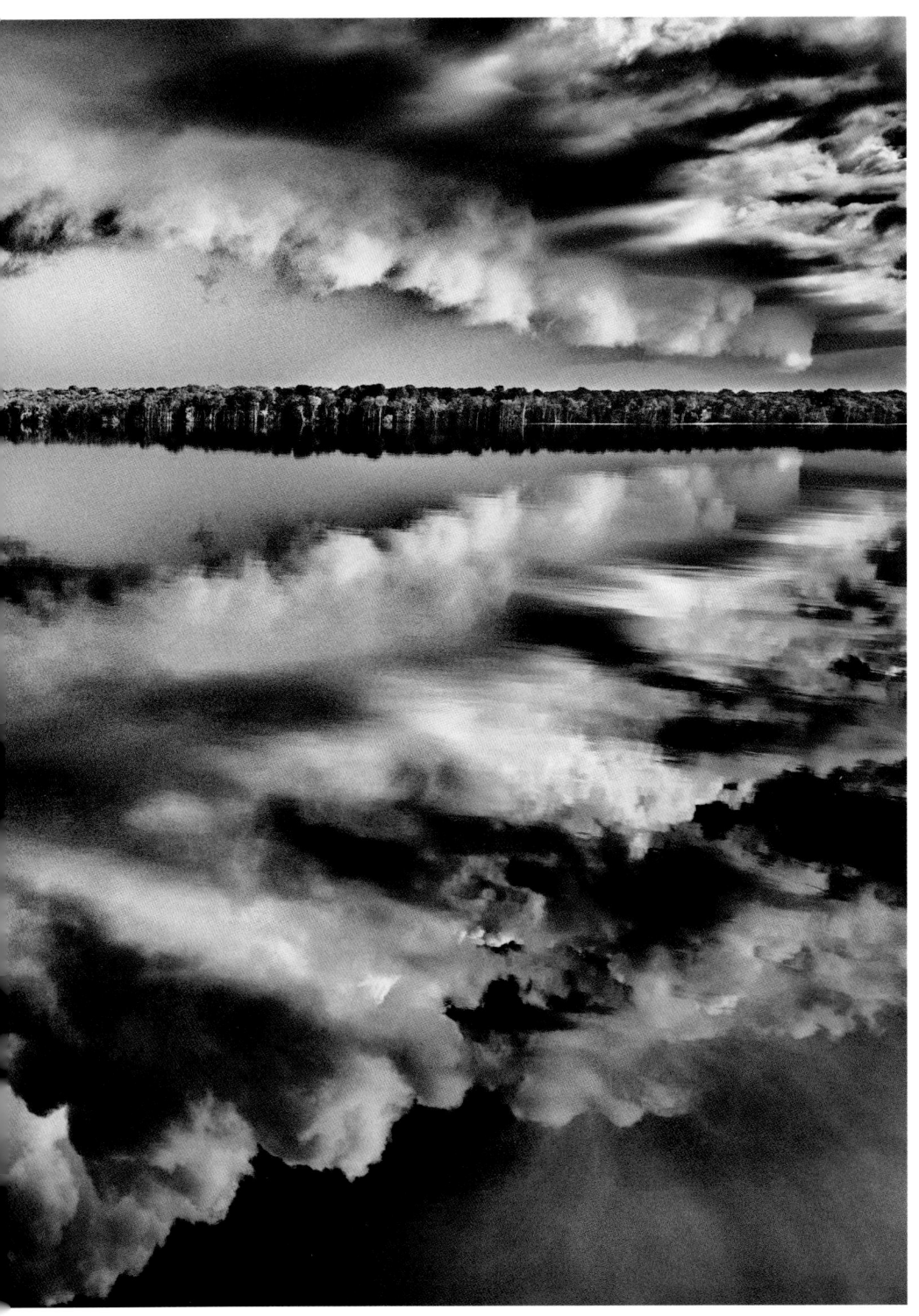

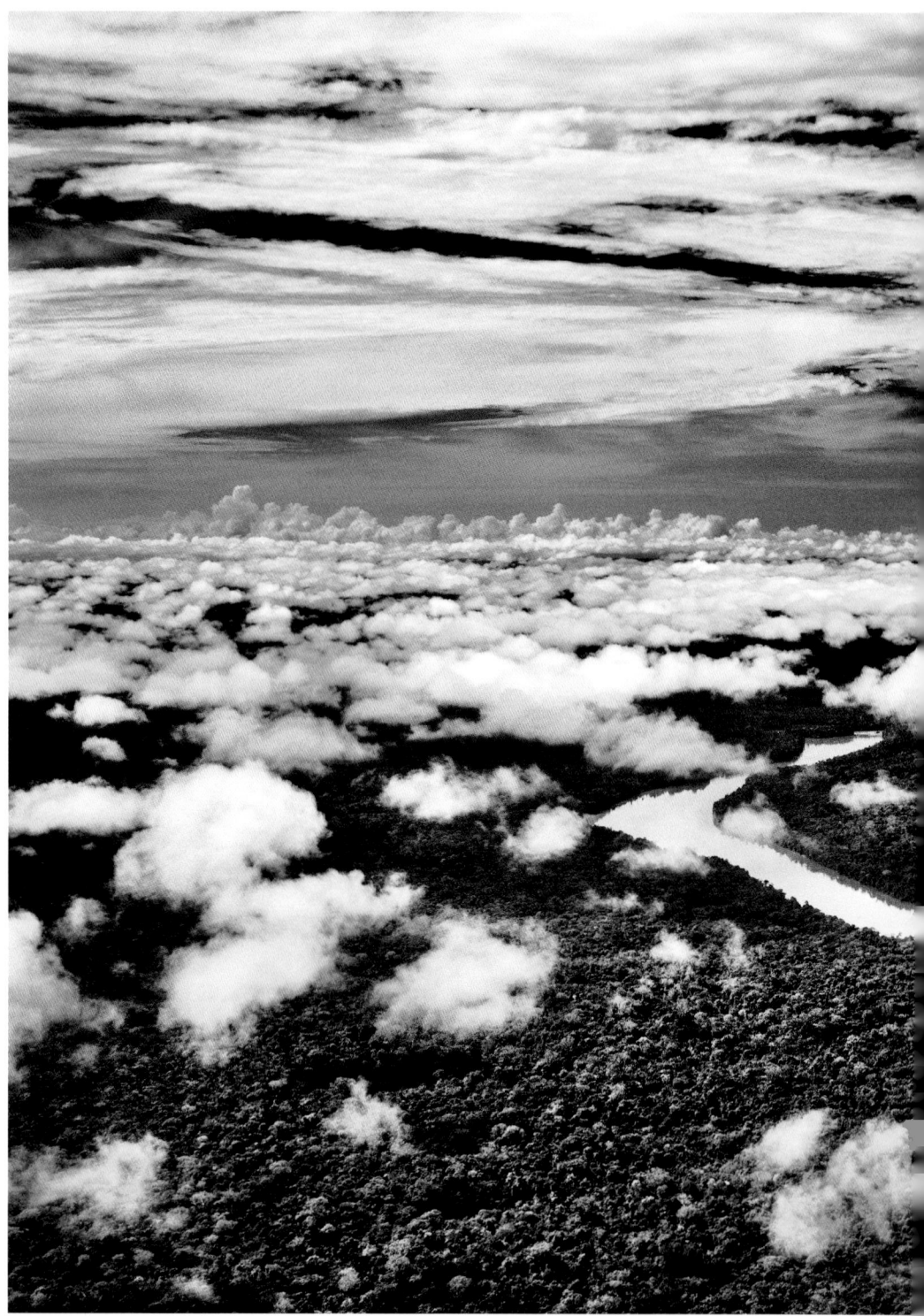

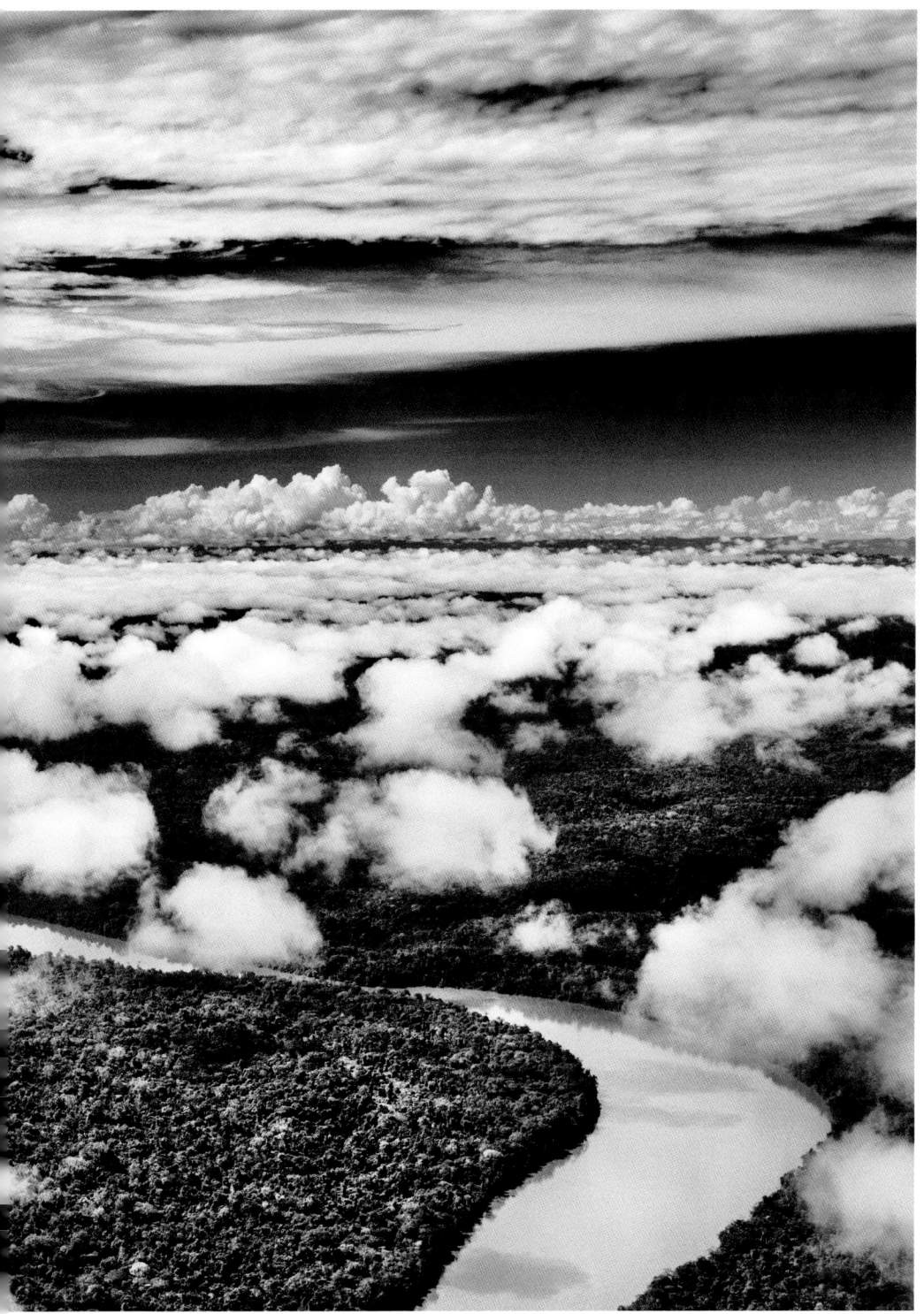

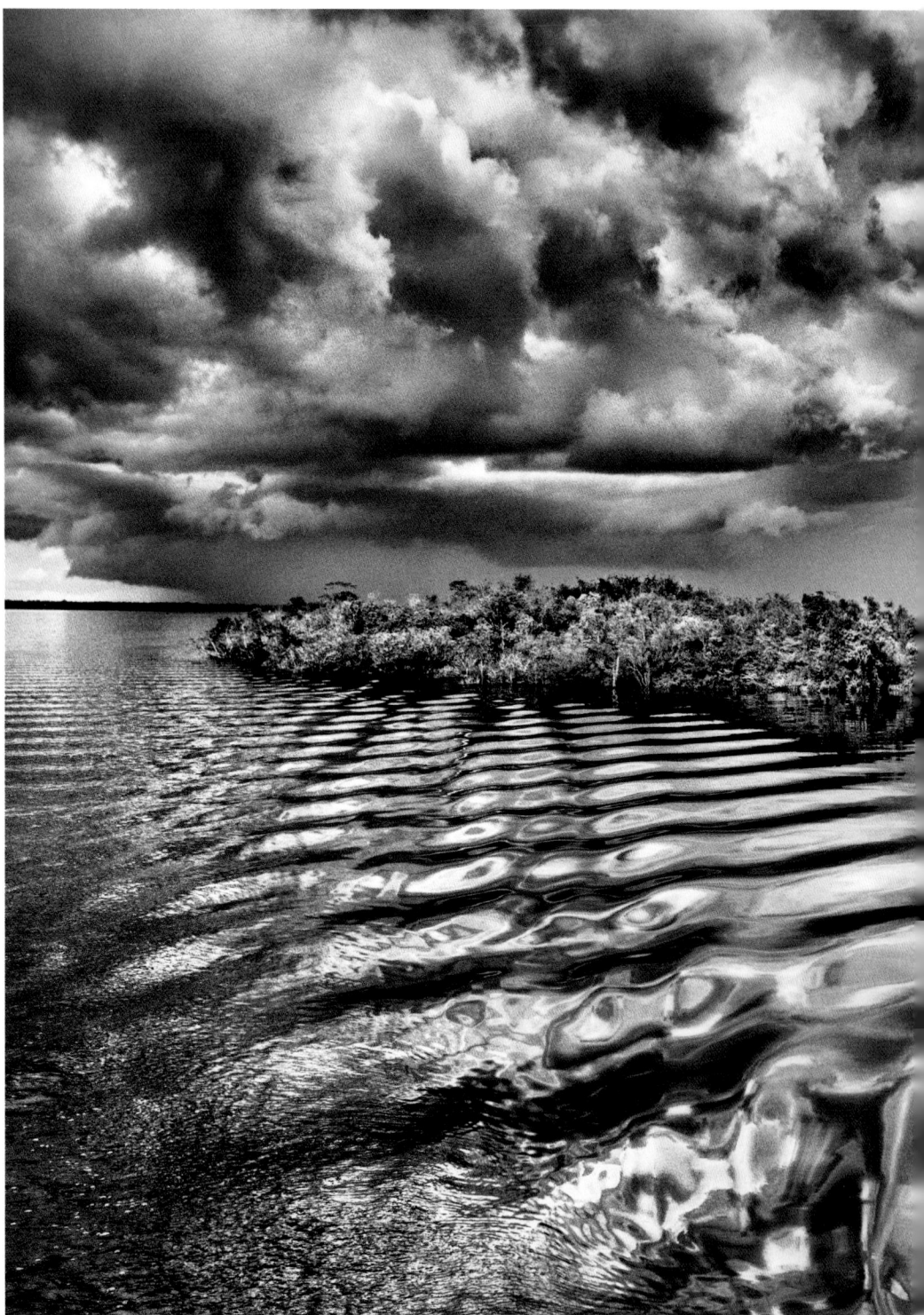

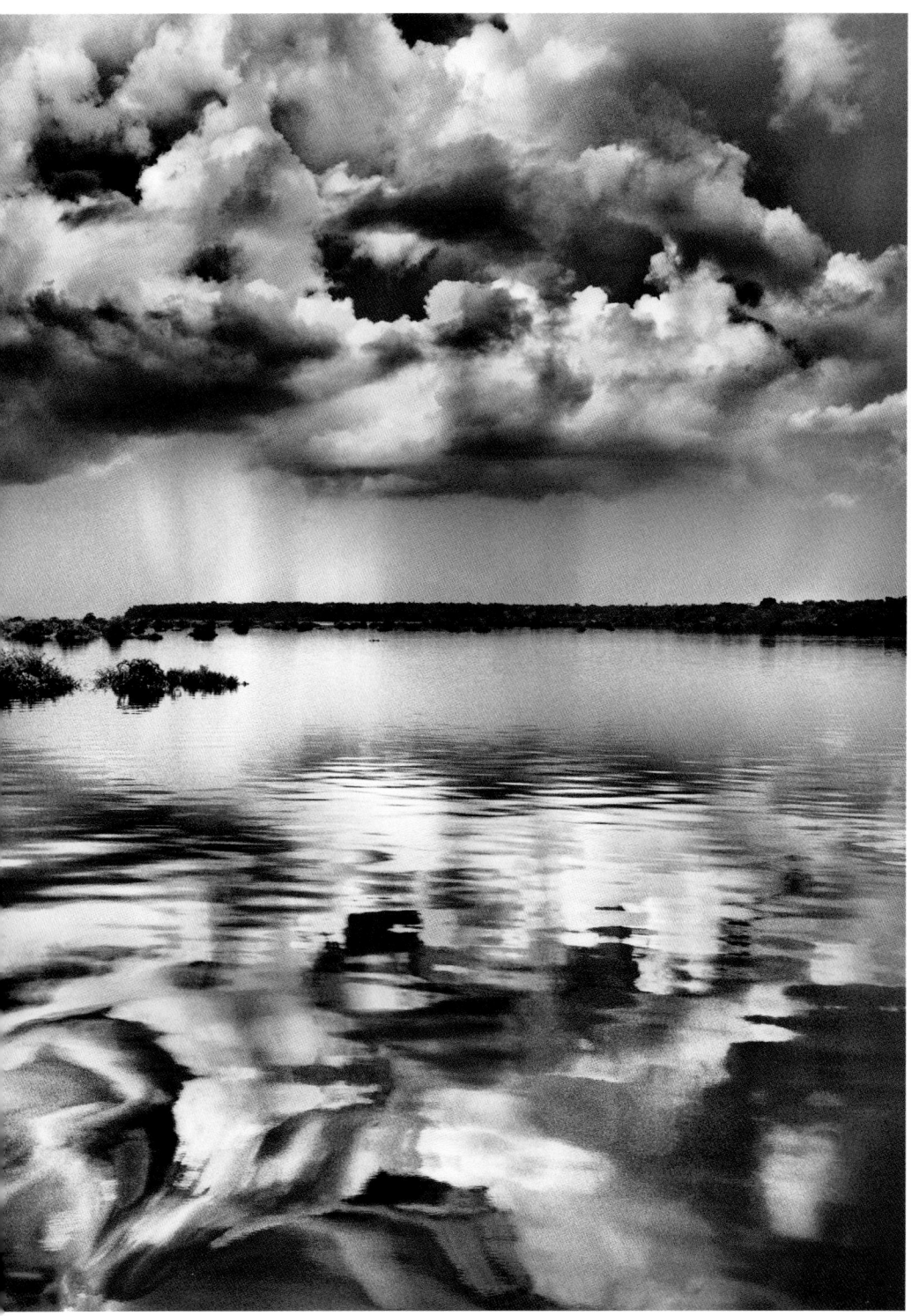

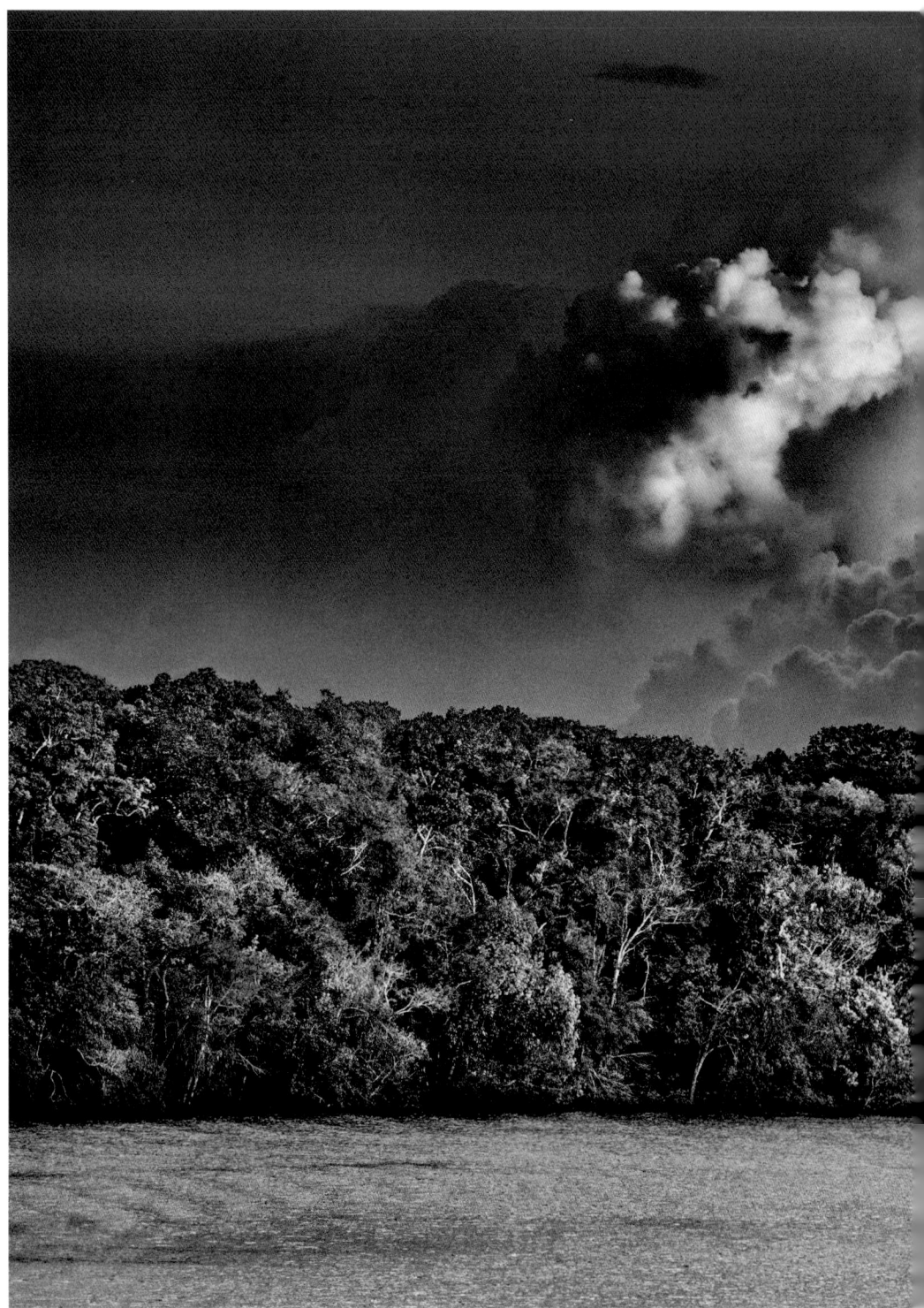

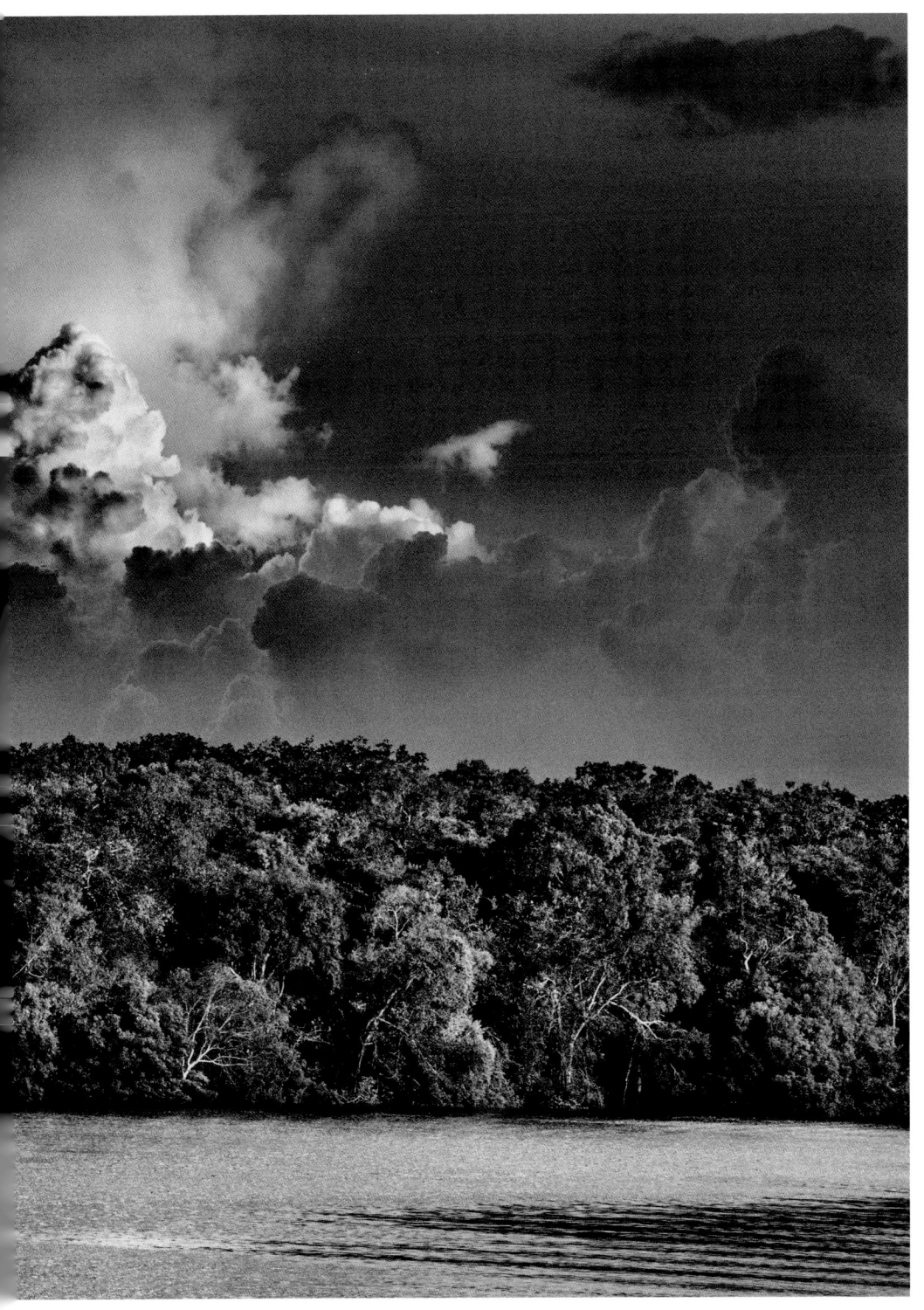

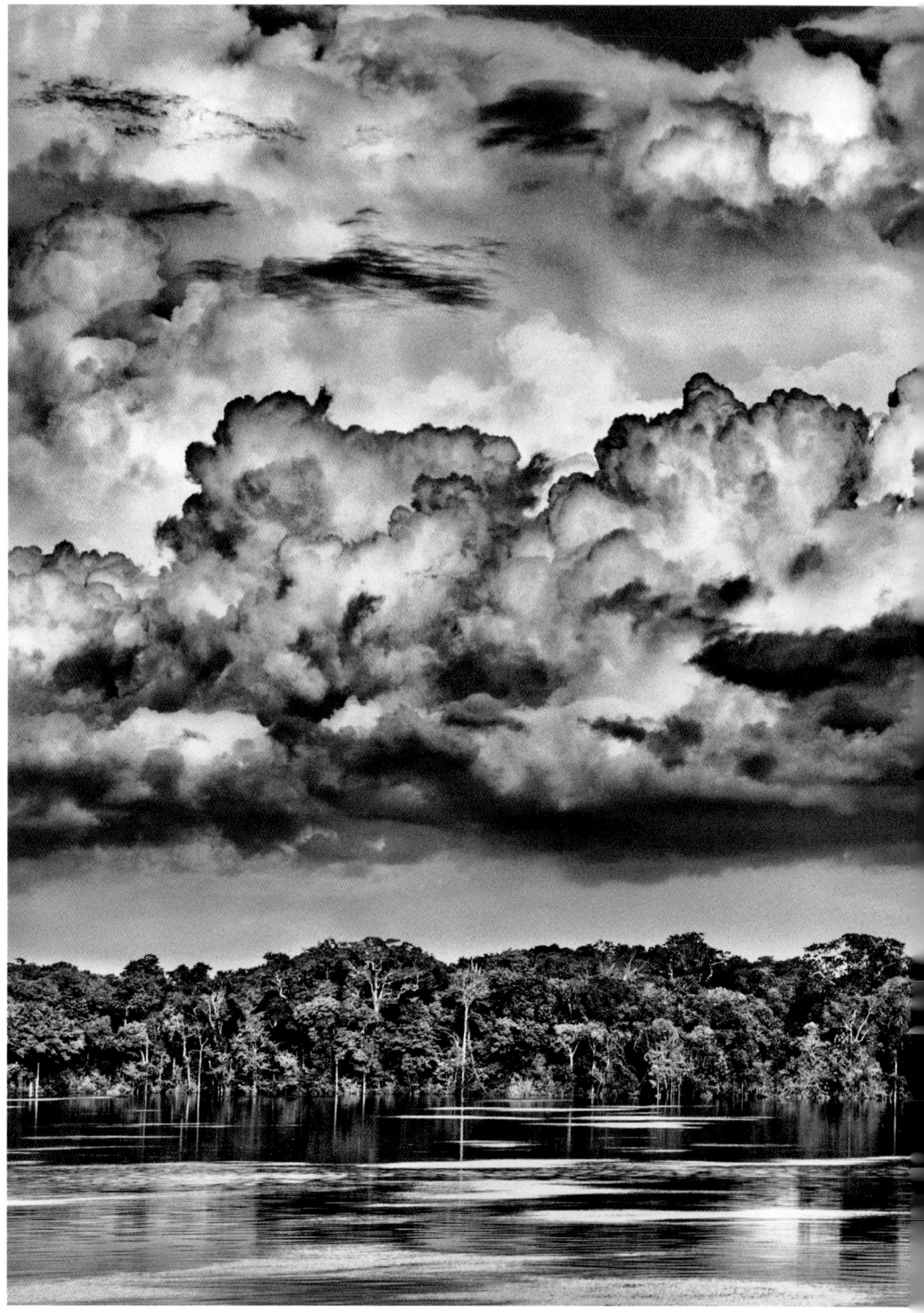

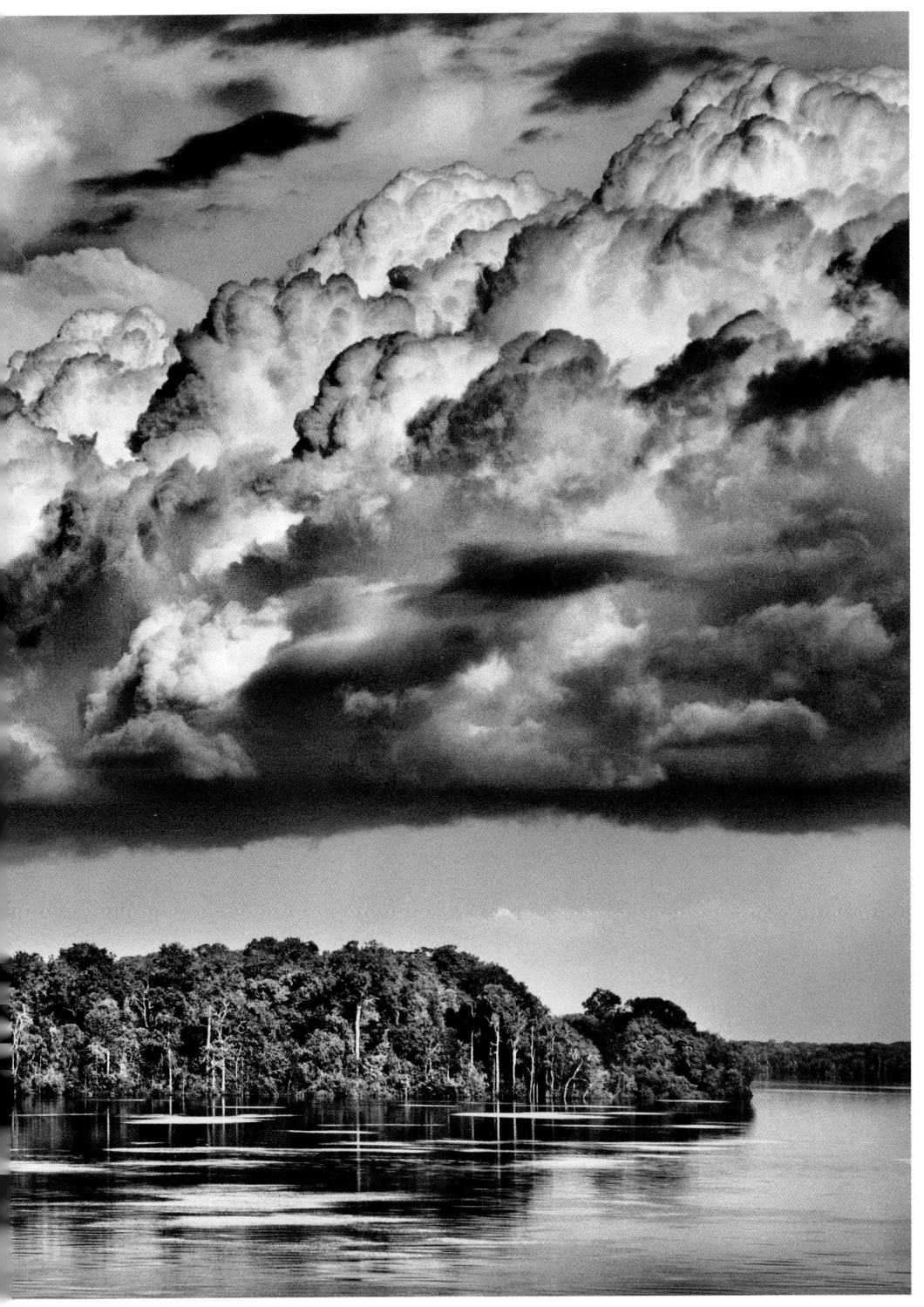

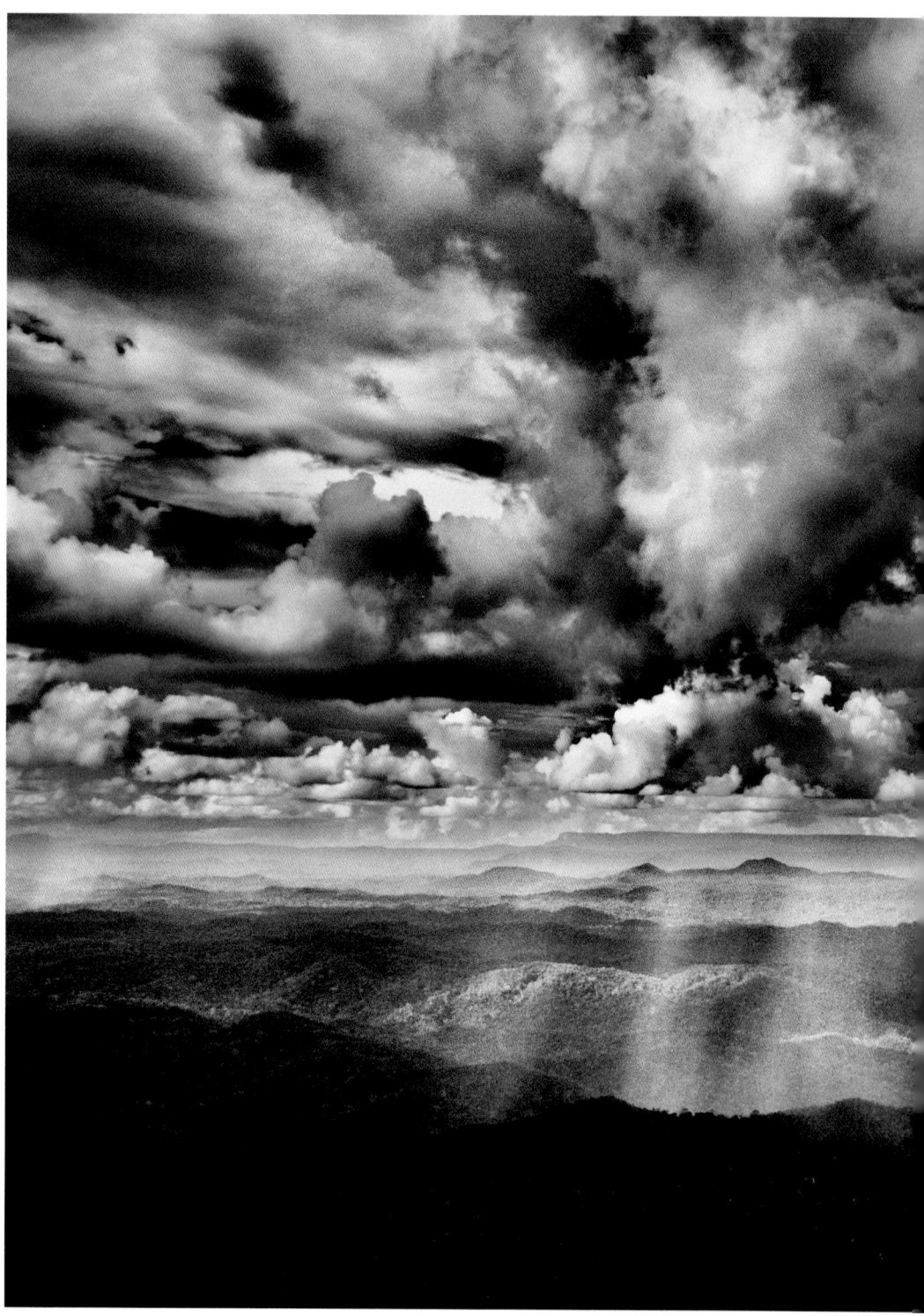

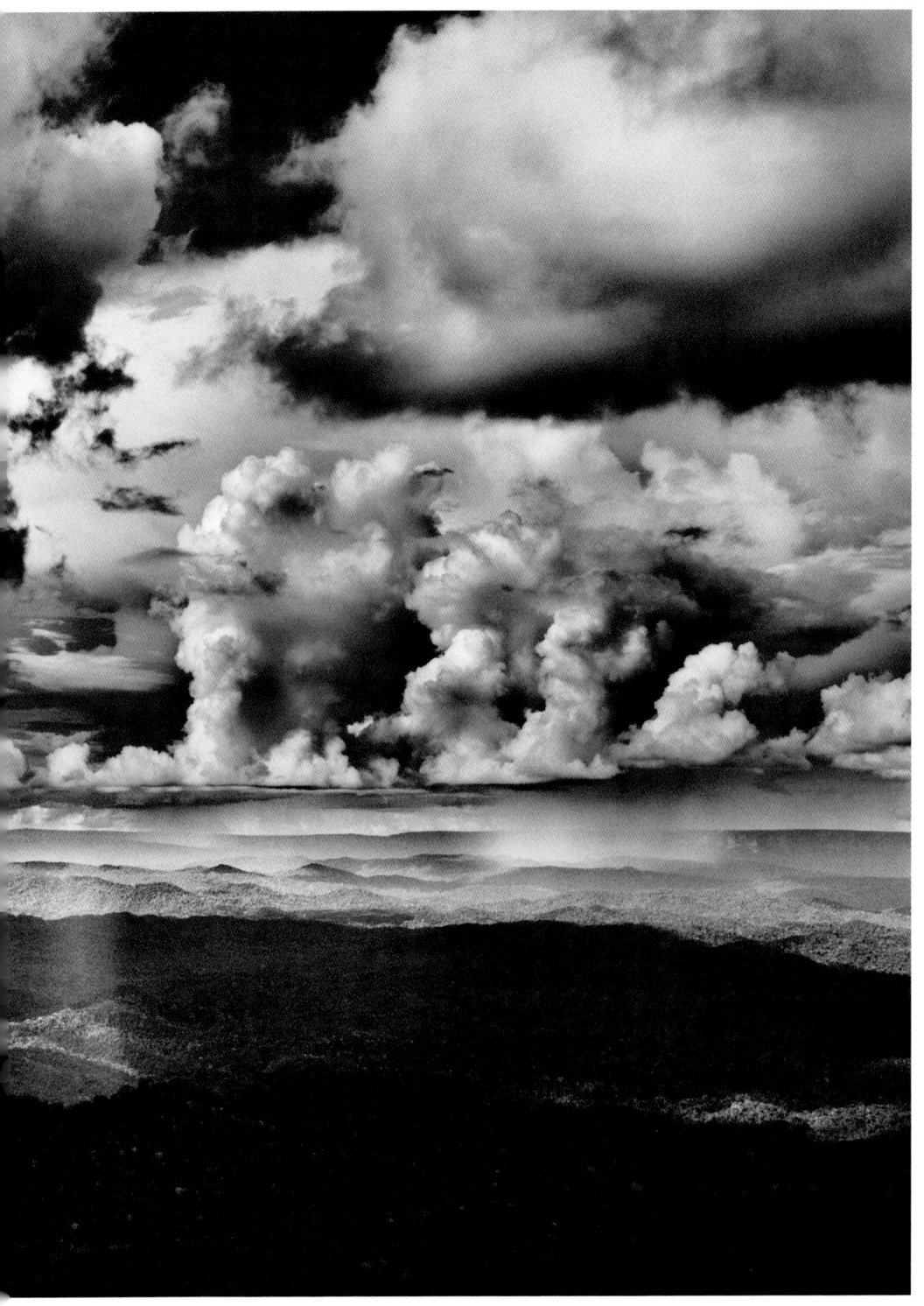

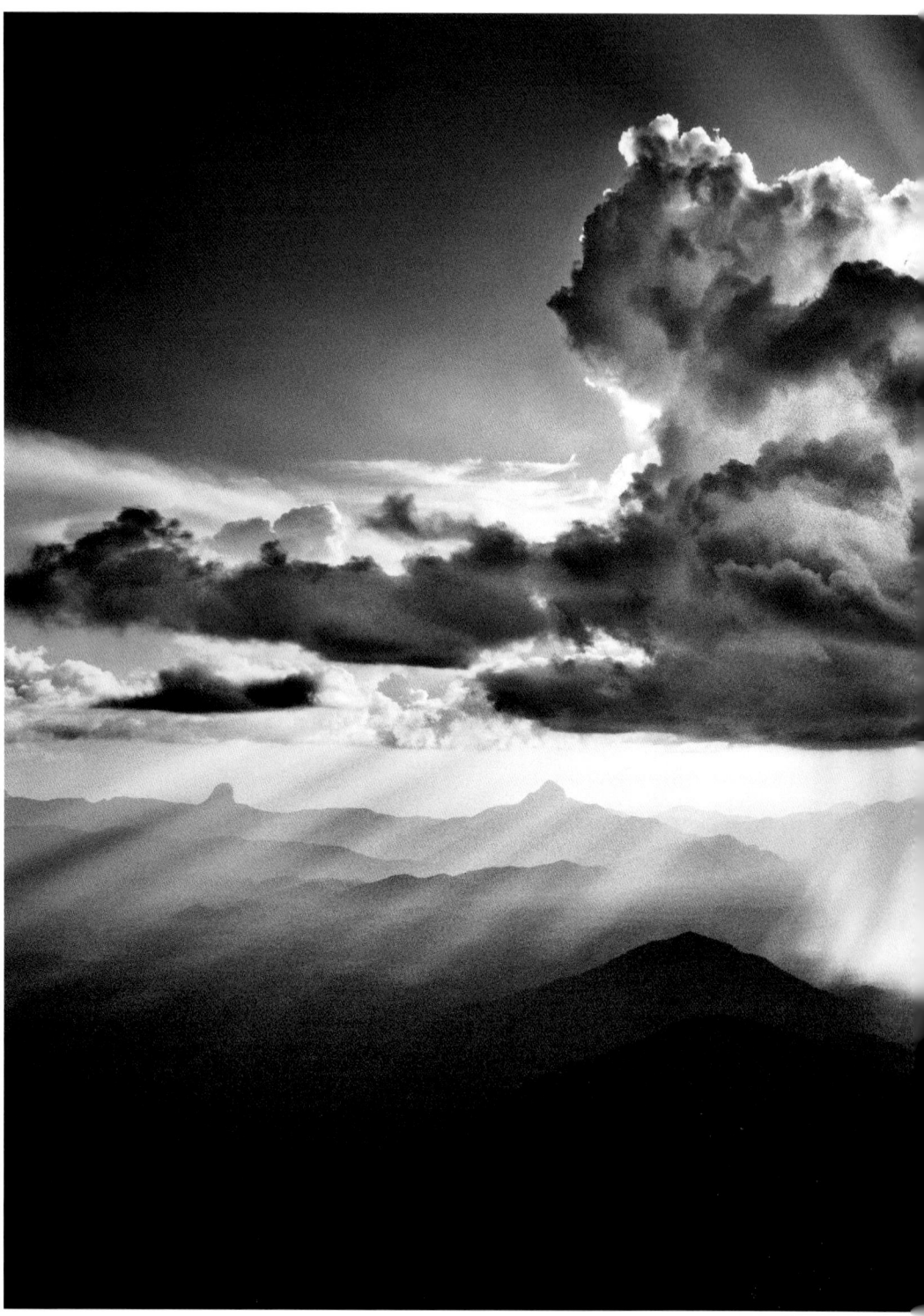

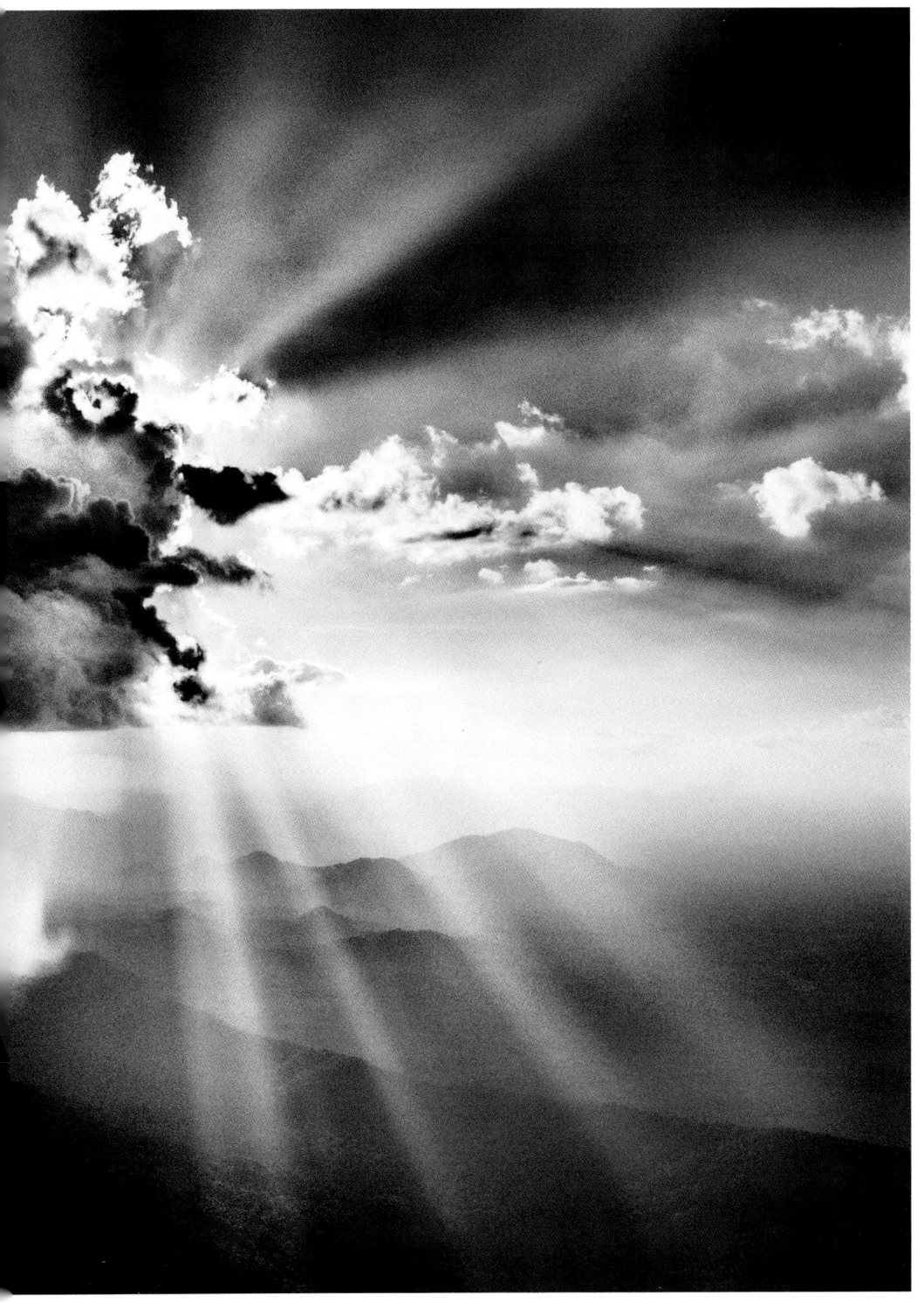

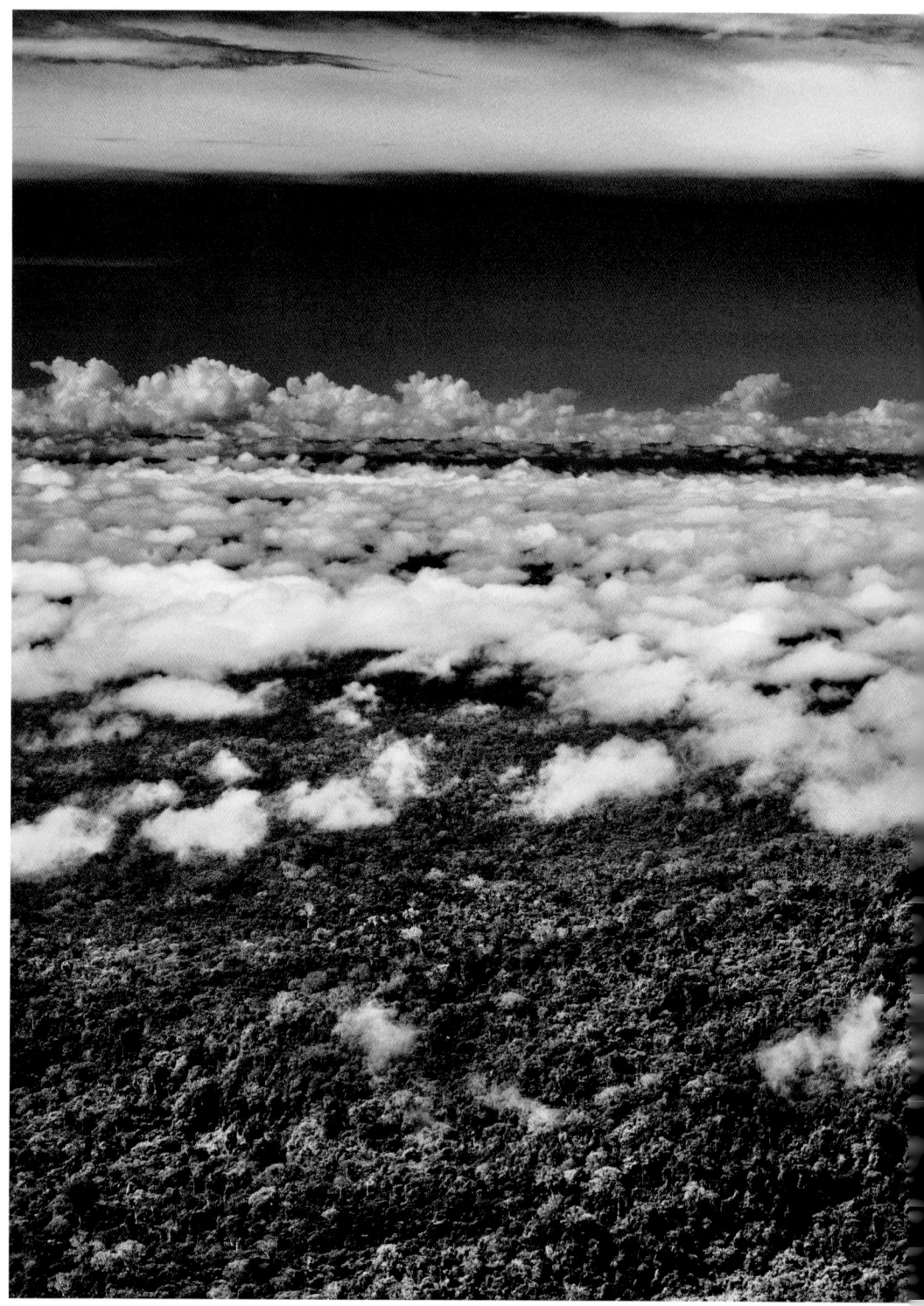

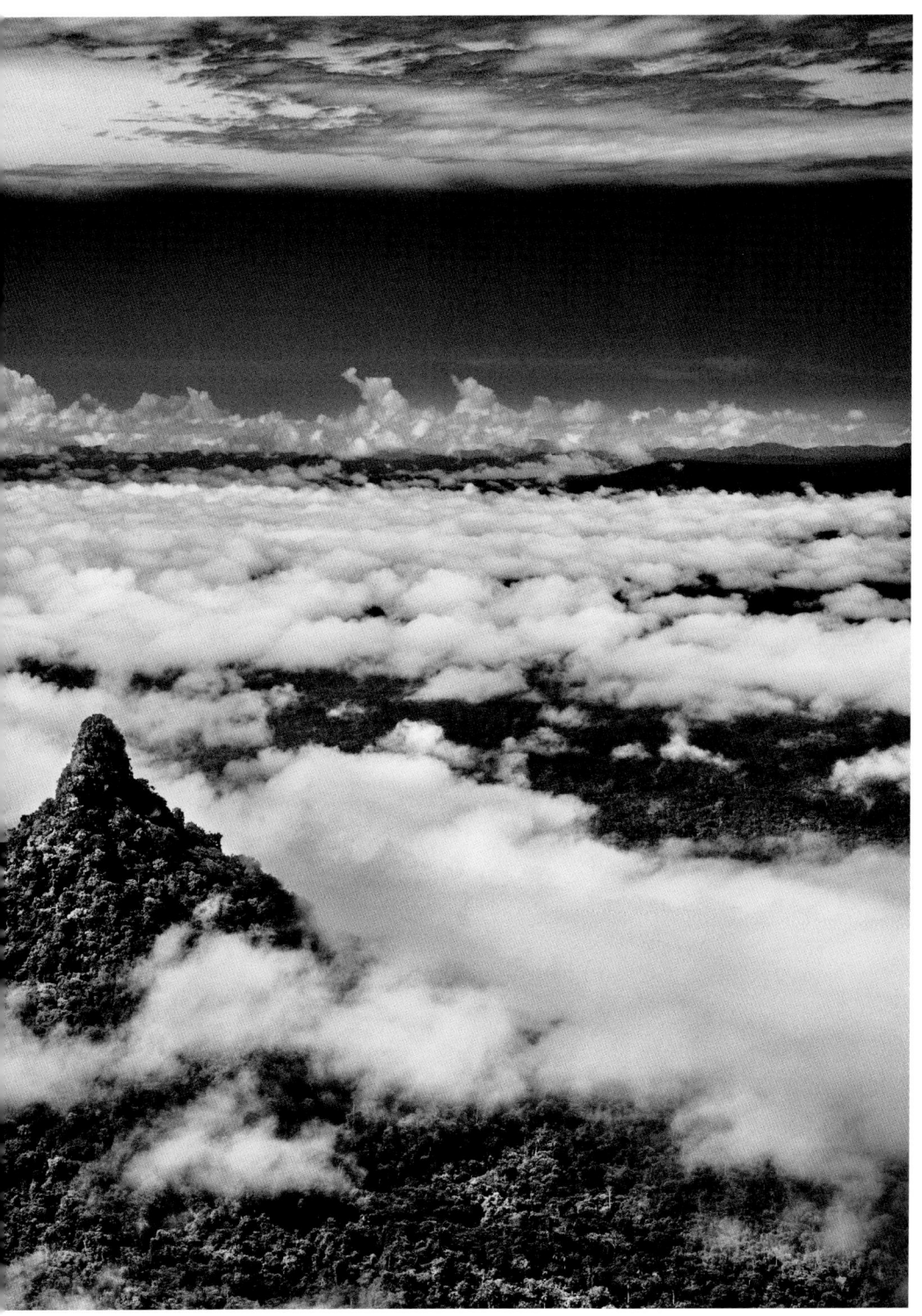

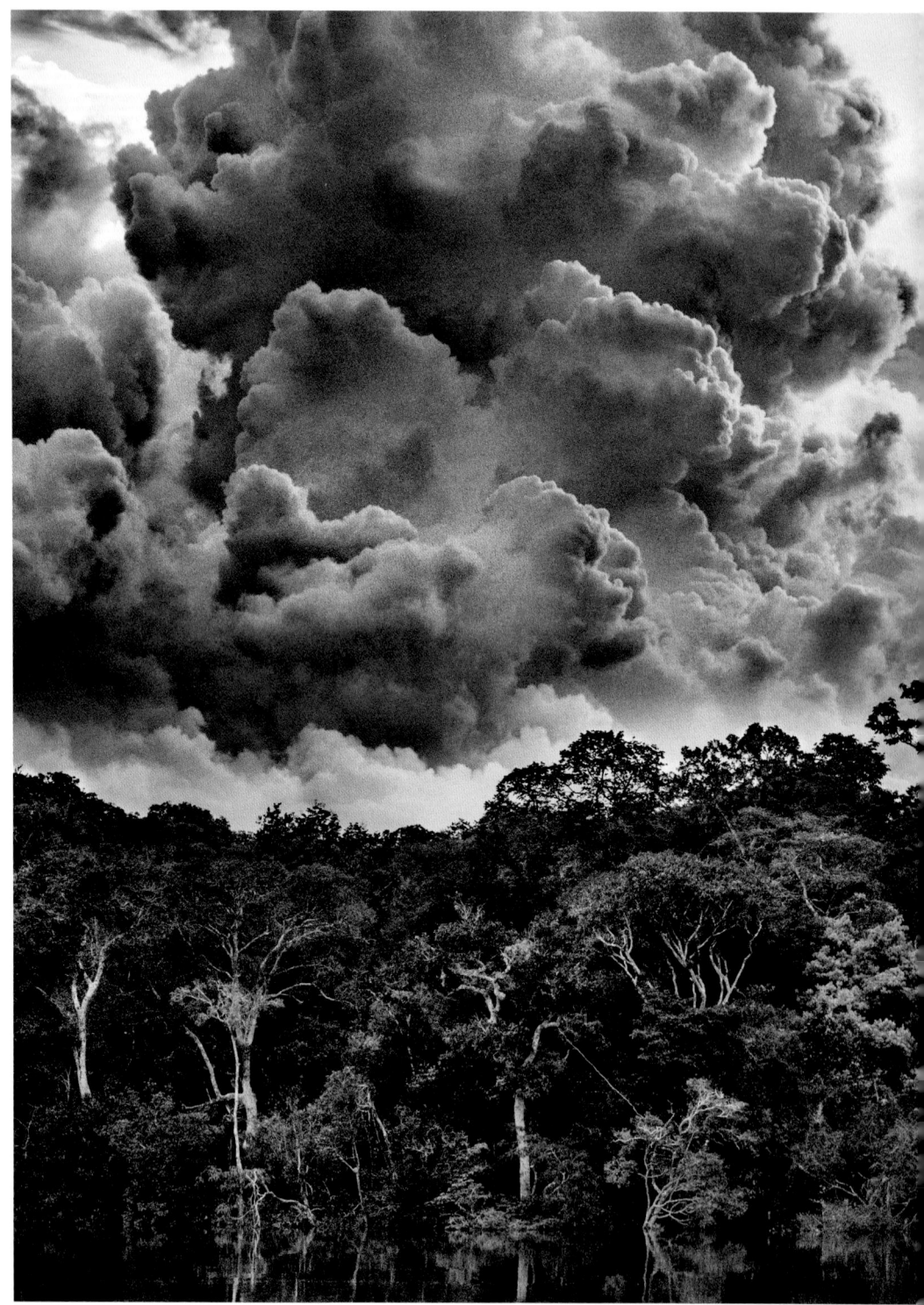

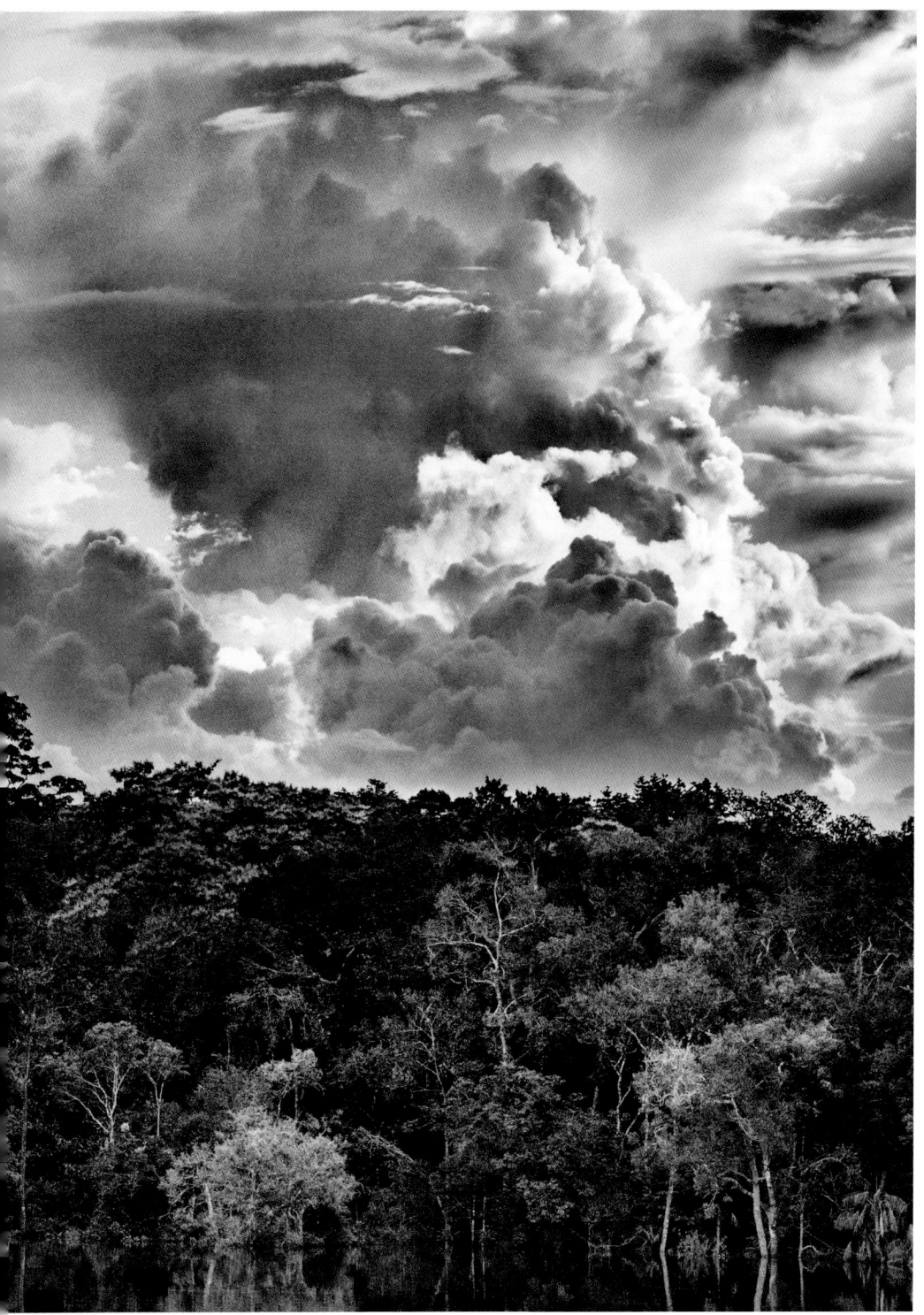

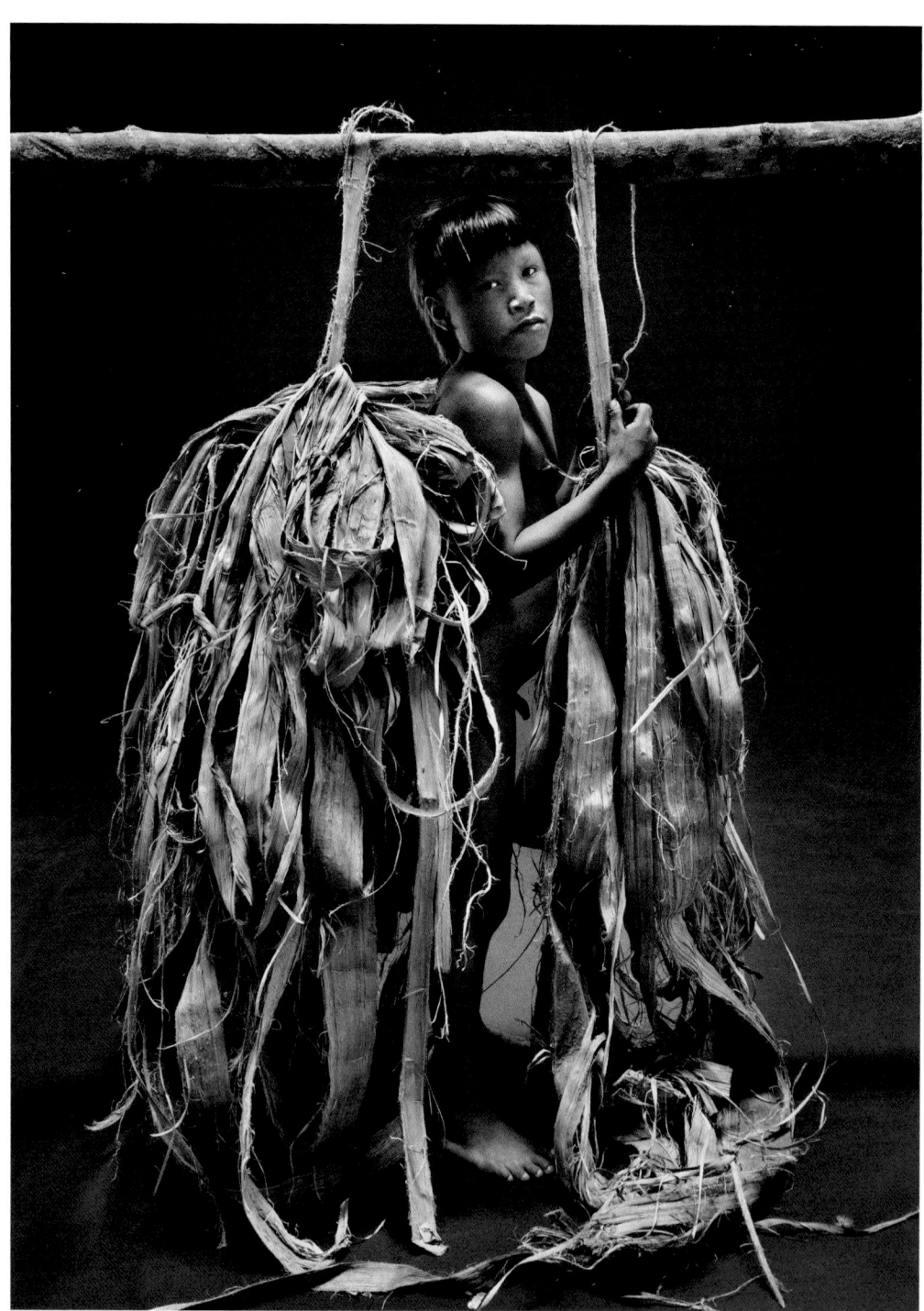

SURUWAHÁ

Their population of 154 continues to grow (there were just one hundred of them in the 1980s). This singularly healthy community produces all the foods its members consume and are very proud of their well-honed farming techniques. They hunt with traditional weapons, the bow and arrow or blowgun, using poison-tipped arrows. The Suruwahá are experts in the use of potions. They have no chiefs, though their great hunters—always recognized by the number of tapirs they have killed (the more tapirs, the more the admiration of others)—are revered, considered *madi iri karuji*, "people of valor" in their language.

The Suruwahá are the closest to what the first Europeans must have seen when they reached Brazil. They have chosen to live in a state of near total isolation and have strongly preserved their customs and the visual expression of their cultural tradition.

A strong sign of health, which they seek to emphasize, is a strong body. Group activities highlight muscular strength, such as the ritual of carrying grated cassava from the *maloca* (the community's large, one-room communal house) to the river for fermentation. They make an immense basket or pannier about 2.5 meters (8 feet) tall and fill it with 600 to 800 kilograms (1,300 to 1,800 pounds) of peeled cassava. Once fermented, the cassava dough will be consumed as a delicacy at celebrations. To carry the basket, all the men work together and take turns being the one in front who carries the most weight. They bind their muscles to avoid muscle tears.

The Suruwahá speak a language from the Arawá family, like several other groups that inhabit the same region (all of the ethnic groups that speak Arawá-family languages live in the interfluve between the Purus and Juruá Rivers). Originally, until the Amazon rubber boom in the second half of the 19th century, there were 11 groups that spoke the same language spoken today by the Suruwahá, who lived around the Cuniuá, Tapauá, and Purus Rivers in the south of the state of Amazonas. Each of them was identified by the name of the river closest to where they lived: the Jukihidawa (who resided where they all live today, near the Pretão stream, which they call Jukihi); the Tabosorodawa, Adamidawa, Nakydanidawa, Sarakoadawa, Yjanamymady, Korobidawa, Masanidawa, Ydahidawa, Zamadawa, and a group called the Suruwahá. These old Suruwahá and the Masanidawa interacted with rubber tappers, from whom they learned to use metal tools but from whom they also caught diseases and ended up nearly extinct. All the other groups suffered massacres by white people (whom they call Jara) and other indigenous peoples, whom they call Abamady (identified as being the Paumari, who lived as nomads on the banks of rivers in the Purus River basin).

The successive massacres and epidemics led the few survivors from the other groups to seek protection from the inhabitants of the Pretão, who lived on high ground, far from the movements of other peoples and therefore more shielded. So although many individuals there prefer to call themselves Jukihidawa, they all still retain the memory of their original *dawa*.

After that merger occurred around the 1920s, those who became known as the Suruwahá had no contact with other groups, indigenous or otherwise, until the early 1980s. In that era, fishers, hunters, and rubber tappers began to threaten this region, where indigenists recognized signs that isolated indigenous people were present. Indigenists from the Indigenous Missionary Council (CIMI, affiliated with the Catholic Church) made contact with them. Having confirmed their existence, they began the official process of obtaining recognition of the indigenous territory, enshrined in law by the Brazilian government in 1991. The Suruwahá are located six days by boat from the municipality of Lábrea, 850 kilometers (530 miles) south of Manaus, Amazonas.

Since the early 2000s, these indigenous peoples have benefited from the so-called no-contact policy: the office for isolated or recently contacted indigenous people, part of the FUNAI (Fundação Nacional do Índio, the National Indian Foundation), maintains just one post several kilometers away from their *maloca* by boat, plus another seven hours of travel. When authorized by FUNAI, a visitor must first undergo a 12-day quarantine at the bureau's post, to make sure there is no prior illness that could infect them.

The Suruwahá have a high death rate from ingesting *timbó* (*Derris elliptica*), a highly toxic substance the indigenous people use to stun fish while fishing. To us it may sound like suicide, but not to them: lives are simply taken by the aggressive spirit of a plant. They have no concept of self-harm, such as suicide. Most of the cases involve people aged 14 to 28, at the height of youthful vigor. Their mythology contributes to this. The Suruwahá believe there are three planes that people go to when they die. Of these, the one where life is best is the one for people who die strong and healthy, as opposed to the other two: one for those bitten by cobras and one for those who die in old age.

The Suruwahá are also a completely anarchic society. They have no leaders and do not submit to leadership. Their radical egalitarianism permits no forms of authority, which distinguishes them from other peoples: decisions of common interest are made at night, after supper, in open conversations. Individual attitudes are a matter of personal responsibility: criticism may take the form of isolating a person, by no one speaking to them, for instance. There are, however, no punishments, for there is no leadership with a mandate to do things like restrict or censure anyone.

They do have people who become role models: the great hunters of tapirs, the builders of the houses where they live, those who distinguish themselves at festivals by carrying the heavy loads of cassava to be fermented. A communal house takes a long time to build: the one they now occupy for most of the year was built by a man named Kwakway, after the men of the community helped him sink its trunk pillars into the ground. These conical houses are 30 meters (100 feet) tall—the height of a ten-story building—and as imposing as a cathedral. Covering it entirely requires three or more years of work, always performed by a mature man.

Page 154 Huwaxi Suruwahá with tree bark fibers, whose thread is used in items such as rope and hammocks. Suruwahá Indigenous Territory, state of Amazonas, 2017.

Pages 158/159 Cousins Hahani, Tiniru, and Ugunja at the SESAI health post near the Pretão stream (which they call Jukihi). Ugunja died a few months after this photograph was taken. The Suruwahá have a high death rate from ingesting *timbó* (*Derris elliptica*), a highly toxic substance that the indigenous people use for hunting and fishing. To us it may sound like suicide, but not to them: lives are simply taken by the aggressive spirit of a plant. They have no concept of self-harm, such as suicide. Most of the cases involve people aged 14 to 28, at the height of youthful vigor. Their mythology contributes to this. The Suruwahá believe there are three planes that people go to when they die. Of these, the most pleasant is the one for those who die strong and healthy, as opposed to the other two: one for those bitten by snakes and one for those who die in old age. Suruwahá Indigenous Territory, state of Amazonas, 2017.

Pages 160/161 Giani (short for Gianzubuni, meaning "heart"), whose body is painted with urucum, holds a blowgun in his right hand and a bow in his left, while his right shoulder holds the strap of his quiver of poisoned darts. The quiver also holds the cotton used to fit the arrows firmly into the blowgun. Suruwahá Indigenous Territory, state of Amazonas, 2017.

Pages 162/163 In the house of Kwakway Suruwahá, with its still incomplete roof, young people prepare a basket about 2.5 meters tall (more than 8 feet high). It will hold up to 800 kilograms (1,800 pounds) of moist cassava dough. Banana leaves line the inside of the container so the cassava will not leak through the basket. Once full, the basket will be carried into the waters of the river, near the *maloca*, where the cassava will ferment over the course of weeks. This accentuates the slightly bitter taste typical of the baked cassava cakes that the Suruwahá consider one of the most delicious of delicacies. Suruwahá Indigenous Territory, state of Amazonas, 2017.

Pages 164/165 Waiubi Suruwahá, from the Uhuzai family, plays an instrument: a *huriatini*, which is used to send warnings over distances between the various *malocas*. Suruwahá Indigenous Territory, state of Amazonas, 2017.

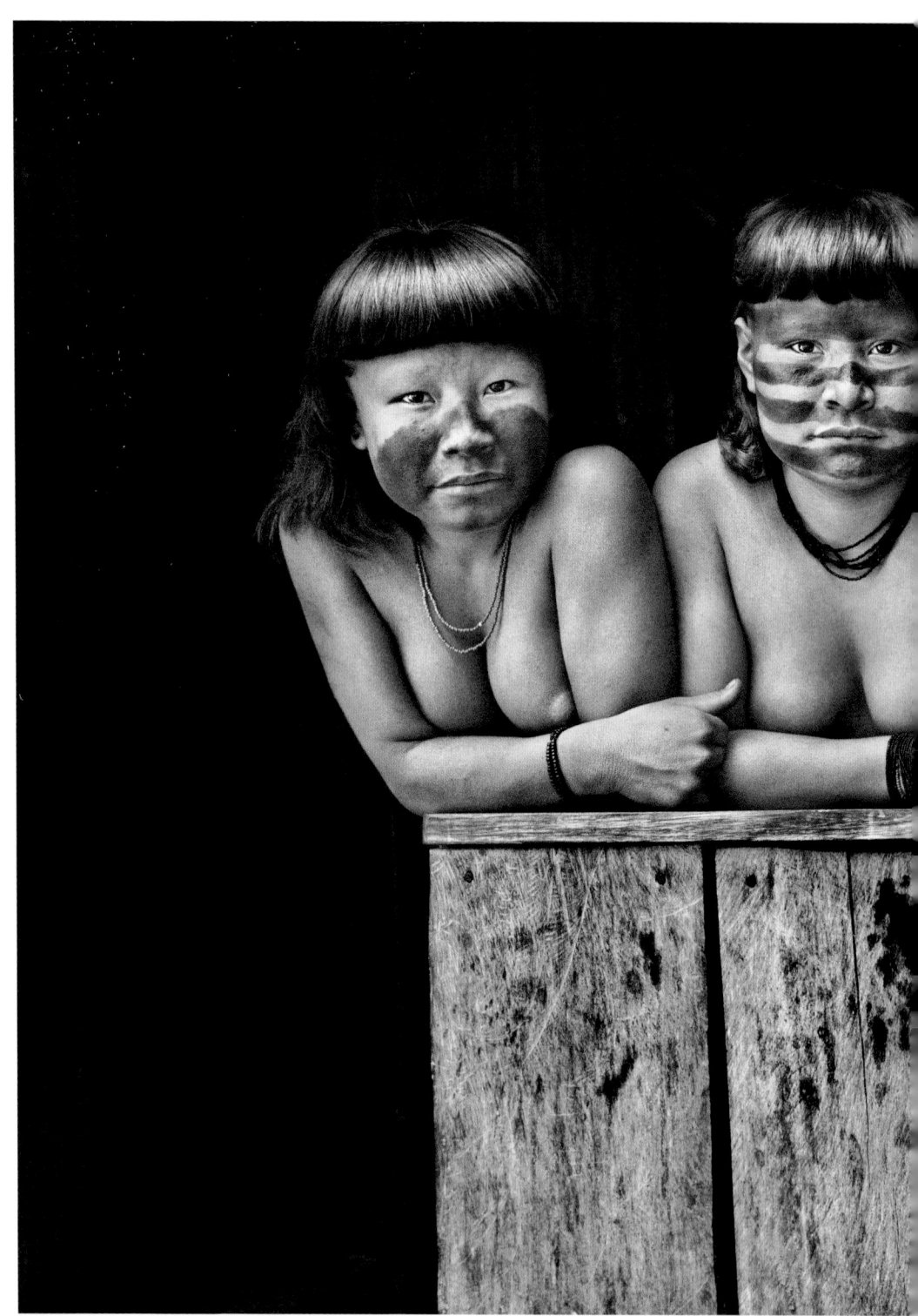

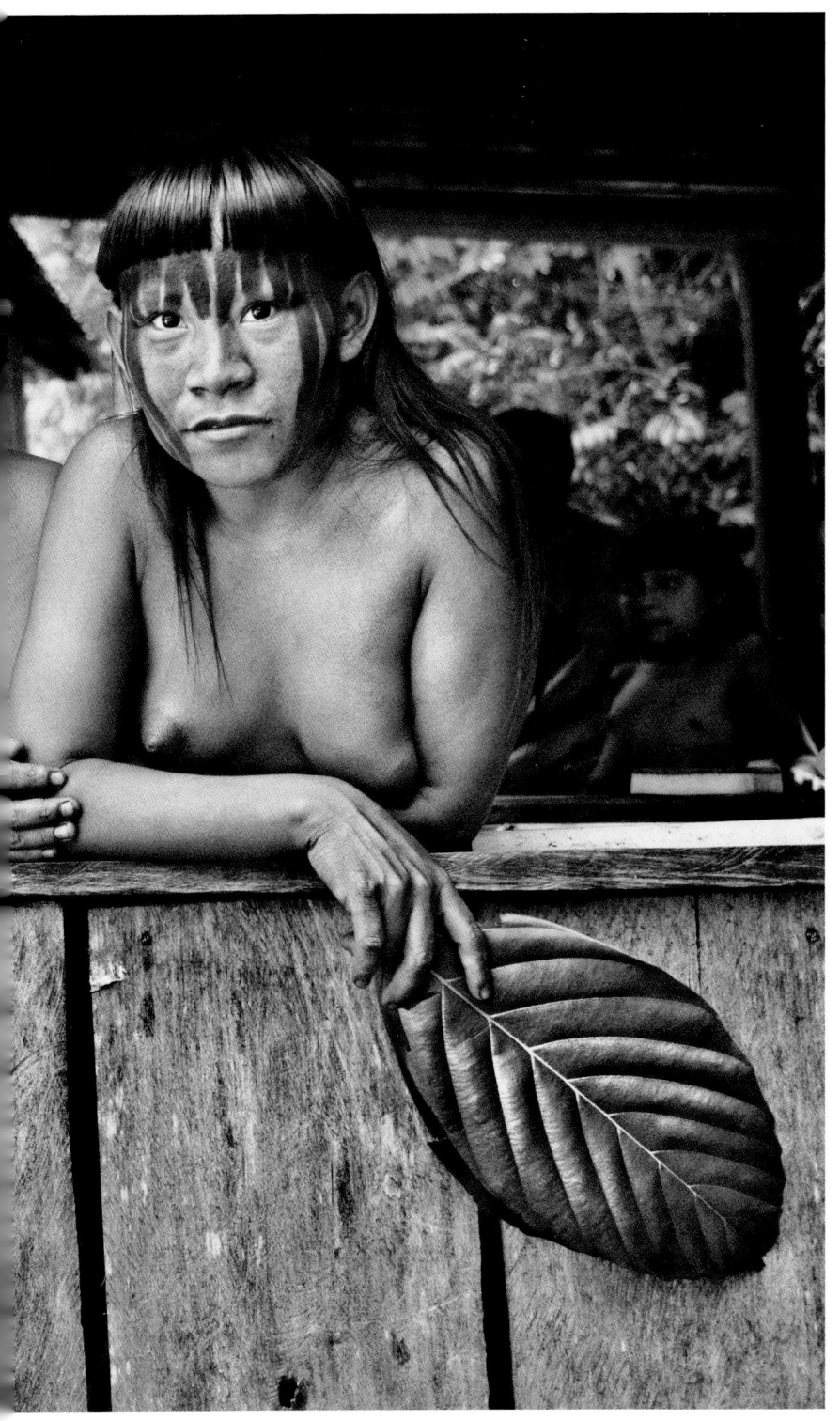

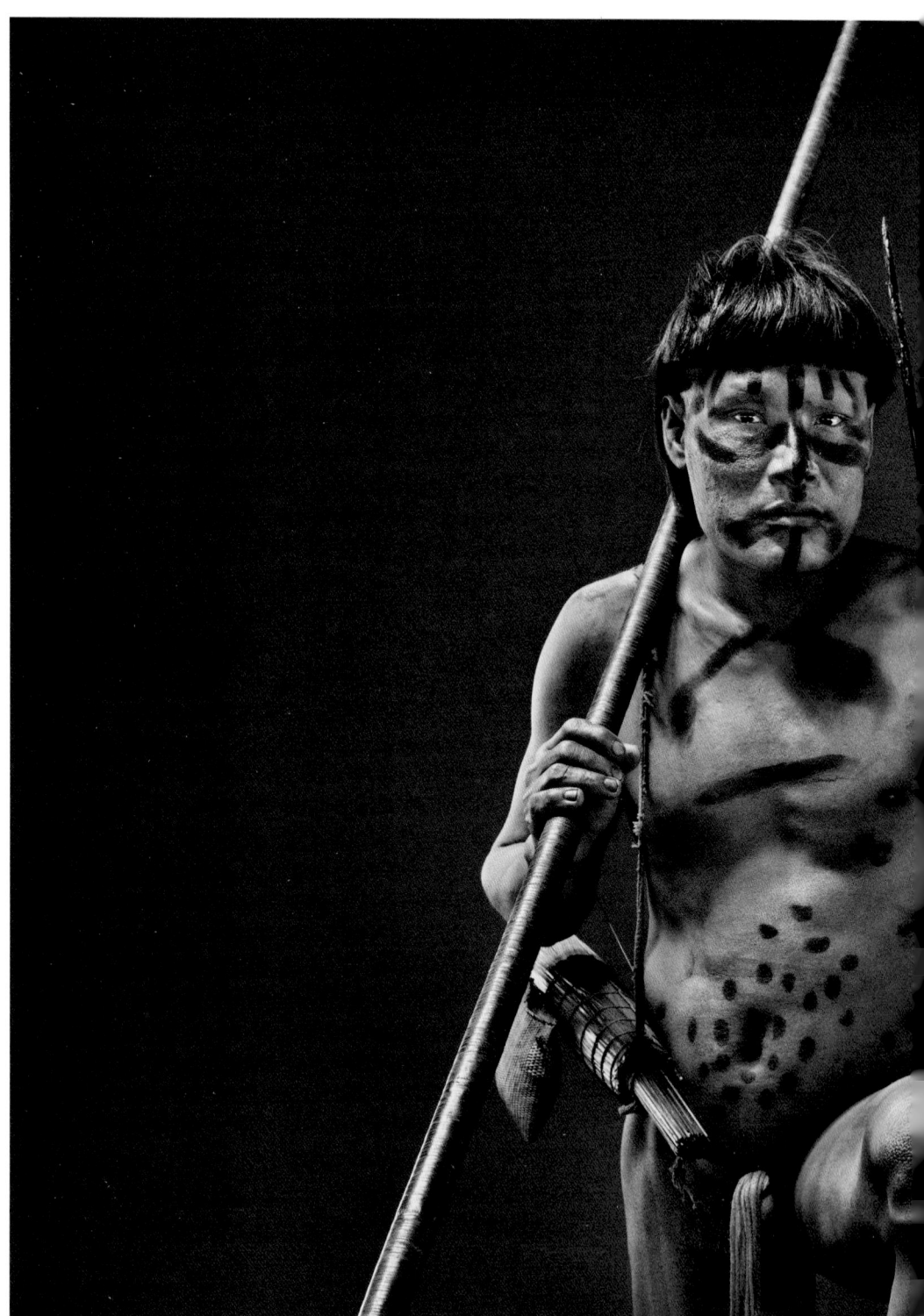

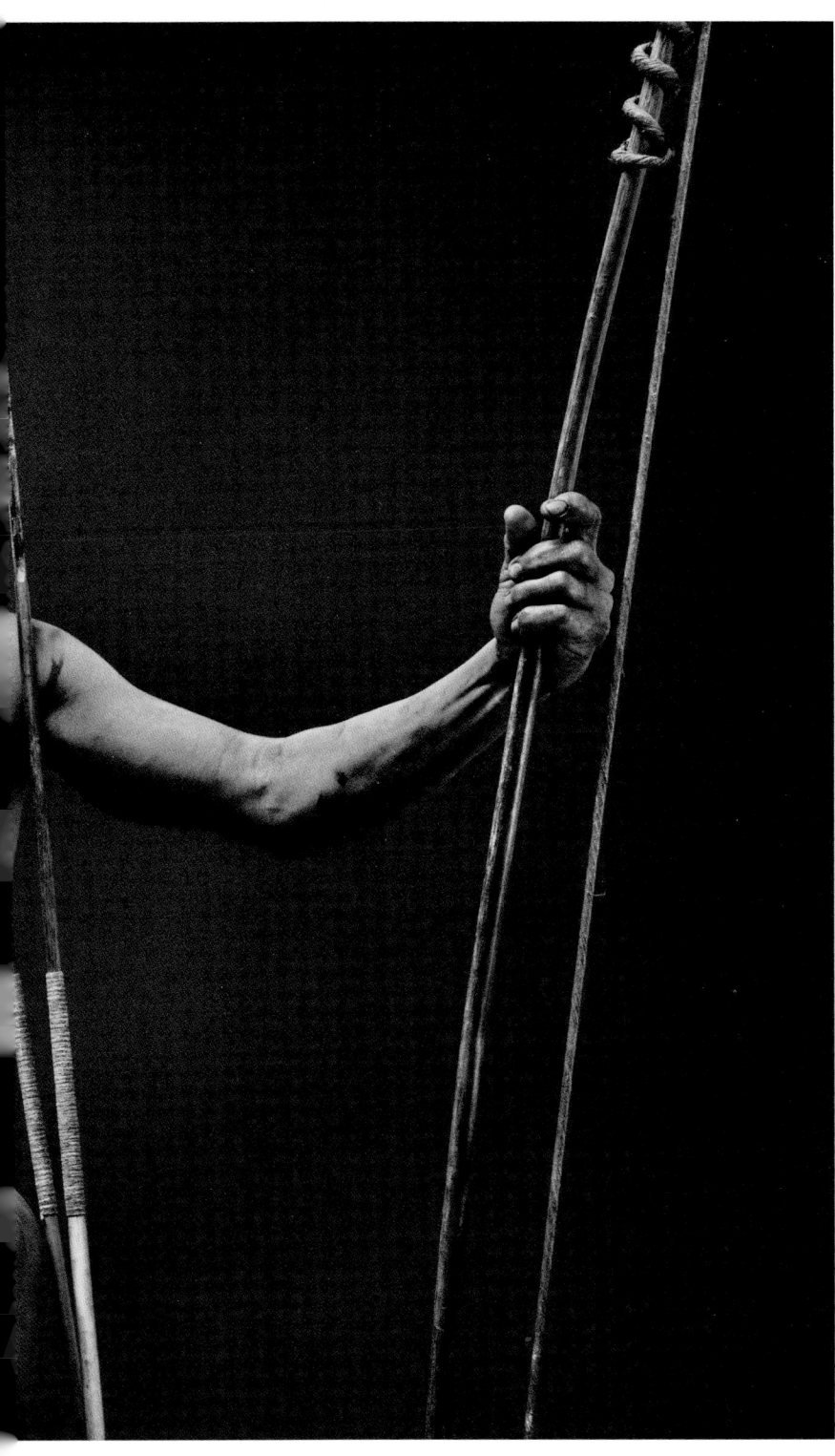

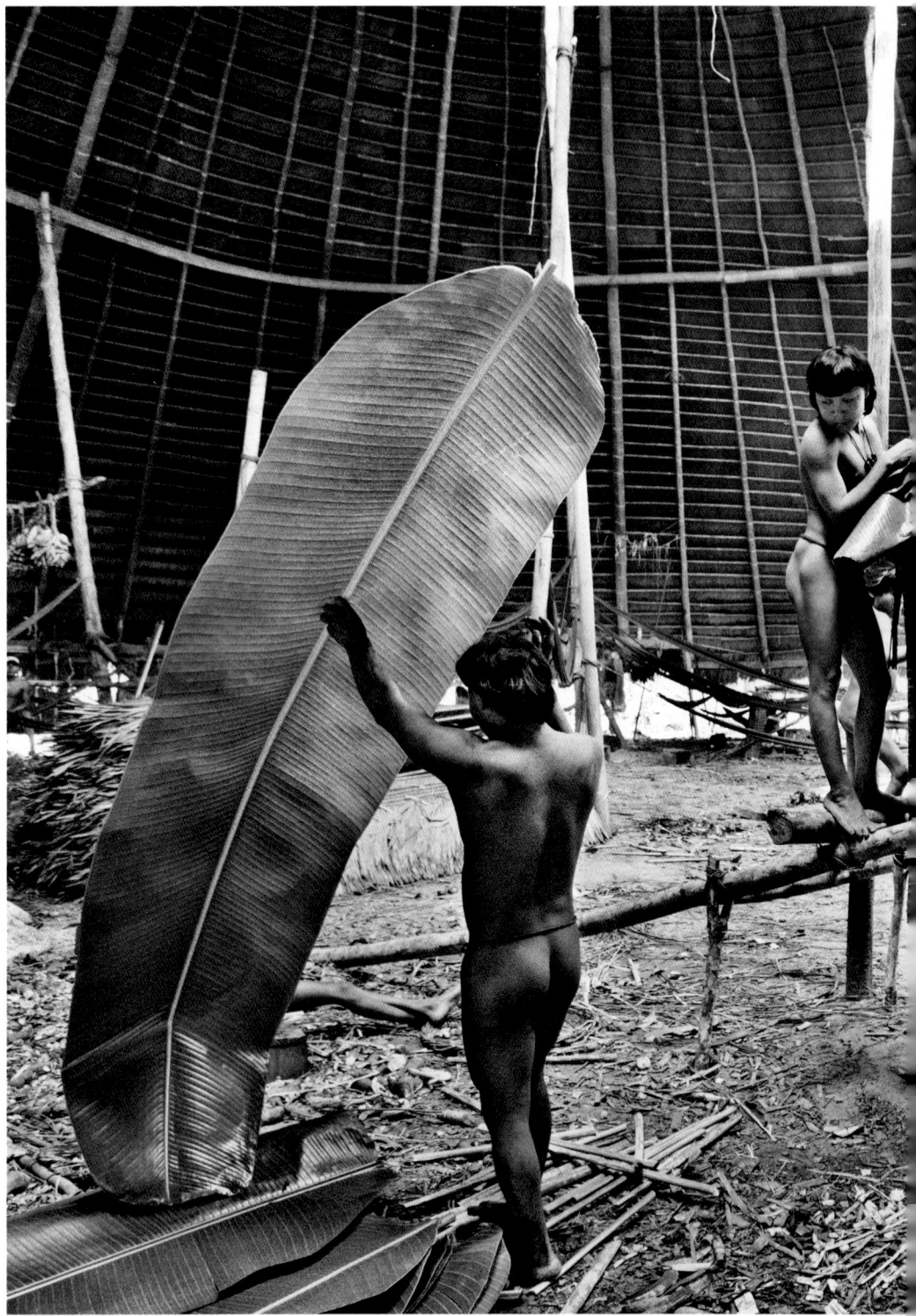

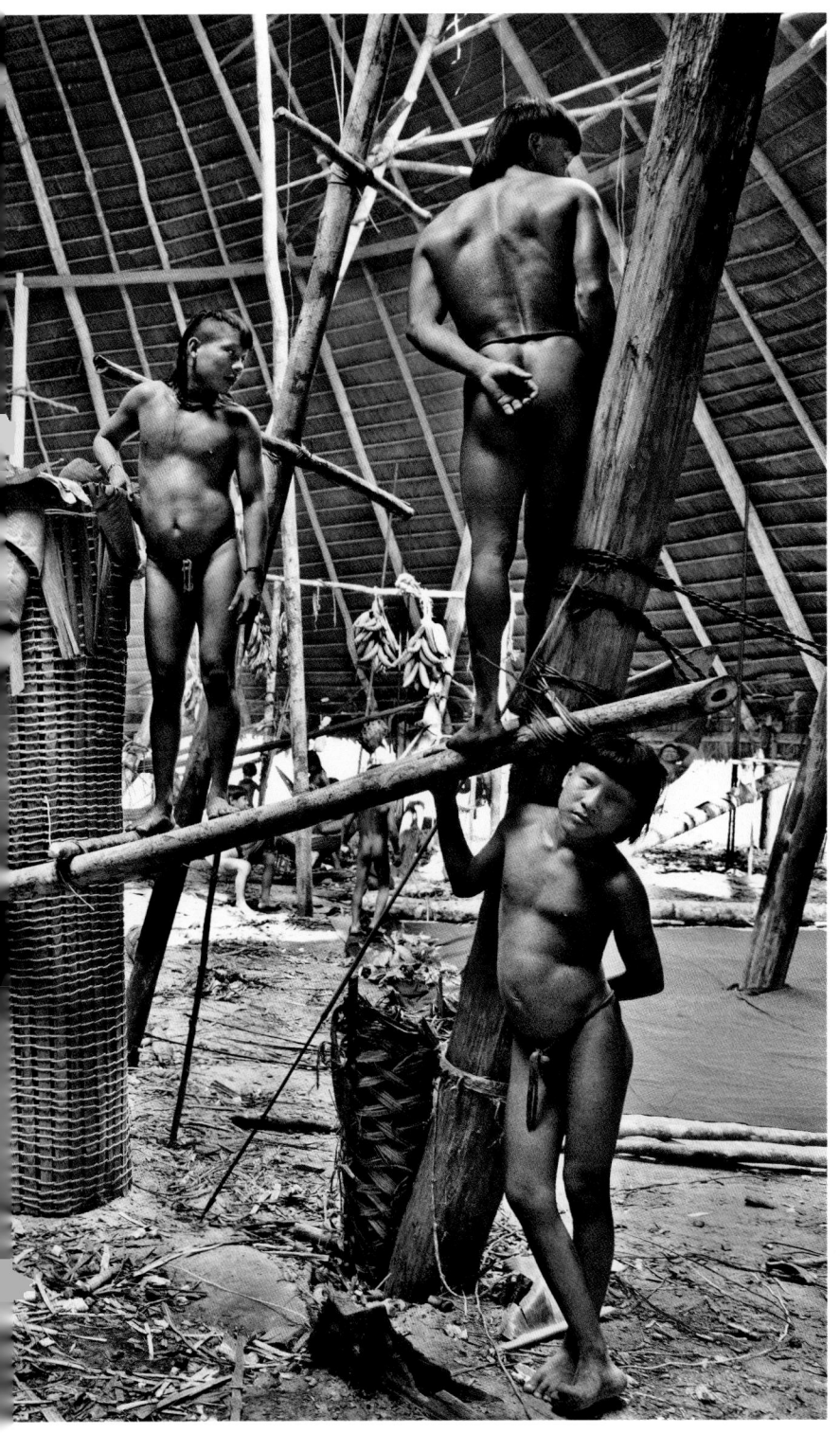

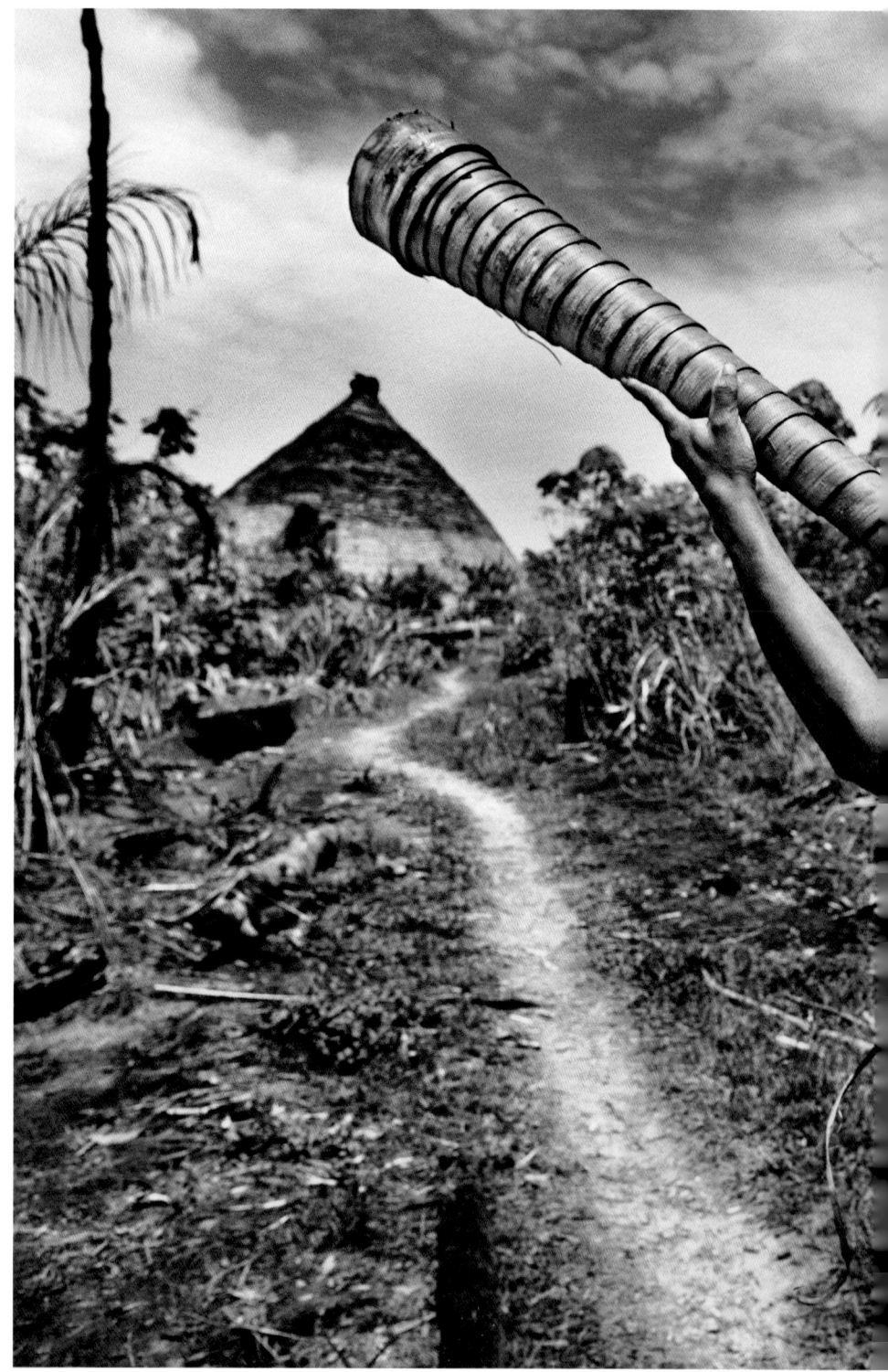

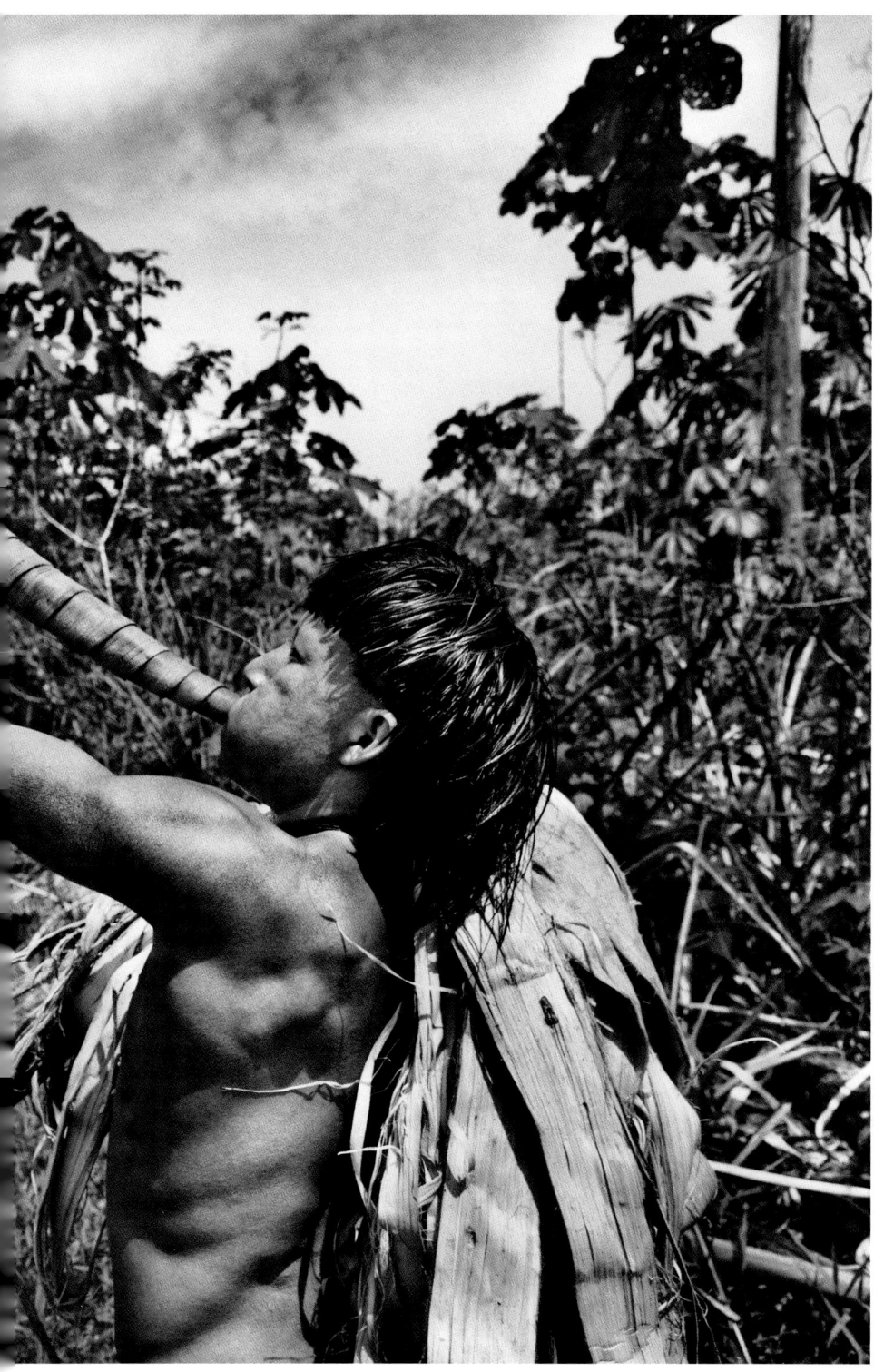

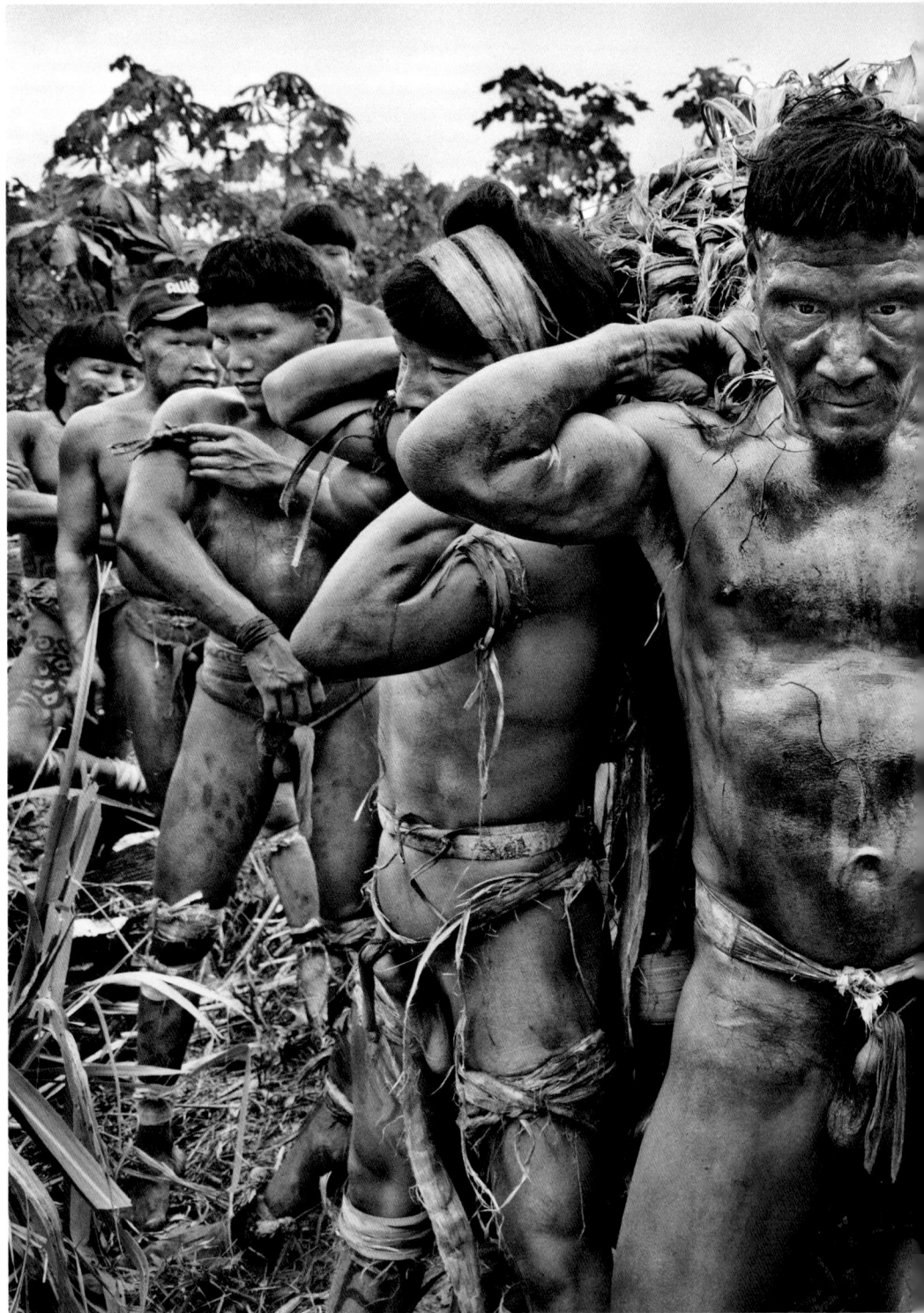

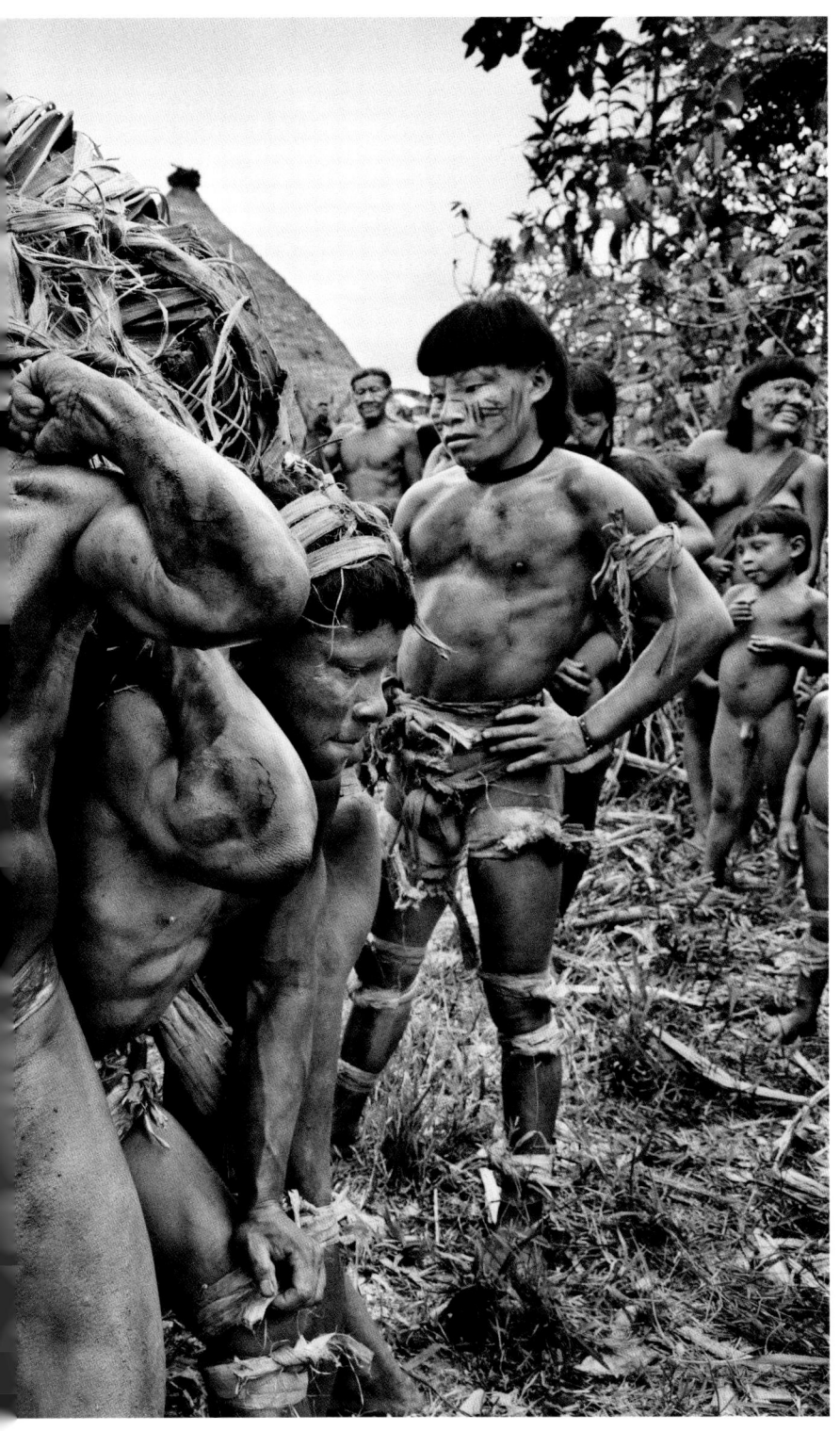

Pages 166/167 Front center: Kwakway. To his right: Baxihywy and Warubi. Suruwahá Indigenous Territory, state of Amazonas, 2017.

Opposite Young Hatiri bathes in a backwater of the Pretão stream, which the indigenous people call Jukihi. Suruwahá Indigenous Territory, state of Amazonas, 2017.

Pages 170/171 In a fishing encampment in Riozinho, Bambuhwa Suruwahá (son of Namijaru and Dawiniawa) and Xamuwa Suruwahá tend the stove where the fish are cooked (roasted over coals to dry them, to allow consumption over a longer period of time). Suruwahá Indigenous Territory, state of Amazonas, 2017.

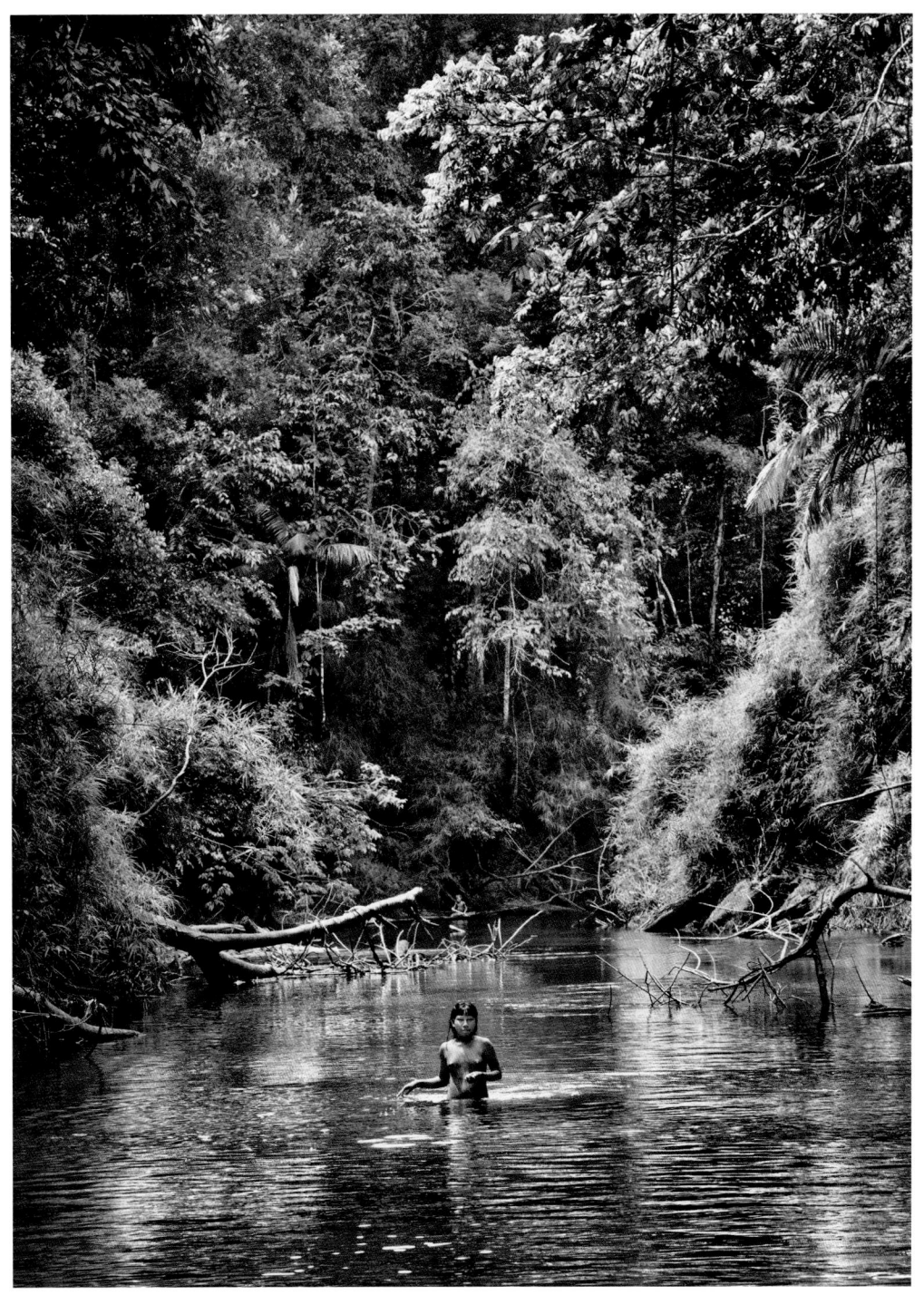

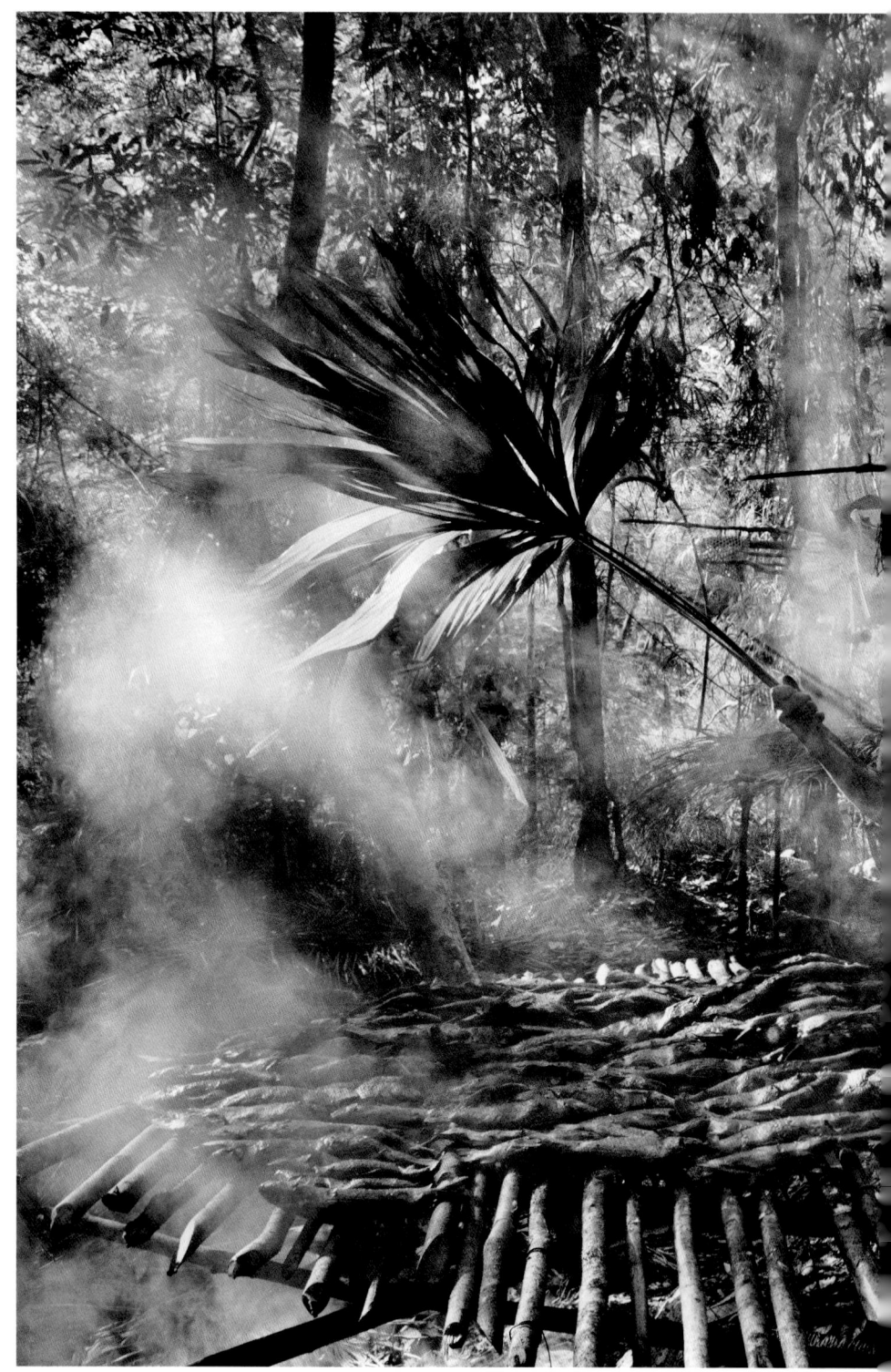

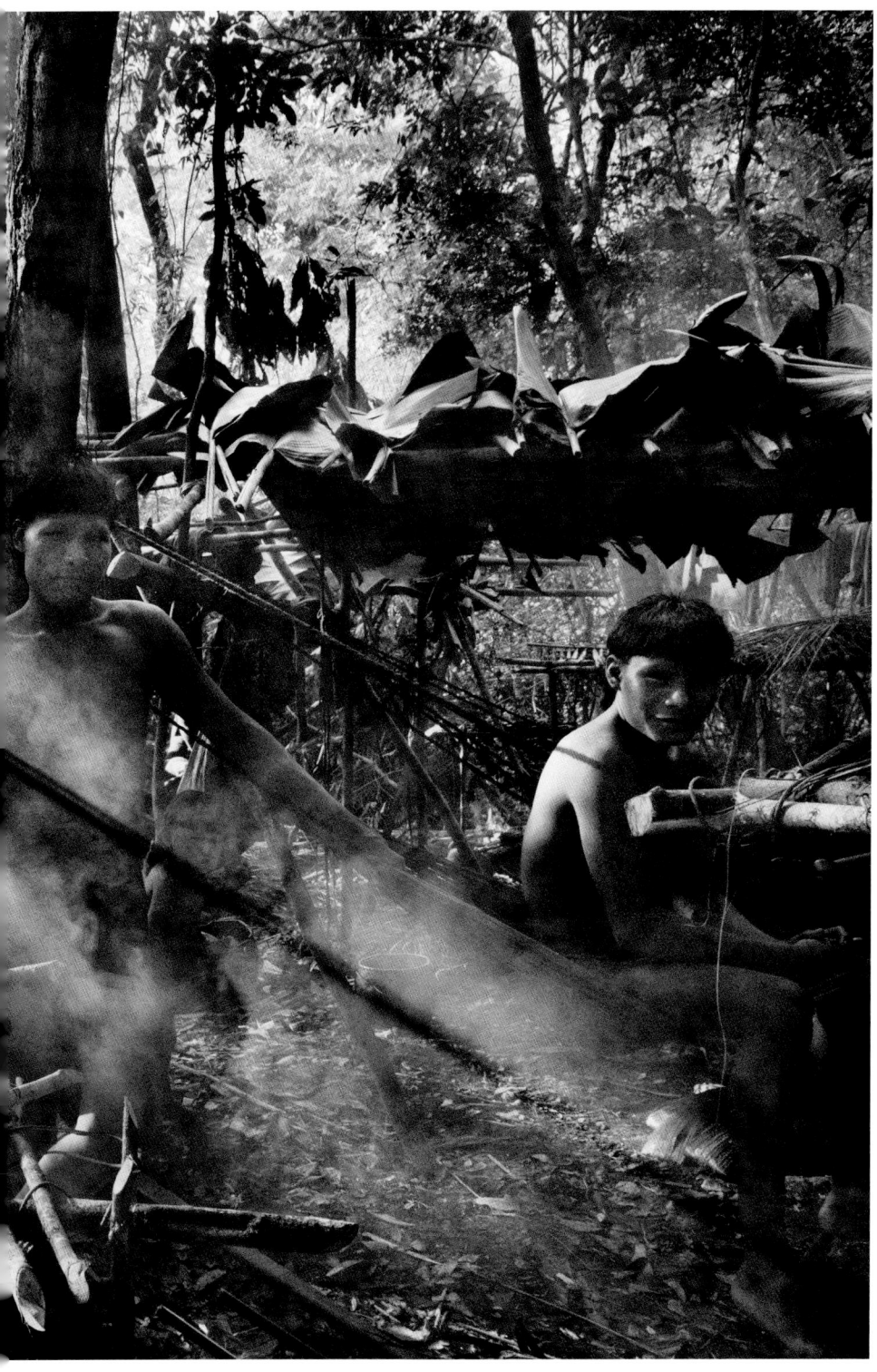

ASHÁNINKA

The Asháninka are one of the indigenous groups with the longest known history: there are records of their economic and cultural relations with the Inca Empire (15th and 16th centuries) that ruled much of the Andes from its capital in the mountains of Peru until the arrival of the Spaniards. Back then, the Asháninka were called "Antis," and they sold forest products to the Incas, such as feathers, animal skins, cotton, fabrics, plants (grains, wood), and in exchange received metal objects (copper axes, gold jewelry), perhaps semiprecious stones, other fabrics, and wool.

The stories told by the Europeans who controlled Peru from the 1530s onward described them as warriors of the hot forest who, because of their braveness and loyalty, served as guards for the last Inca nobles. After losing the capital city, Cuzco, these nobles took refuge in an area near the Amazon rainforest. There, protected by their soldiers, who were accustomed to life in the mountains, and by the local indigenous people from the Amazon, the Inca court survived 40 years in the hidden city of Vilcabamba. When the Spanish captured the last Inca in 1572, he was surrounded by Asháninka warriors. The tribe's own name for themselves contains the name of their former partners.

Known as "Antis" or "Andes" (depending on pronunciation in the Quechua language), their name survives in the geography of the continent as a remembrance of the pre-Columbian era. The area where they lived, on the slopes of the chain of mountains north of Cuzco, was called "Antisuyo," land of the Antis. The Spaniards assumed this was the name of the mountains and so they applied it to the entire mountain range, from Patagonia to Colombia. The Andes therefore reflect the history of the Asháninka.

Anyone arriving in the village of Apiwtxa sees right away that it is an Asháninka community: they seem to have been in the same position for a long time. That permanence is expressed in cultural elements, such as clothing, the style of the houses, eating habits, and the stories they tell, in which the defeat of the Incas sounds like a recent event.

Men and women still wear the *kushma*, the tunic of handmade cloth described by travelers in the past. Men plant cotton and women spin and weave. Men's clothing is made of different colored threads, with vertical stripes woven into the cloth. A well-worn *kushma* whose colors have faded or lost their vividness is dyed a dark brownish color. Women's tunics are different: the cloth is smooth and brown and their stripes are horizontal, painted on with black paint made from river sand. Besides this garment, the men also wear a rigid straw hat, with feathers, and a band of fabric that looks like a tie.

The relationship between the Asháninka and the Incas is so old and deep that it even appears in myths about the creation of the world and of men, as if these two peoples were born from each other. According to one such myth, as told by the shaman Moisés Piyãko:

One day, a very long time ago, there was an Asháninka community, and in the middle of it was a pond. From within the pond, they could hear the cries of a chicken. One day, someone took a hook and went fishing. Each piece of bait he used caught something: a chicken or creatures that did not exist. One of the times that he put the hook in the water, he caught an Inca. That is why they originally lived with the Asháninka. But one day they went off to live farther away, and that is where the Inca people came to exist. Whatever my people needed, they sought in the cities of the Incas. And whatever they needed, they bought from the Asháninka. The Incas did not know how to get around in the forest, they did not come down into the forest, they stayed only in the mountains.

Also according to their mythology, after the territory was conquered by the Spanish, whom they call *Wiracocha*, the supreme god of the Asháninka, Pawa, decided to hide knowledge and keep the sages from telling the invaders the secrets of his powers. Pawa hid wisdom by turning the wise men into animals. But he needed to preserve a way for some men to access that knowledge. So he created *ayahuasca*, a drink that puts men in touch with the spirit world. It is "the key that lets us successfully reach all the spells that are locked away."

The Asháninka consider the knowledge of *ayahuasca* essential. It is now present in several indigenous cultures in Acre and in forms of religious worship in big cities in Brazil and elsewhere.

Among the Asháninka, the ritual consumption of *kamarampi* takes place in small groups and discreet gatherings around a shaman, such as Moisés, with five or six people. The aim is to hear the spiritual world, receive teachings, understand situations.

Communal celebrations (called *piarentsi*) bring together the whole village and guests, who consume *caiçuma*, a slightly fermented drink made from cassava or potato. These celebrations play a very important role in the life of the Asháninka as expressions of joy, gratitude, and closeness among the people of the community. At the same time, they are a thermometer to measure the mood of the gods: when taking part in an indigenous celebration, if the god that owns the rain (Inkaniteri) gets drunk, he will make it rain hard; if it does not rain, it is because he did not have much fun. If, however, there are soft rains after a celebration, it is a sign that the female spirits got merry and drunk.

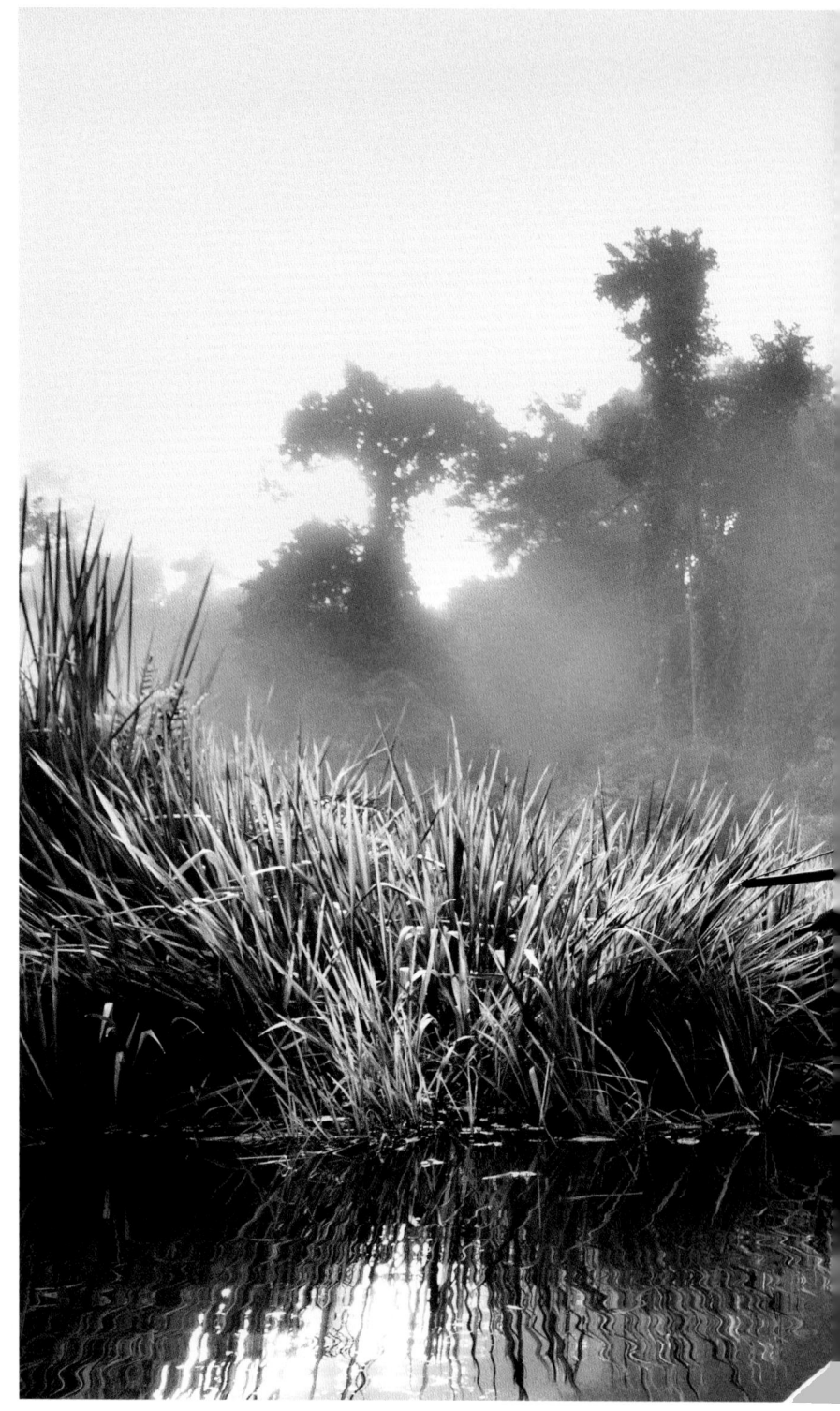

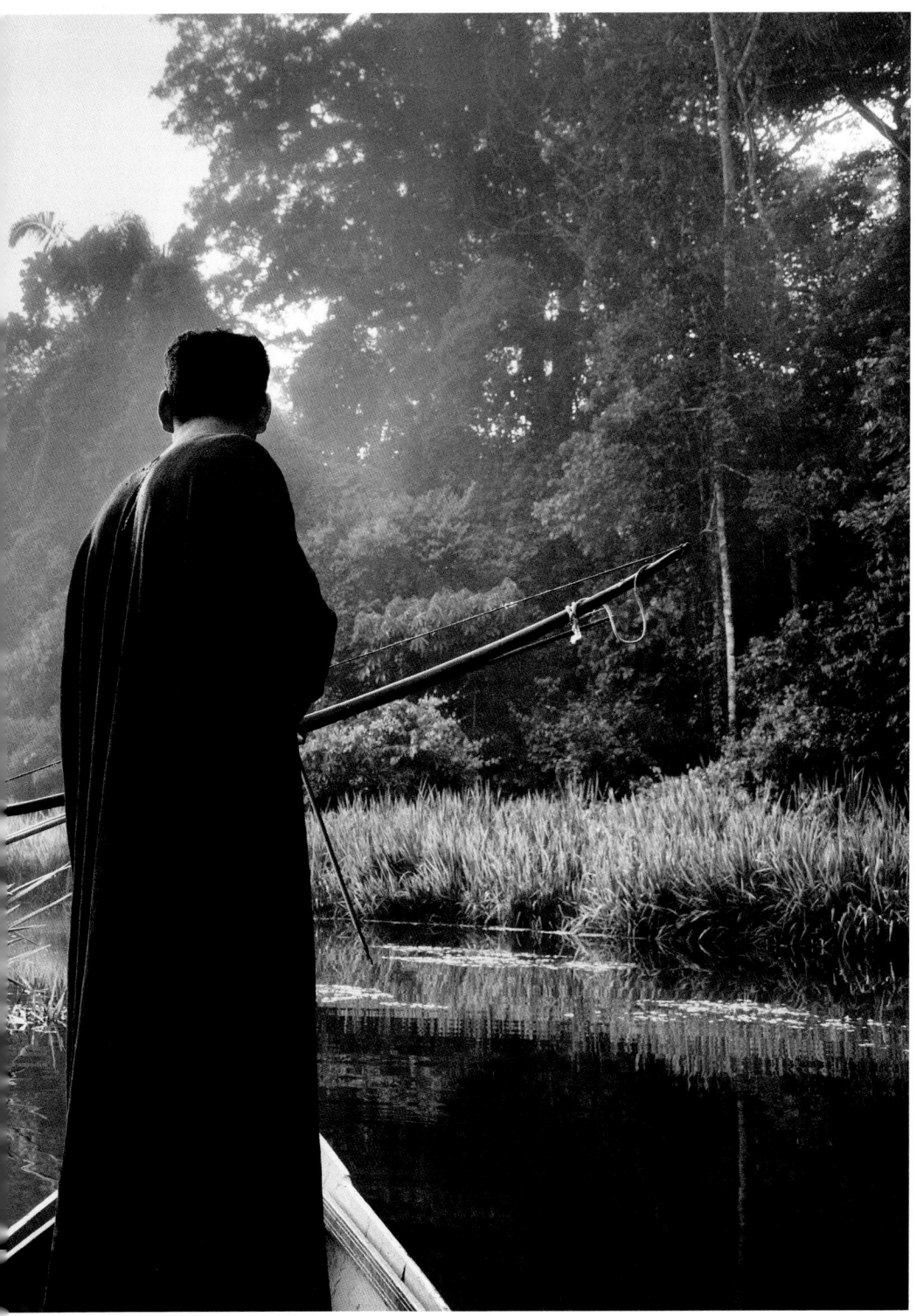

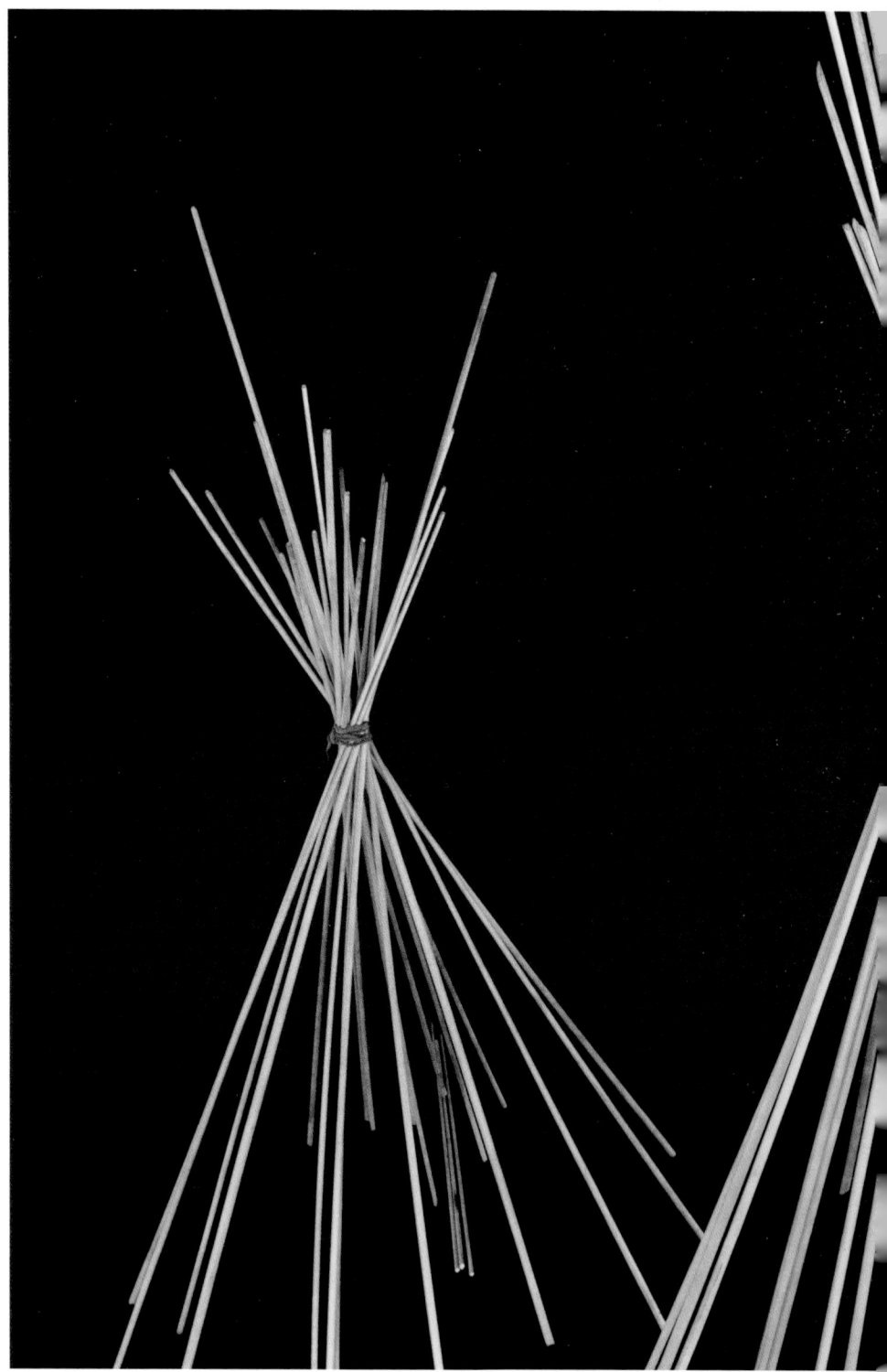

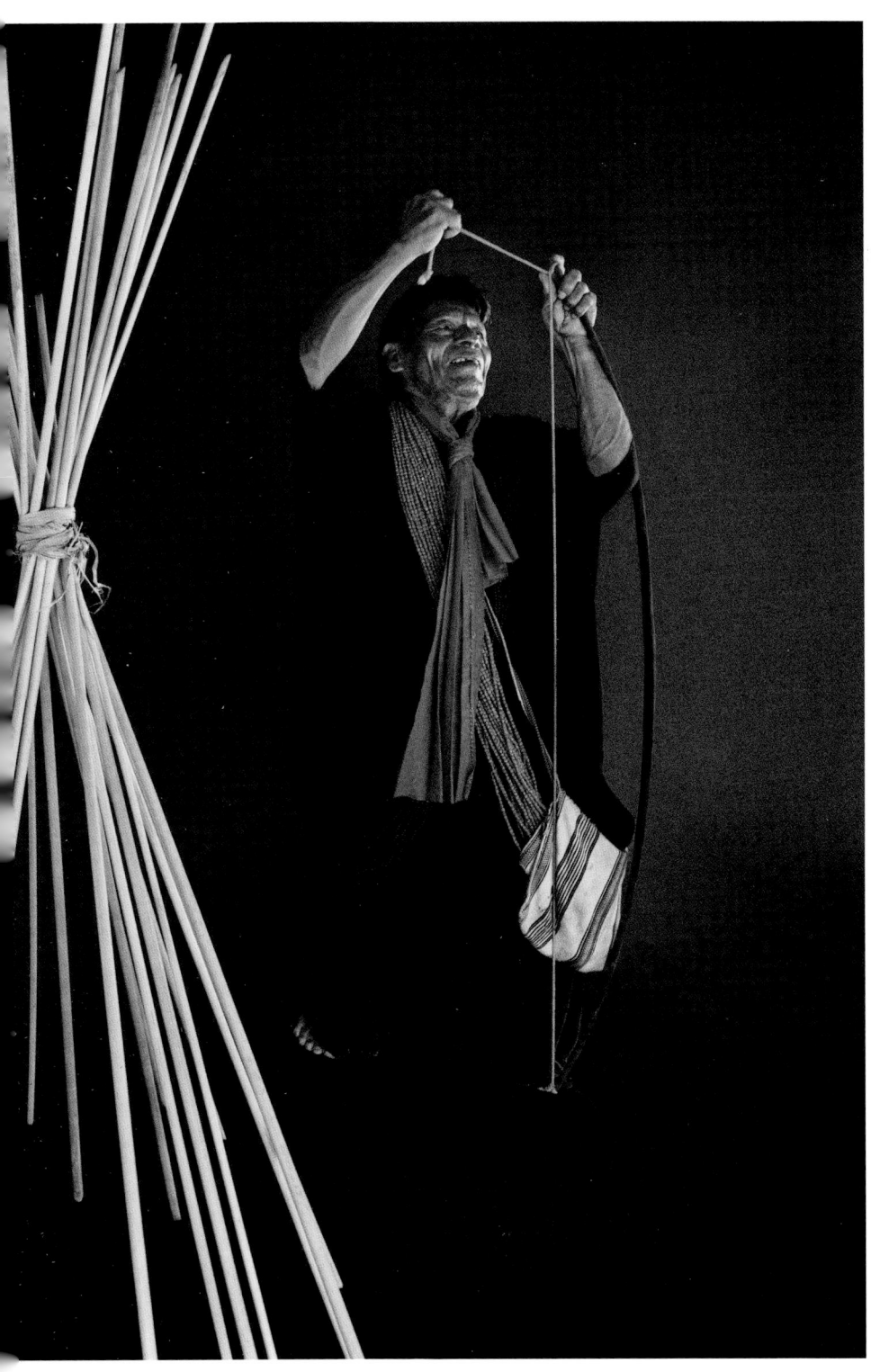

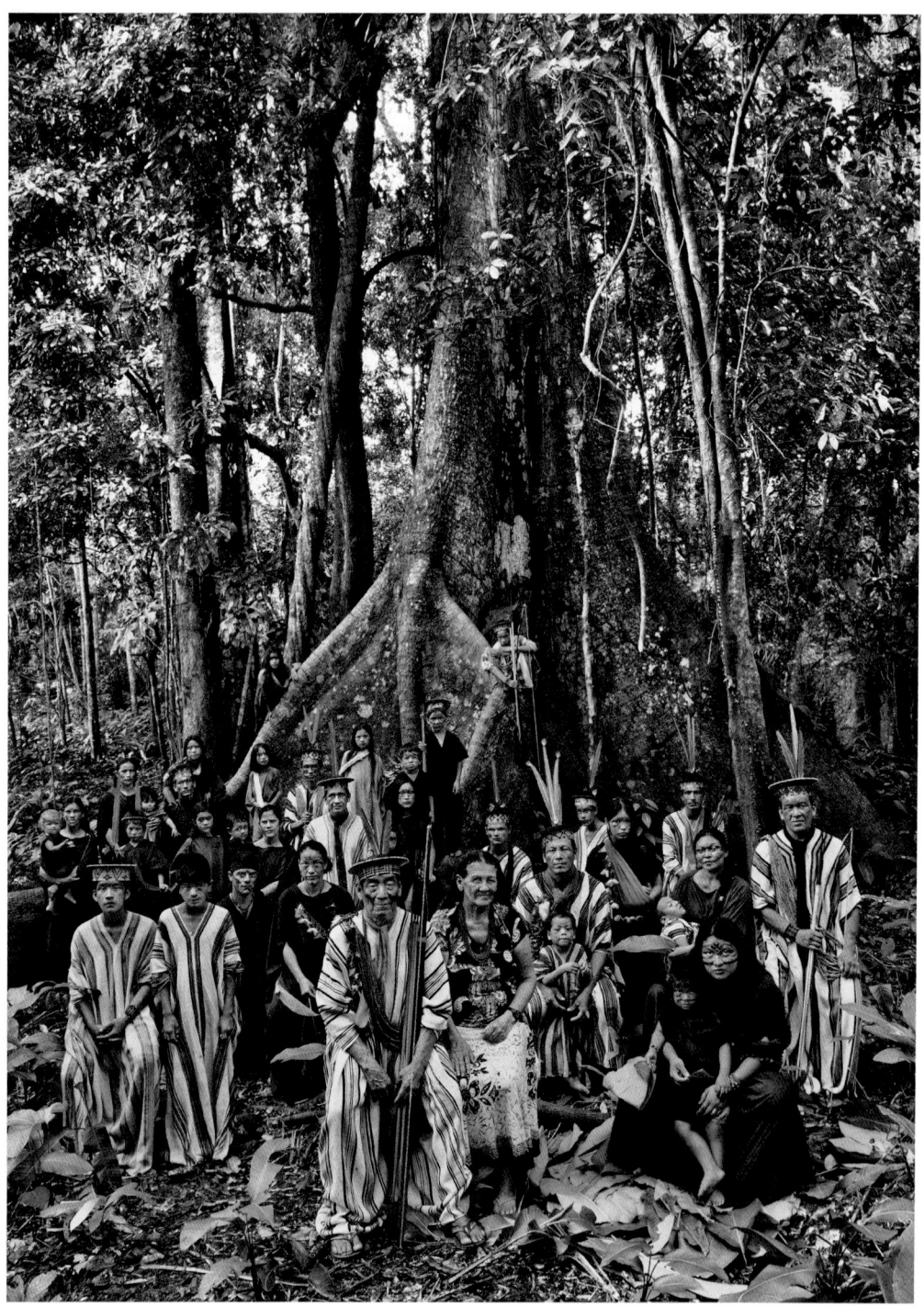

Pages 174/175 Standing in a canoe, Wewito Piyāko Asháninka fishes with a bow and arrows. Kampa do Rio Amônea Indigenous Territory, state of Acre, 2016.

Pages 176/177 Pishiro finishes producing a bow by tying the string to the ends. He trains young Asháninka to make bows and arrows, in this case from a type of lightweight bamboo called *chicosa*. Kampa do Rio Amônea Indigenous Territory, state of Acre, 2016.

Opposite Family of Antônio Piyāko (center, foreground) and his wife, Francisca ("Dona Pity" is white and never adopted traditional Asháninka clothing). They had seven children: Francisco, 49; Moisés, 48; Isaac, 46; Bênki, 44; Dora, 42; Wewito, 40; and Alexandrina, 38. Then they raised seven more. Kampa do Rio Amônea Indigenous Territory, state of Acre, 2016.

Pages 180/181 Eliane, from the Yawanawá tribe, is married to Asháninka leader Francisco Piyāko. She continues to wear traditional Yawanawá face paint, different from that of Asháninka women. In her hair, she wears a pin with macaw feathers arranged like flowers. Kampa do Rio Amônea Indigenous Territory, state of Acre, 2016.

Pages 182/183 Wewito Piyāko Asháninka examines the arrow he is making. His son Owyari is behind him, his daughter Kamorishi opposite him, and further back, his wife, Auzelina (left). Also in the photo: Wewito's sister Dora and his niece Êrishi. Kampa do Rio Amônea Indigenous Territory, state of Acre, 2016.

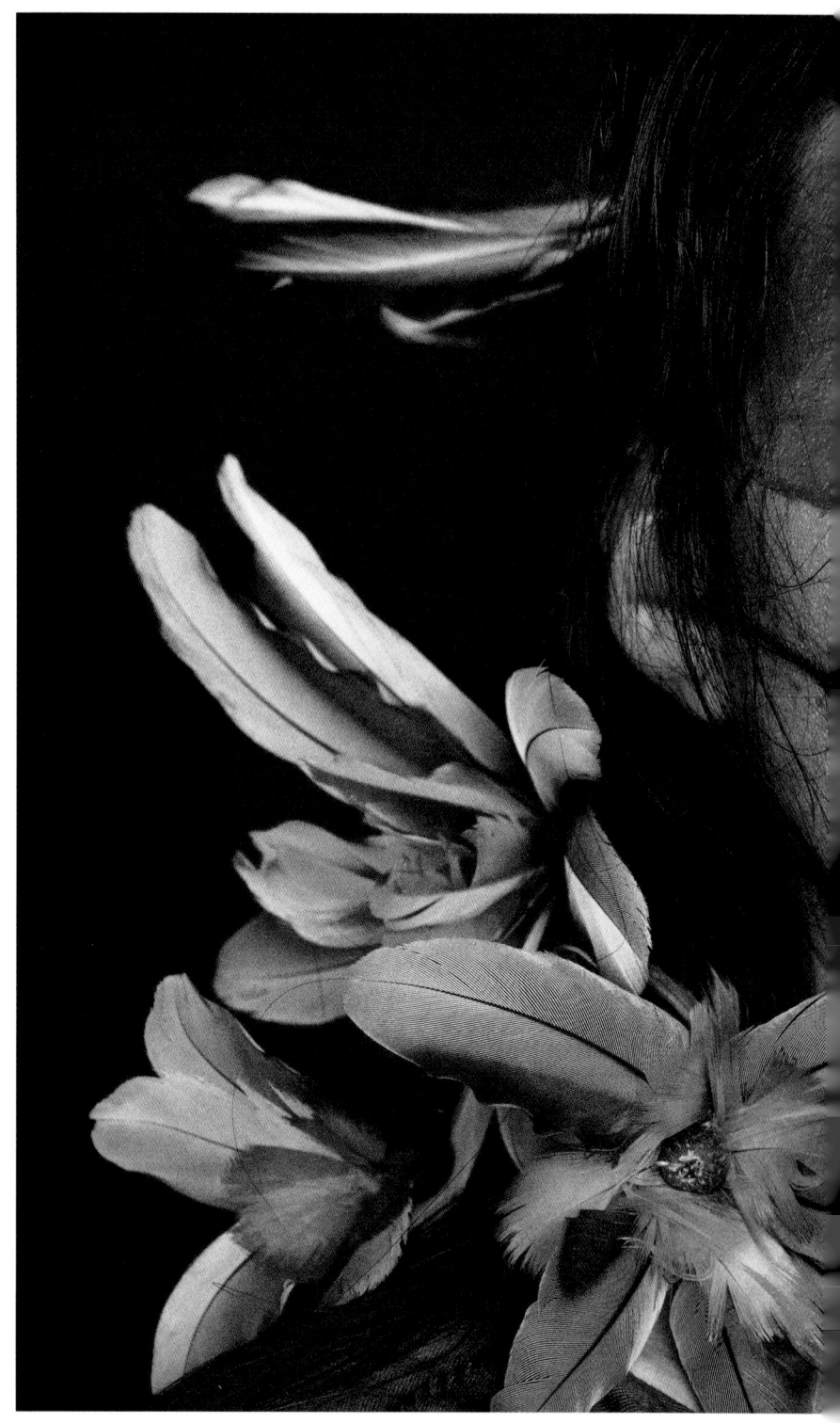

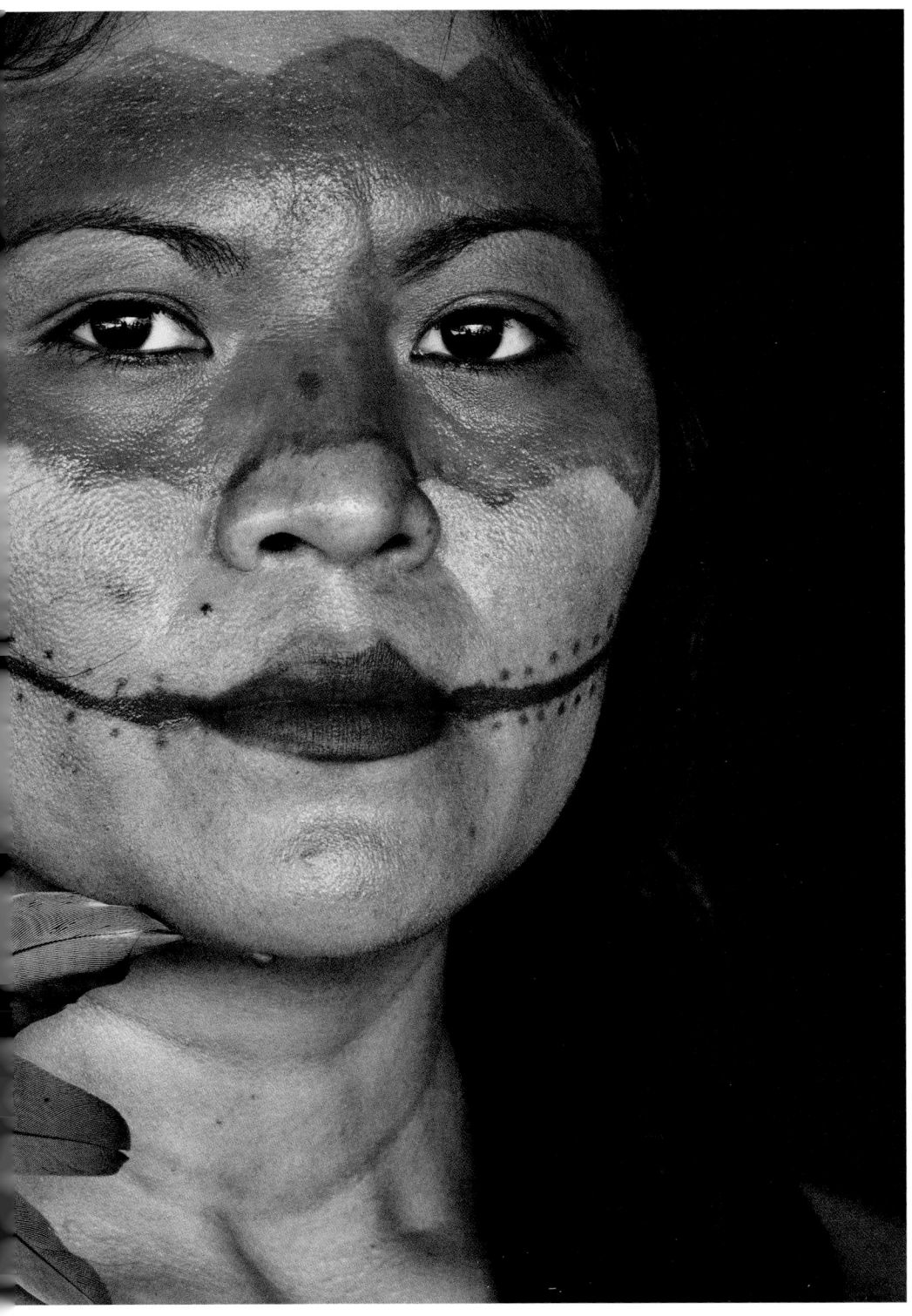

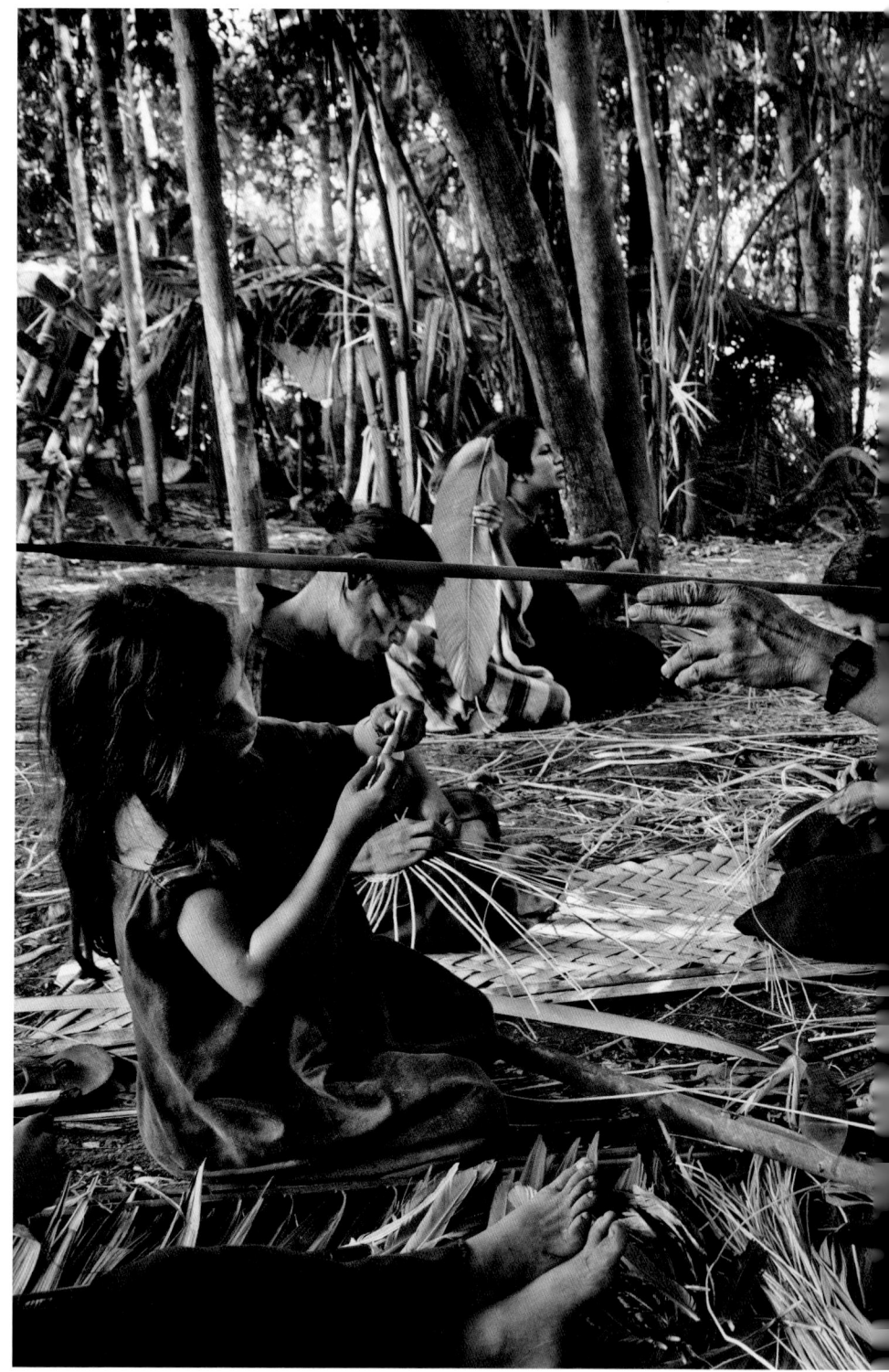

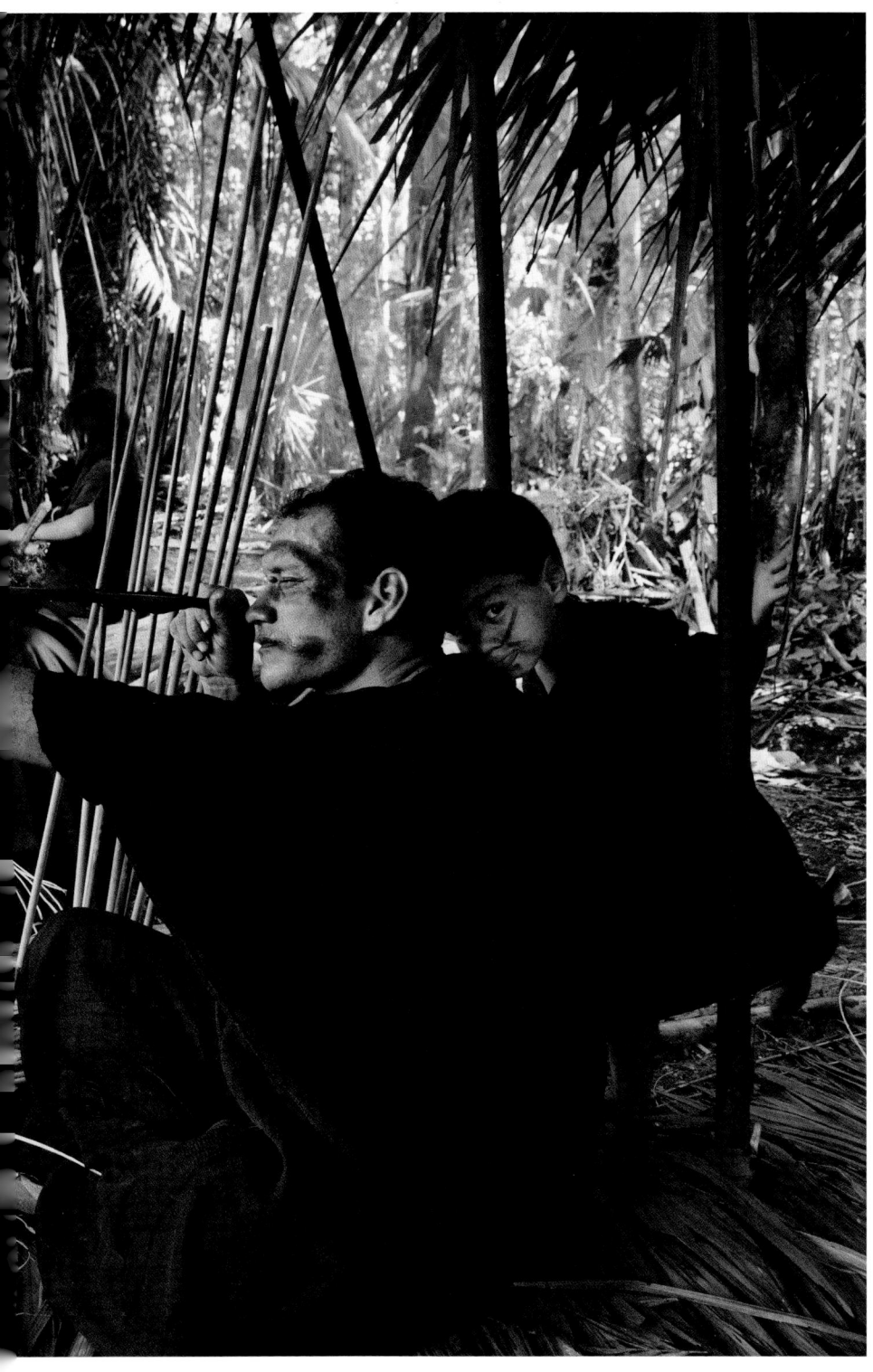

Opposite Yara Asháninka. She is the eldest daughter of Wewito Piyāko and Auzelina. The small paint designs on her face indicate that a girl is not yet engaged. Kampa do Rio Amônea Indigenous Territory, state of Acre, 2016.

Pages 186/187 Onātxo and Thōwero, Winko Asháninka's daughter and granddaughter, with little children. Kampa do Rio Amônea Indigenous Territory, state of Acre, 2016.

Pages 188/189 Manitzi Asháninka (right) and son Tchari, or Davizinho (left). *Manitzi* means "jaguar." Kampa do Rio Amônea Indigenous Territory, state of Acre, 2016.

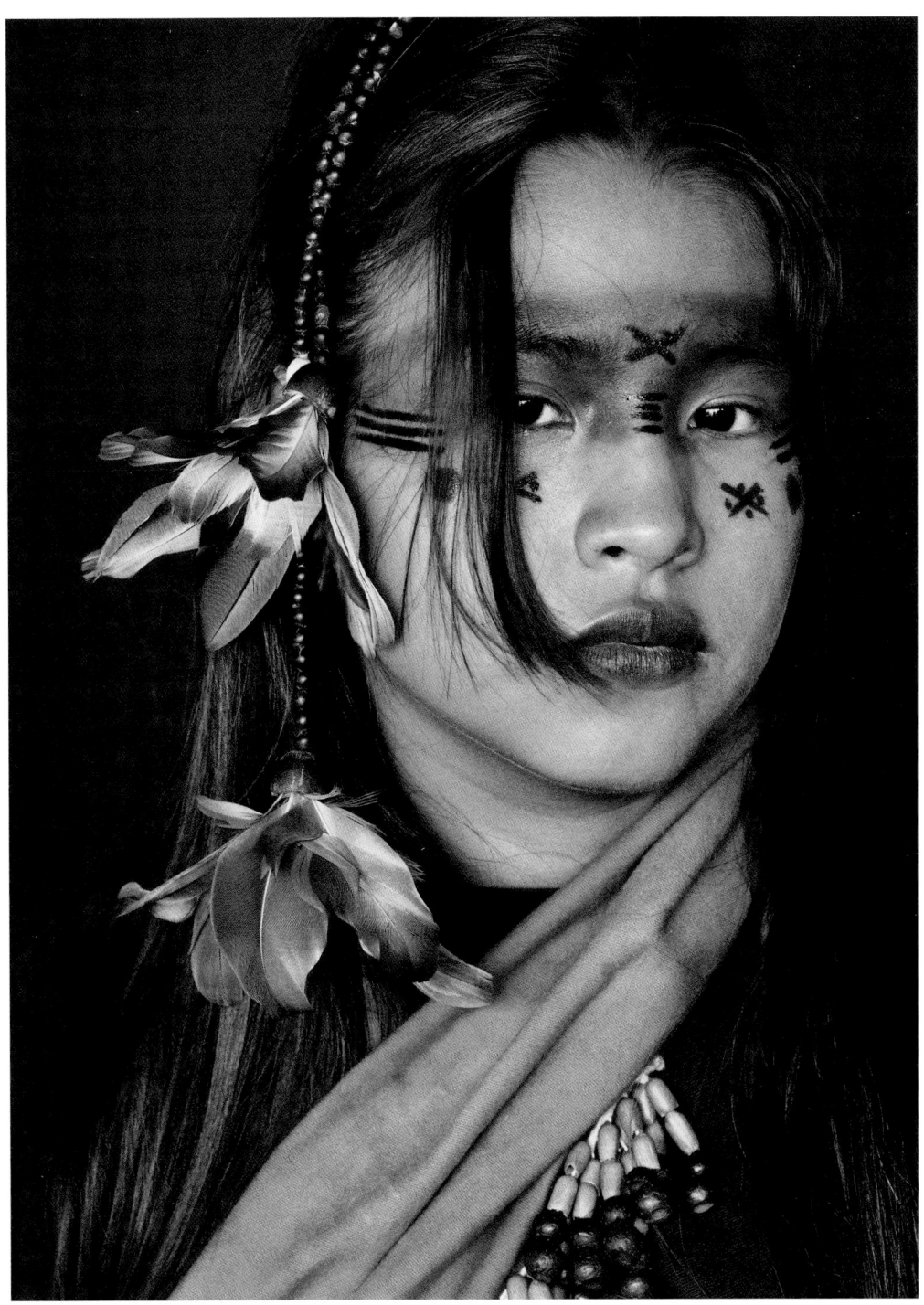

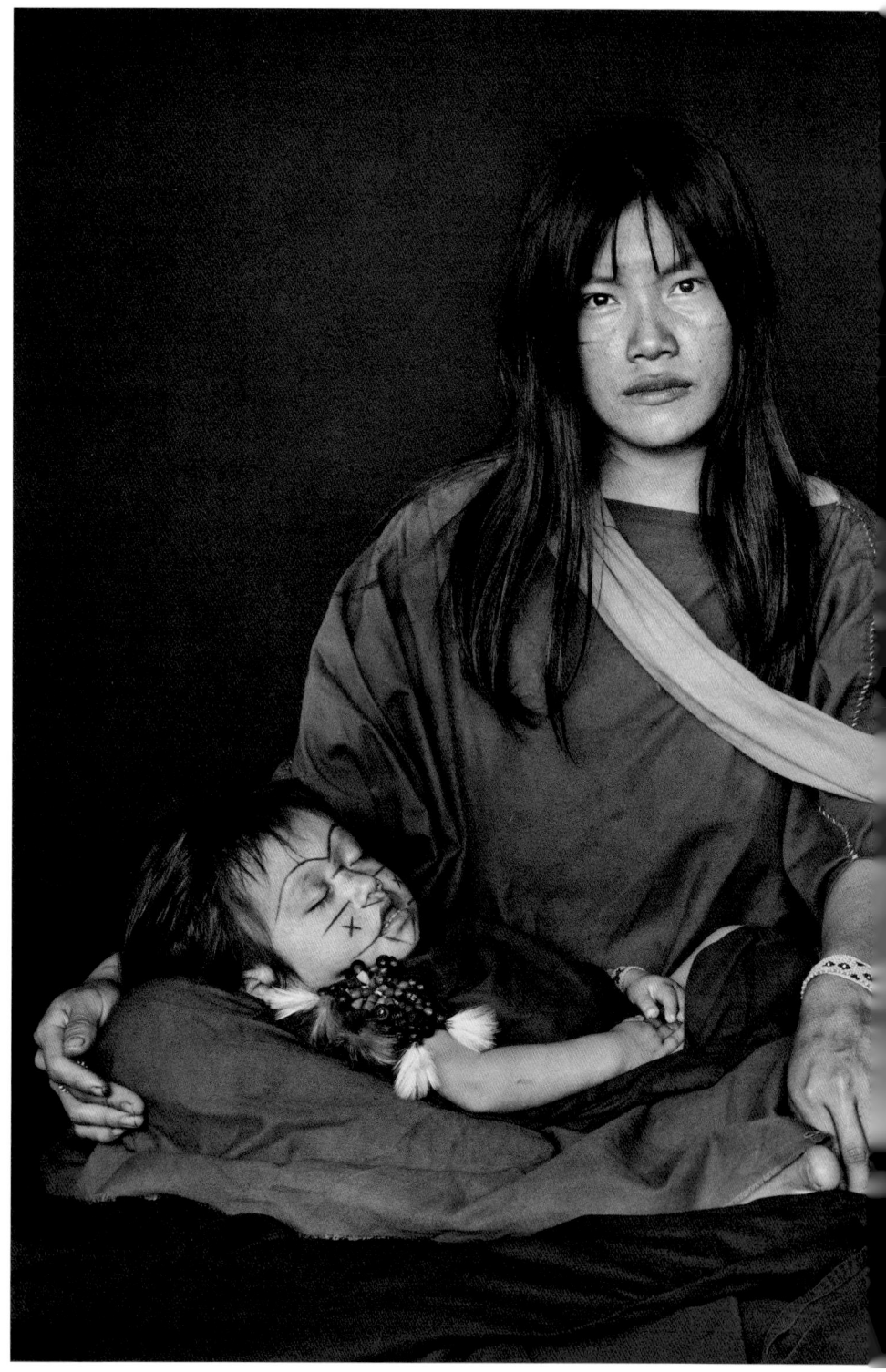

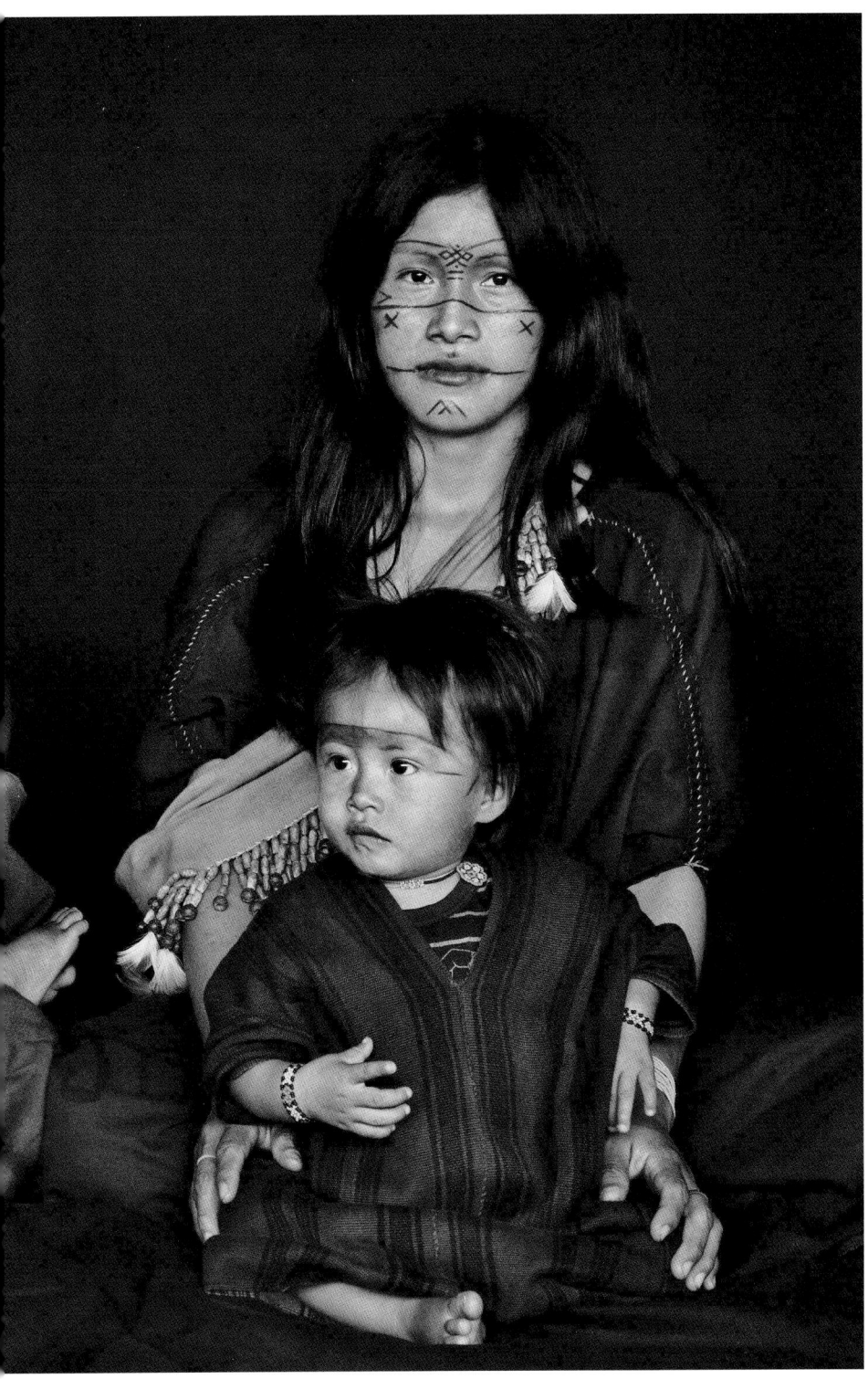

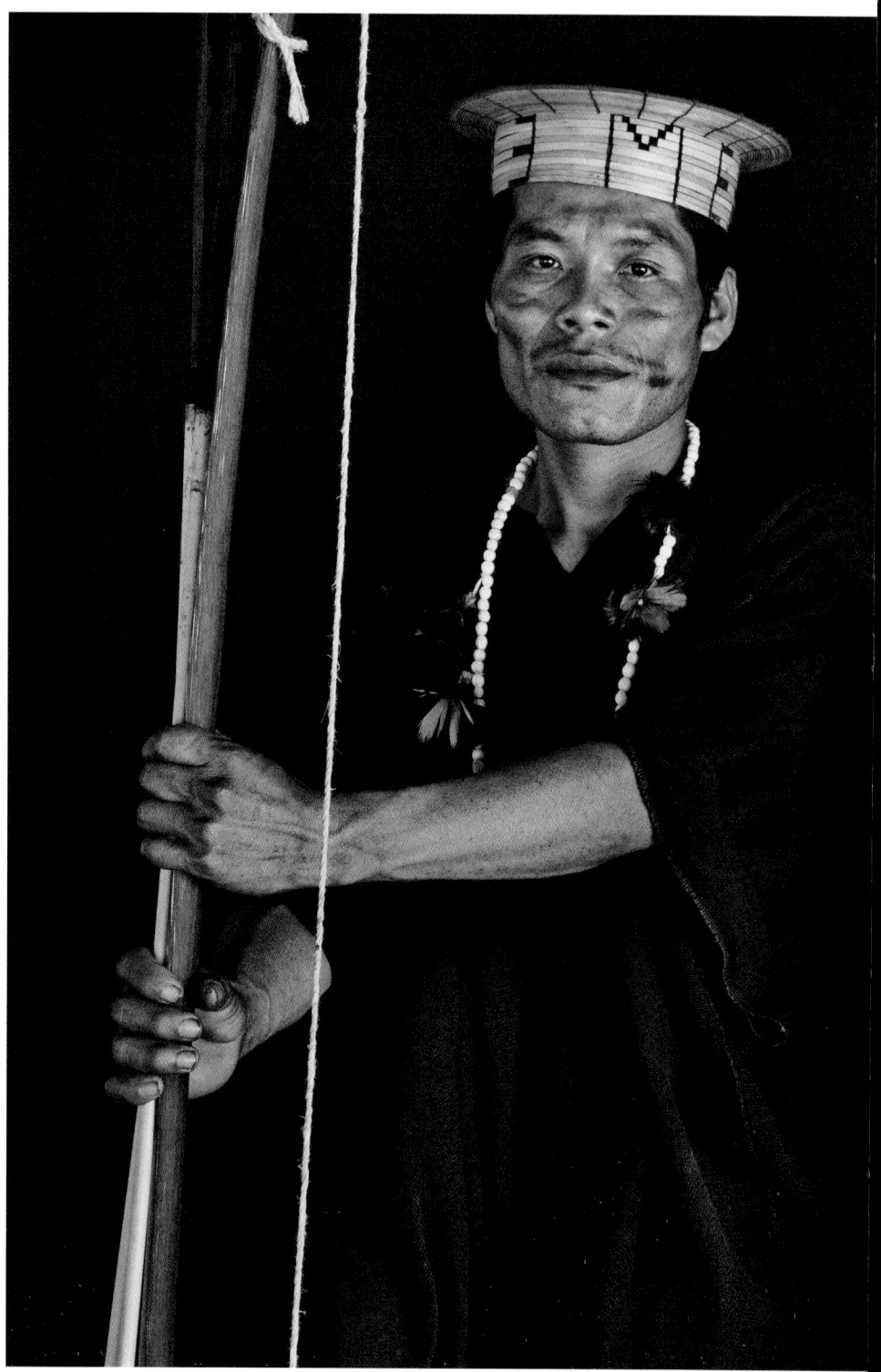

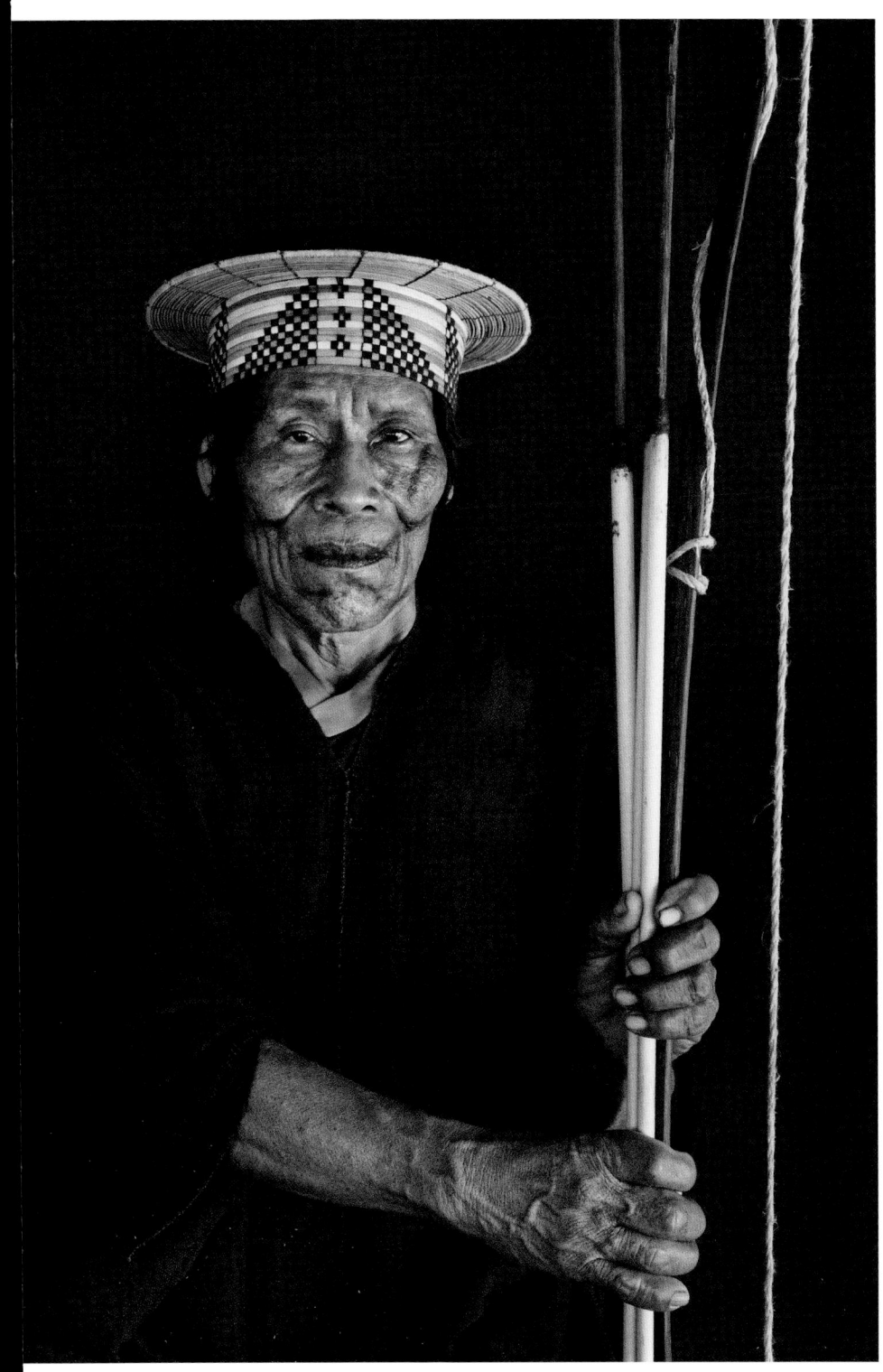

Opposite Julieta Piyāko, sister of Antônio Piyāko. Her brother is the most important leader of the Asháninka. Kampa do Rio Amônea Indigenous Territory, state of Acre, 2016.

Page 192 In Brazil, the Asháninka are spread across several indigenous territories. The most populous is the Rio Amônea Indigenous Territory. Wiyōya, with her daughter in her arms, lives in the Rio Envira Indigenous Territory, where Asháninka indigenous people also live. Kampa do Rio Amônea Indigenous Territory, state of Acre, 2016.

Page 193 Luísa, daughter of Moisés Piyāko Asháninka, paints herself in the mirror. Kampa do Rio Amônea Indigenous Territory, state of Acre, 2016.

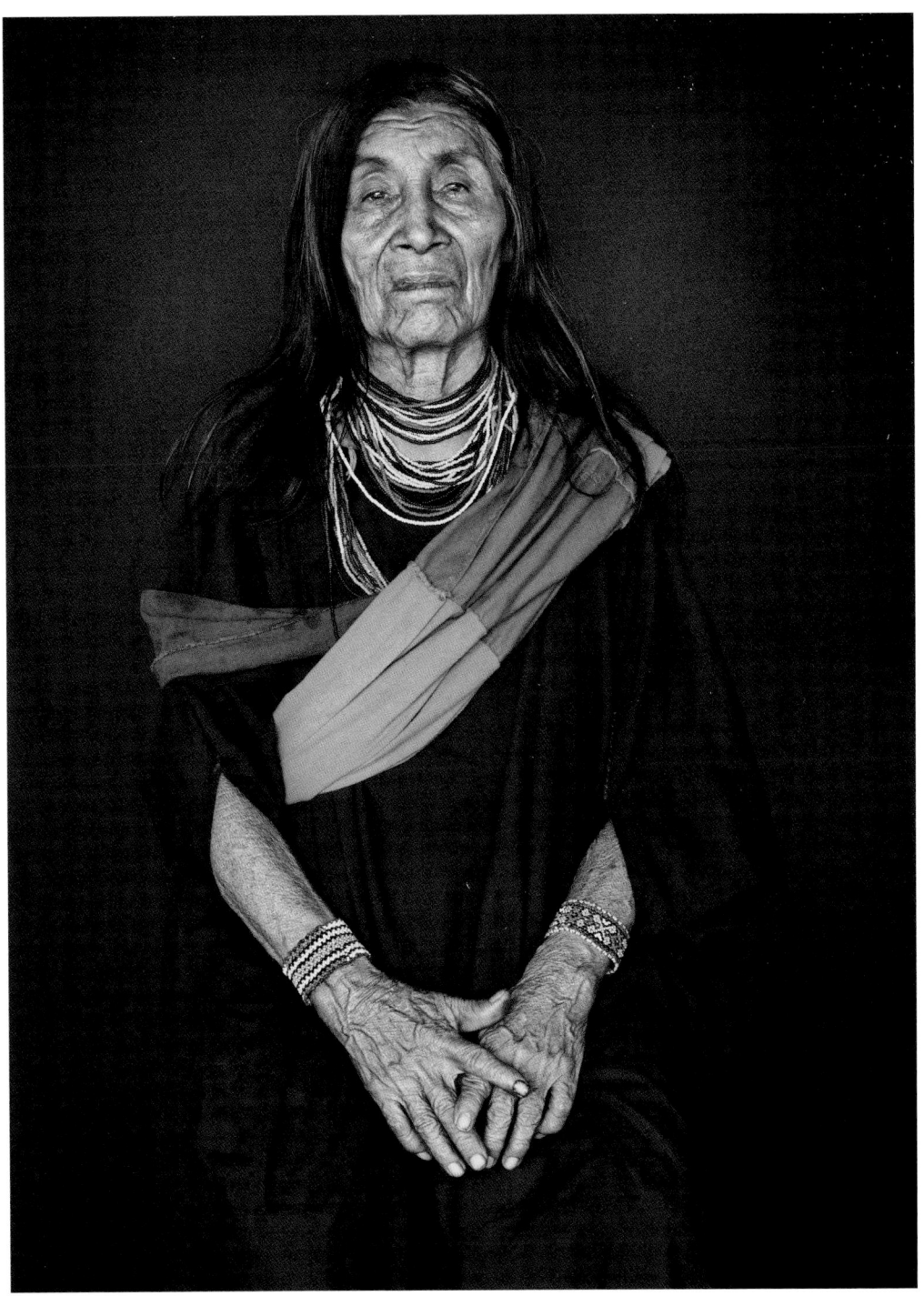

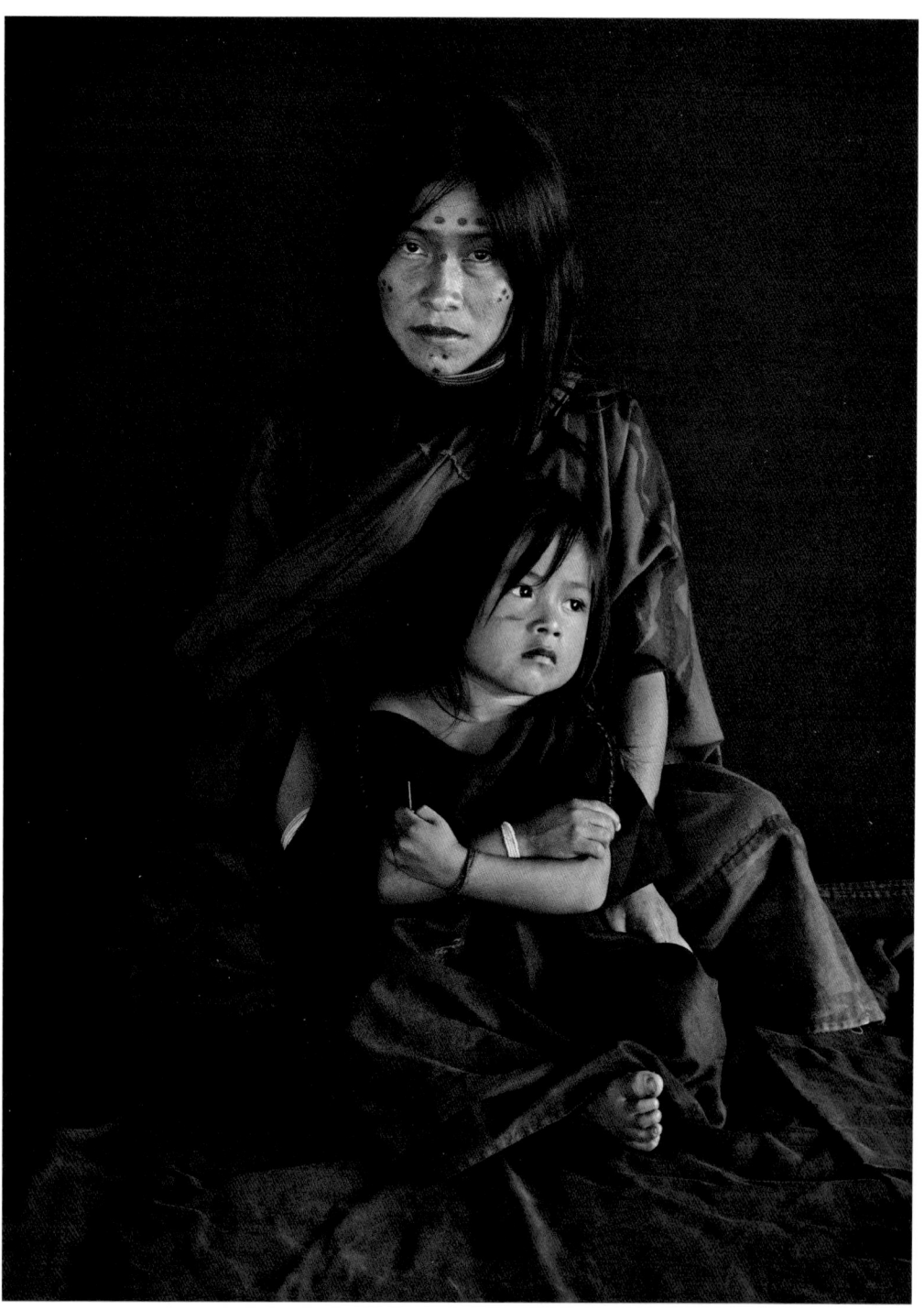

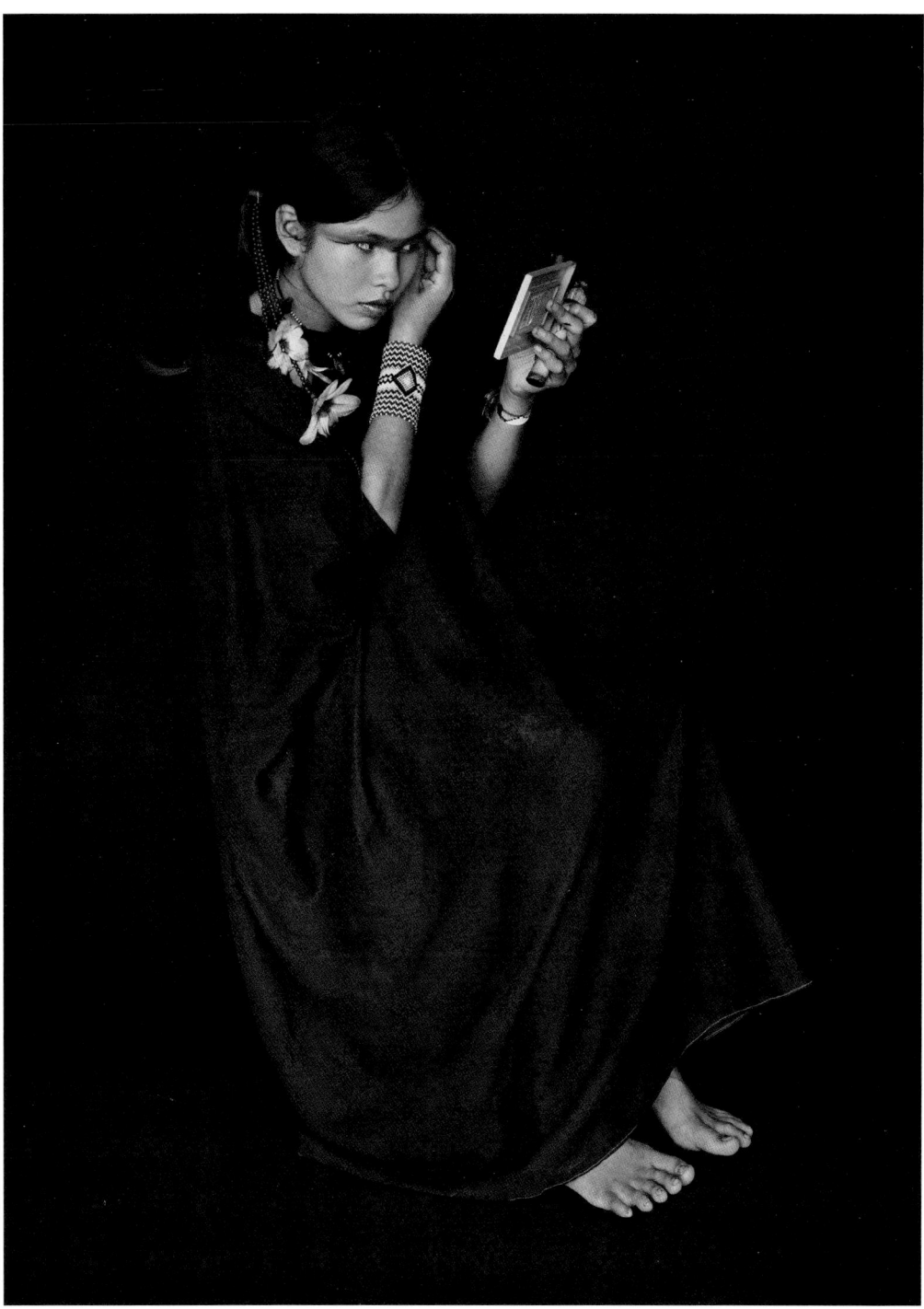

Opposite Boys painting themselves among the roots of a big kapok (*Ceiba pentandra*, also called sumauma or silk-cotton), a huge tree that can reach a height of 50 meters (165 feet) and is considered sacred by the Asháninka and in several other indigenous cultures. Kampa do Rio Amônea Indigenous Territory, state of Acre, 2016.

Pages 196/197 Standing in a canoe, Wewito Piyãko Asháninka casts a throw net for fishing. Kampa do Rio Amônea Indigenous Territory, state of Acre, 2016.

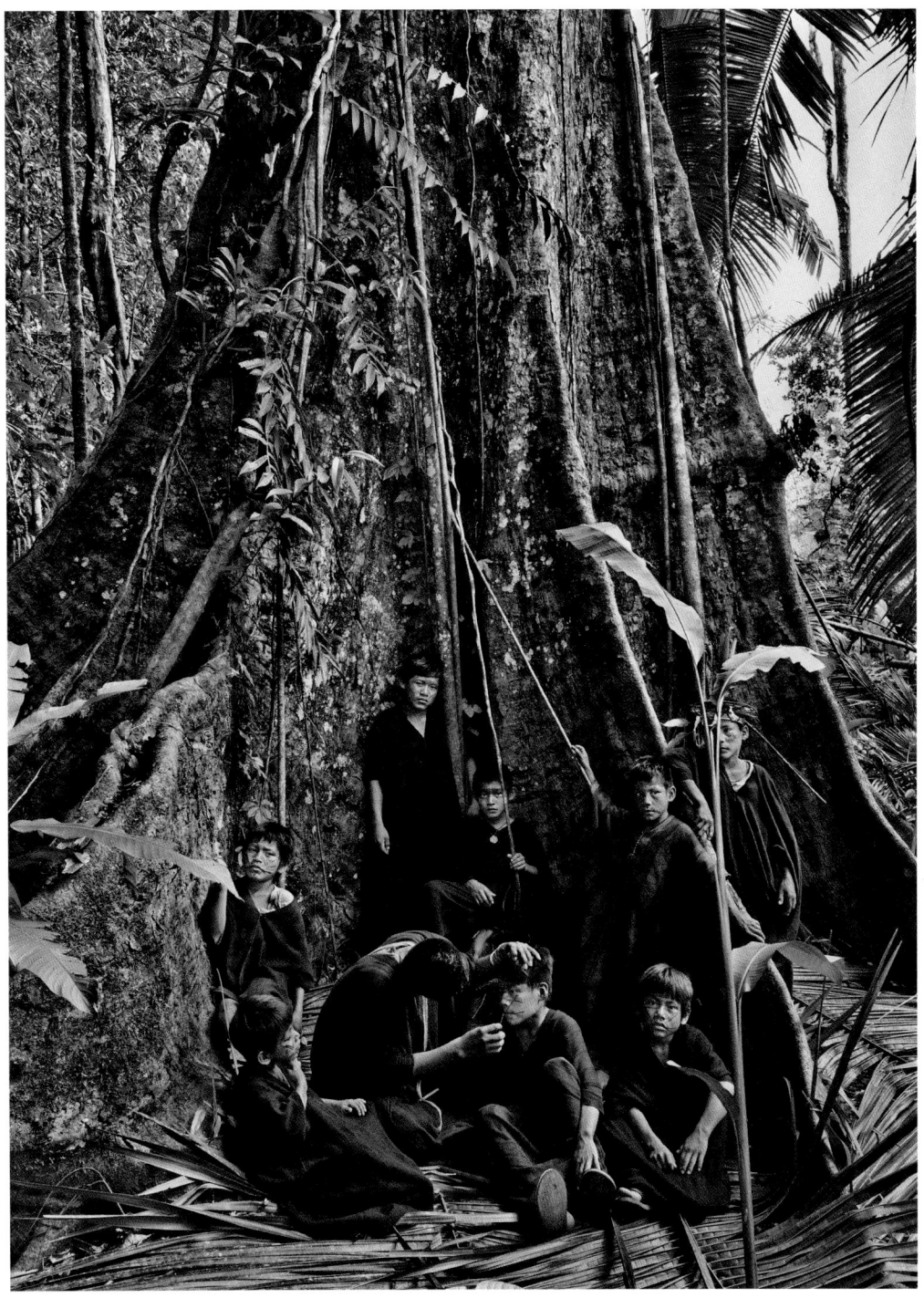

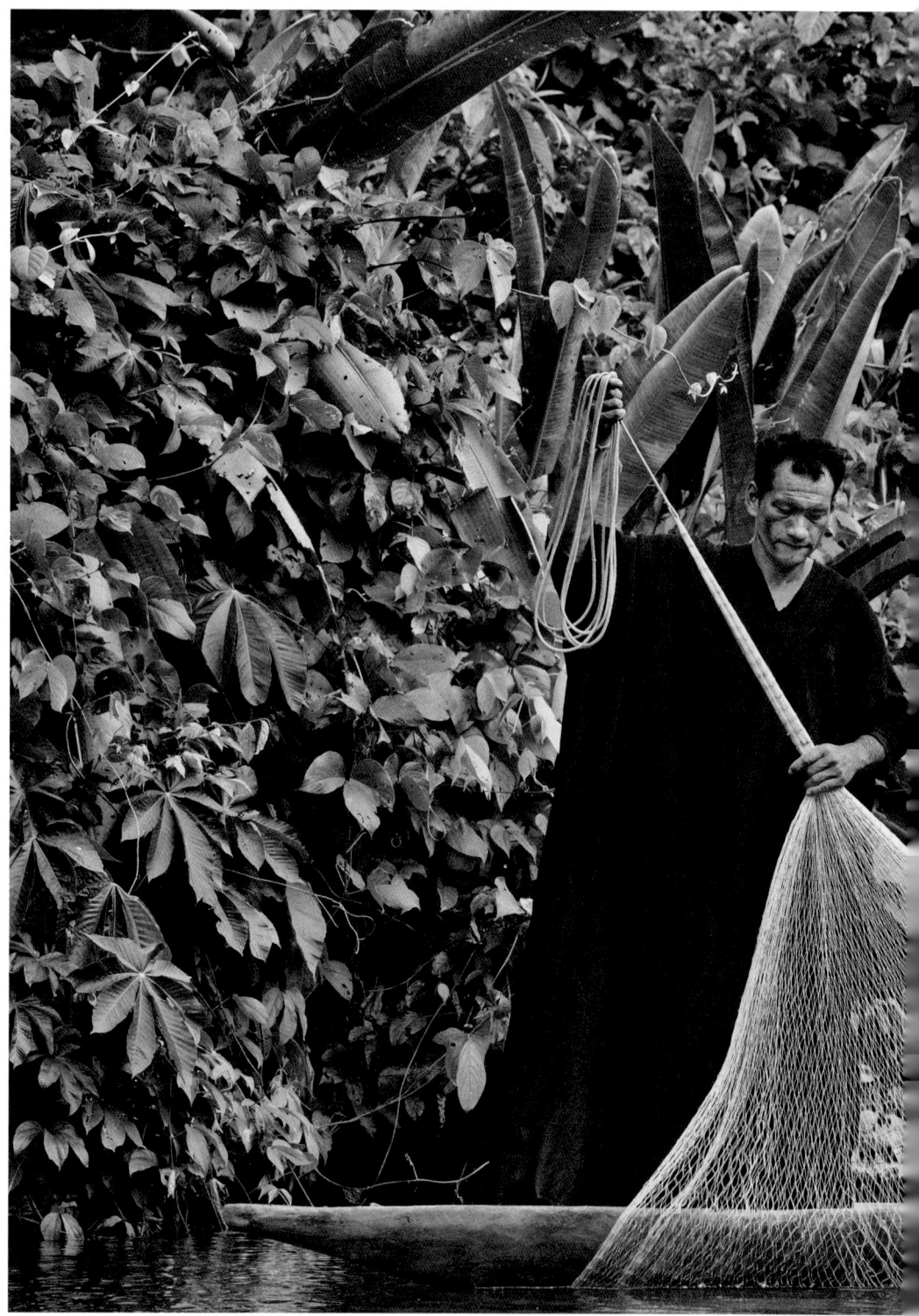

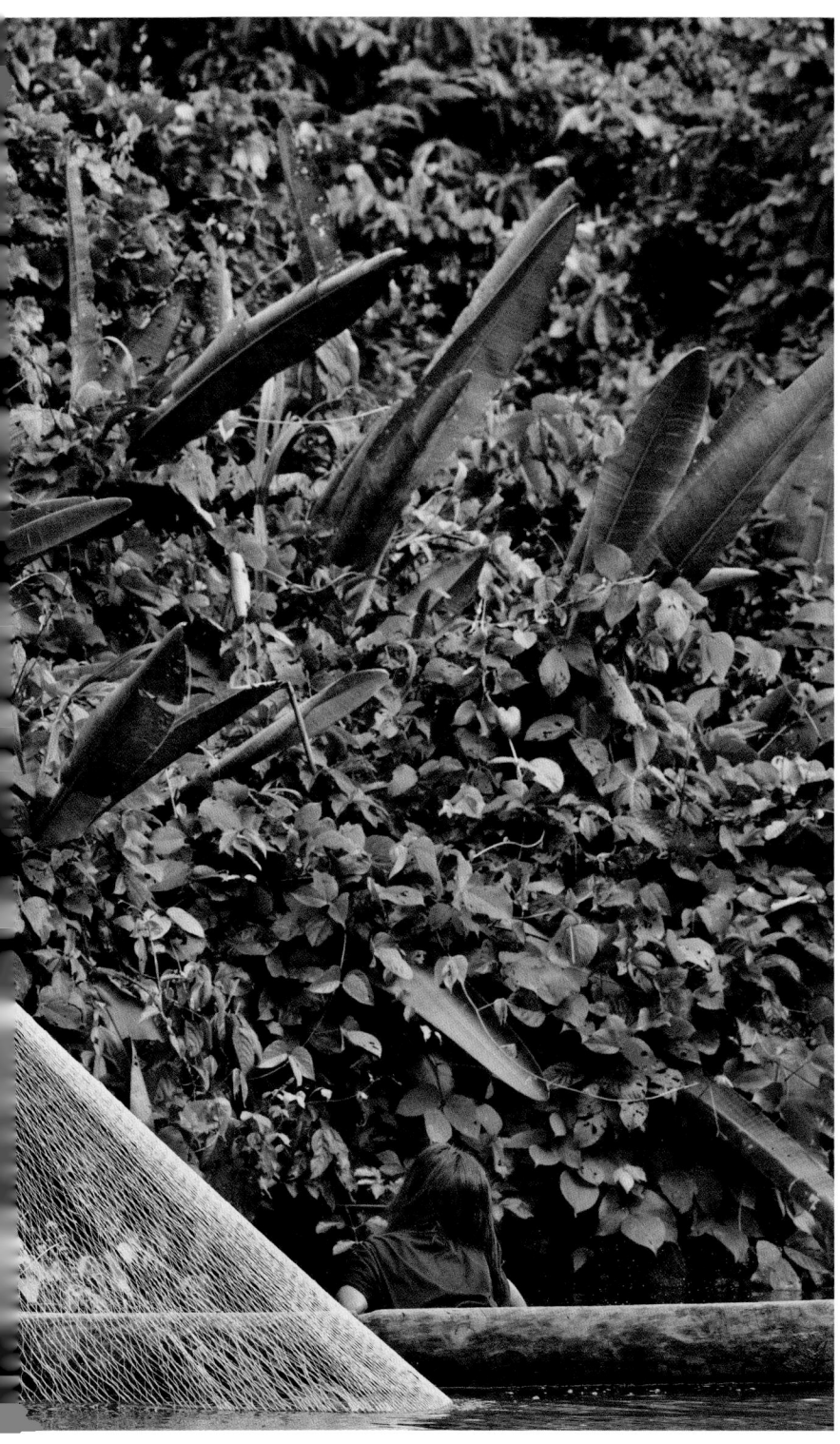

MOUNTAINS

The mountain range that defines the life of the Amazon basin lies far to the west of Brazil. But if the Andes provides most of the water that flows through hundreds of tributaries into the Amazon River, Brazil too can boast mountains. To the southeast lie the Brazilian Highlands, which include the mineral rich state of Minas Gerais. Heading north towards the heart of the rainforest, the landscape remains undulating, with a hilltop known as Serra Pelada in the state of Pará drawing one of the country's biggest-ever gold rushes in the 1980s. Even closer to the Amazon River, occasional large rock formations appear like intruders into the quiet order of the lowlands.

Brazil's most important chain of mountains, the Imeri, serves almost like a natural border with Venezuela in the far north of the state of Amazonas. Its dominant feature is the sharply pointed Pico da Neblina, or Mist Peak, which at over 3,000 meters (10,000 feet) is Brazil's highest mountain. As its name suggests, it is often shrouded in clouds, making climbing it a slippery and perilous experience. Then, not far away, the Pico 31 de Março rises almost as high to 2,900 meters (9,500 feet). And in the same region, the Pico Guimarães Rosa, named after a renowned Brazilian writer, stands 2,105 meters (7,000 feet) above sea level. What is striking about these mountains is how the rainforest covers their lower slopes, with vegetation gradually thinning out until it is halted by sheer rock.

To the east in the state of Roraima, Monte Roraima, or Mount Roraima, which forms part of the Pacaraima mountain range, is a quite different geological formation. Rising to 2,800 meters (9,000 feet), this tabletop mountain standing on the border with Guyana and Venezuela belongs to a category called *tepuis*. What makes the *tepuis* interesting beyond their striking shape is that the microclimate on their flattops has spawned its own endemic plant species and even a so-called Roraima bush toad. Fed by almost daily rain, dramatic waterfalls spill out on several sides.

Immediately to the south of the Pacaraima mountains, the rainforest is suddenly replaced by a strangely arid landscape, the *Lavrado*, that might more comfortably fit into the Mongolian outback. Here erosion has carved thick crevices into hillsides, with edges that resembled lava flows. The only interruption in the dull brown panorama are narrow lines of green where trees hug the banks of rivers. Yet this too belongs to the basin and the water from its modest rivers also ends up in the Amazon River.

One mountainous massif of exceptional beauty is protected as the Serra do Aracá State Park. Situated some 400 kilometers (250 miles) north of Manaus, its rugged structure is again formed largely by *tepuis* and, while rising only to a maximum of 1,700 meters (5,600 feet), it stands out dramatically against the jungle. It is also home to El Dorado Falls and Desabamento Falls, Brazil's highest waterfalls, with water tumbling 360 meters (1,180 feet) past a bare mountain façade.

Some 600 kilometers (370 miles) to the east, close to the border with Suriname in the state of Pará, is still another range of mountains which gives its name to the National Park of Tumucumaque. Stretching 135 kilometers (85 miles) north to south, it is thought to be immensely rich in metals and minerals which large mining corporations have expressed interest in exploiting. So far they have been denied permission because it lies too close to the territories legally reserved for the exclusive use of the Zo'é and Tiriyó indigenous tribes.

Pages 200/201 Mount Roraima. Monte Roraima National Park. Raposa–Serra do Sol Indigenous Territory, state of Roraima, 2018.

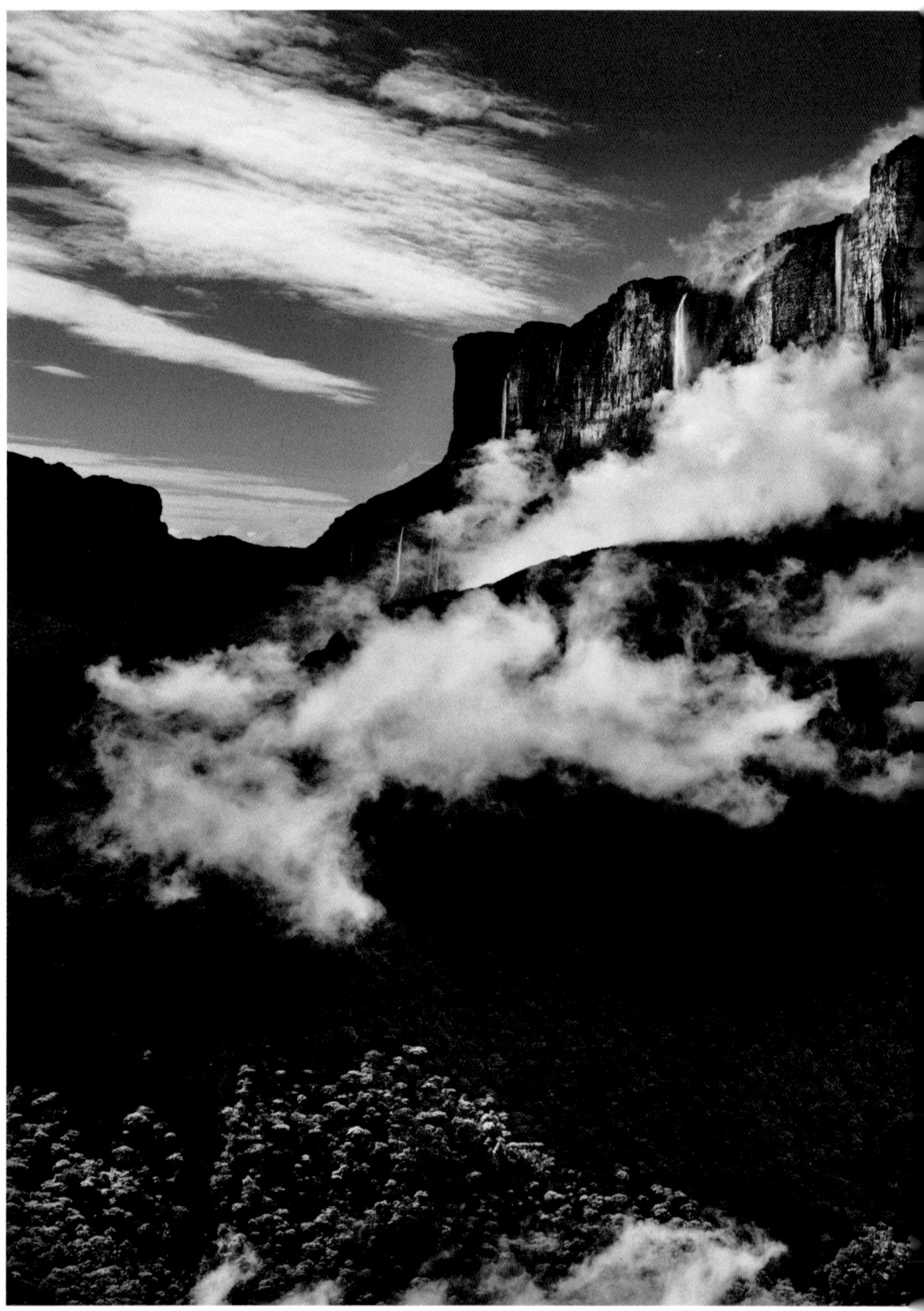

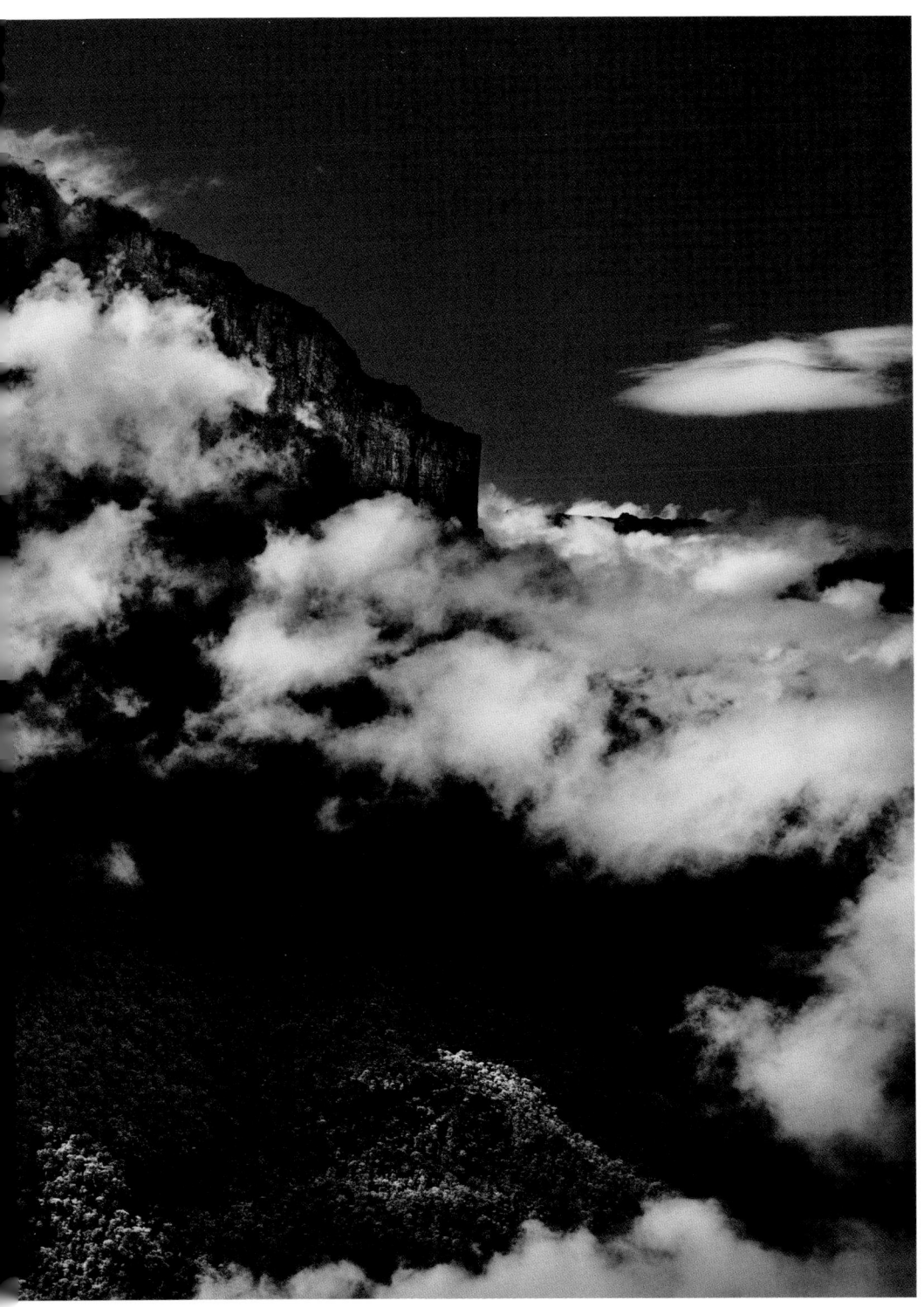

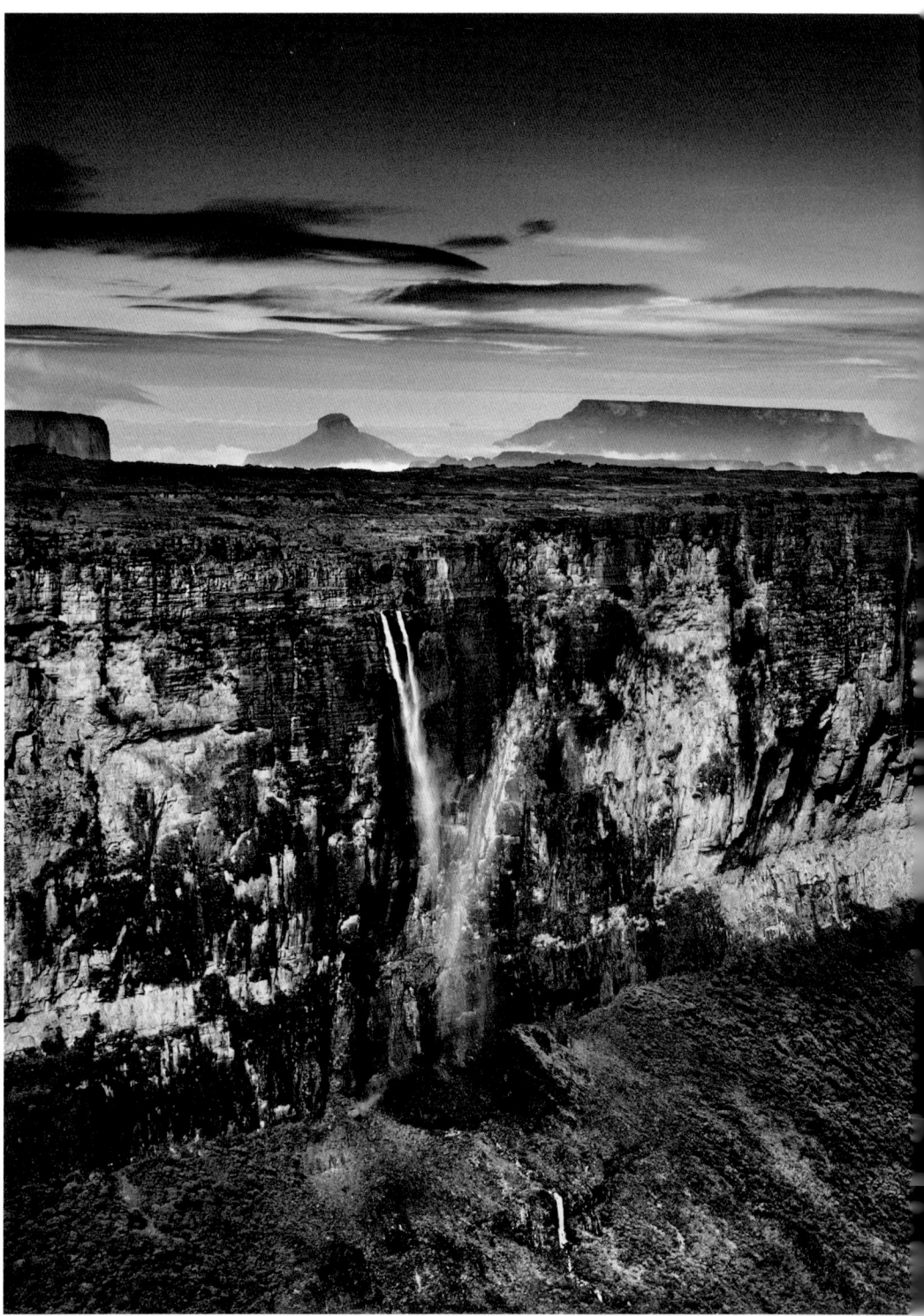

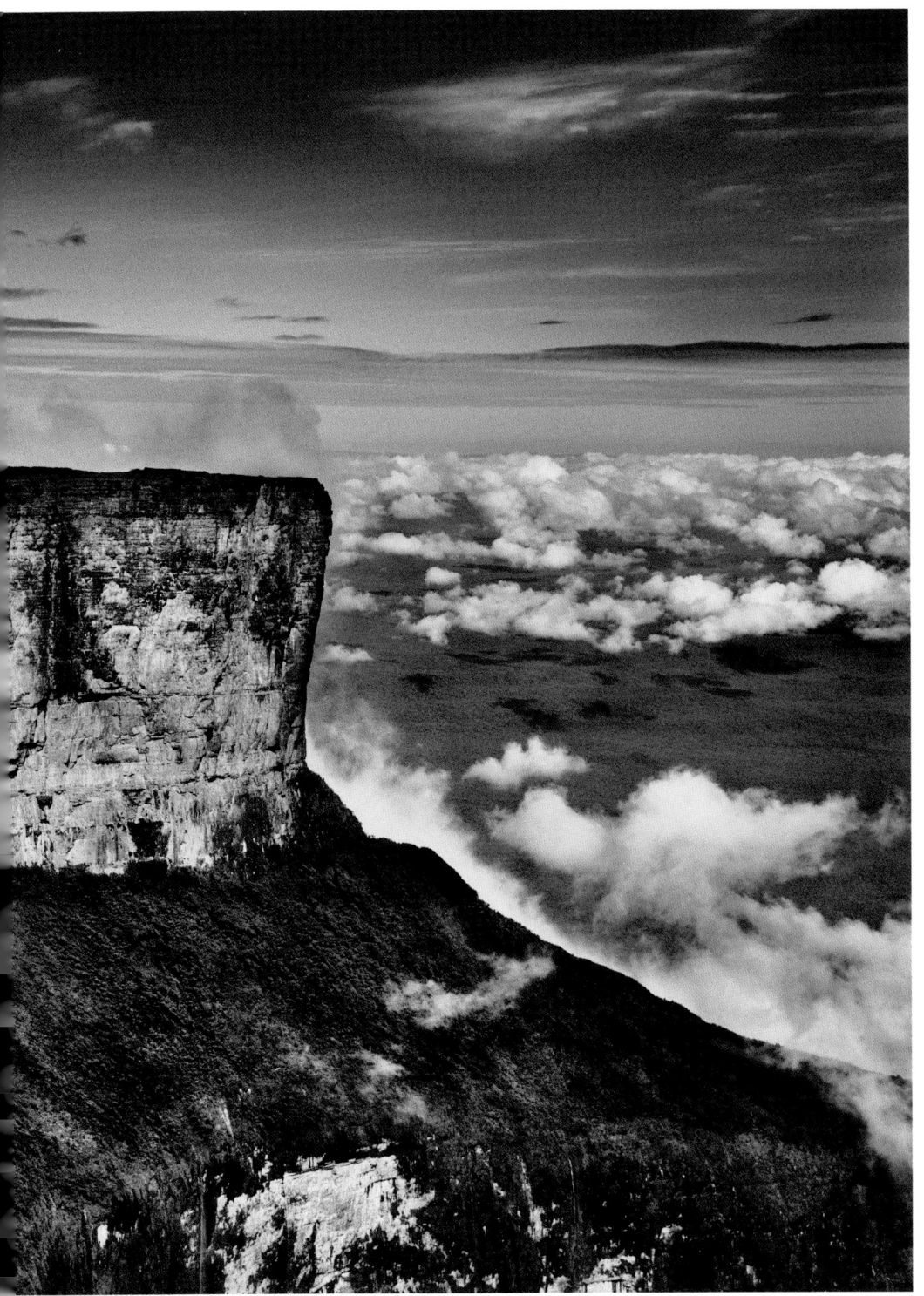

Opposite and pages 202/203 Mount Roraima. Border between Brazil and Guyana. Monte Roraima National Park. Raposa–Serra do Sol Indigenous Territory, state of Roraima, 2018.

Pages 206/207 Mount Roraima, located at the triple border between Brazil, Venezuela, and Guyana. Raposa–Serra do Sol Indigenous Territory, state of Roraima, 2018.

Pages 208/209 and 210/211 Marauiá mountain range. Yanomami Indigenous Territory. Municipality of São Gabriel da Cachoeira, state of Amazonas, 2018.

Pages 212/213 Neblina Mountains, in the Yanomami Indigenous Territory. Municipality of São Gabriel da Cachoeira, state of Amazonas, 2018.

Pages 214/215 Pico da Neblina, elevation 3,107 meters (10,194 feet), as seen from the forest during an ascent to the summit. The highest mountain in Brazil, it is part of the Imeri mountain range and stands out from the jungle as a jagged crag, but is often shrouded in clouds as its name suggests (*neblina* is Portuguese for "fog" or "mist"). Yanomami Indigenous Territory. Municipality of São Gabriel da Cachoeira, state of Amazonas, 2014.

Pages 216/217 Pico da Neblina in the Yanomami Indigenous Territory. Municipality of São Gabriel da Cachoeira, state of Amazonas, 2009.

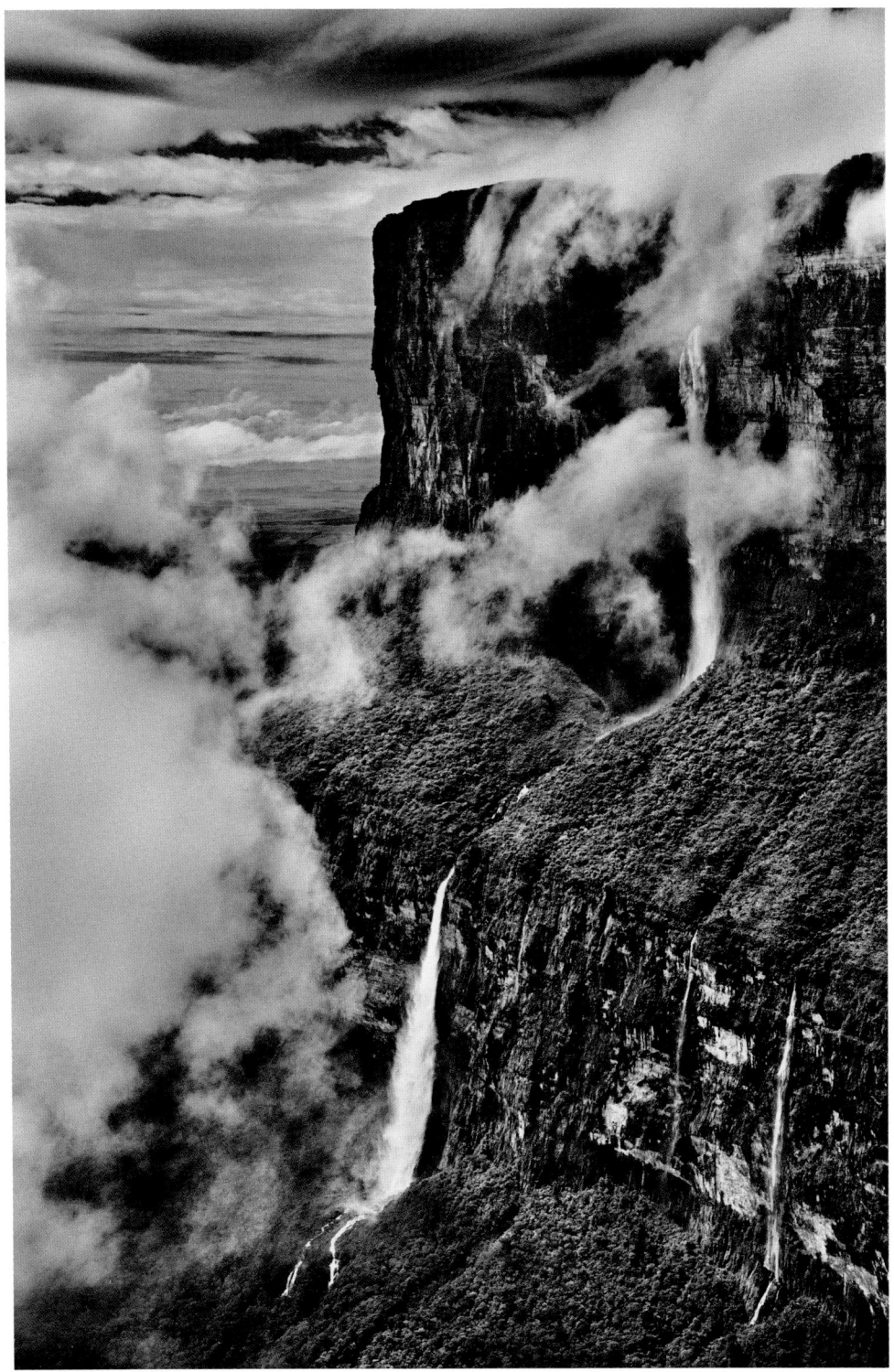

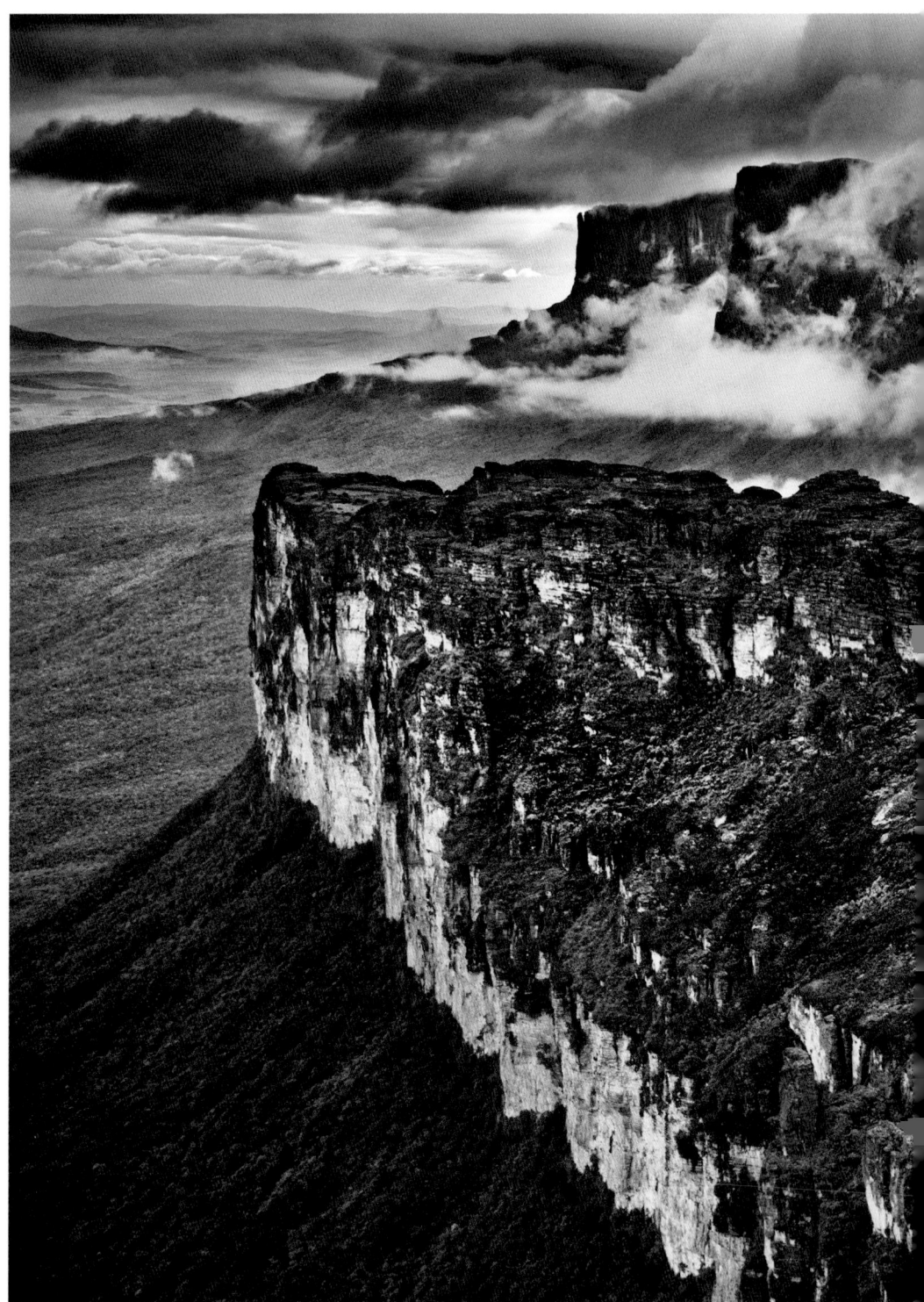

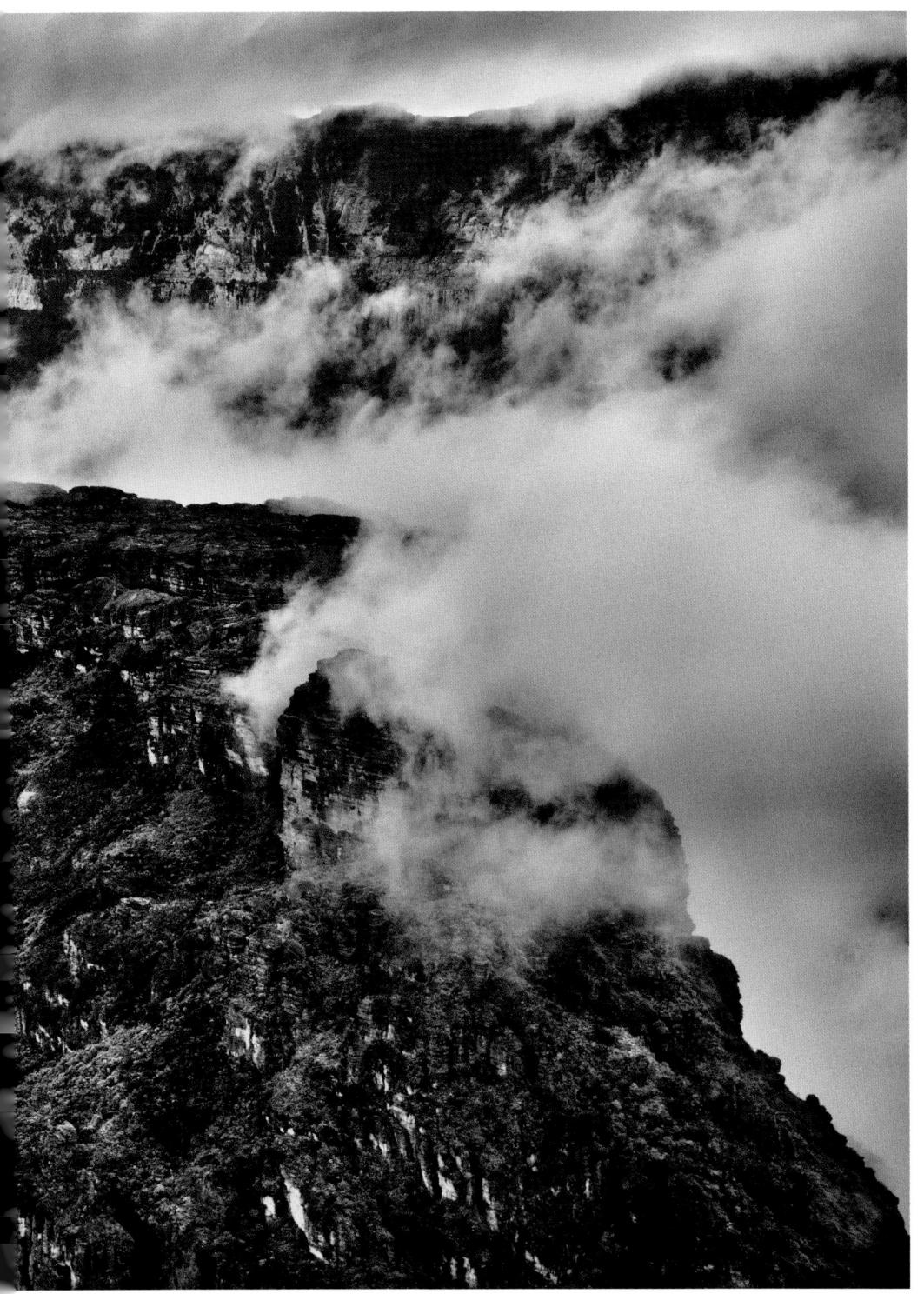

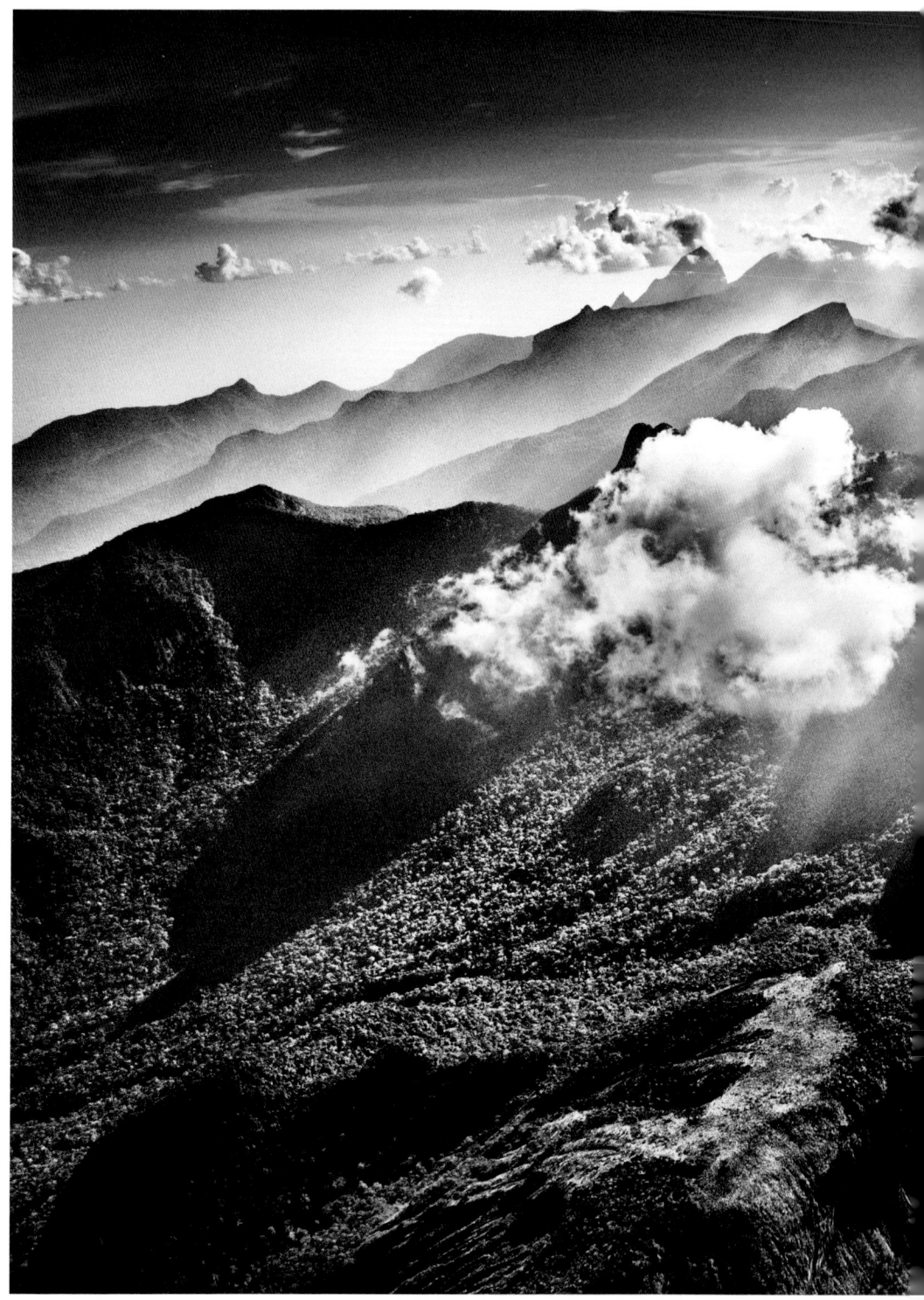

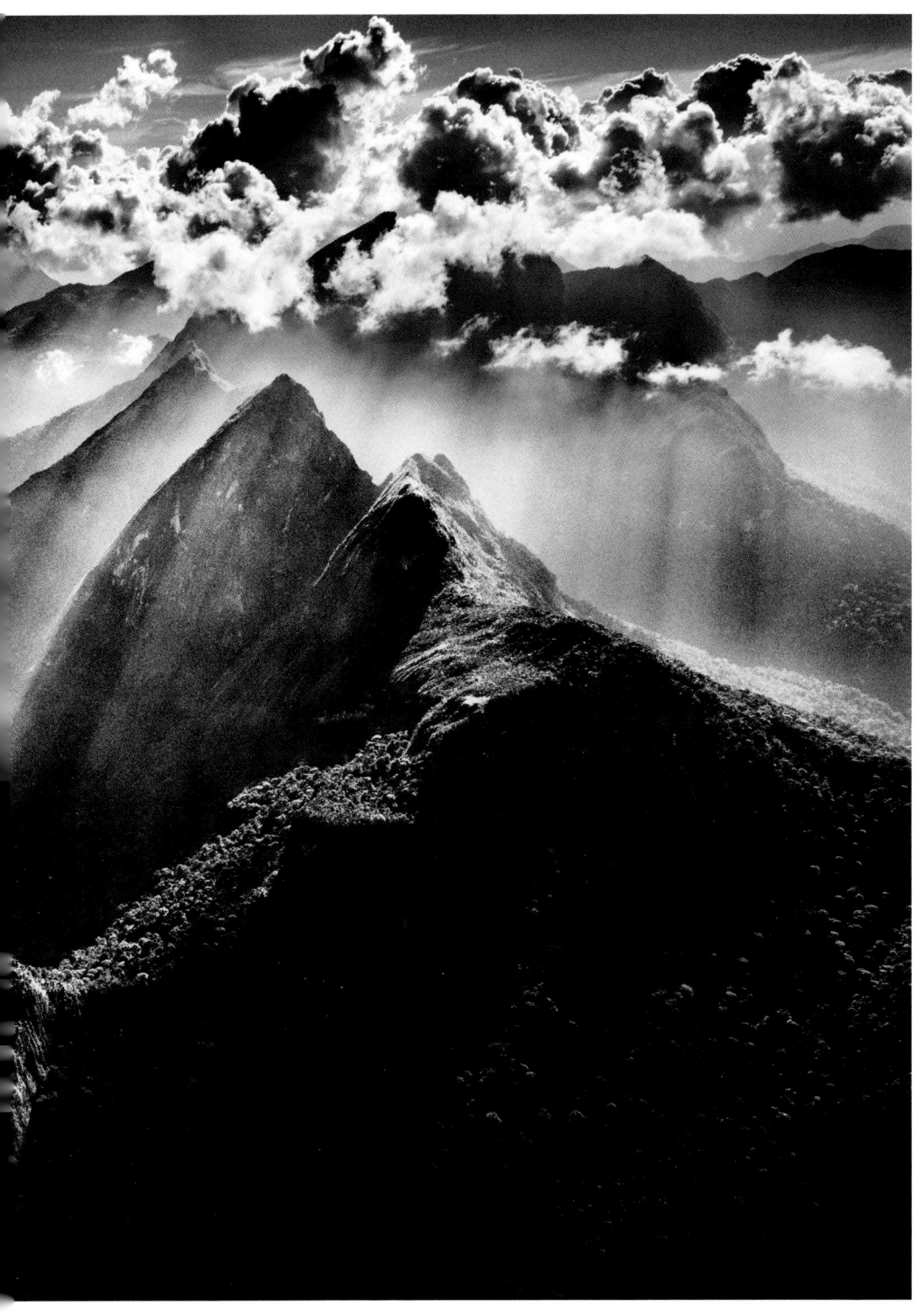

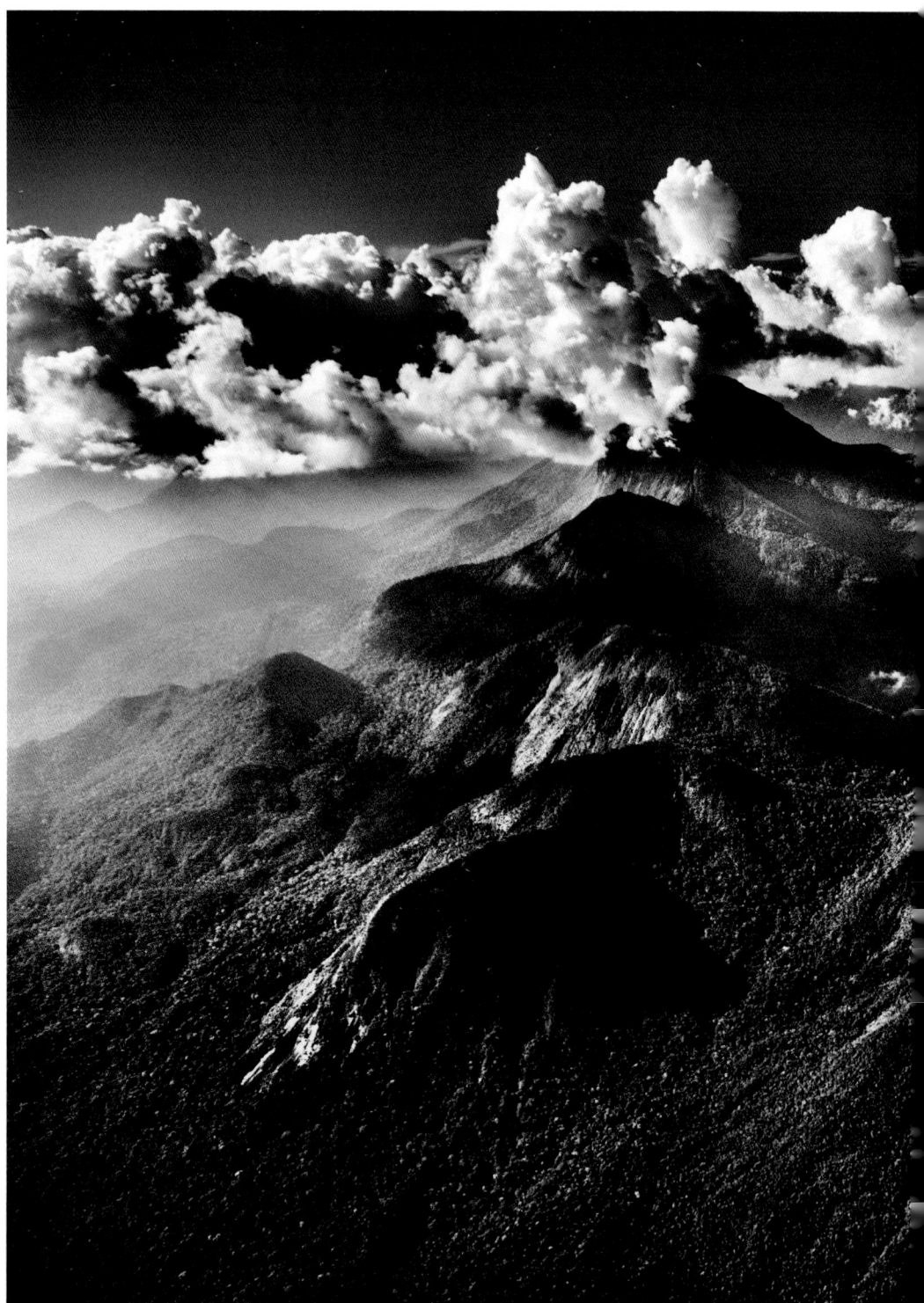

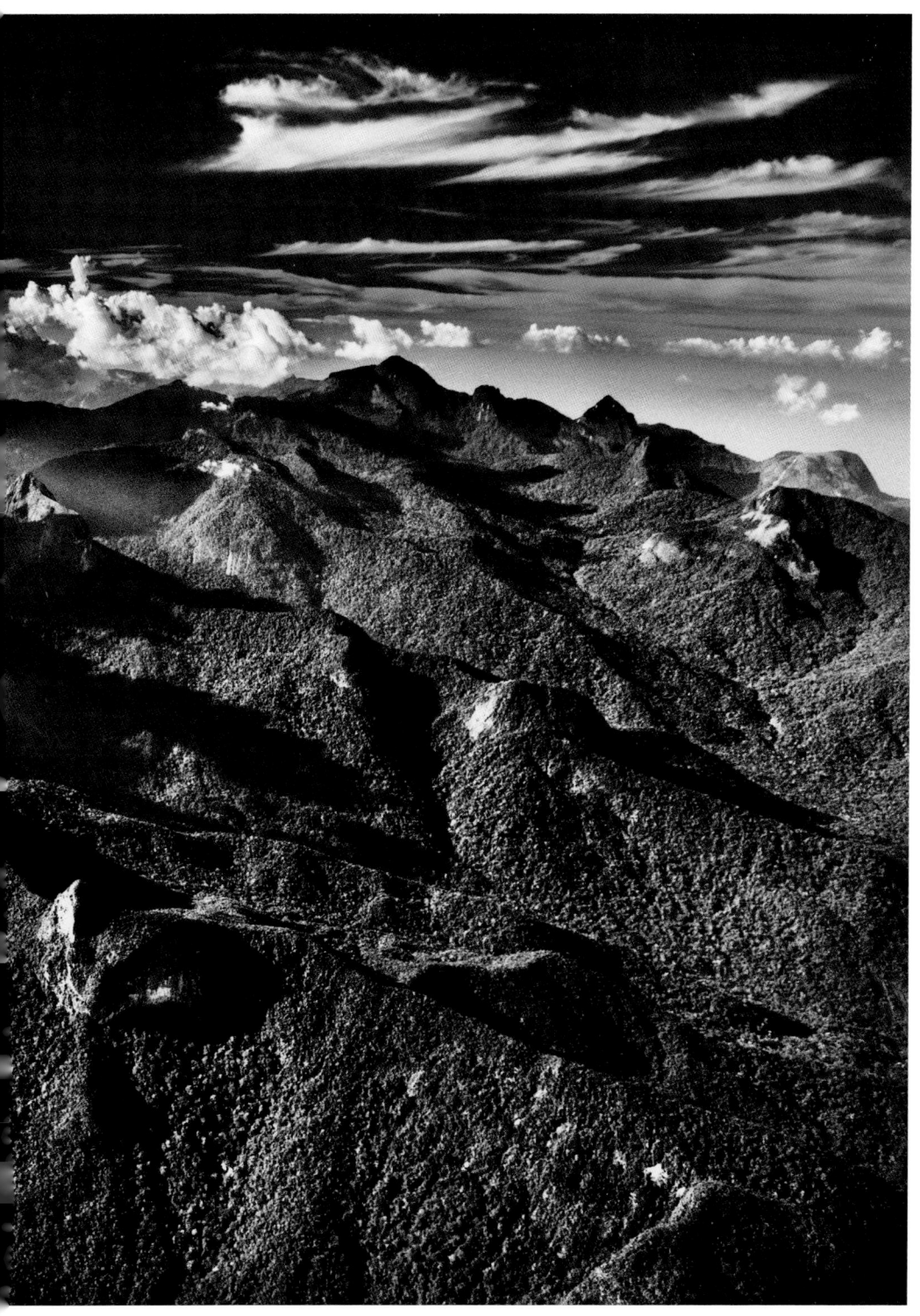

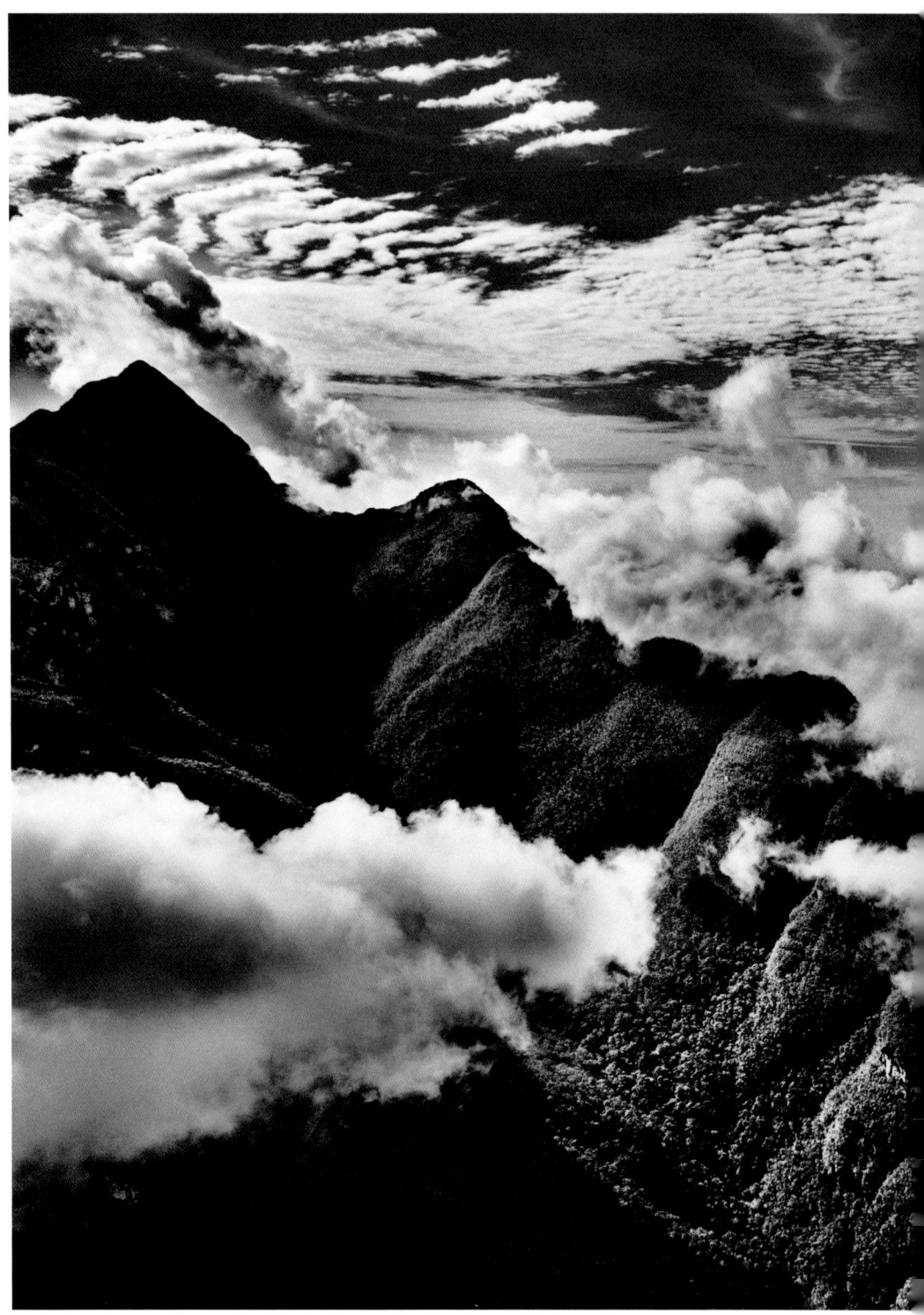

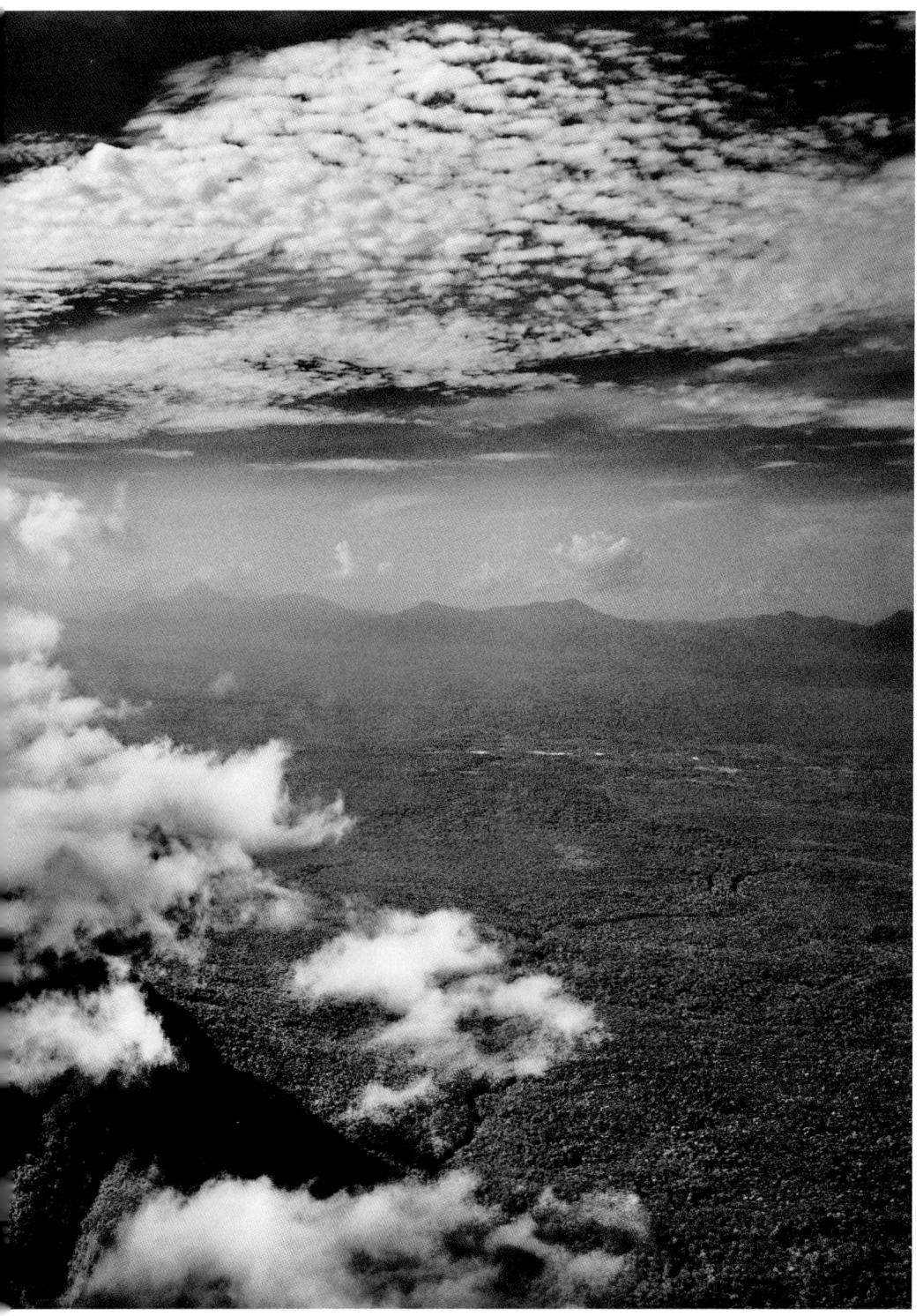

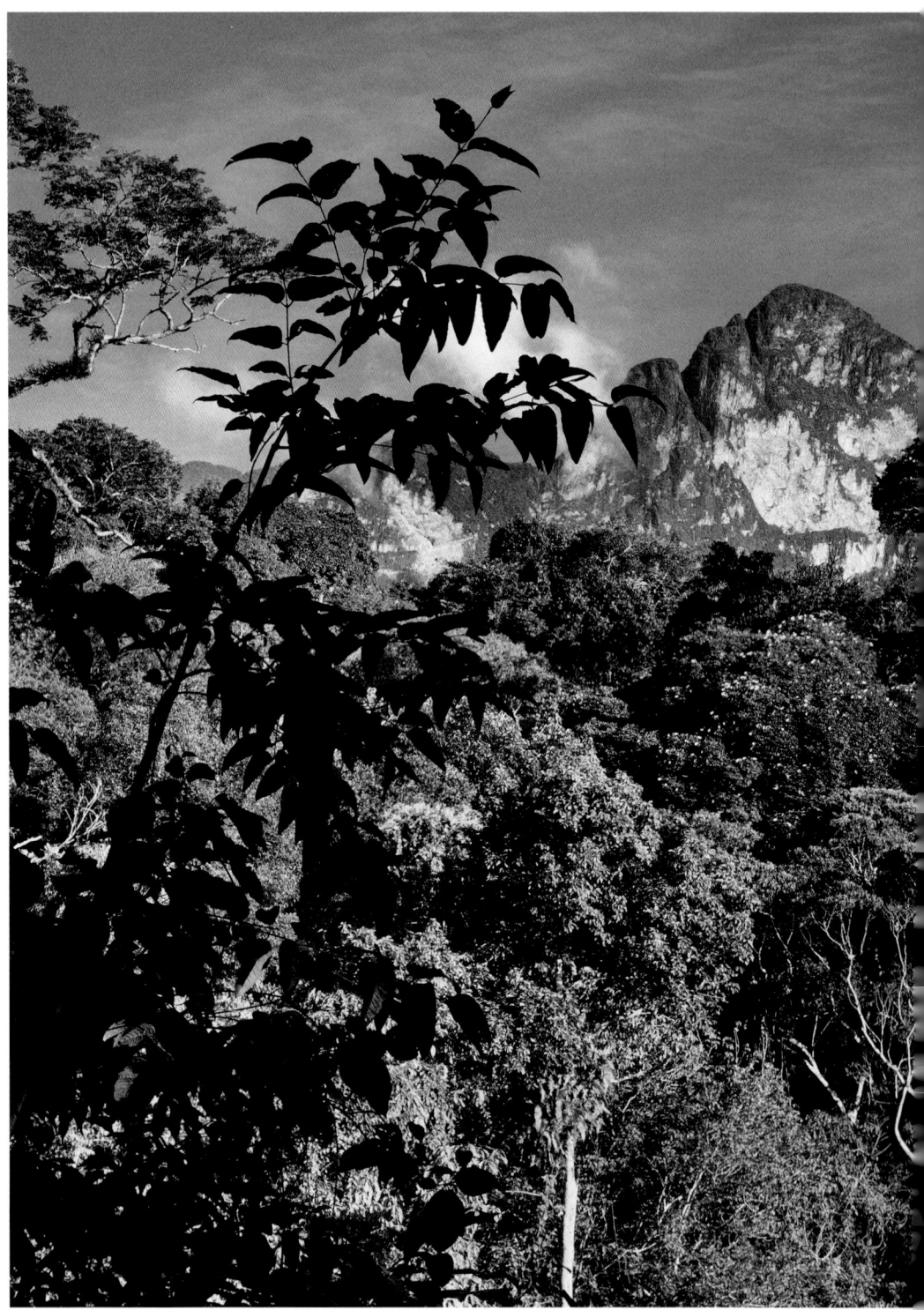

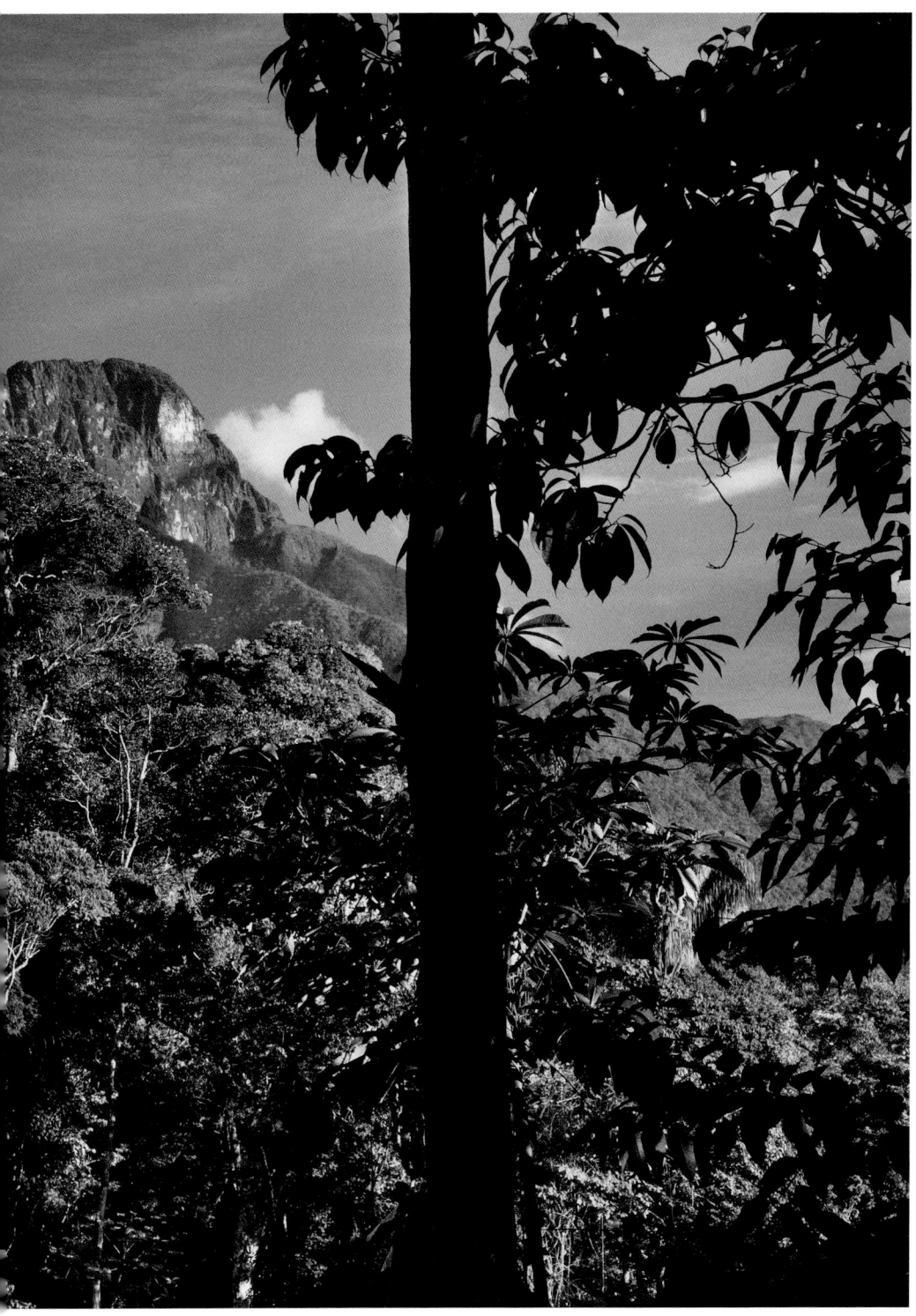

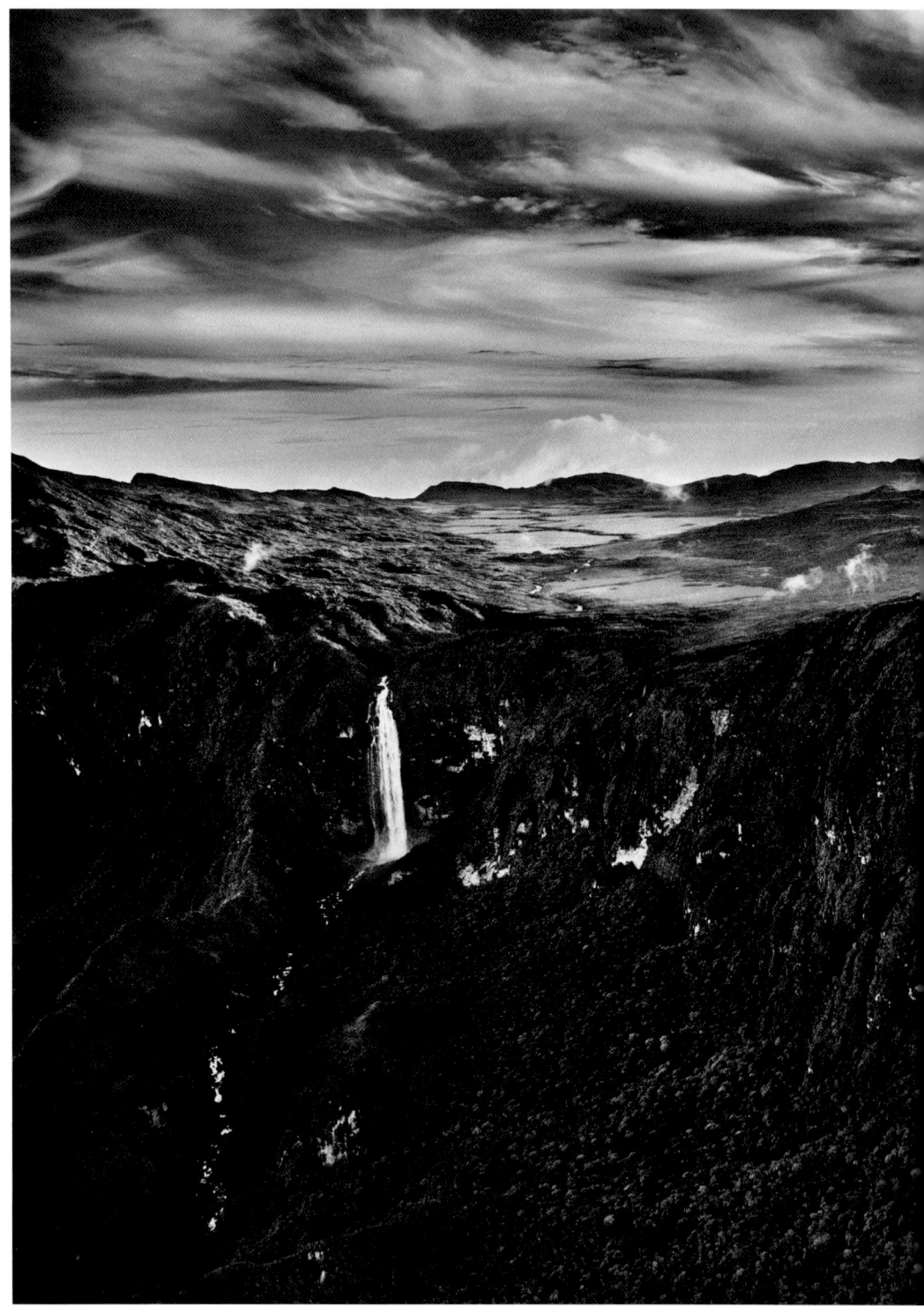

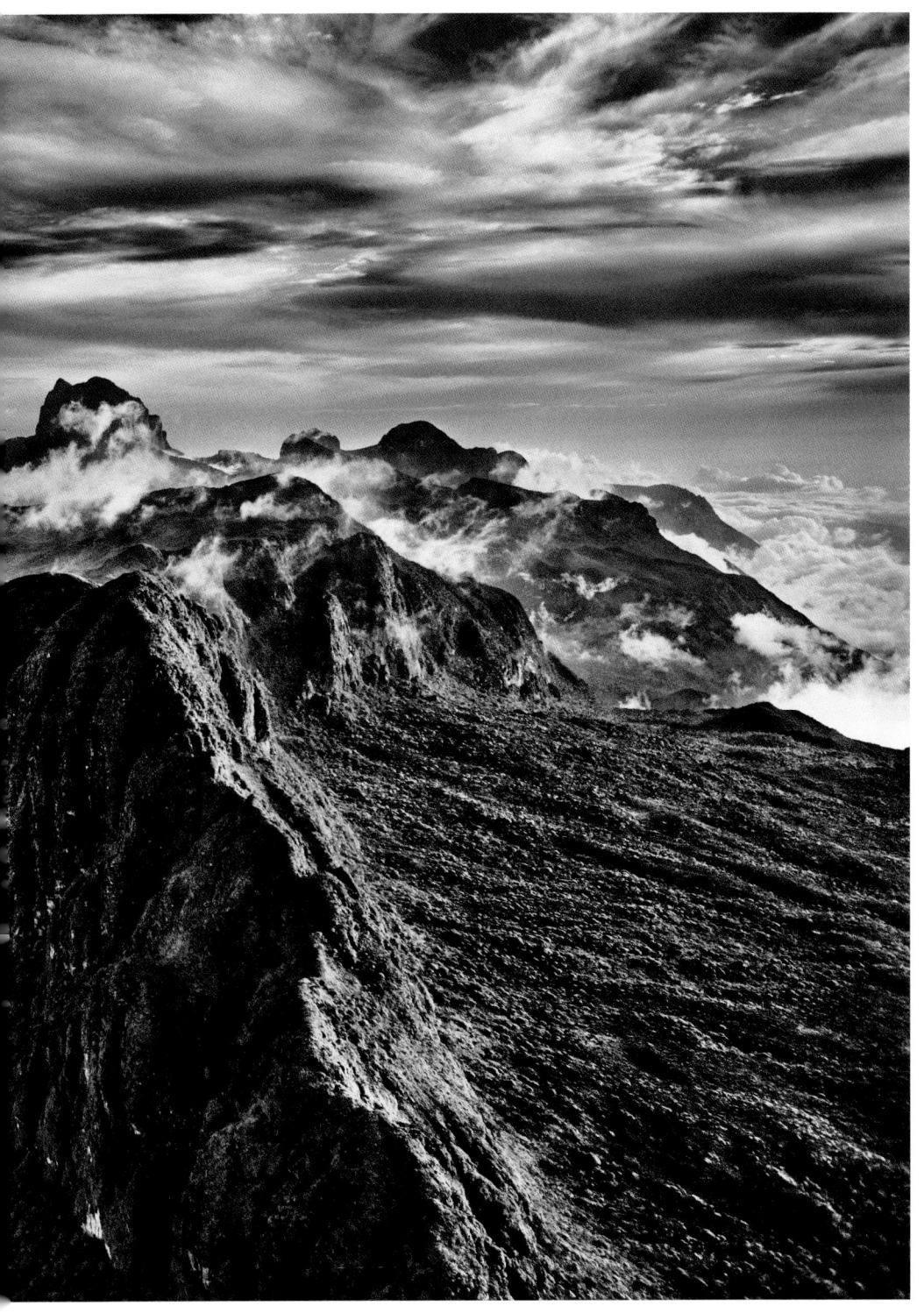

YAWANAWÁ

In the course of some 50 years, the Yawanawá have emerged from complete invisibility into a period of exuberant cultural activity, becoming a reference point for sustainable living and indigenous culture for travelers from all over the world. In 1970, there were just 120 of them, with rampant alcoholism and the resulting social and cultural breakdown, to the point where their language was about to disappear. They were pressured not to use their language in front of whites, mainly by the owners of the rubber plantations, who controlled the forests of Acre from the late 19th century. The plantation owners treated them as slaves and did not want the language to reveal the existence of native tribes who might claim ownership of the land. Another threat was posed by Evangelical missionaries who had enforced Christian worship and attacked traditional indigenous rites as "demonic."

"Our language was forbidden. Only the old people knew it, but the children only learned Portuguese. Our beliefs and traditions were considered demonic by the missionaries and a lot of us believed it. We began to live as slaves, at work and culturally," says Biraci Brasil Yawanawá, better known as Bira, who assumed leadership of the group in the early 1990s. The new leader expelled the missionaries, got rid of the bibles, reestablished teaching of the traditional language, which belongs to the Pano language family, and began encouraging study of the old myths and stories as a way to pass down the old people's knowledge and memories to the new generations. In three decades, the population has grown to about 1,200 people. The Yawanawá became the living proof that when indigenous people control their own lands, they can combine traditional culture with entrepreneurship. At the same time, they rehabilitated the tradition of the old rituals and speak their ancestral language, but they connect to the contemporary world through smartphones and computers, using Wi-Fi antennas installed in their villages.

Just like their Asháninka neighbors, the Pano-speaking peoples must have had intense interactions with the Inca Empire, as seen in the frequent mythical references to heroes called "Inka" or to a long-ago time when they lived under Inca rule. Such stories exist among the Yawanawá and other ethnic groups in the same language family, such as the Kashinawá and Marubo. Their collective memory holds that contact with the "whites" occurred at the height of the Amazon rubber boom, in the late 19th and early 20th centuries. The rubber tappers settled there and stayed in the area until the demarcation of the indigenous territory in the 1980s.

The Yawanawá are one of many Pano-speaking peoples of the western Amazon who make up what scholars call the "Pano corridor" that originated about 2,000 years ago. They spread out around the Javari, Juruá, and Purus Rivers, with some moving into the region of Ucayali, Peru, to the slopes of the Andes, becoming the lords of that vast, humid plain around the 9th century CE, when one or more groups of Arawak speakers (like the Asháninka) came from the north and the west and conquered parts of the region.

The Pano groups have names ending in *nawá* and *bo*, such as Yawanawá, Yaminawá, Kashinawá, Marubo, Korubo, Shipibo, and Conibo. The Yawanawá have also been called Yawabo or Yawavo. They are proud of their name, which means "the peccary people": the white-lipped peccary is one of the most feared animals in the forest, for they travel in cohesive herds and, as a group, can defeat their predators. That trait served as an inspiration for their group cohesion in reviving their culture.

One striking aspect of their revived traditions is their feather art: the Yawanawá produce some of the most elegant feather work anywhere in the Amazon, usually made of white feathers from an eagle, a sacred animal for them.

Pages 220/221 Biraci Brasil (Nishiwaká), leader of the Yawanawá of the Upper Rio Gregório, at center, with his son Shanáihu, left, and nephew Táikuru, right, from the village of Nova Esperança. Rio Gregório Indigenous Territory, state of Acre, 2016.

Pages 222/223 Biraci Brasil (Nishiwaká), leader of the Yawanawá of the Upper Rio Gregório, with Tênpu in back and Tchanu and João kneeling, burning *sepá* (resin from a *protium* tree) as incense to produce smoke for a ritual in Aldeia Sagrada (the Sacred Village). Rio Gregório Indigenous Territory, state of Acre, 2016.

Pages 224/225 Paná (Saulo) Yawanawá. Rio Gregório Indigenous Territory, state of Acre, 2016.

Pages 226/227 Kanamashi Yawanawá (foreground) with her friends in a fishing encampment near the village of Amparo. Rio Gregório Indigenous Territory, state of Acre, 2016.

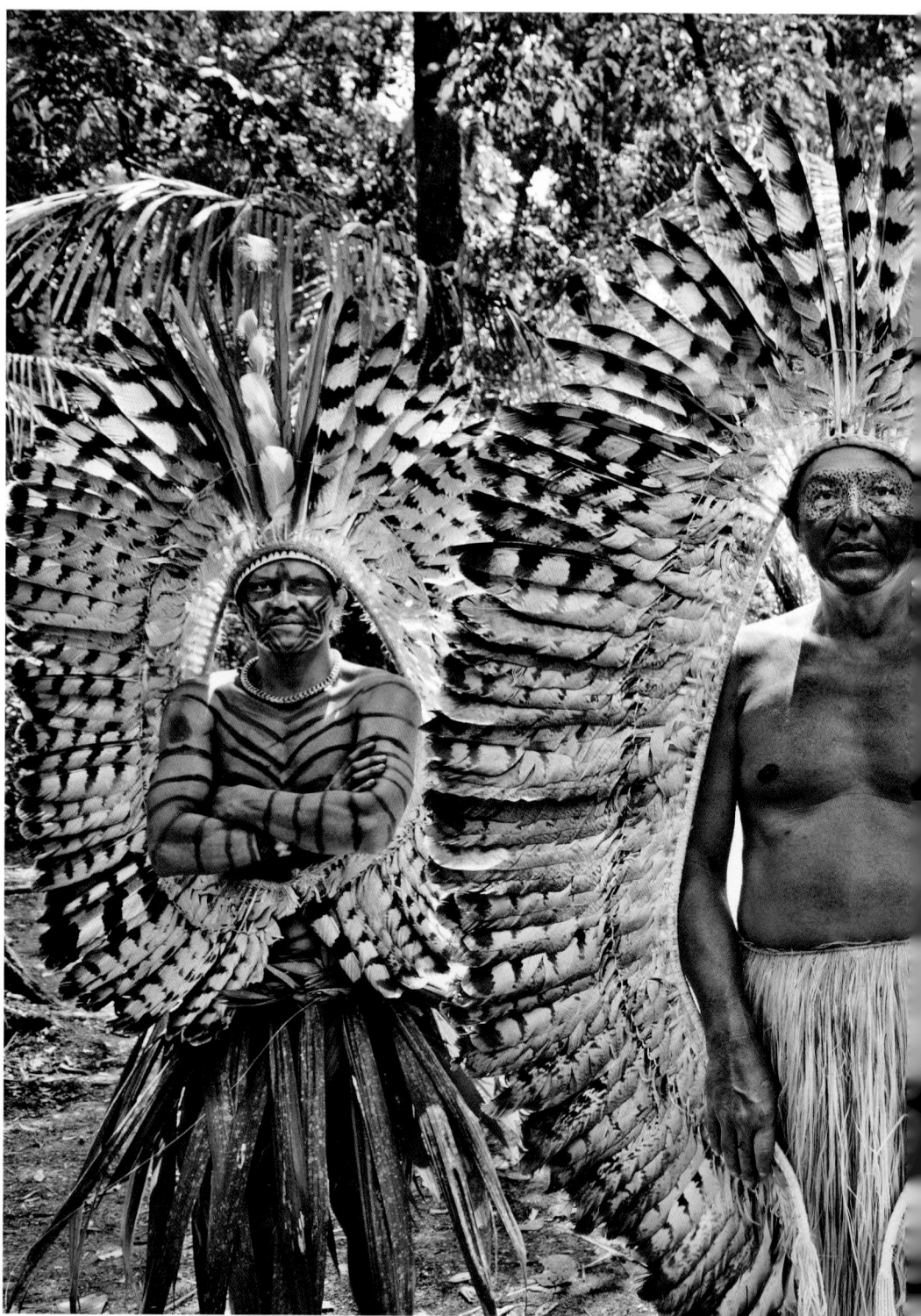

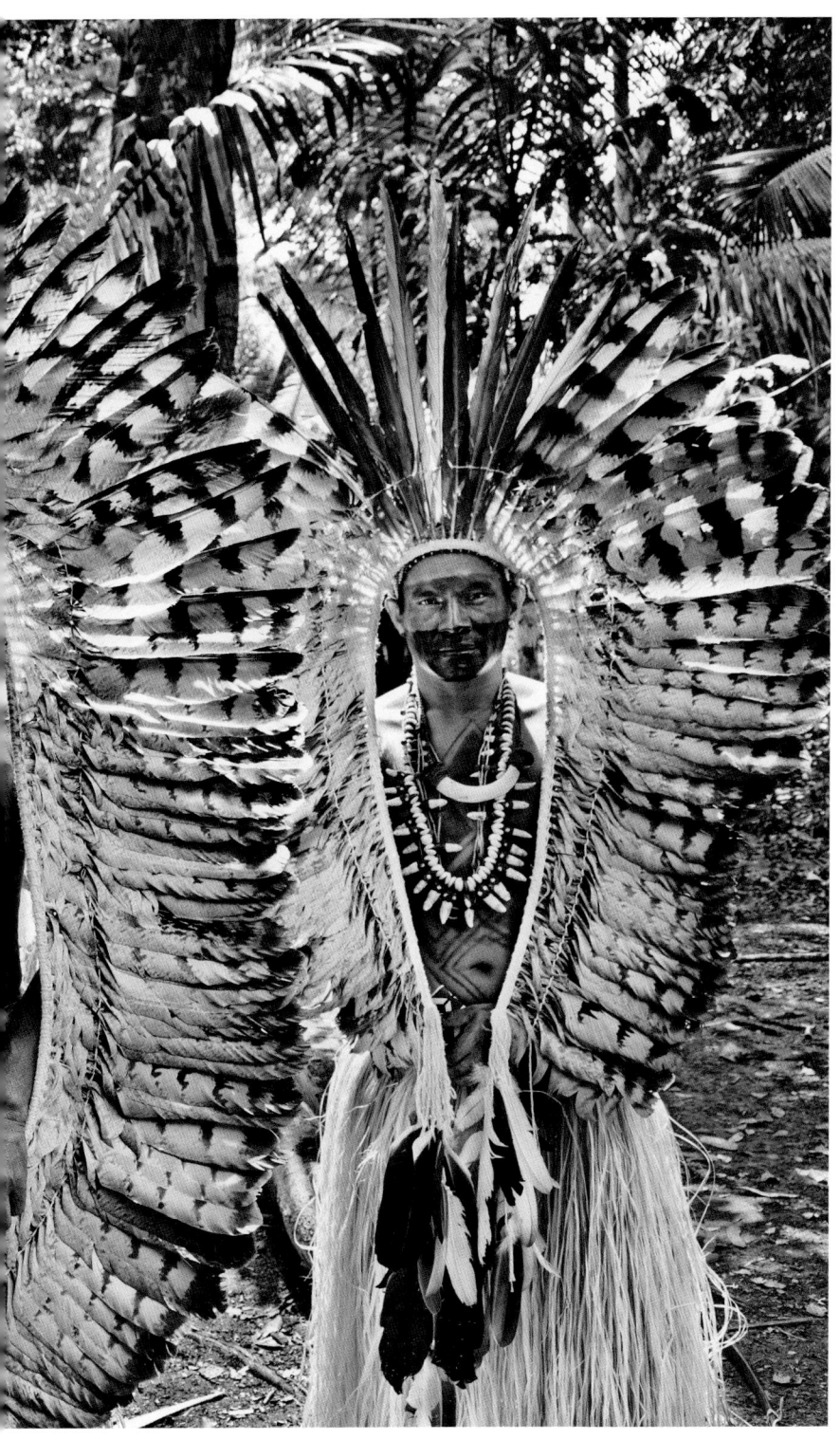

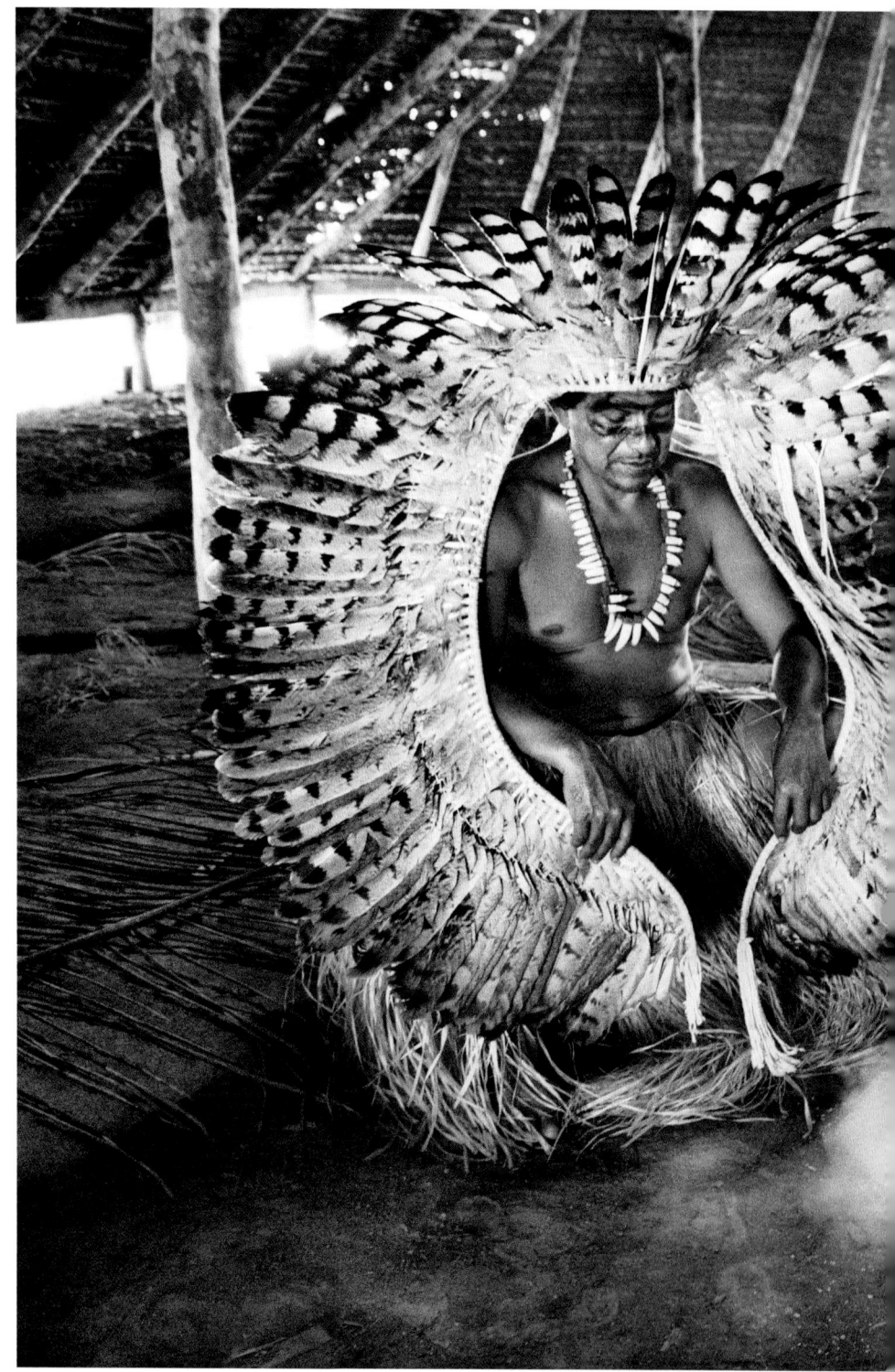

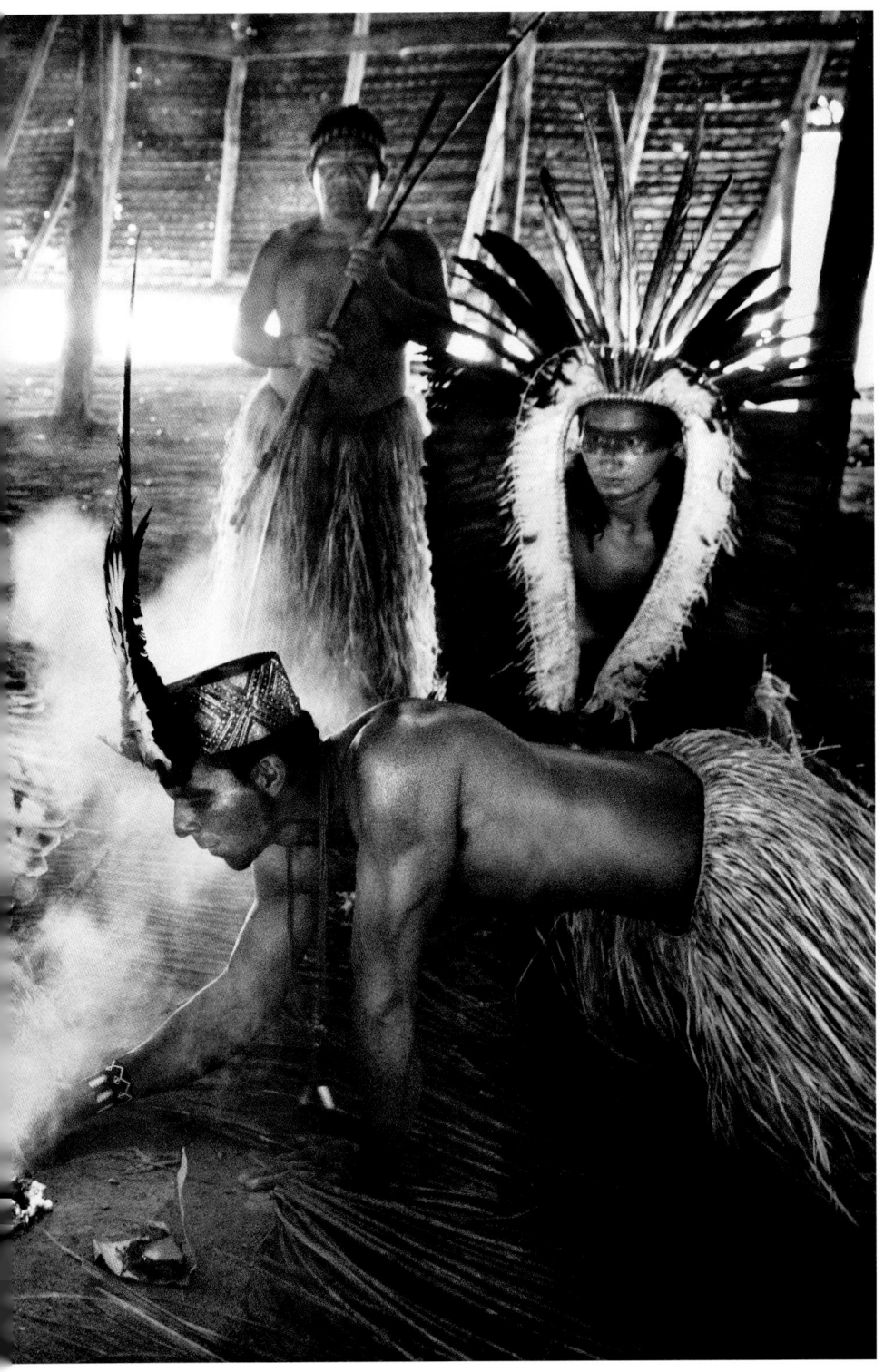

223

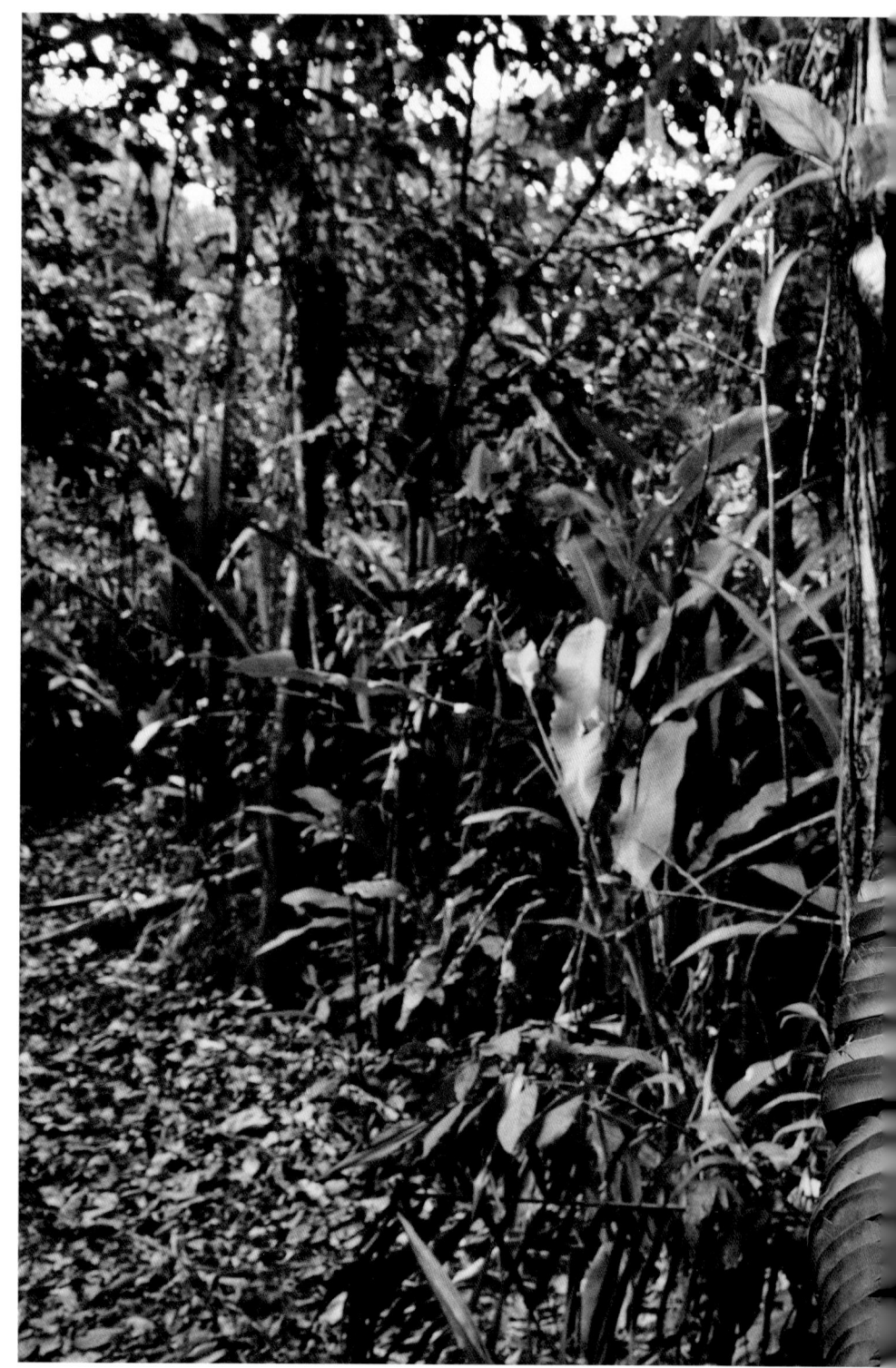

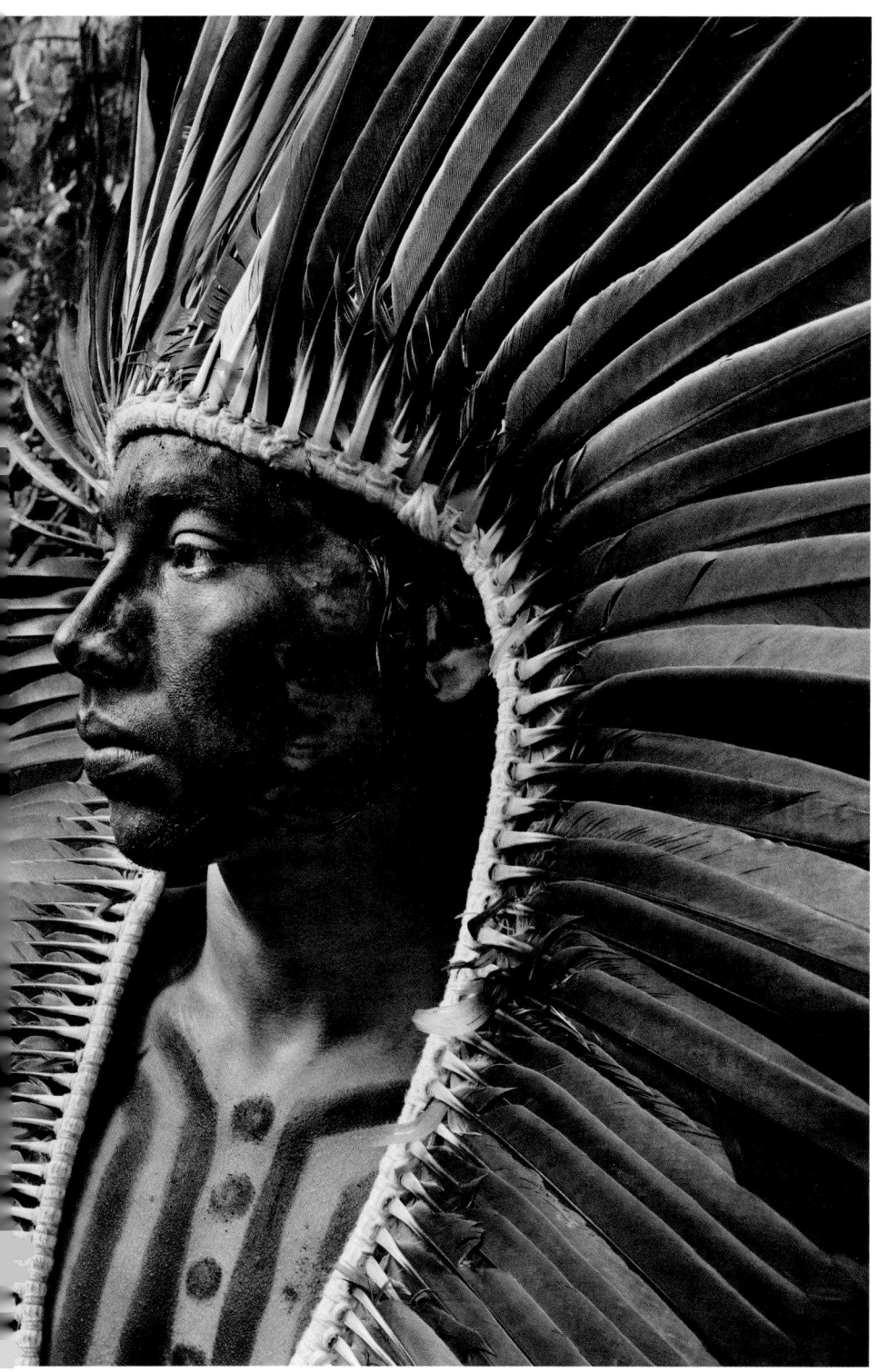

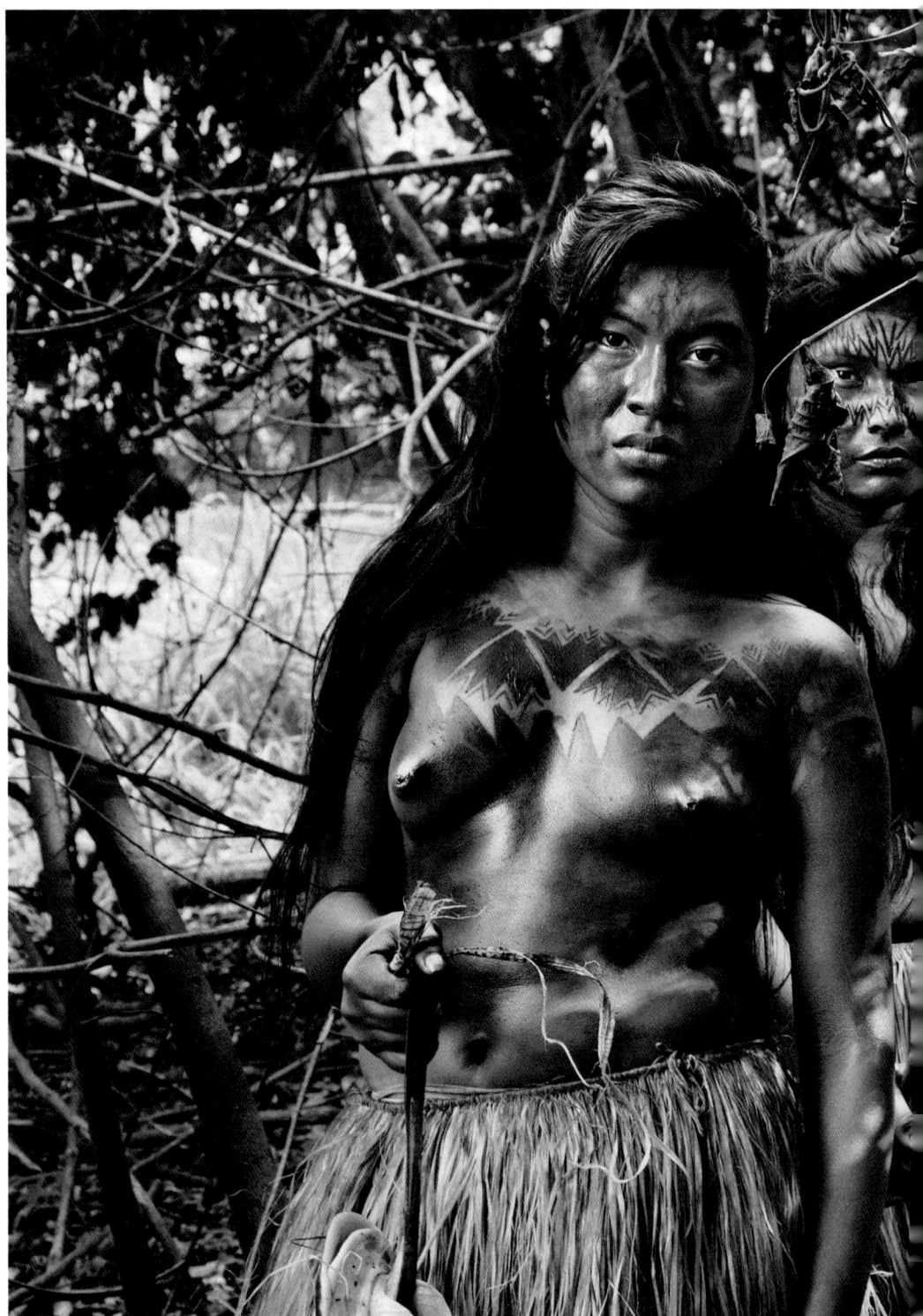

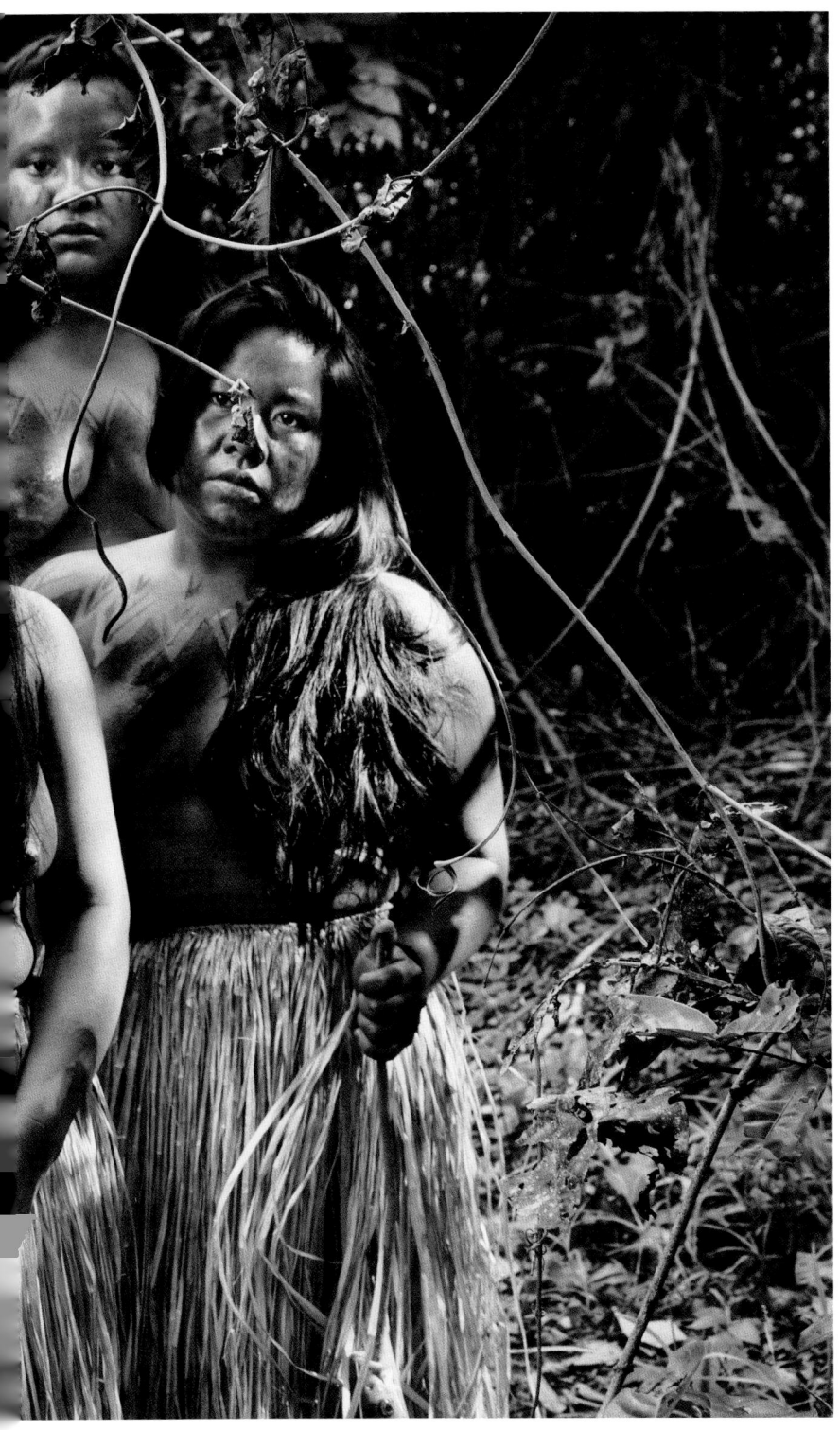

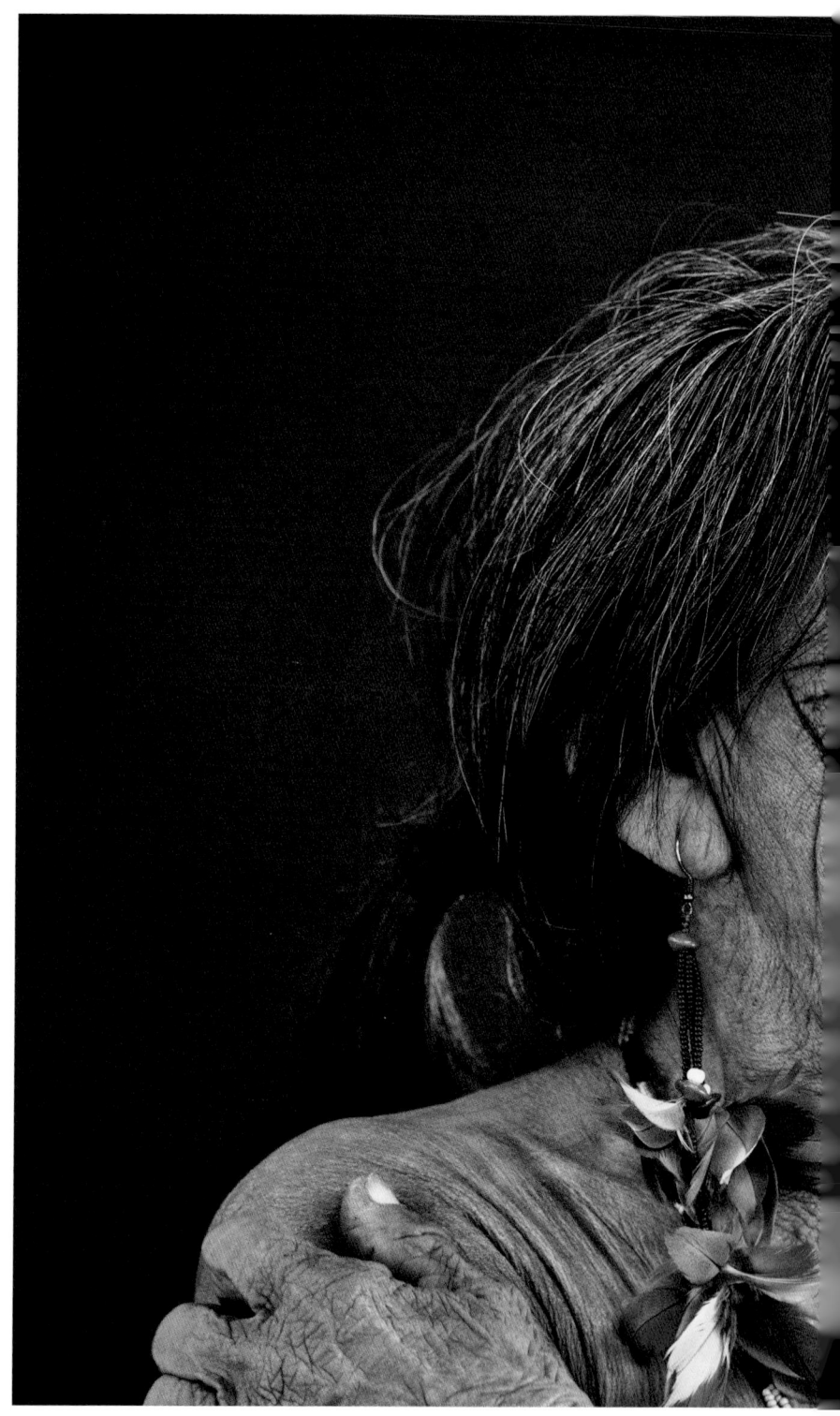

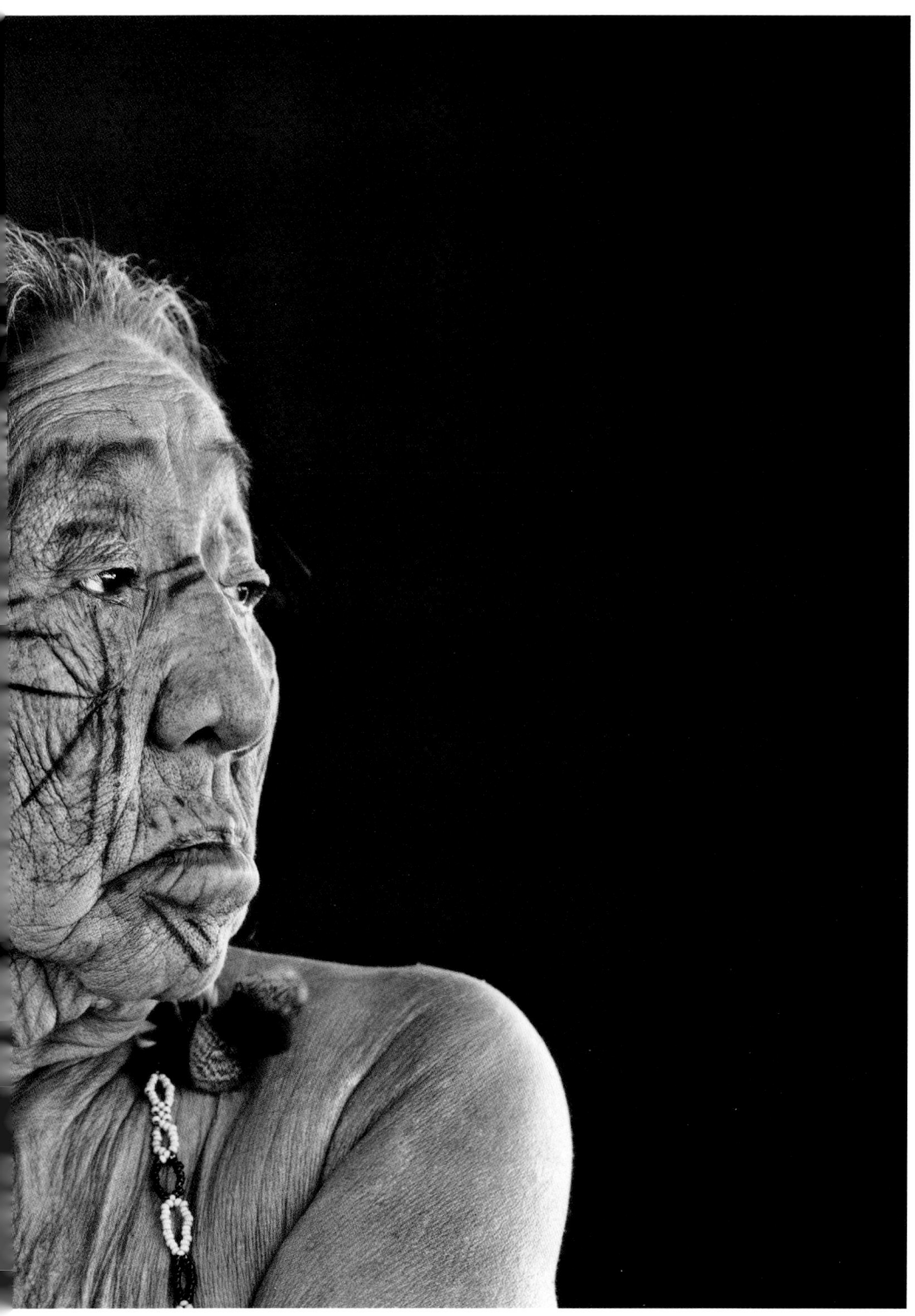

Pages 228/229 Alzira, village of Mutum. Rio Gregório Yawanawá Indigenous Territory, state of Acre, 2016.

Opposite Maria Yawanawá, with her body painted dark, holding a clay pot. Village of Mutum, Rio Gregório Indigenous Territory, state of Acre, 2016.

Pages 232/233 Keiá from the village of Mutum, paints the back of young Kanamashi, from the village of Amparo. The flower-shaped ornament in her hair is made of bird feathers. Village of Mutum, Rio Gregório Yawanawá Indigenous Territory, state of Acre, 2016.

Pages 234/235 Shaná Yawanawá painting the face of daughter Makashê. Village of Nova Esperança, Rio Gregório Yawanawá Indigenous Territory, state of Acre, 2016.

Page 236 Bela Yawanawá, from the village of Mutum, with a headdress and painted face. Rio Gregório Yawanawá Indigenous Territory, state of Acre, 2016.

Page 237 Kanamashi Yawanawá, daughter of Toata Yawanawá, from the village of Amparo. Rio Gregório Yawanawá Indigenous Territory, state of Acre, 2016.

Pages 238/239 Adão Yawanawá in a headdress of eagle feathers, wearing face paint made from the fruit of the genip tree (*Genipa americana*). Village of Nova Esperança, Rio Gregório Yawanawá Indigenous Territory, state of Acre, 2016.

Pages 240/241 Left to right: Para Yuva Yawanawá, Yawatume Yawanawá, Mane Yawanawá, and Tuduyuman Yawanawá with their children. Village of Nova Esperança, Rio Gregório Indigenous Territory, state of Acre, 2016.

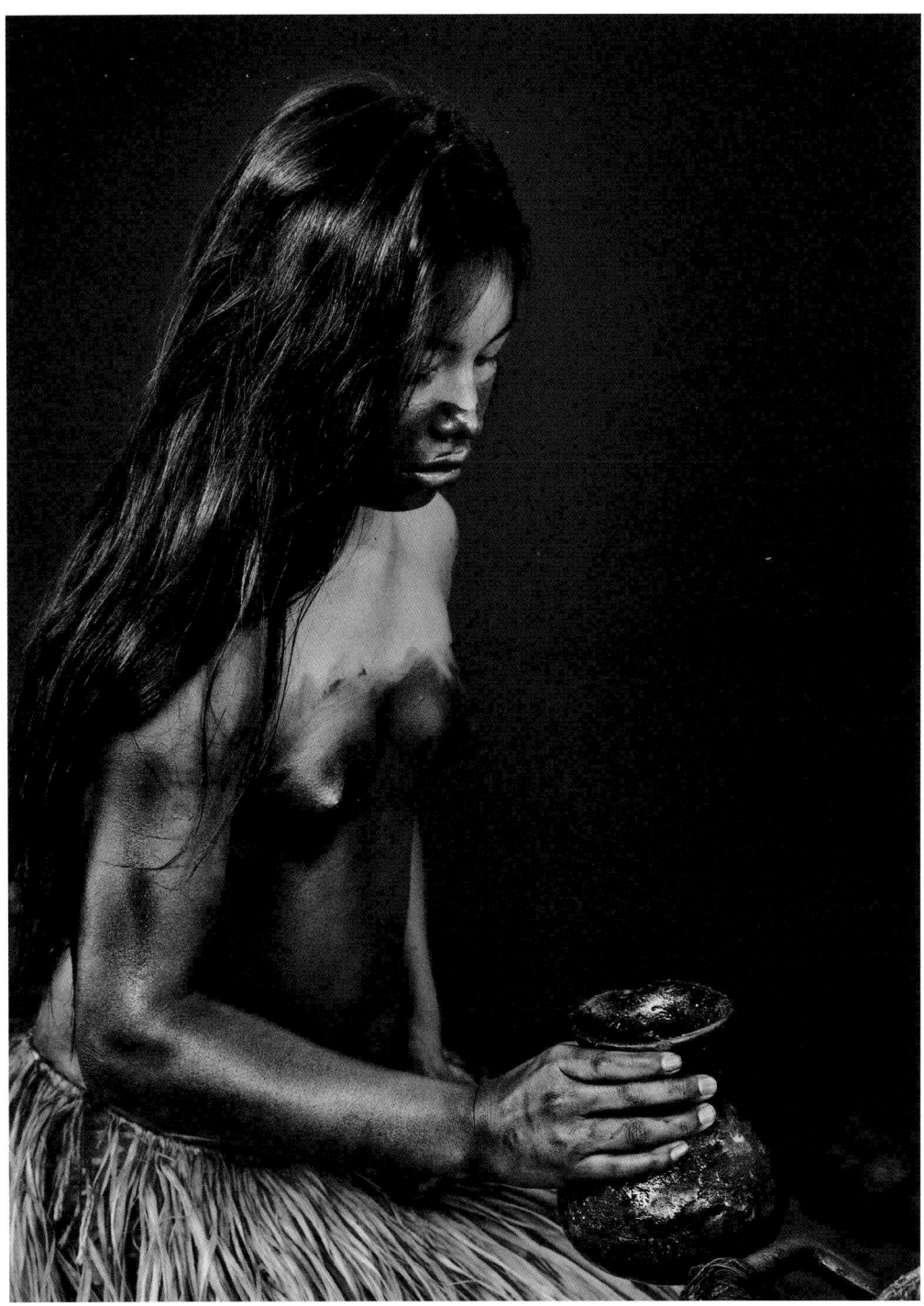

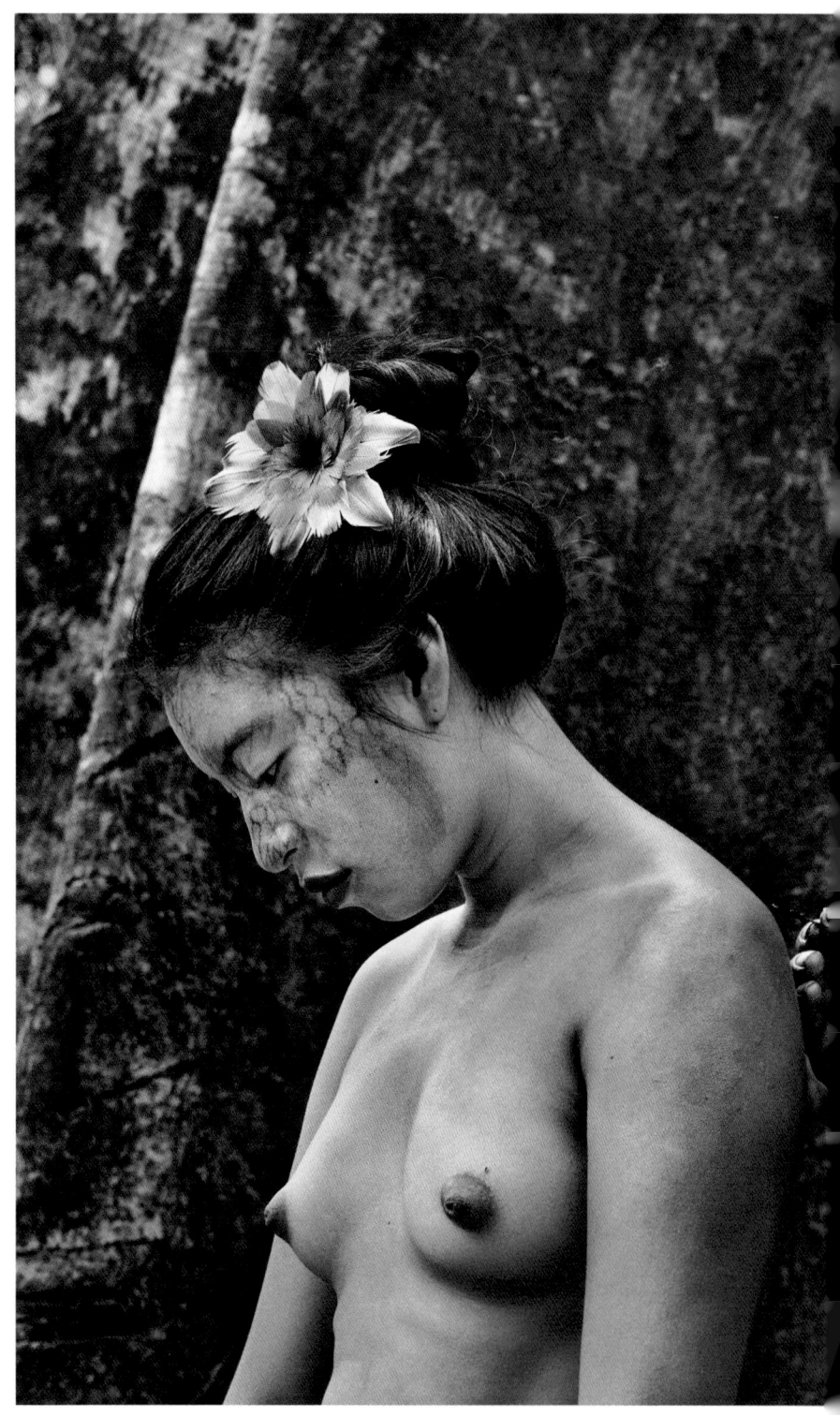

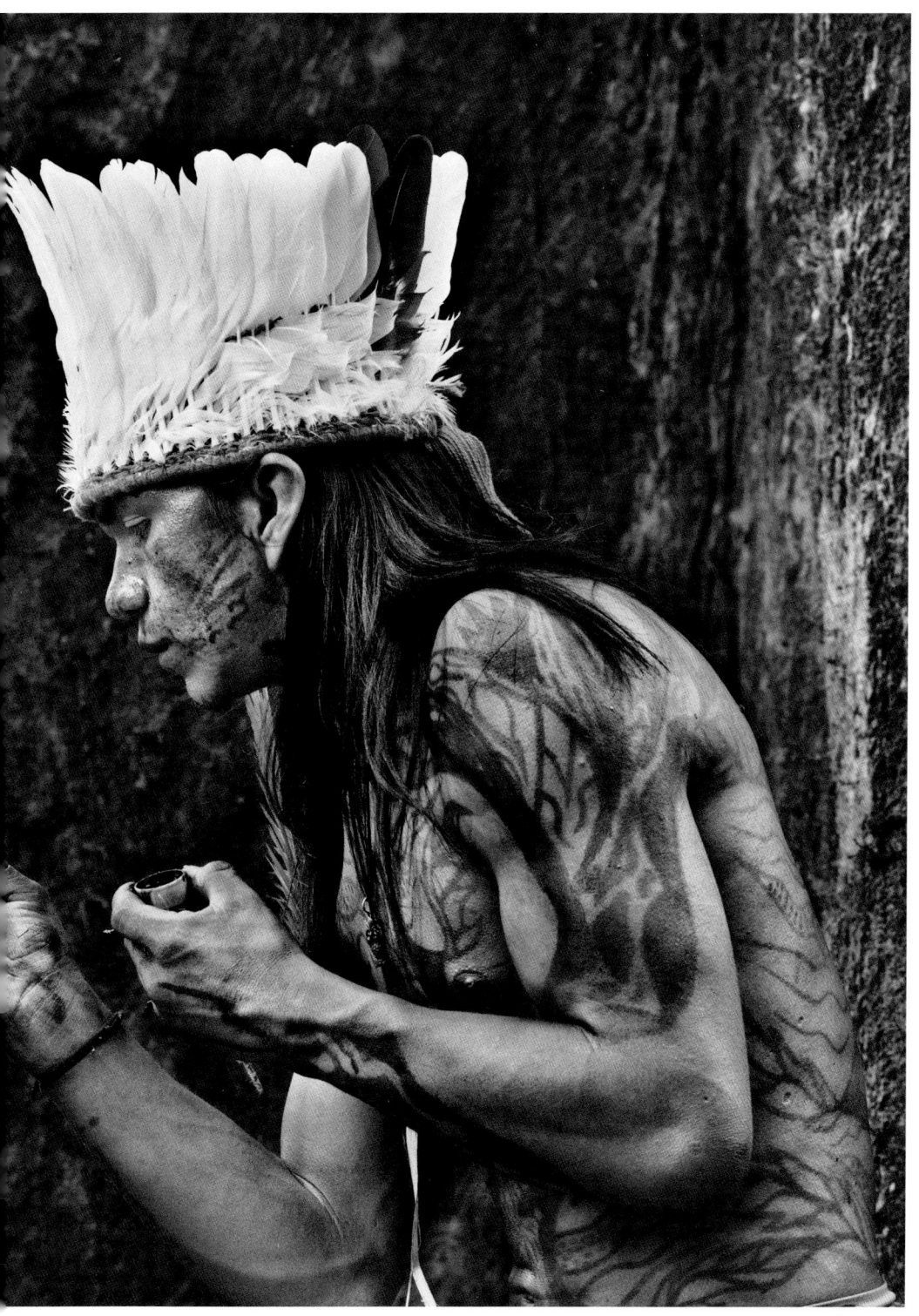

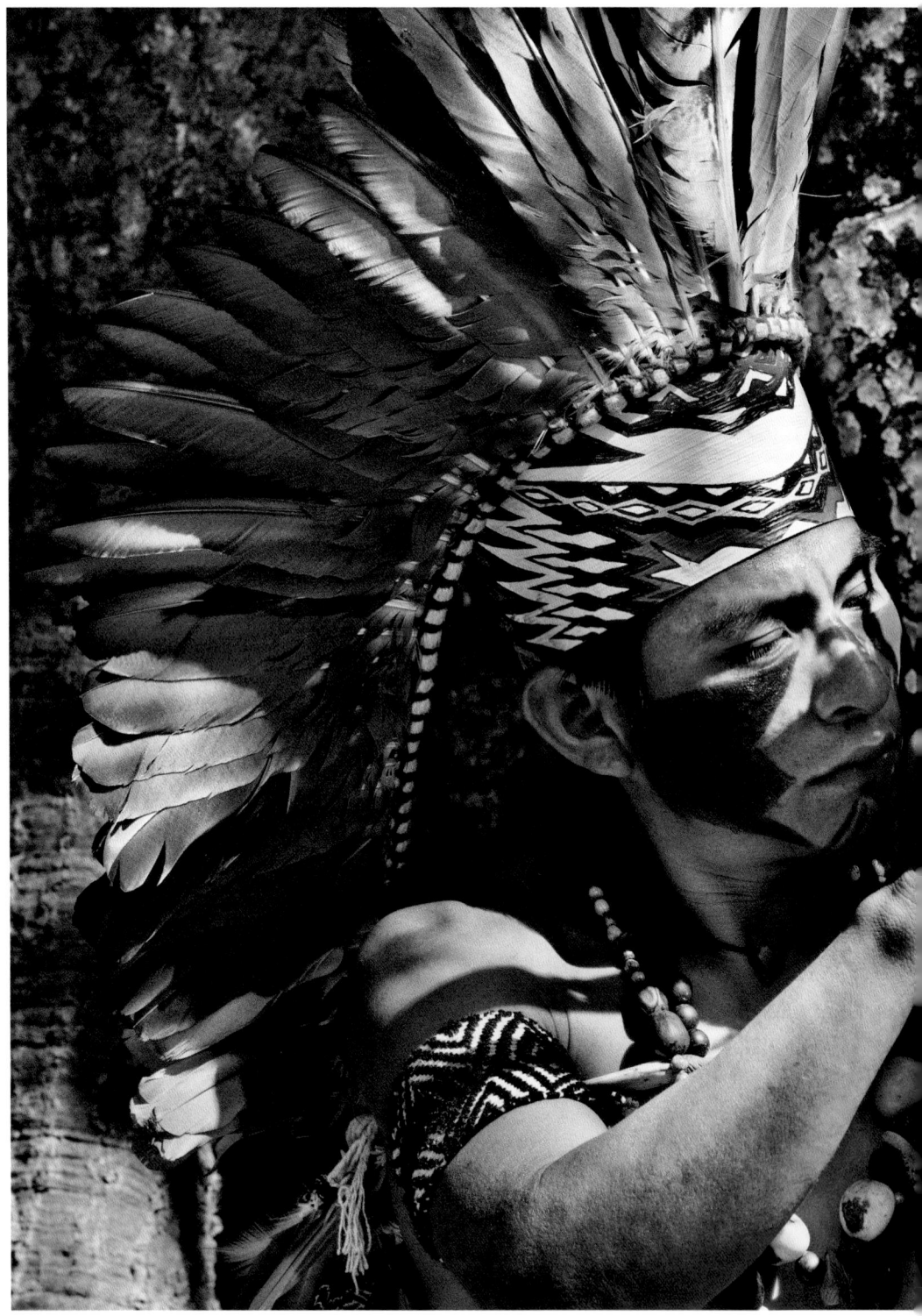

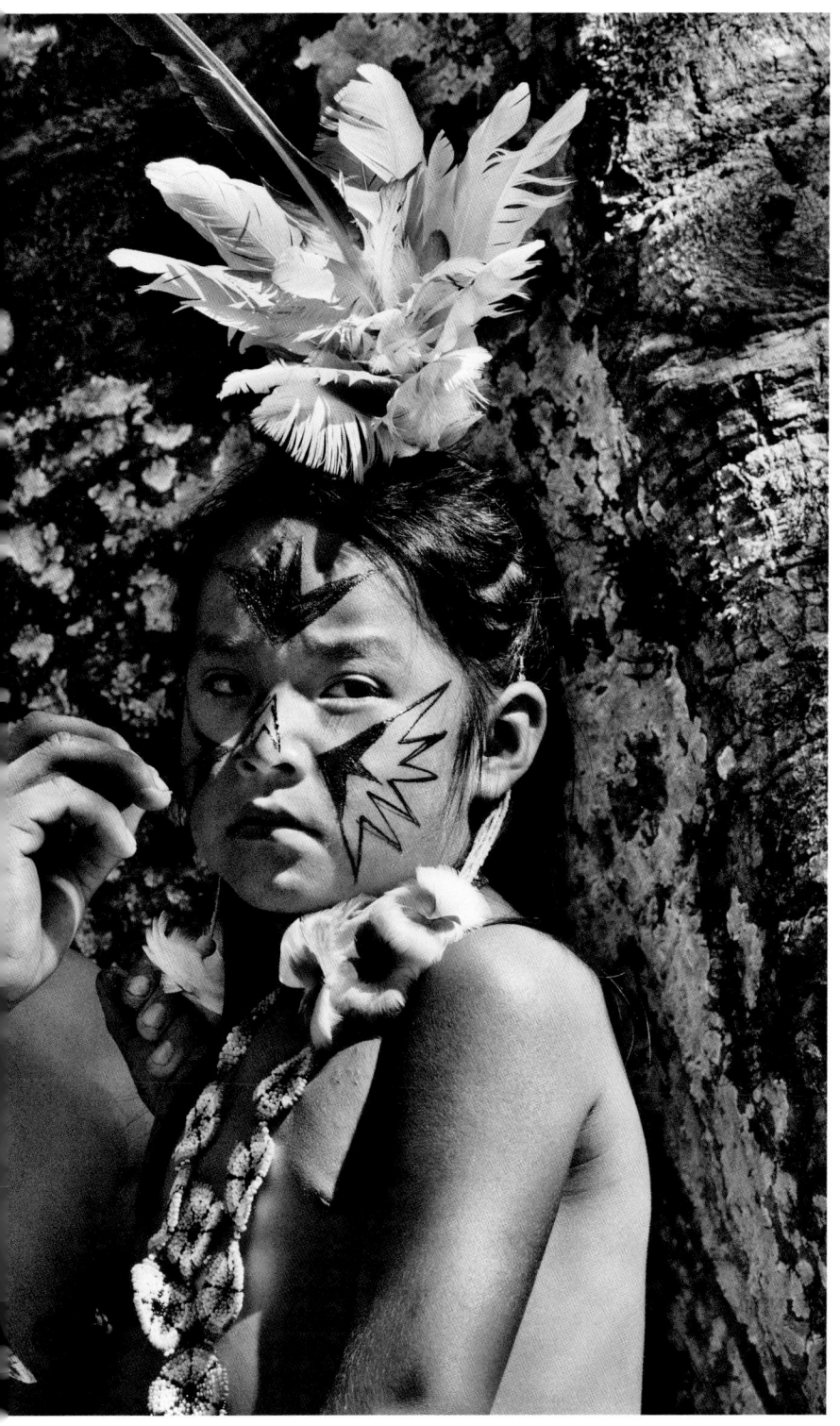

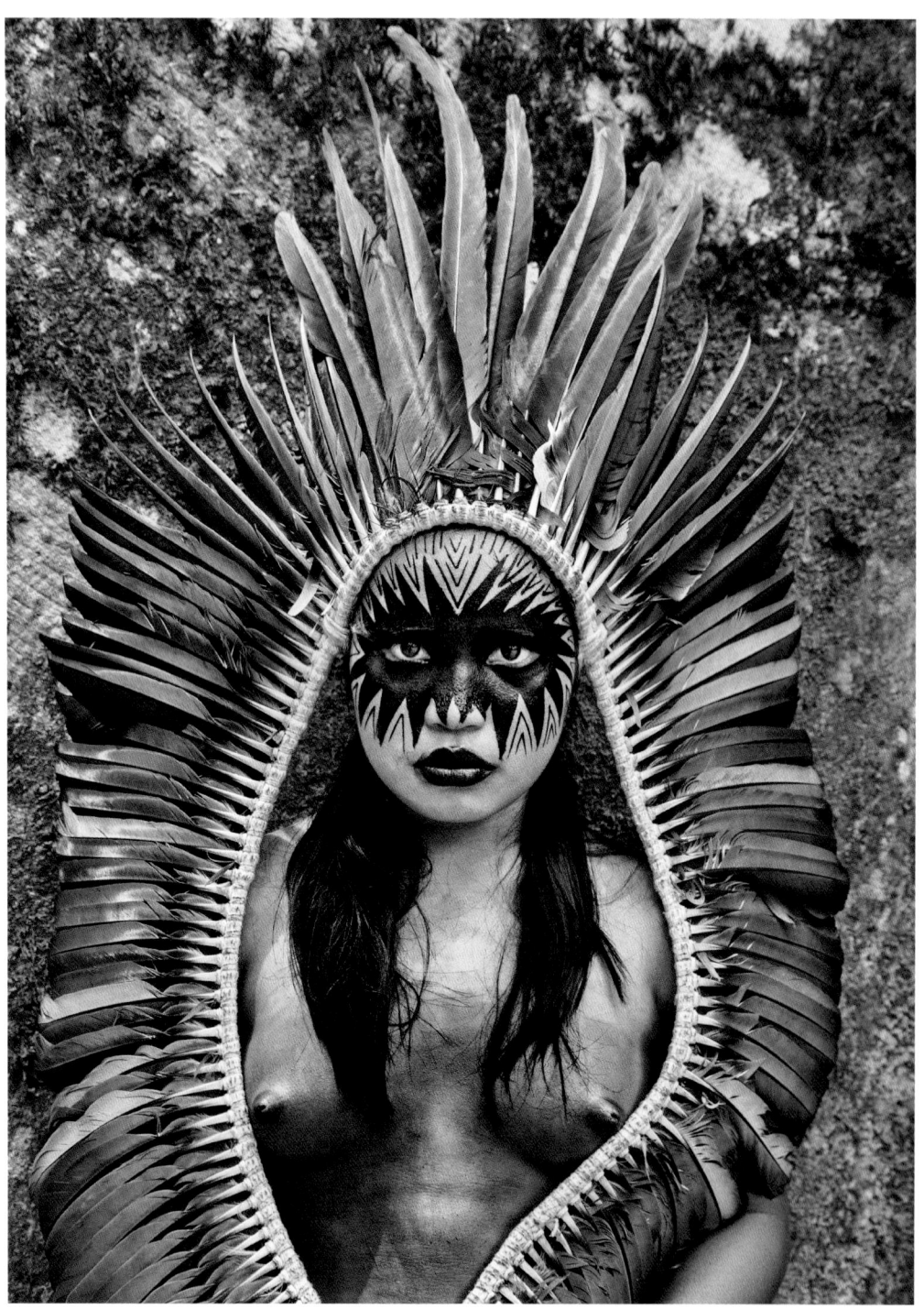

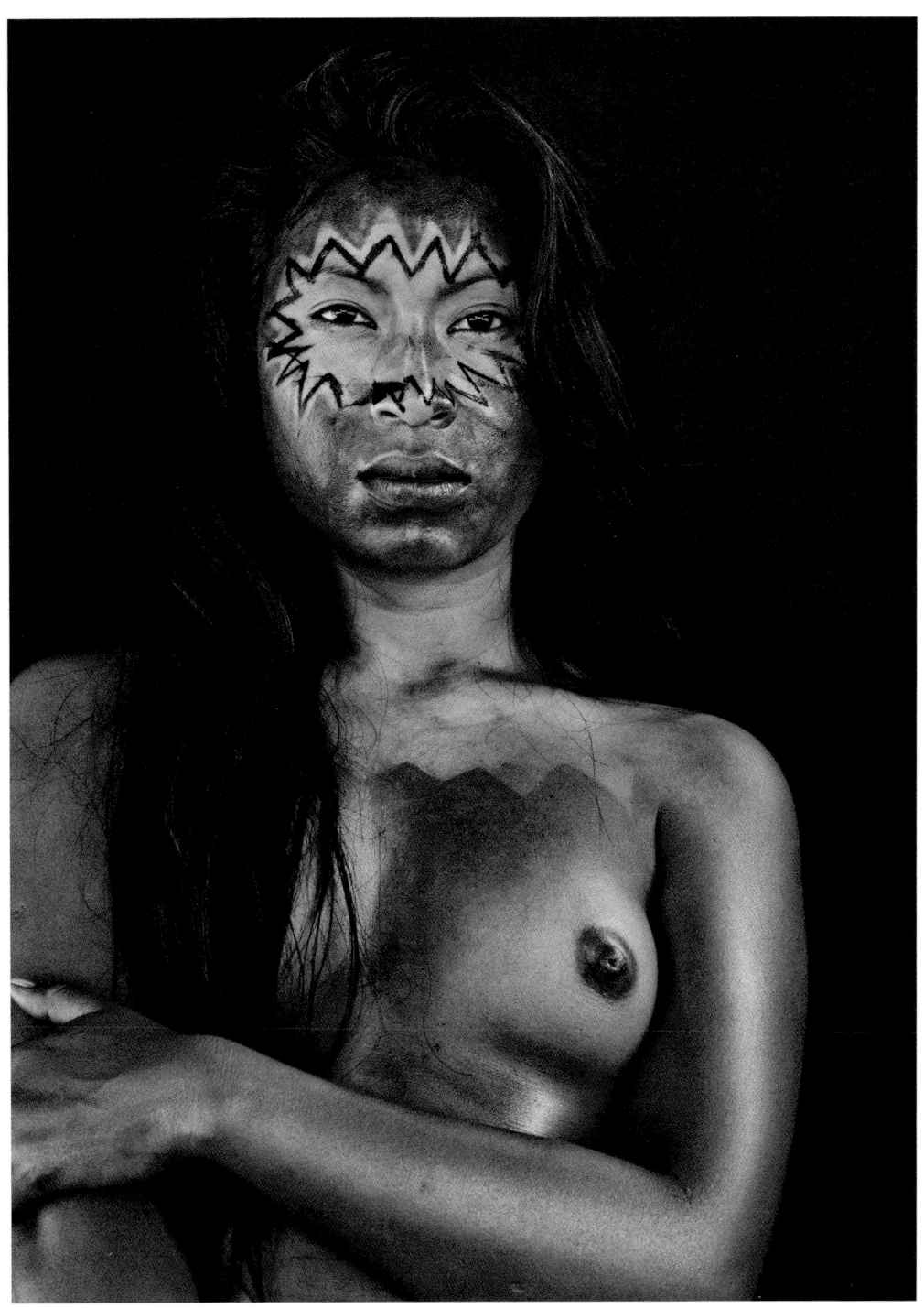

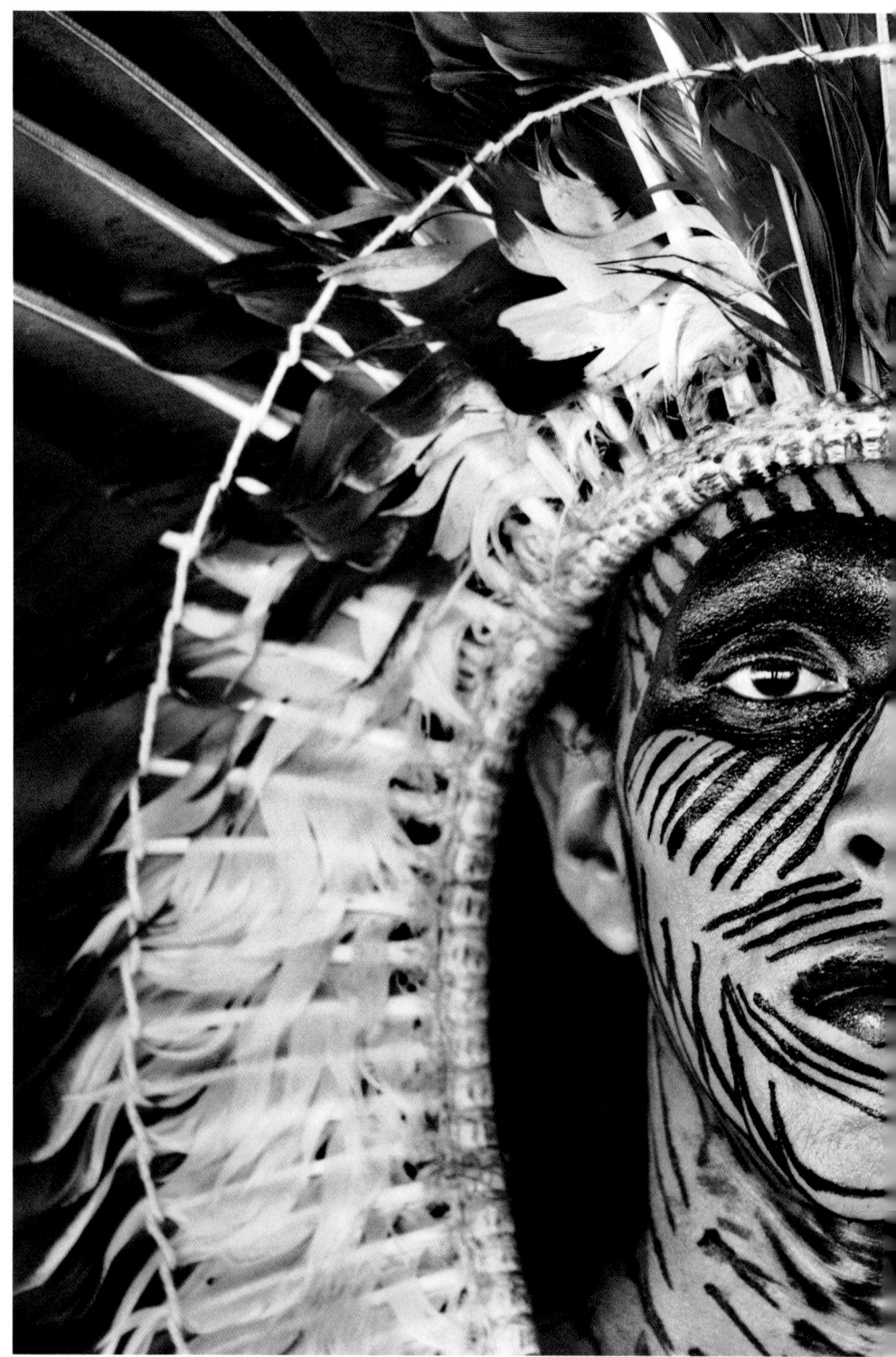

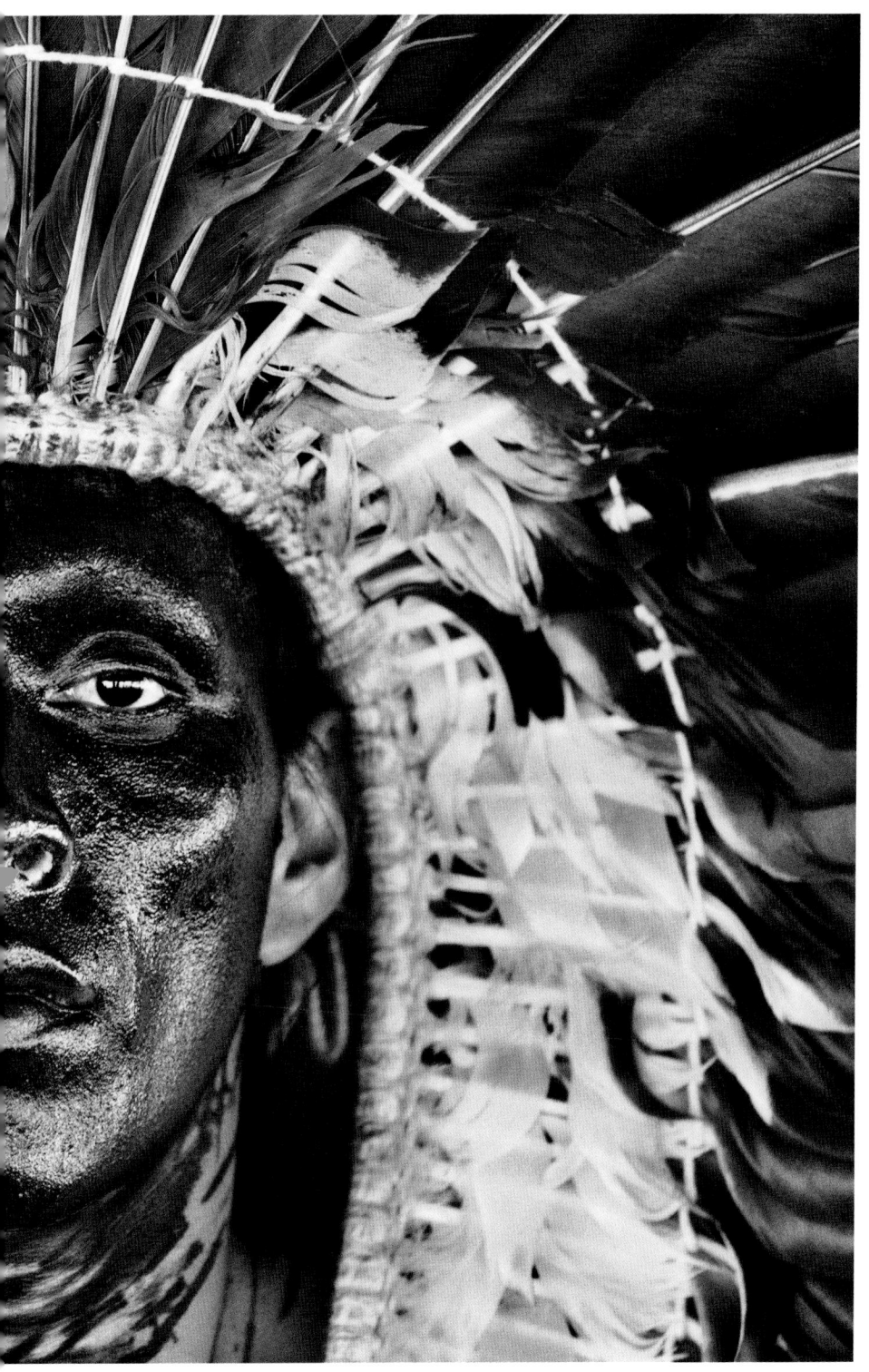

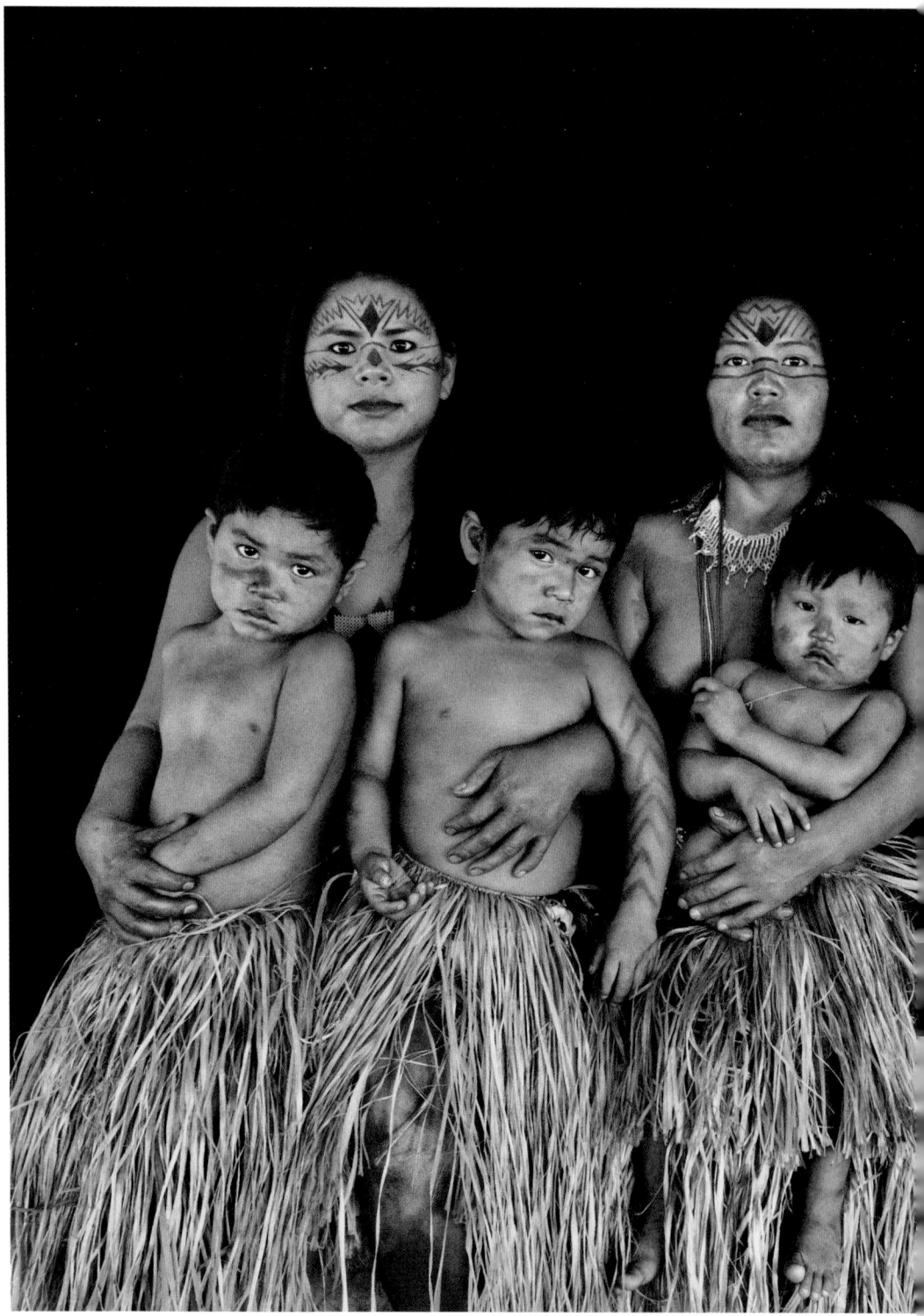

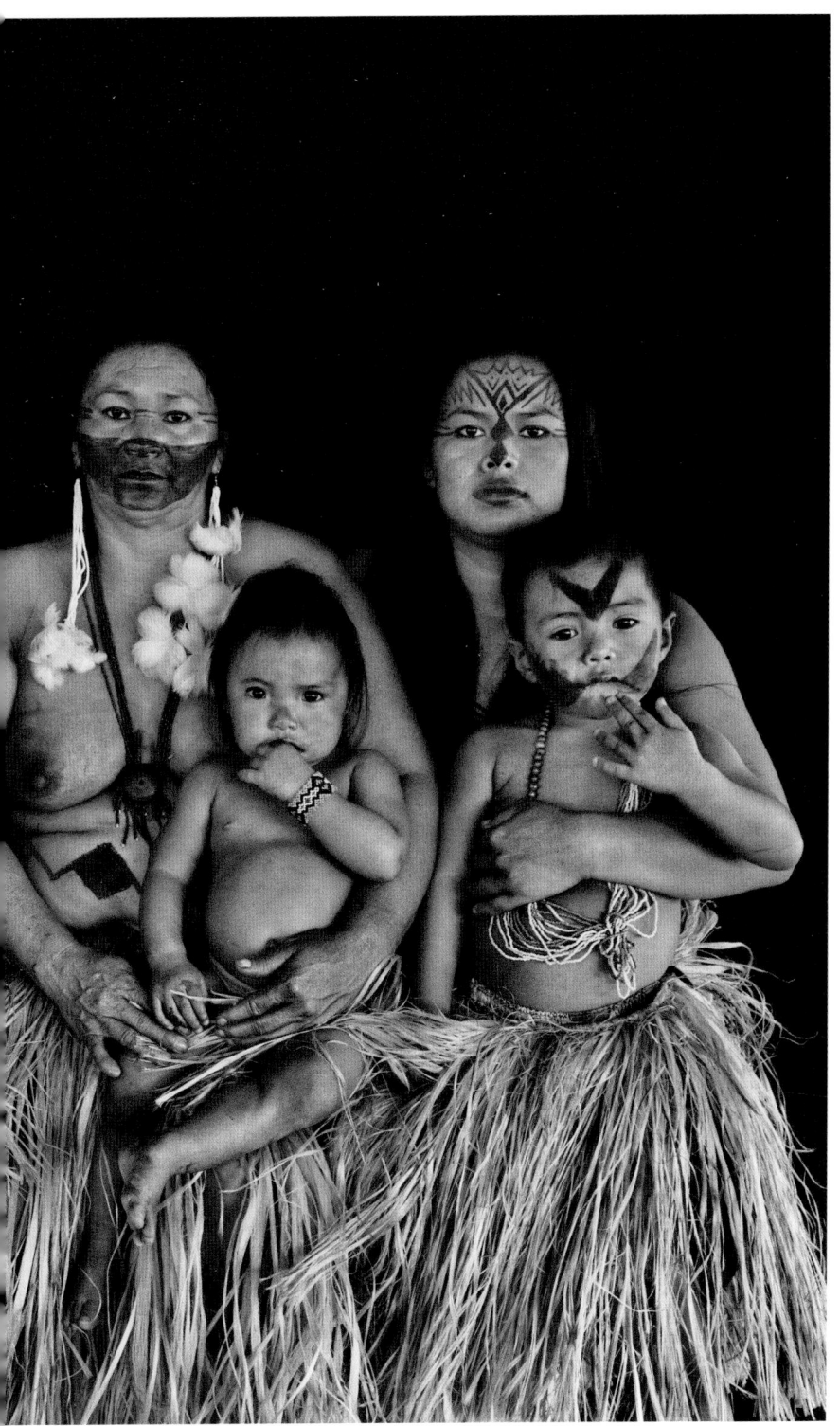

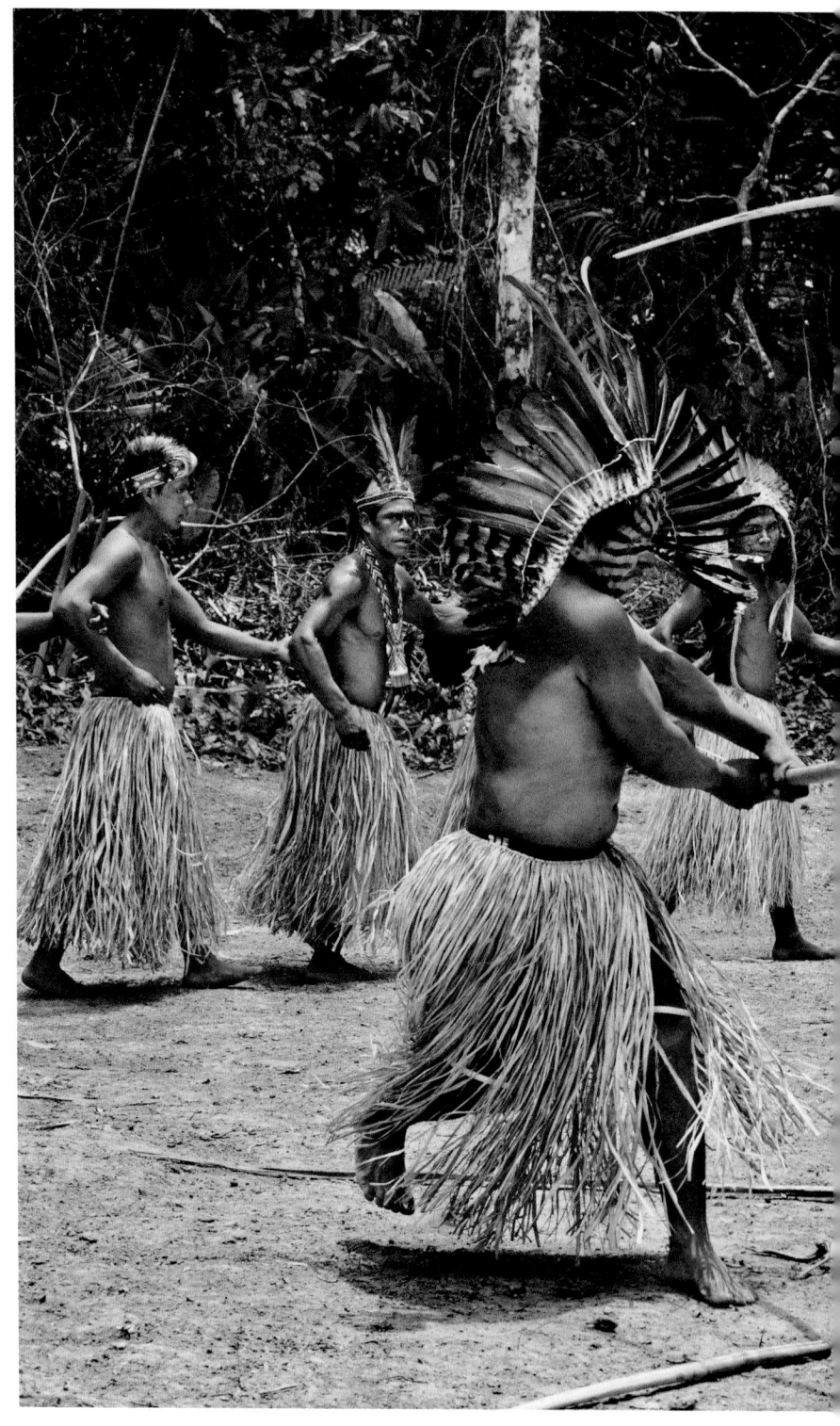

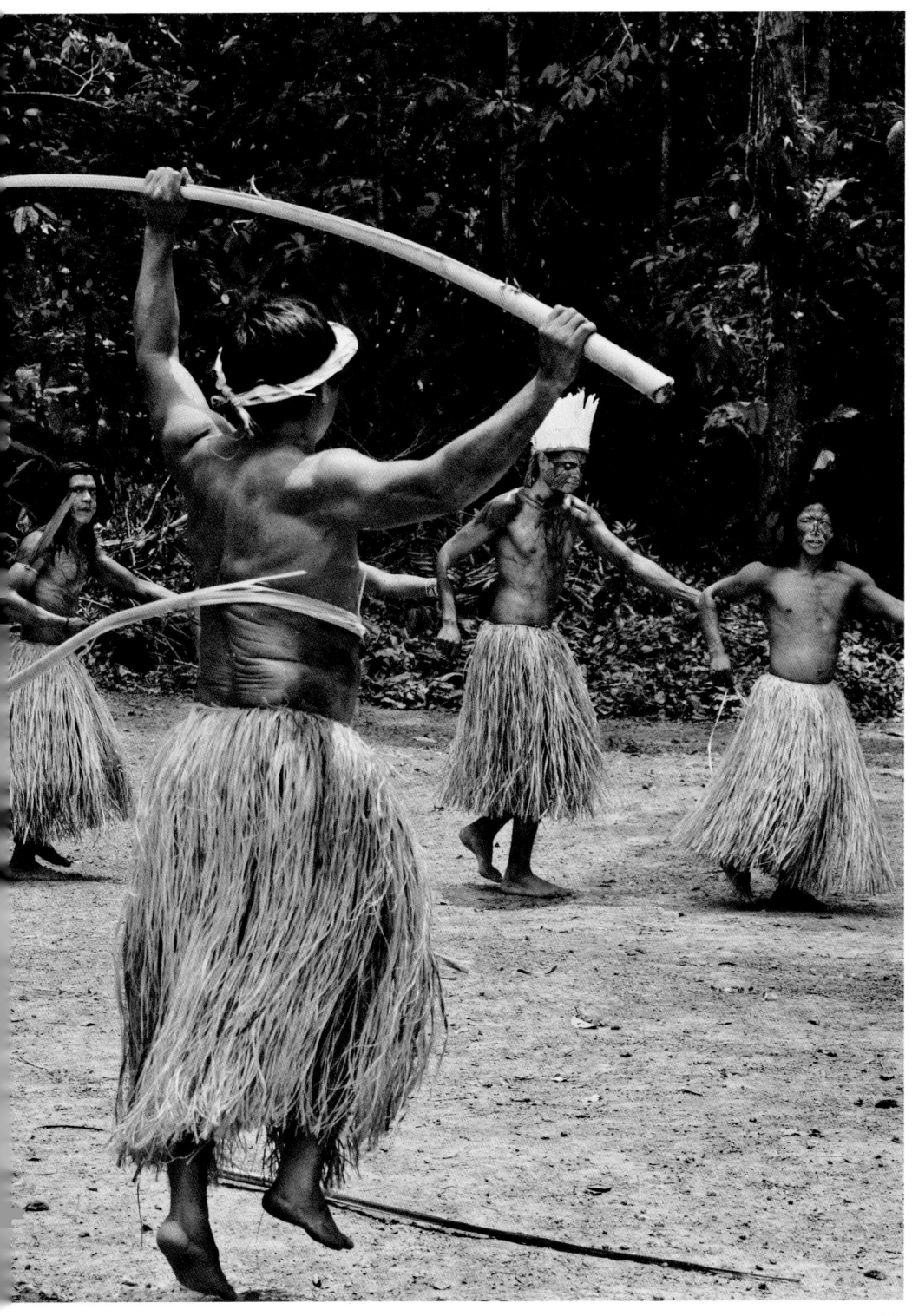

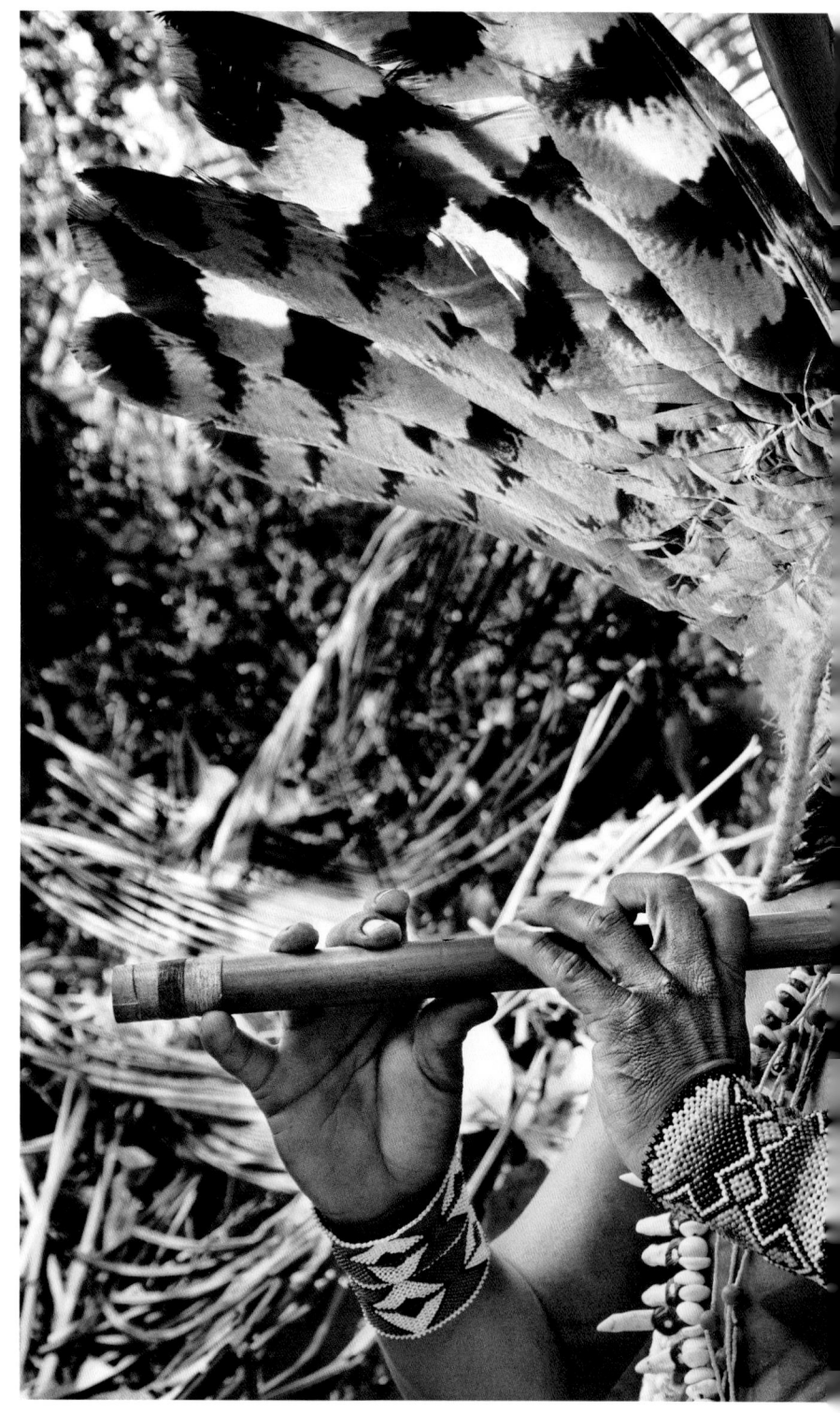

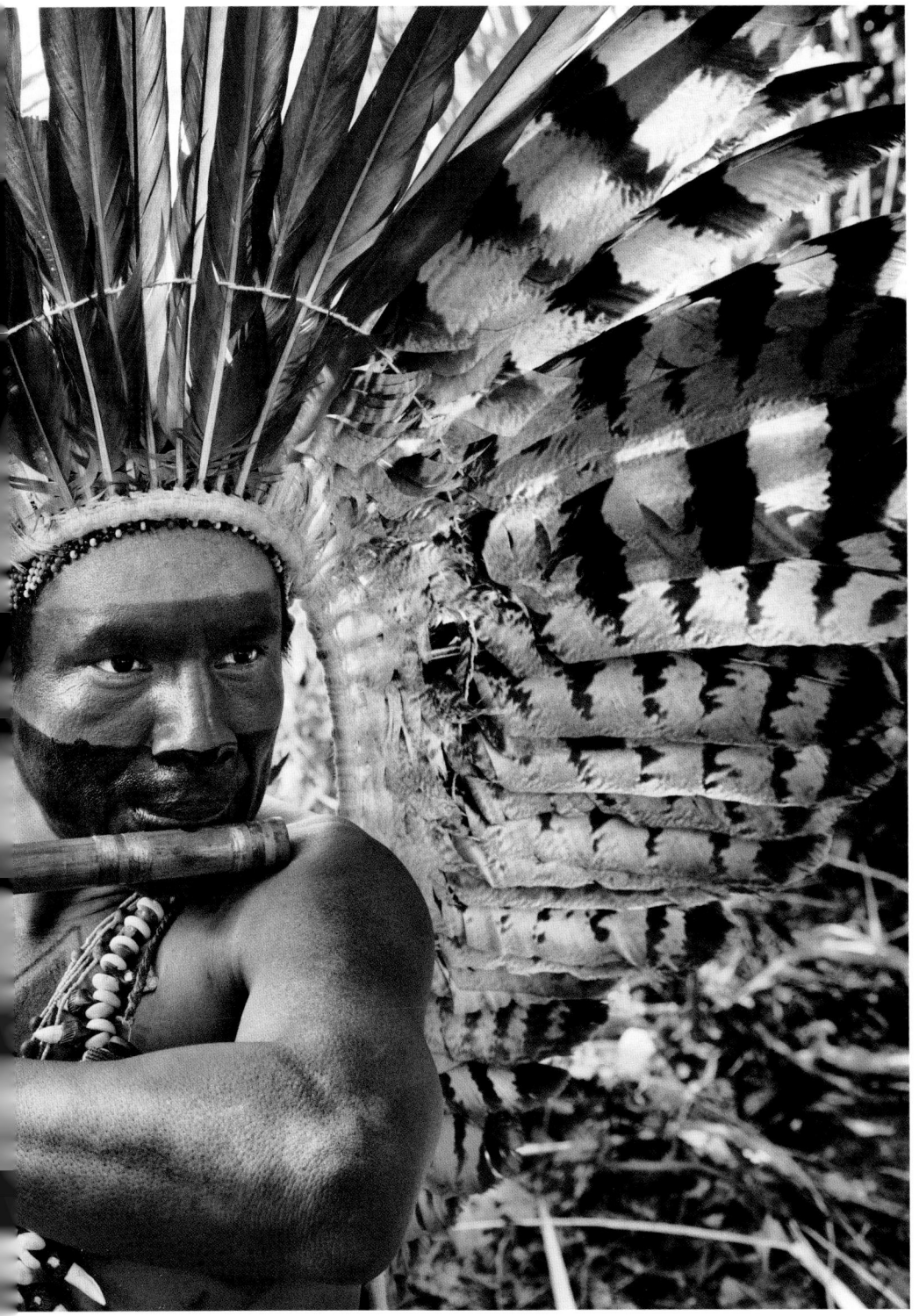

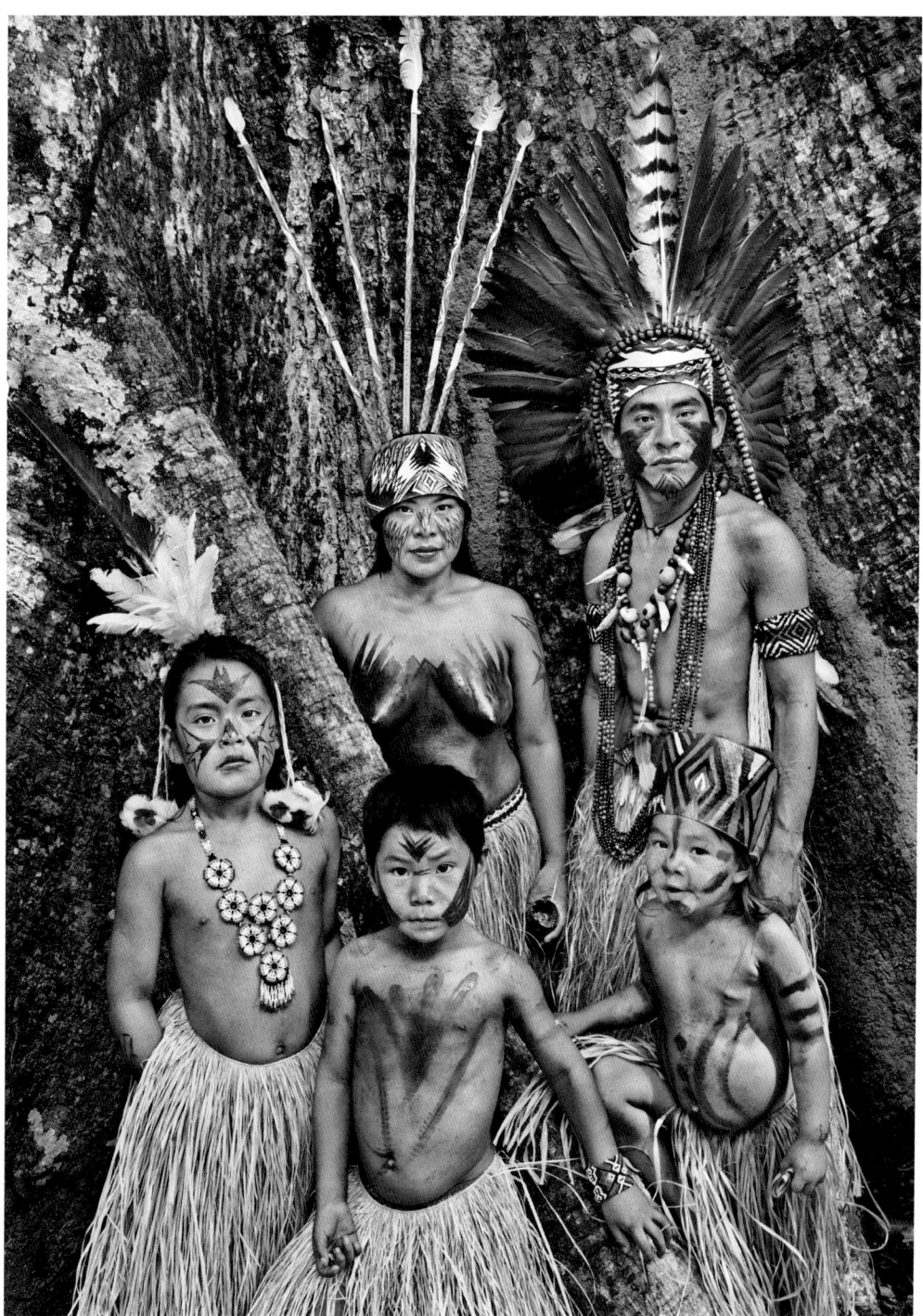

246

Pages 242/243 Yawanawá festival: the revival of their culture and language included reestablishing traditional celebrations. Along with their language, the ancient rites and the production techniques for feather art had become known only to the aged. In teaching the traditions to younger people the Yawanawá have become a benchmark in feather art and also in sharing indigenous traditional culture with tourists from various parts of the world, who seek out their festivals. Rio Gregório Indigenous Territory, state of Acre, 2016.

Pages 244/245 Tuim Kuru Yawanawá, teacher in the Nova Esperança community. The Yawanawá revived techniques for creating their feather art. Things had reached the point where only old people still held that knowledge. Now, however, younger people have begun creating some of the most striking work in the Amazon region, generally made with feathers from eagles (*Harpia harpyja*, which they call "royal hawks"), which are sacred to them. Rio Gregório Indigenous Territory, state of Acre, 2016.

Opposite Shanã Yawanawá (top right) with wife Taiana (top center) and their small children, left to right: daughter Makashê, son Verá, and son Tauá, all from the Yawanawá village of Nova Esperança. Rio Gregório Indigenous Territory, state of Acre, 2016.

Pages 248/249 Manda Yawanawá, daughter of Jeré (Yawakashahu) Yawanawá, from the village of Escondido. Rio Gregório Indigenous Territory, state of Acre, 2016.

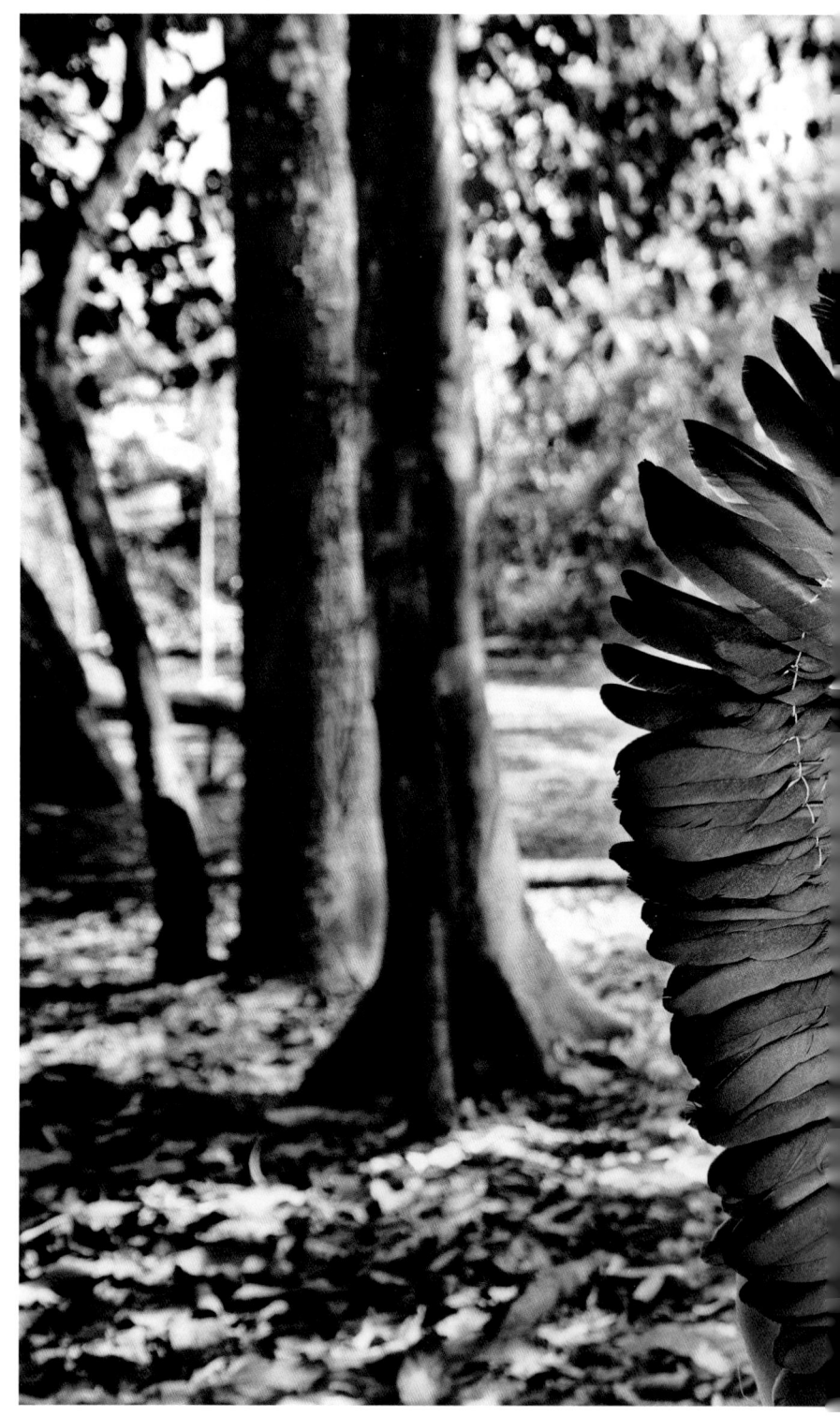

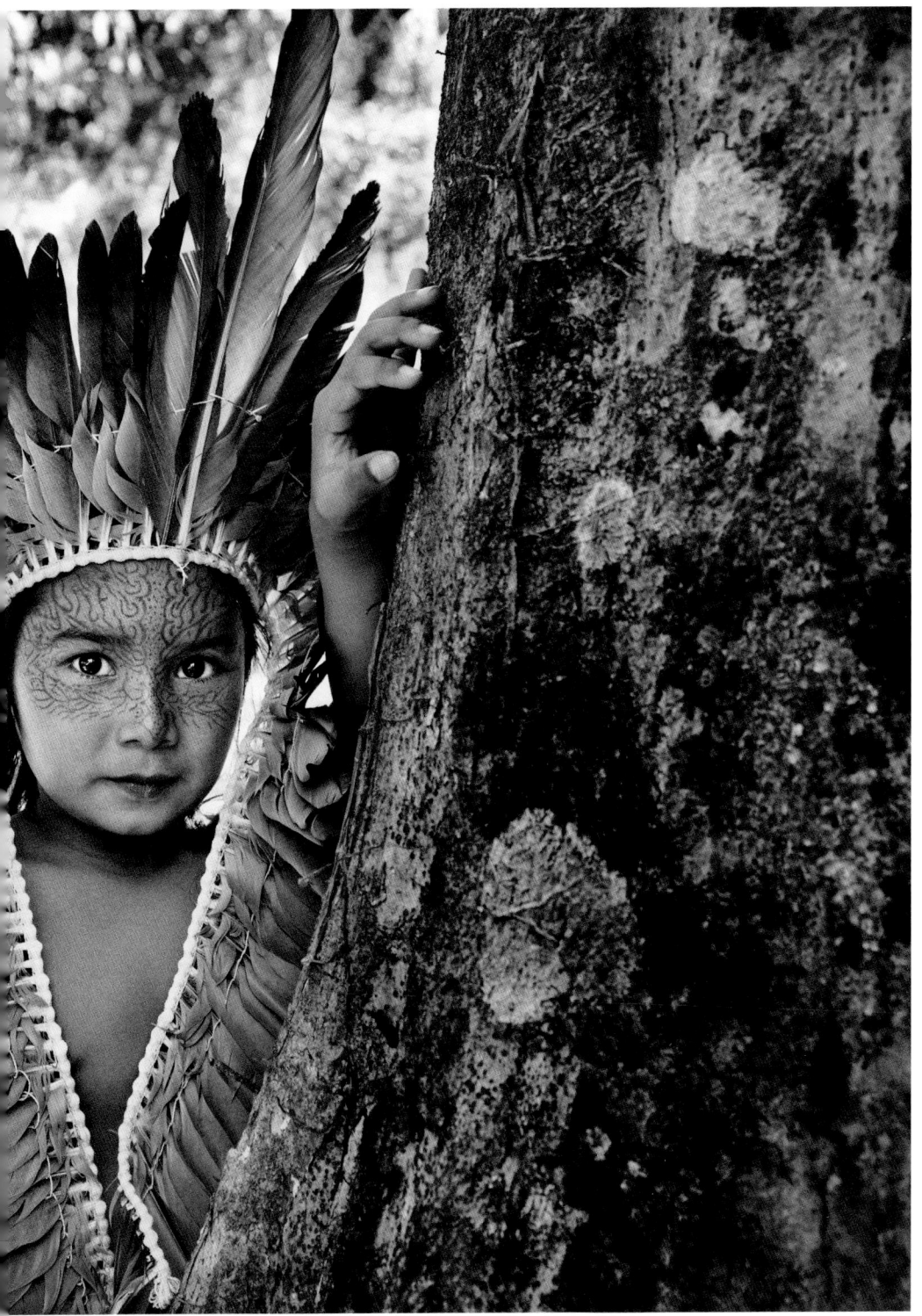

YANOMAMI

The Yanomami are the largest low-contact indigenous ethnic group in the world. They have a population of around 40,000 people, with 28,000 in Brazil and the rest in Venezuela. They live in mountains ranges and valleys in the far north of Brazil, in the country's largest indigenous territory, bordering Venezuela. The land extends from the north of the state of Roraima to the Rio Negro in the state of Amazonas. The Yanomami include at least one isolated group.

For about 1,000 years, they have lived around the highest mountain range in Brazil. They used to live on the mountaintops of this range. Over the centuries, contact with nonindigenous people devastated the inhabitants of the valleys and allowed the Yanomami to expand into the lowlands.

Only in the second half of the 20th century did they become more exposed to nonindigenous representatives: religious missionaries, envoys from Brazilian federal agencies in charge of marking the borders, and the first explorers. Starting in the 1970s, amid a big push for development, the Brazilian military dictatorship (1964–85) decided to build a set of highways through their lands. Unprepared for the diseases that white people brought there, the indigenous population suffered successive epidemics of flu, malaria, measles, and sexually transmitted diseases.

In the late 1980s, President José Sarney's administration proposed creating dozens of small reserves for the Yanomami, which recognized as indigenous land only the area around their largest communities. Indigenous people and indigenist agencies called for recognition of the whole area where they lived and wandered. At that time, as the National Constituent Assembly was debating the new Brazilian constitution that would expand indigenous rights, a wave of prospectors invaded the region, numbering an estimated 30,000 to 40,000 (five times the indigenous population of the invaded area), with tacit consent from the federal agencies tasked with protecting indigenous peoples. Over a short period, 15 percent of the affected indigenous population died. At the time, Prince Charles, heir to the British throne, described the occurrence as a "genocide."

The federal government expelled the prospectors during the term of President Fernando Collor (1990–92), who also recognized as indigenous territory the entire 96,000 square kilometer (37,000 square mile) area indicated by anthropological studies. Illegal prospecting decreased but the prospectors who remained became more violent. In 1993, Haximu, a Yanomami community, suffered a massacre by illegal miners. This led to the only conviction for the crime of genocide in the entire history of Brazilian justice. Some 30 years later, the only convicted perpetrator still alive continues to work in illegal mine prospecting, which made him a wealthy businessman. The prospectors returned. Starting in the early 2010s, they began to act freely, unhindered by any moves to dislodge them.

Shamanism is central to Yanomami culture. Their main leader is the shaman Davi Kopenawa, a pioneer in the campaign to establish the Yanomami Indigenous Territory, starting in the late 1970s. During the mining invasion crisis, in 1988, he won a United Nations Environment Programme award. Later, amid another wave of invasions, he won the Right Livelihood Award, popularly known as the "Alternative Nobel Prize."

Yanomami houses are circular communal *malocas*, some of which, such as Piaú and Watoriki, are built in a ring shape with a large central courtyard for celebrations and communal rituals. Other groups have circular houses with roofs over the entire circle.

The Yanomami tongue is actually a language family divided into six languages. Until lately, five languages were known, but recently the linguist Helder Perri Ferreira identified a sixth one.

Pages 252/253 Tainá, in a hammock in the community of Watoriki, in the Demini River region. It is a cultural taboo to address the Yanomami by their names. Therefore, since non-indigenous people are not aware of this custom and address them by name, these indigenous people began adopting names or nicknames from "white" culture as a way to avoid the use of indigenous names. Yanomami Indigenous Territory, state of Amazonas, 2014.

Pages 254/255 The communal *maloca* of Watoriki, a community founded and led by shaman Davi Kopenawa in the region of the Demini River. Yanomami Indigenous Territory, state of Amazonas, 2014.

Pages 256/257 In the community of *Piaú*, pajés (shamans) Cláudio, Gilberto, and Person (left to right), from other communities, visit and perform shamanic treatment on an older resident. Yanomami Indigenous Territory, state of Amazonas, 2019.

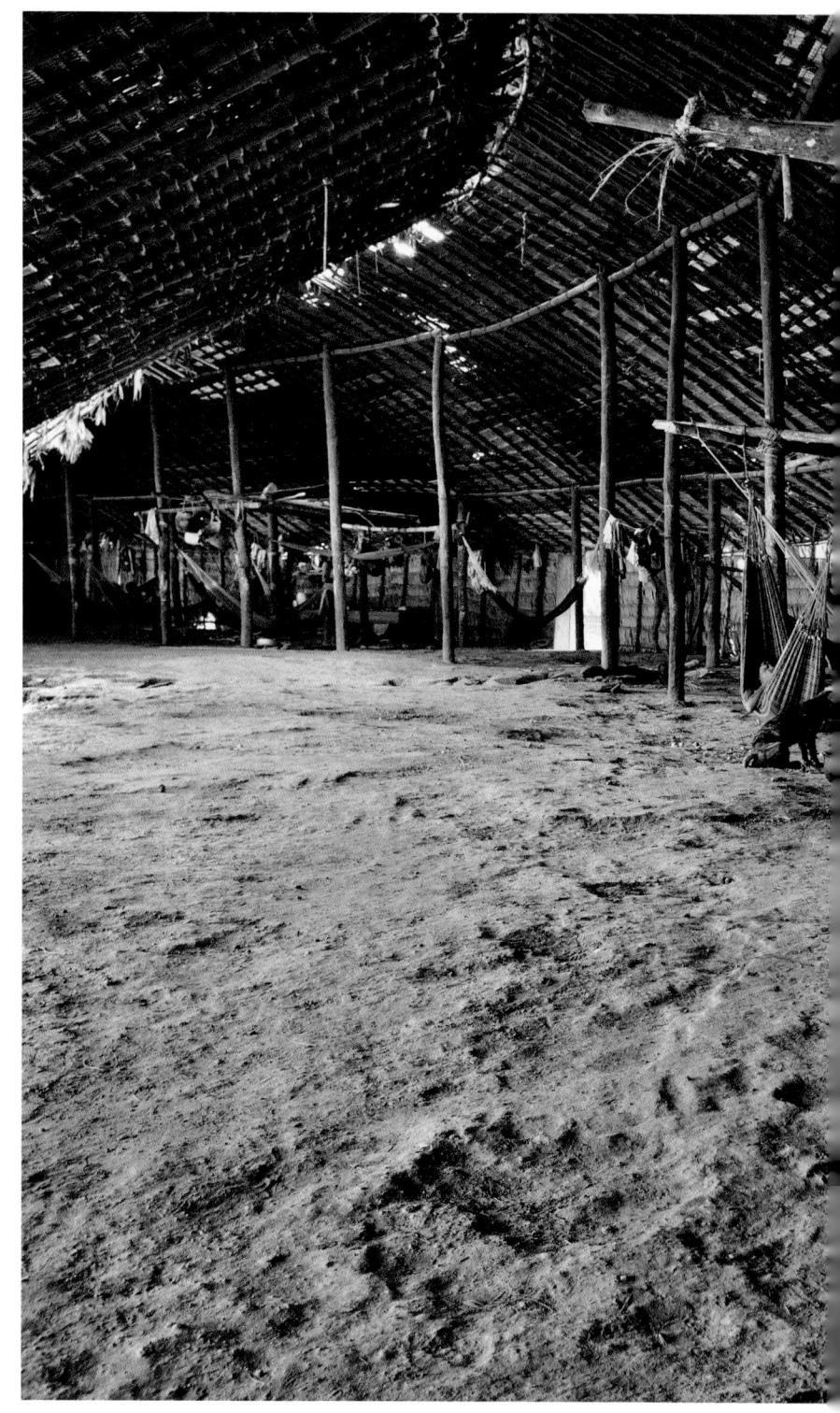

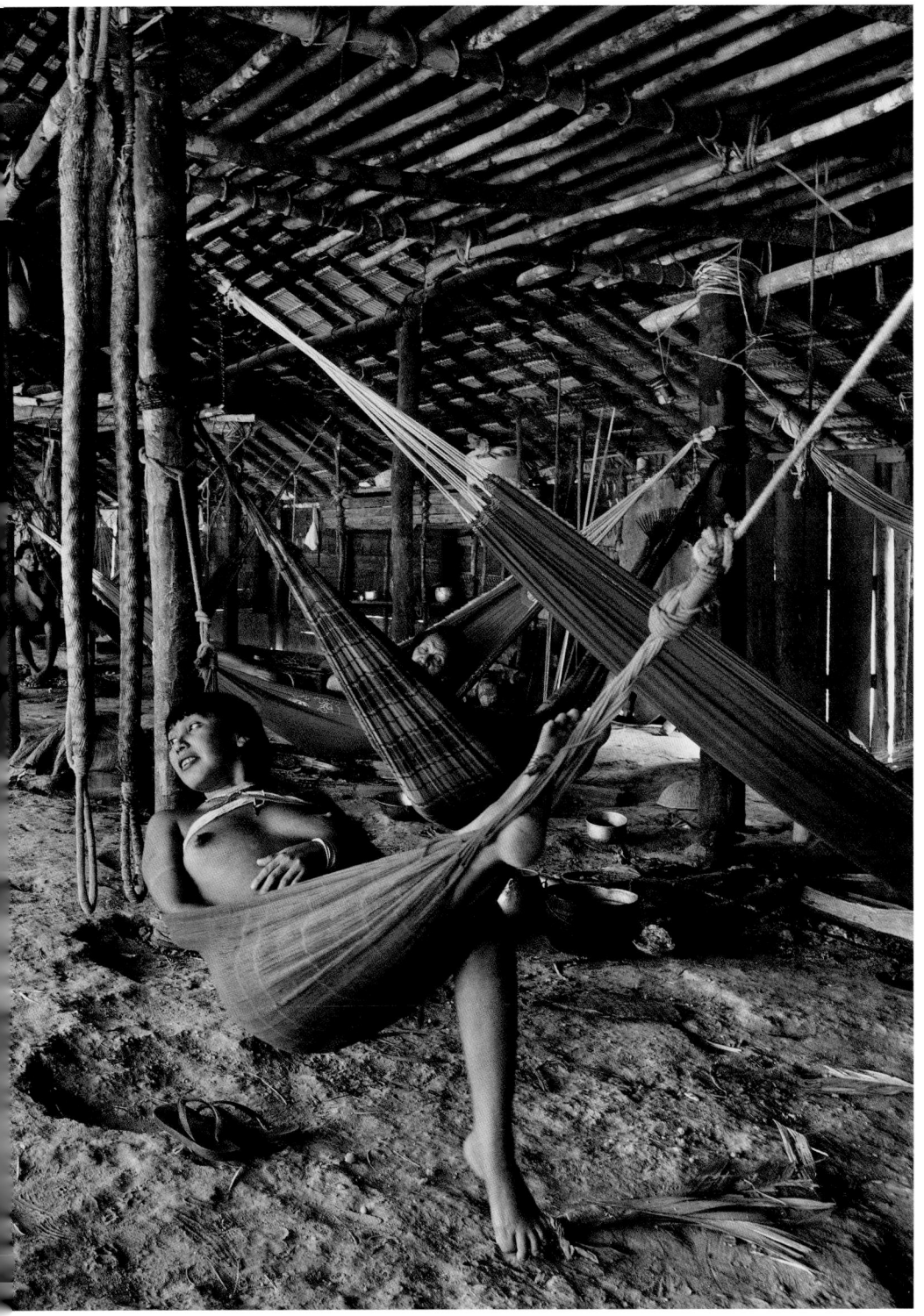

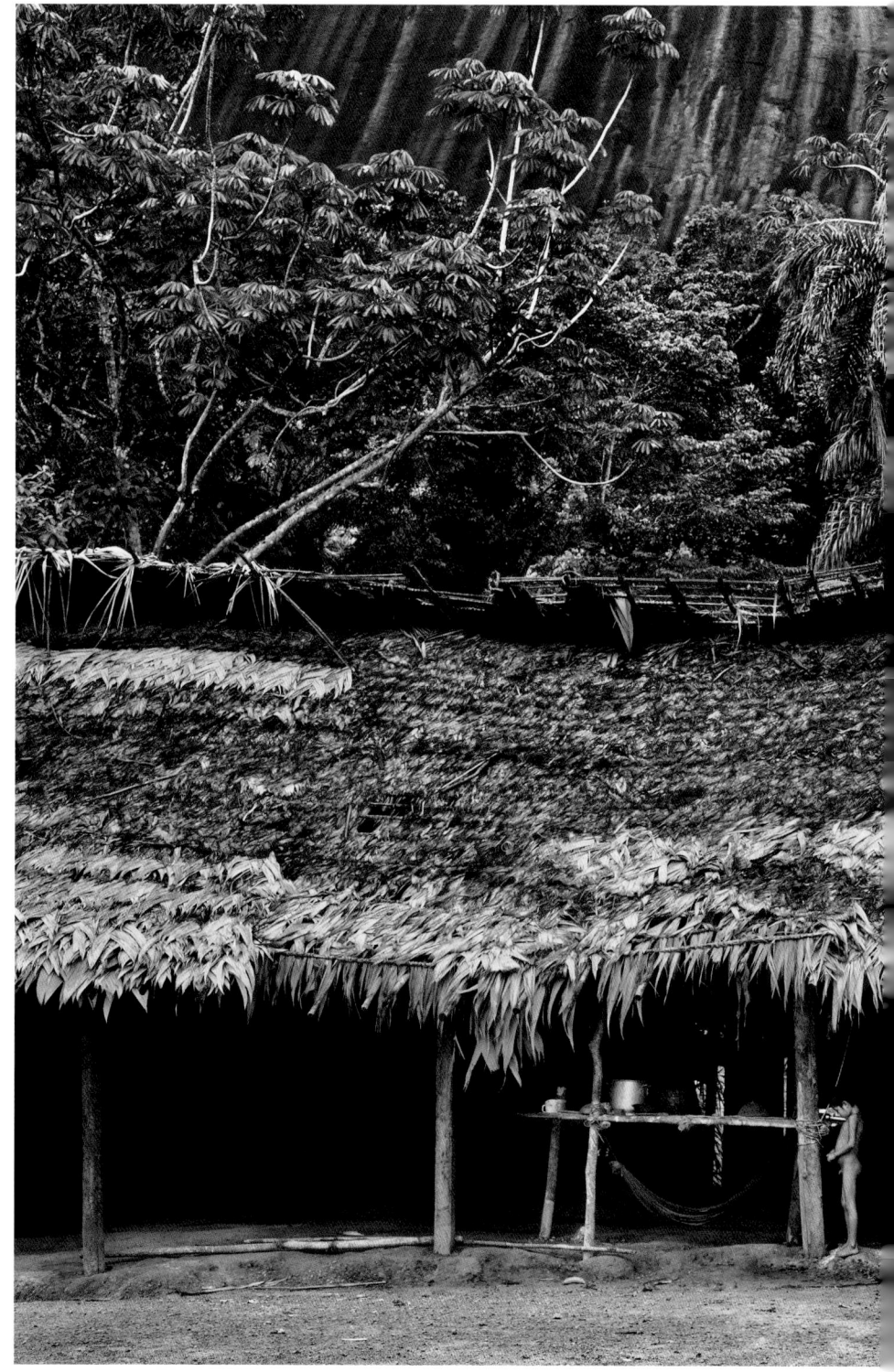

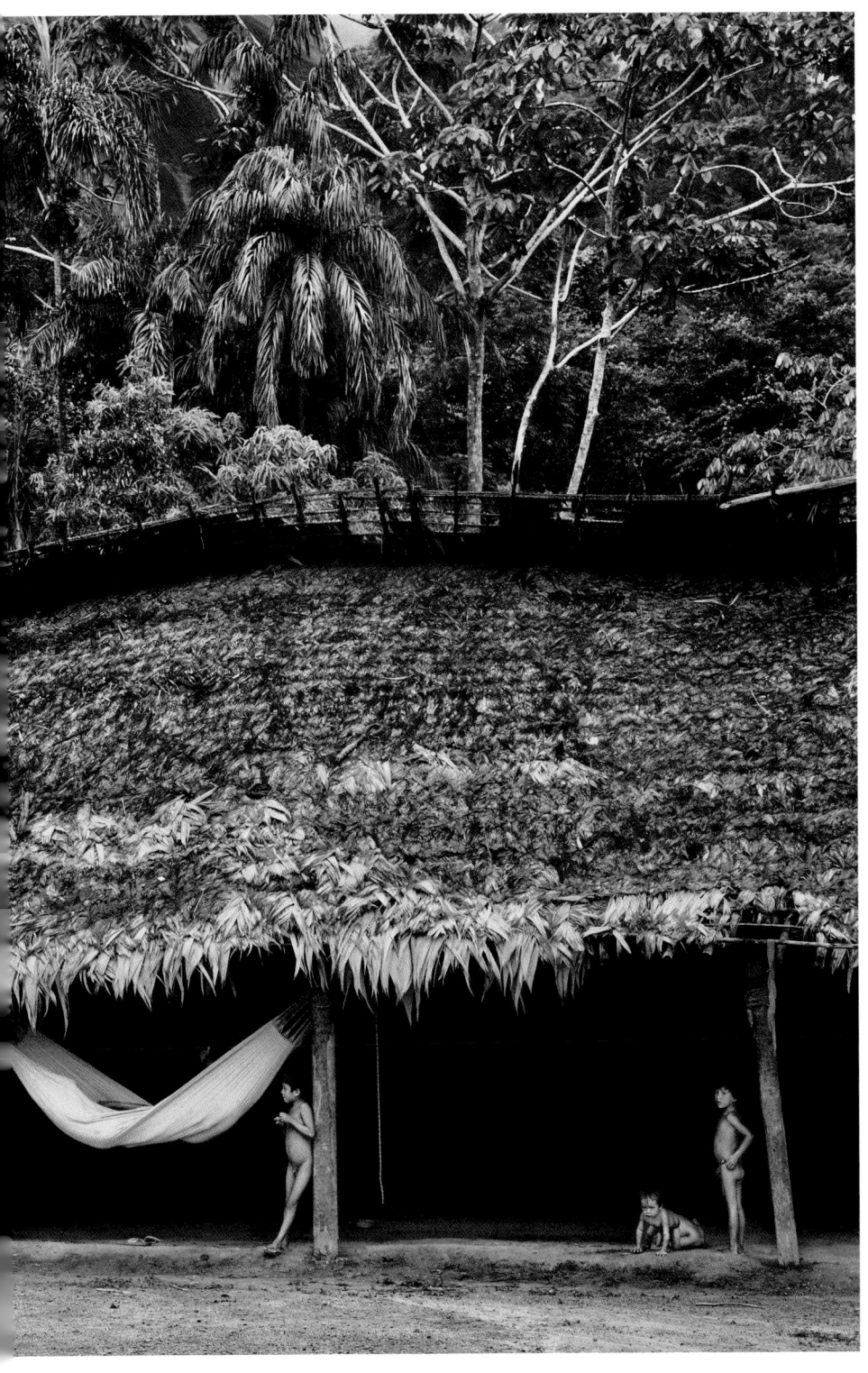

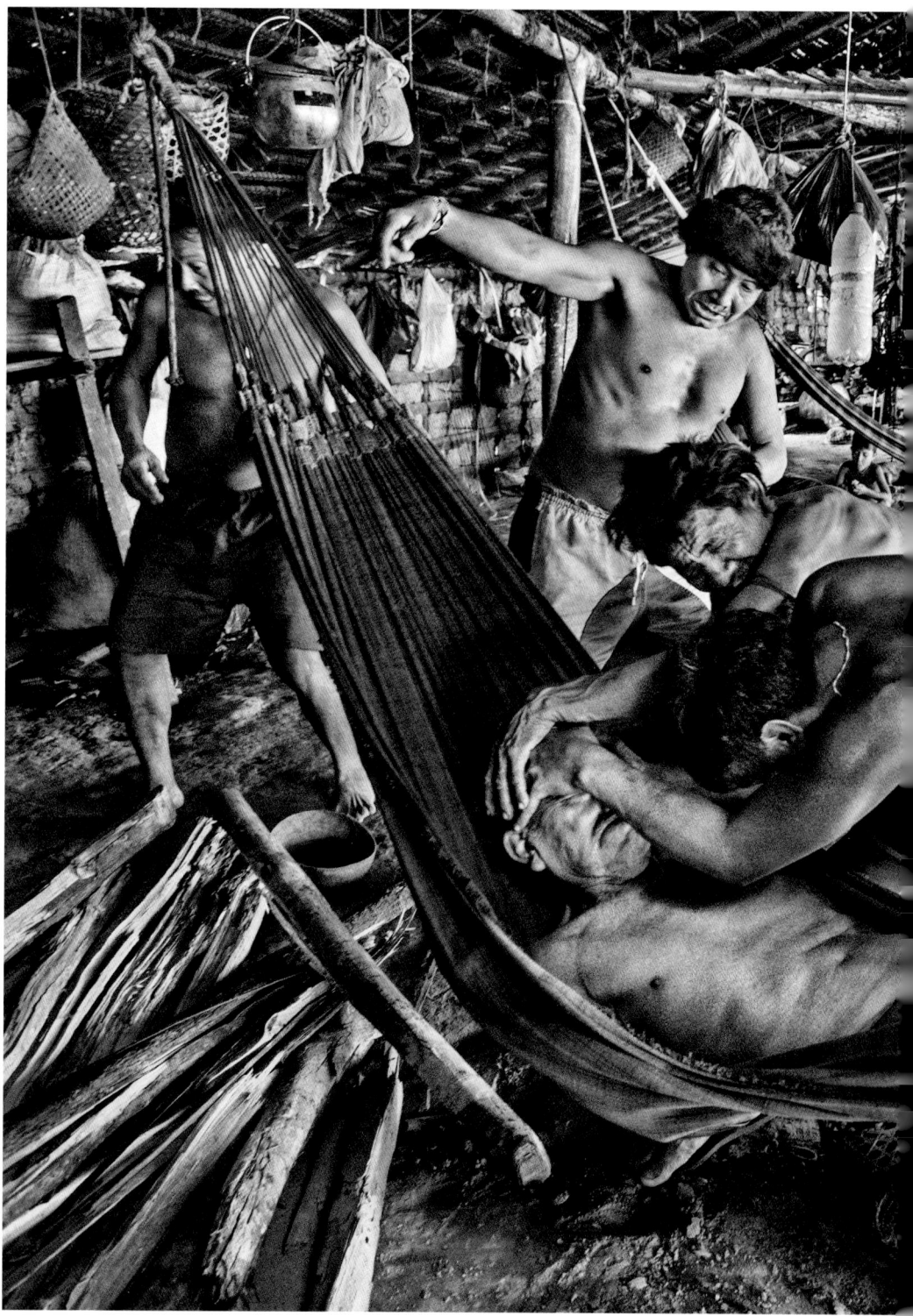

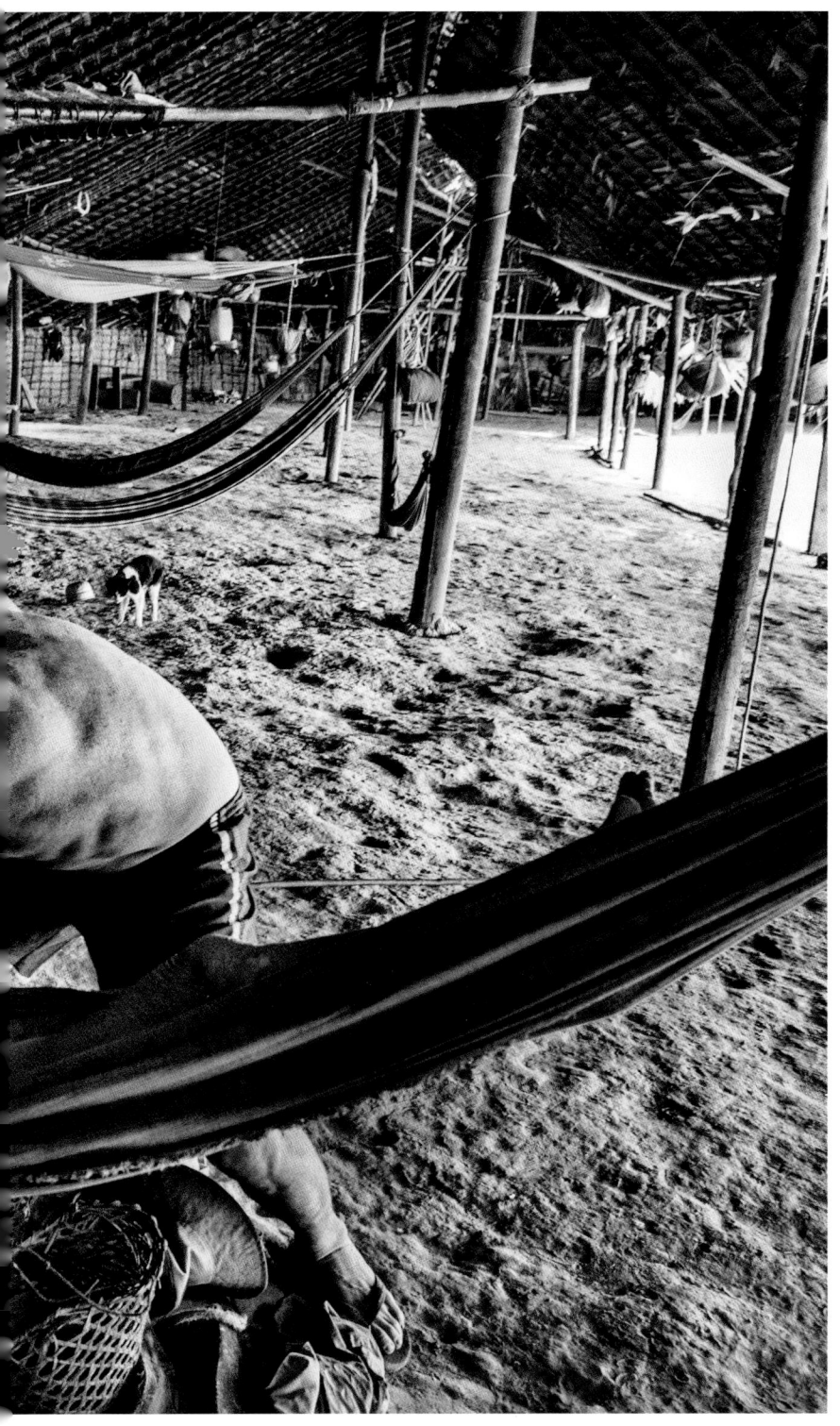

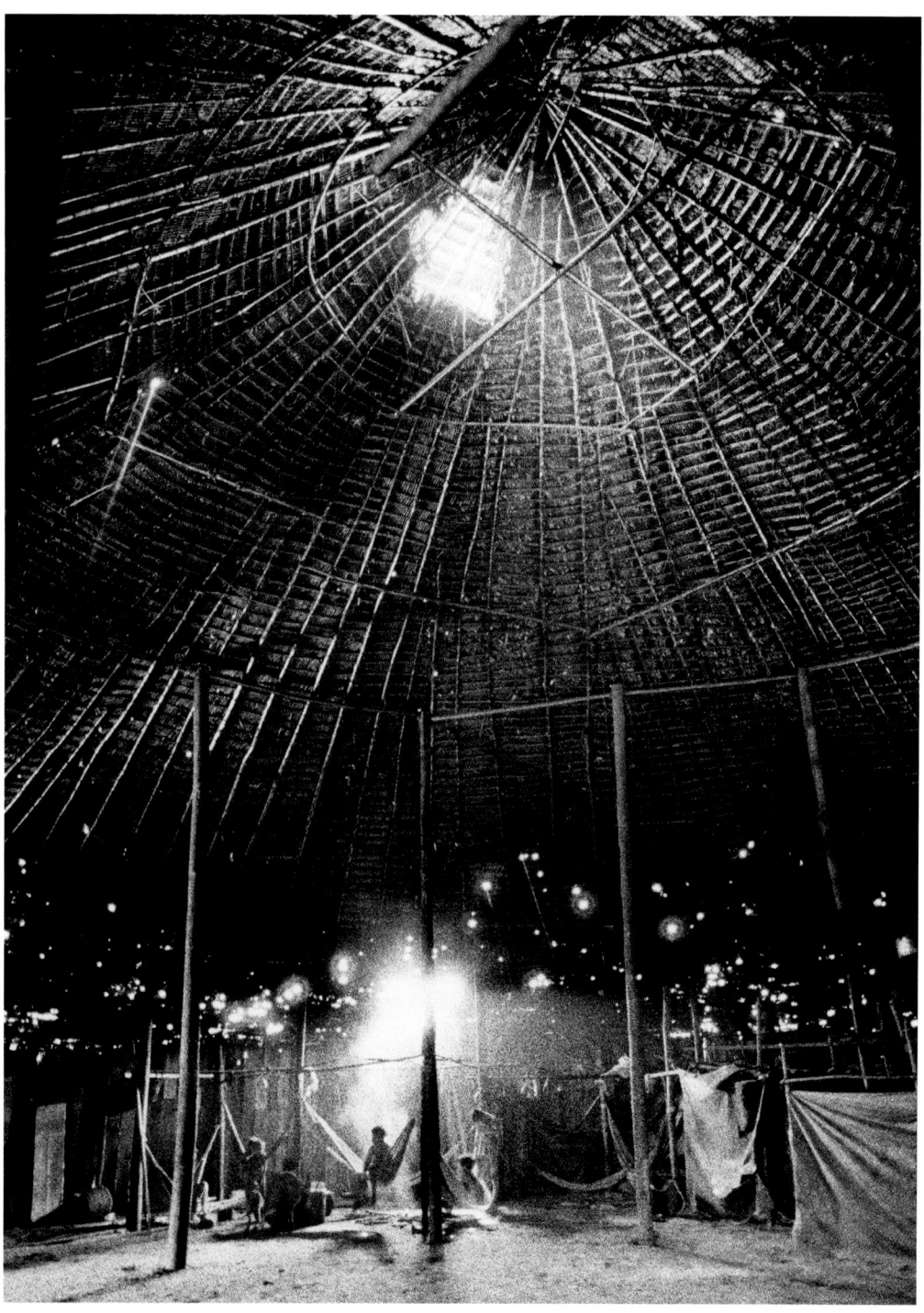

Opposite Communal *maloca* in Tototobi, where the houses' architecture differs from the communal houses in the Demini region: here, the entire central courtyard is covered by a roof, creating permanent darkness broken only by a few beams of light, producing an effect like a starry sky even during the day. Yanomami Indigenous Territory, state of Amazonas, 1998.

Pages 260/261 The women of the Watoriki community grate cassava to make large *beiju* cakes, which once baked, will be distributed to nourish visitors on their way home after the festivals. Yanomami Indigenous Territory, state of Amazonas, 2014.

Pages 262/263 Elisangela in her hammock in the Piaú community's main *maloca*. Yanomami Indigenous Territory, state of Amazonas, 2019.

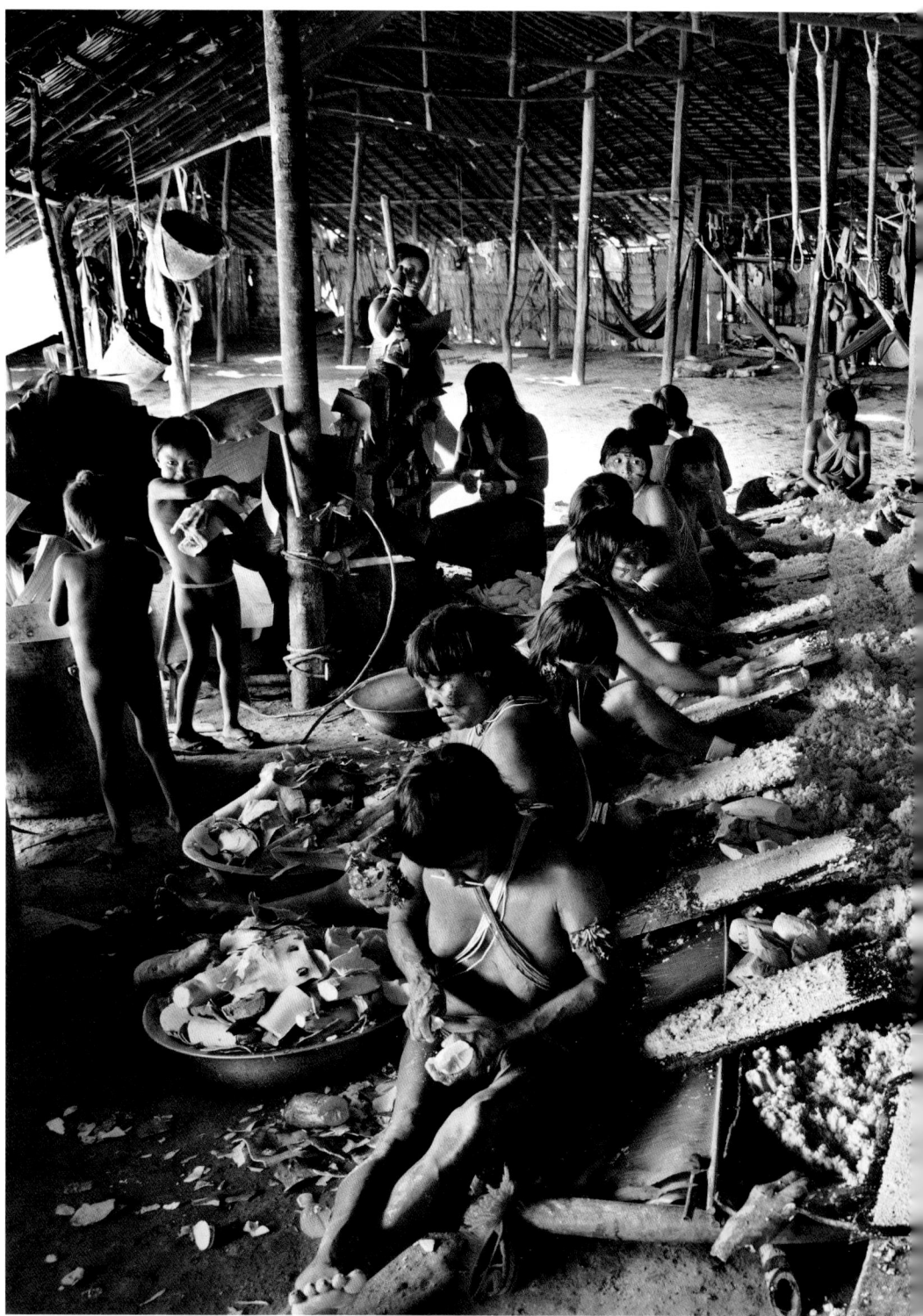

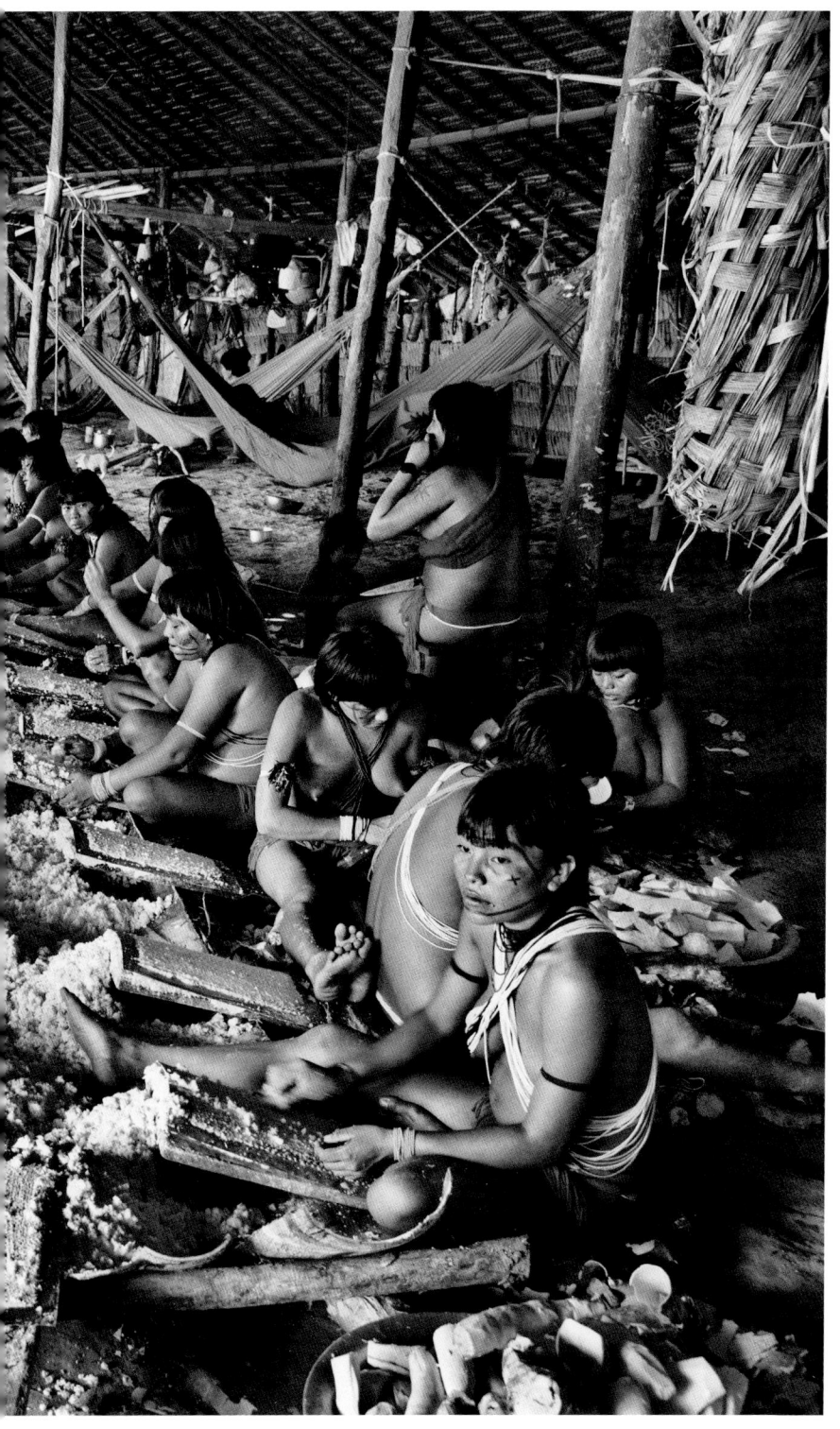

261

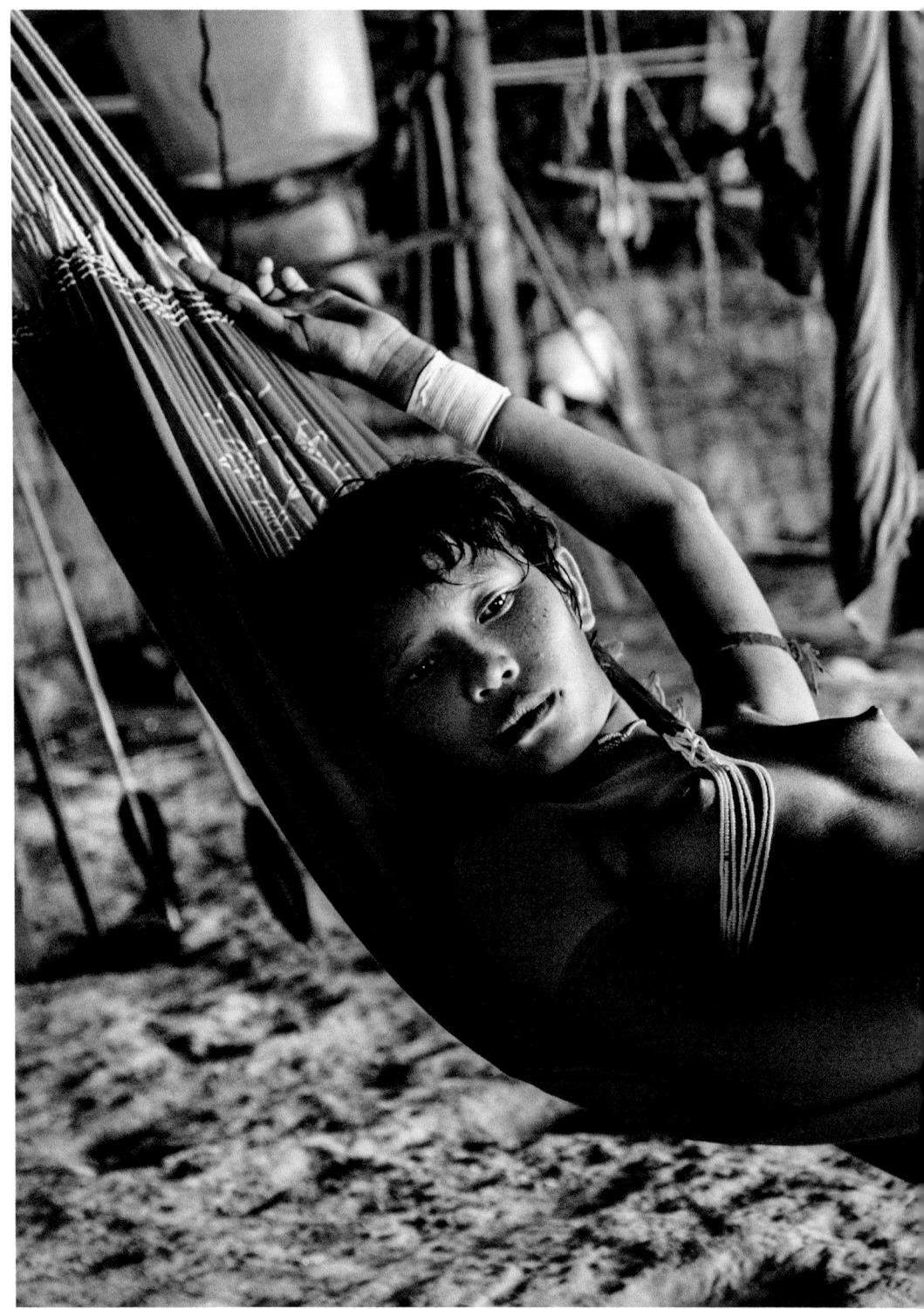

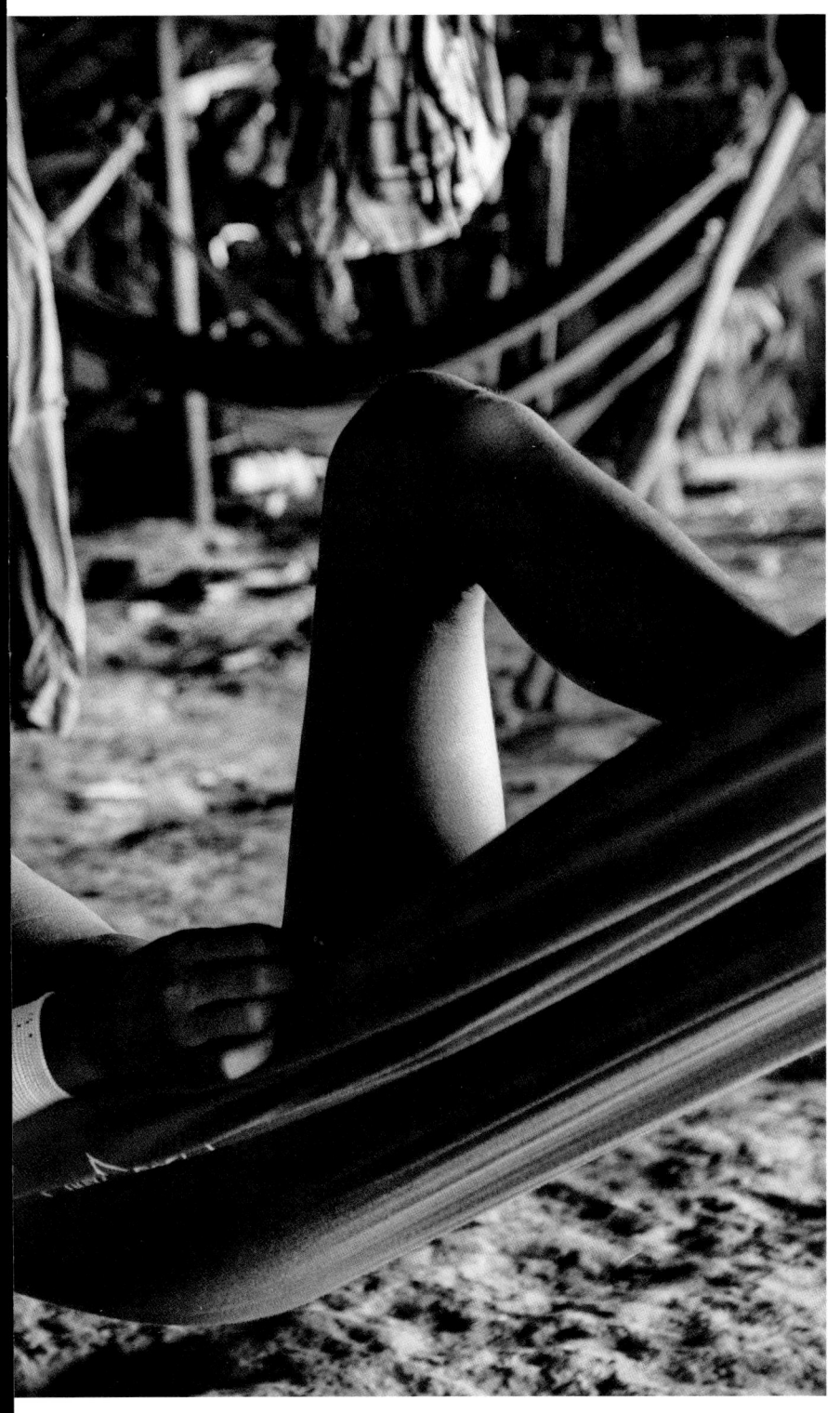

Opposite Edneuza, community of Piaú. The face adornments are typical of Yanomami groups: small pieces of wood used as piercings, called *pirimahiki*. The armbands are made with branches from plants tied to strings of beads, also used in making the necklaces worn across the chest. Yanomami Indigenous Territory, state of Amazonas, 2019.

Pages 266/267 Josane (foreground) and Aldeni, residents of communities in the Demini River region. Josane lives in the village of Ponto Quebrado, and Aldeni in the community of Watoriki. Yanomami Indigenous Territory, state of Amazonas, 2014.

Pages 268/269 Moko dressed for a festival. Community of Tototobi. Yanomami Indigenous Territory, state of Amazonas, 1998.

Pages 270/271 Mother and infant in a hammock. Community of Surucucu. Yanomami Indigenous Territory, state of Roraima, 1998.

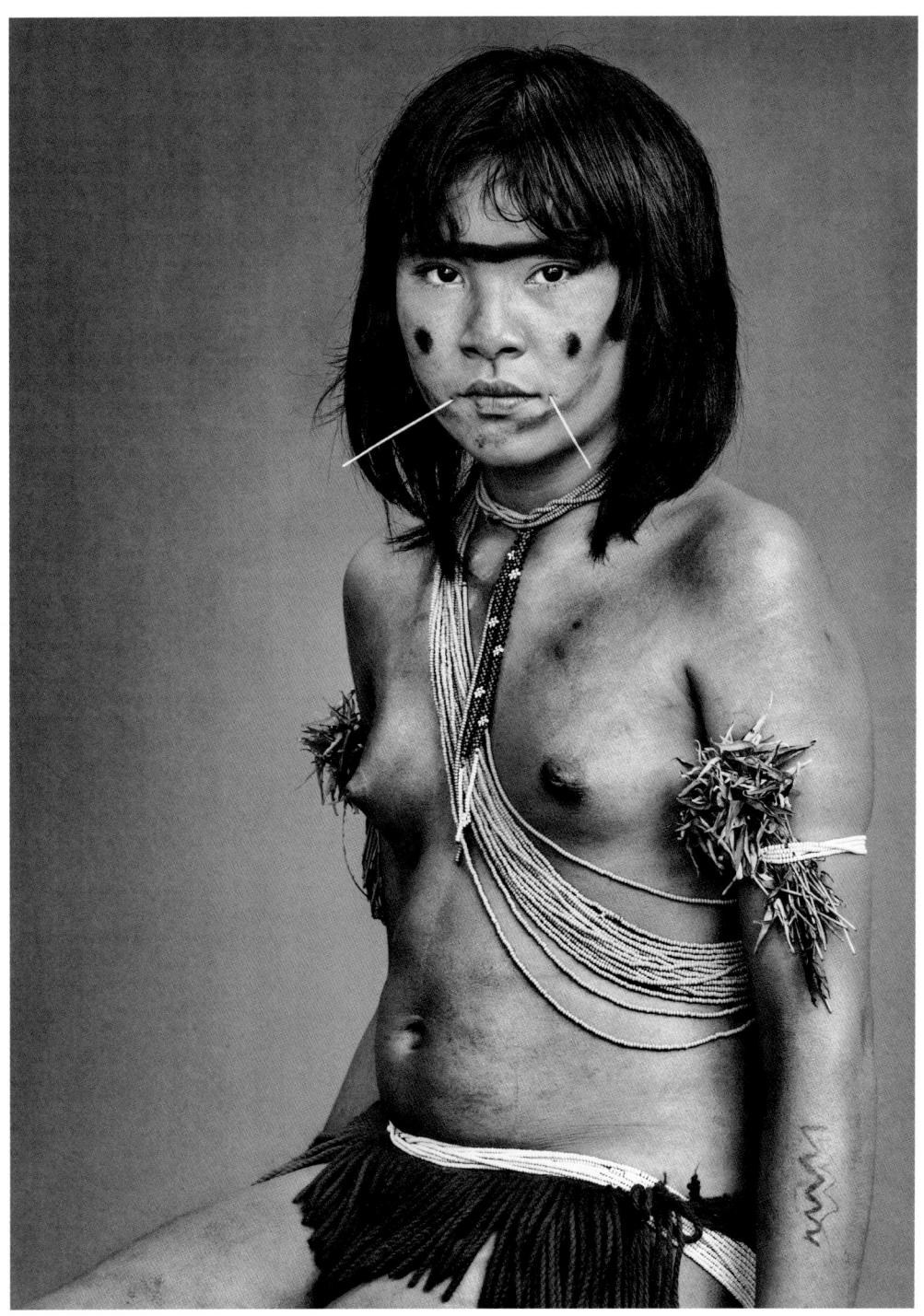

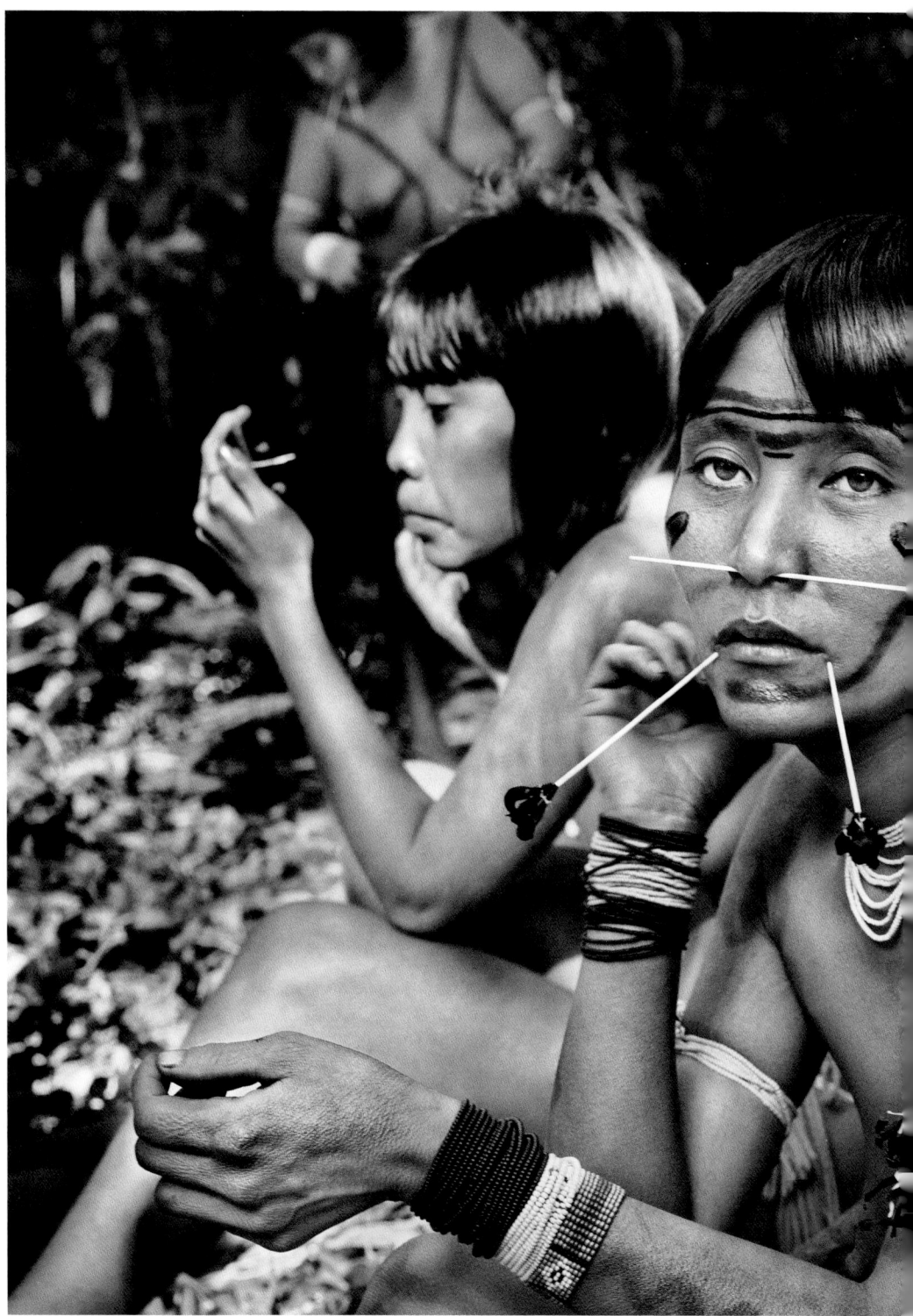

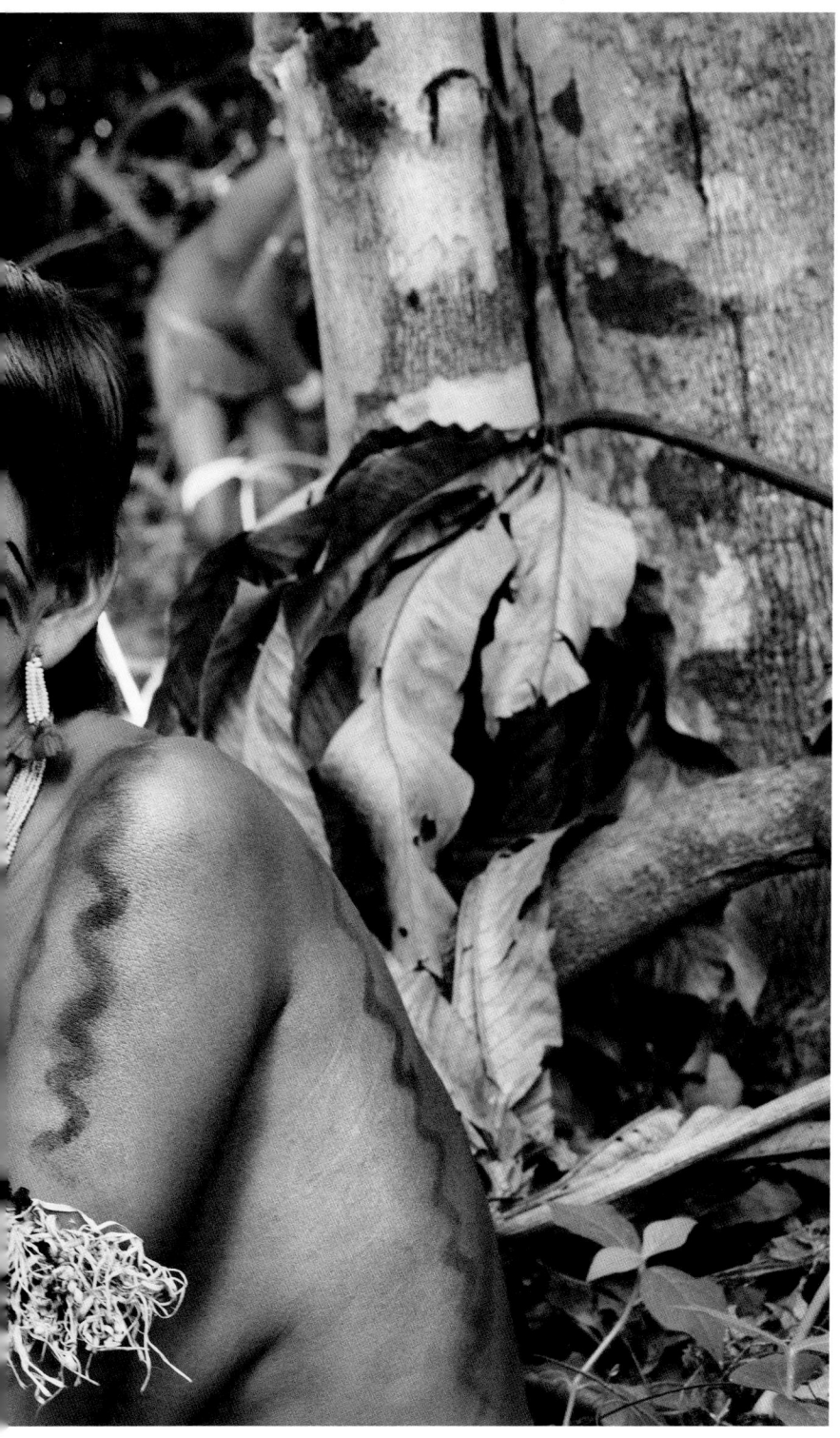

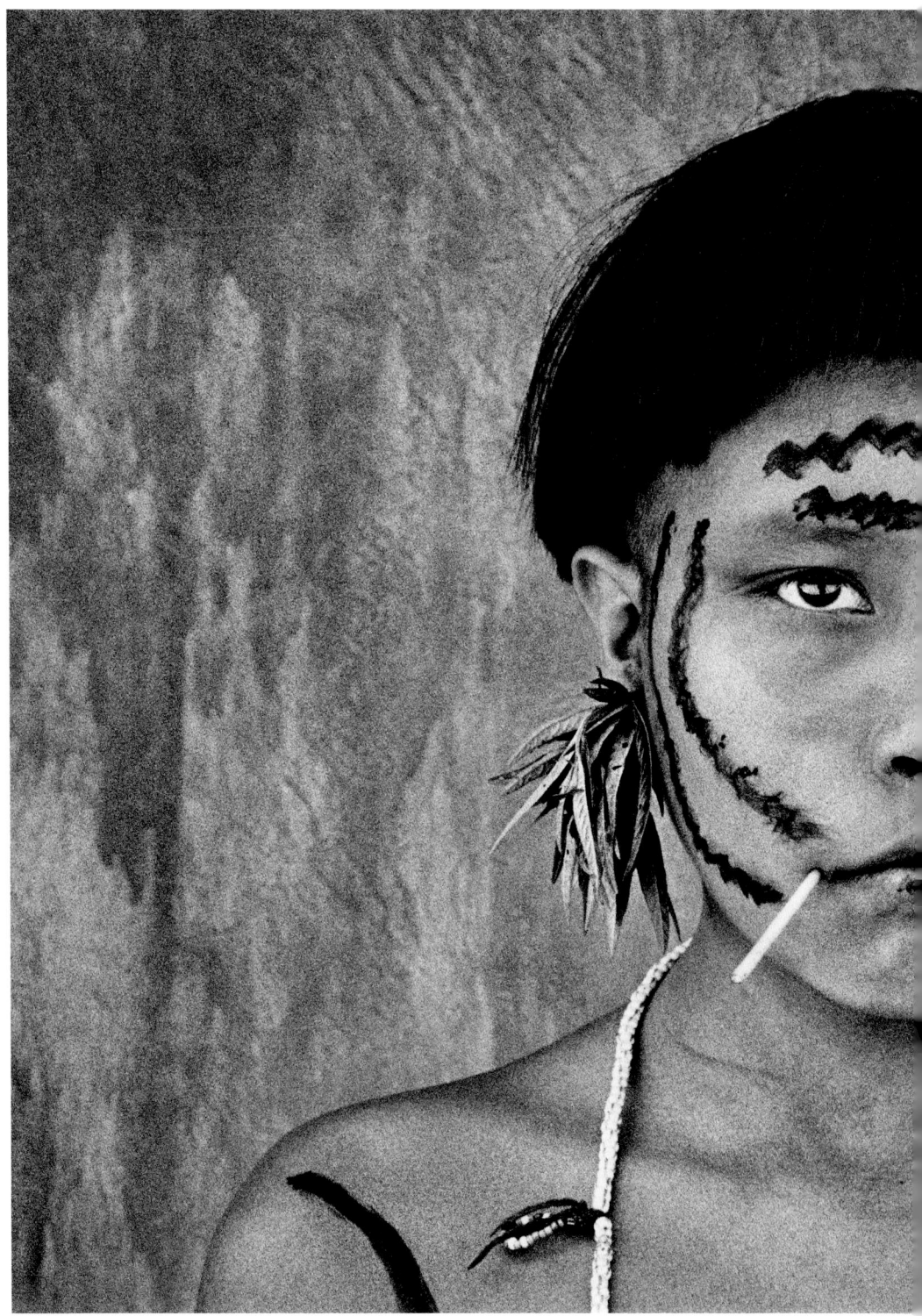

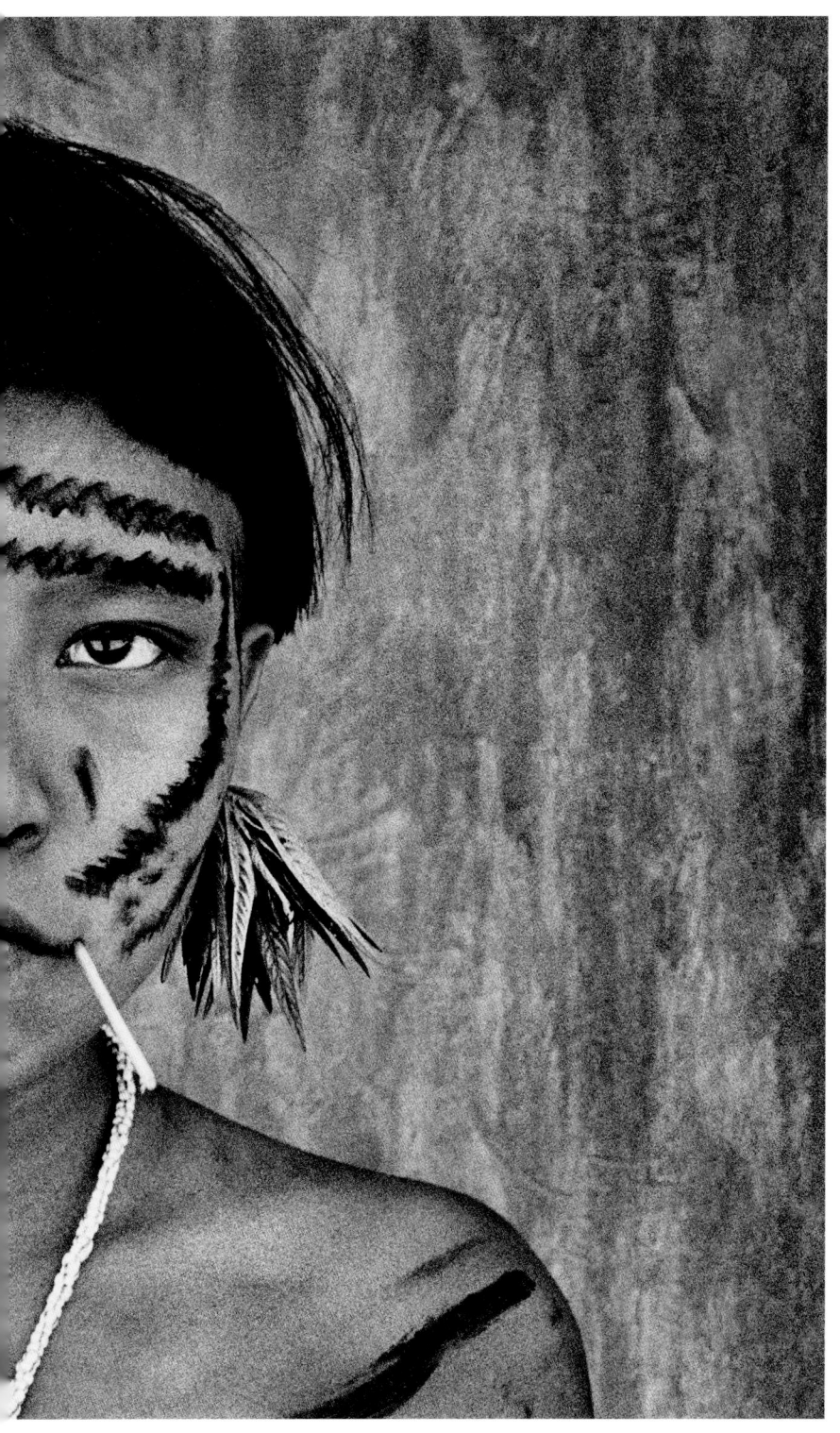

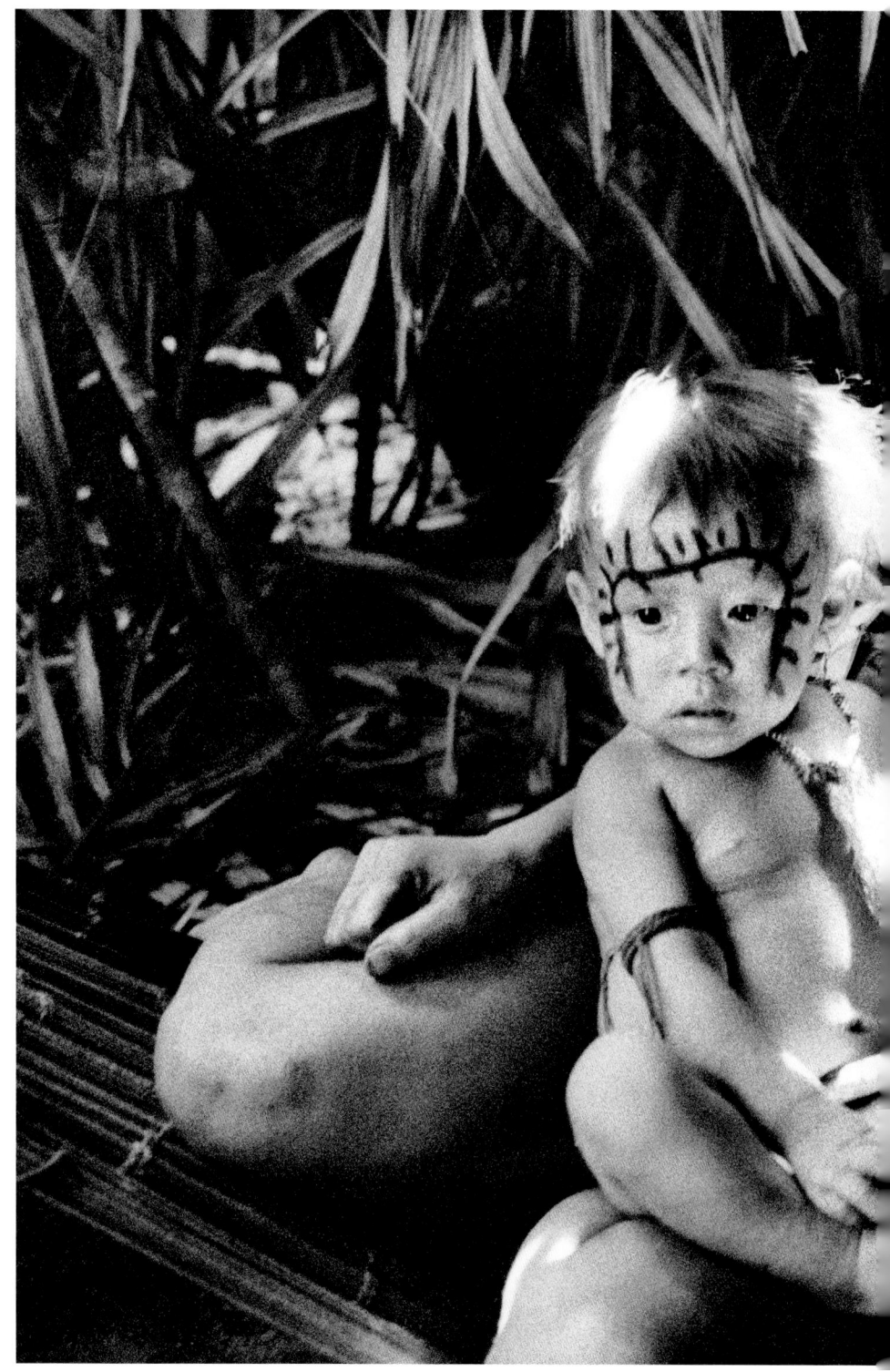

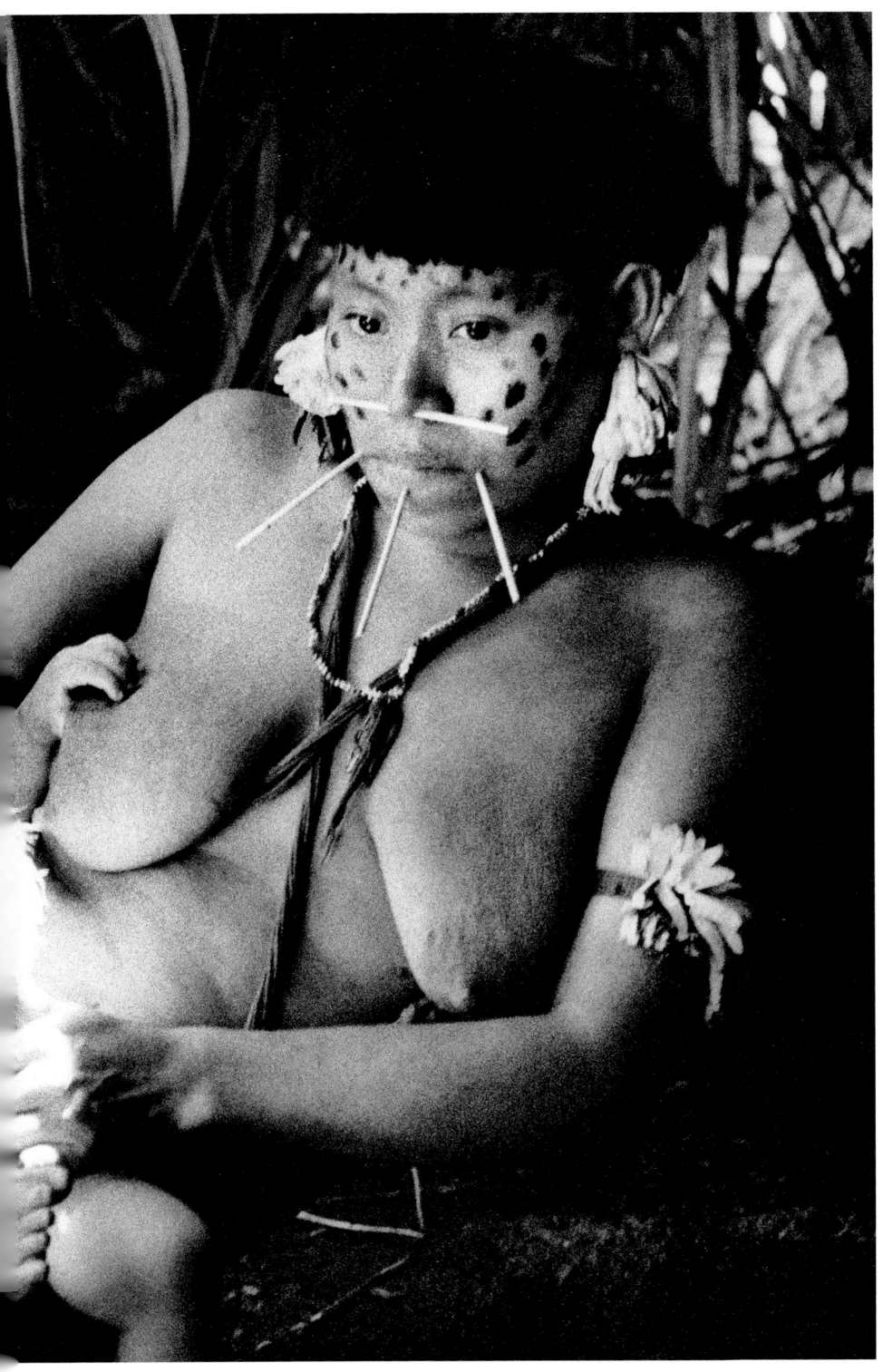

Opposite Ricardo, community of Piaú. Yanomami Indigenous Territory, state of Amazonas, 2019.

Pages 274/275 Residents of Watoriki—a community in the Demini region, founded by leader Davi Kopenawa Yanomami—walk past the large kapok (*Ceiba pentandra*), a sacred tree decorated with paintings, near the main *maloca*. Yanomami Indigenous Territory, state of Amazonas, 2014.

Pages 276/277 Shaman Ângelo Barcelos (Koparihewë, which means "Head of Song" or "Voice of Nature"), from the community of Maturacá, interacts with *Xapiri* spirits in visions during an ascent to Pico da Neblina, the highest mountain in Brazil. For the Yanomami, it is a sacred place called *Yaripo*. Tied to his arms are two feather arrangements typical of shamans, in addition to the crown of white bird feathers (men and shamans put beeswax in their hair and then stick these downy feathers to it). Yanomami Indigenous Territory, state of Amazonas, 2014.

Pages 278/279 Yanomami from the community of Maturacá, looking at *Yaripo*, the summit of Pico da Neblina. The peak is covered by the clouds that give it its name (Portuguese for "Mist Peak"). They are pausing on their way to the summit of Brazil's highest mountain. Yanomami Indigenous Territory, state of Amazonas, 2014.

Pages 280/281 Two men engaging in *waymou* dialogue in the central courtyard of the community of Watoriki. The language is very difficult to understand, even for the most learned linguists. A local dignitary is receiving a visitor during a celebration; they face each other, squatting, and speak at flabbergasting speed. The visitor relates his adventures, the events of his several days of journeying, and the host offers information about his village, in words that are 2,000 years old, words from the beginnings of this language that emerged in the highlands of the Parima mountains. The ring-shaped *maloca* was built near a hill formed by a vast rock that thrust out of the Earth. Yanomami Indigenous Territory, state of Amazonas, 2014.

Pages 282/283 The community of Watoriki is surrounded by lush forest, enriched by nearby fruit-bearing species and towered over by the large dark rock. Yanomami Indigenous Territory, state of Amazonas, 2014.

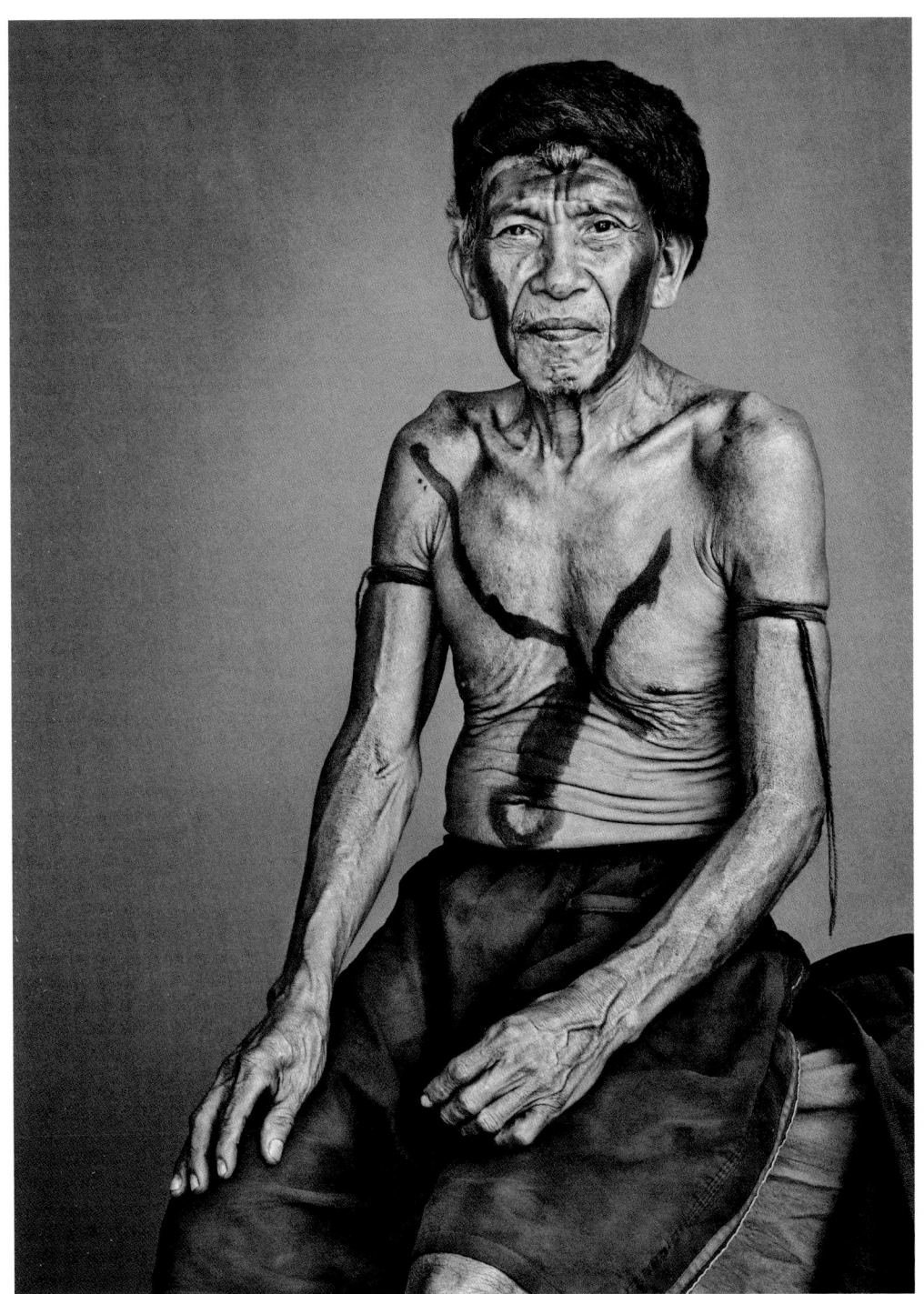

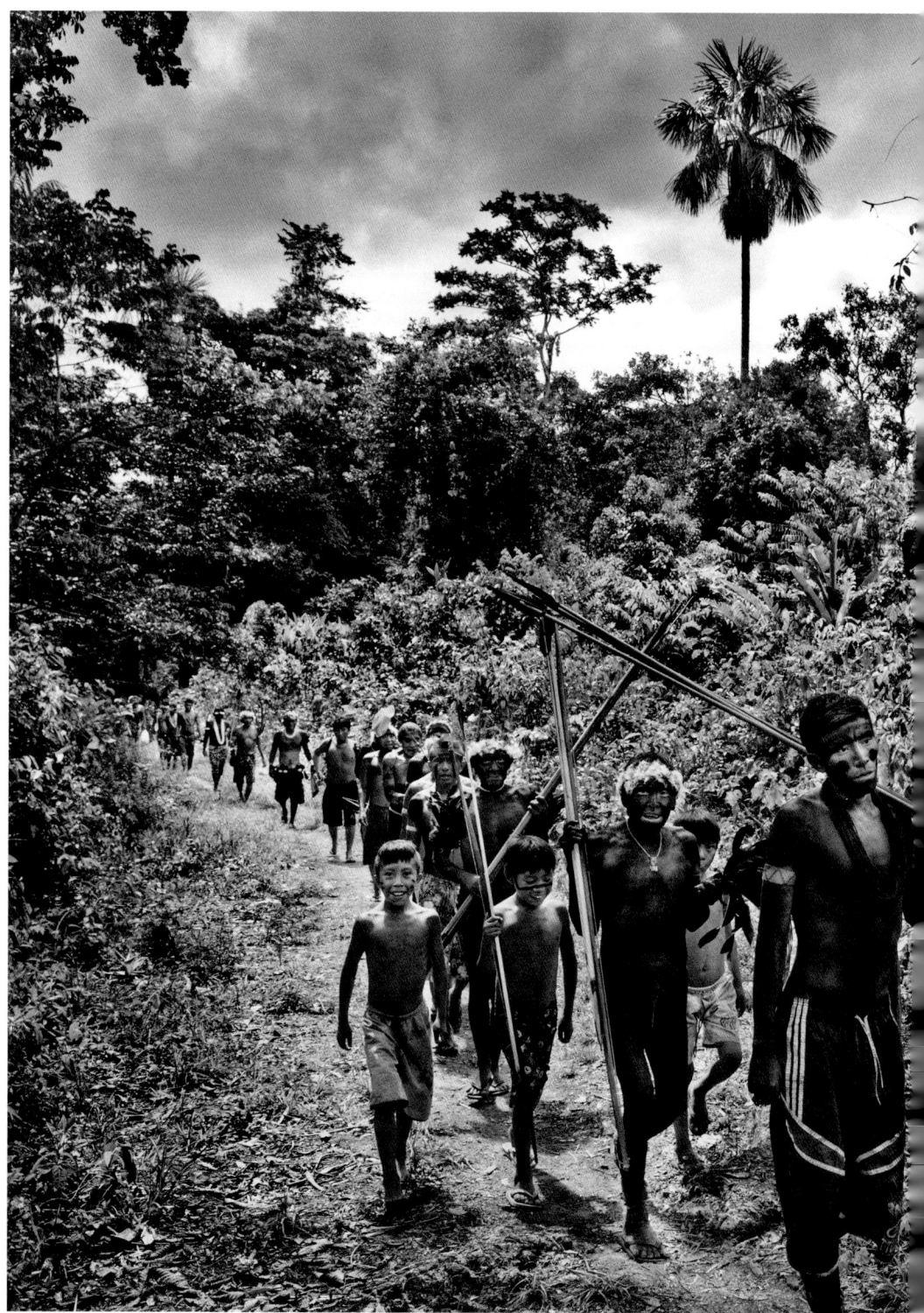

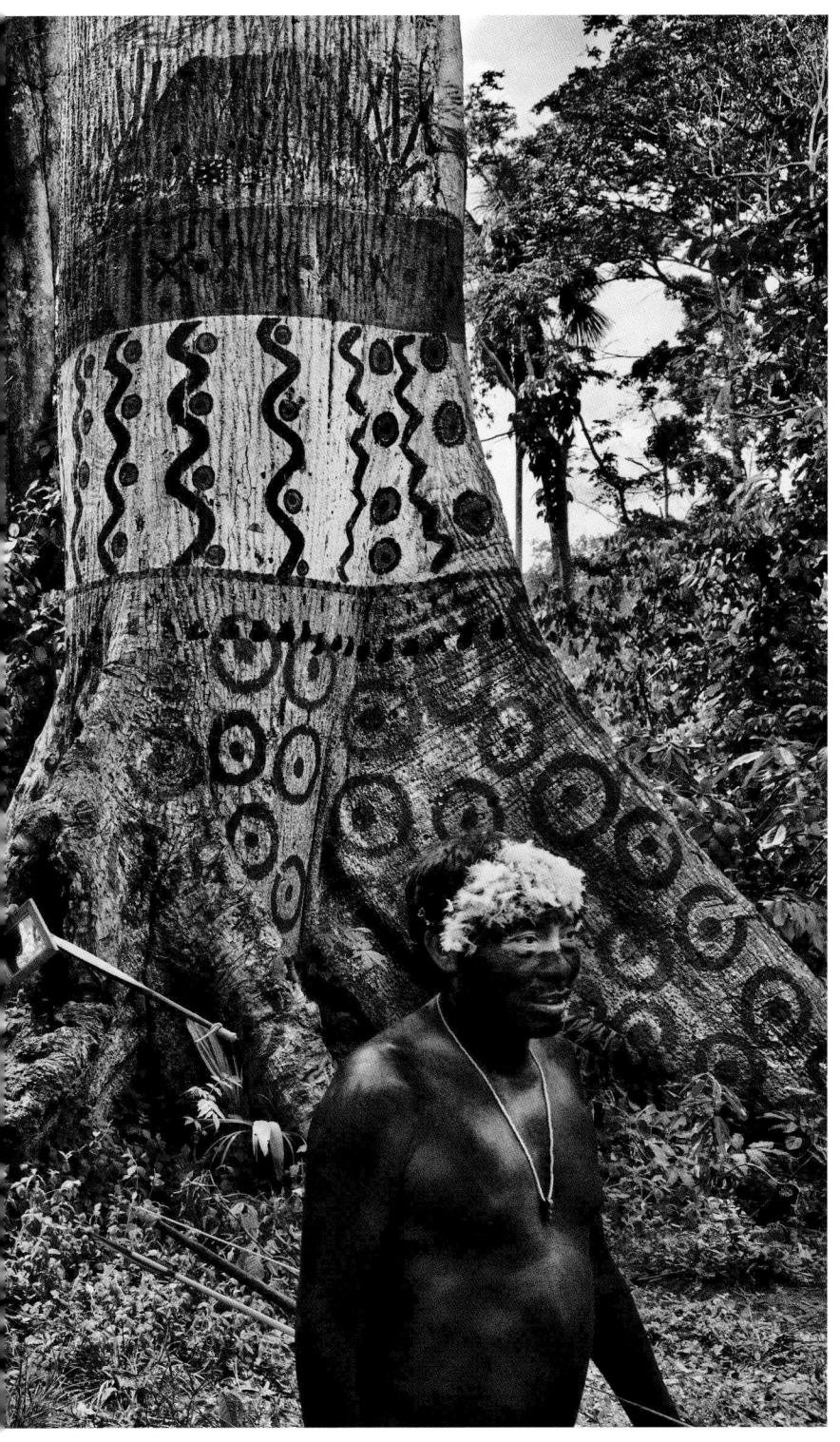

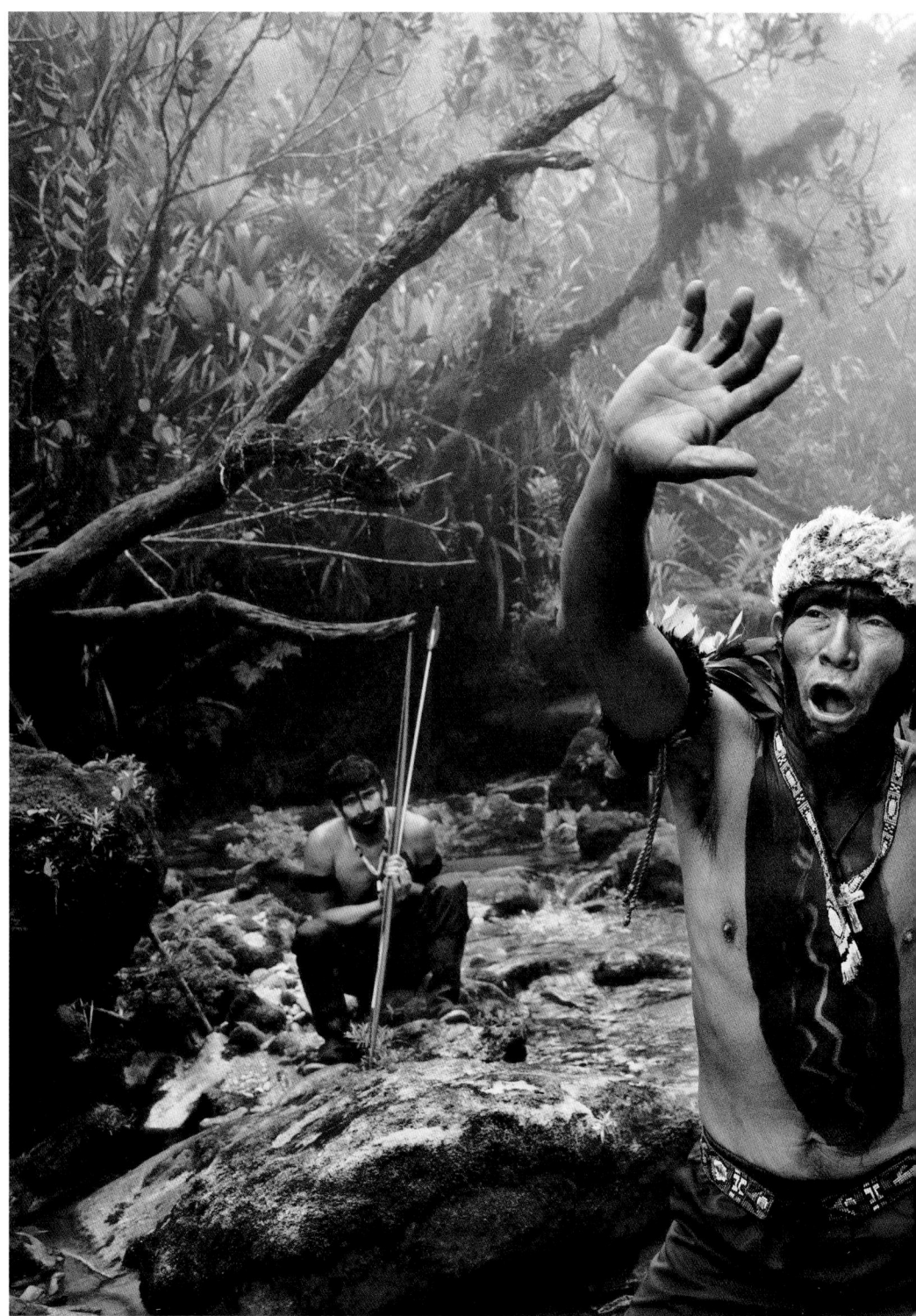

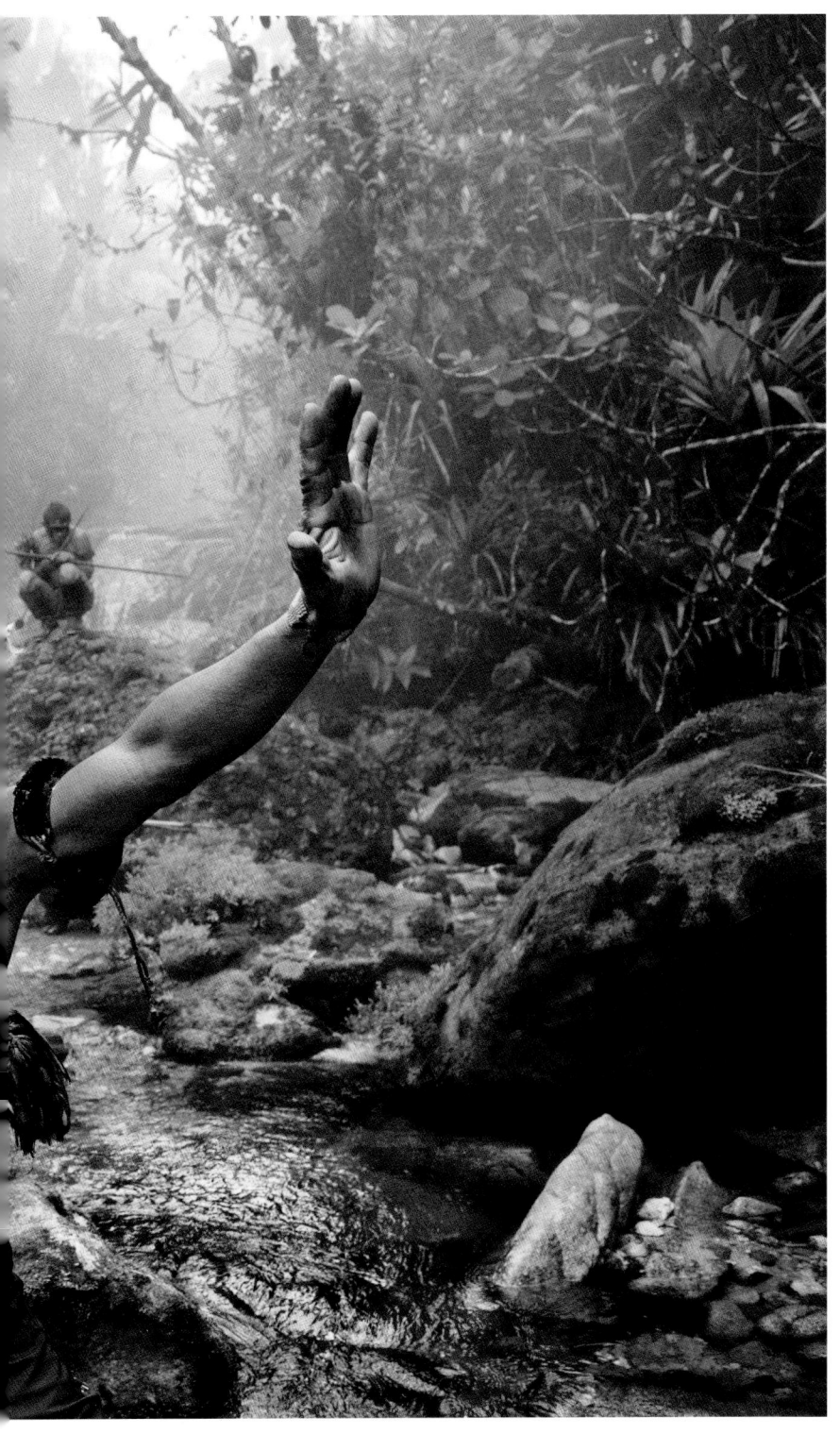

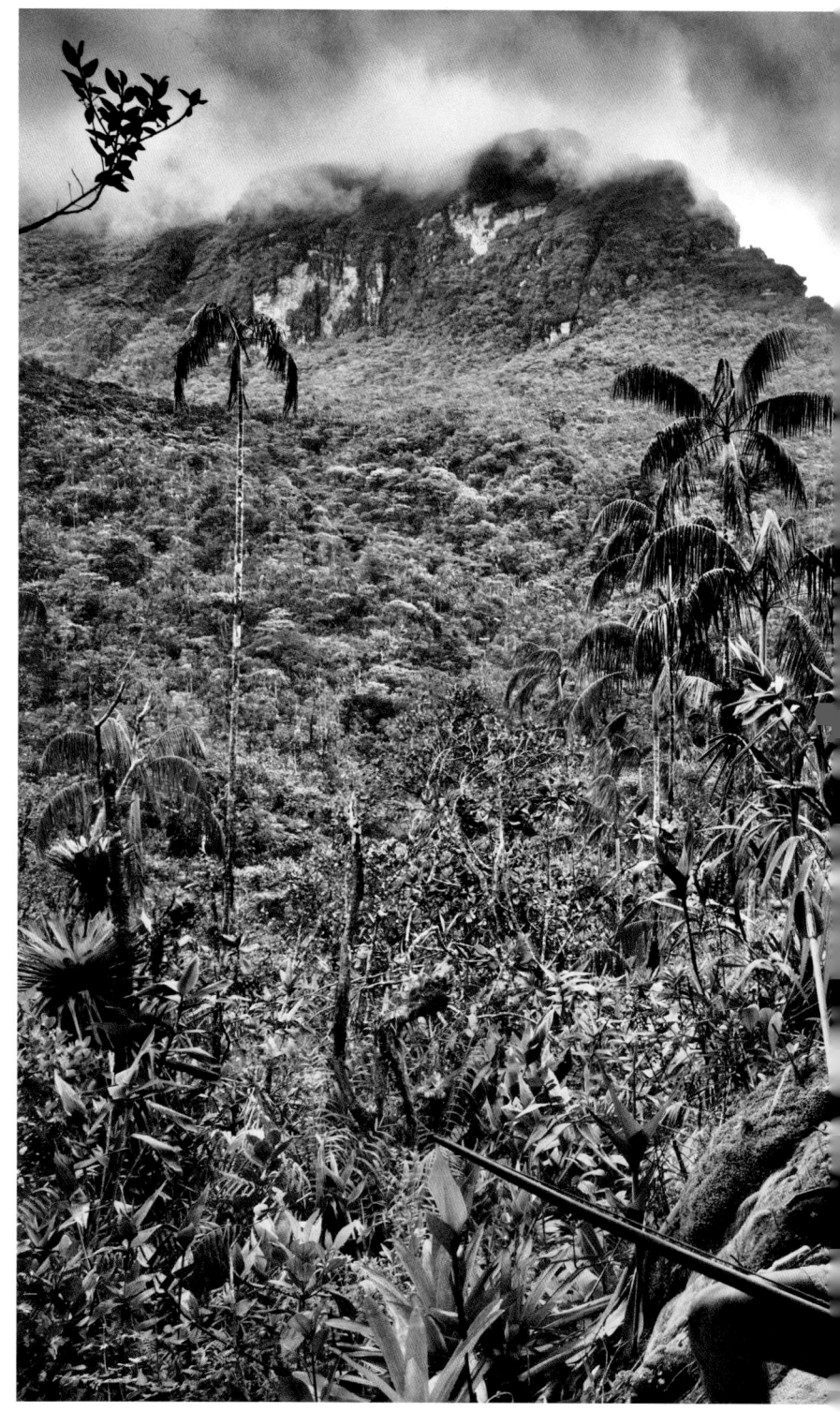

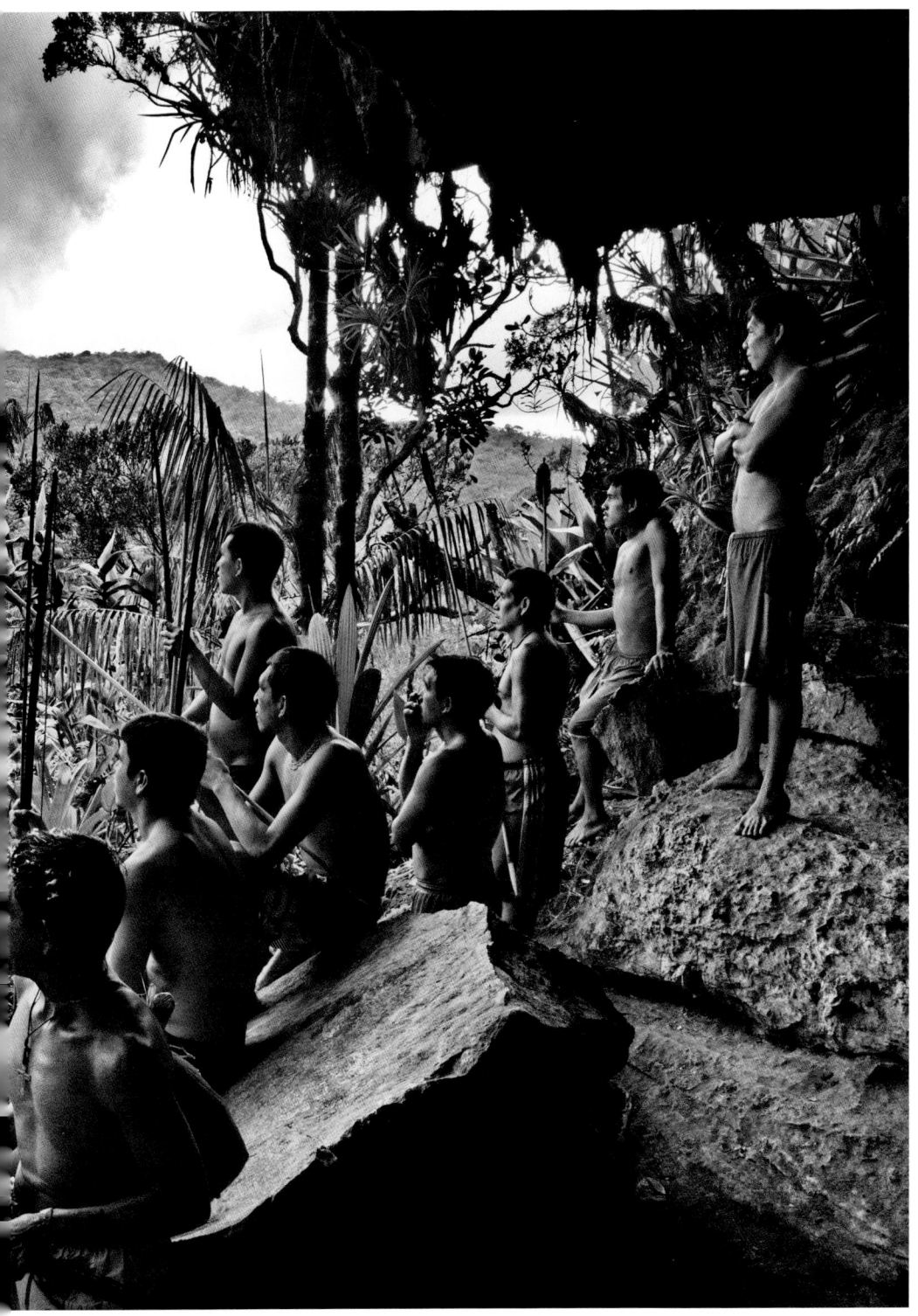

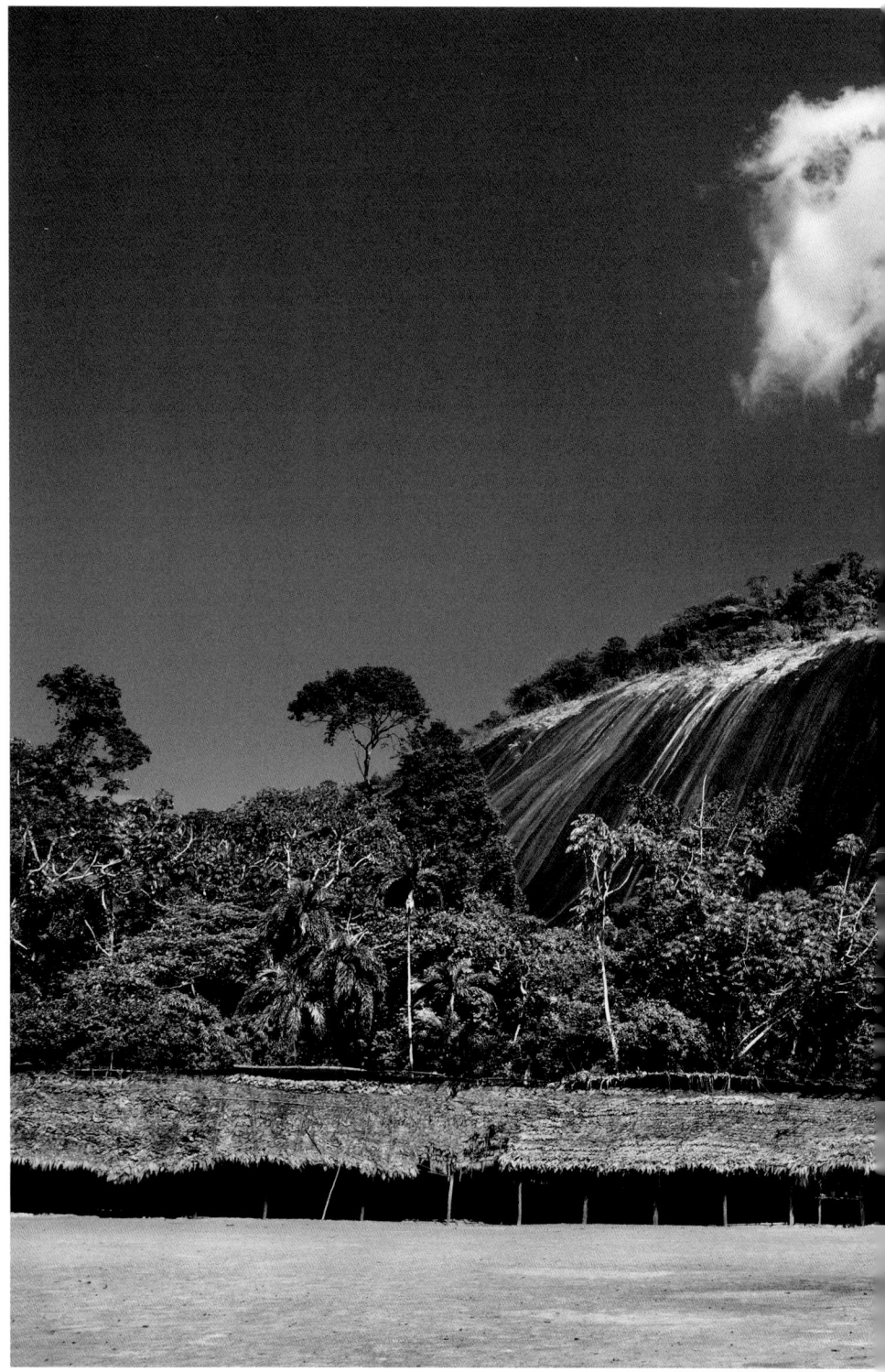

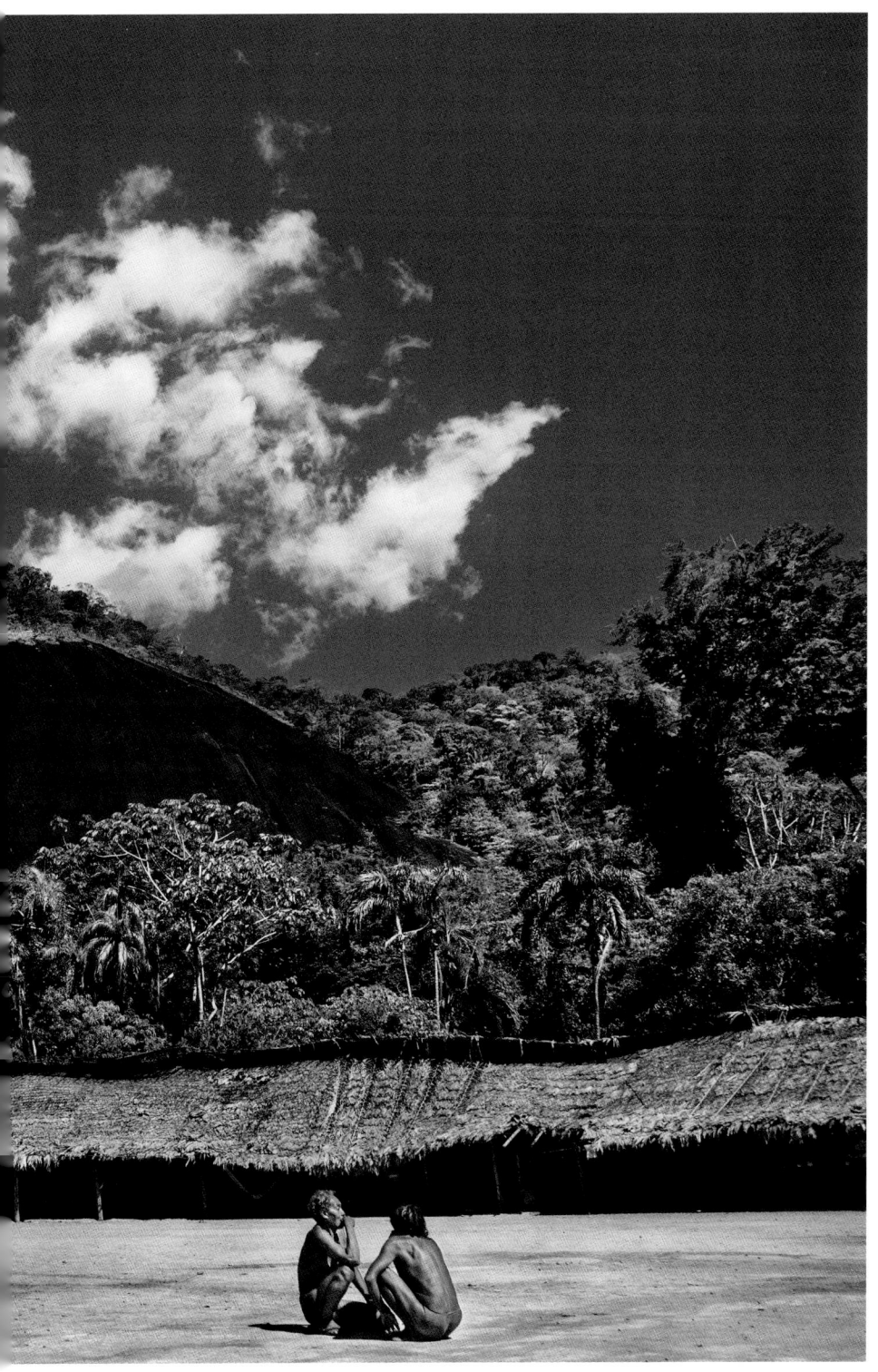

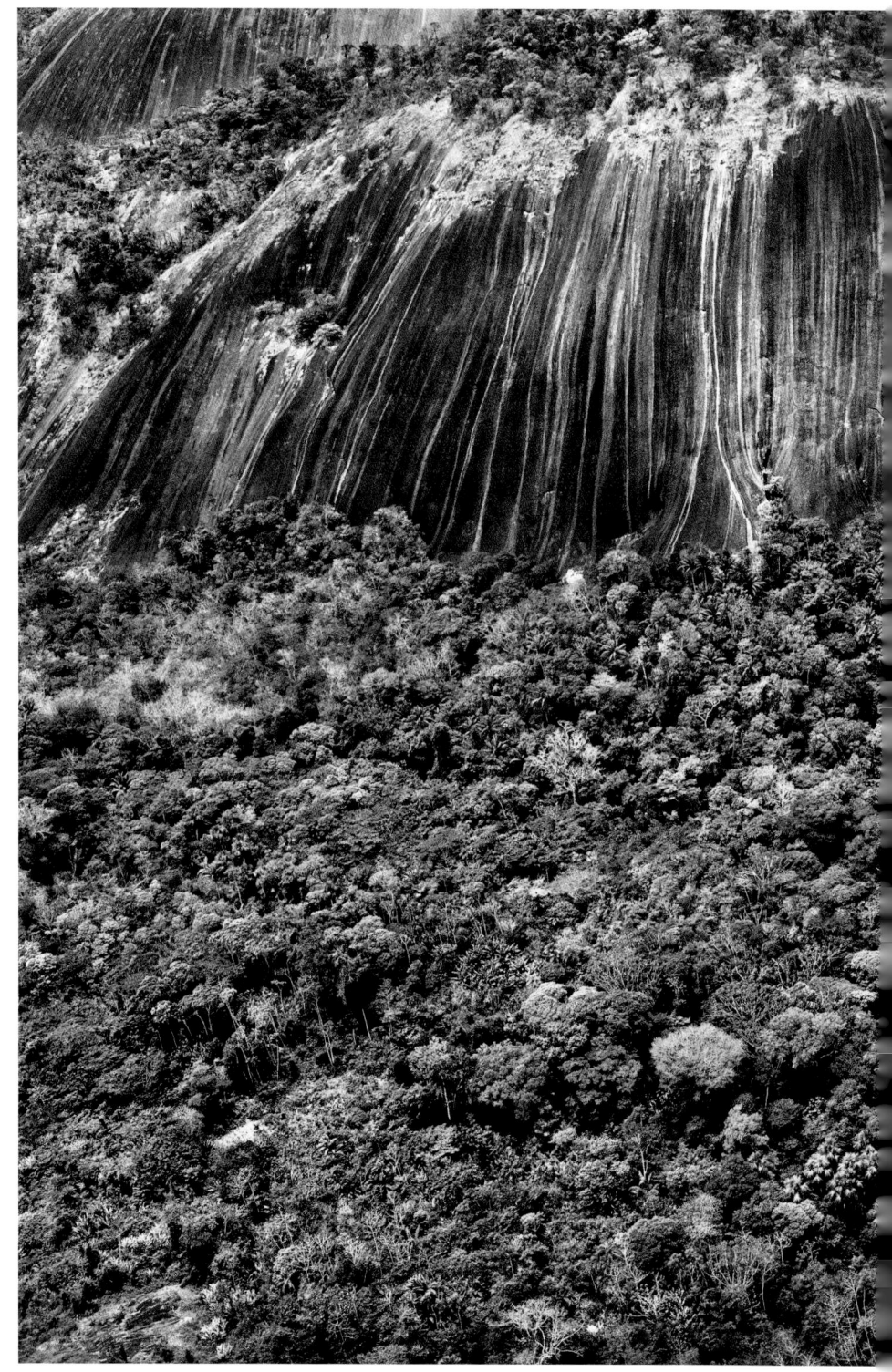

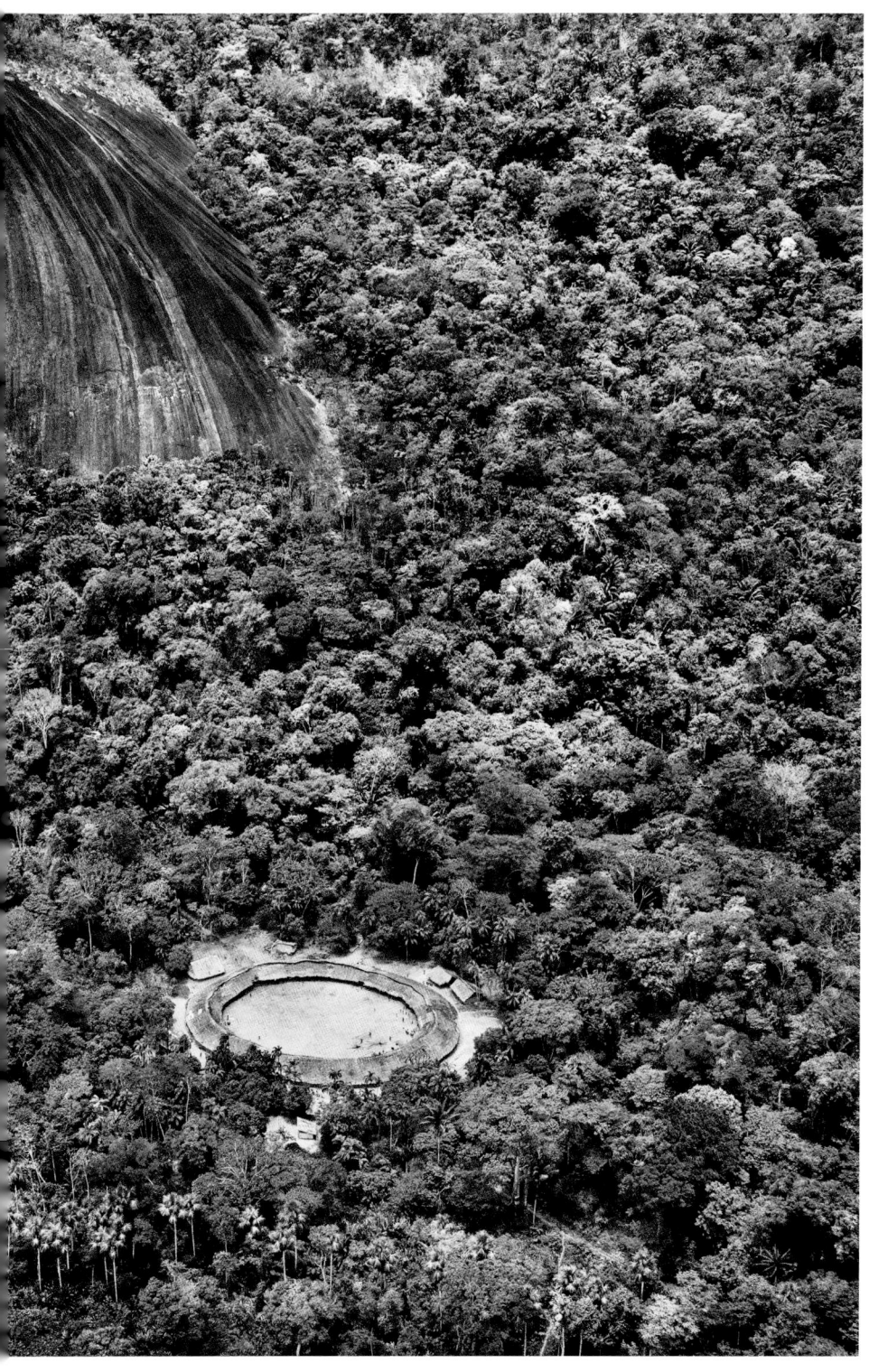

FORESTS

For centuries after Portugal colonized Brazil, the Amazon rainforest was nicknamed the Green Hell, an impenetrable rain-sodden jungle that offered only danger to outsiders. Those who survived to tell their story gained fame, from the Spanish conquistador Francisco de Orellana and the German explorer Alexander von Humboldt to Theodore Roosevelt and Marshal Cândido Rondon, a Brazilian army cartographer in the last century who is considered the greatest protector of indigenous peoples in Brazil. But many expeditions, above all those hoping to find gold in the mythical lost city of El Dorado, never returned. Some may have been killed by hostile native tribes or died of snake bites or starvation, but a surprisingly large number of explorers chose to settle down with indigenous tribes and share their bucolic way of life.

Today, the rainforest is viewed more benignly, sometimes even romantically, as the Green Paradise, more often simply as an extraordinary treasure of nature, one with the planet's largest concentration of botanical species, including some 16,000 species of trees and innumerable plants with remarkable medicinal potential. Further, this unparalleled concentration of vegetation absorbs greenhouse gases and breathes out oxygen. It also offers a traditionally secure home to hundreds of indigenous tribes, some of whom have never had contact with the outside world.

Instead of fear, then, the Amazon now evokes marvel and, for most people, a wish to protect it and its native inhabitants from deforestation, fires, illegal logging and mining, and "imported" diseases.

To spend time in the forest, above all in the company of indigenous tribespeople, is to experience it still another way. For a start, the undergrowth is all embracing. Thick trunks thrust their way through creepers towards the canopy, on their way spinning off branches to intertwine with those of other trees, offering an aerial playground for the forest's 15 species of monkeys. The appeal of the canopy is its access to the sun. On the ground, except where a fallen tree has opened a small glade, the forest is dark, with barely visible footpaths opened by natives on their hunting and fishing outings. The ground is soft with fallen leaves and branches and moist with the all too frequent rain.

Rivers provide the indigenous communities with essential high protein food, but the tribes also know to keep a safe distance from natural floodplains which are invaded by major rivers up to a distance of 100 kilometers (60 miles) during the high water season. Much of this water originates as melted snow and rain in the Andes and swells the rivers as it reaches the lowlands between April and June. The resulting flooding is a constant reminder that most of the Amazon basin was once under the sea. That accounts for the sandy quality of the soil of the forest, which depends on the nutrients of dead leaves for sustenance. It also explains why, lacking the roots of trees and natural nutrients, deforested land is quickly exposed to erosion and loss of soil quality.

Native tribespeople have an extraordinary talent for moving quickly through the undergrowth, sometimes walking for several days and sleeping in the forest in order to visit relatives in a distant village. But traveling by river offers an easier means of transport. Riverboats act like buses on the Amazon and larger rivers, but going upstream on a smaller tributary often involves switching to a dugout with an outboard motor that can handle rapids. Then if a waterfall appears, those on board quickly close ranks to carry the canoe to a safer spot upriver. To voyage through the rainforest is a thrill and a privilege, but it is also always a challenge.

Pages 286/287 Imeri mountain range, the highest region of Brazil. Yanomami Indigenous Territory, municipality of São Gabriel da Cachoeira, state of Amazonas, 2018.

Pages 288/289 São Gabriel da Cachoeira, Yanomami Indigenous Territory, near the Maru River, state of Amazonas, 2018.

Pages 290/291 View of one of the peaks of the Imeri mountain range, in the Maturacá region. Yanomami Indigenous Territory, state of Amazonas, 2018.

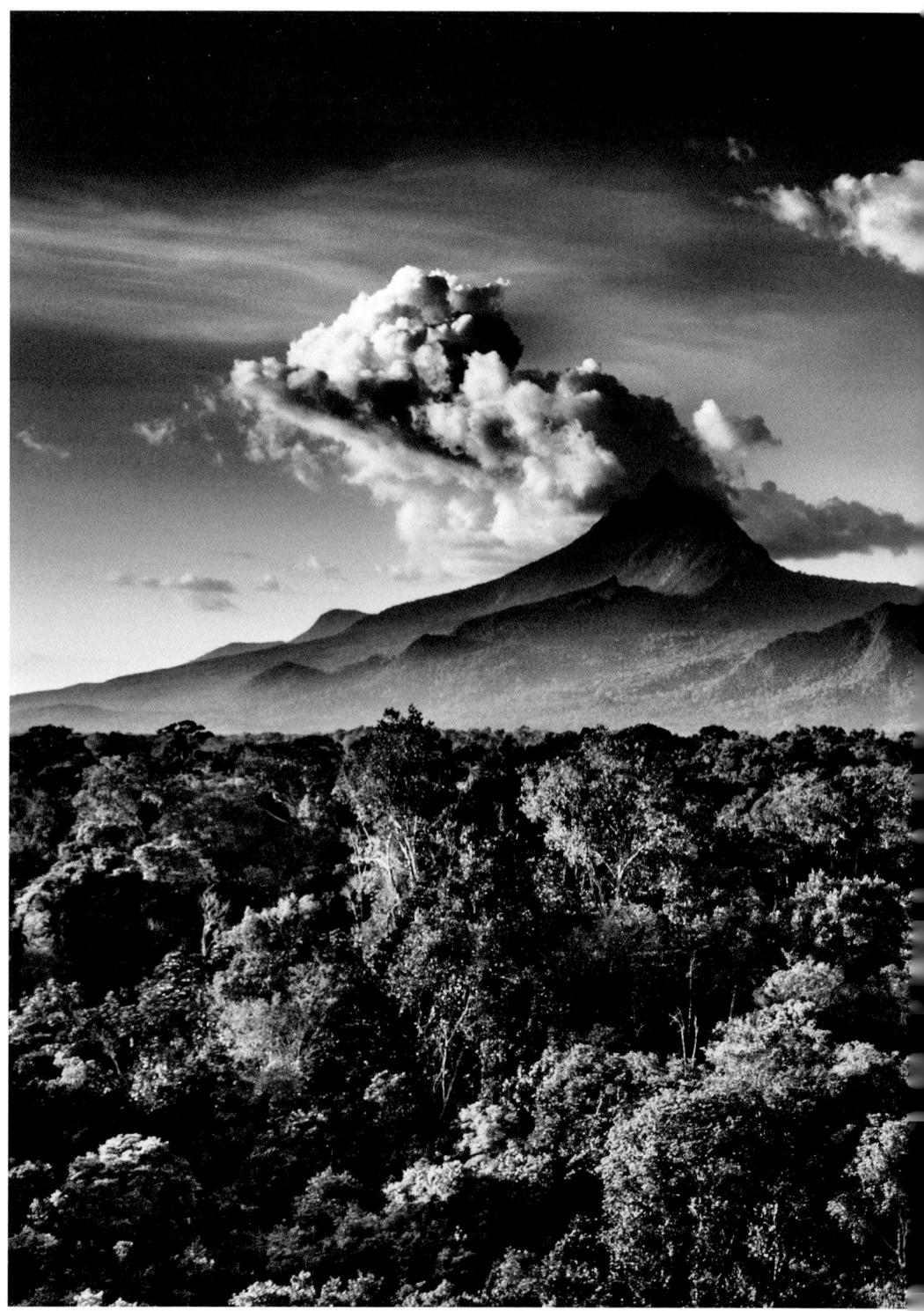

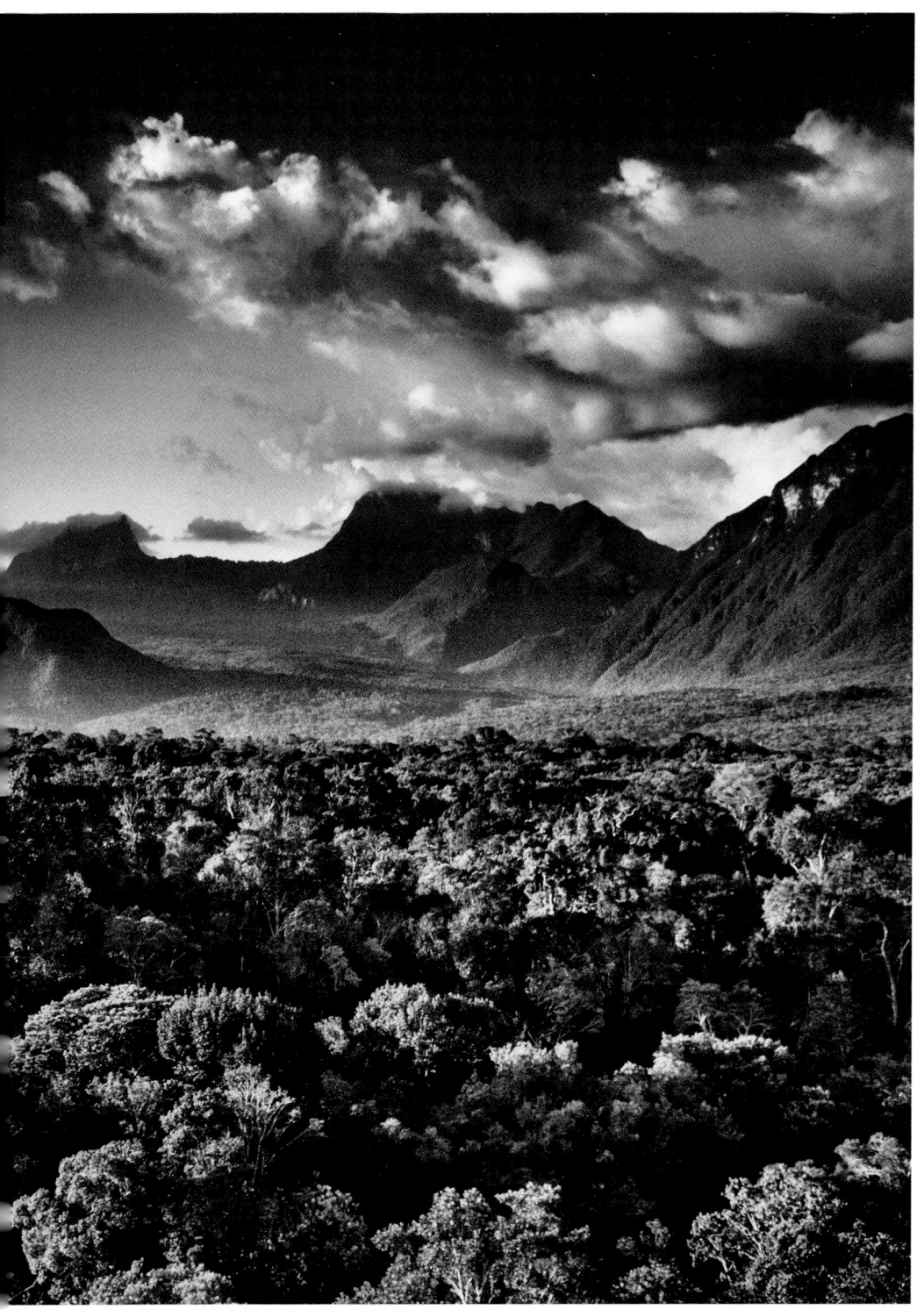

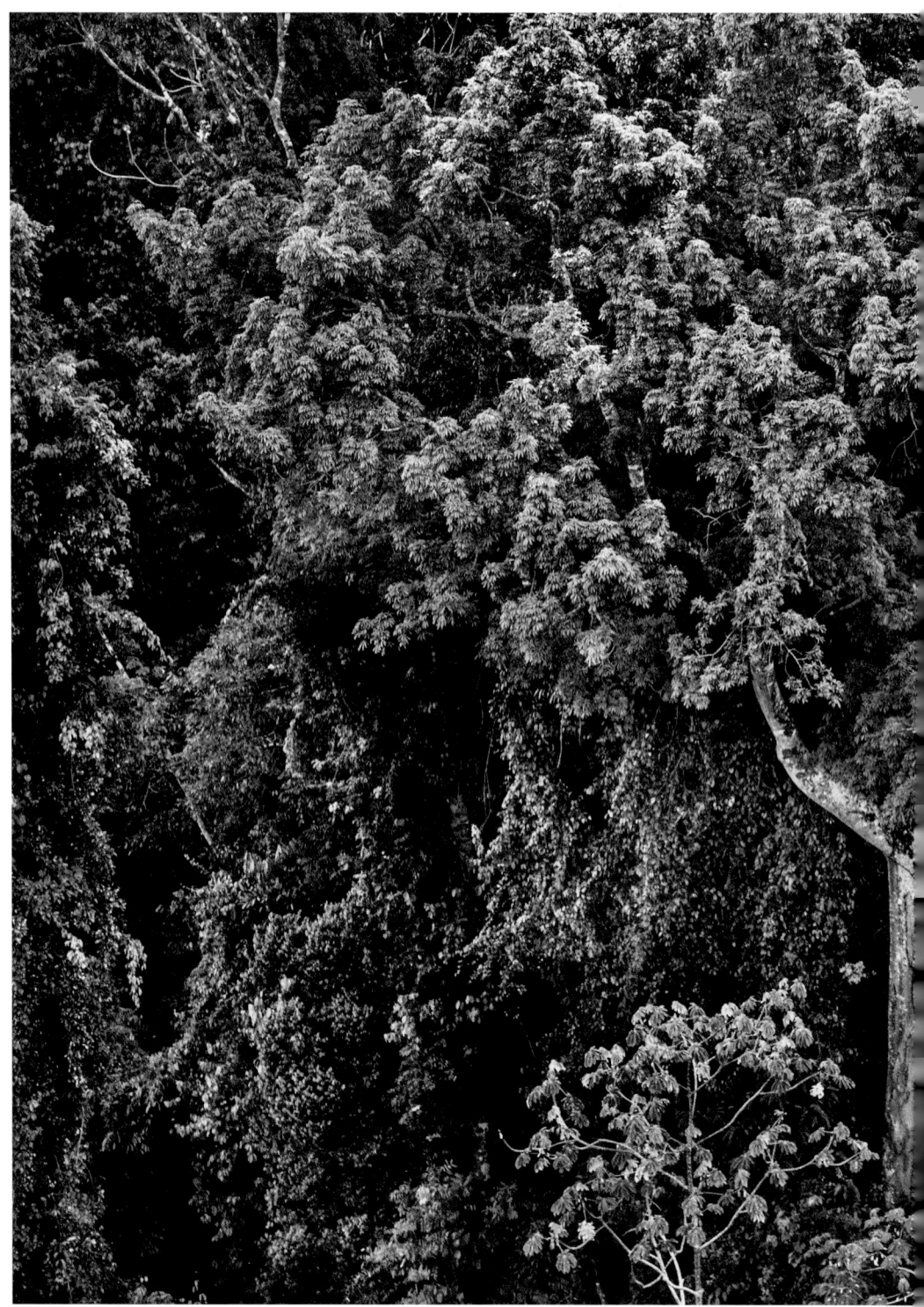

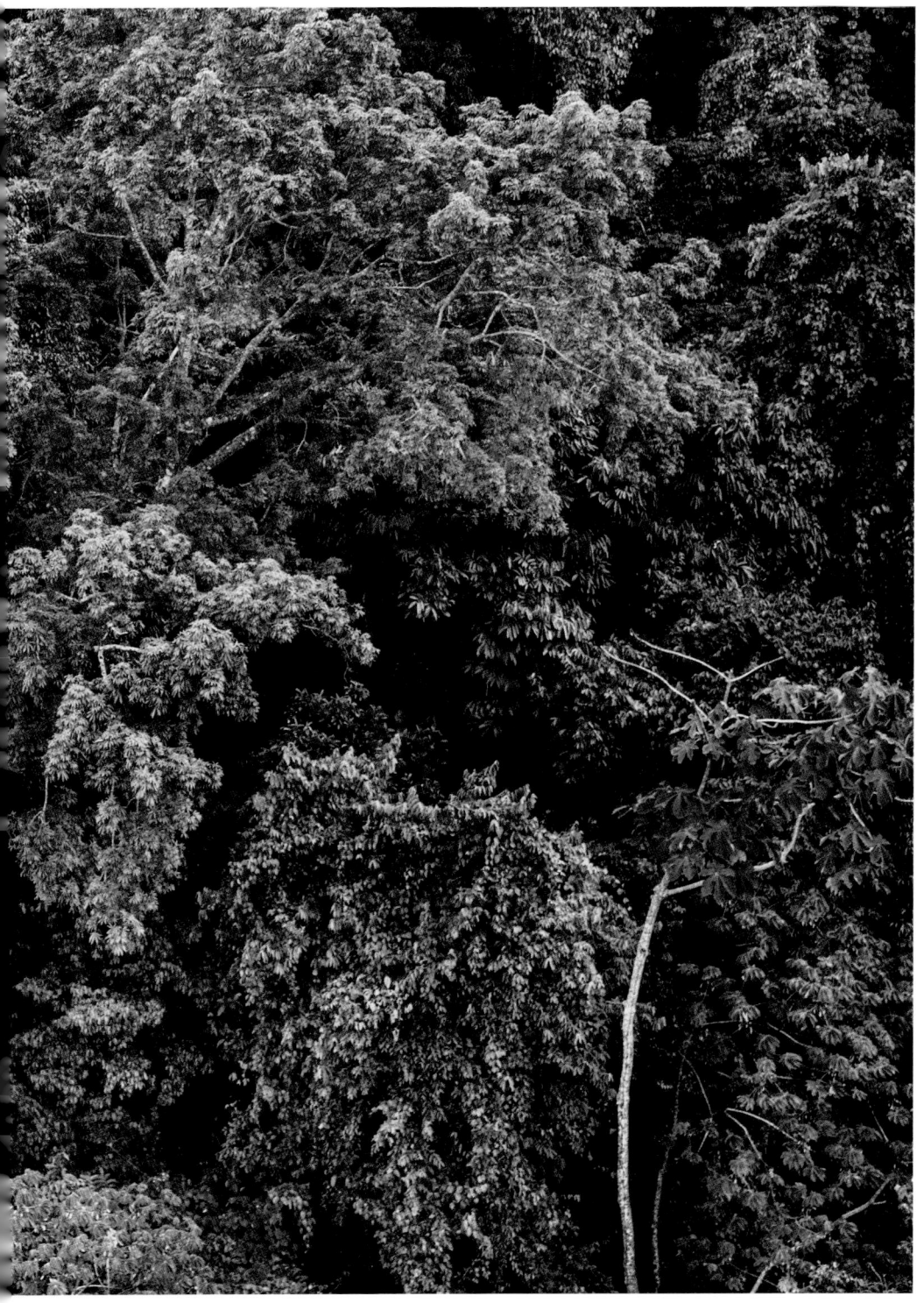

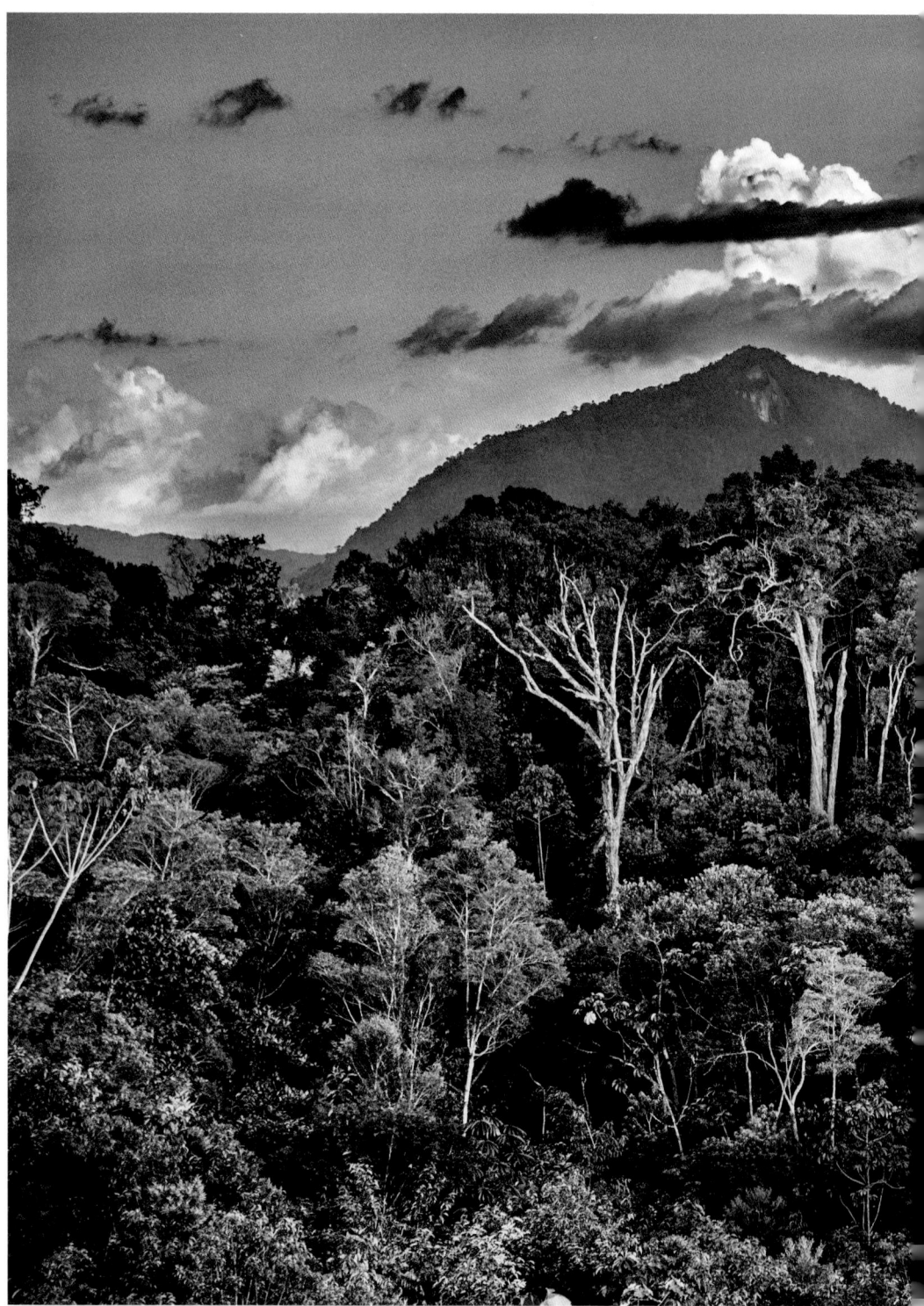

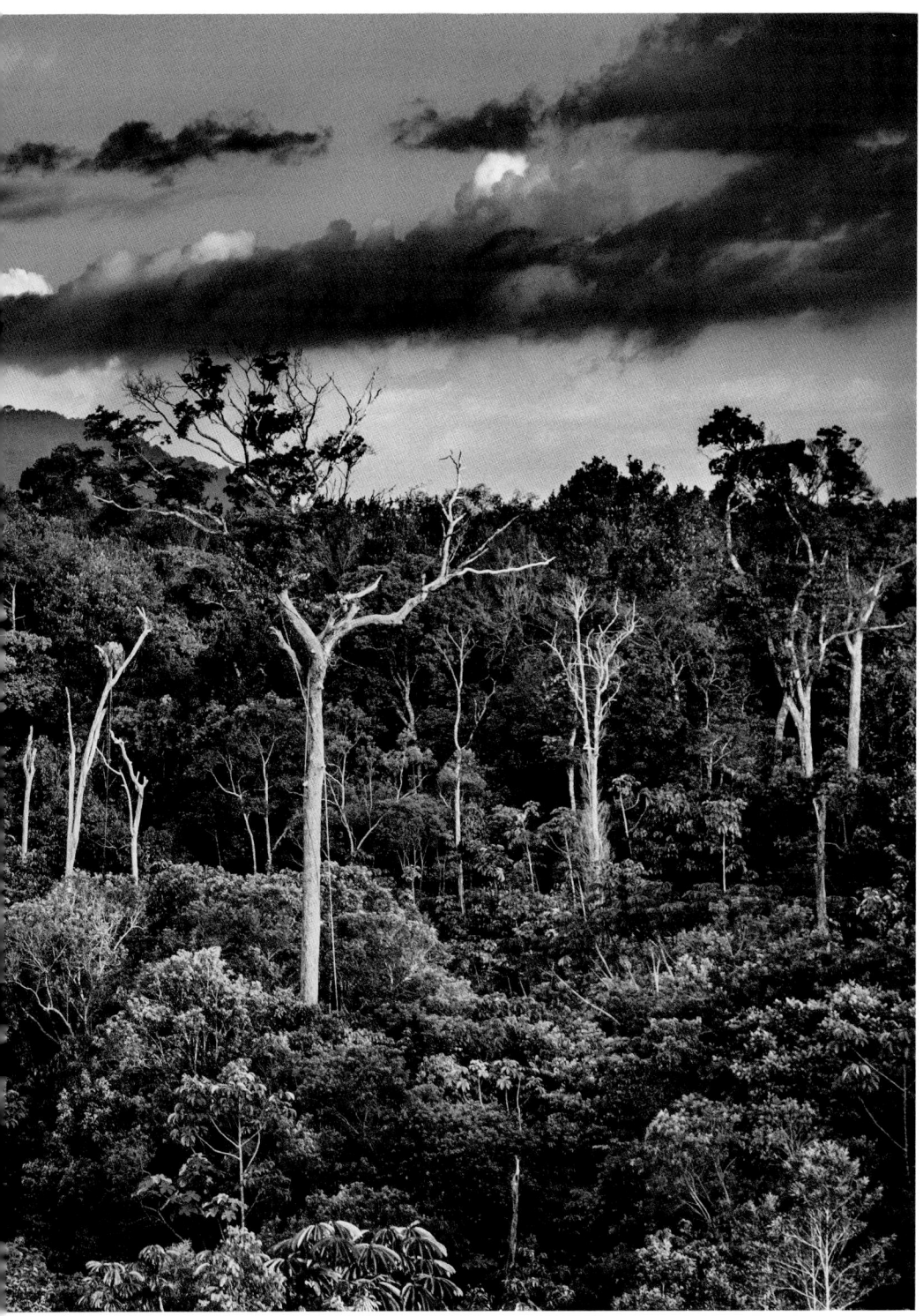

Opposite At center, a tree rises out of the black water of the Rio Negro. It is a type of *Aldina* tree (*Aldina latifolia*) typical of that *igapó* forest, which lives with its trunk covered with water for much of the year. At the top of the trunk, towards the top of the photo, the epiphytic plant tumbling towards the ground is a type of philodendron (*Philodendron solimoesense*). Epiphytic plants have commensal relationships in which they benefit from the support of a tree's branches without harming the tree. Lower Rio Negro, downstream from the confluence with the Rio Branco and near the Anavilhanas Archipelago, state of Amazonas, 2019.

Pages 294/295 Landscape of an *igapó*, a type of forest frequently flooded by blackwater rivers, on the banks of the Jaú River, Jaú National Park, state of Amazonas, 2019.

Pages 296/297 Green-winged macaws (*Ara chloropterus*). These birds from the *Psittacidae* family mate for life and so are normally seen flying in pairs. Generally, if they are flying in threes, it is the parents and their offspring. Jaú National Park, state of Amazonas, 2019.

Pages 298/299 Rain in the Anavilhanas Archipelago; an *igapó*, meaning a type of forest frequently flooded by river water. Anavilhanas National Park, Lower Rio Negro, state of Amazonas, 2019.

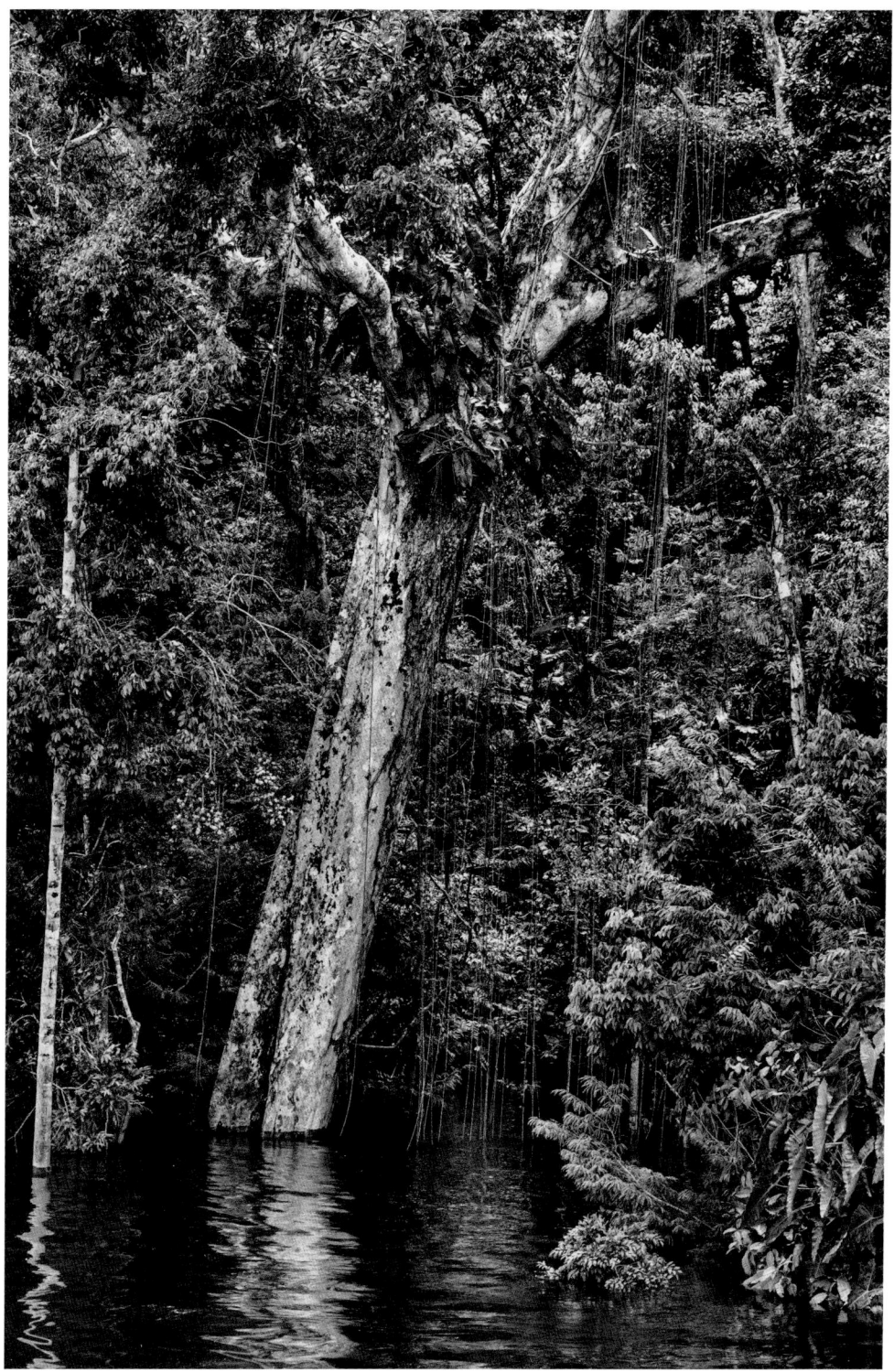

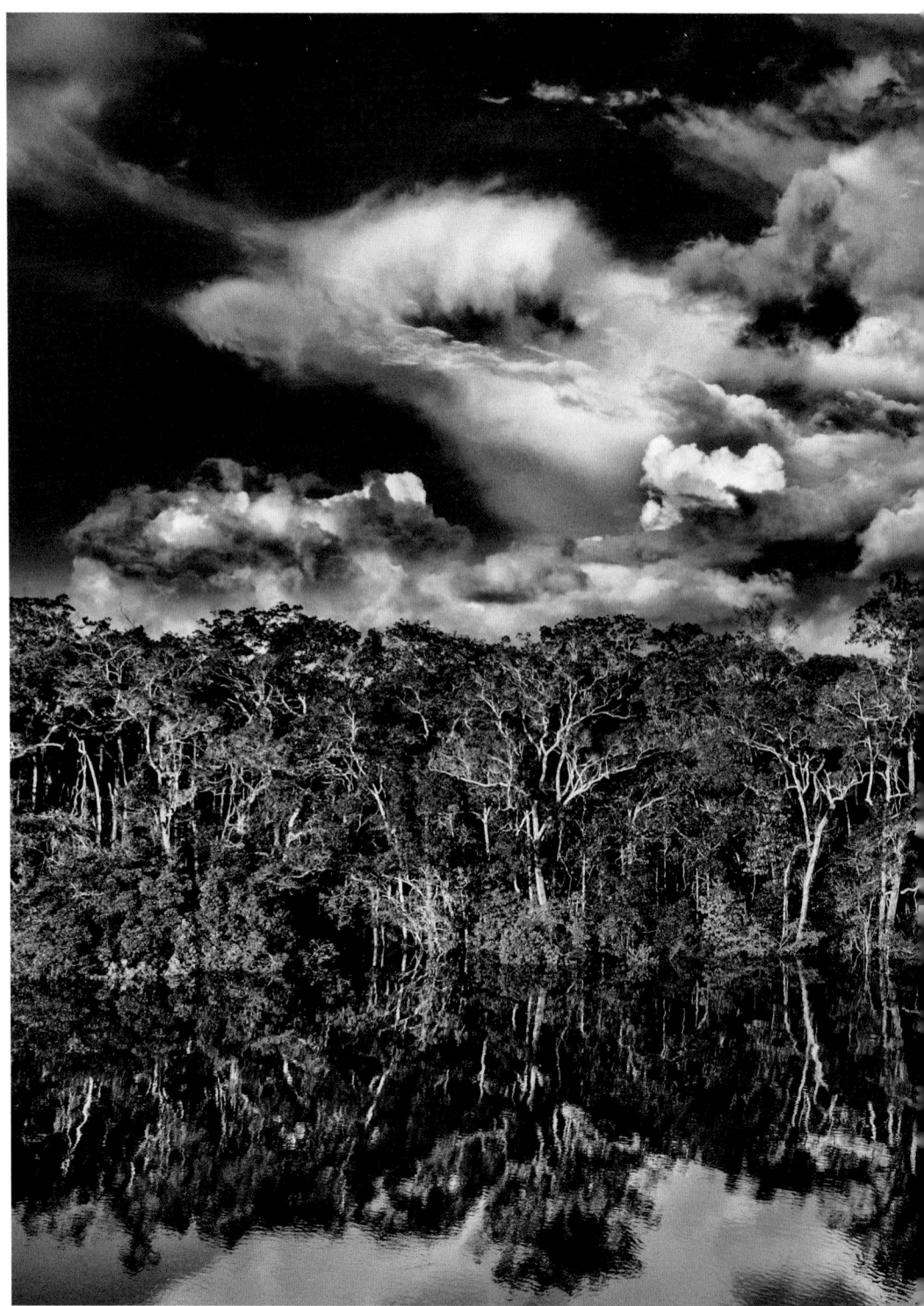

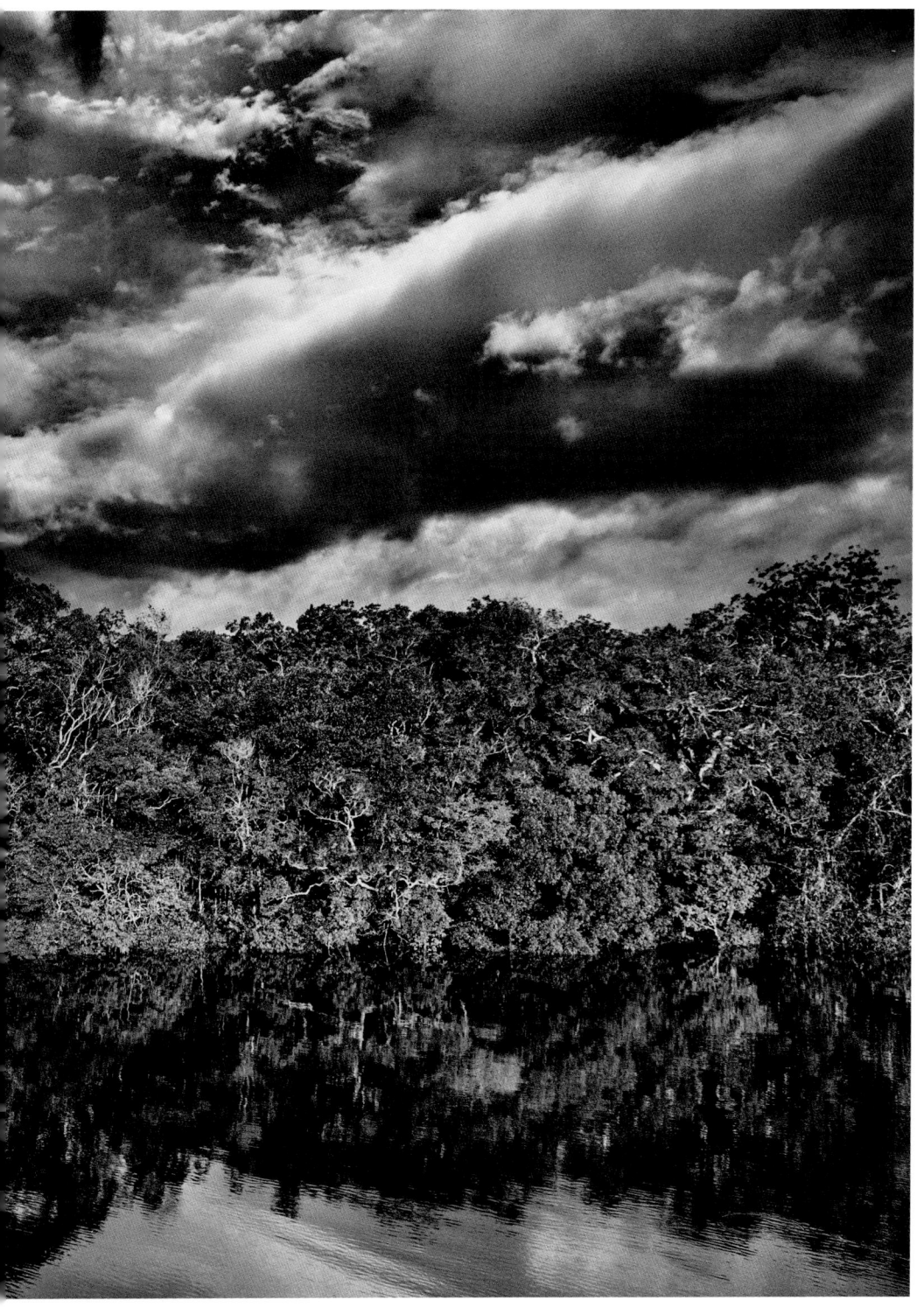

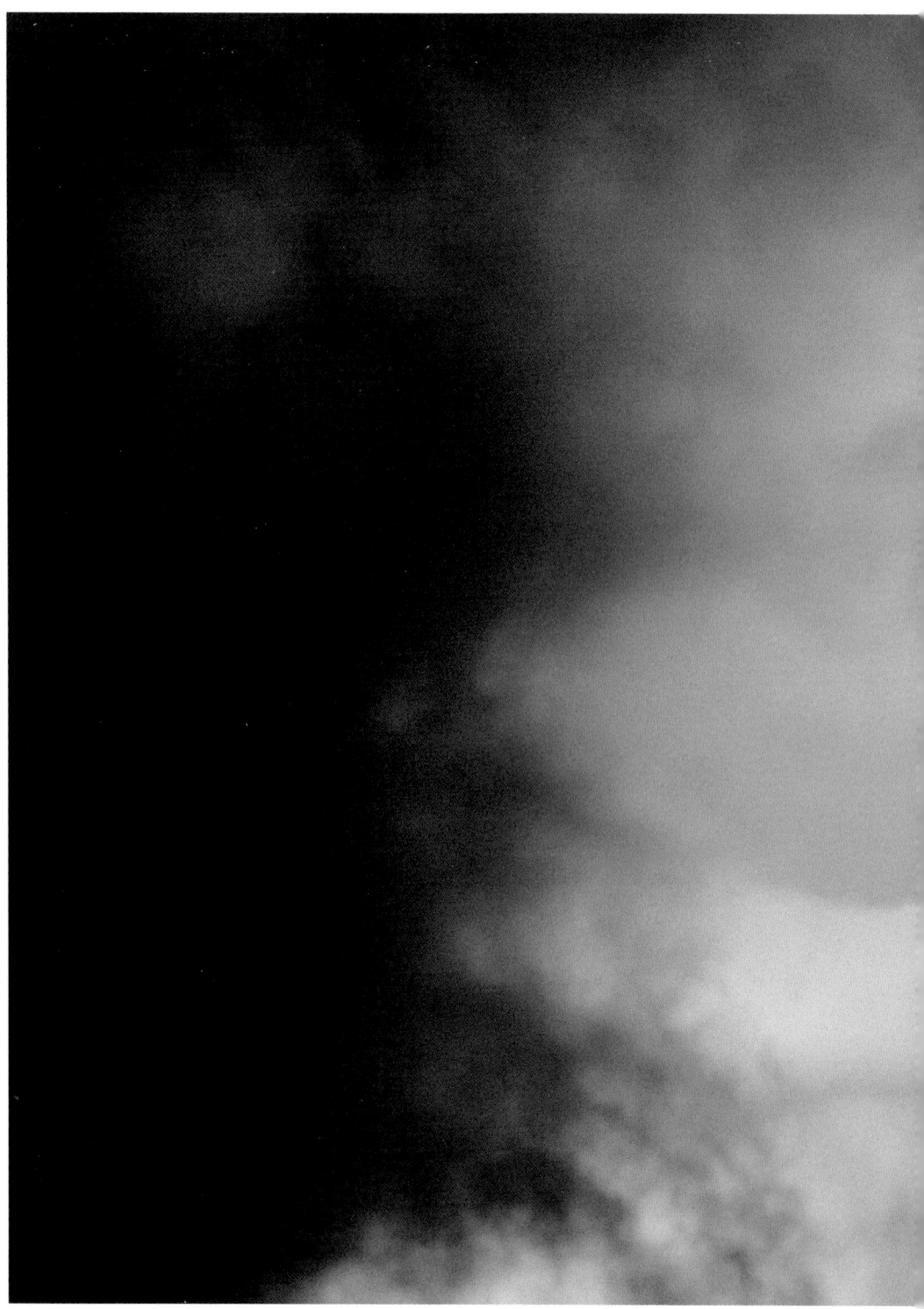

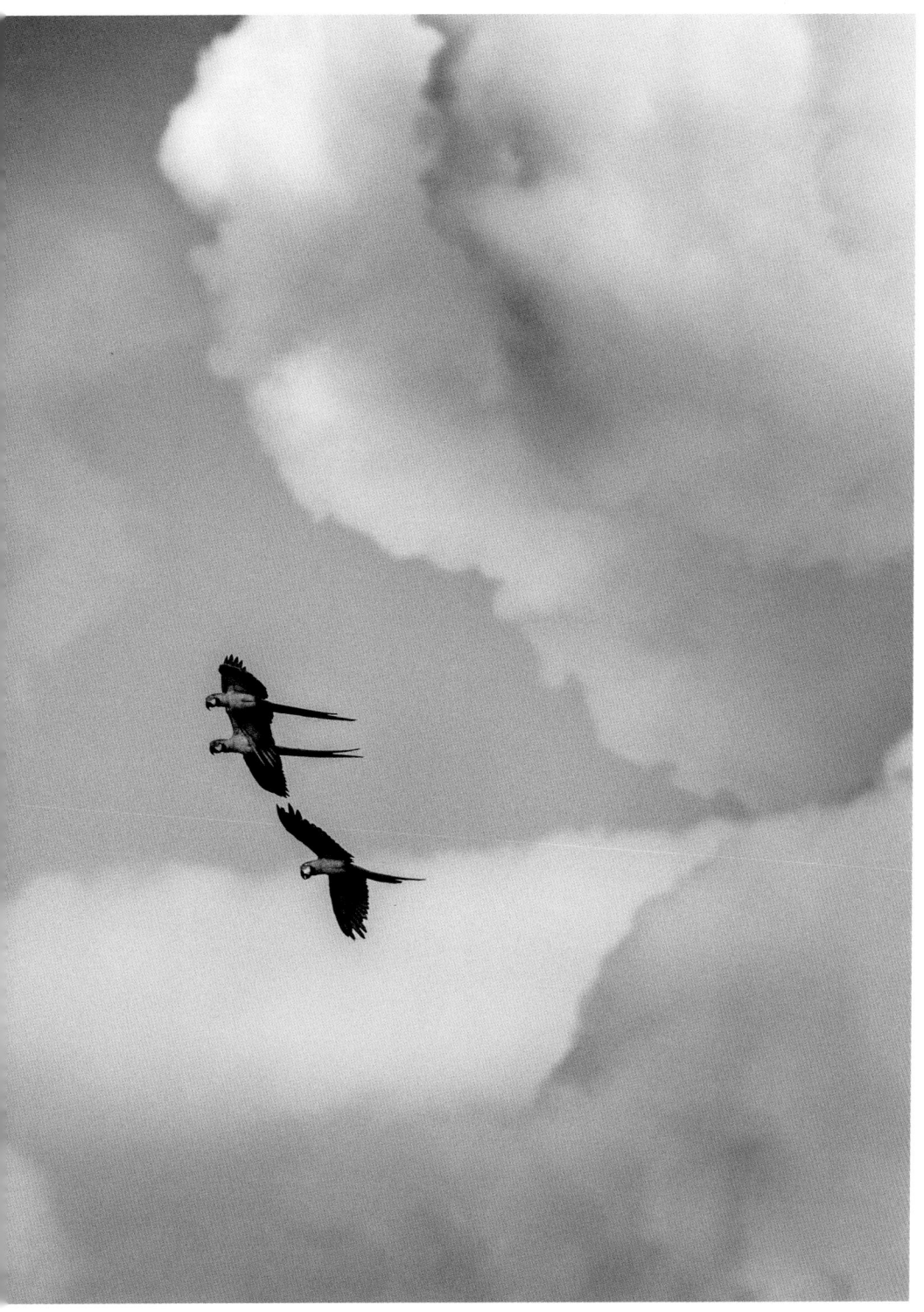

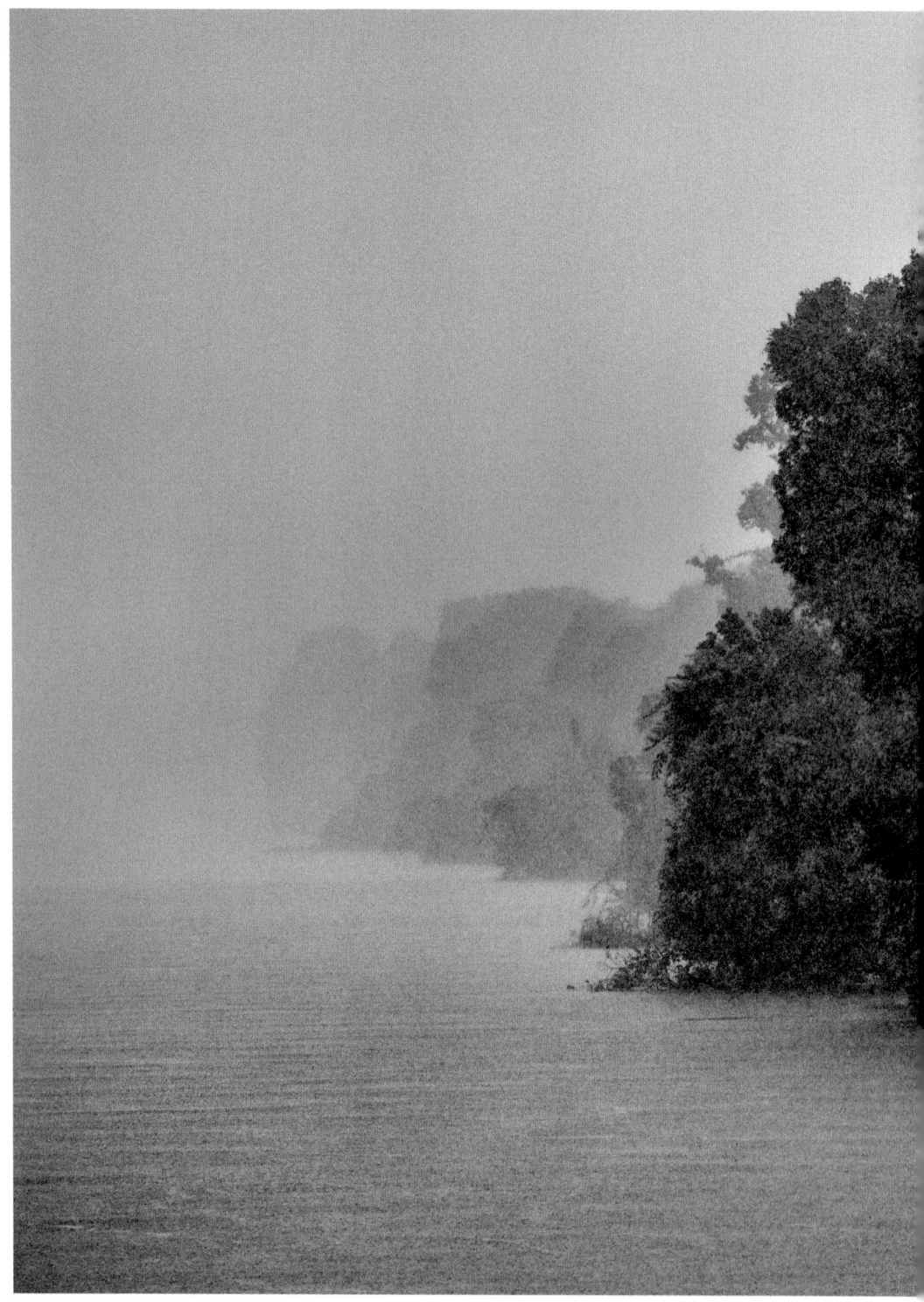

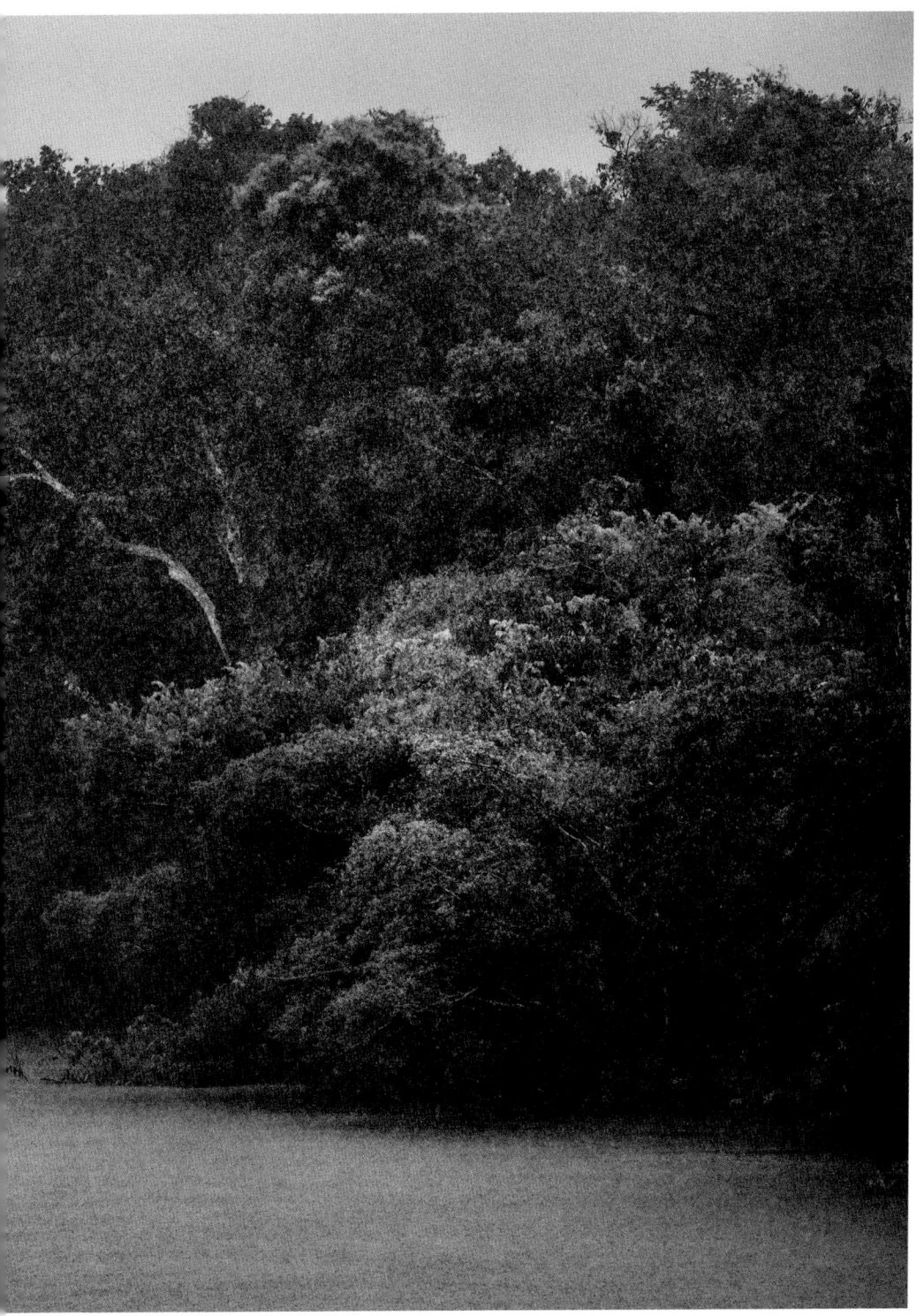

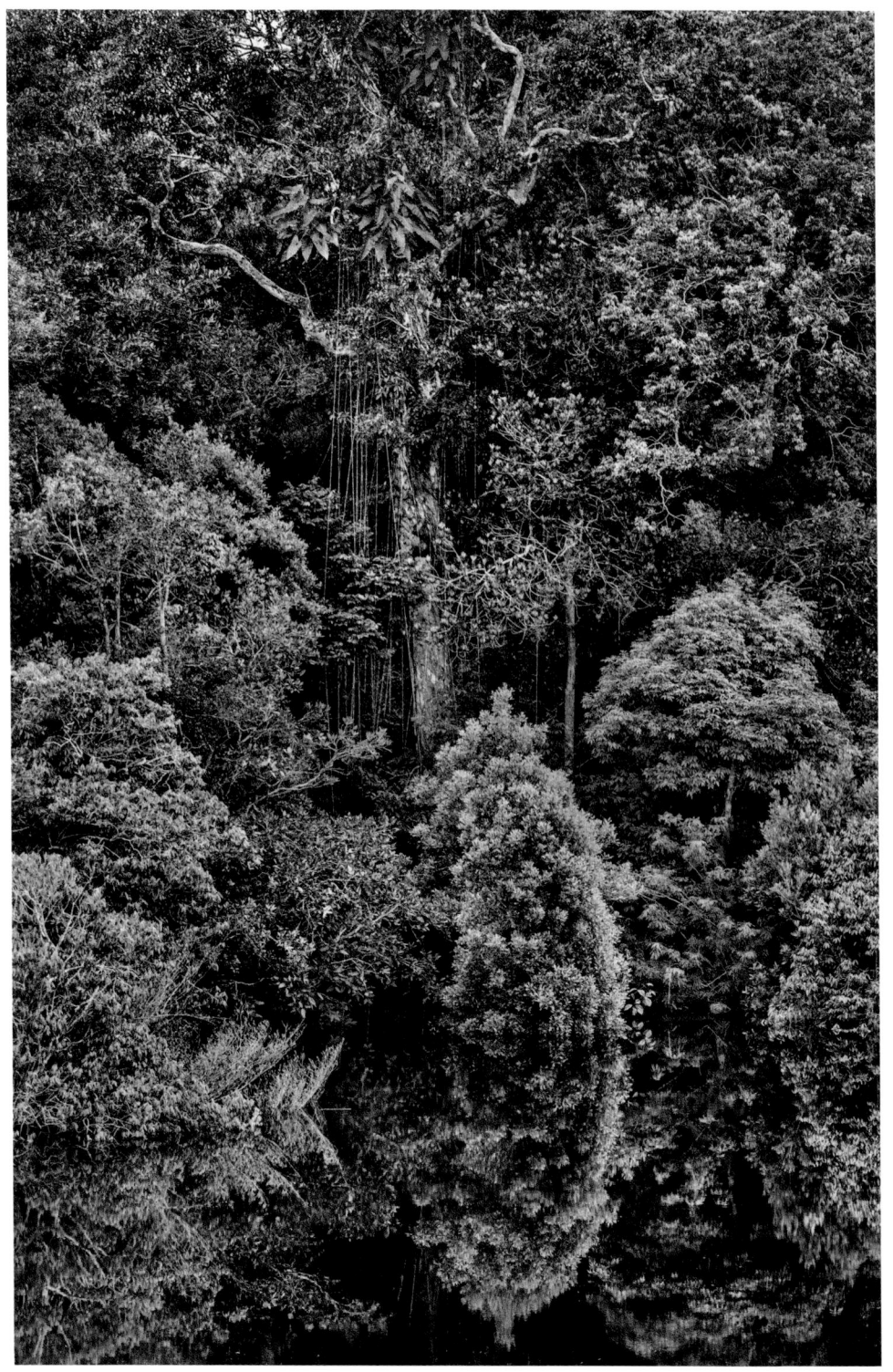

Opposite An *igapó*, a type of forest frequently flooded by blackwater rivers. The epiphyte at center top is a type of philodendron (*Philodendron solimoesense*) whose long roots tumble towards the ground, ensconced in the branches of an *Aldina* tree (*Aldina latifolia*). Jaú River, Jaú National Park, state of Amazonas, 2019.

Pages 302/303 In an *igapó* forest, water from a blackwater river overflows the banks, covering trees' roots and trunks. The tree prominent in the foreground is a *jauari* palm (*Astrocaryum jauari*). In the middle ground, the two prominent trees at left and right with lighter-colored leaves are a type of *cecropia* known in Brazil as *embaúba-da-várzea* or *embaúba-do-igapó* (*Cecropia latiloba*). Jaú River, Jaú National Park, state of Amazonas, 2019.

Pages 304/305 A great white egret (*Ardea alba*) on a branch in an *igapó*, a seasonally flooded blackwater forest. Jaú River, Jaú National Park, state of Amazonas, 2019.

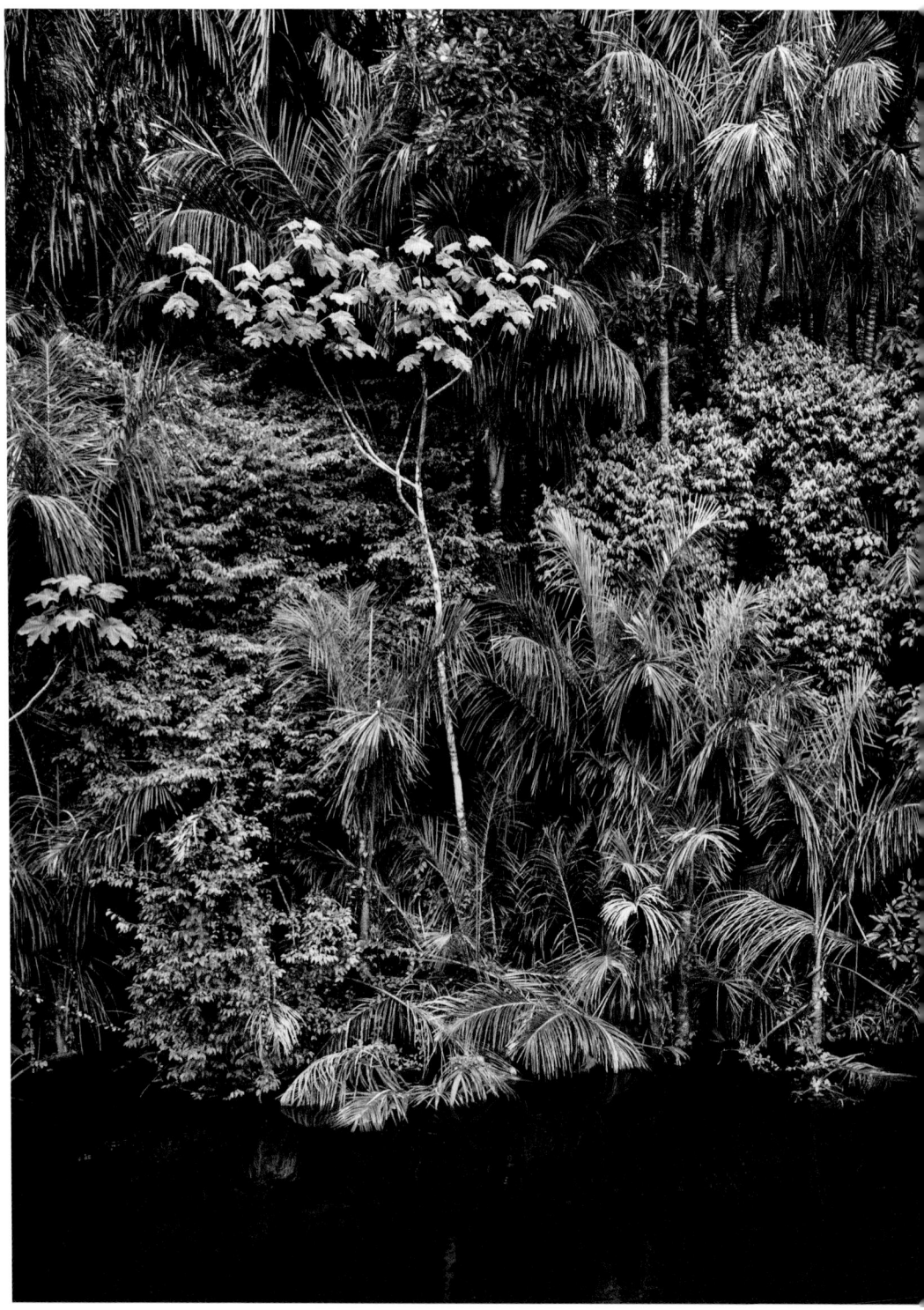

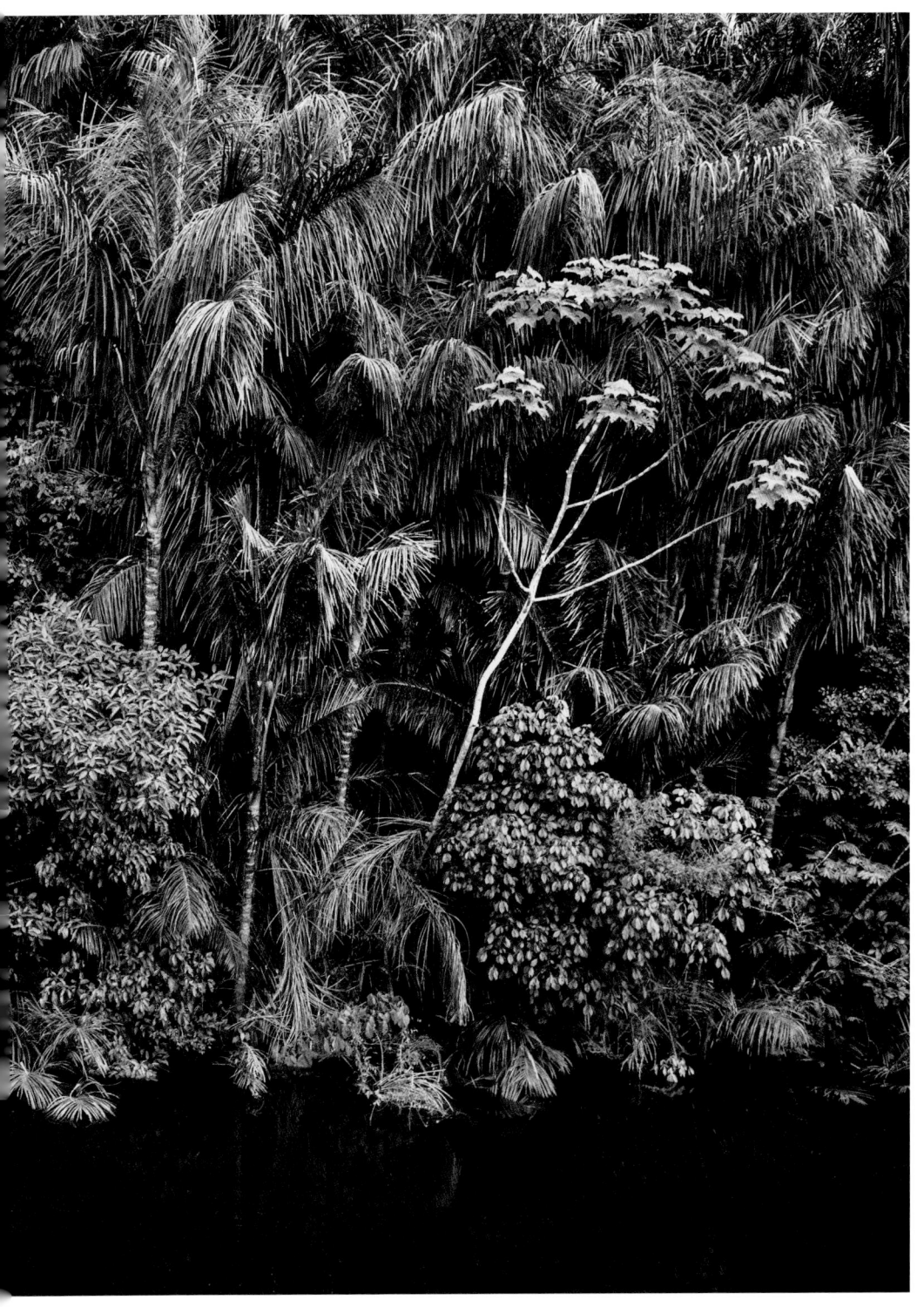

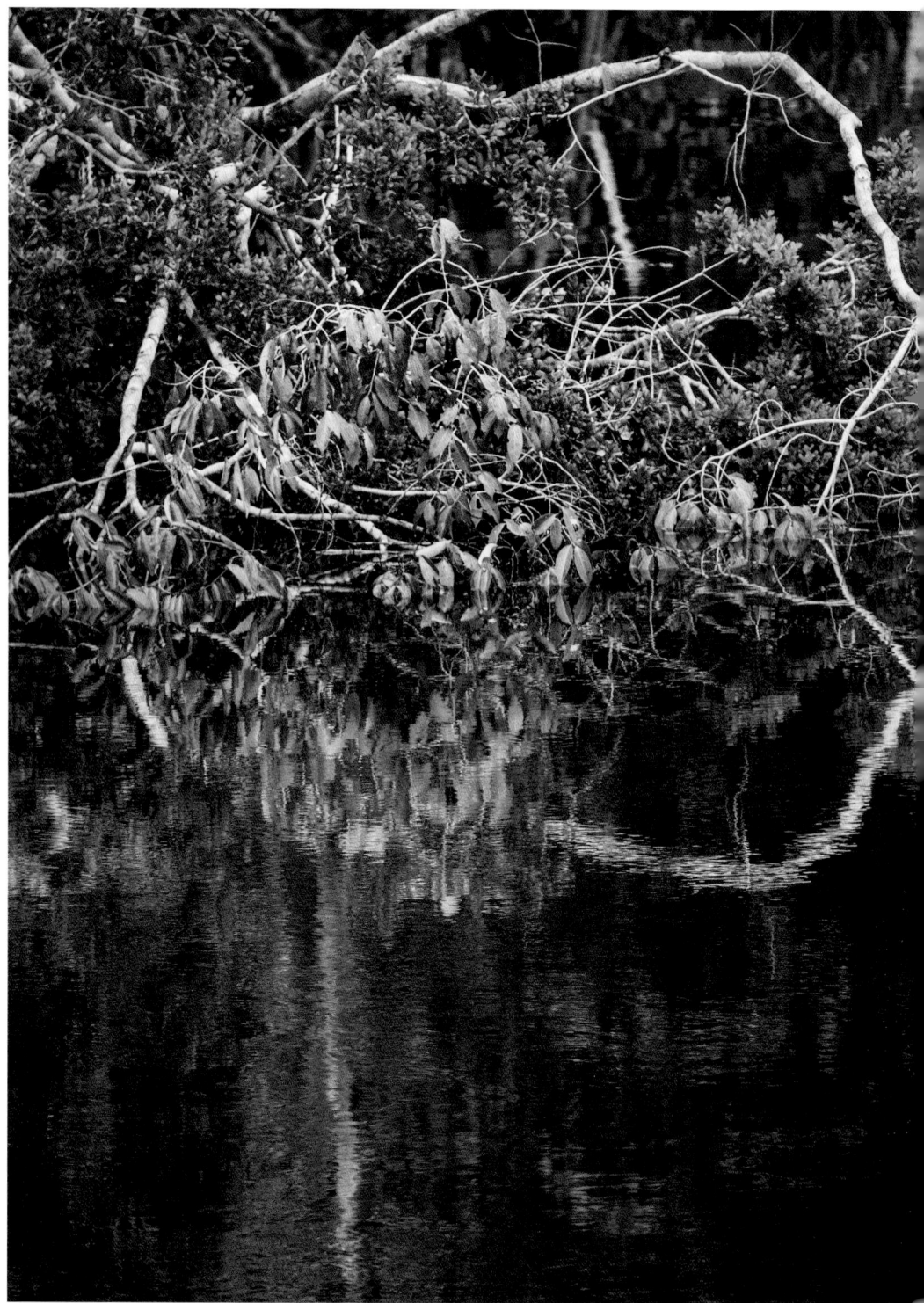

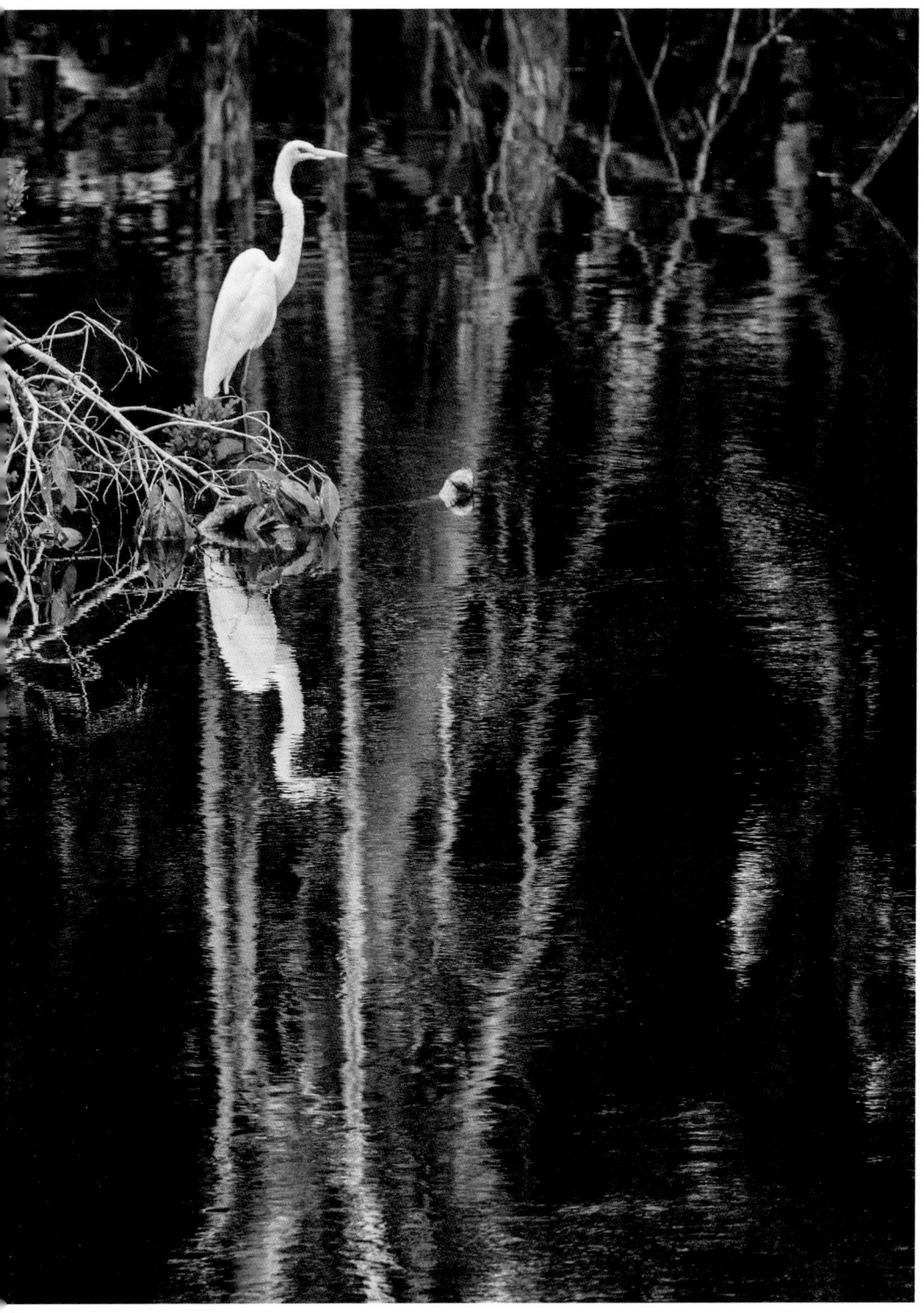

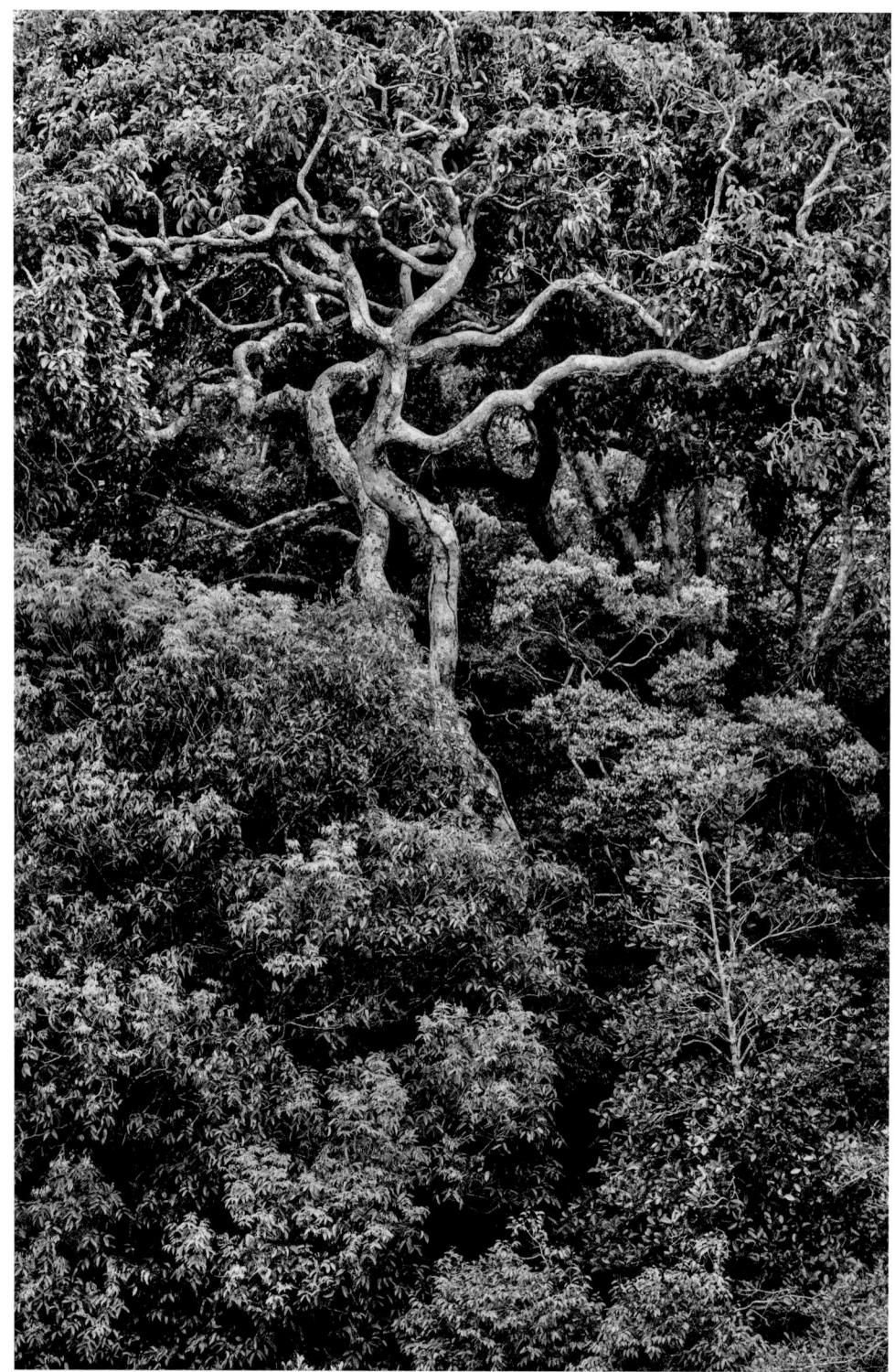

Opposite The main tree in the photo, emerging from behind the others, is an *Aldina* (*Aldina latifolia*). Jaú River, Jaú National Park, state of Amazonas, 2019.

Pages 308/309 Crôa River, Cruzeiro do Sul region, state of Acre, 2018.

Pages 310/311 View of an *igapó*, a type of forest frequently flooded by blackwater rivers. Jaú River, Jaú National Park, state of Amazonas, 2019.

Pages 312/313 An *igapó* with palms and other emerging trees. In the center of the photo, a tree whose trunk is covered with water: an *Aldina* (*Aldina latifolia*). At right, a *jauari* palm tree (*Astrocaryum jauari*). Anavilhanas Archipelago, Anavilhanas National Park, Lower Rio Negro, state of Amazonas, 2019.

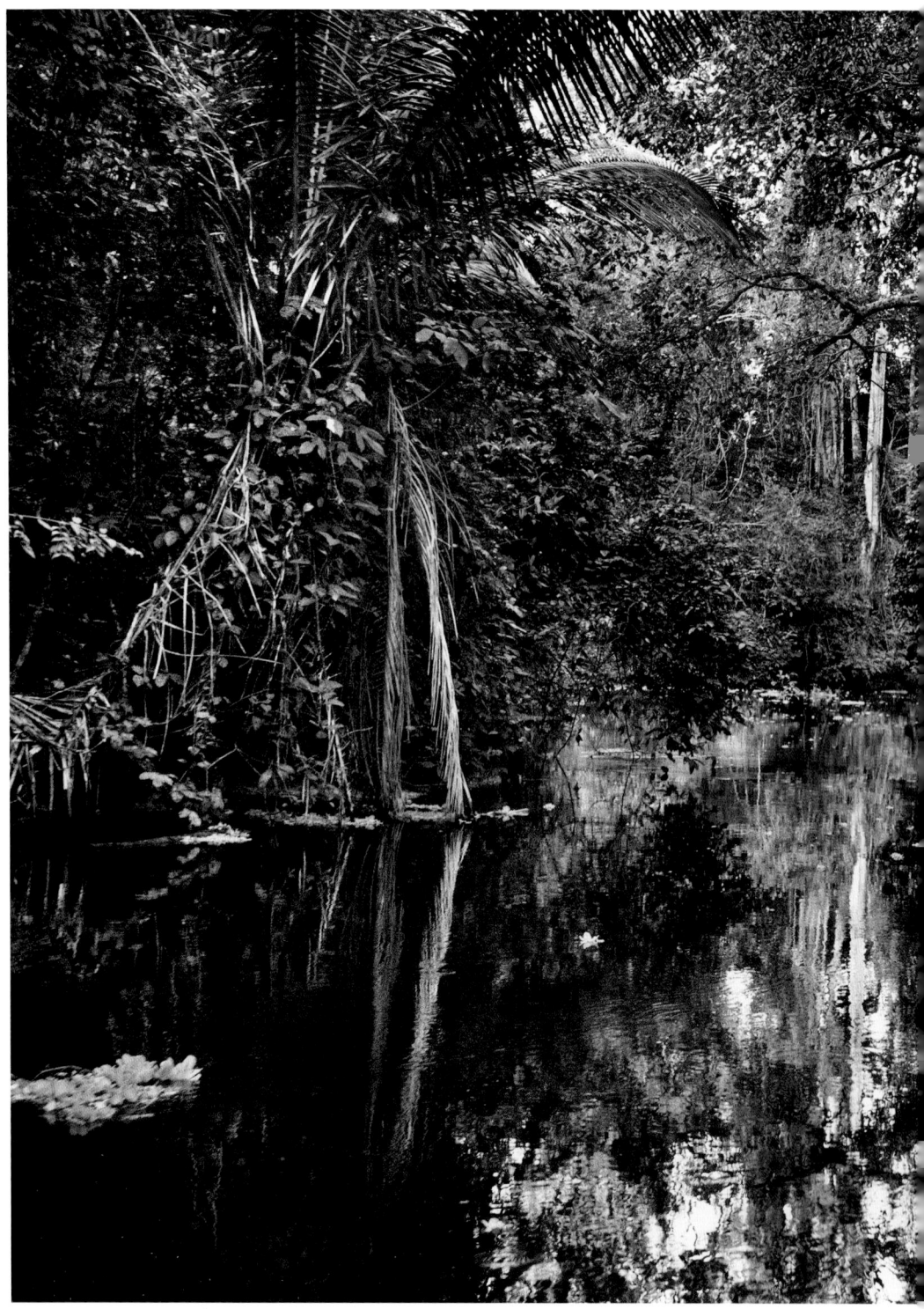

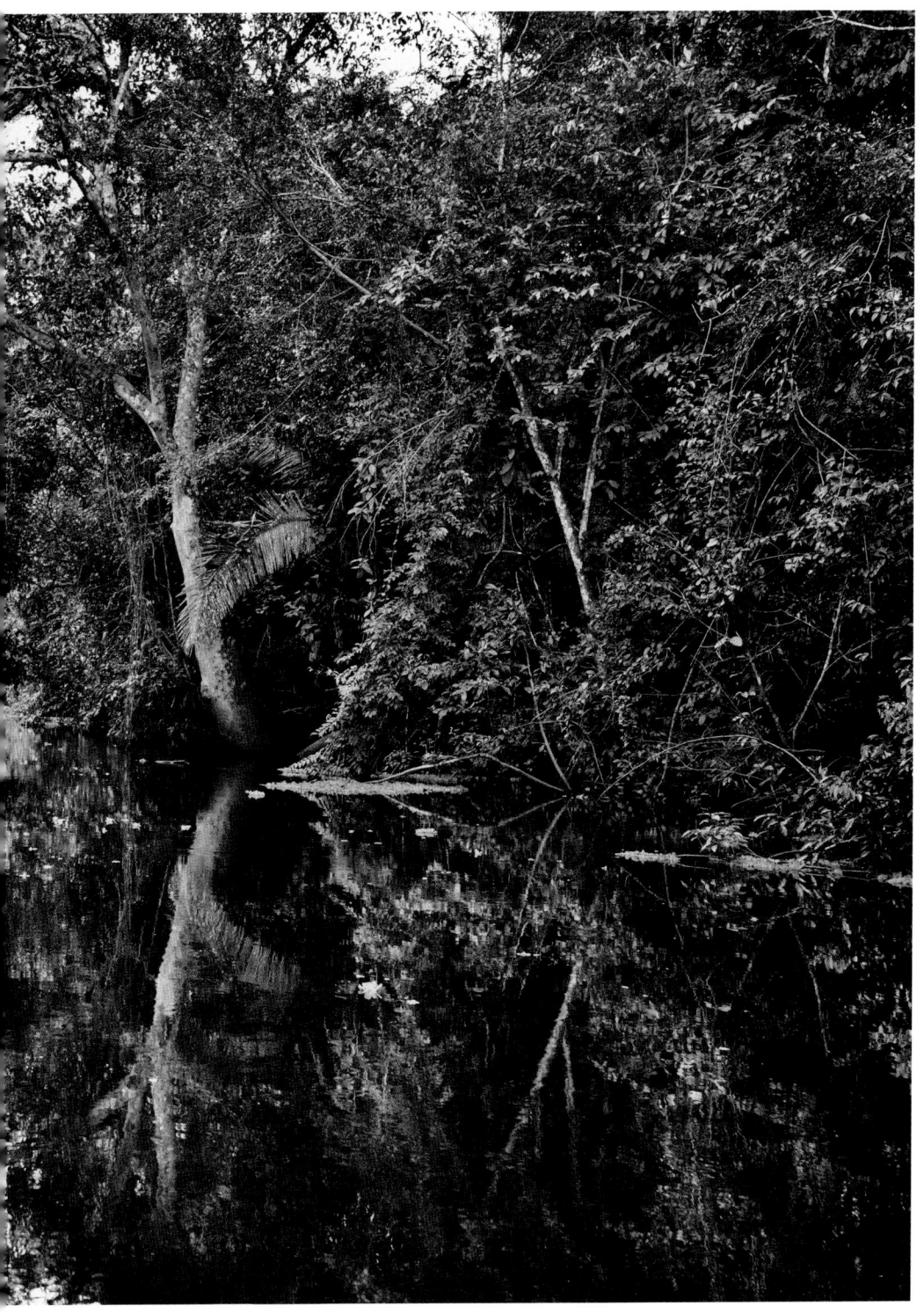

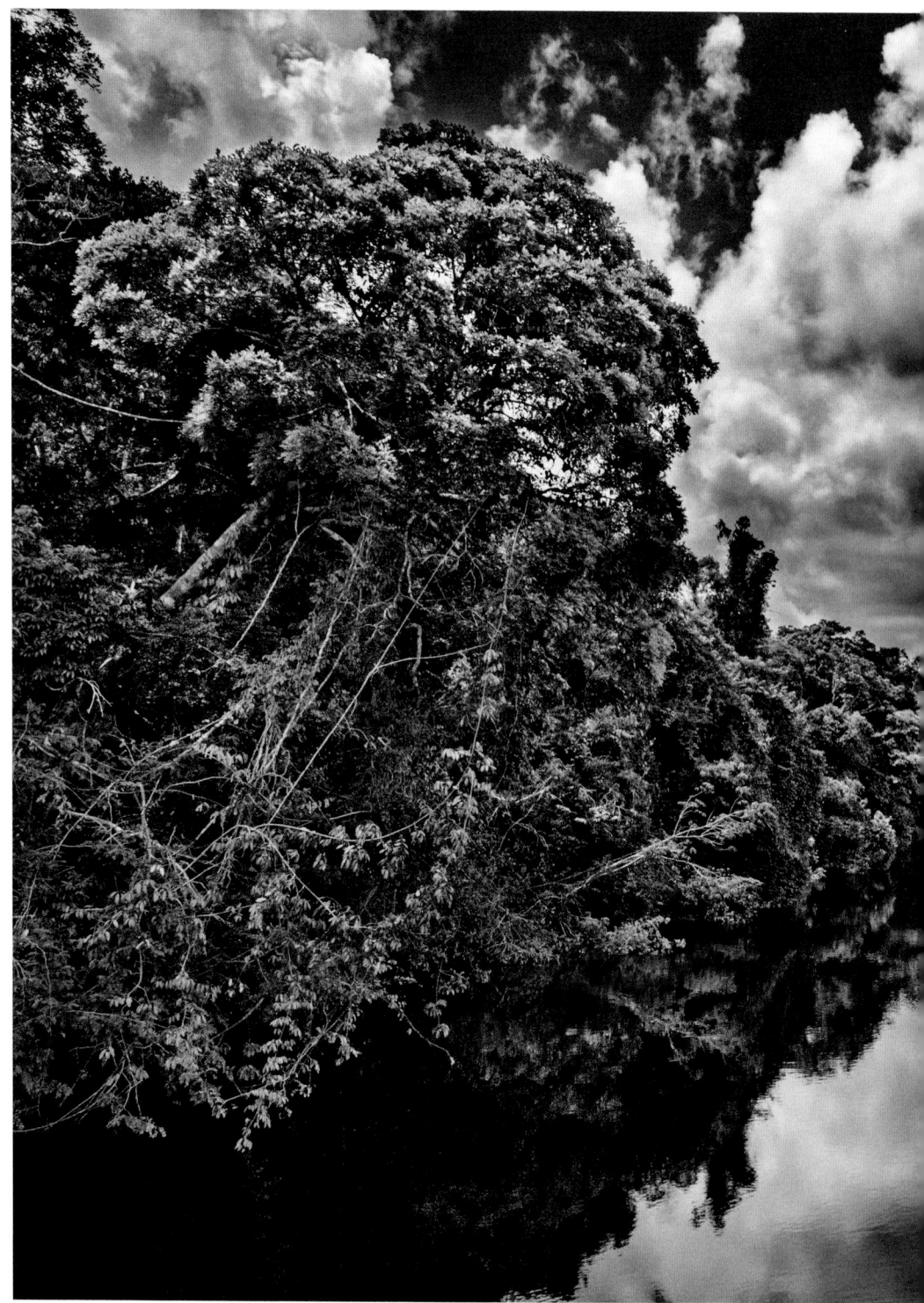

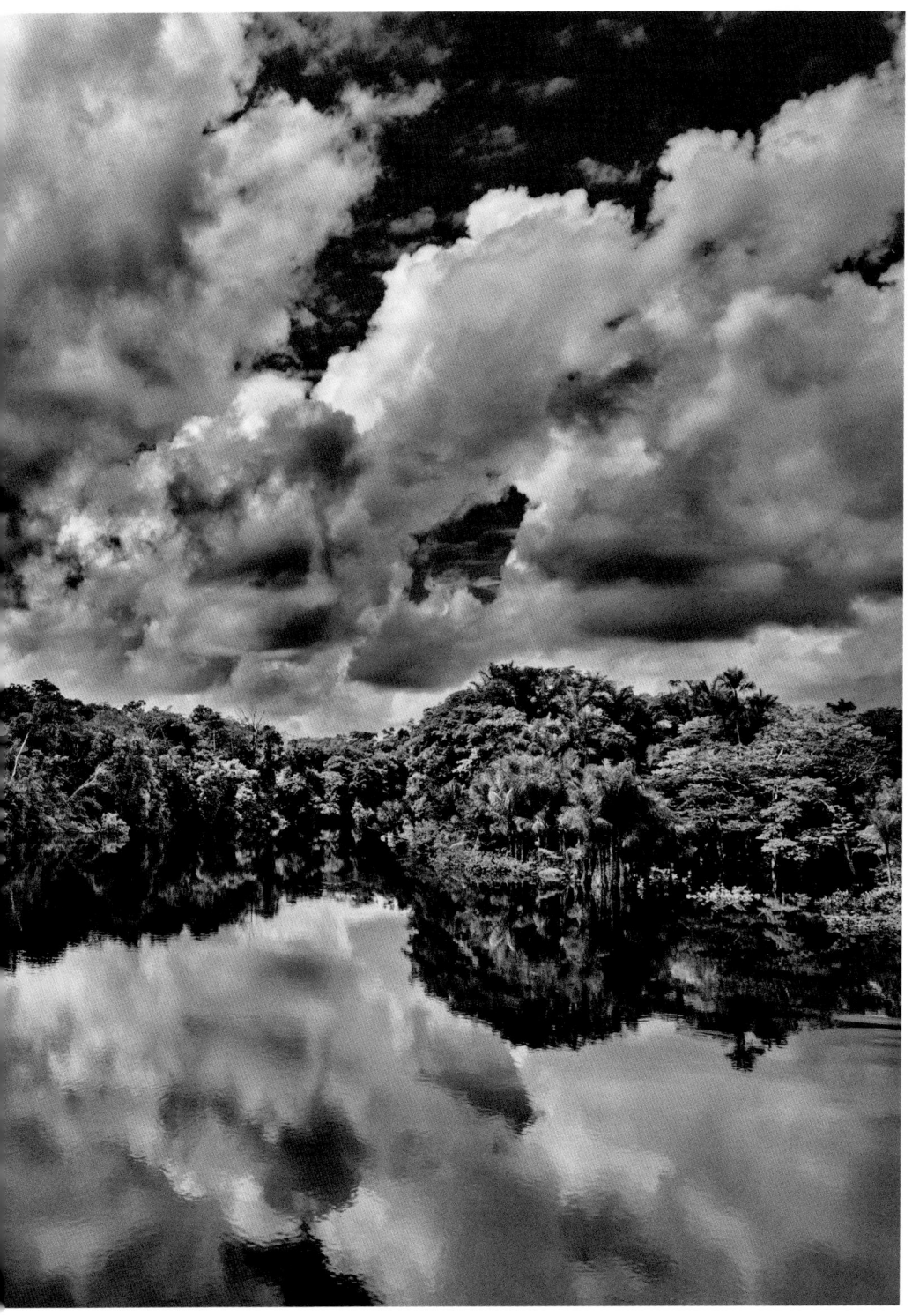

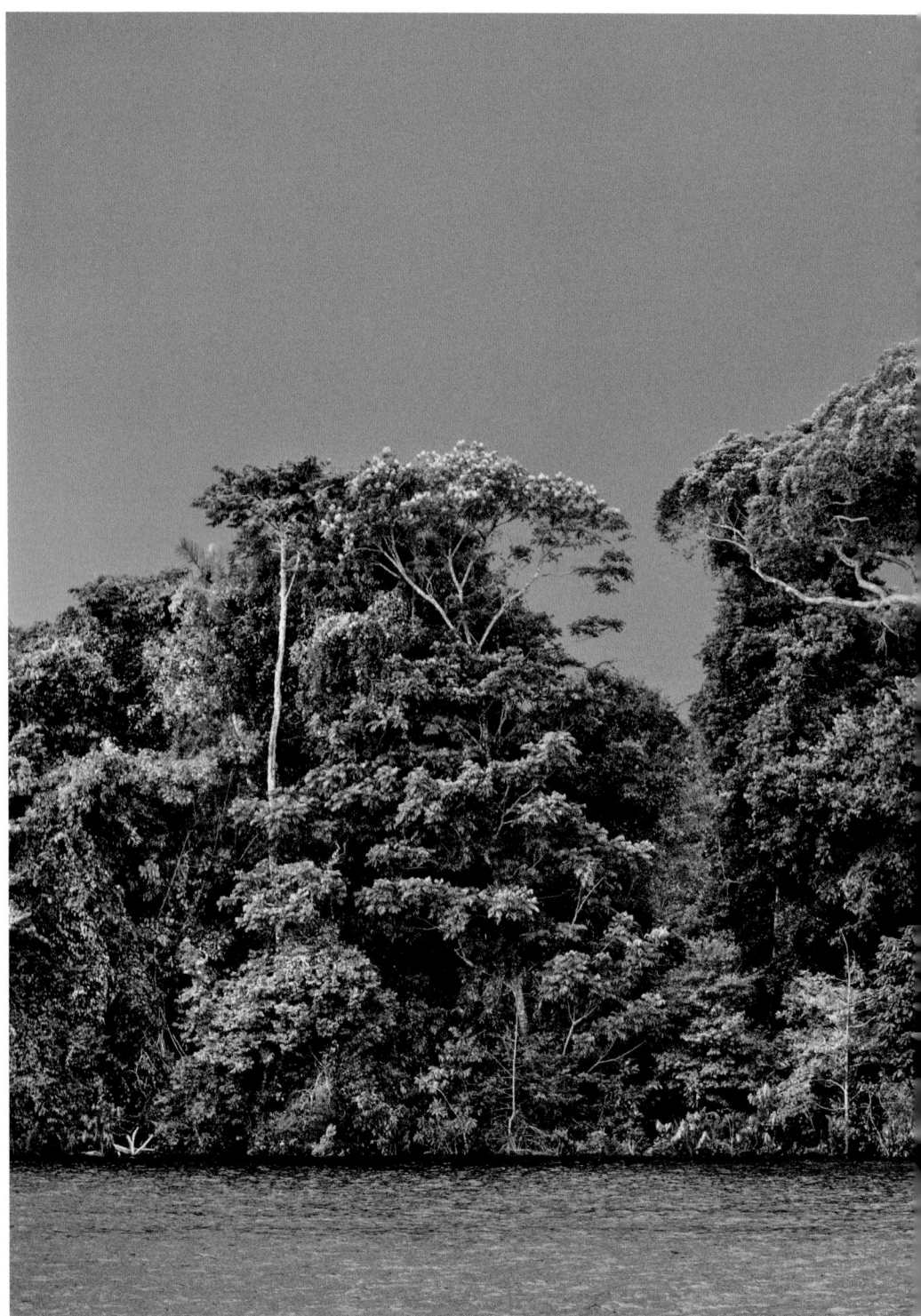

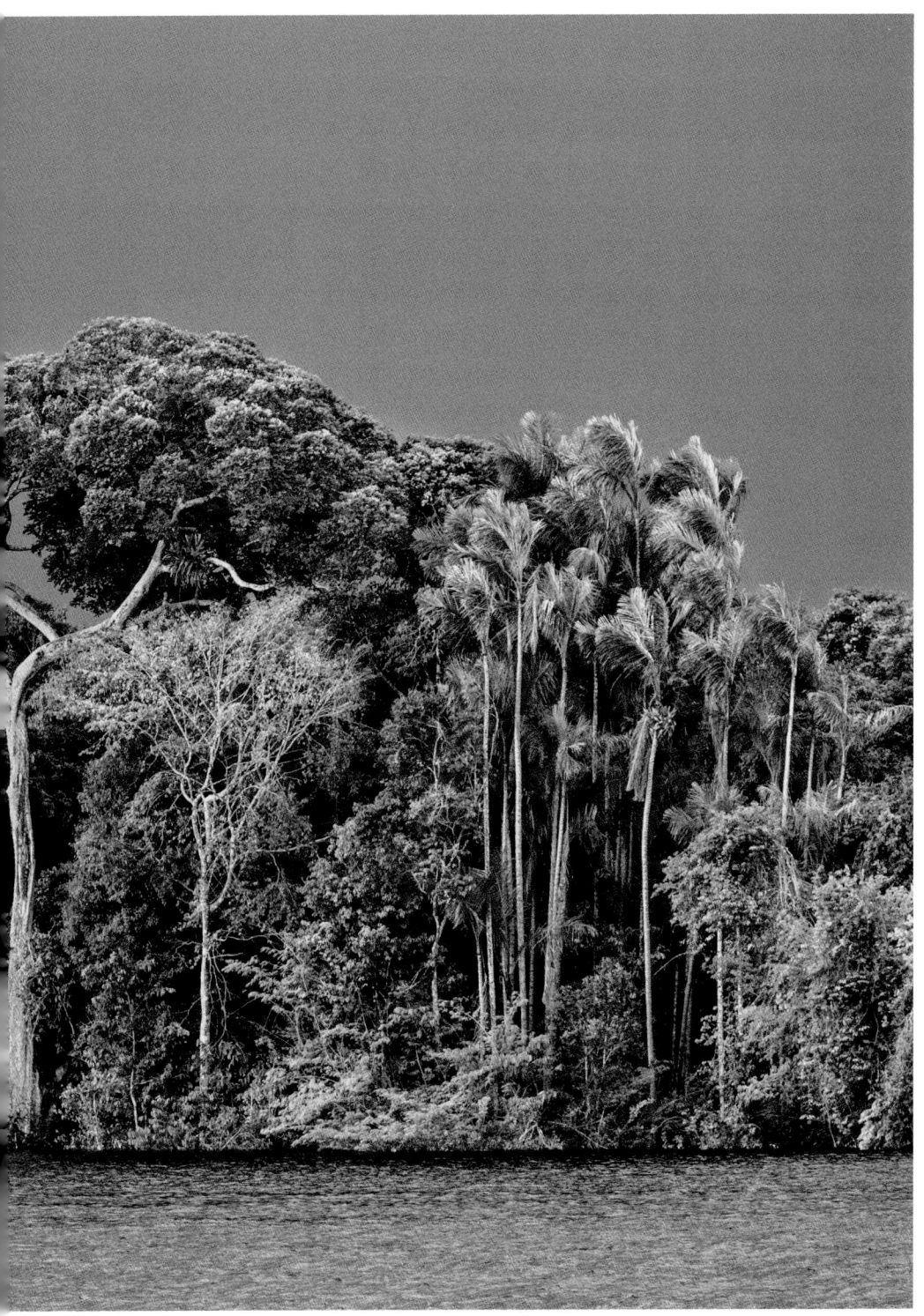

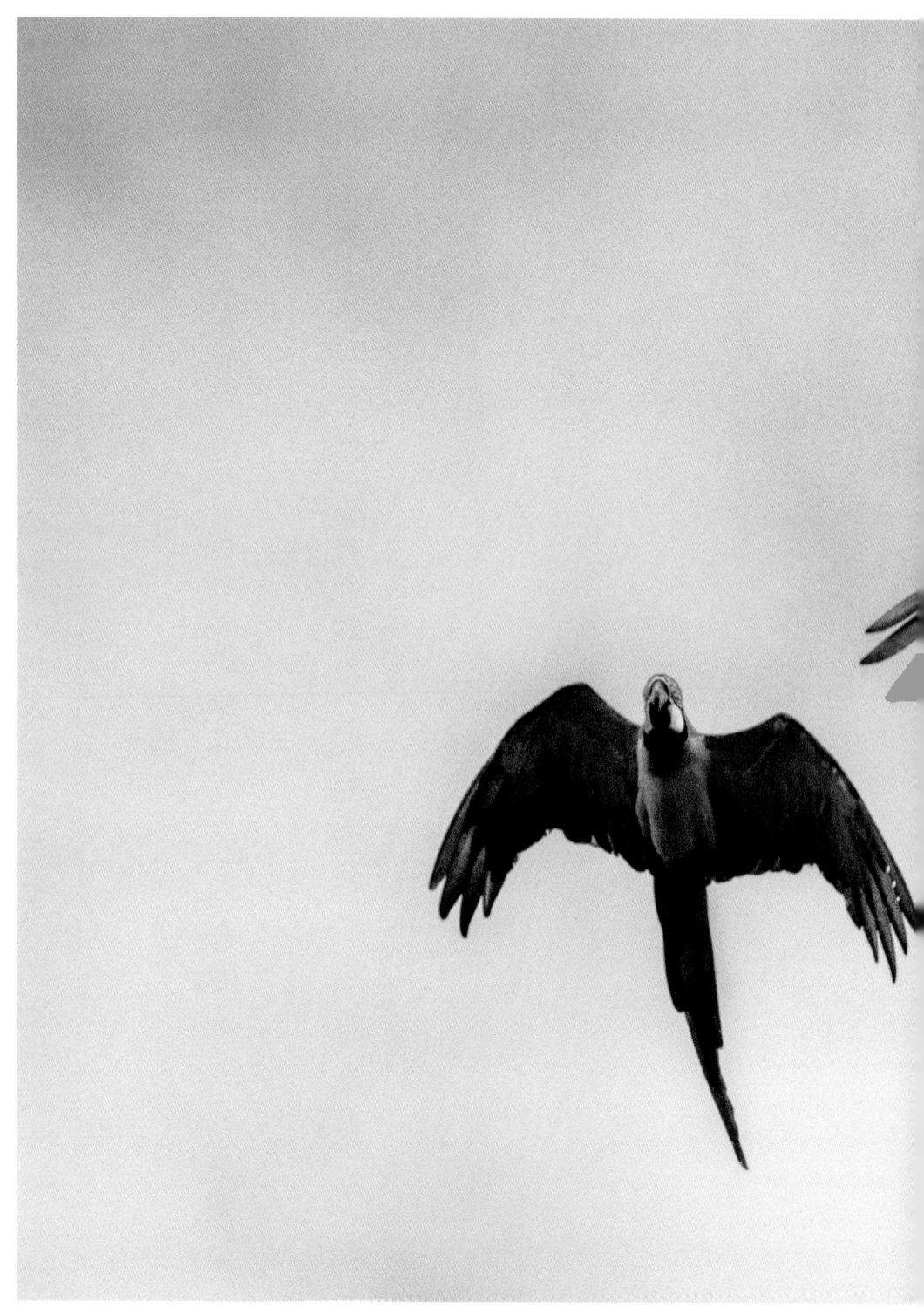

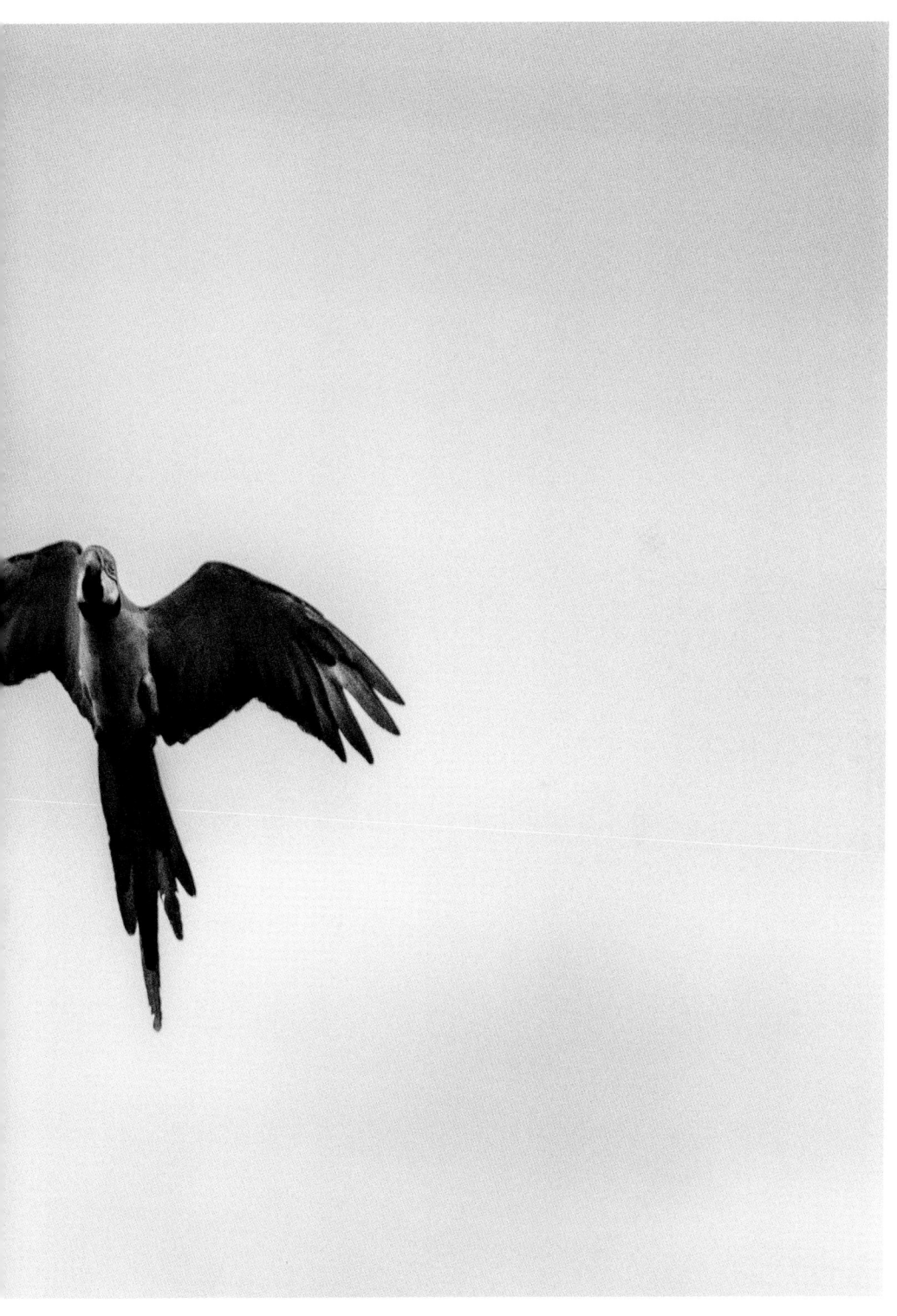

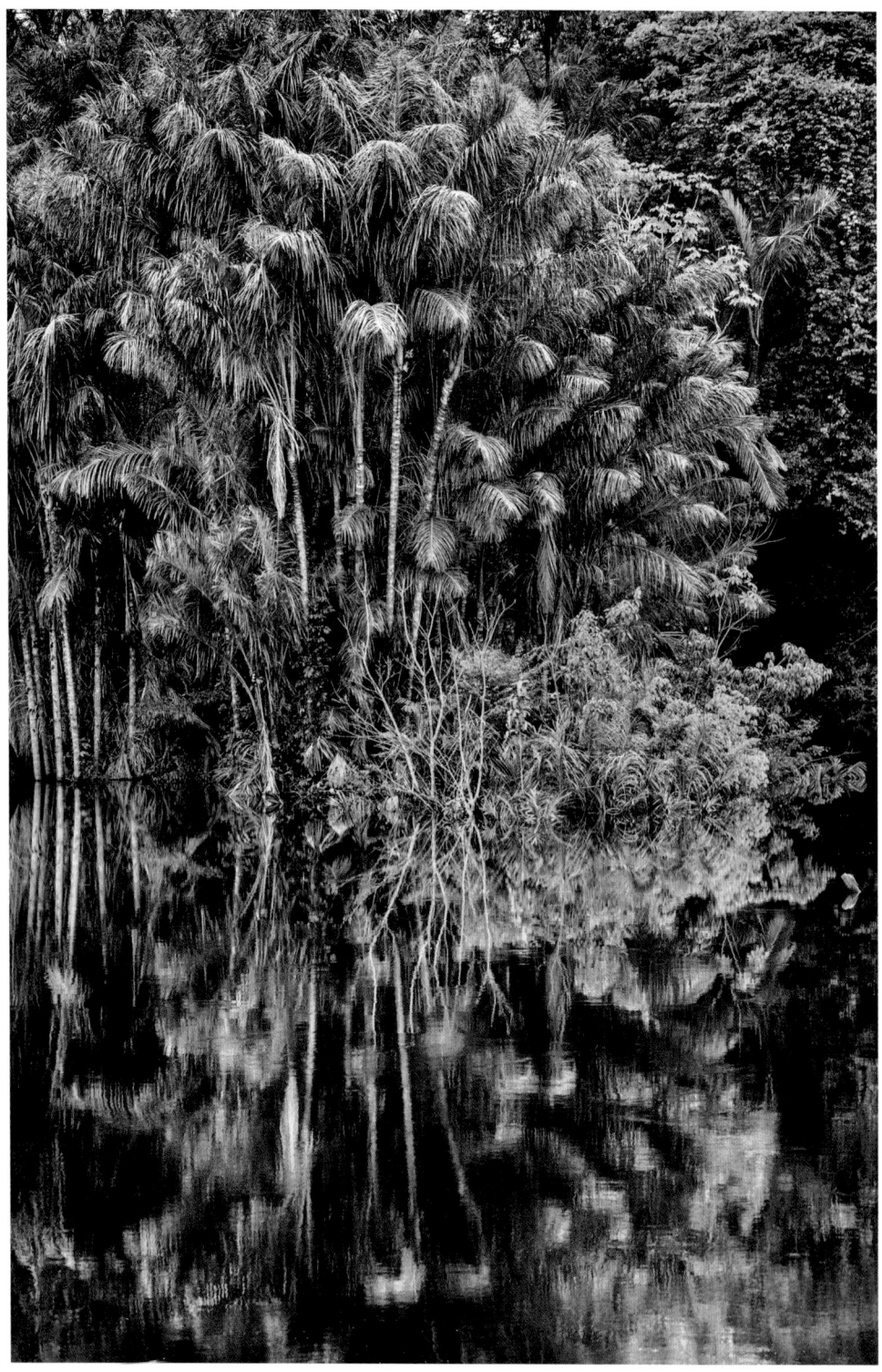

Pages 314/315 Green-winged macaws (*Ara chloropterus*). Jaú River, Jaú National Park, state of Amazonas, 2019.

Opposite A formation of *jauari* palm trees (*Astrocaryum jauari*). Jaú River, Jaú National Park, state of Amazonas, 2019.

Pages 318/319 Edge of an *igapó* forest with palm tree formations, including *jauaris* (*Astrocaryum jauari*). Jaú River, Jaú National Park, state of Amazonas, 2019.

Pages 320/321 An *igapó* forest: in the foreground, a leaning *jauari* palm (*Astrocaryum jauari*). In the middle ground, also leaning, is a type of *cecropia* known in Brazil as an *embaúba-da-várzea* (*Cecropia latiloba*). *Embaúbas* are considered pioneer trees, the first to grow in devastated areas, creating an environment for the establishment of other trees. That is why they

are so common in *igapó* areas, where severe flooding tends to move the riverbanks. Jaú River, Jaú National Park, state of Amazonas, 2019.

Pages 322/323 A great white egret (*Ardea alba*) perched elegantly near the edge of an *igapó* forest. Common in the Amazon rainforest, egrets are *pelecaniform* (pelican-like) birds that live in flocks and feed on fish and other river species. Jaú River, Jaú National Park, state of Amazonas, 2019.

Pages 324/325 A bend in the Gregório River, under the hill where the Yawanawá village of Nova Esperança is located. This region of Acre consists of "new lands," as the river's course changes often due to the force of floodwaters. Rio Gregório Yawanawá Indigenous Territory, state of Acre, 2016.

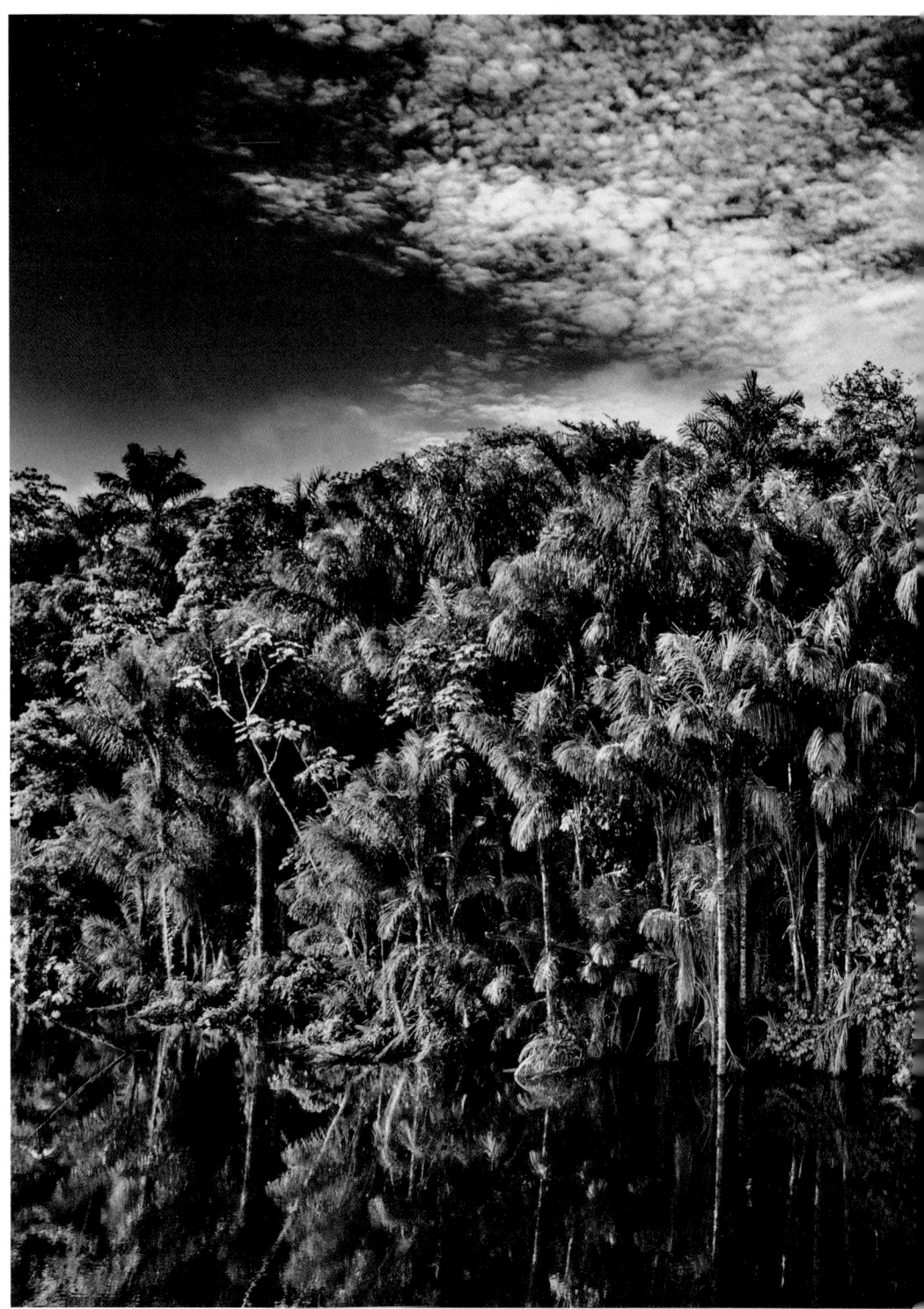

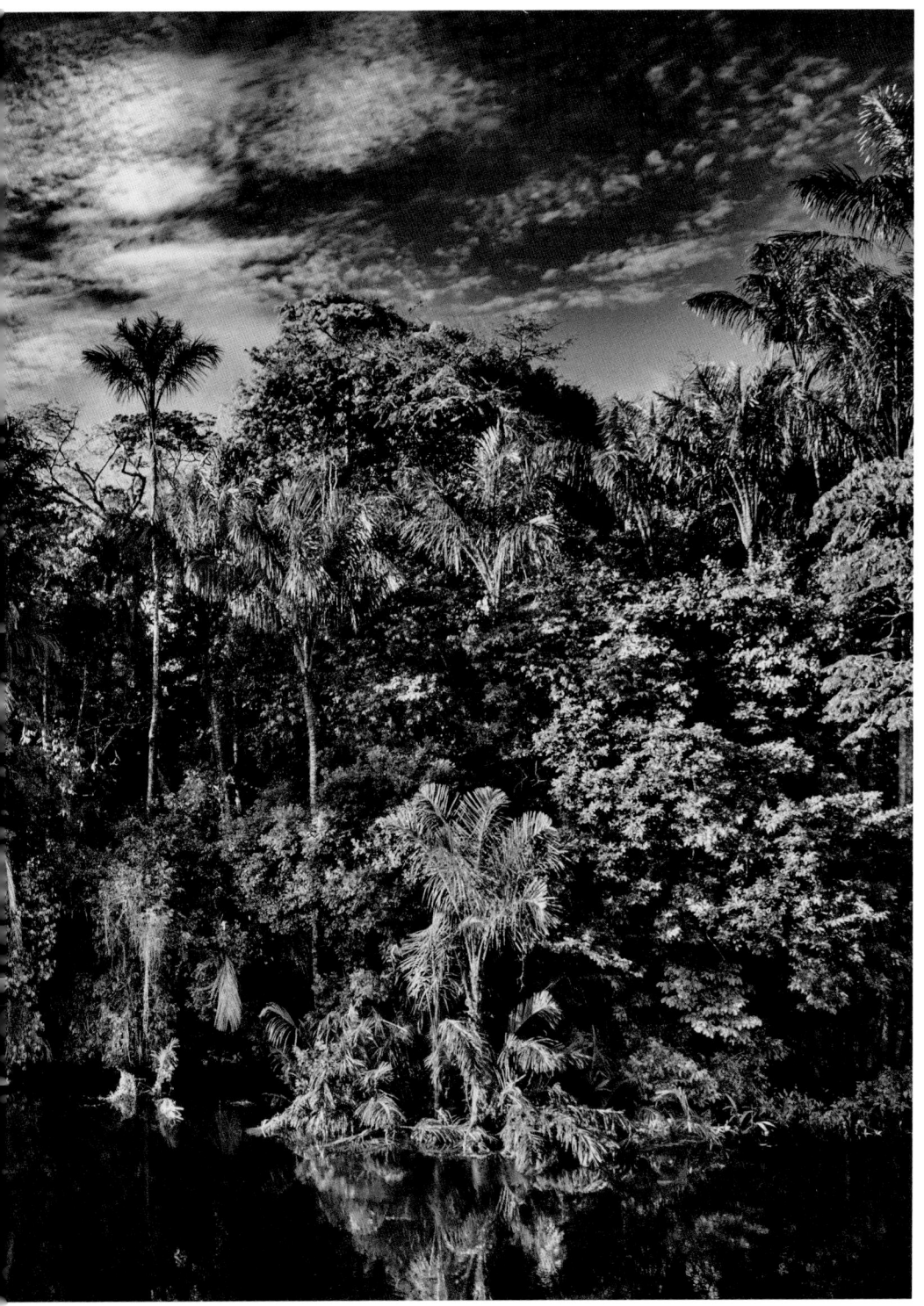

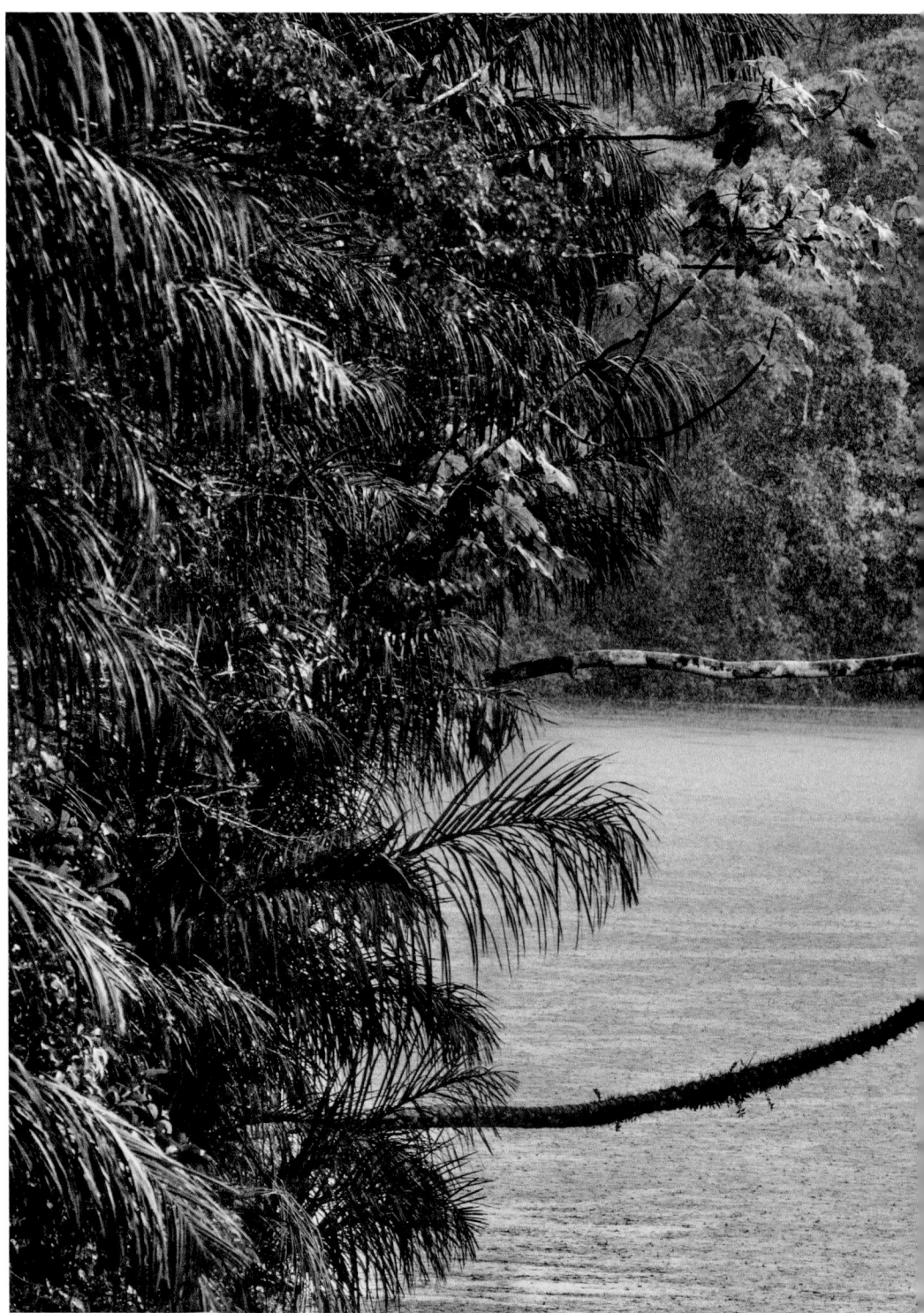

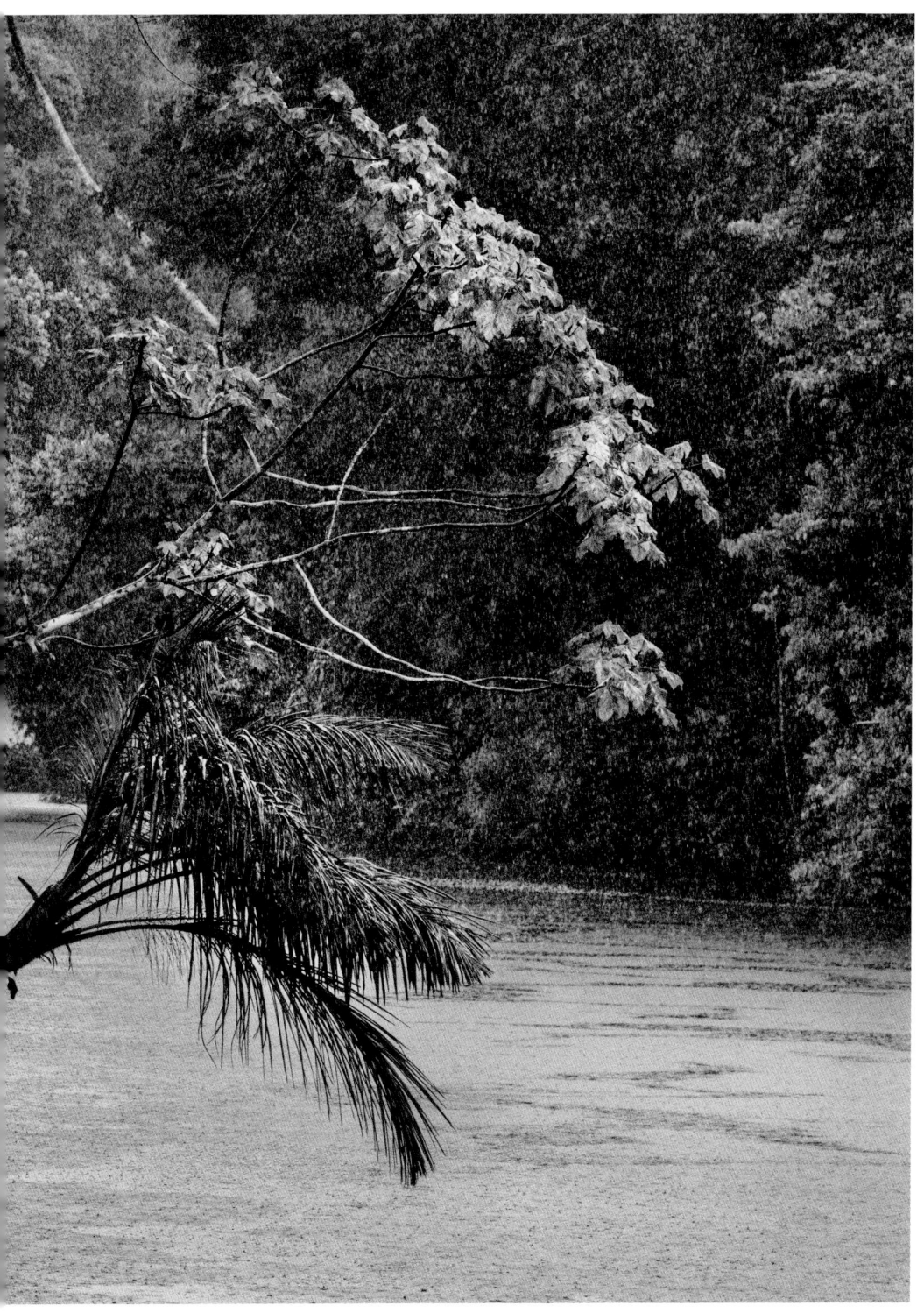

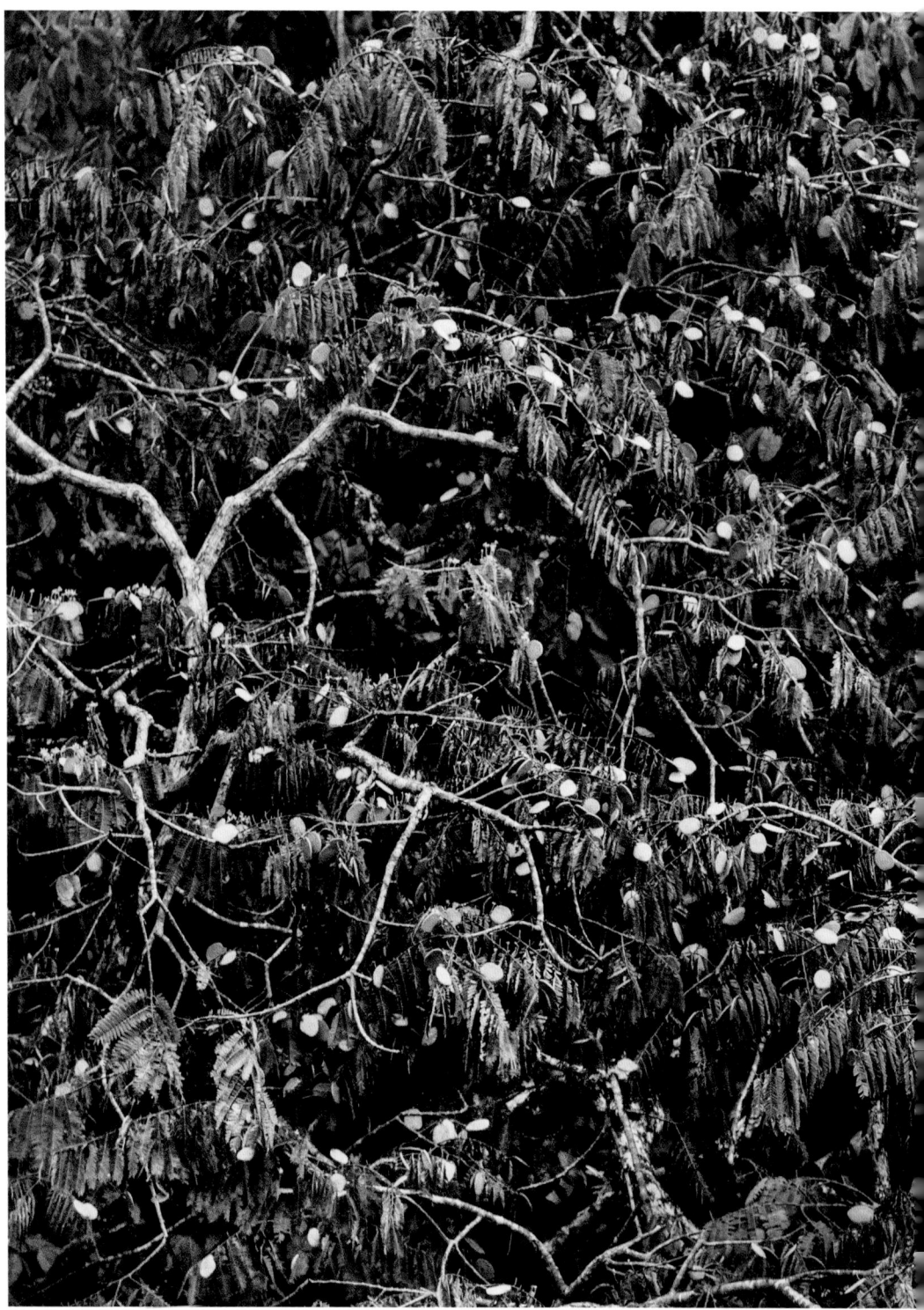

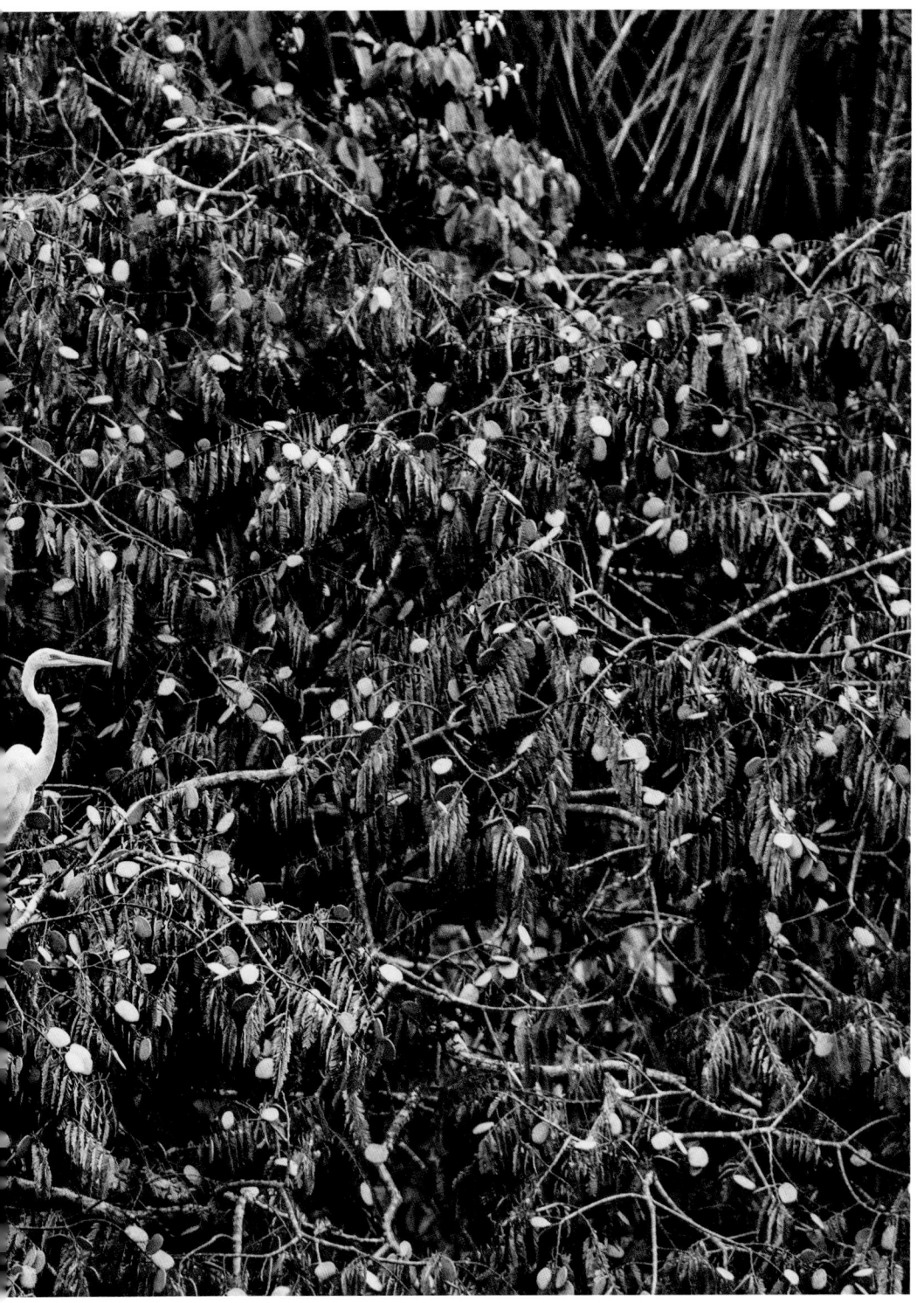

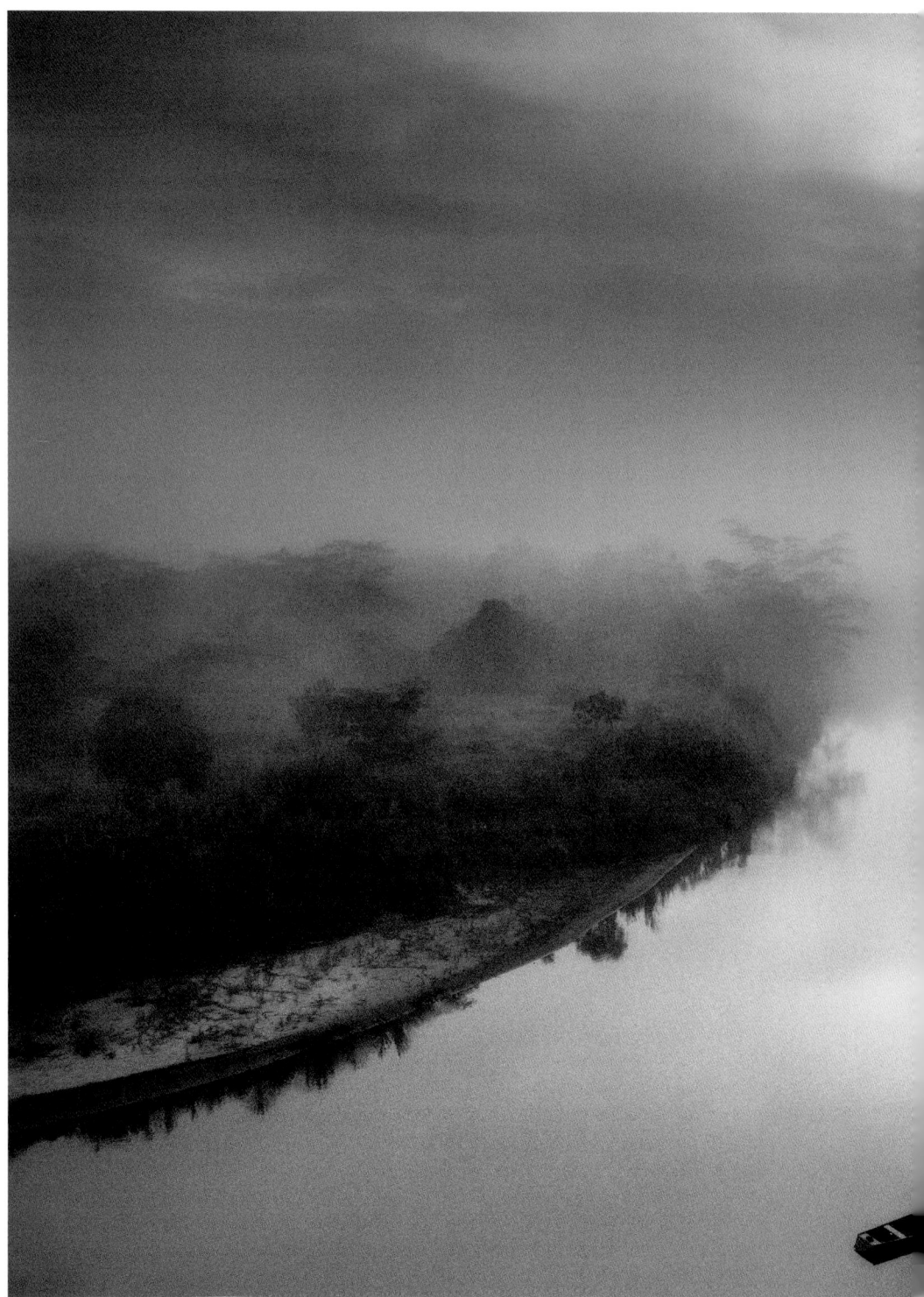

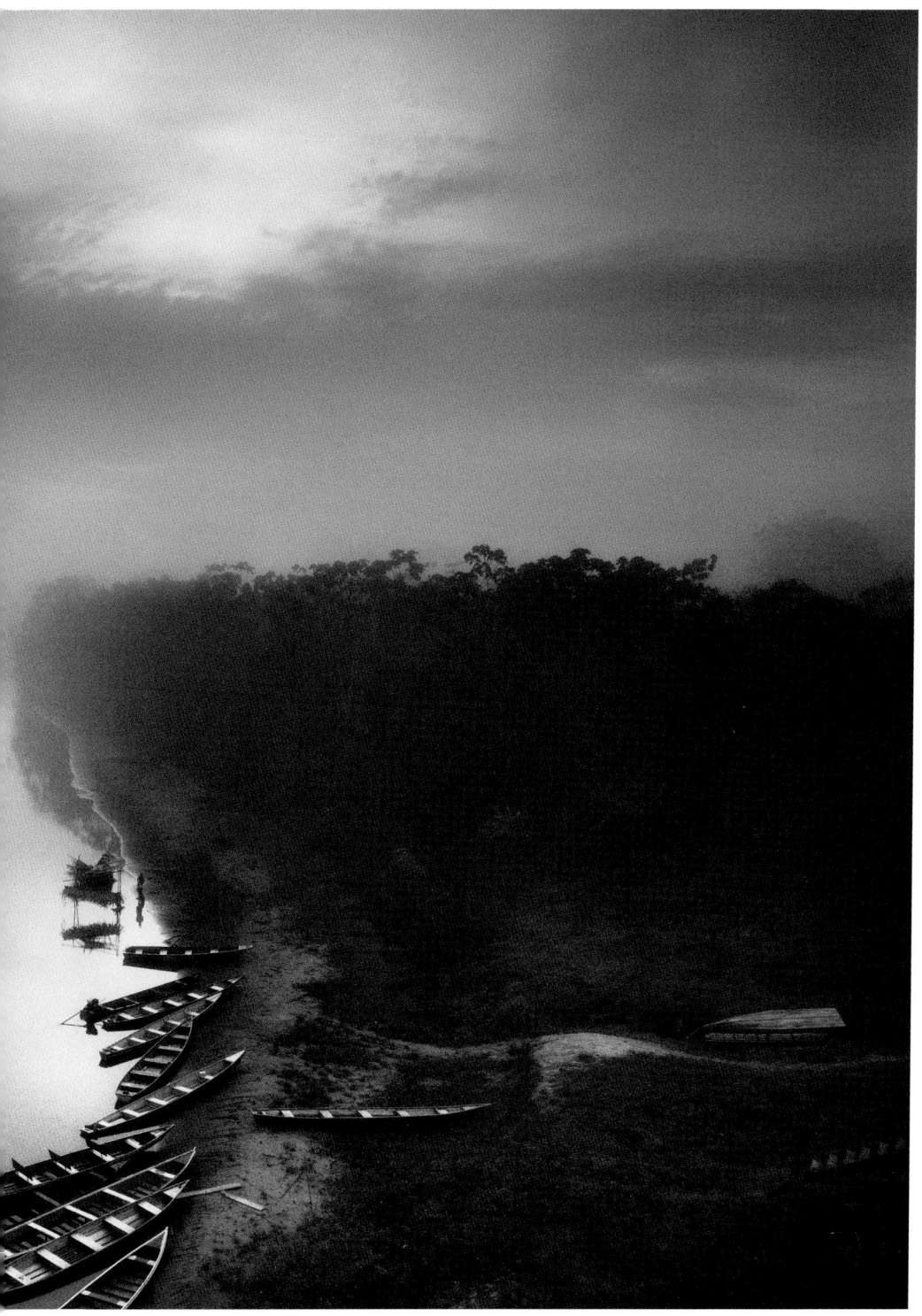

Opposite Cloud forest on the way up Pico da Neblina, in the Imeri mountain range, Maturacá region, municipality of São Gabriel da Cachoeira, state of Amazonas, 2014.

Pages 328/329 Waterfall on the Erepecuru River (also called the Paru de Oeste River), in the north of the state of Pará, near the mountains that mark the border between Brazil and Suriname. Zo'é Indigenous Territory, state of Pará, 2009.

Pages 330/331 Landscape of an *igapó*, a type of forest frequently flooded by blackwater rivers, with *jauari* palm trees (*Astrocaryum jauari*). Jaú River, Jaú National Park, state of Amazonas, 2019.

Pages 332/333 Thick branches of a rubber fig tree (*Ficus clusiifolia*) strangle the trunk of a kapok tree (*Ceiba pentandra*) on the banks of the Crôa River, in Cruzeiro do Sul. State of Acre, 2018.

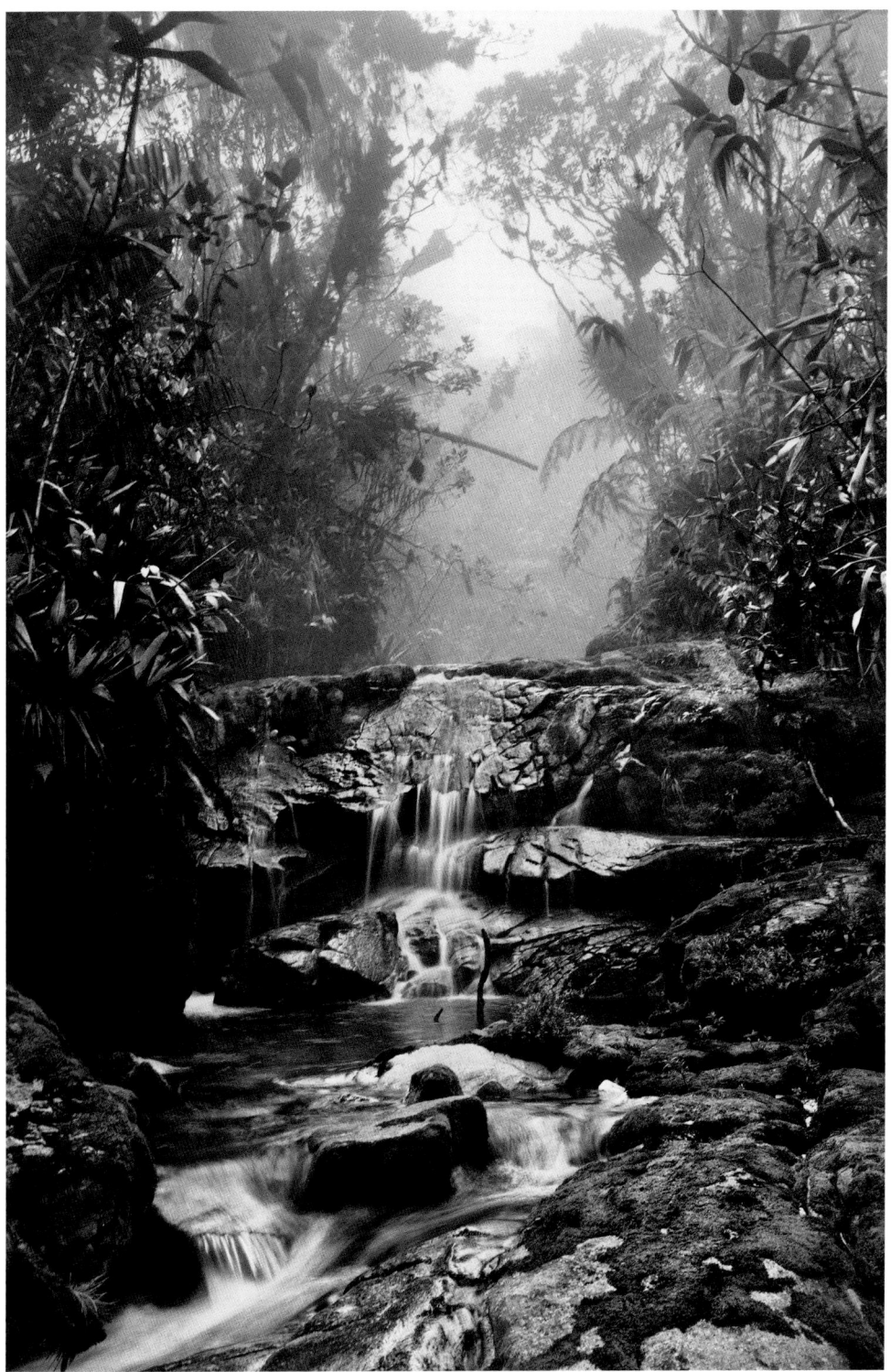

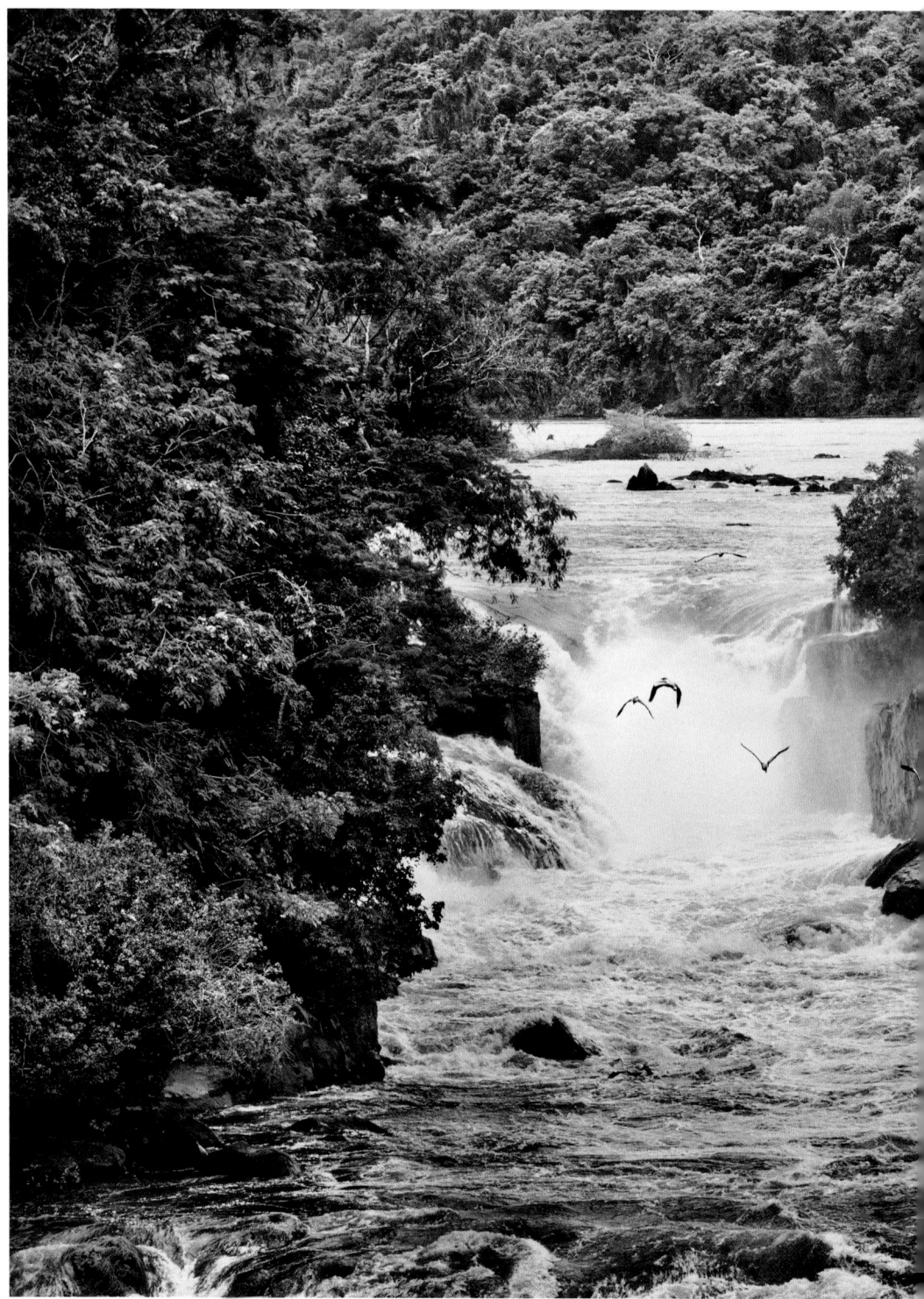

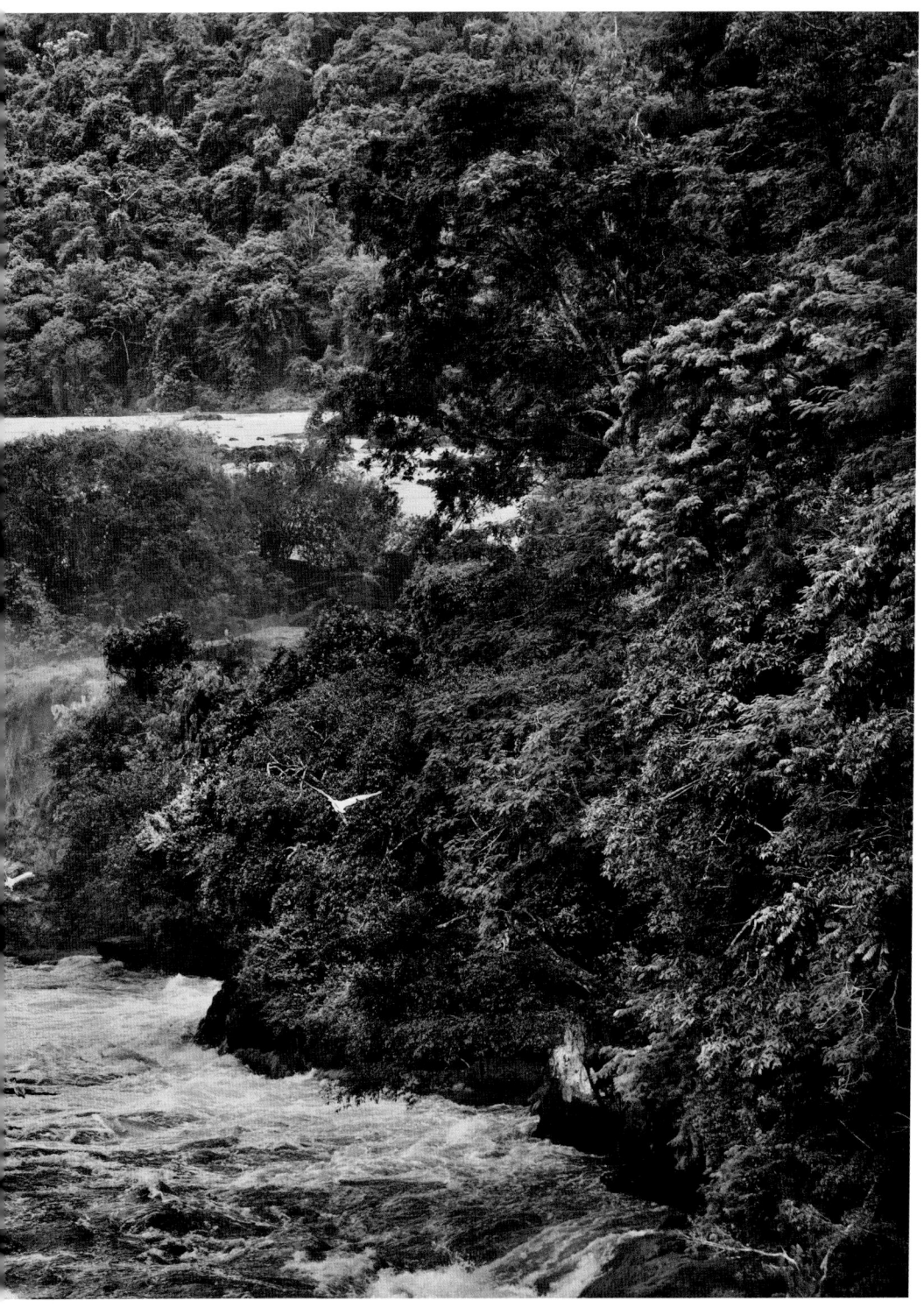

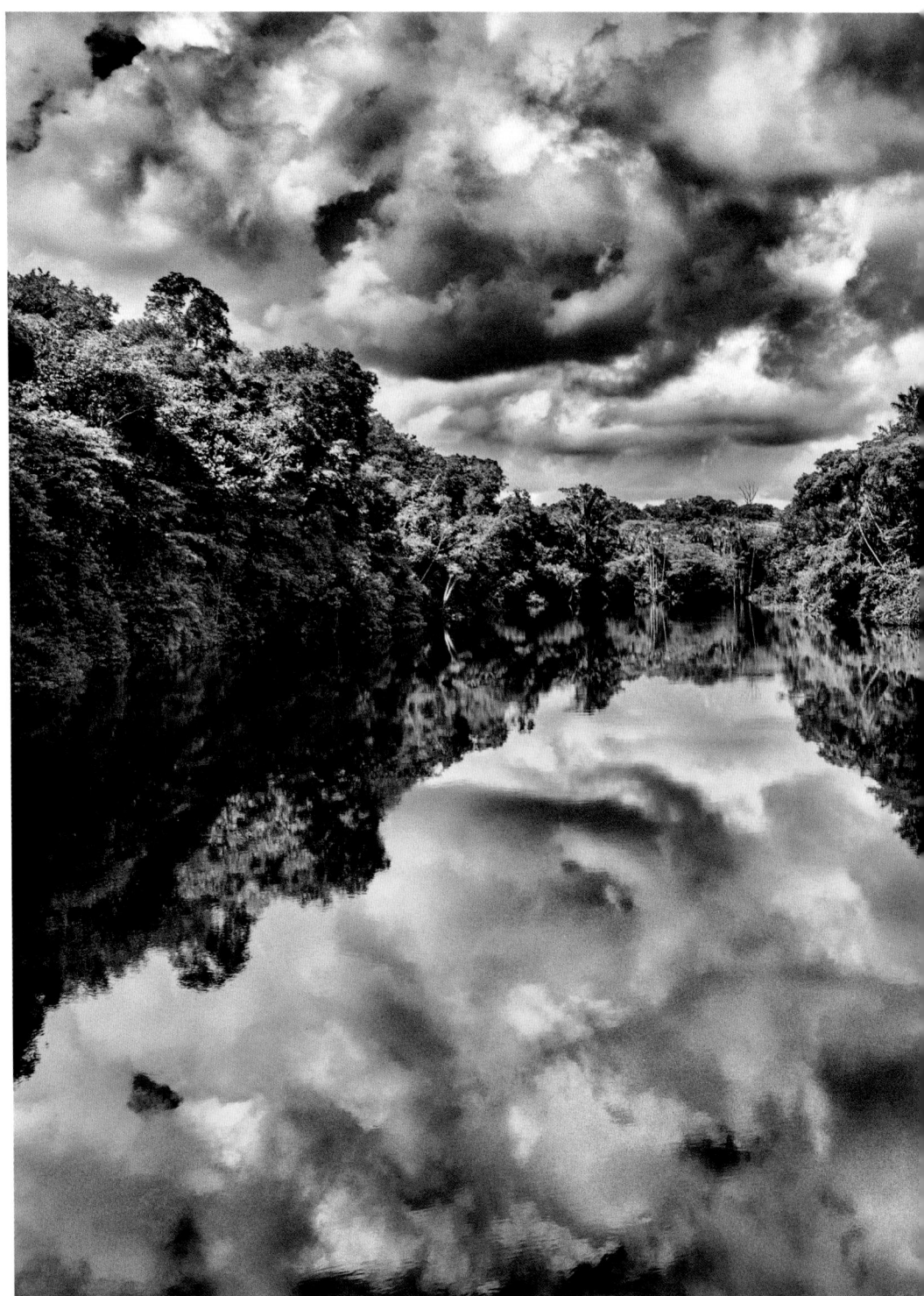

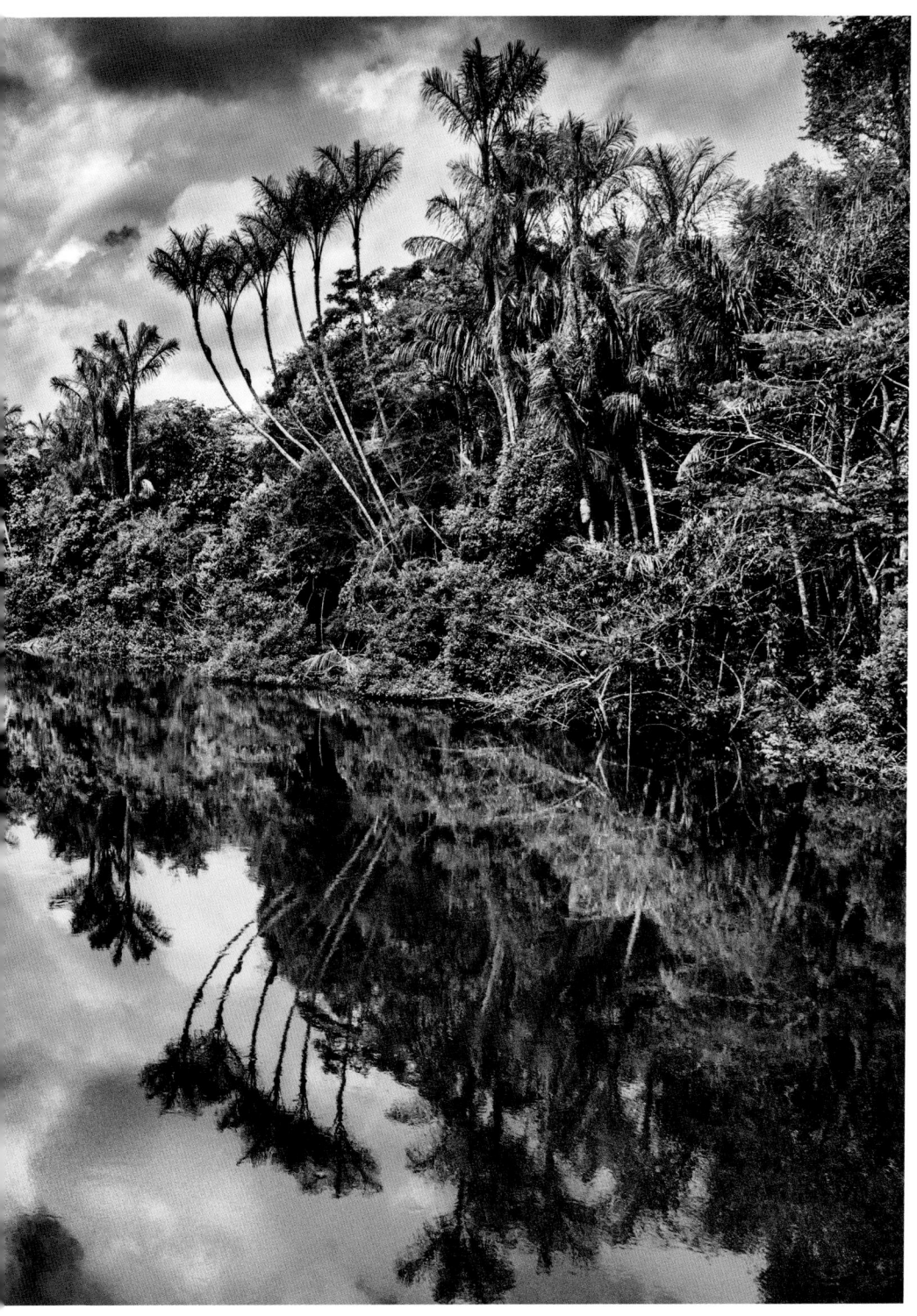

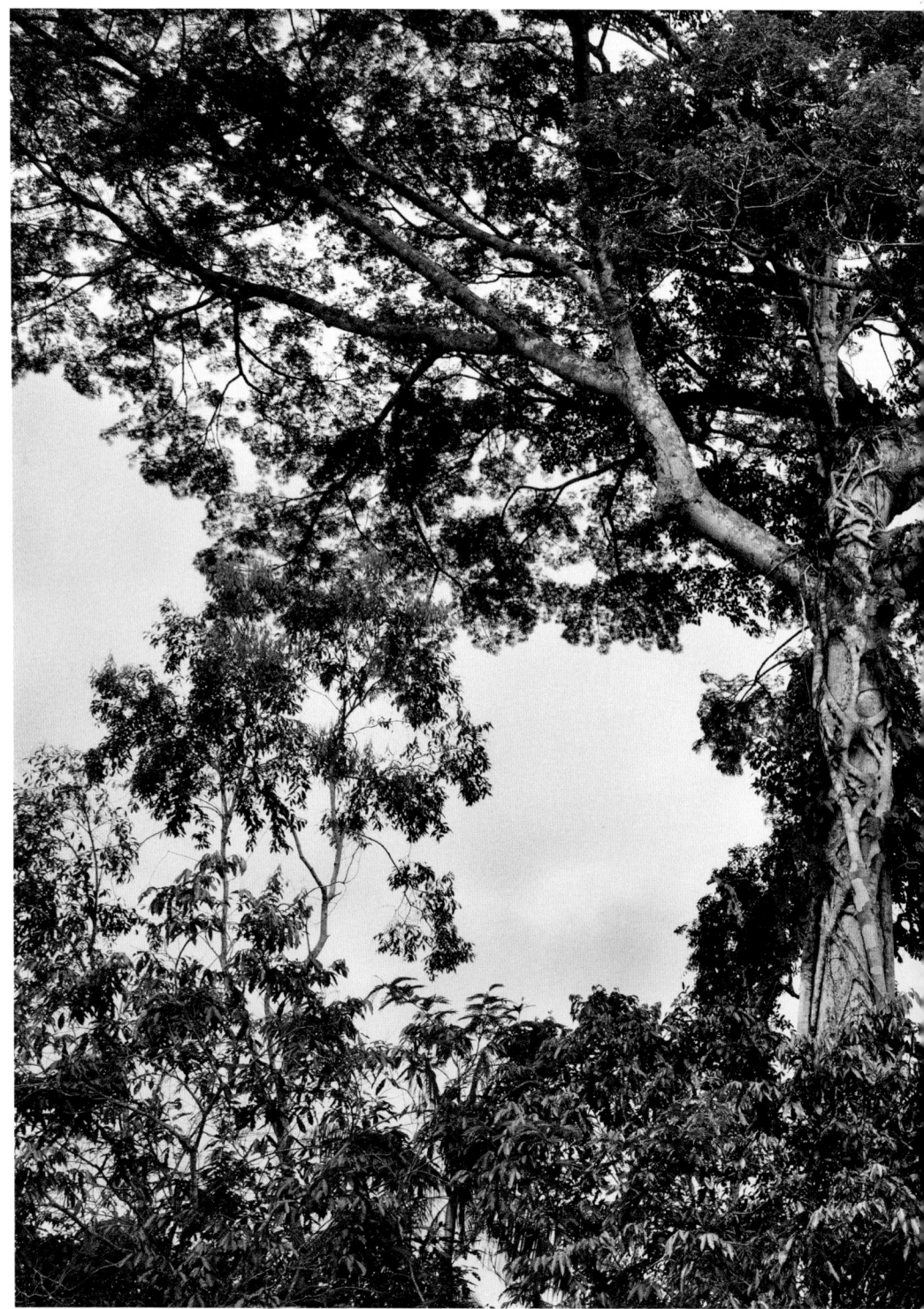

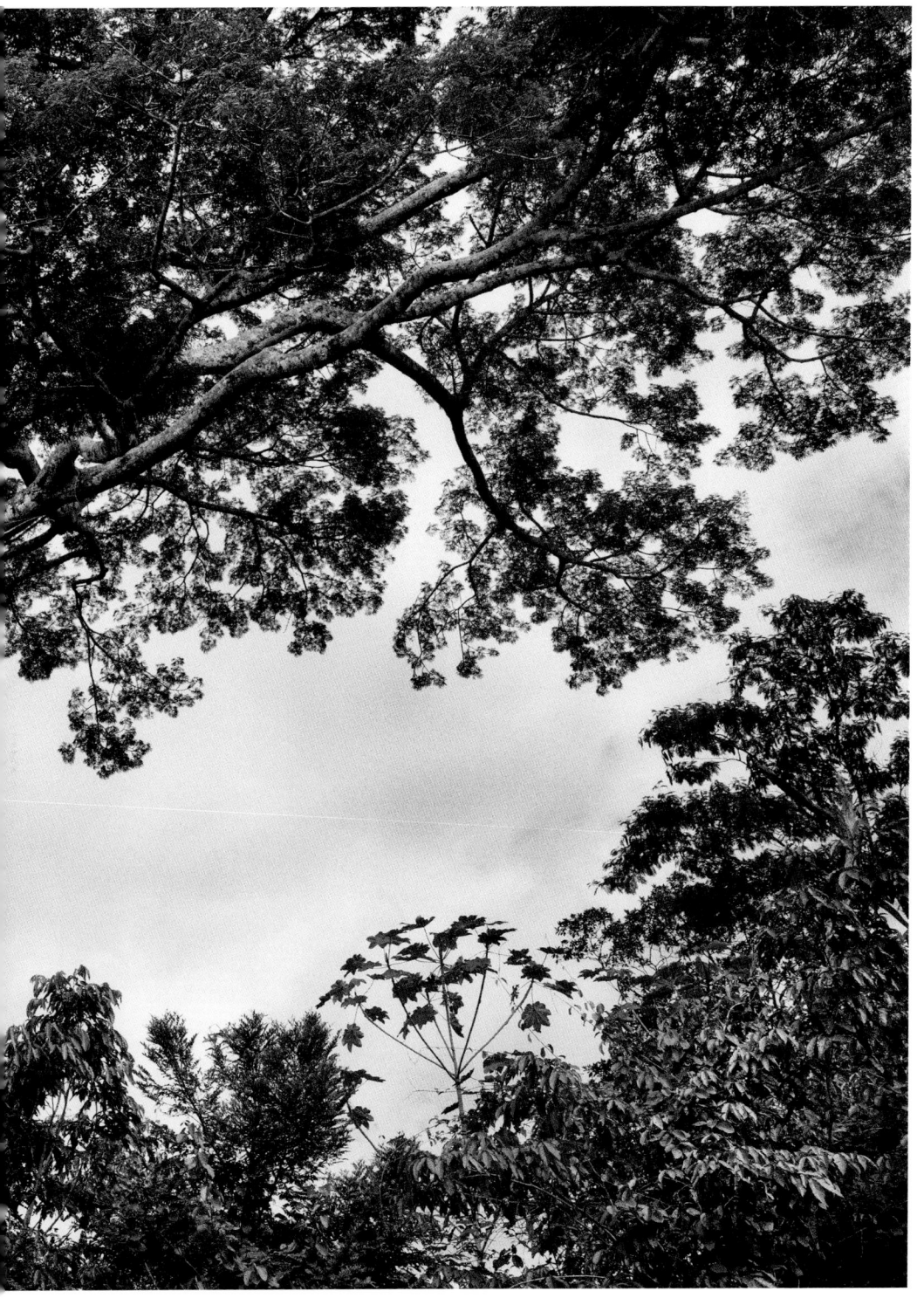

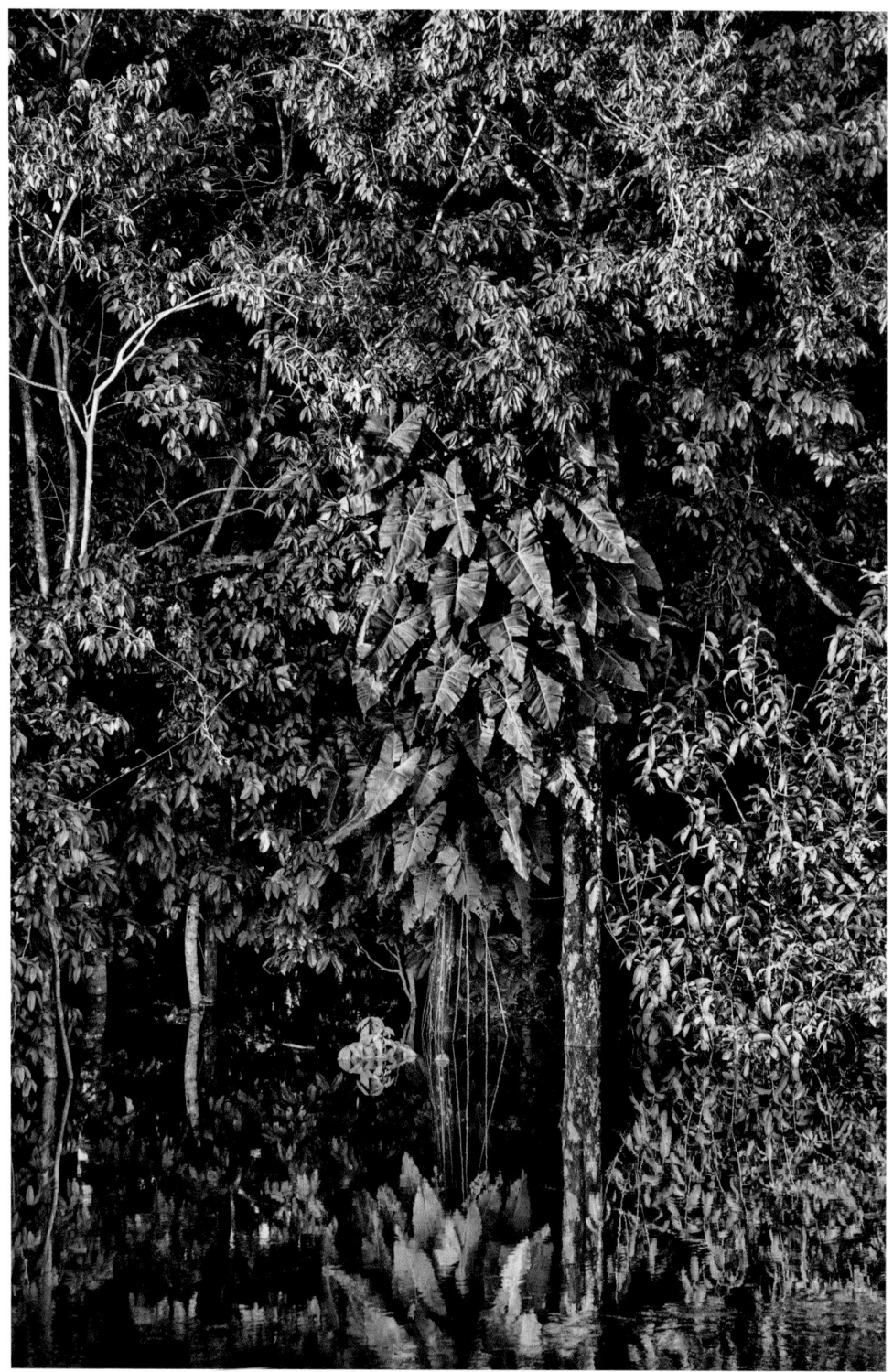

Opposite A philodendron (*Philodendron solimoesense*) is prominent in this view of an *igapó*, a type of forest frequently flooded by blackwater rivers. Jaú River, Jaú National Park, state of Amazonas, 2019.

Pages 336/337 In an *igapó*, a treetop on the banks of the Jaú River is almost completely covered by water during the flood season. Jaú National Park, state of Amazonas, 2019.

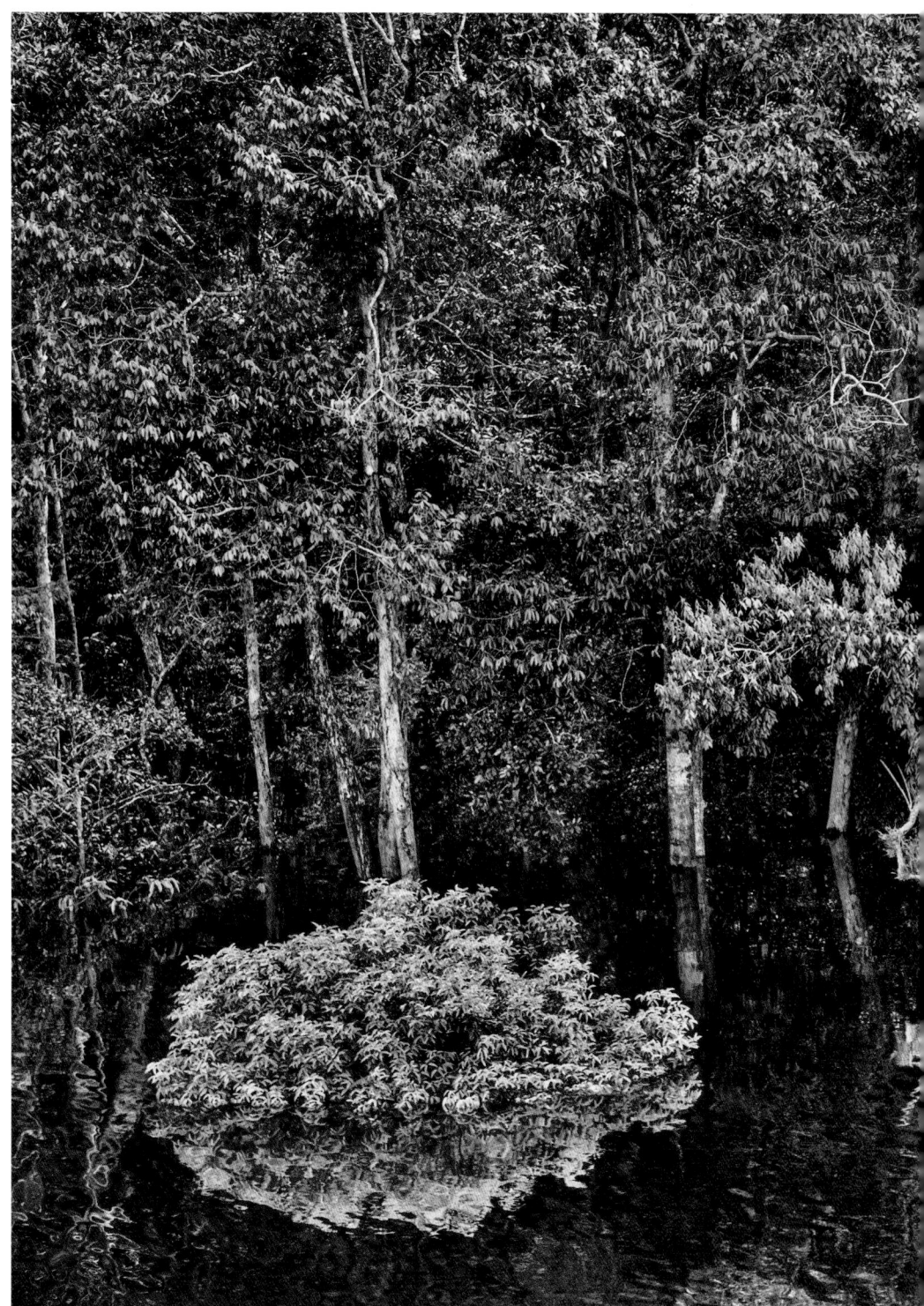

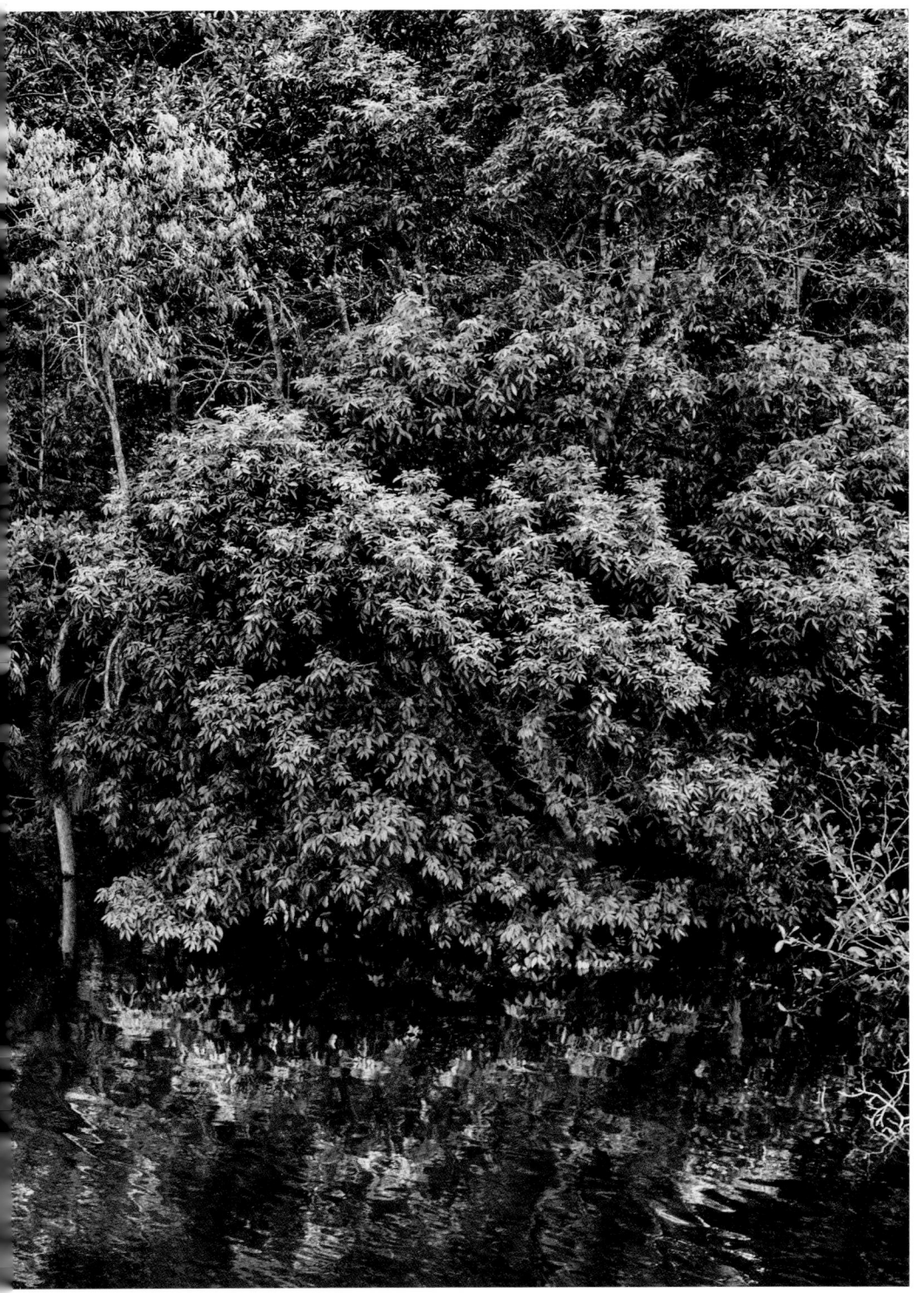

Opposite Water covers the trunks almost to the treetops in an *igapó*, a type of forest often flooded by blackwater rivers. Jaú River, Jaú National Park, state of Amazonas, 2019.

Pages 340/341 An *igapó*, prominent in the photo: a *jauari* palm (*Astrocaryum jauari*). Jaú River, Jaú National Park, state of Amazonas, 2019.

Pages 342/343 Tapajós River area, near Santarém, state of Pará, 2009.

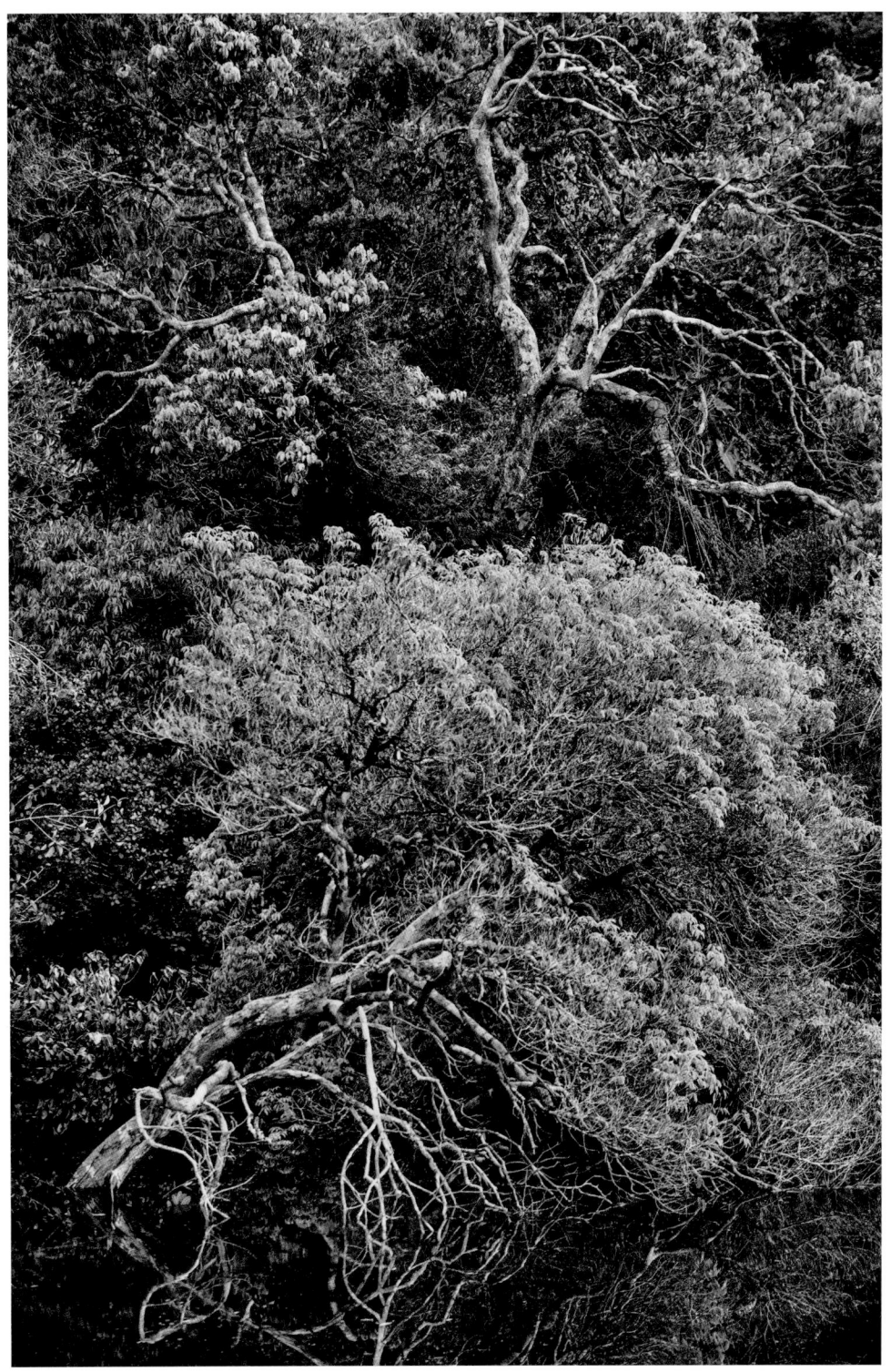

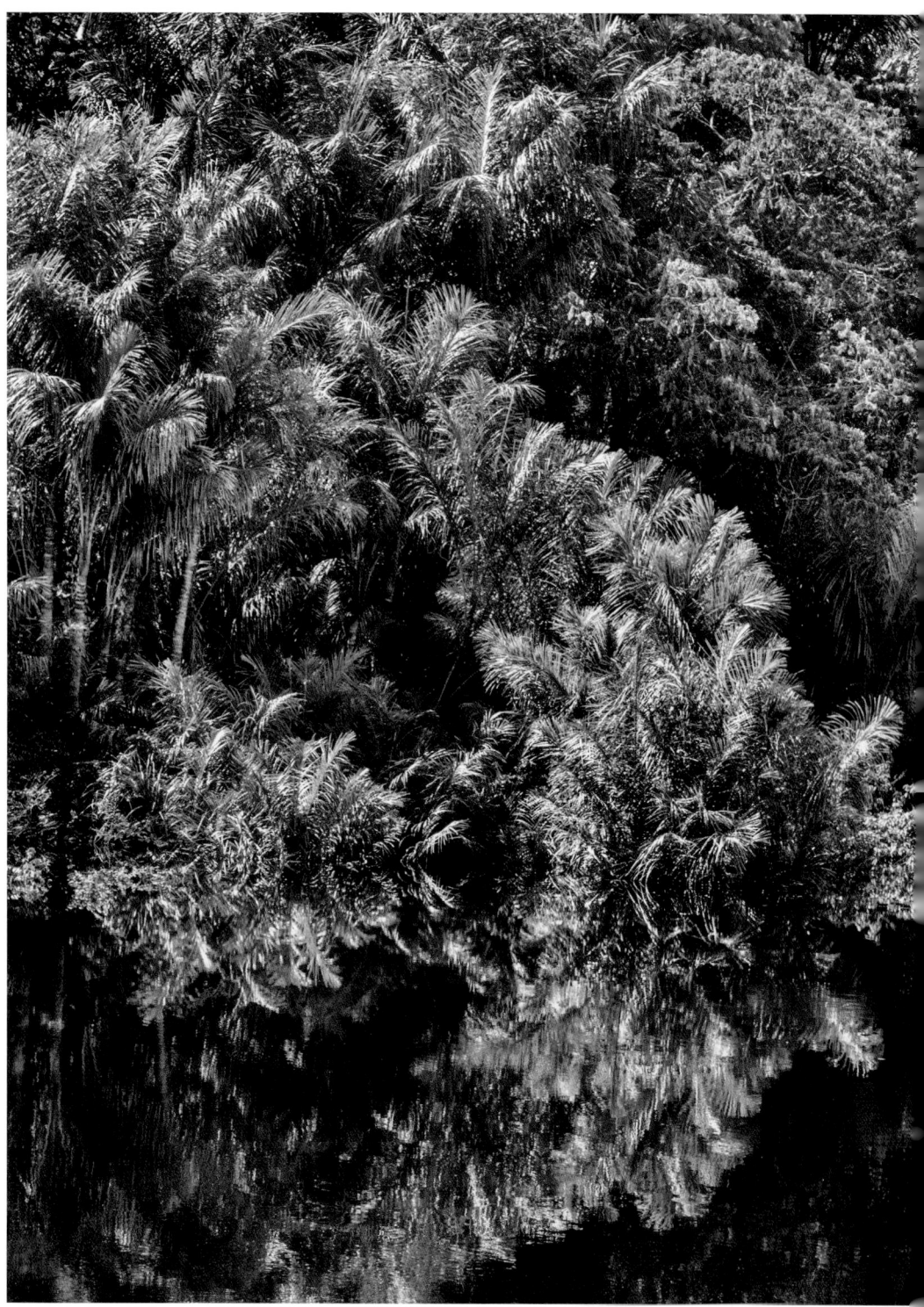

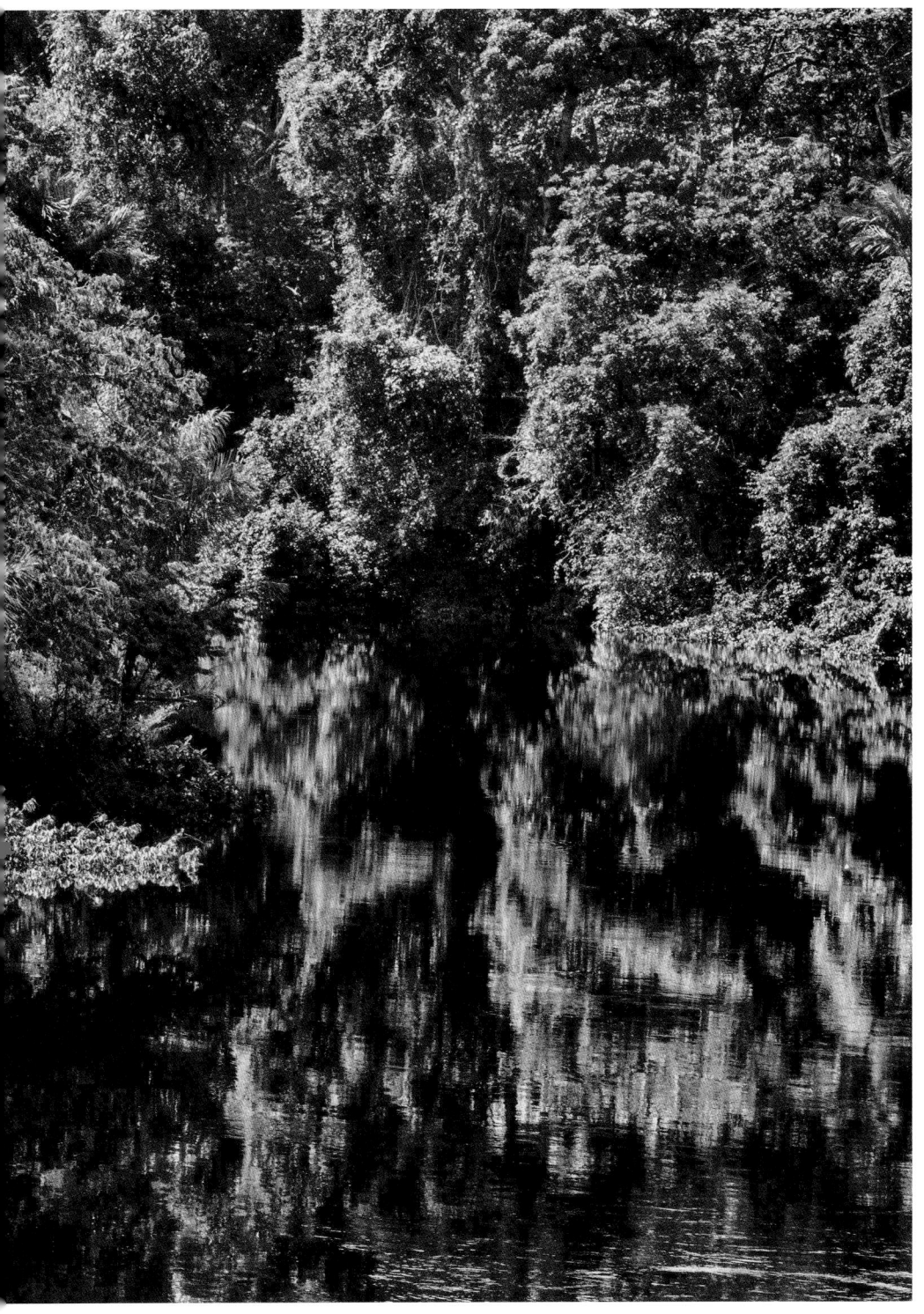

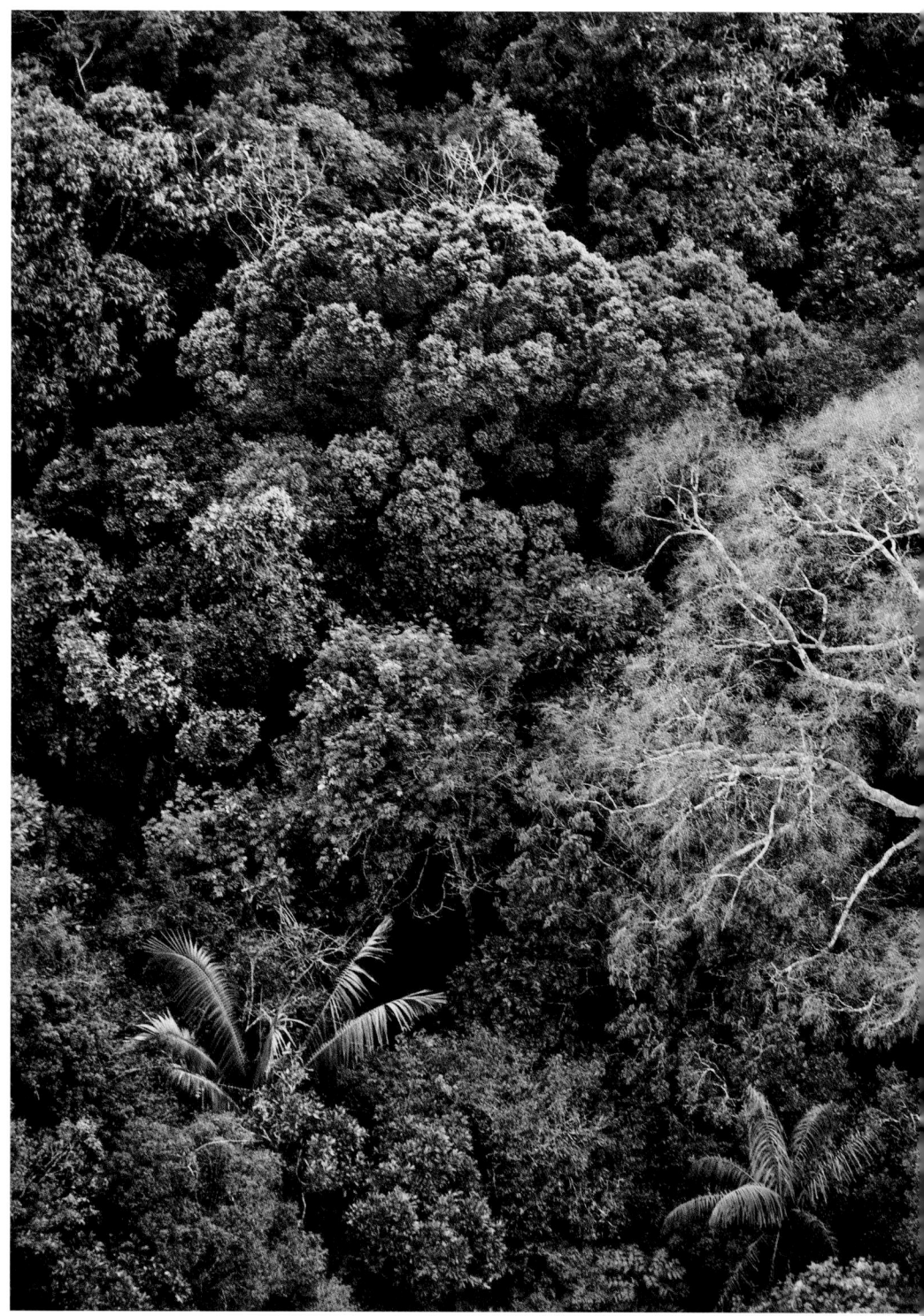

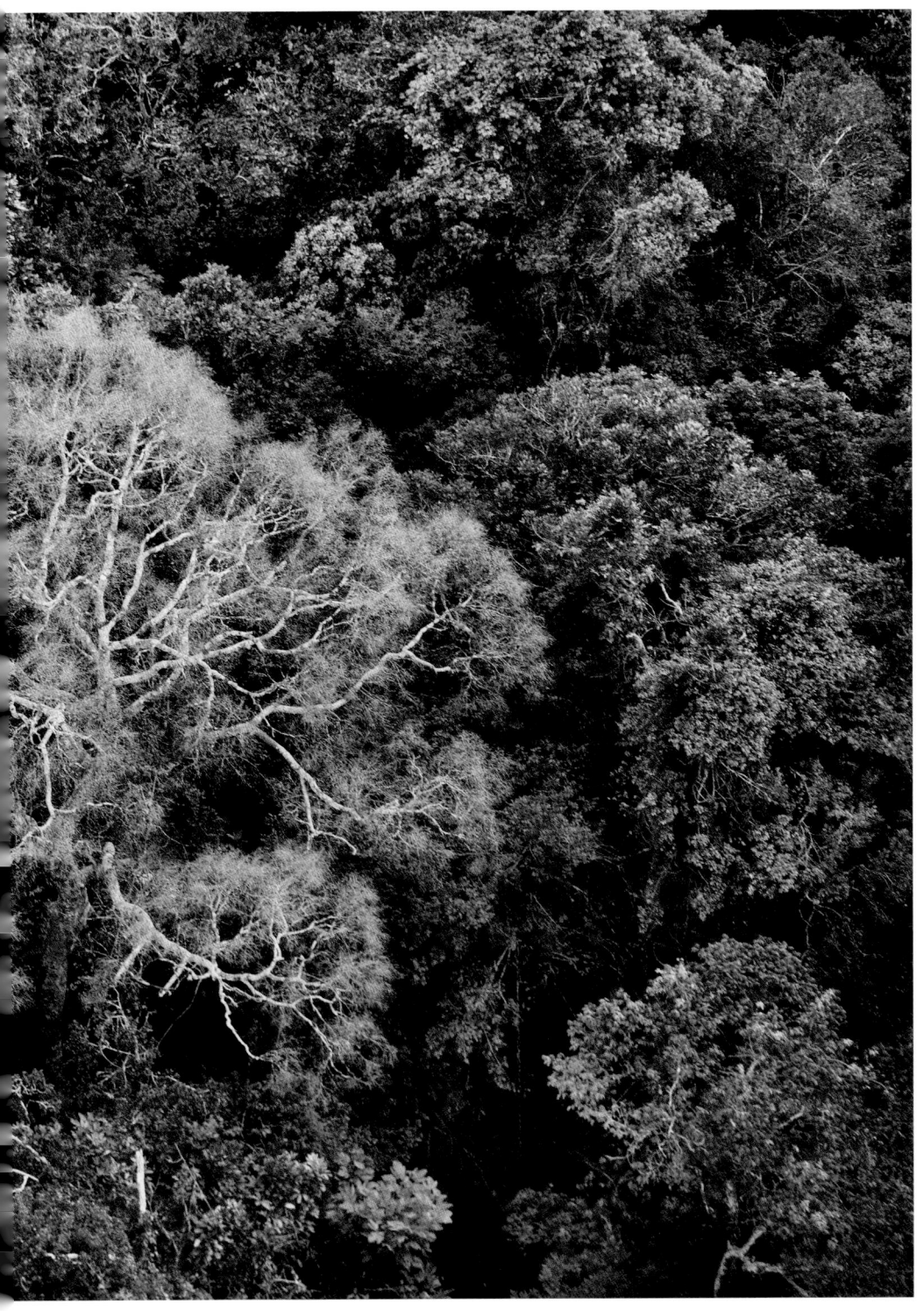

MACUXI

Demarcation of the Macuxi land, one of Brazil's oldest recognized indigenous territories, began in 1919 as indicated by a marker placed in the village of Maturuca by the pioneer of Brazilian indigenism, Marshal Cândido Rondon. Their land was gradually expropriated throughout the 20th century, occupied by ranchers and rice farmers. At first, this was described as a loan of land, but then it was taken by force, and finally, the indigenous people were expelled from most of the territory.

By the late 1970s, the indigenous people had lost ownership of the land to ranchers who refused to recognize their historic right to it. The indigenous people lived concentrated in towns, constantly threatened by violent, gun-toting agents of the ranch owners. There was a prolonged movement, begun in 1980, called "Ou Vai ou Racha" (which means, roughly, "All or Nothing") that started mobilizing indigenous people and demanding recognition of their land rights.

When I visited them in 1998, the areas where indigenous people lived were being watched and surrounded. The small plane I was traveling in was encircled by gunmen when we landed in a nearby town. They refused to sell us fuel.

New leadership emerged in that era, with the goal of reviving cultural elements, pride, and, right from the start, their language. That is precisely why many of the young leaders were and still are teachers. They trained the new generation that reconquered their right to the land. These photographs document that moment at the start of the movement to regain their territory.

The final decision came with recognition of the Raposa–Serra do Sol Indigenous Territory and its approval by the administration of President Luiz Inácio Lula da Silva in 2005, and confirmation of the decision by the Federal Supreme Court in 2009.

As its name suggests, the Raposa–Serra do Sol Indigenous Territory is divided into two areas with different climates: to the south, the fields (called *Lavrado*) occupy about 70 percent of the area; to the north, the mountain areas, with denser forest, make up the other 30 percent of this 1,747,460-hectare (4,318,070-acre) territory, with an indigenous population of some 26,000 from five peoples: Macuxi, Ingarikó, Patamona, and Taurepang, who are part of the same group, called Pémon, speak Carib (a language that gave its name to the Caribbean Sea, where it originated). There are also Wapichana indigenous people living in this territory, who speak Arawakan, a language from Central America.

The mountain range features one of the most impressive mountains in all Brazil, Mount Roraima, at the confluence of the triple border between Brazil, Venezuela, and Guyana. Rising to 2,810 meters (9,220 feet), it represents one of the oldest geological formations on Earth: a type of mesa called a *tepui*, typical of the Pacaraima range. Rain is abundant on the mountaintop, hence the waterfalls that pour down its slopes.

Pages 346/347 Mount Roraima near the Macuxi community of Maturuca, the largest village in the Raposa–Serra do Sol Indigenous Territory. In these mesa-like mountains, the terrain changes suddenly and completely as the jungle gives way to a strangely arid landscape that reminds me of far-off Central Asia. Erosion has sculpted thick crevasses into the hillsides, their edges resembling lava flows. The only break in this dull brown landscape is the sight of narrow lines of green where trees crowd together along the course of the water. This is the *Lavrado*, also part of the Amazon rainforest but completely different from what I had seen before. Raposa–Serra do Sol Indigenous Territory, state of Roraima, 2018.

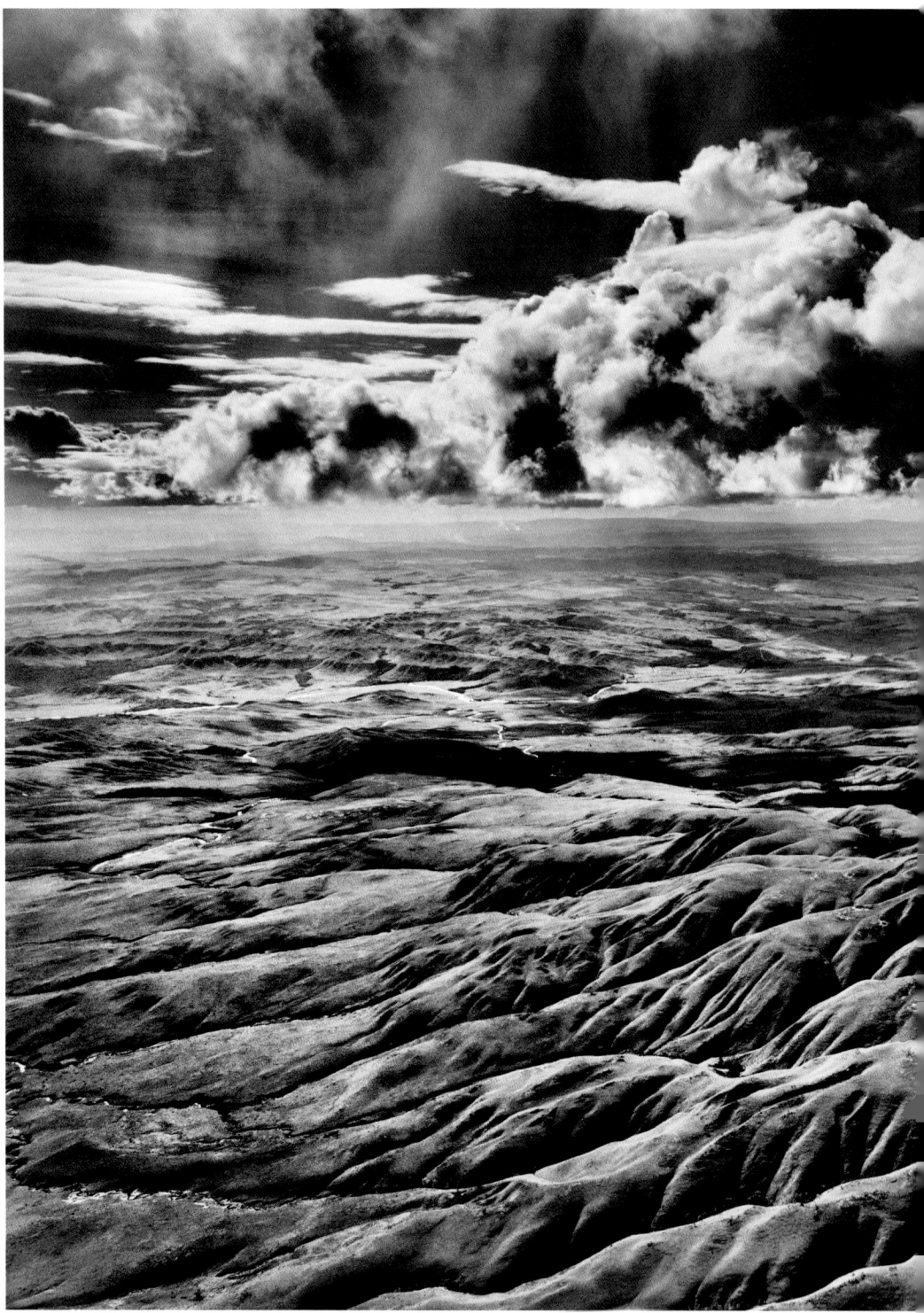

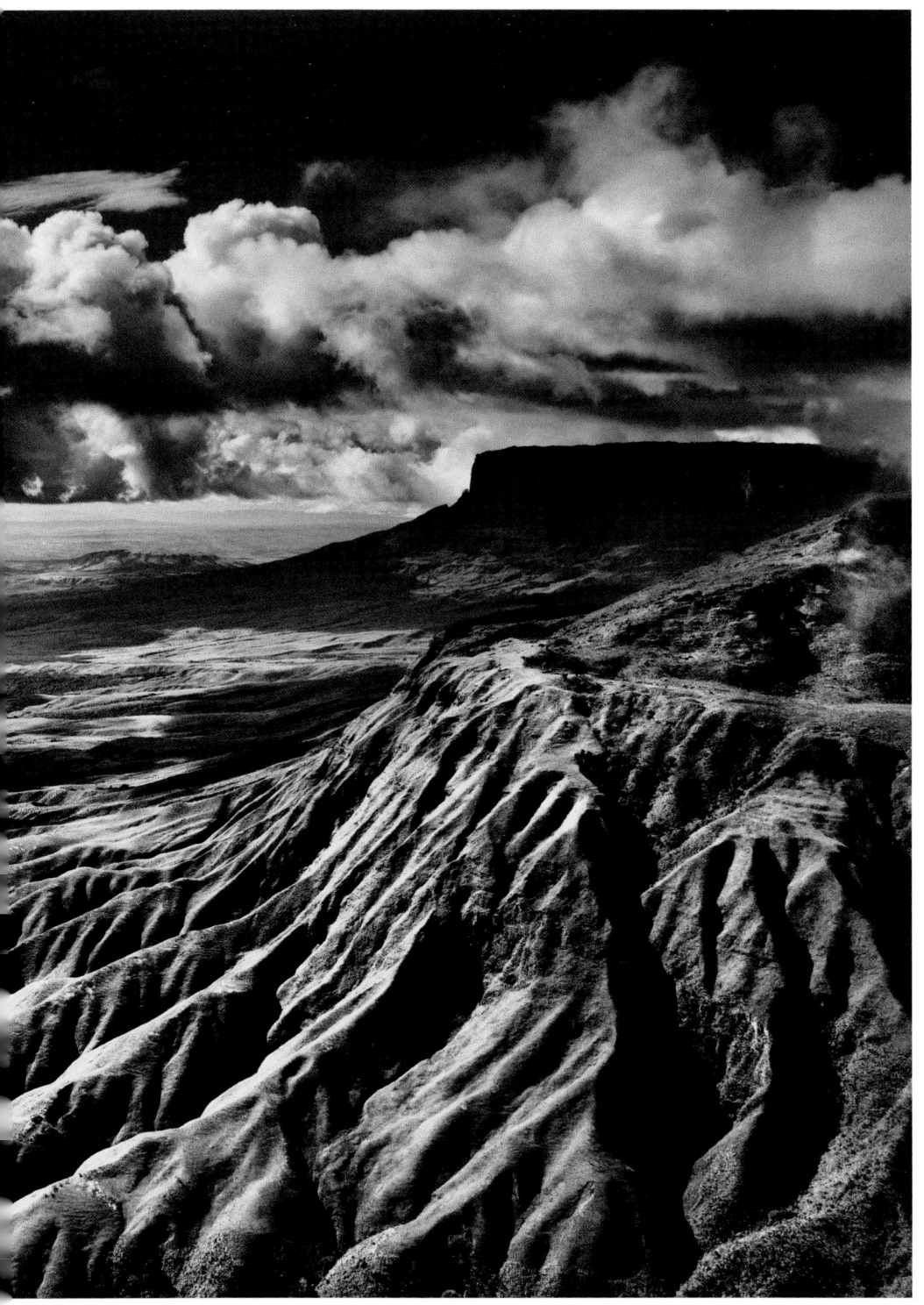

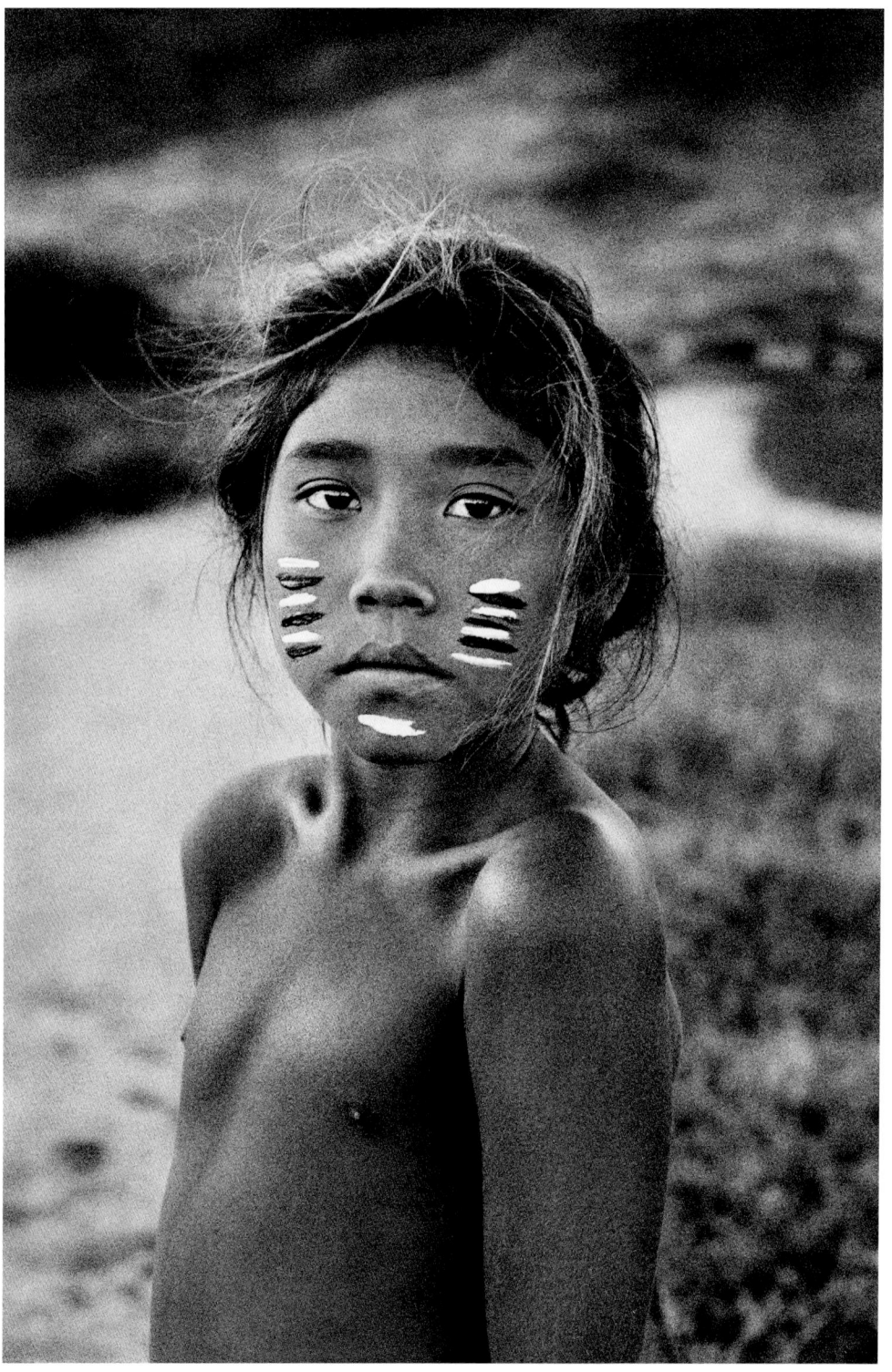

Opposite Valderlania Macuxi, resident of the community of Maturuca. Raposa–Serra do Sol Indigenous Territory, state of Roraima, 1998.

Pages 350/351 This indigenous land consists of two very distinct environments: the mountains with their denser forest and the plains with their characteristic meadows, known locally as *Lavrado*, meaning "plowed land." Raposa–Serra do Sol Indigenous Territory, state of Roraima, 2018.

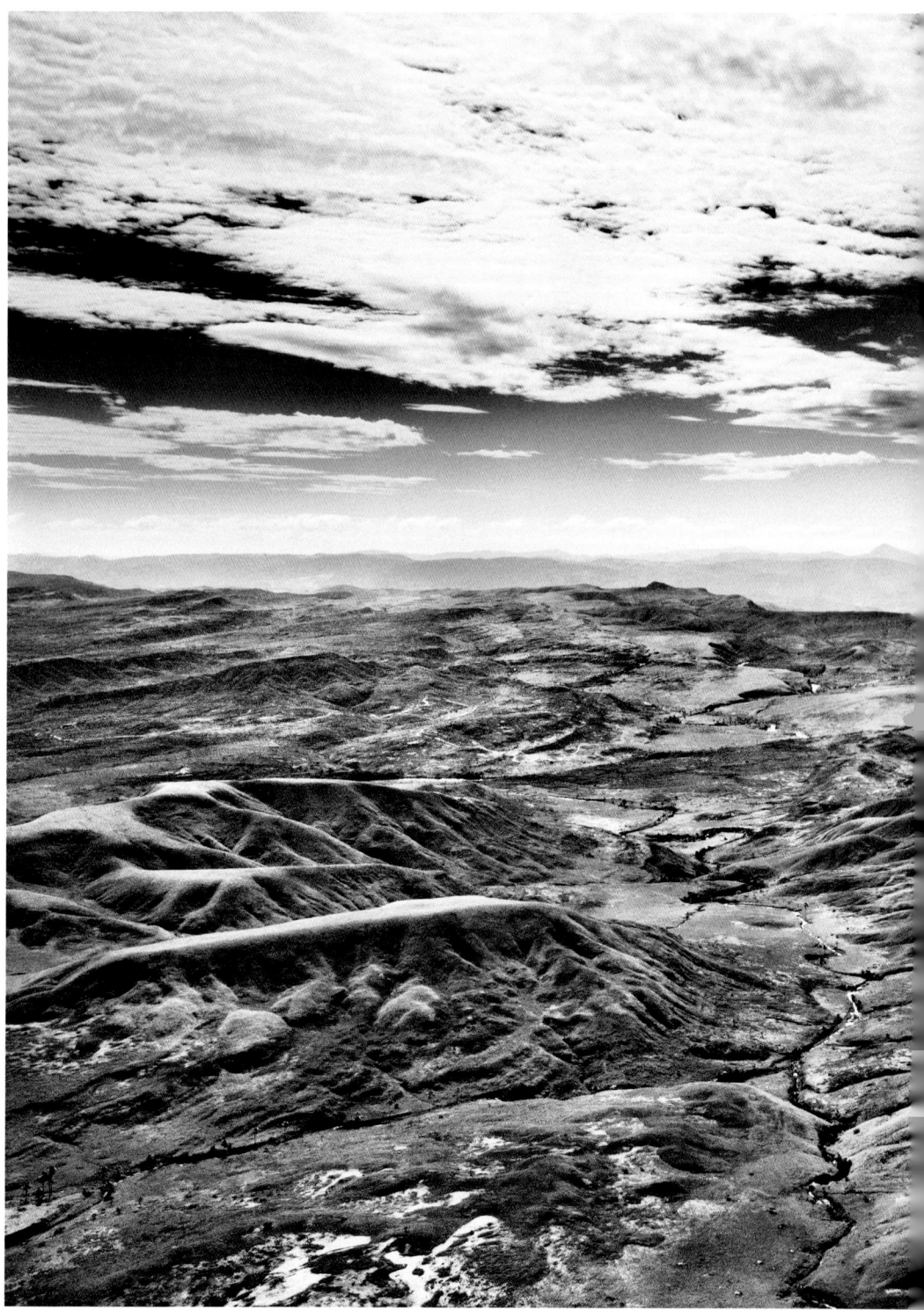

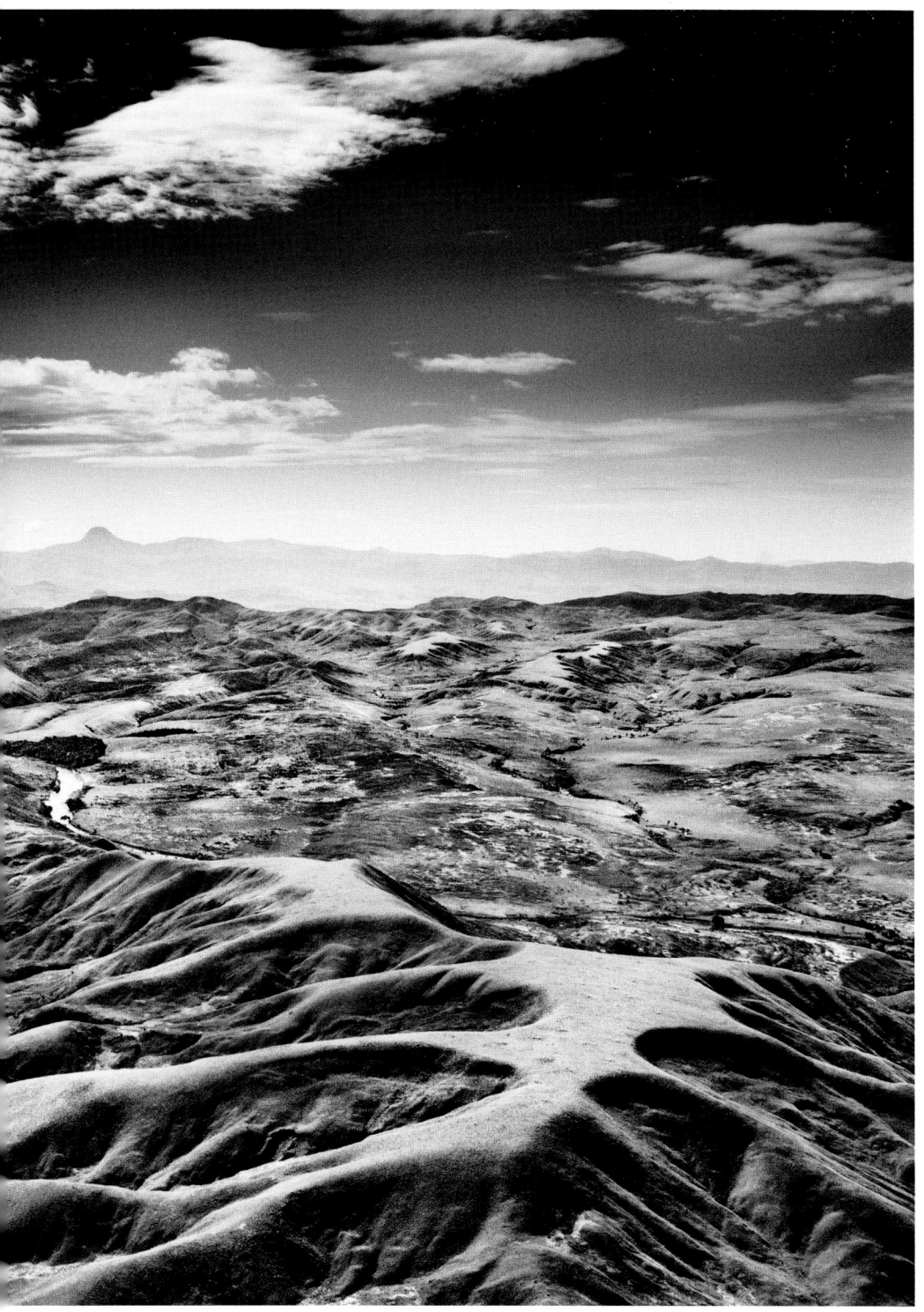

Opposite Elaine Afonso da Silva Macuxi, from Camararem, in the Raposa–Serra do Sol Indigenous Territory, state of Roraima, 1998.

Pages 354/355 The indigenous territory has two well-defined environments: one is the mountains, with denser forest. The other is the plains with their characteristic fields, which in the region are called *Lavrado*. Raposa–Serra do Sol Indigenous Territory, state of Roraima, 2018.

Pages 356/357 The Macuxi have coexisted frequently with whites for a longer time, and long ago began having dogs as pets. Raposa–Serra do Sol Indigenous Territory, state of Roraima, 1998.

Pages 358/359 Members of the Macuxi indigenous community of Eremutaken. Raposa–Serra do Sol Indigenous Territory, state of Roraima, 1998.

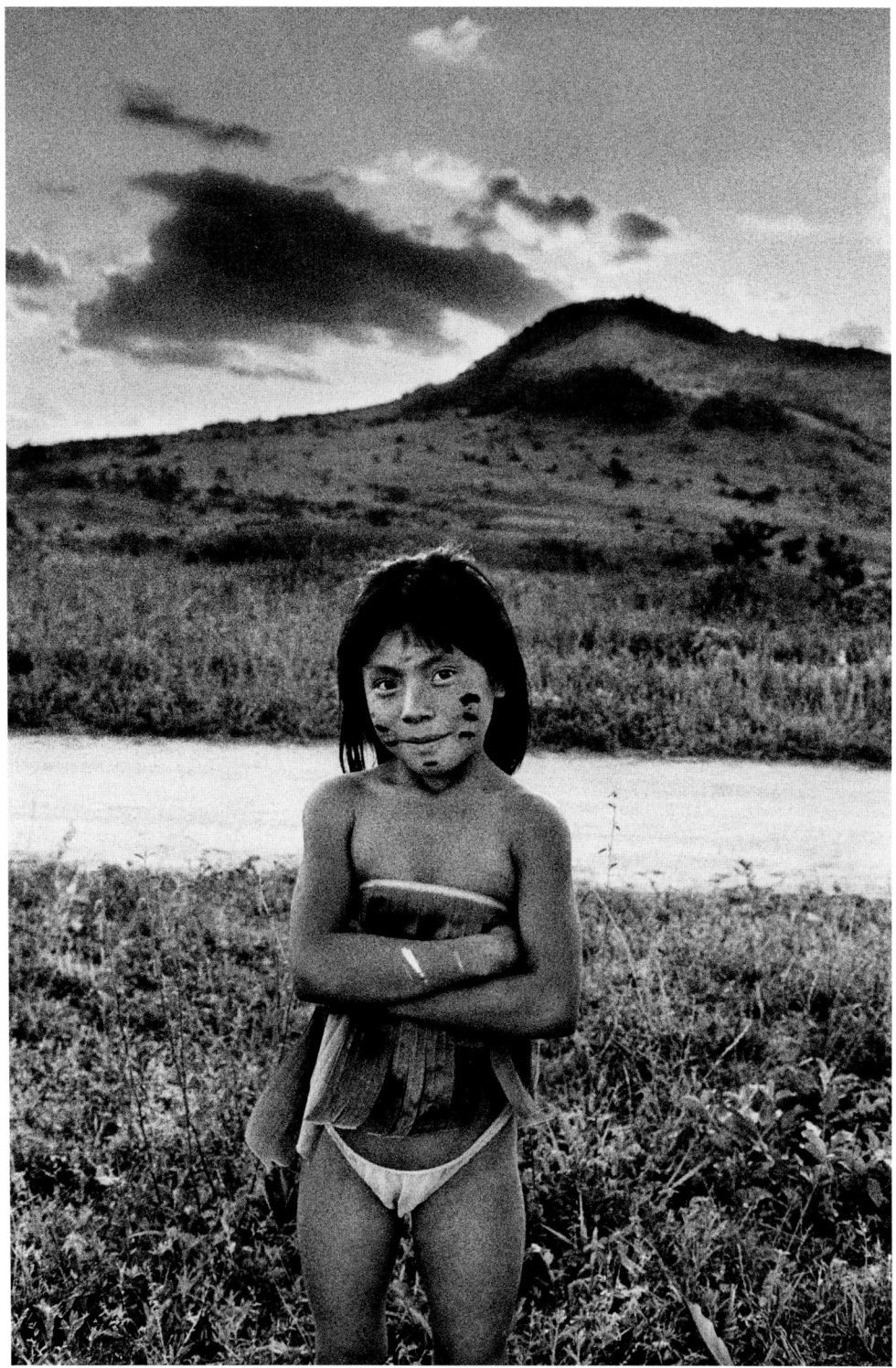

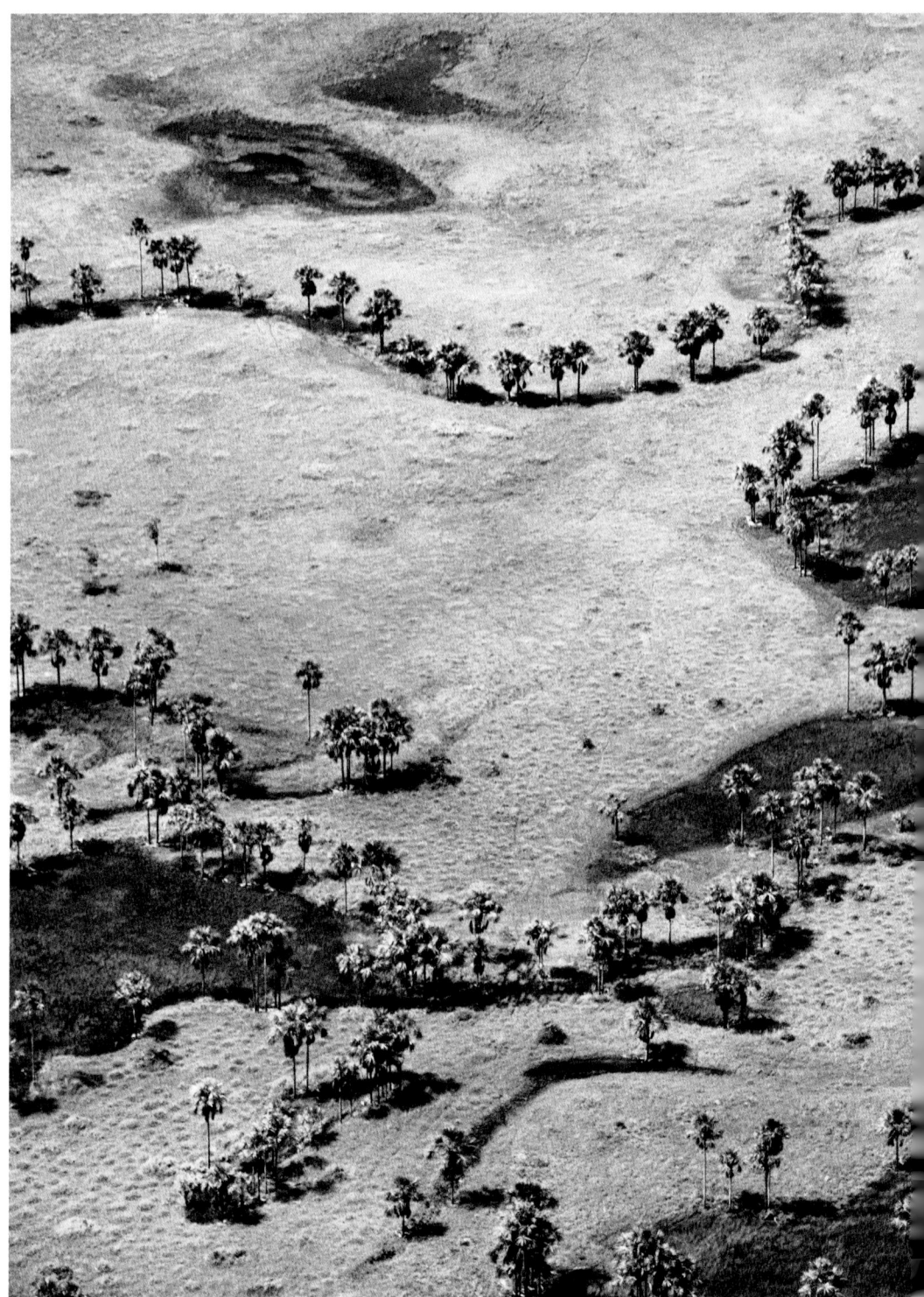

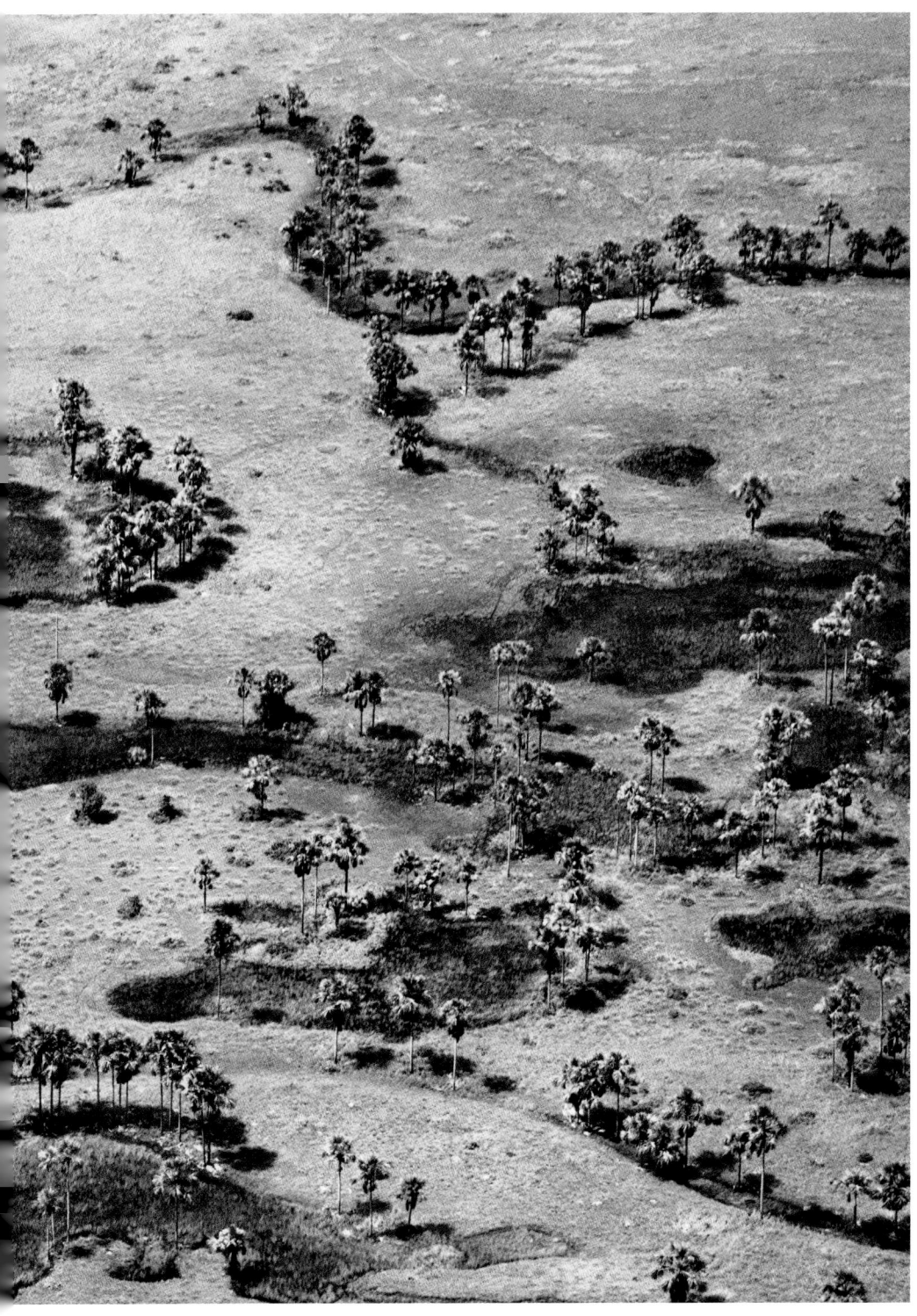

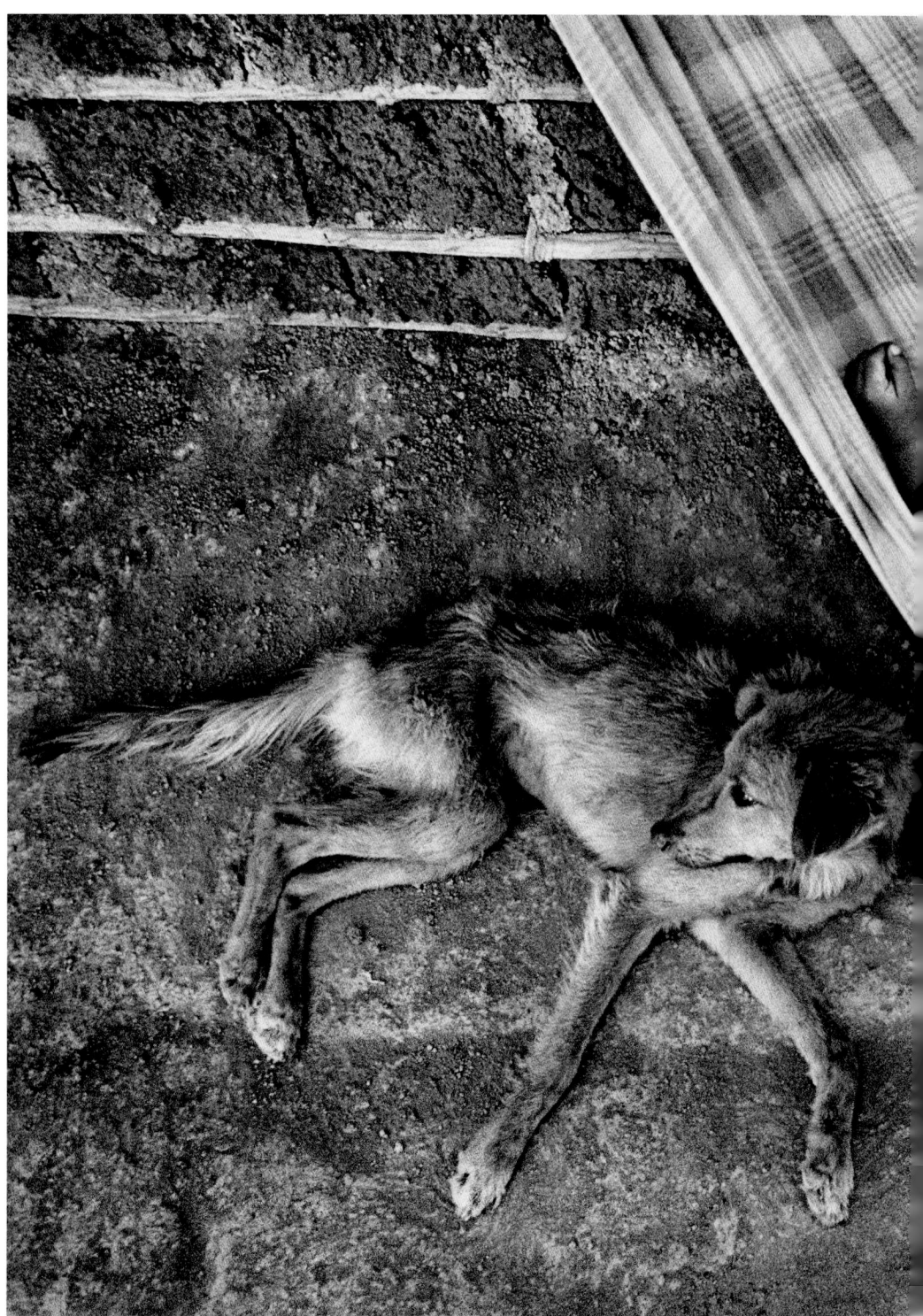

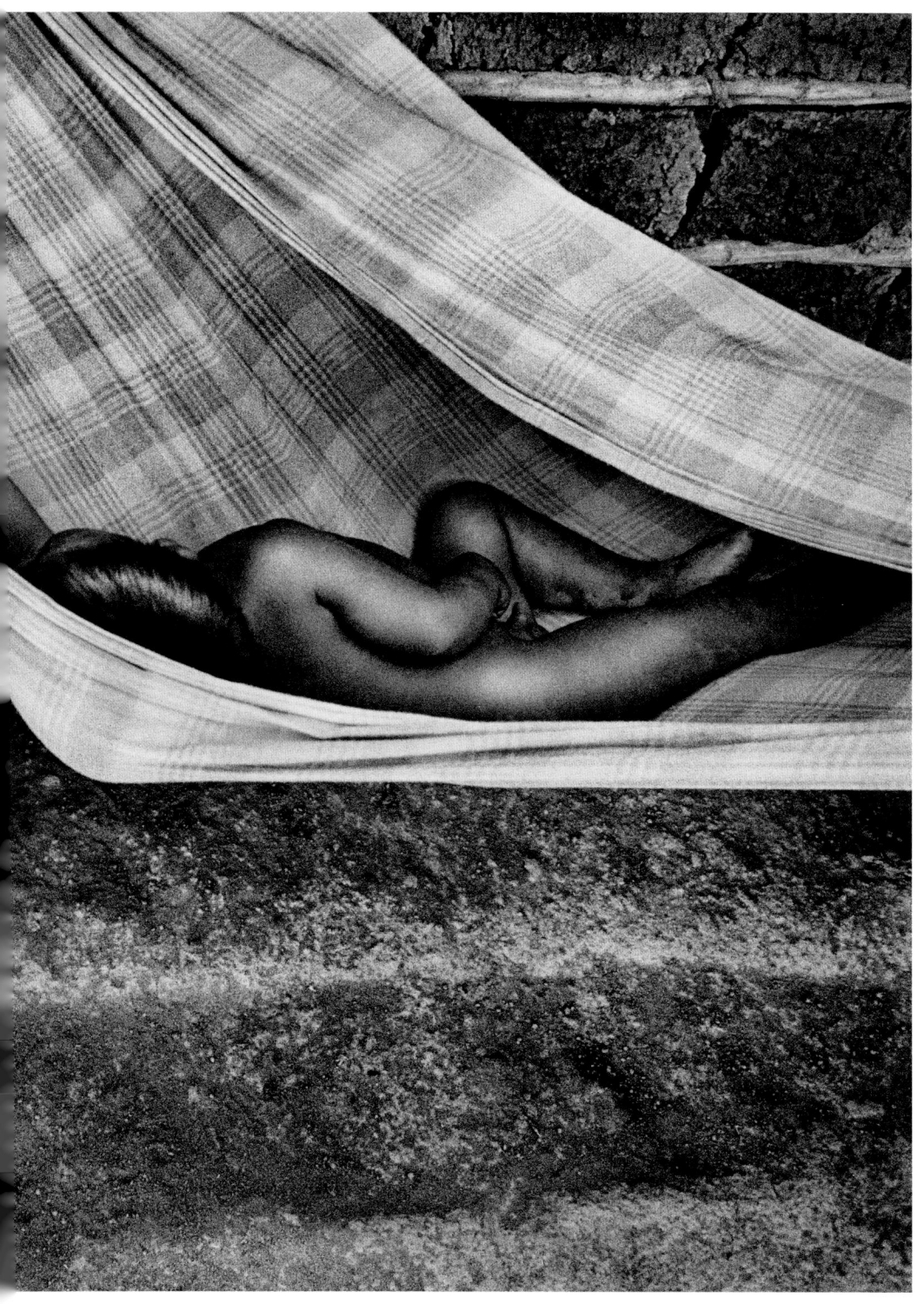

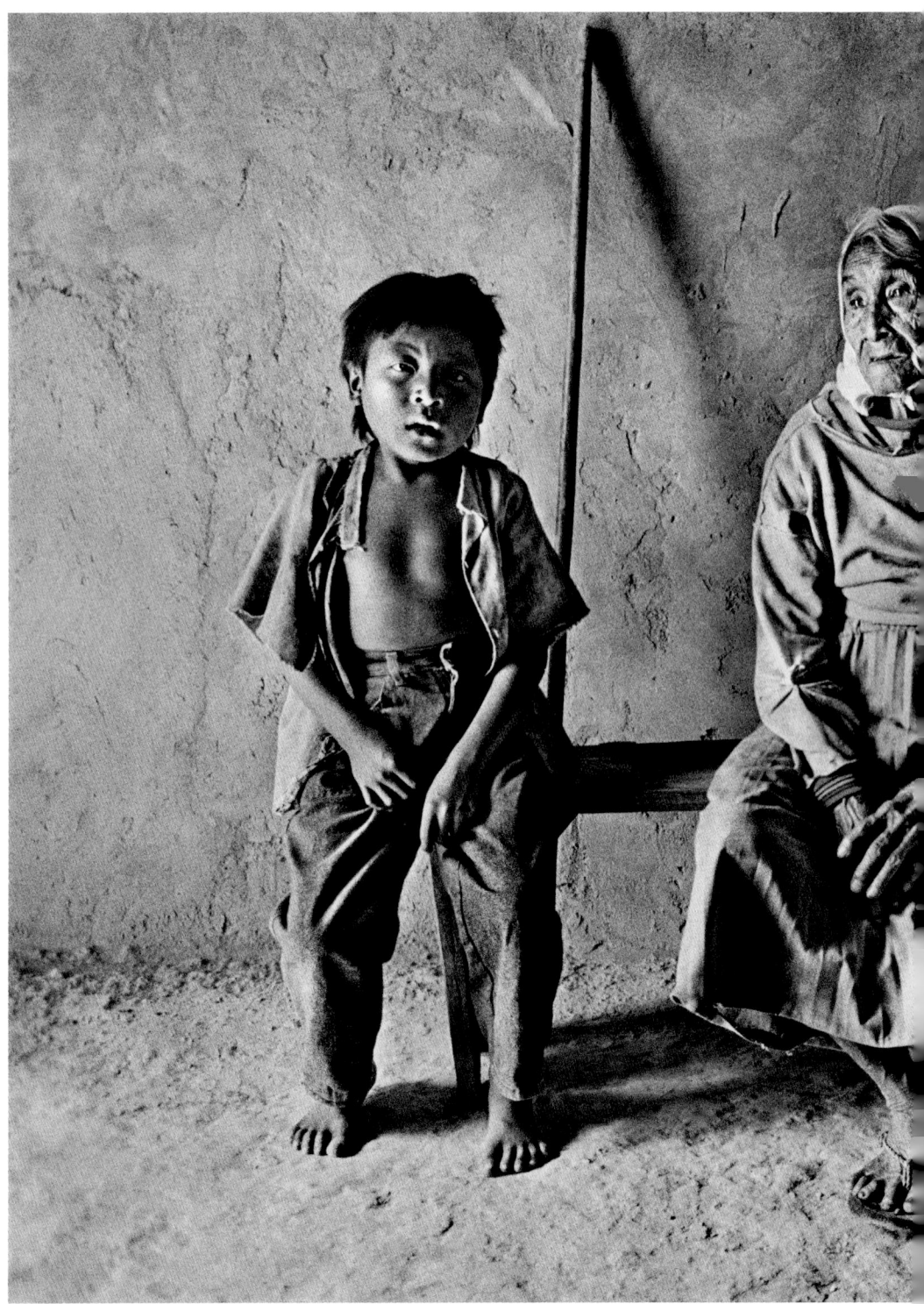

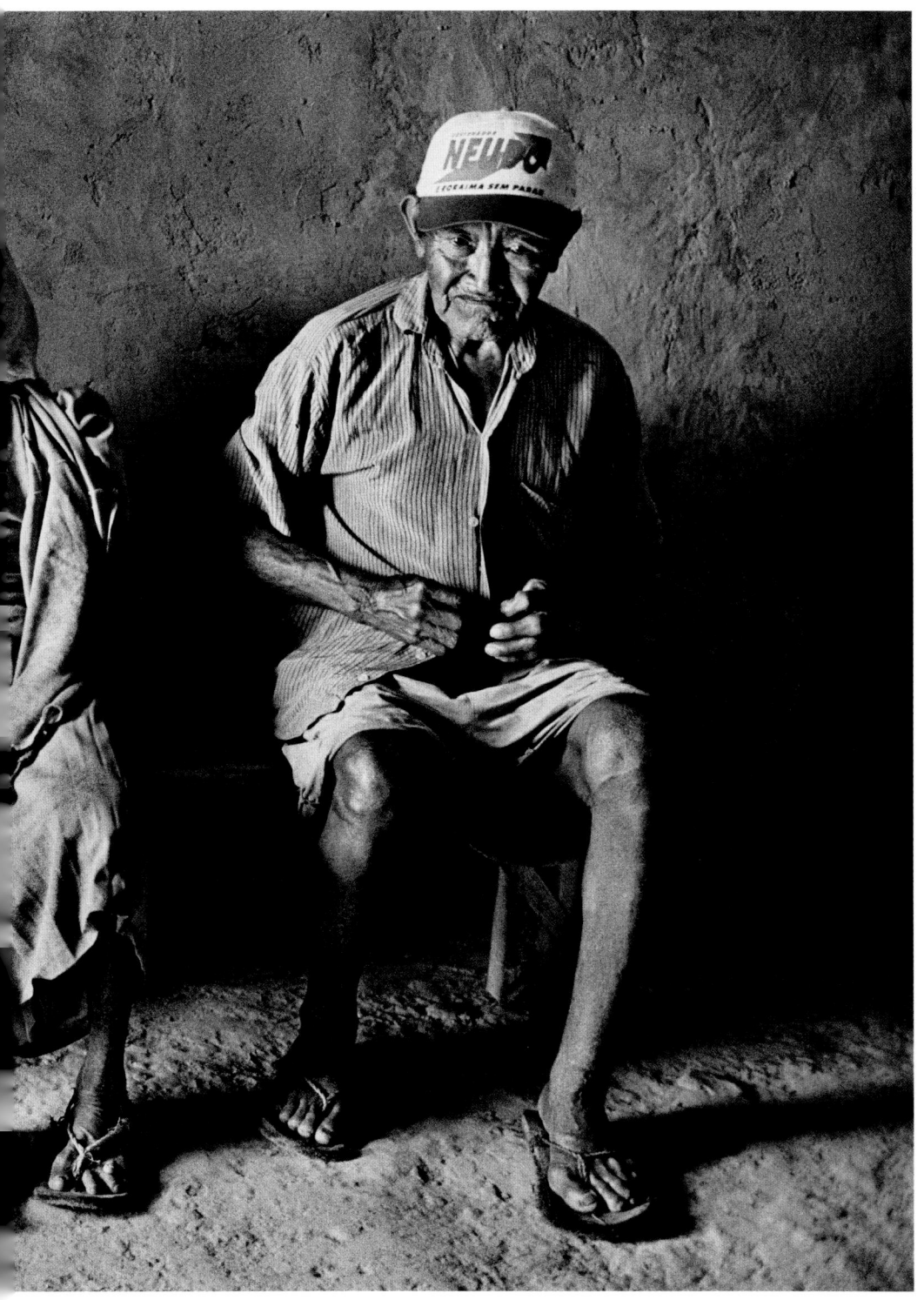

Opposite Members of the Macuxi indigenous community of Eremutaken. Raposa–Serra do Sol Indigenous Territory, state of Roraima, 1998.

Pages 362/363 Aerial view of the Raposa–Serra do Sol region. Foreground: Onça Falls on the Maú River. Top of the photo, far background: two large *tepuis*. At right: Mount Roraima to the left of Mount Kukenán. Raposa–Serra do Sol Indigenous Territory, state of Roraima, 2018.

Page 364 Ronaldo Almeida André Macuxi, a resident of the town of Eremutaken. Raposa–Serra do Sol Indigenous Territory, state of Roraima, 1998.

Page 365 Elisneide Macuxi, who lives in Maturuca. Raposa–Serra do Sol Indigenous Territory, state of Roraima, 1998.

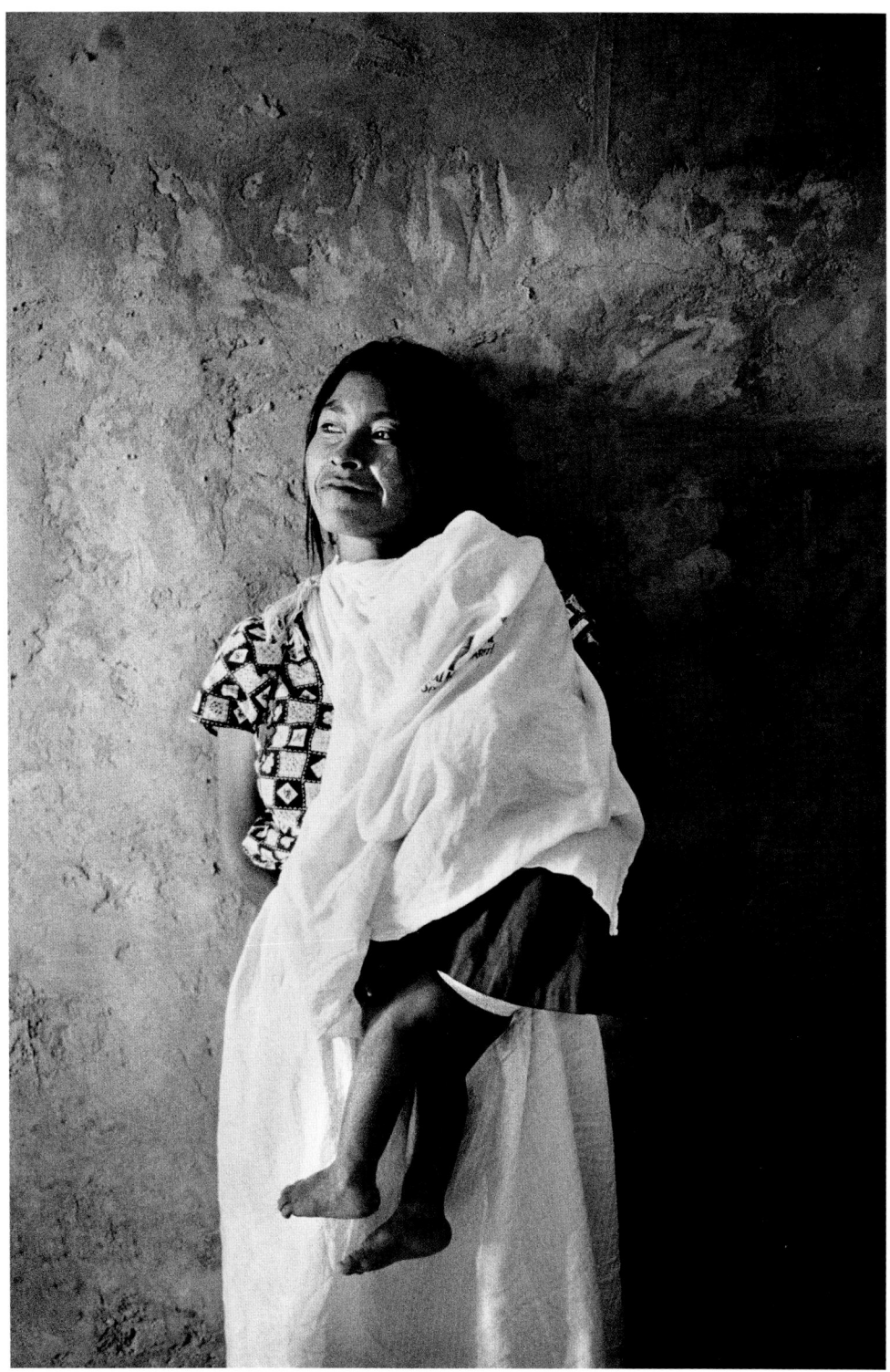

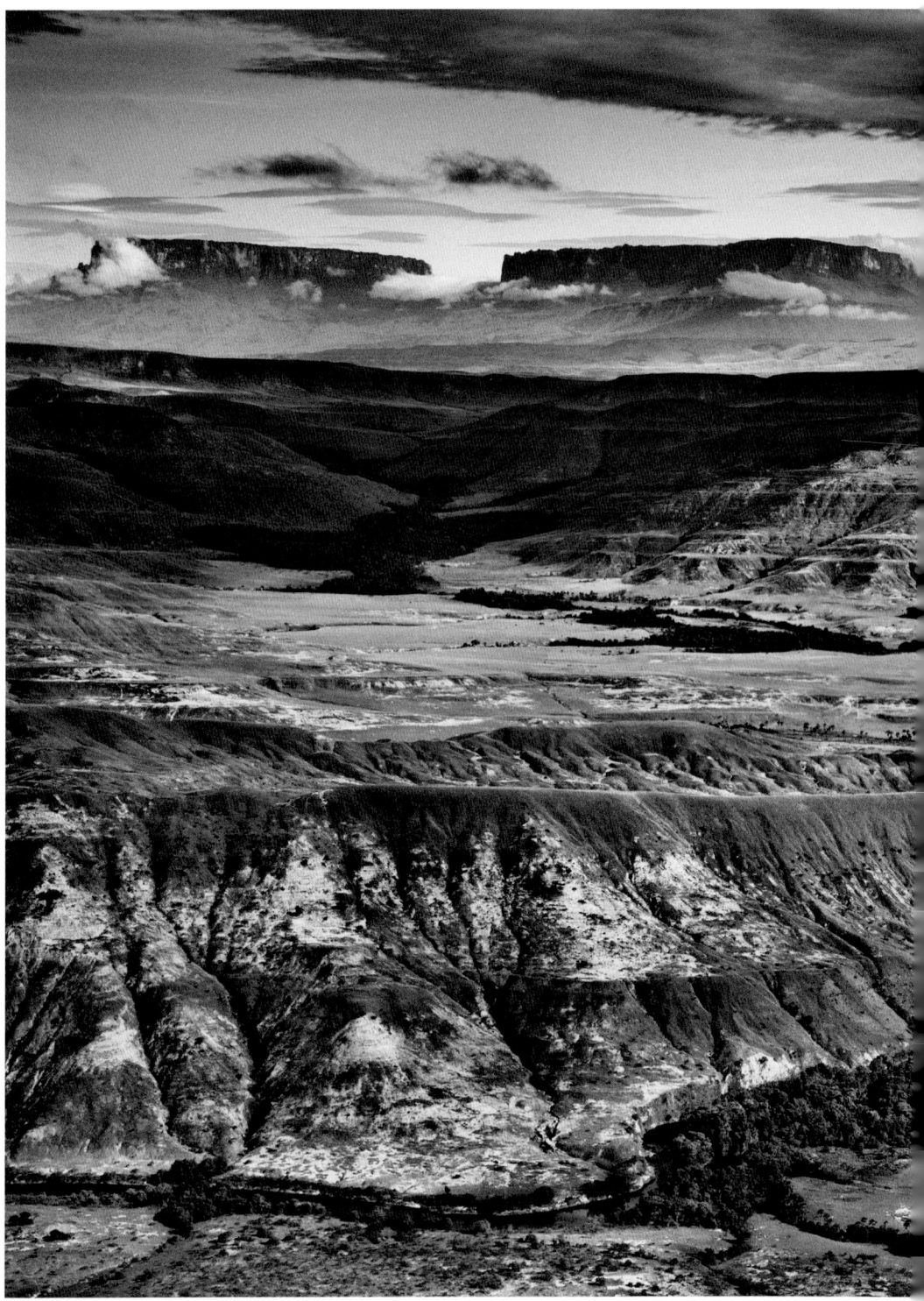

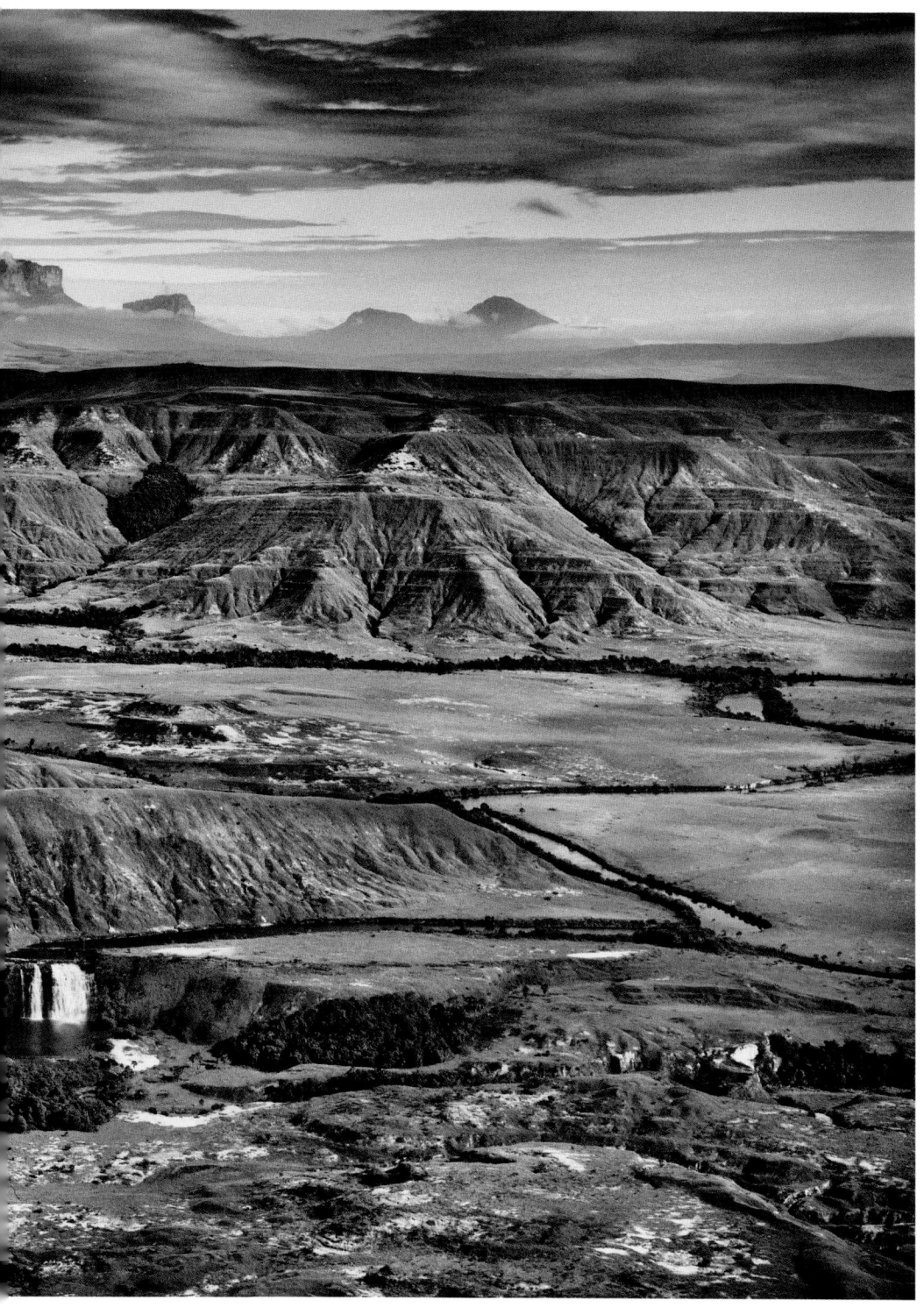

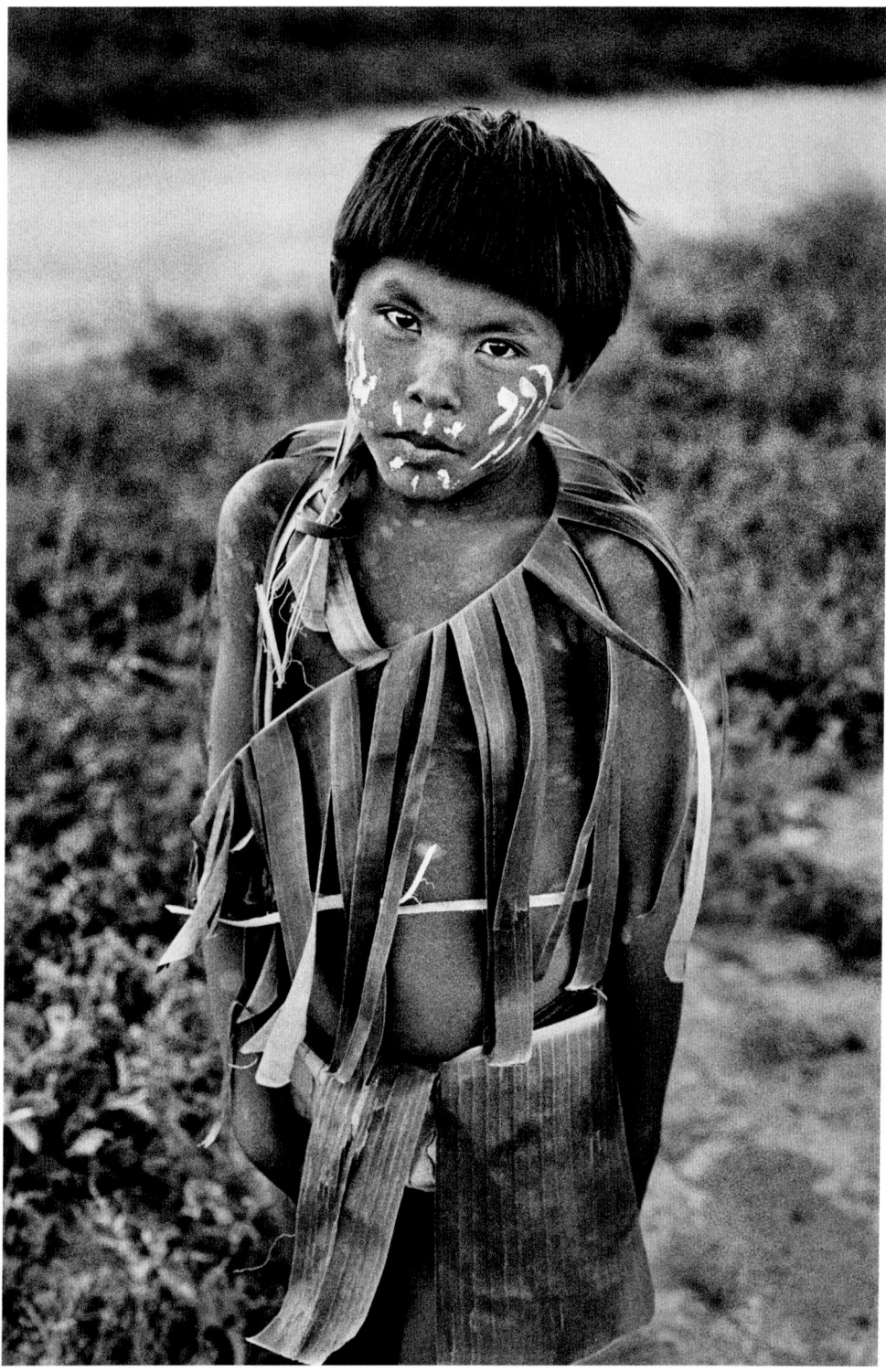

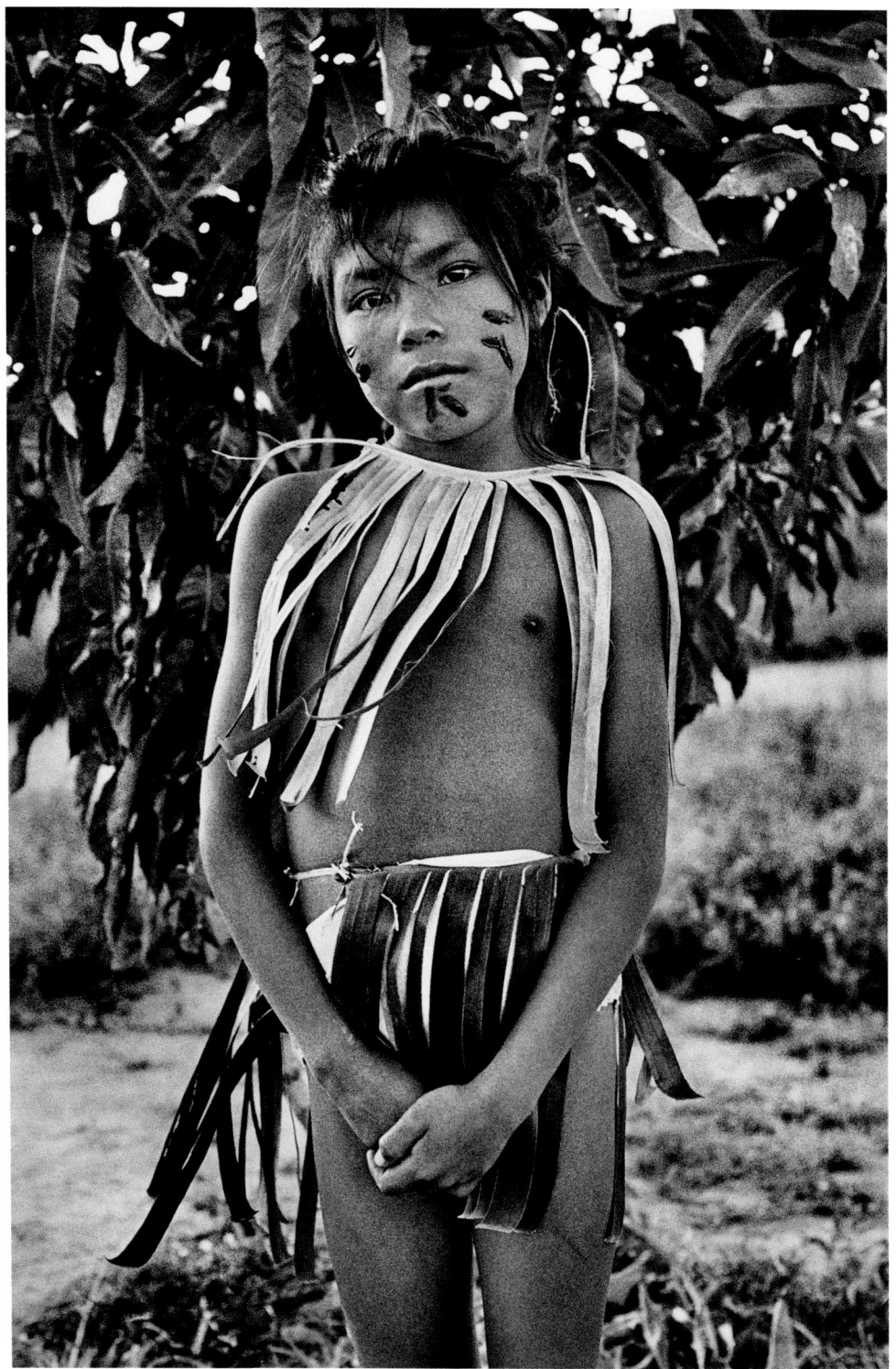

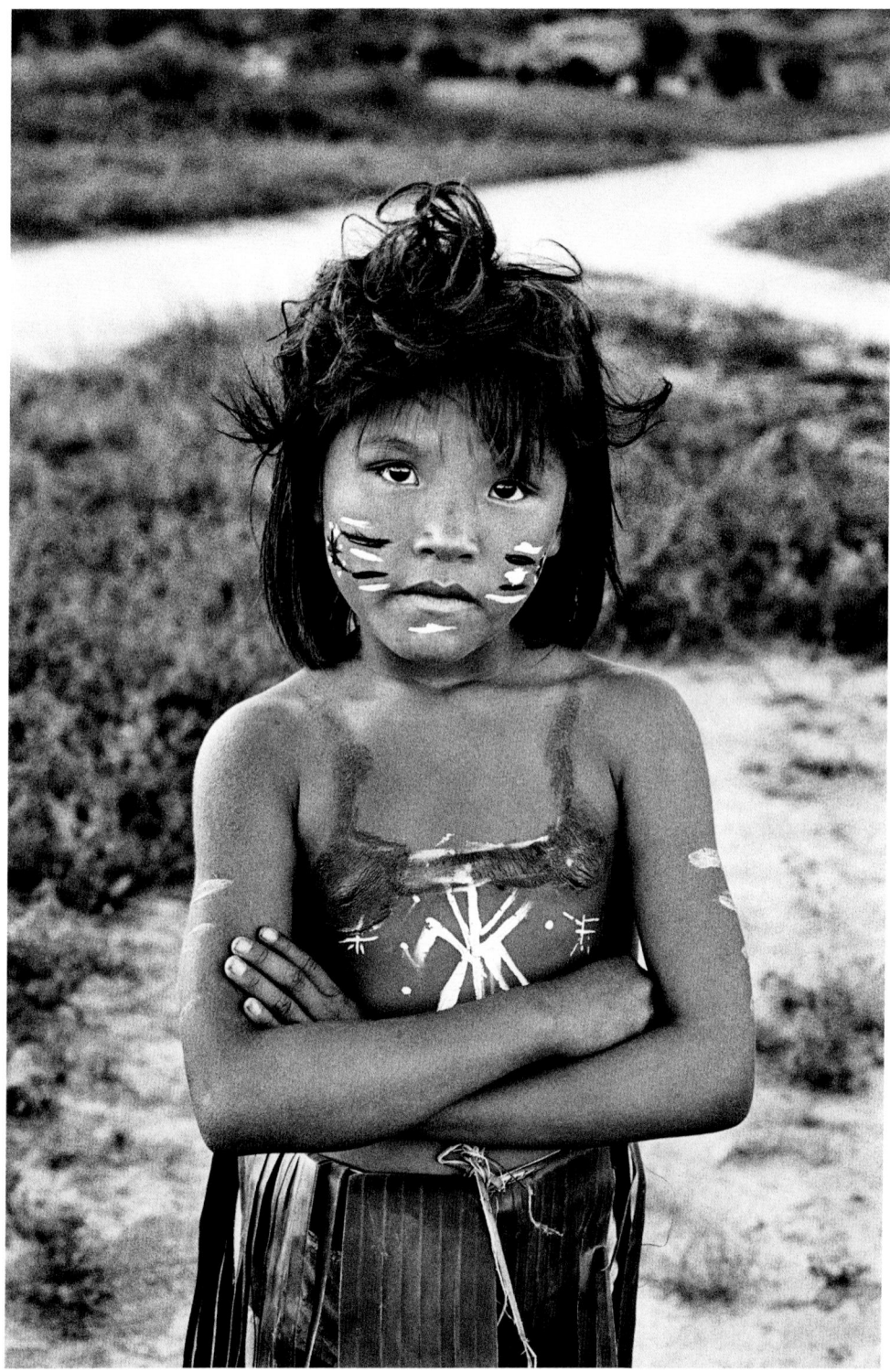

Opposite Andecleia Macuxi, photographed in 1998 in the town of Maturuca, now lives in the village of Mutum. Raposa–Serra do Sol Indigenous Territory, state of Roraima, 1998.

Pages 368/369 Aerial view of the Sol mountain range area, with *tepuis* and the fields below. Raposa–Serra do Sol Indigenous Territory, state of Roraima, 1998.

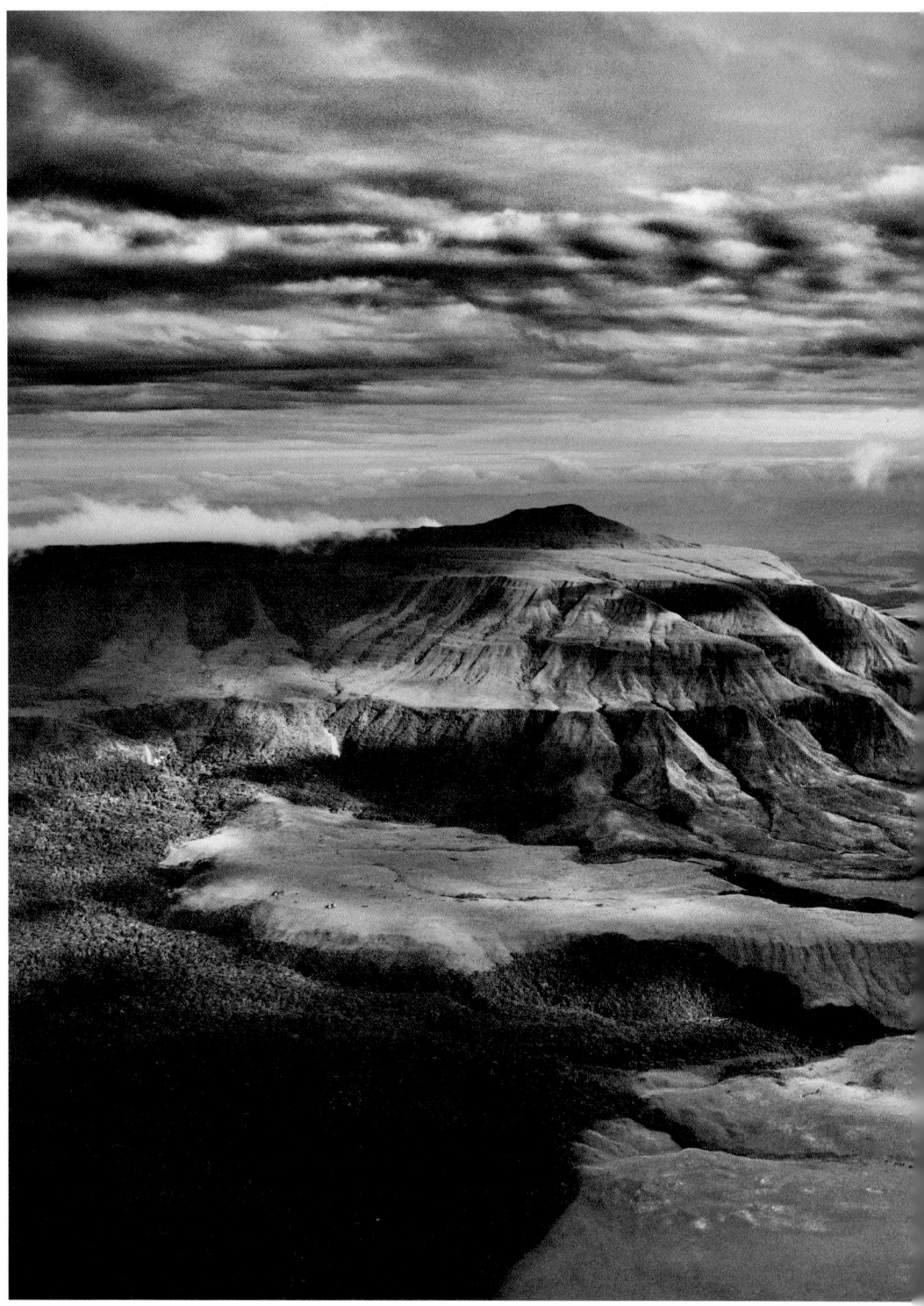

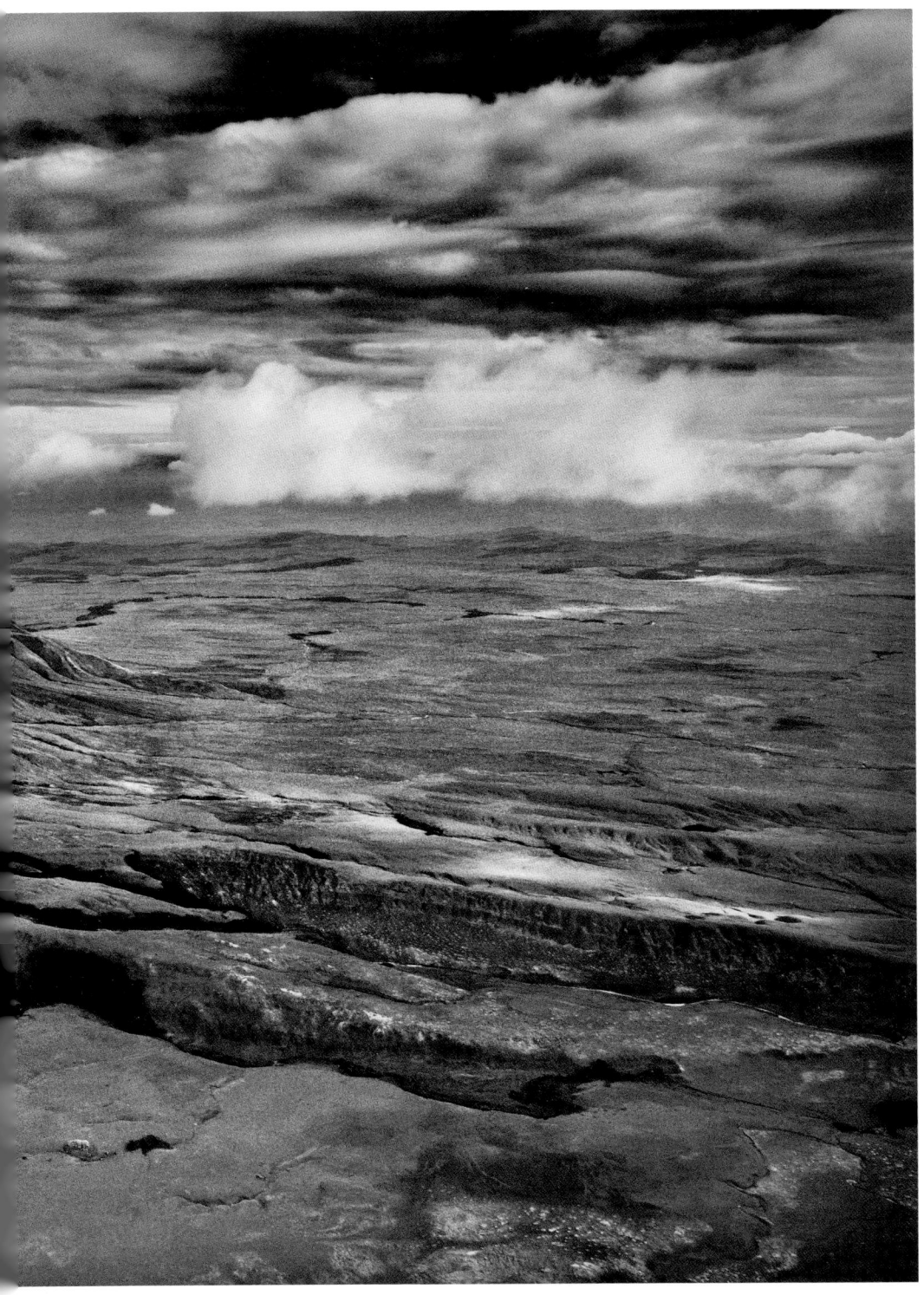

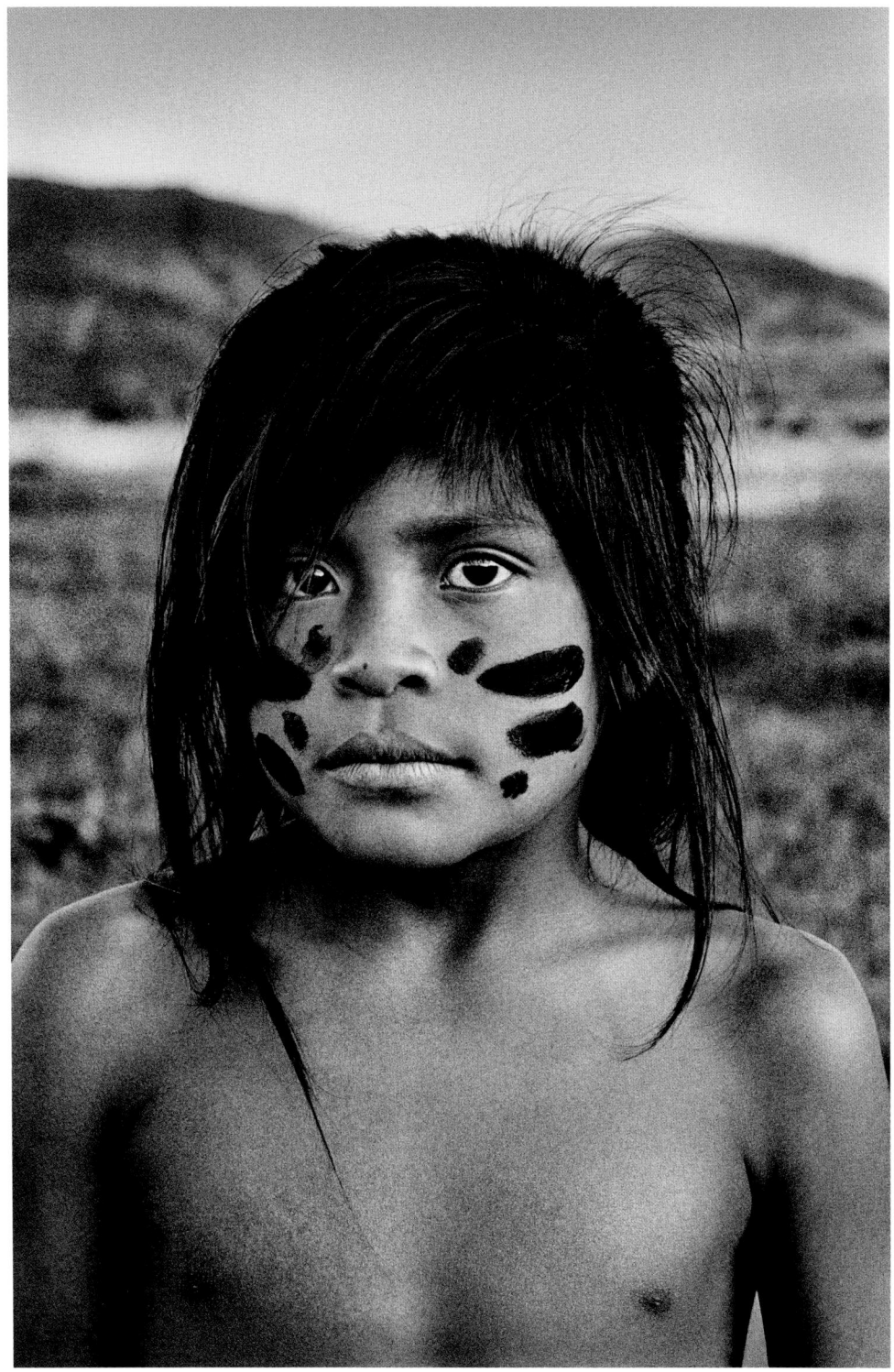

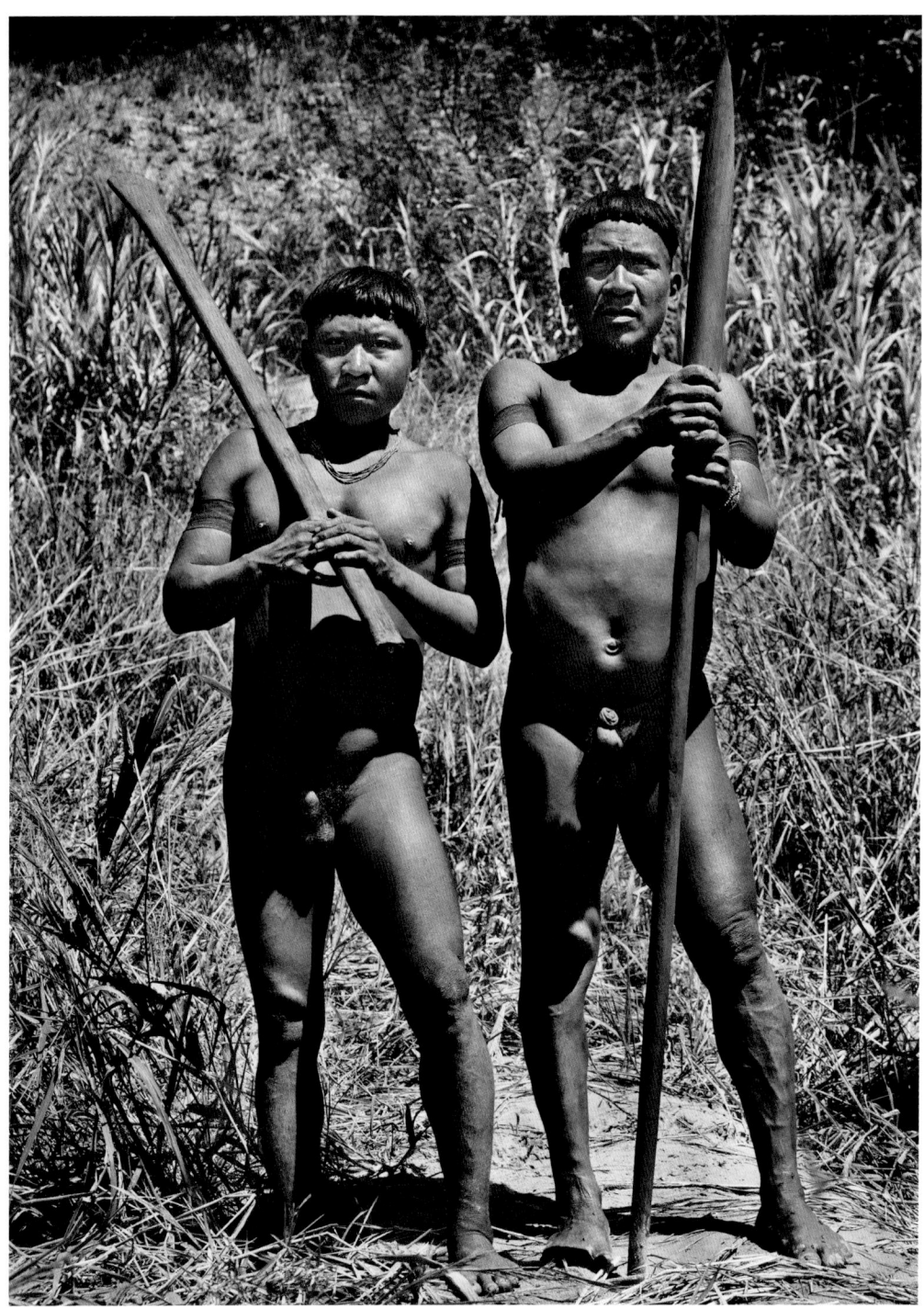

KORUBO

The Korubo have been equally famous and feared by indigenous and nonindigenous people alike in the Javari Valley region since the 1970s, when Brazilian government agents began mineral prospecting in the region. The Korubo gained attention for their violent response to invasions of their territory. They became known as *índios caceteiros* (club-wielding indigenous people) because of how they attack their victims, armed with large clubs (*cacetes* in Portuguese).

Their skin is always painted red with a dye made from urucum seeds, but it was the color of mud that earned them their name (in the Pano language, which they share with the nearby Marubos, Matsés, and Matis). They are a highland people, living far from the rivers and from the mosquitos that swarm along their banks. When they approach the riverbanks, bothered by all those insect bites, they cover their skin with mud to try to protect themselves. On seeing them like that, their Matis neighbors nicknamed them "Koru-bo," mud-covered people.

Until contacted, they did not use bows and arrows, so common among other indigenous groups. They hunt small animals with blowguns, which they use with great precision. They attack large animals with spears and clubs.

The Korubo lived in isolation until the mid-1990s when a group of them, nearly all suffering from malaria, approached some whites for help. By then, all the older men had died of the disease and the group felt disoriented. A woman called Mayá had assumed leadership. This group comprised just 21 people. Two other groups, also victims of diseases or attacks from other indigenous people, joined the first one in 2014 and 2015. A fourth group was contacted by a team of indigenists from the National Indian Foundation (FUNAI) in 2019, to prevent them from being targeted for attack by other indigenous people. Today, there are about 120 Korubo living in two villages on the banks of the Ituí River in the Javari Valley Indigenous Territory, in western Amazonas state near the border with Peru. At least one other group continues to live without contact in the jungle.

To date, they have little contact with other peoples and their traditional culture is very well preserved. Other than the urucum paint, their distinctive haircuts, and two armbands, they have few adornments.

Classified as "recently contacted" or those with little interaction with whites, they live traditionally, few of them speak Portuguese, and they are still highly vulnerable to diseases common among nonindigenous people. Therefore, outsiders are generally kept out of their community. My expedition in October 2017 marked the first time a documentation team and journalists stayed among them.

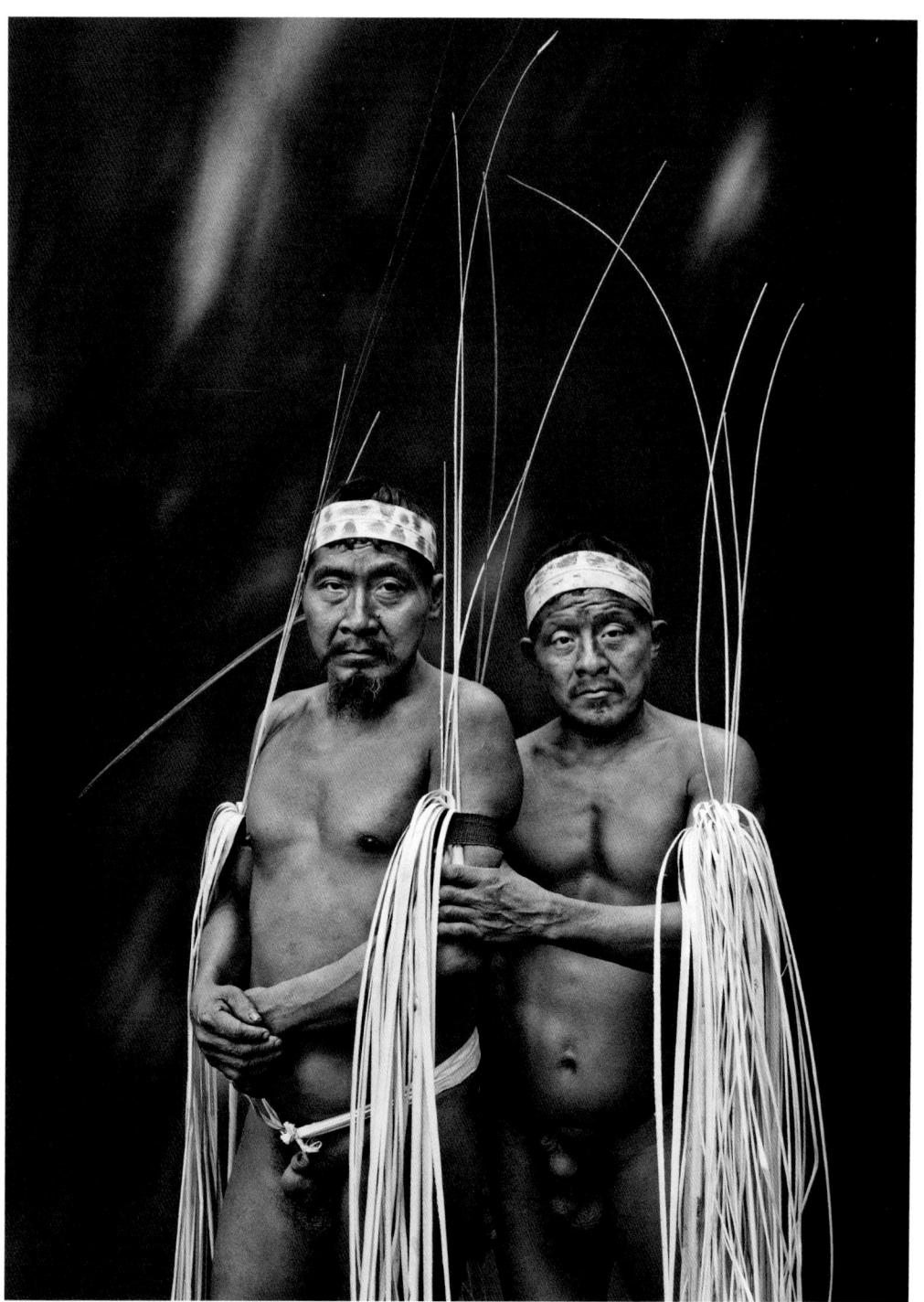

Page 372 Left to right: Visa Korubo, who was part of the Korubo group contacted in 2014, with Takvan Korubo, who was in the 1996 group and today is leading the founding of a new Korubo village called Mário Brasil on the banks of the Ituí River. The look on their faces as they stand on the riverbank to meet visitors reflects the Korubo approach to outsiders: suspicious, prepared for conflict, with a club and spear at the ready. Javari Valley Indigenous Territory, state of Amazonas, 2017.

Opposite Pëxken, at left, was one of the indigenous people contacted in 2015, and Xikxuvo, at right, was part of the first group of Korubo contacted in 1996. Hunting encampment on the Ituí River, Javari Valley Indigenous Territory, state of Amazonas, 2017.

Pages 376/377 Tupa Korubo, left, and Tumi Muxavo Korubo, both children of couples from the Korubo group contacted in 1996. Hunting encampment. Ituí River, Javari Valley Korubo Indigenous Territory, state of Amazonas, 2017.

Pages 378/379 Pinu Korubo family, contacted in 2014. From left to right: the mother, Naylo; son Vali, standing in back; son Wanka Vakwë, seated left of center; the father, Pinu, seated; son Kanikit, standing at right. Hunting encampment. Ituí River, Javari Valley Indigenous Territory, state of Amazonas, 2017.

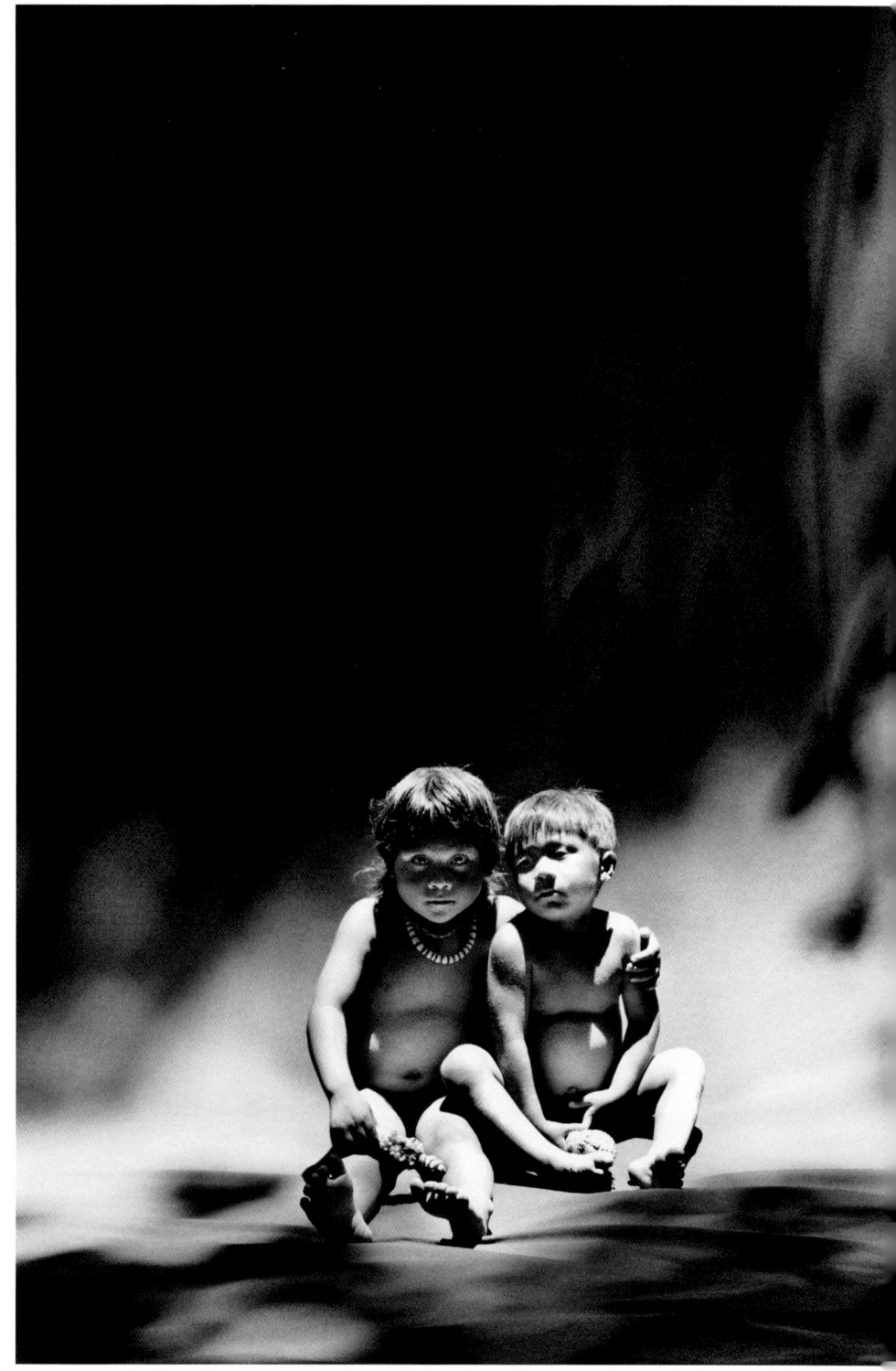

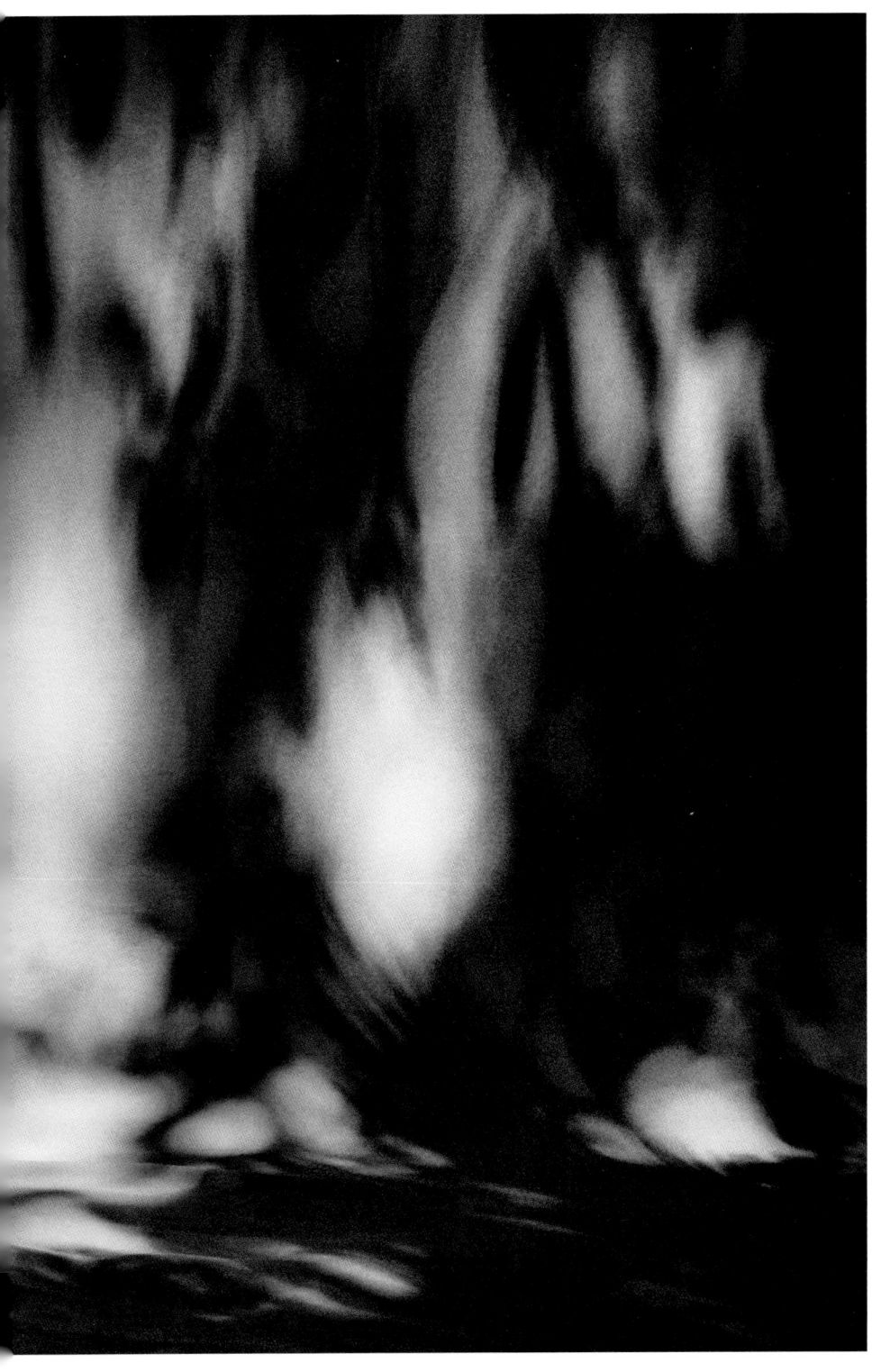

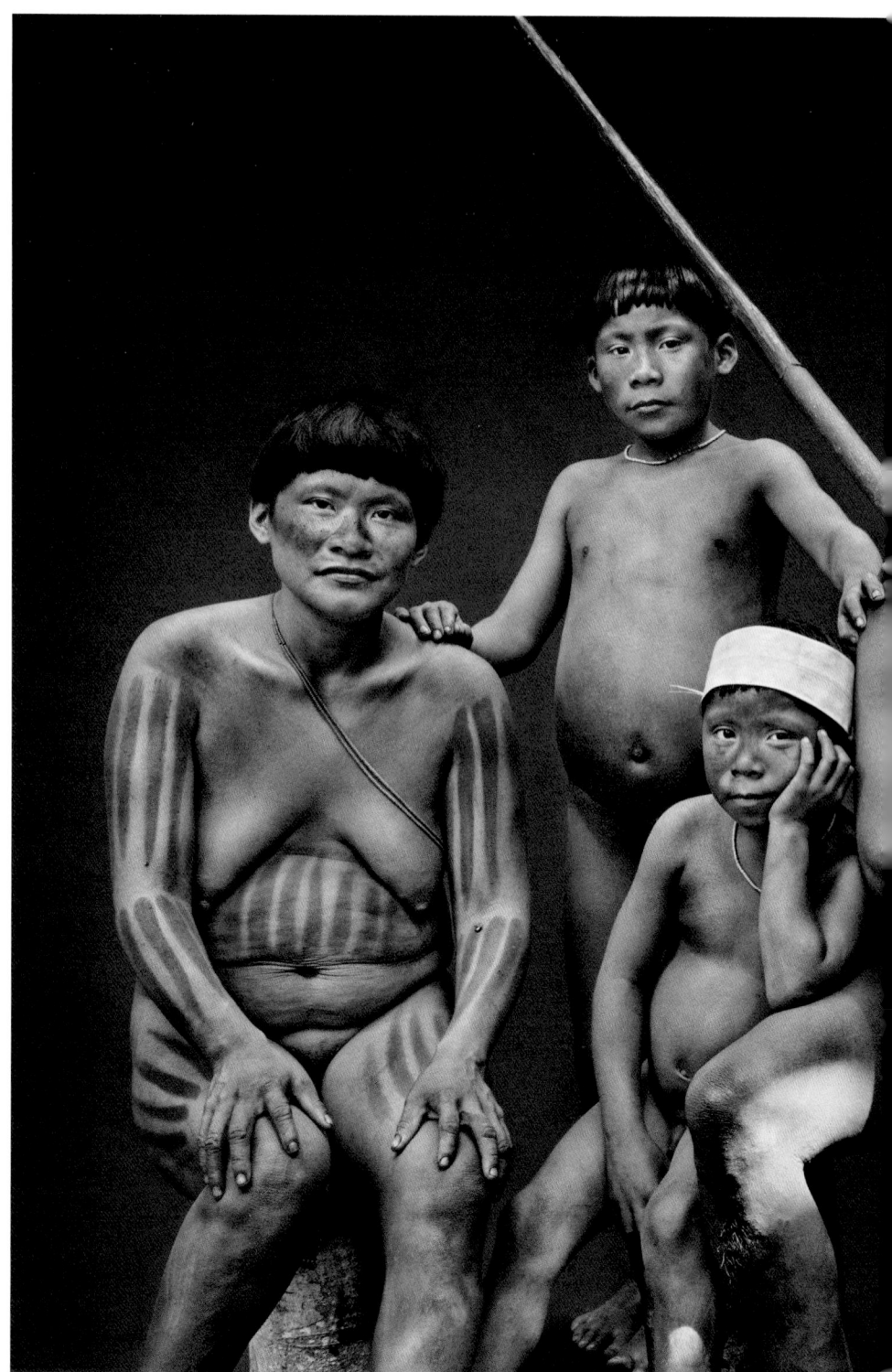

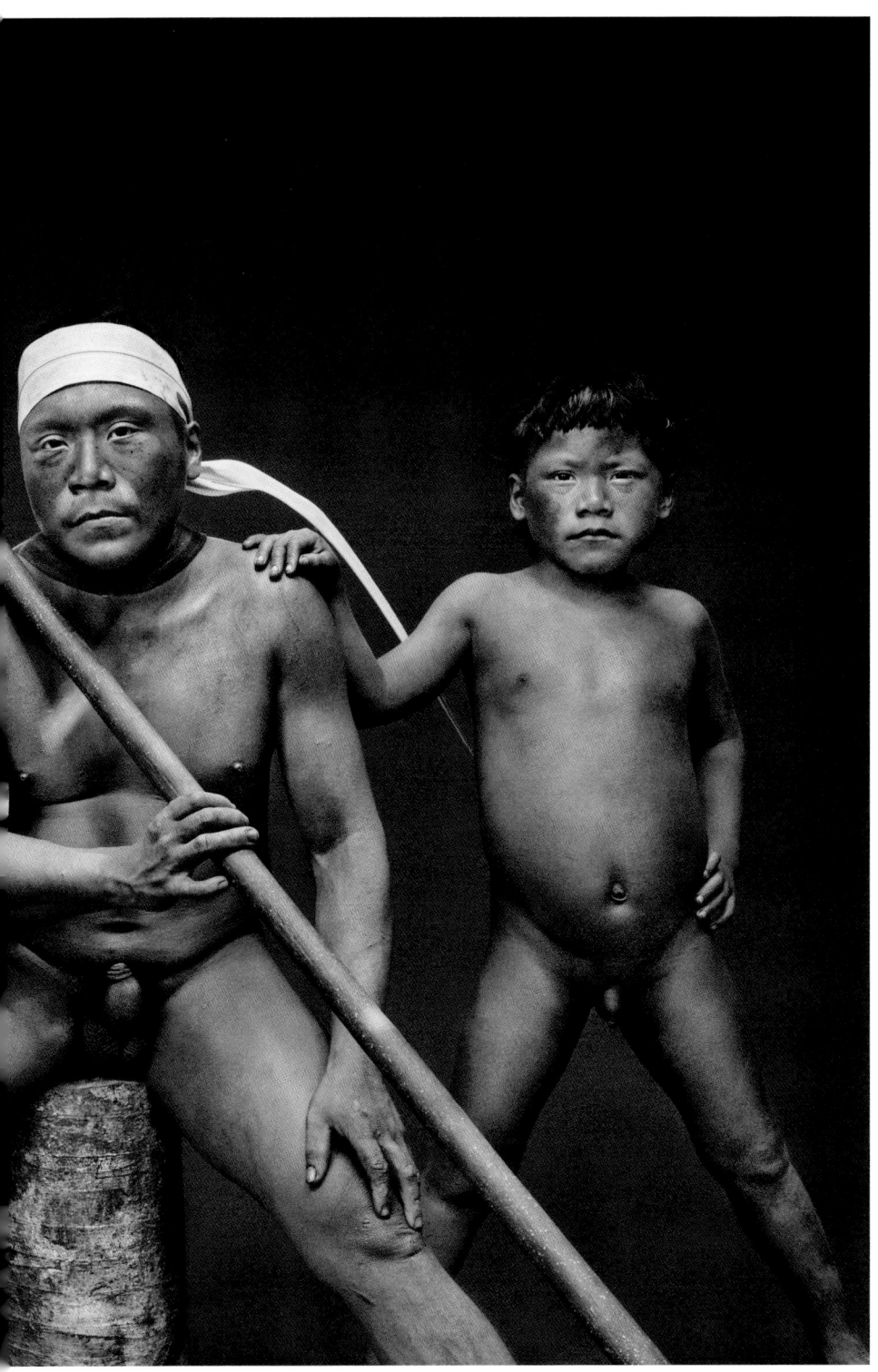

Opposite Tixlavo Korubo, left, and Kontxo Korubo look after pet two-toed sloths (*Choloepus didactylus*, known as *pusën* in the Korubo language). Javari Valley Indigenous Territory, state of Amazonas, 2017.

Pages 382/383 Ayax Punu Korubo, contacted in 2015, and his brown titi monkey (*Callicebus brunneus*; Korubo term: *masoko*). Ituí River, Javari Valley Indigenous Territory, state of Amazonas, 2017.

Pages 384/385 Left to right: Pinu Vakwë Korubo shooting a blowgun, contact in 2014; Pinu with a quiver of arrows hanging from his neck, contact in 2014; Omon holding a child, contact in 1996; Patsinlut, child being held; Vali shooting a blowgun in front, contact in 2014; Wanka Vakwë, front right, contact in 2014; Kanikit in back, contact in 2014; Vali, back right, contact in 1996. Hunting encampment. The Korubo use blowguns to hunt birds and monkeys, and spears for larger creatures such as tapirs. Javari Valley Indigenous Territory, state of Amazonas, 2017.

Pages 386/387 Korubo group. Left to right: Xikxuvo, contact in 1996; Këtsi, contact in 2015; Maya Koluvo, daughter of a couple in the group contacted in 1996; Luni, on whose head is perched a black-headed night monkey (*Aotus nigriceps*; Korubo term: *vëtikit*), contact in 2015; Këtsi Vakwë, contact in 2015; Wanka, contact in 1996; Pëxken, contact in 2015; Lëyu, contact in 1996; Xamalekit, contact in 2014; Mëlanvo, contact in 2015. They have been successfully hunting tapir (*Tapirus terrestris*; Korubo term: *awat*), Brazil's largest wild mammal, weighing up to 300 kilograms (660 pounds) and measuring more than 2.5 meters (8 feet). Javari Valley, Korubo Indigenous Territory, state of Amazonas, 2017.

Pages 388/389 Kulutxia Korubo, contact in 2015. Hunting encampment on the Ituí River. Javari Valley Indigenous Territory, state of Amazonas, 2017.

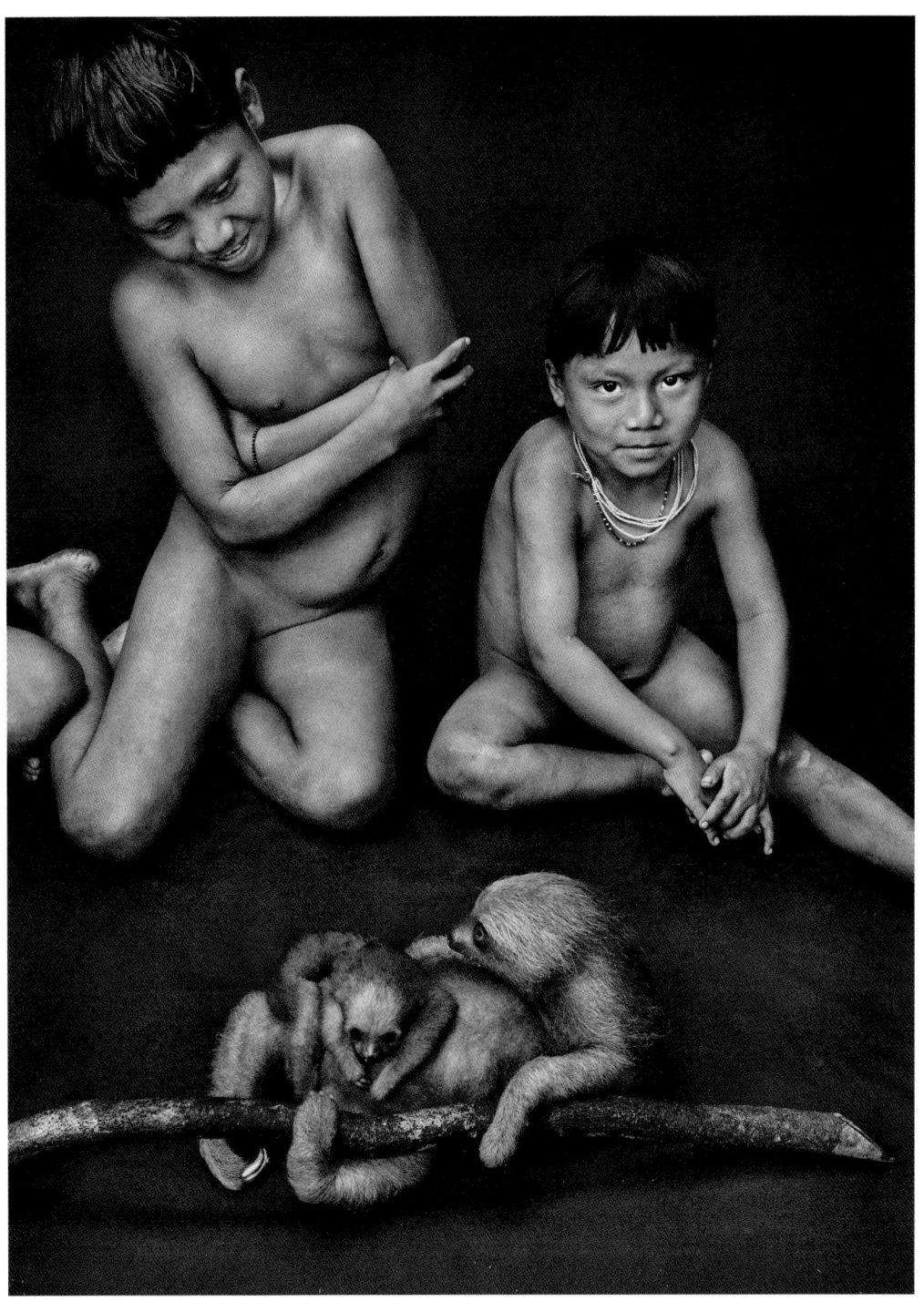

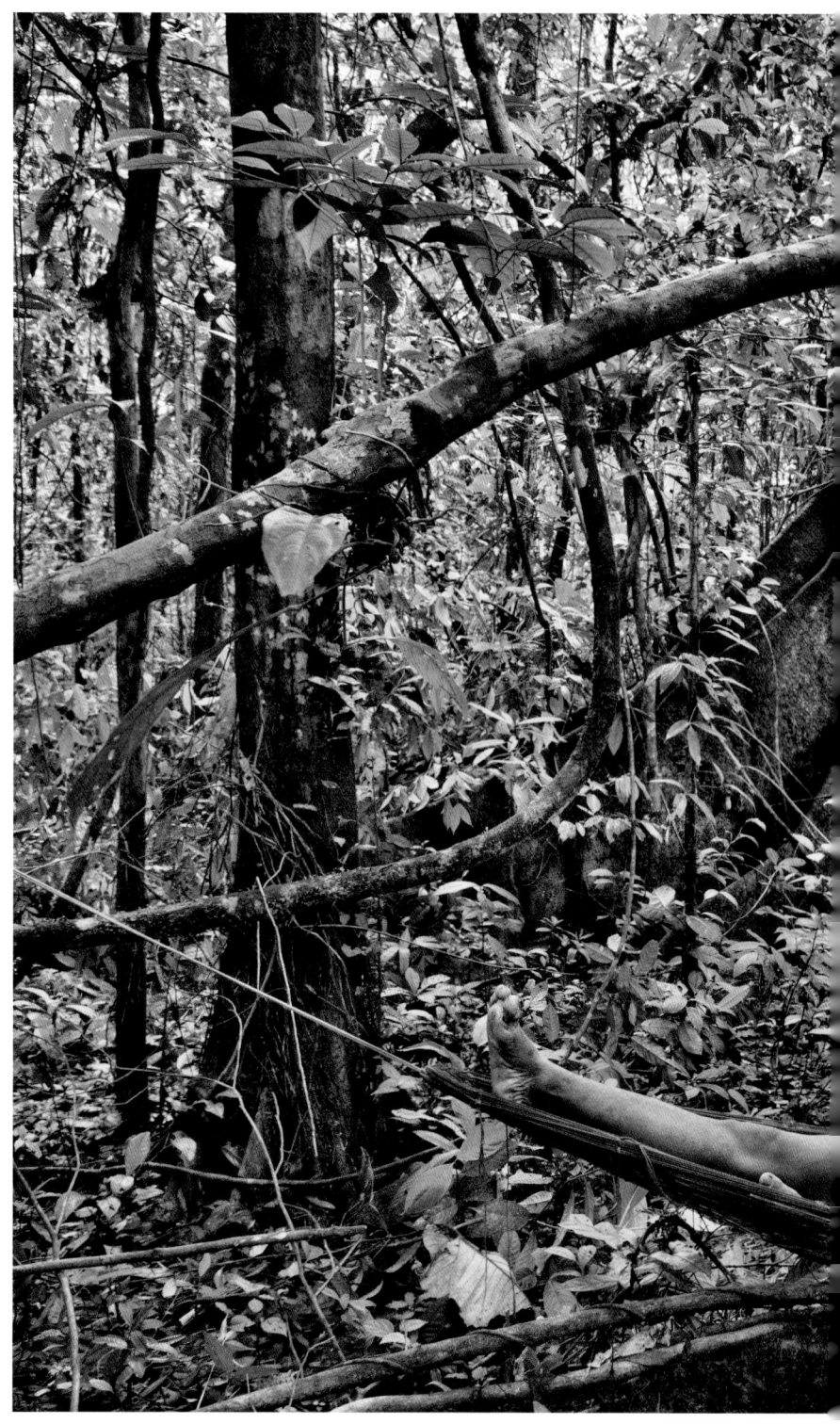

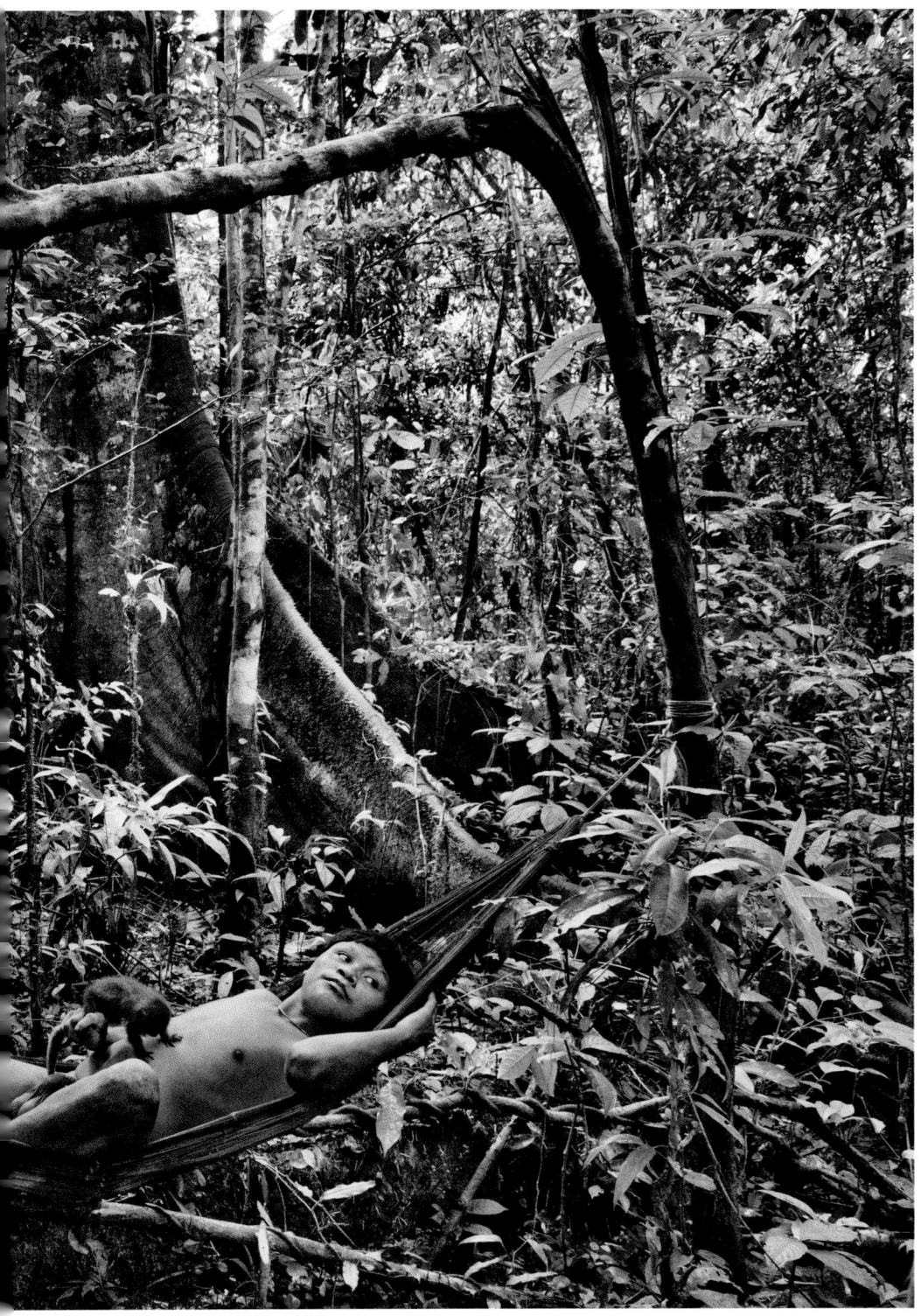

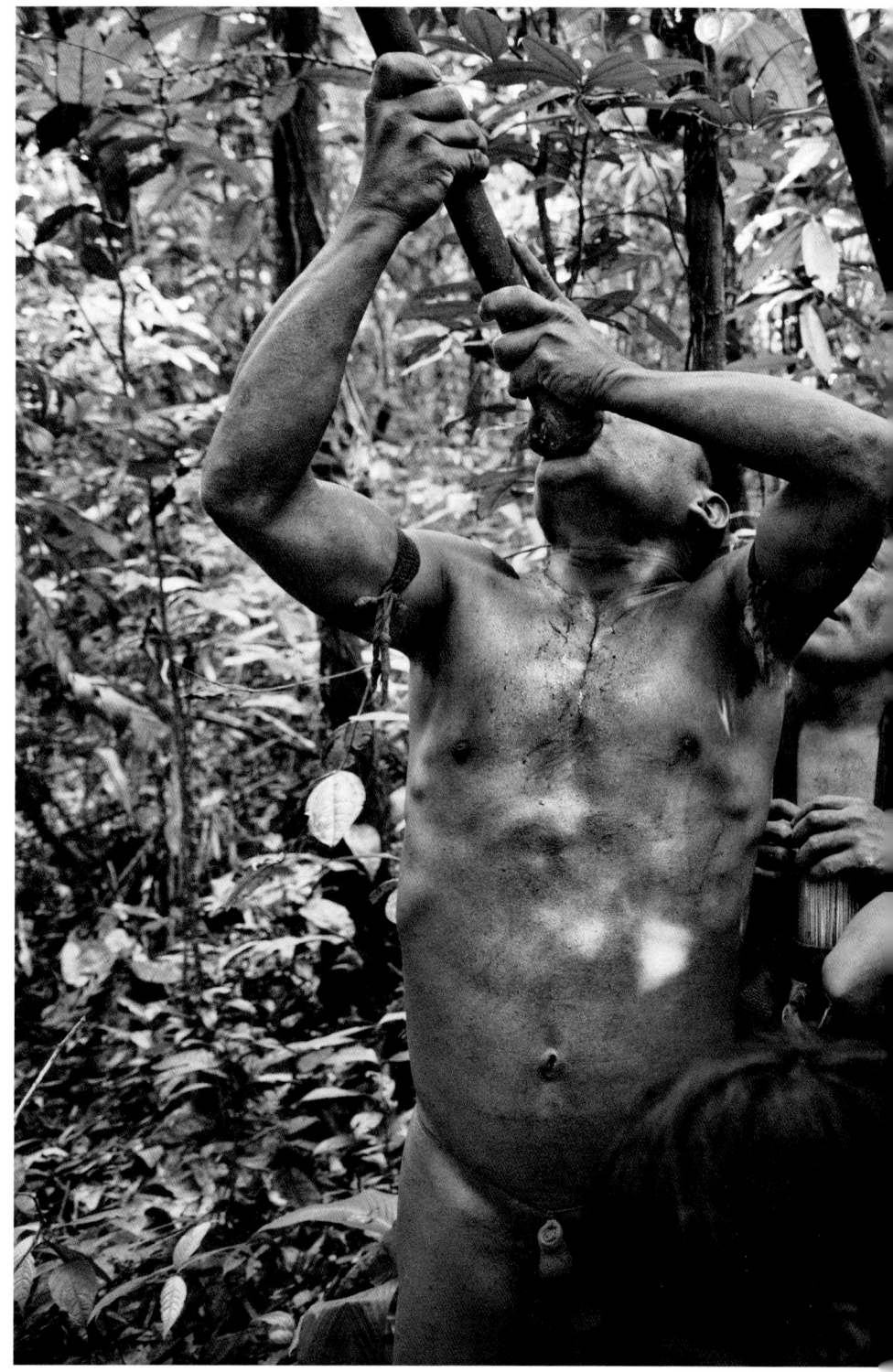

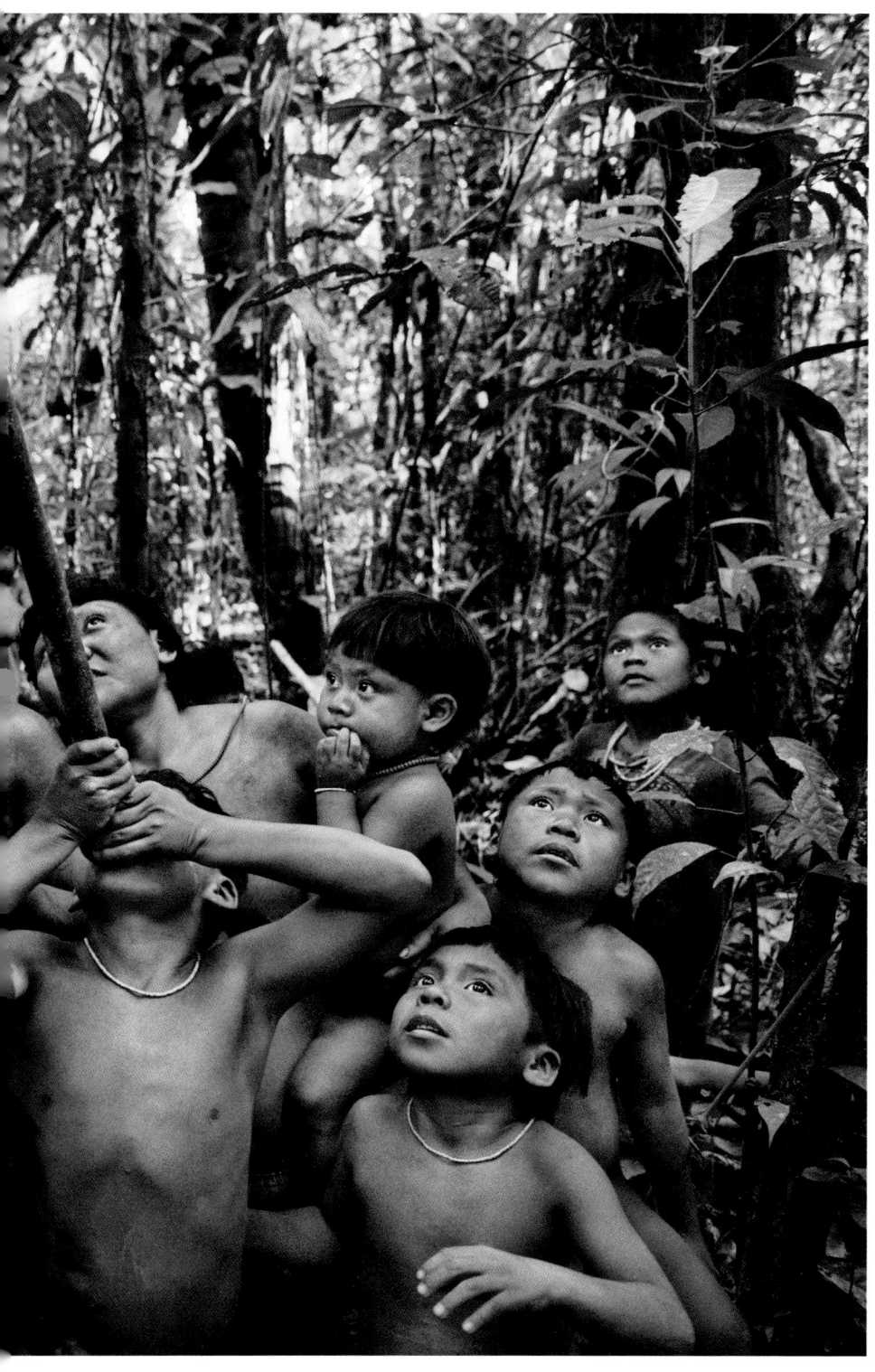

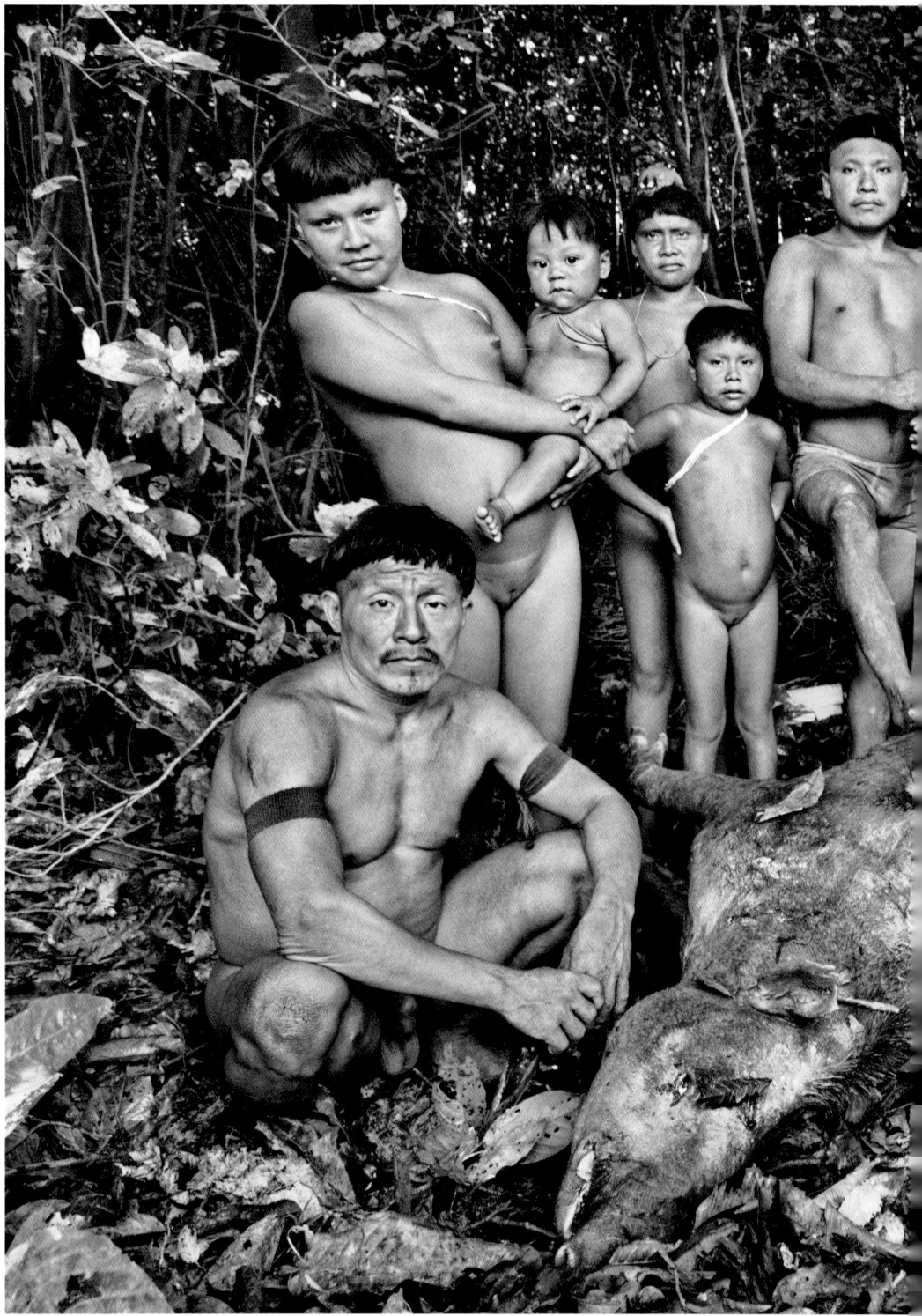

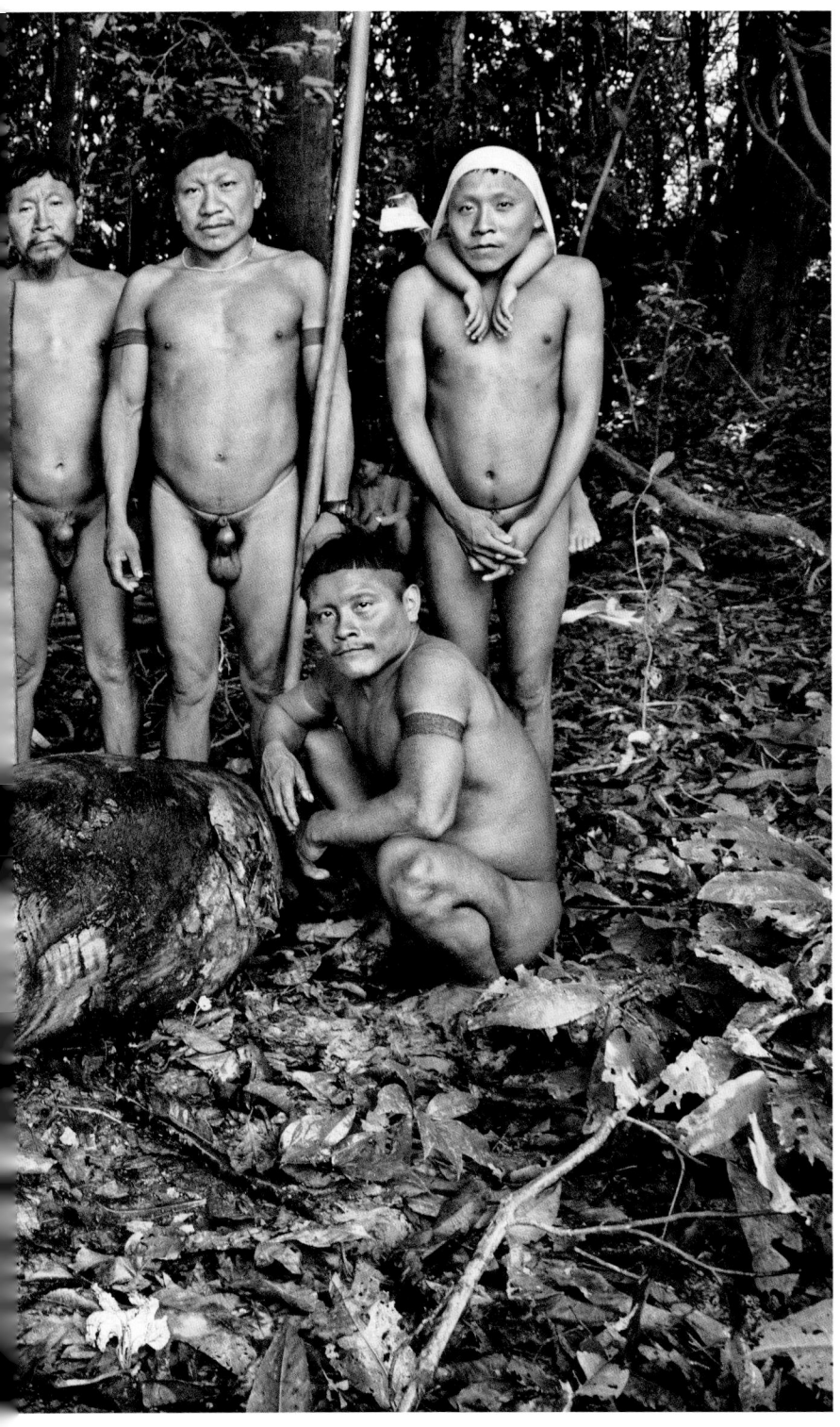

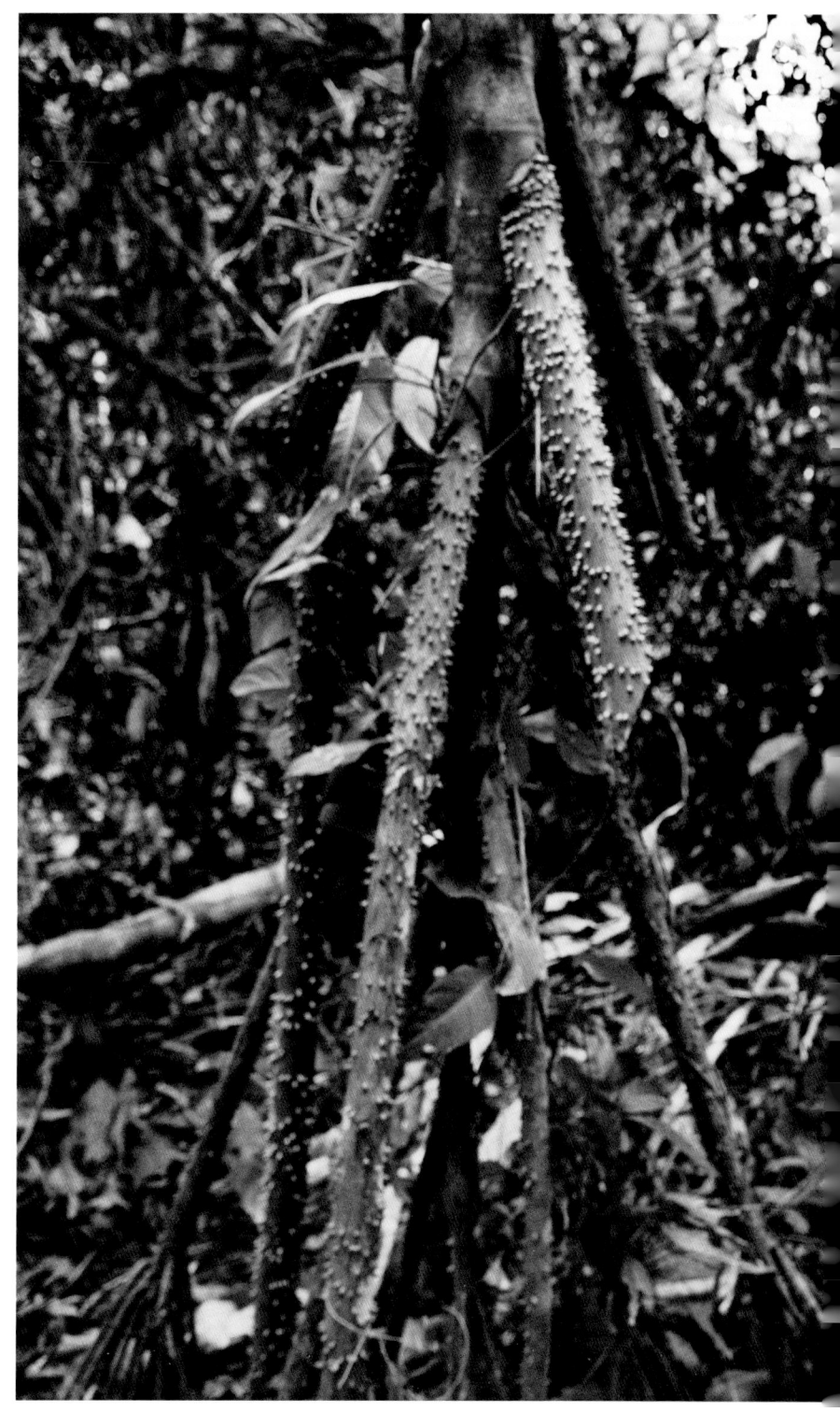

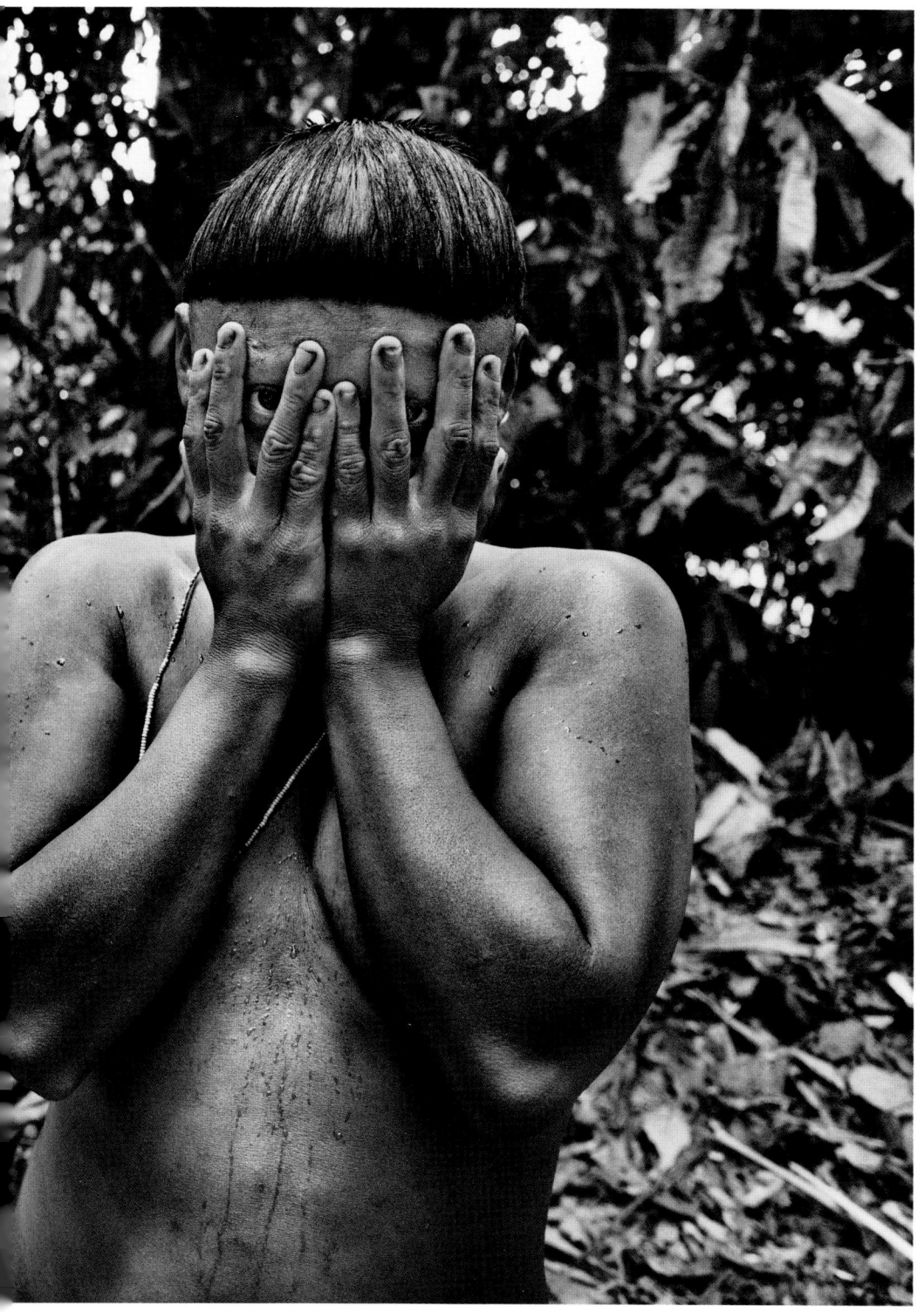

TORRENTIAL RAIN

Clouds are an intrinsic part of the never-ending drama of the Amazon. They can be small or large, friendly or threatening, but from a boat on a river or a plane in the sky, they are always in view. Even in the forest, where vegetation may block them from sight, they remain very present because, before the day is out, heavy rain is more than likely. And if it is a tropical storm, the experience can be both perilous and fearsome. For their own safety, then, anyone spending time in the region, above all anyone flying over the rainforest, must learn to read the clouds as they might a detailed map.

Over the Amazon rainforest, rare is the day when you can see a clear sheet of blue sky or a solid blanket of gray cloud. Rather cloud formations offer an ever-changing spectacle. This begins in the morning, when warm moist air rises from the jungle and makes contact with minuscule particles, which permit the vapor to condense into water droplets and become little clouds resembling cotton balls known locally as *aru*. As the day advances, they rise and join forces and, temperature and wind speed permitting, gather strength to become a storm cloud known as a cumulonimbus.

This is quite the most dangerous meteorological formation, reaching several thousand meters into the sky, spewing out pieces of ice and winds of up to 200 kilometers per hour (125 miles per hour) at the same time as sending lightning, strong winds, and fierce precipitation toward the jungle. Such is its force that even large aircraft will do everything to avoid it, helicopters immediately look for a jungle clearing in order to land and riverboats hurriedly take shelter from the blinding rain. On rare occasions, as most recently in 2005, a storm is so devastating that it fells hundreds of thousands of trees.

The months when it rains with little interruption in the Amazon are March and April, although the massive volume of water flowing down from the Andes keeps rivers swollen until mid-year. Yet in practice, it rains almost every day, with deluges often coming at night when the ground temperature falls and the morning hydrological cycle is reversed. Interestingly, the region's rivers do not form clouds, but storms will nonetheless also raise water levels and their winds set off angry waves.

Whatever its form and intensity, this rain is life-giving for animals, vegetation, river life, and the indigenous population. Alarmingly, though, perhaps as a consequence of climate change, the dry season in the Amazon region has increased by an average of four weeks over the past 40 years, while droughts are occurring with growing frequency and ferocity, most recently in 2005, 2010, and 2015–16. And these can provoke greater damage even than storms, not least because a large part of southern Brazil and of the River Plate basin depend on the water carried by the Amazon's clouds.

Pages 392/393 Heavy rain on the Juruá River. Tefé area, state of Amazonas, 2009.

Pages 394/395 Rain at the meeting point of the Rio Negro and the Demini River, state of Amazonas, 2019.

Pages 396/397 The rain in the region is so dense that it makes this mountain, in the Imeri range, look like a volcano. Municipality of São Gabriel da Cachoeira, Yanomami Indigenous Territory, state of Amazonas, 2018.

Pages 398/399 Rain obscures the horizon in Serra do Divisor National Park, state of Acre, 2016.

Pages 400/401 A rainbow forms as the rains pound the Auaris area, in the Parima mountain range. Parima Forest Reserve, Yanomami Indigenous Territory, state of Roraima, 2018.

Pages 402/403 Lower Rio Negro (downstream from the confluence with the Rio Branco and start of the Anavilhanas), state of Amazonas, 2019.

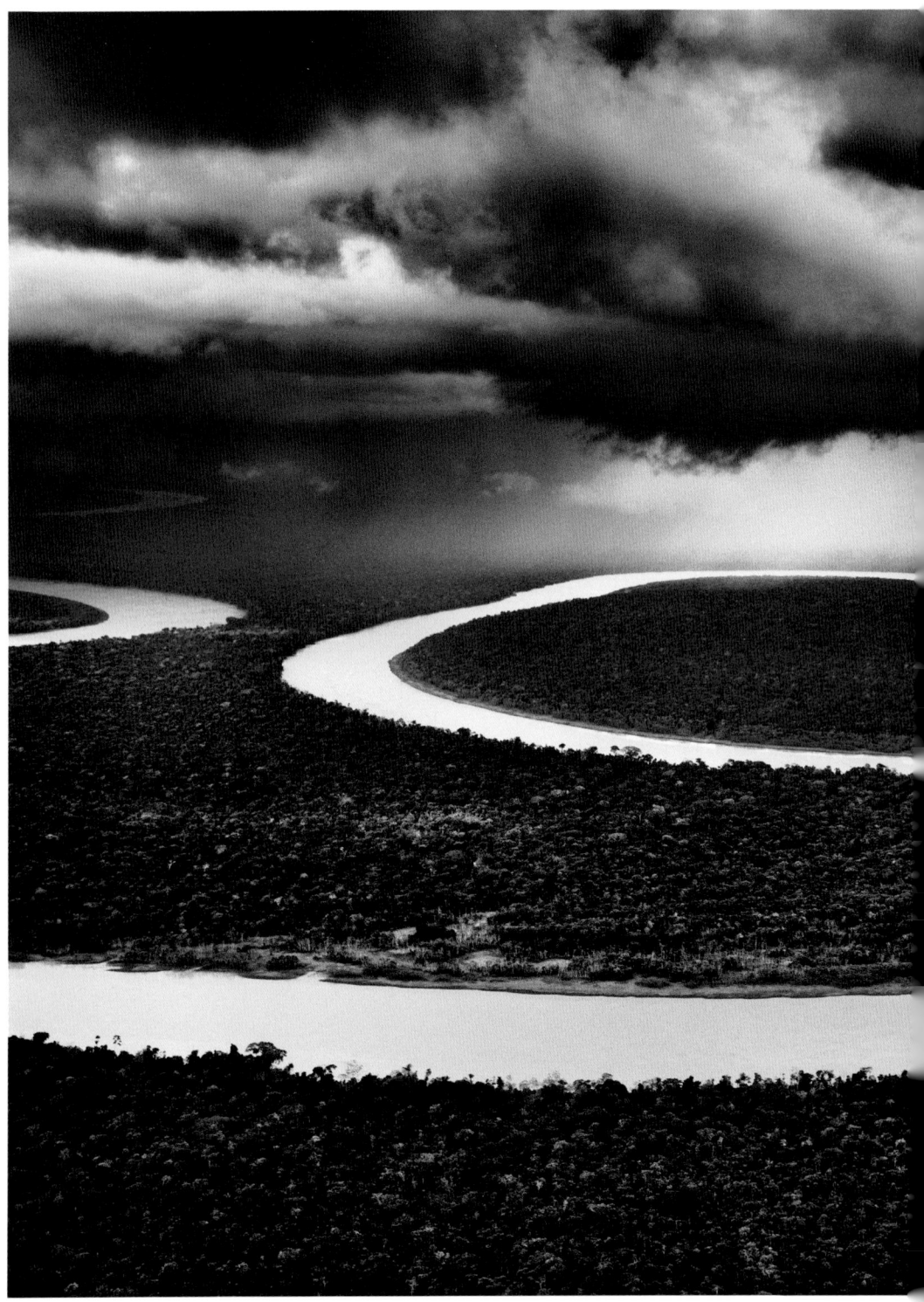

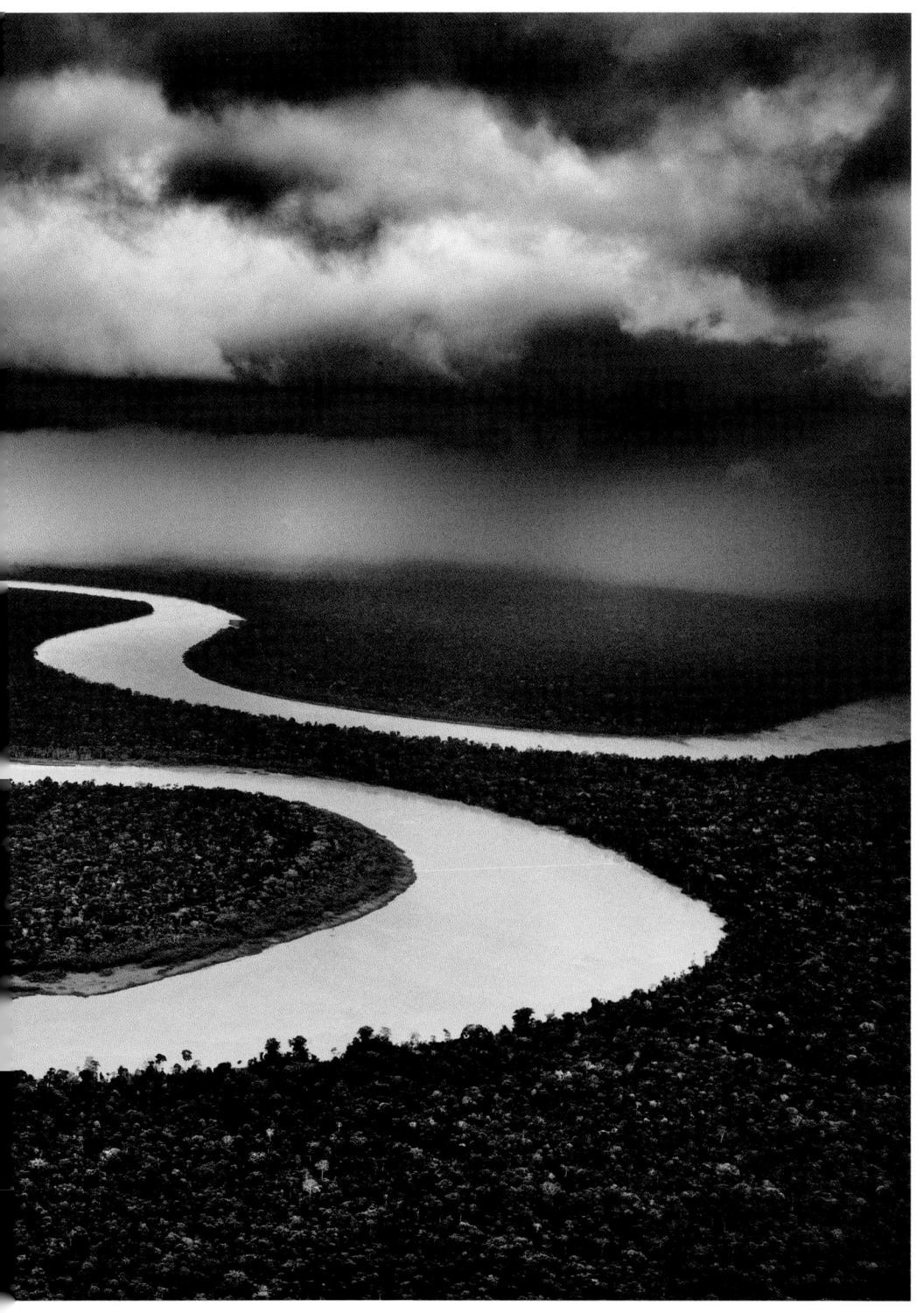

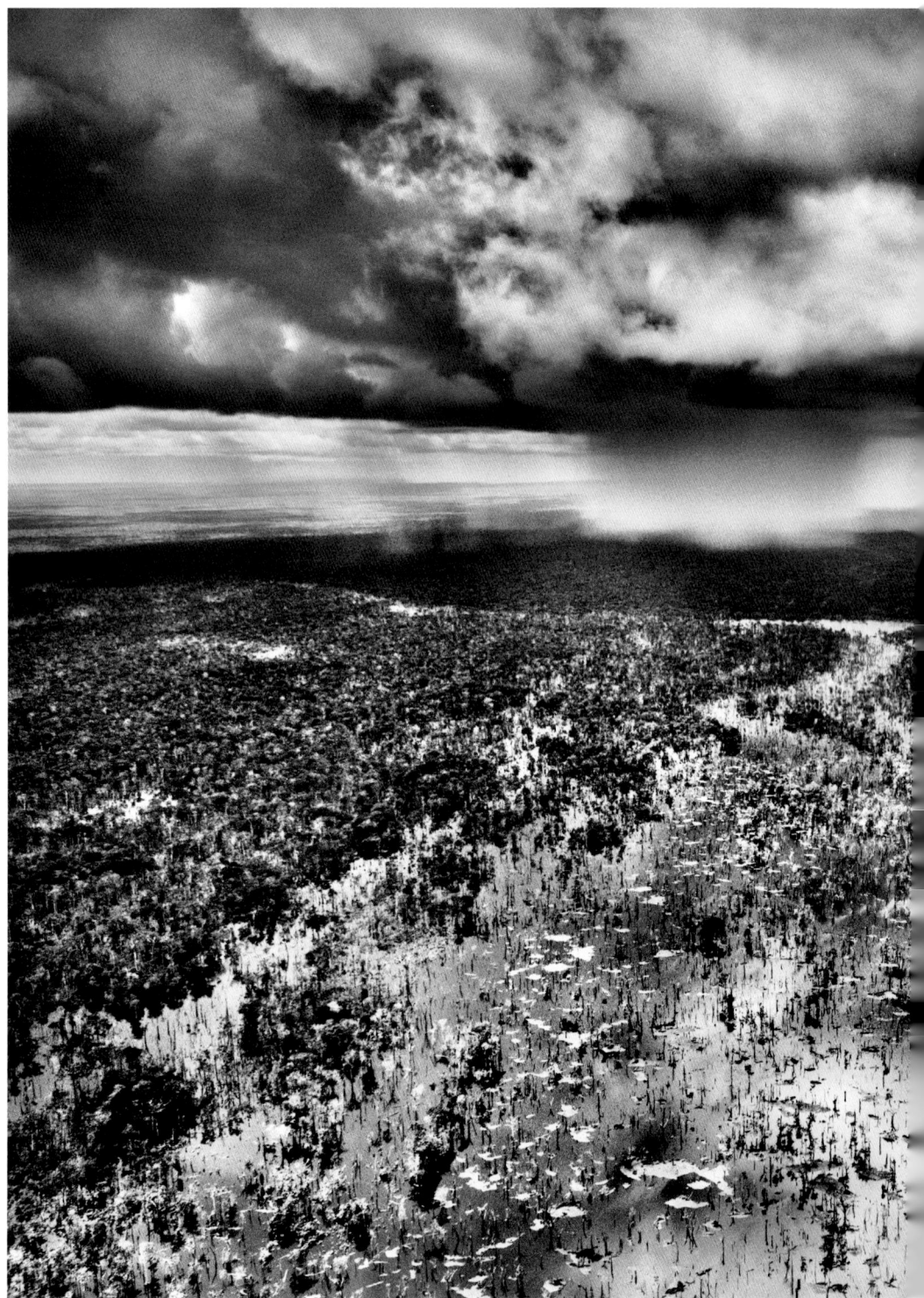

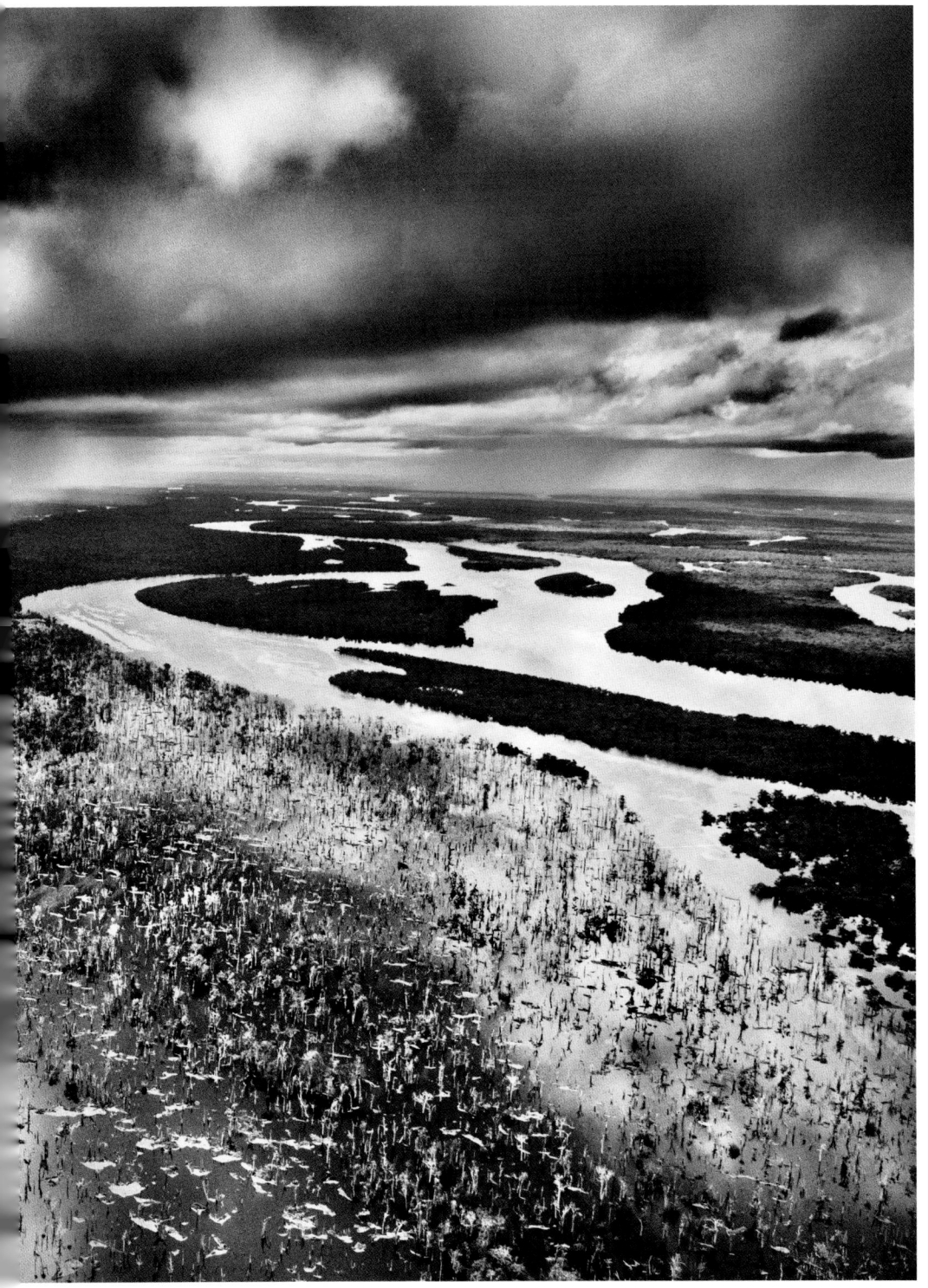

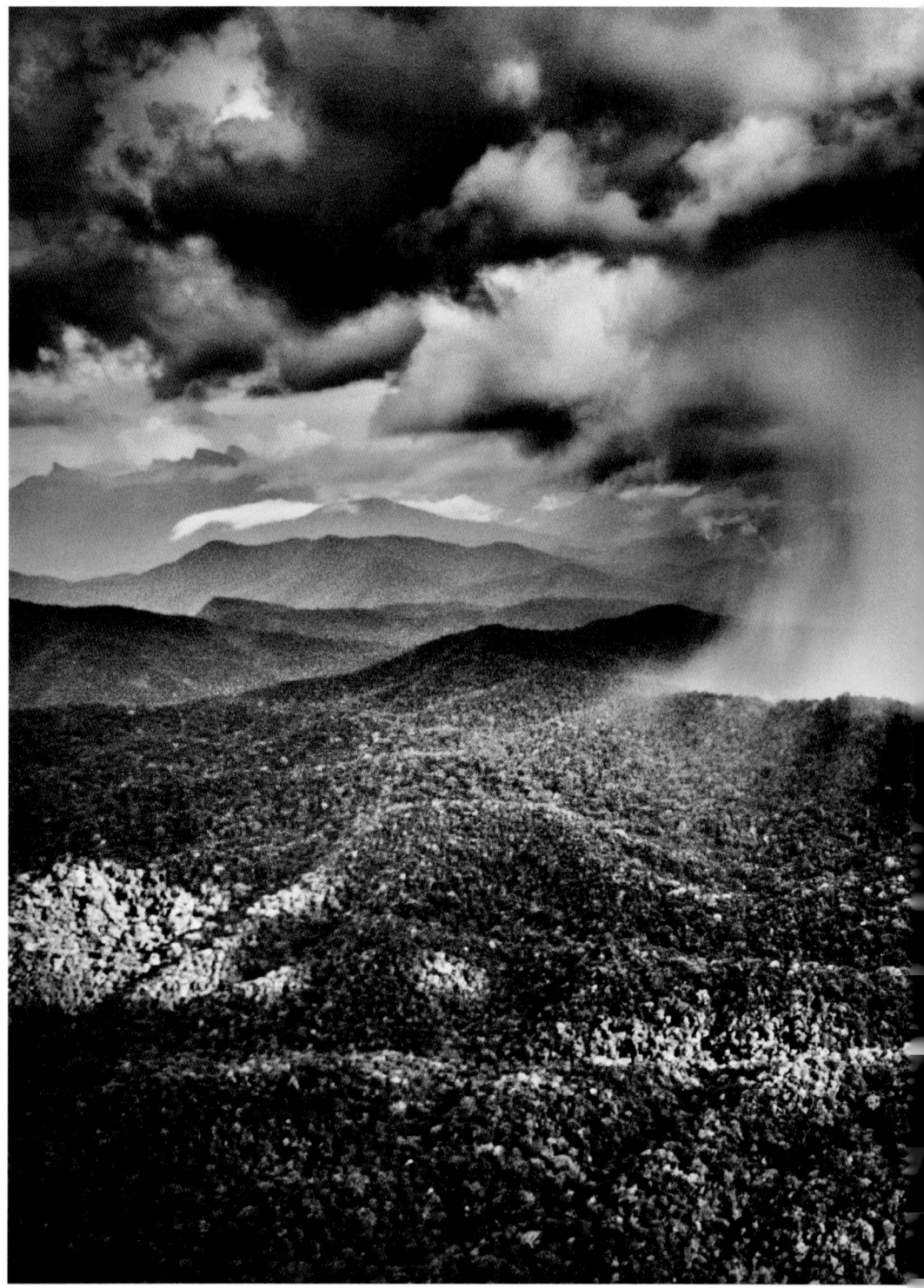

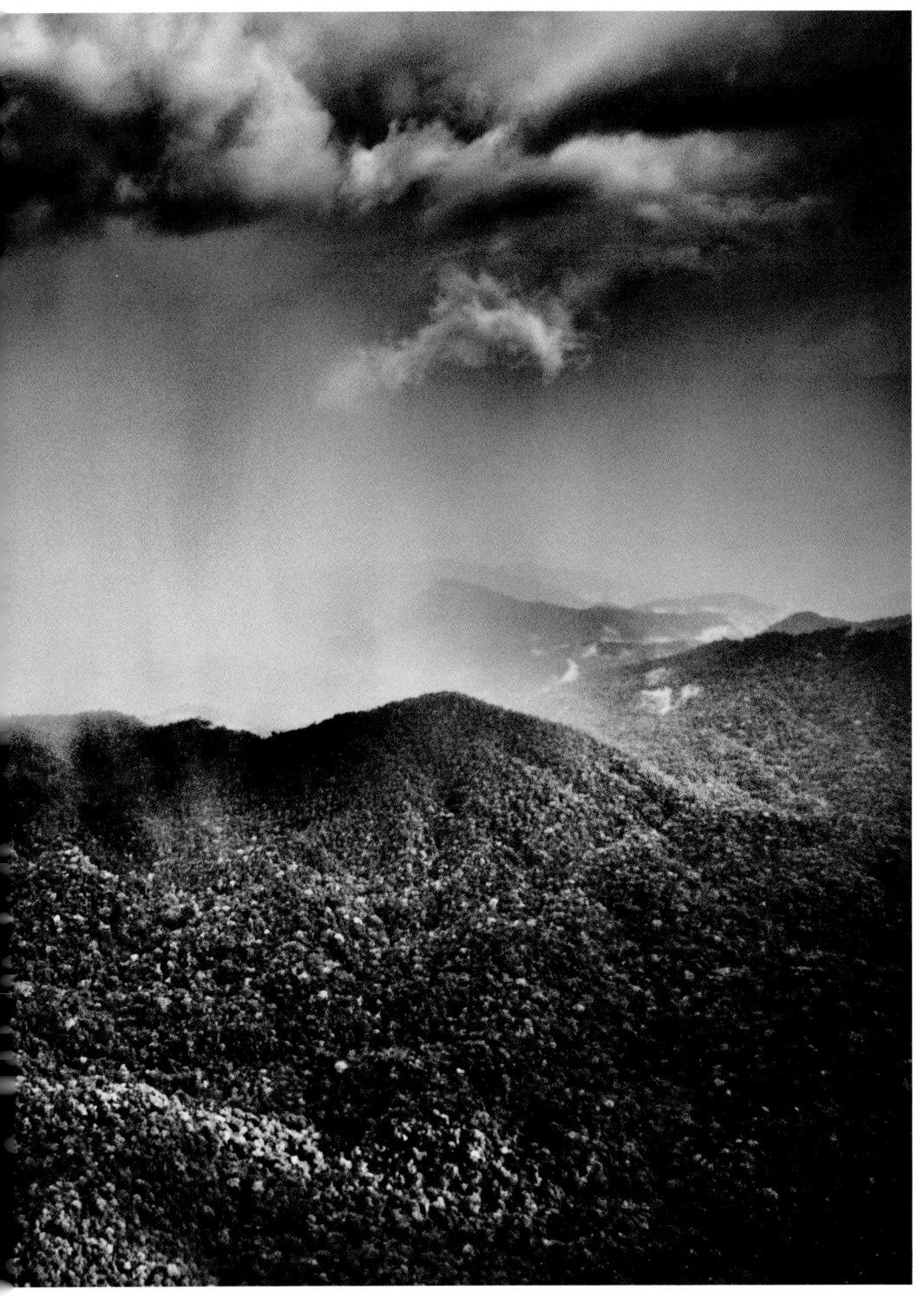

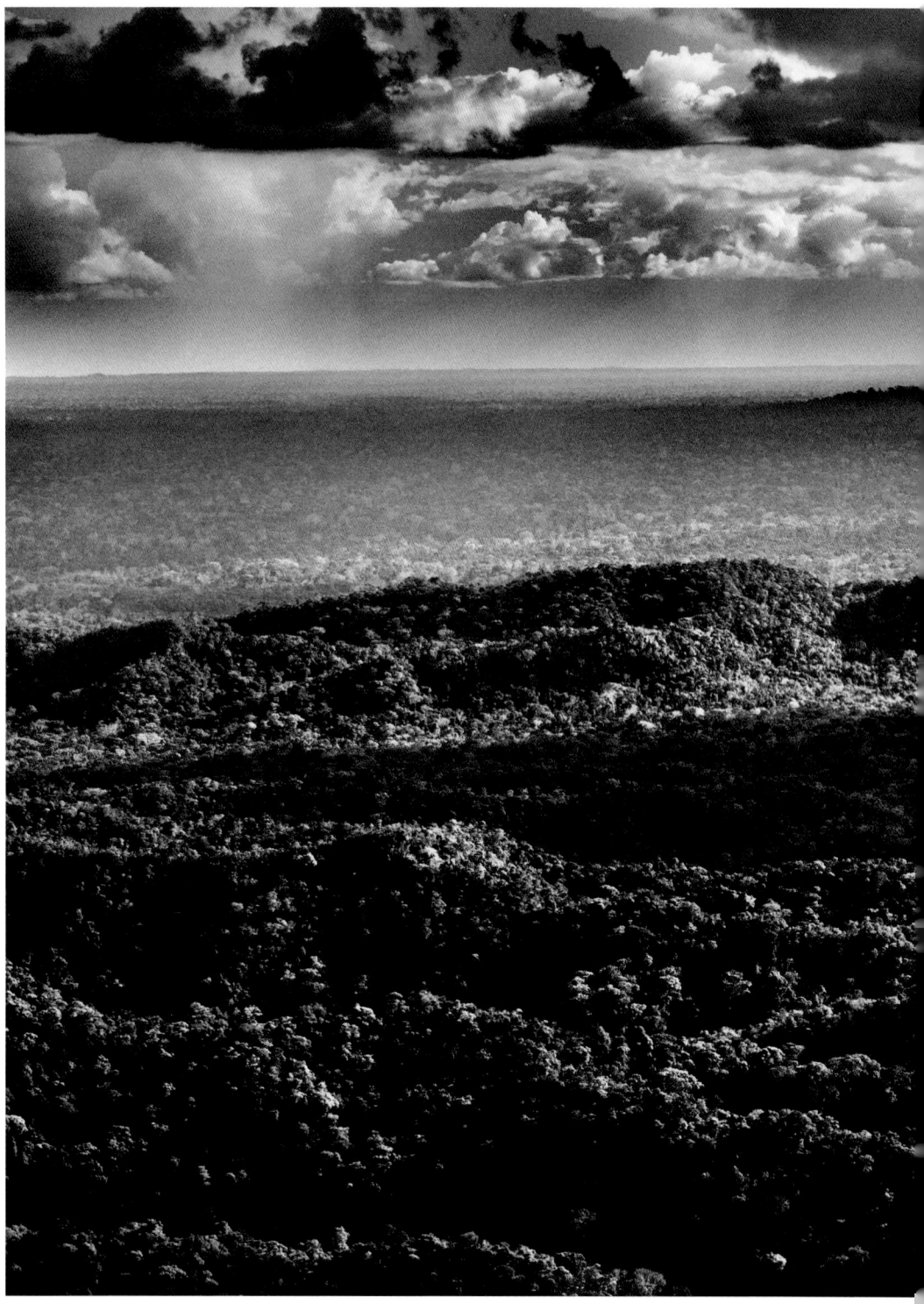

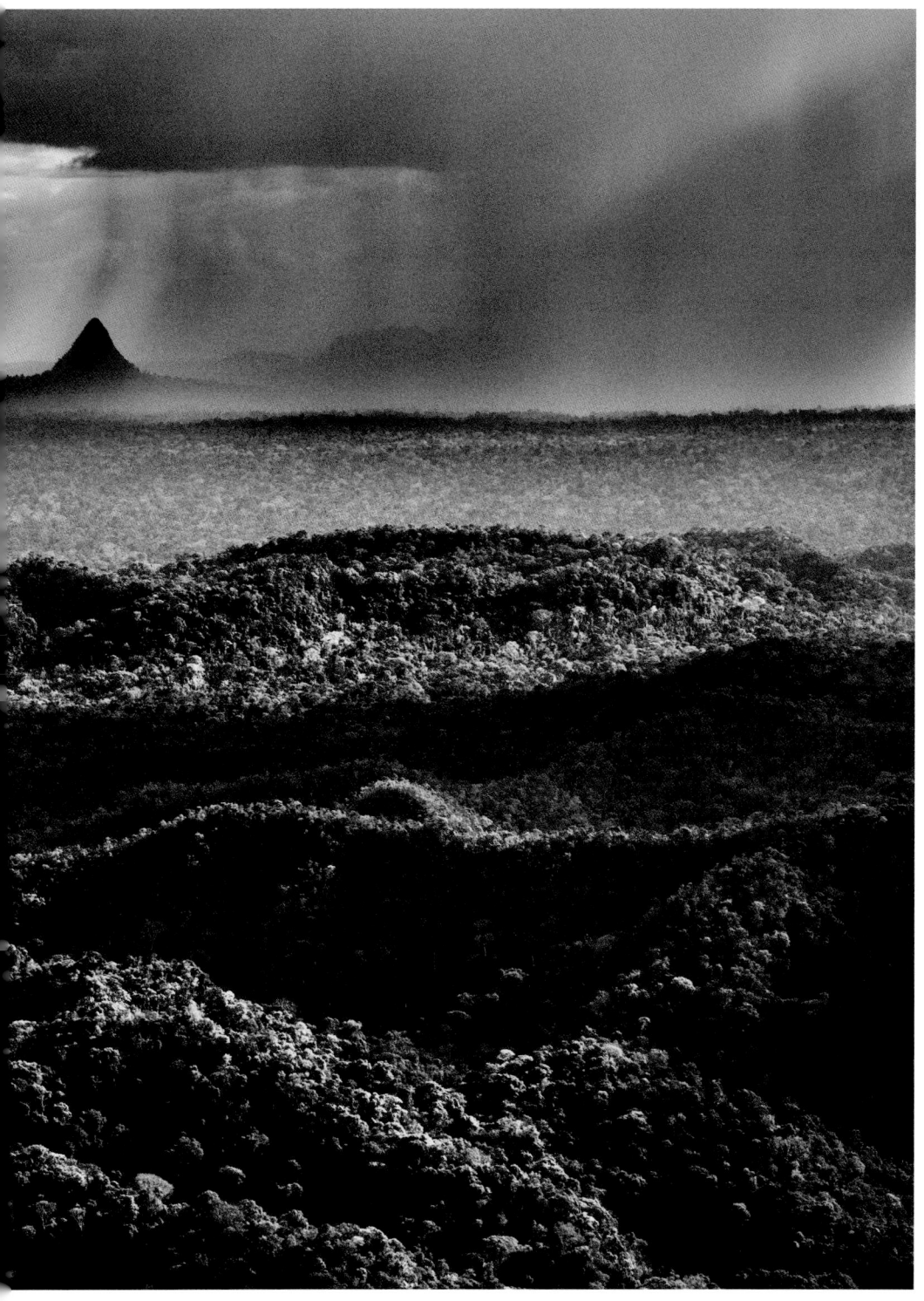

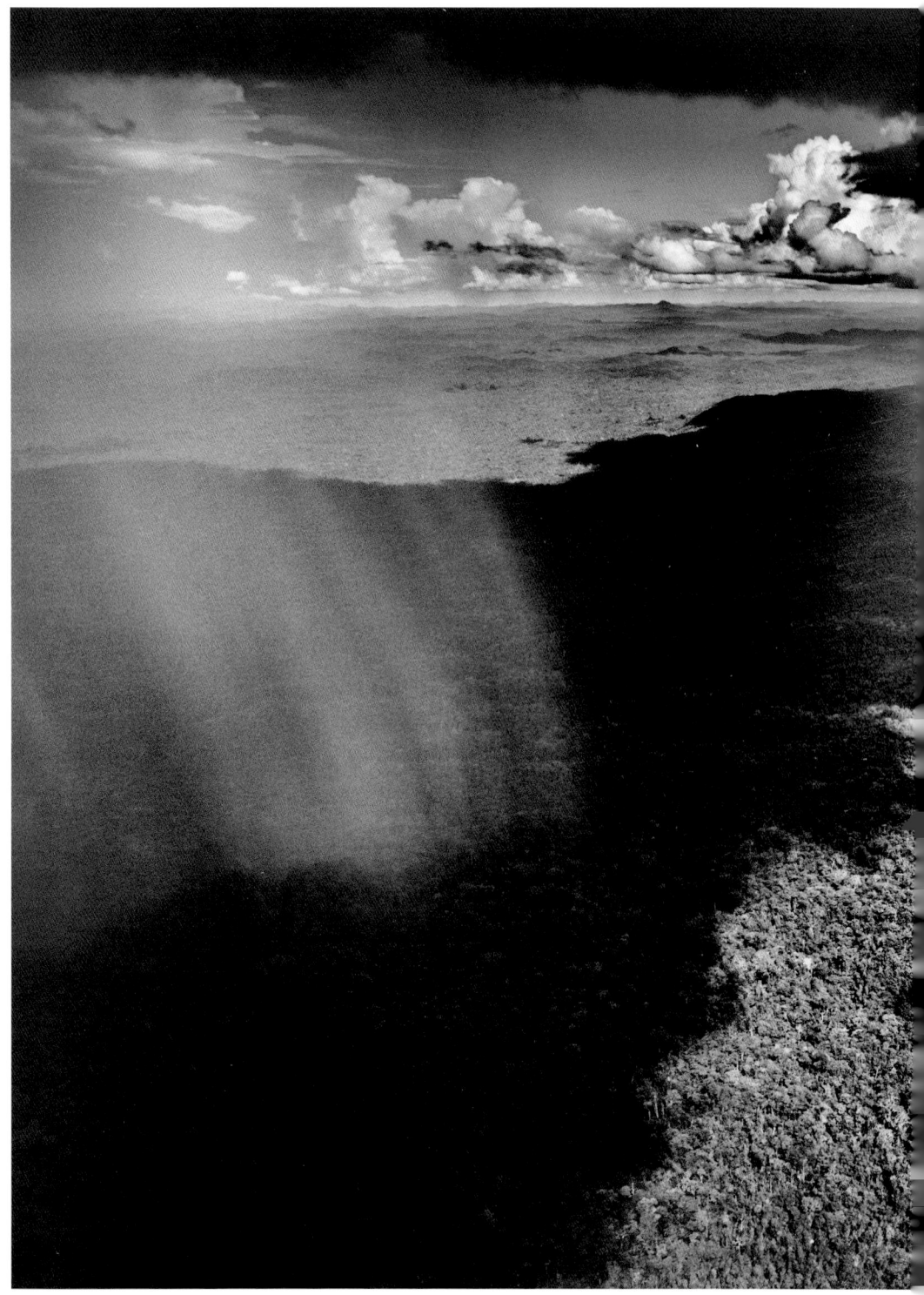

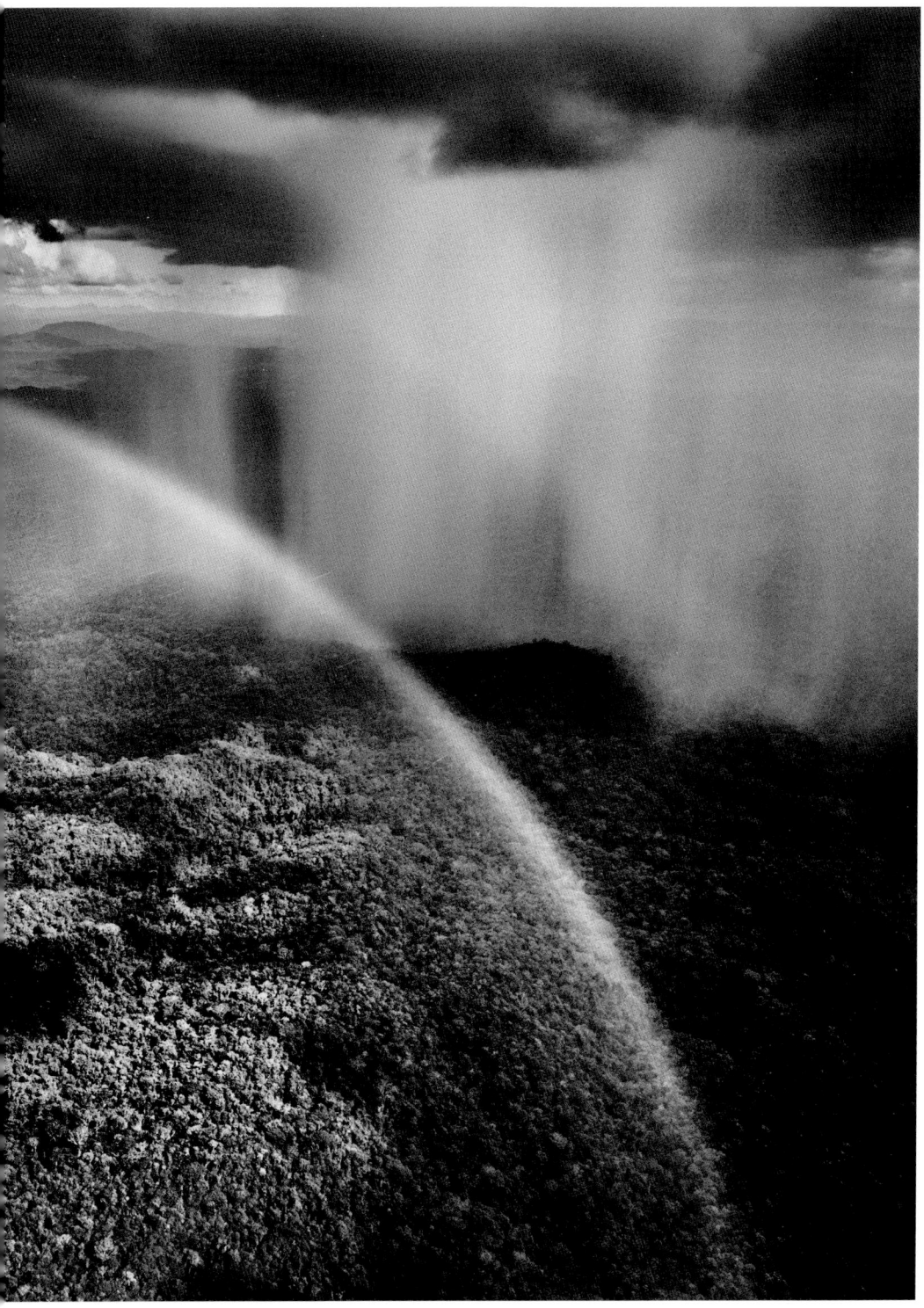

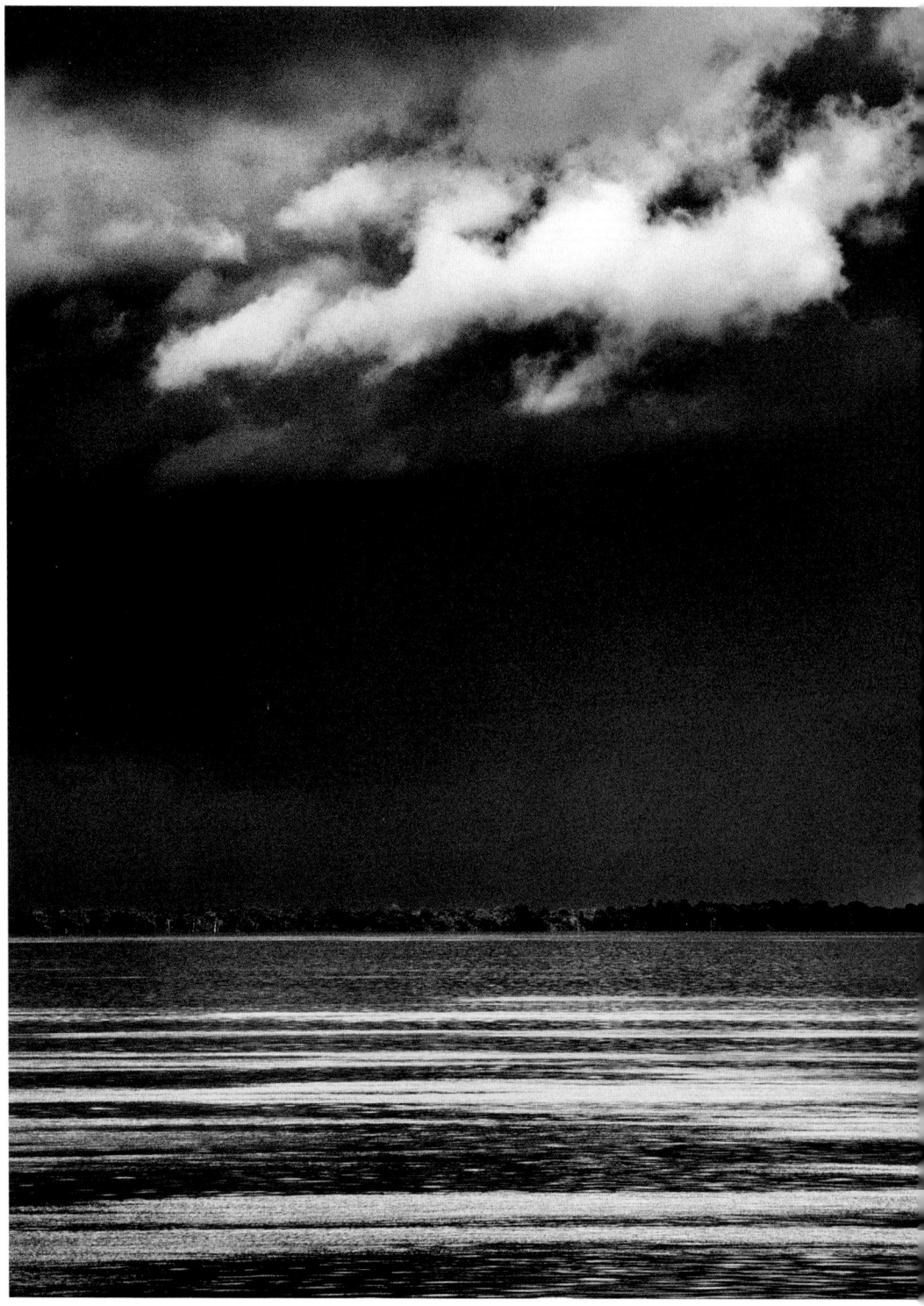

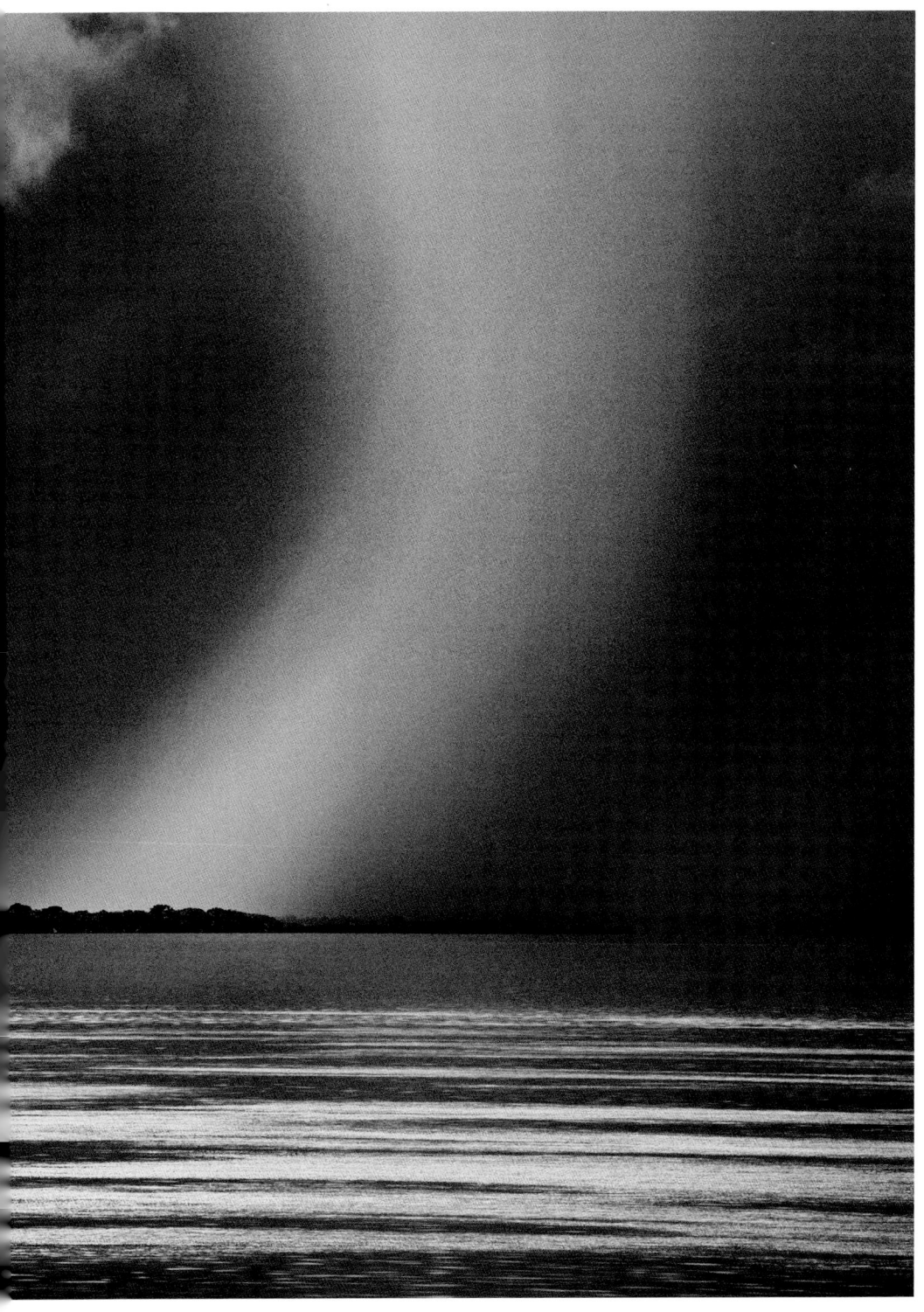

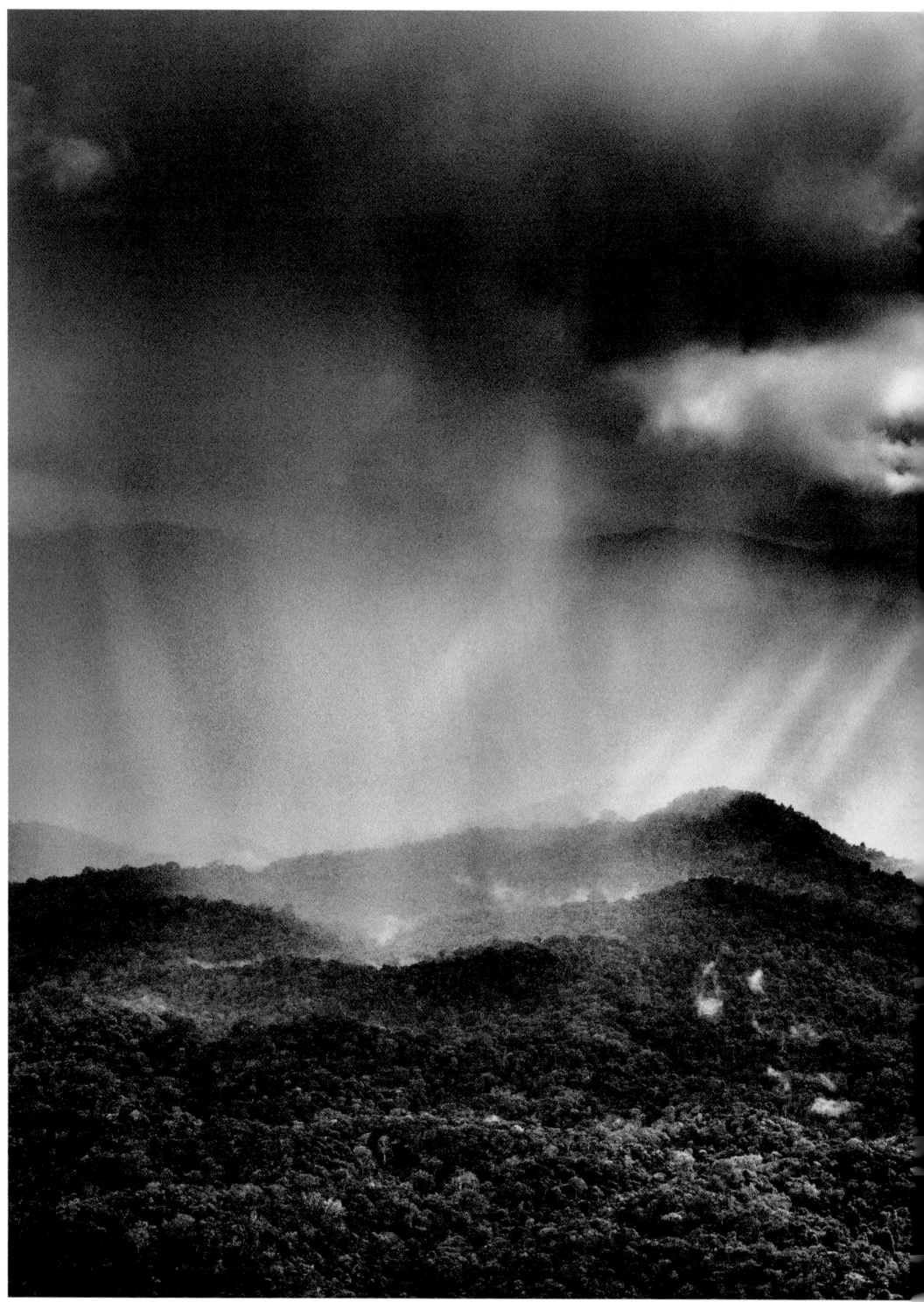

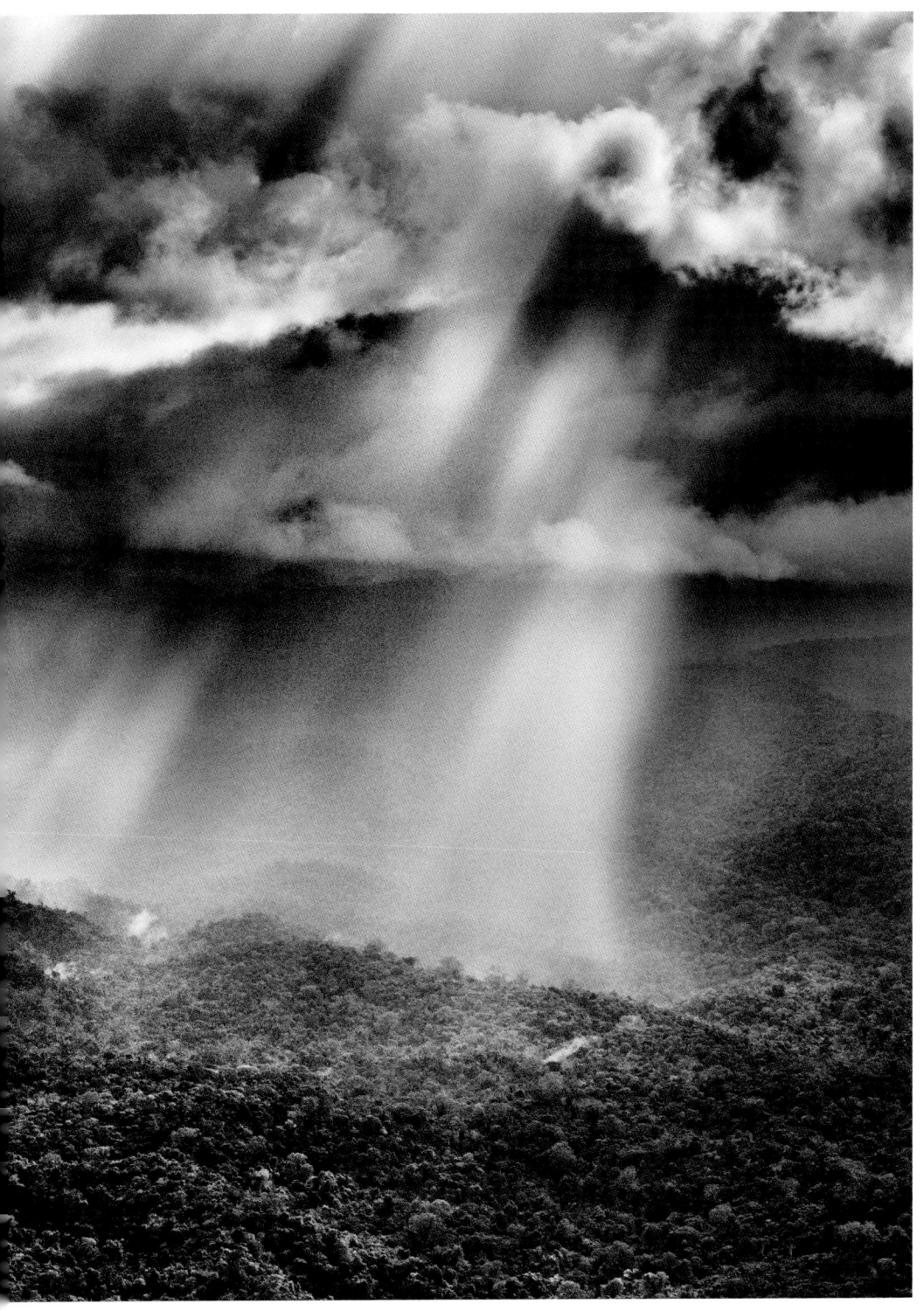

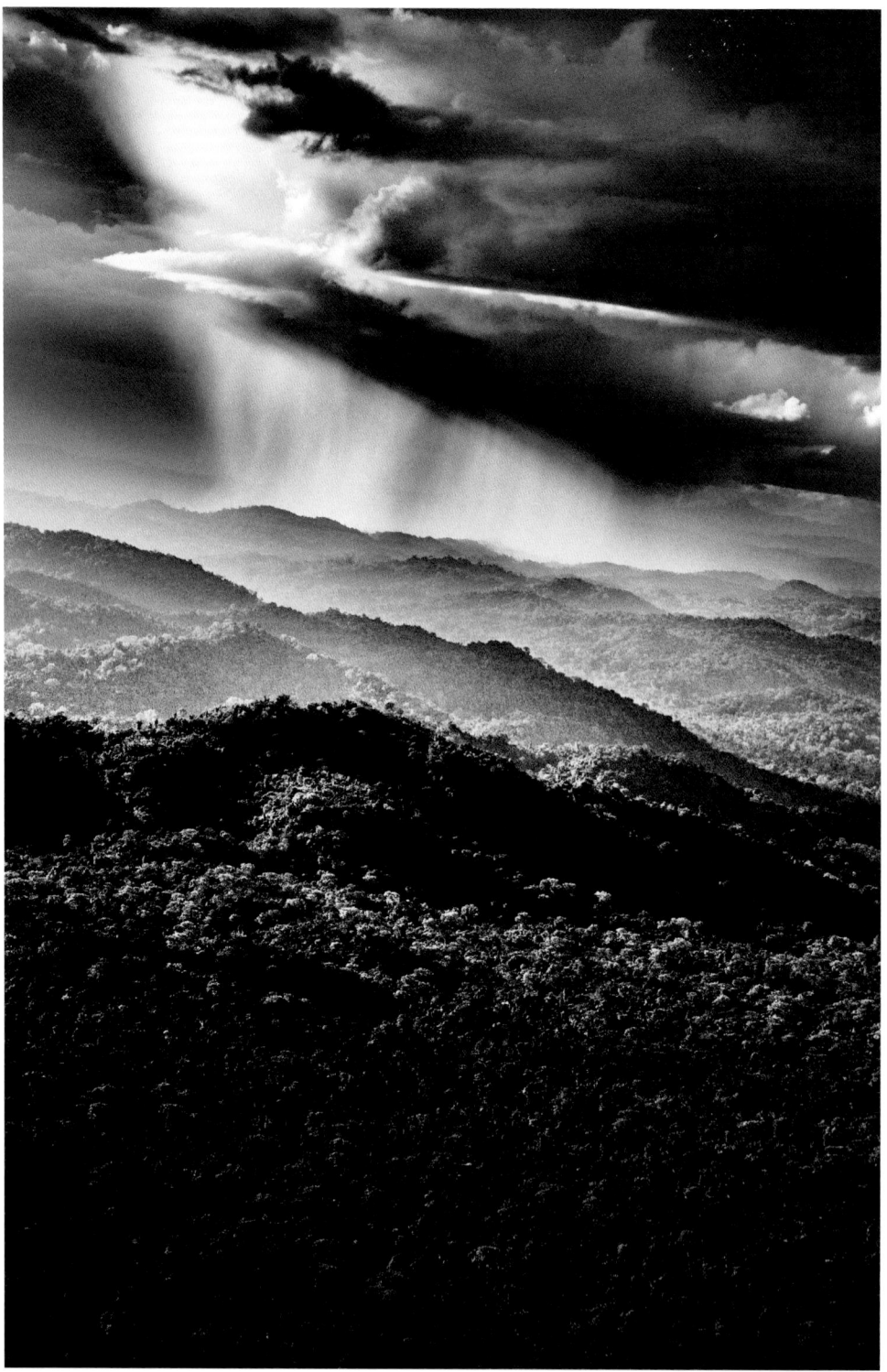

Opposite and pages 404/405 Aerial views of the Auaris area, in the Parima mountain range. Parima Forest Reserve. Yanomami Indigenous Territory, state of Roraima, 2018.

Pages 408/409, 412/413, and 418/419 Parima Forest Reserve. Yanomami Indigenous Territory, state of Roraima, 2018.

Pages 410/411 São Gabriel da Cachoeira area, Yanomami Indigenous Territory, state of Amazonas, 2018.

Pages 414/415 The Padre Mountains are part of the Neblina mountain range, in the Maturacá area, municipality of São Gabriel da Cachoeira, state of Amazonas, 2018.

Pages 416/417 The Inajá stream with rain in the background, falling in the Auaris area. Parima Forest Reserve. Yanomami Indigenous Territory, state of Roraima, 2018.

Pages 420/421 Storm over the Lower Rio Negro, near the confluence with the Rio Branco and with the Anavilhanas Archipelago, state of Amazonas, 2019.

Pages 422/423 Rainbow over the Tucuxim area. Parima Forest Reserve. Yanomami Indigenous Territory, state of Roraima, 2018.

Pages 424/425 The rain is so intense in Serra do Divisor National Park that it looks like an atomic mushroom cloud. State of Acre, 2016.

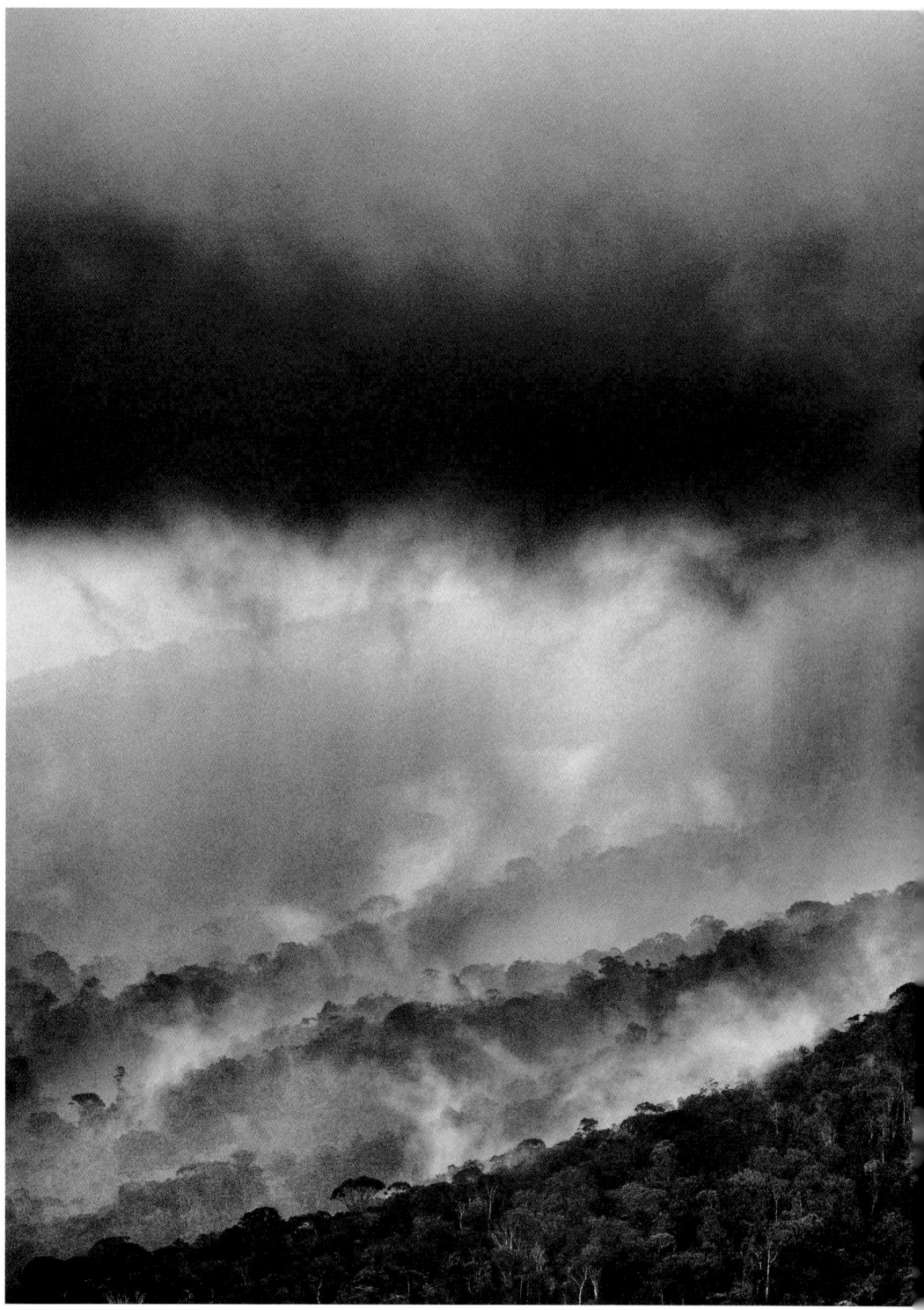

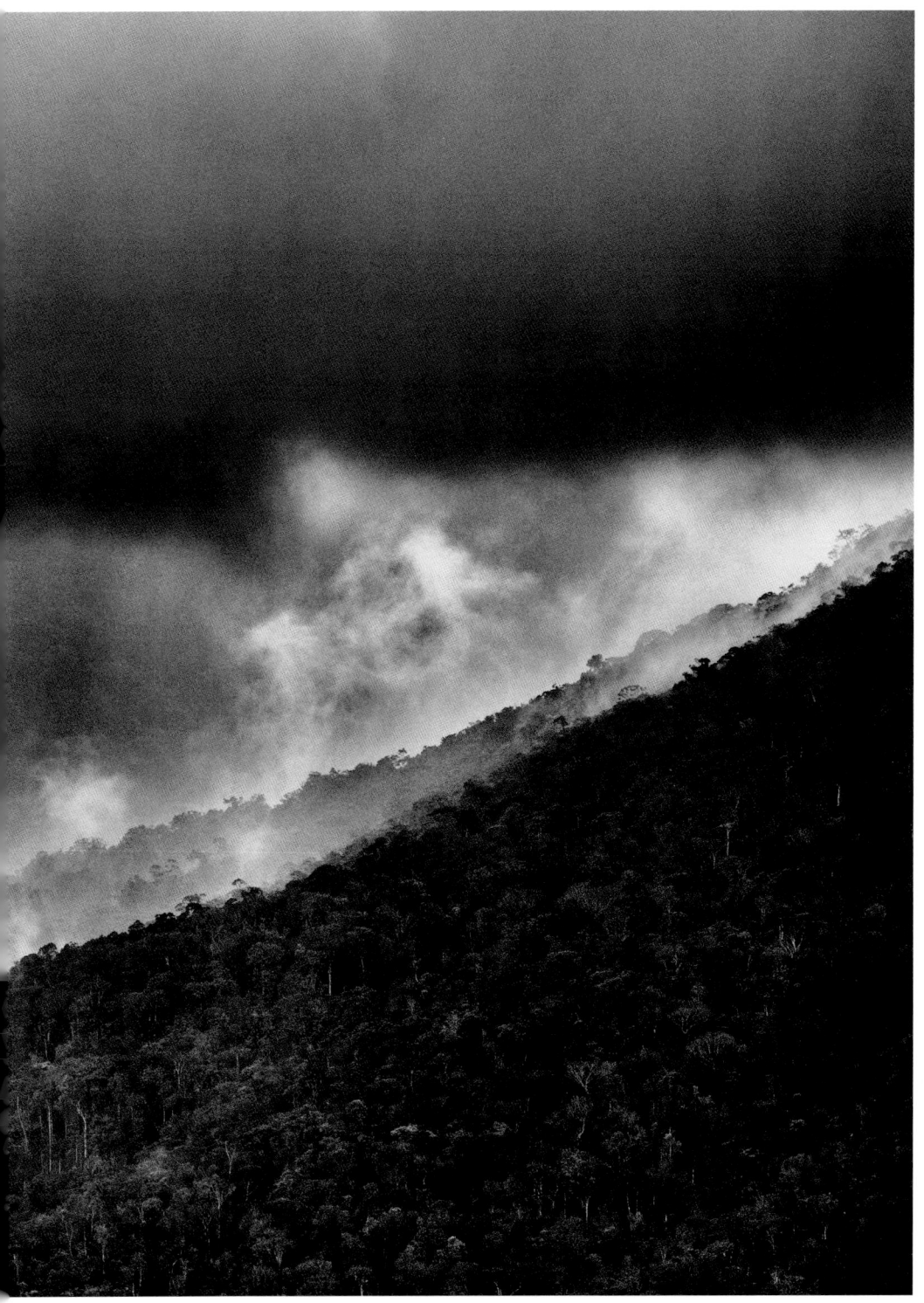

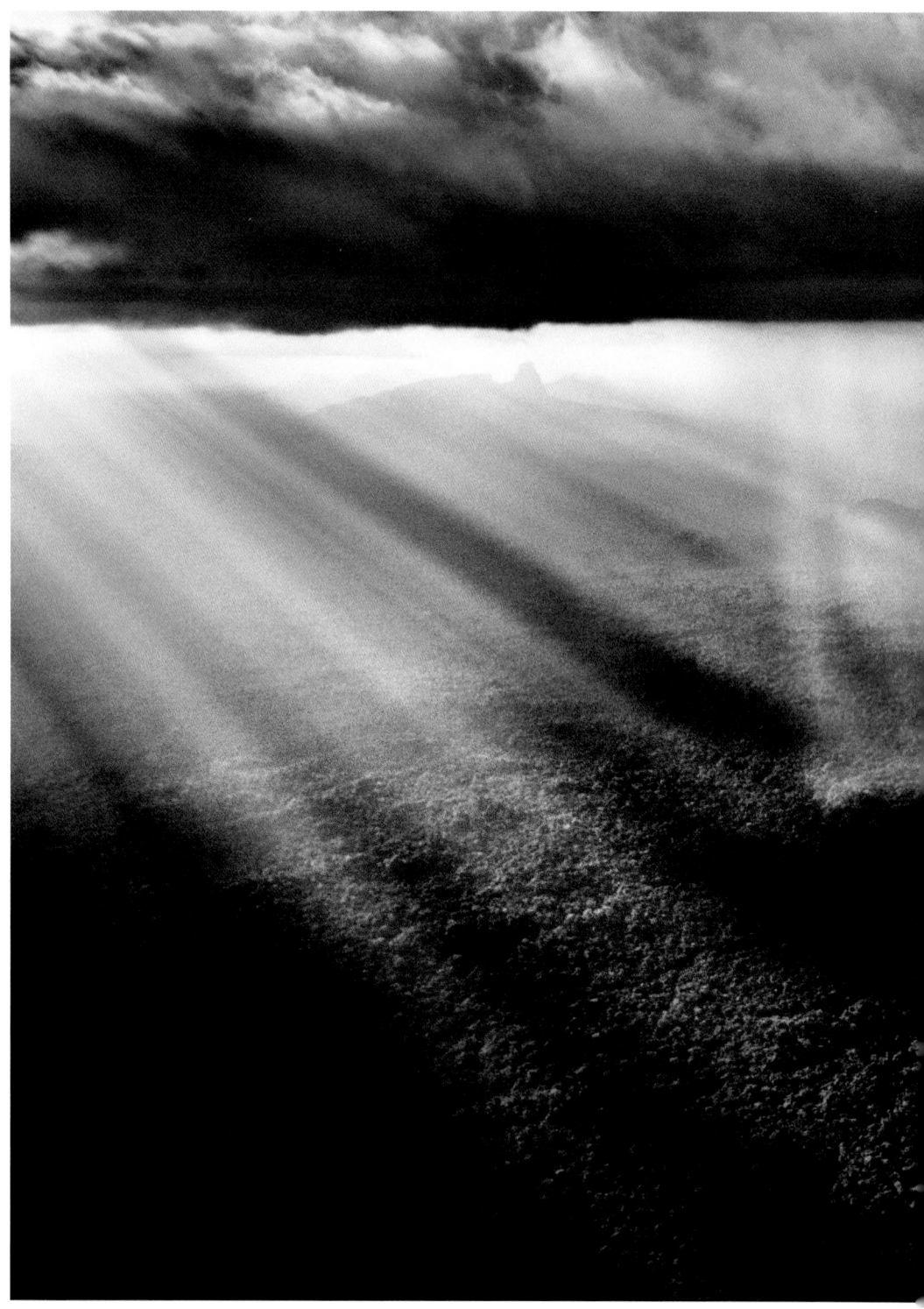

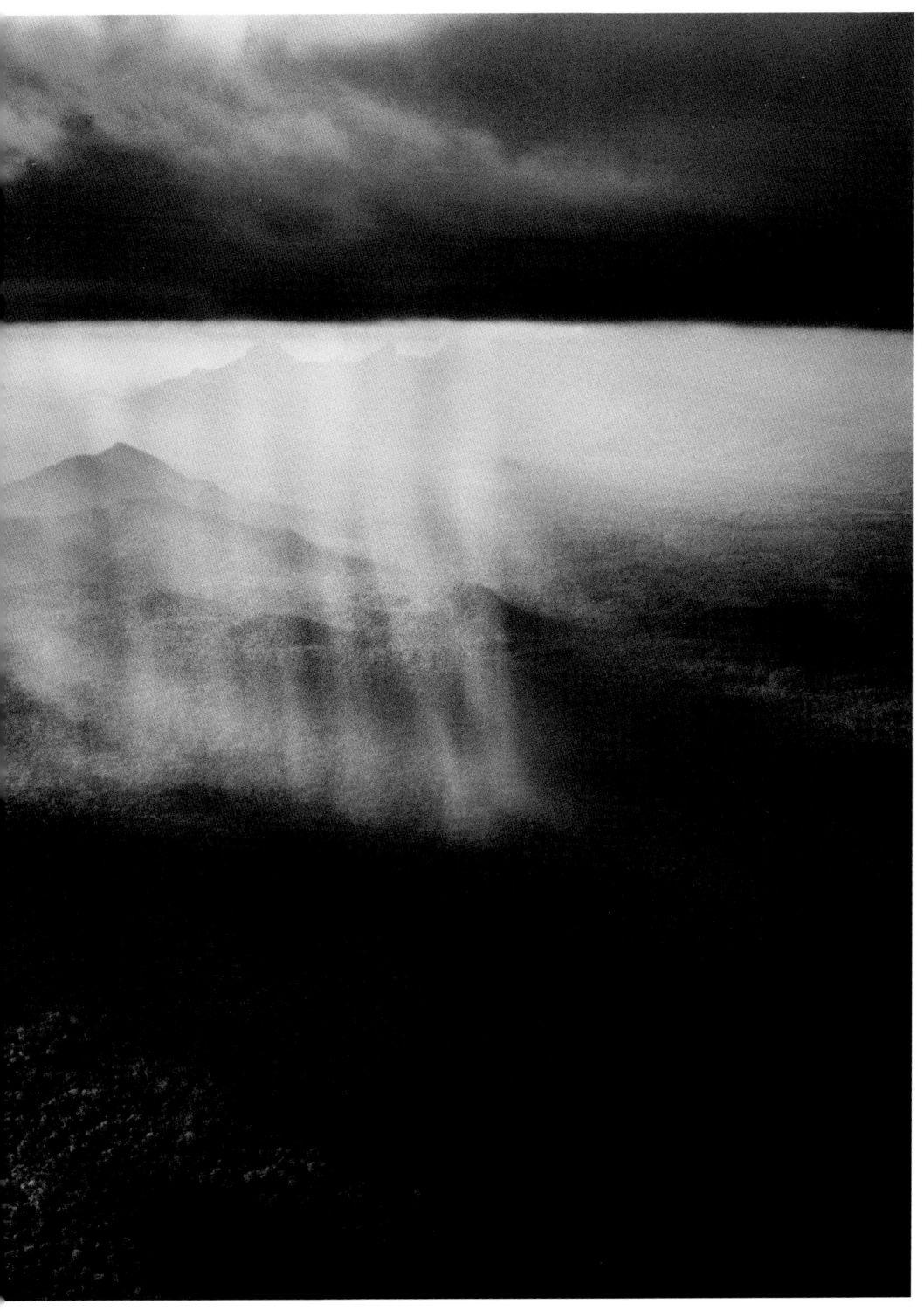

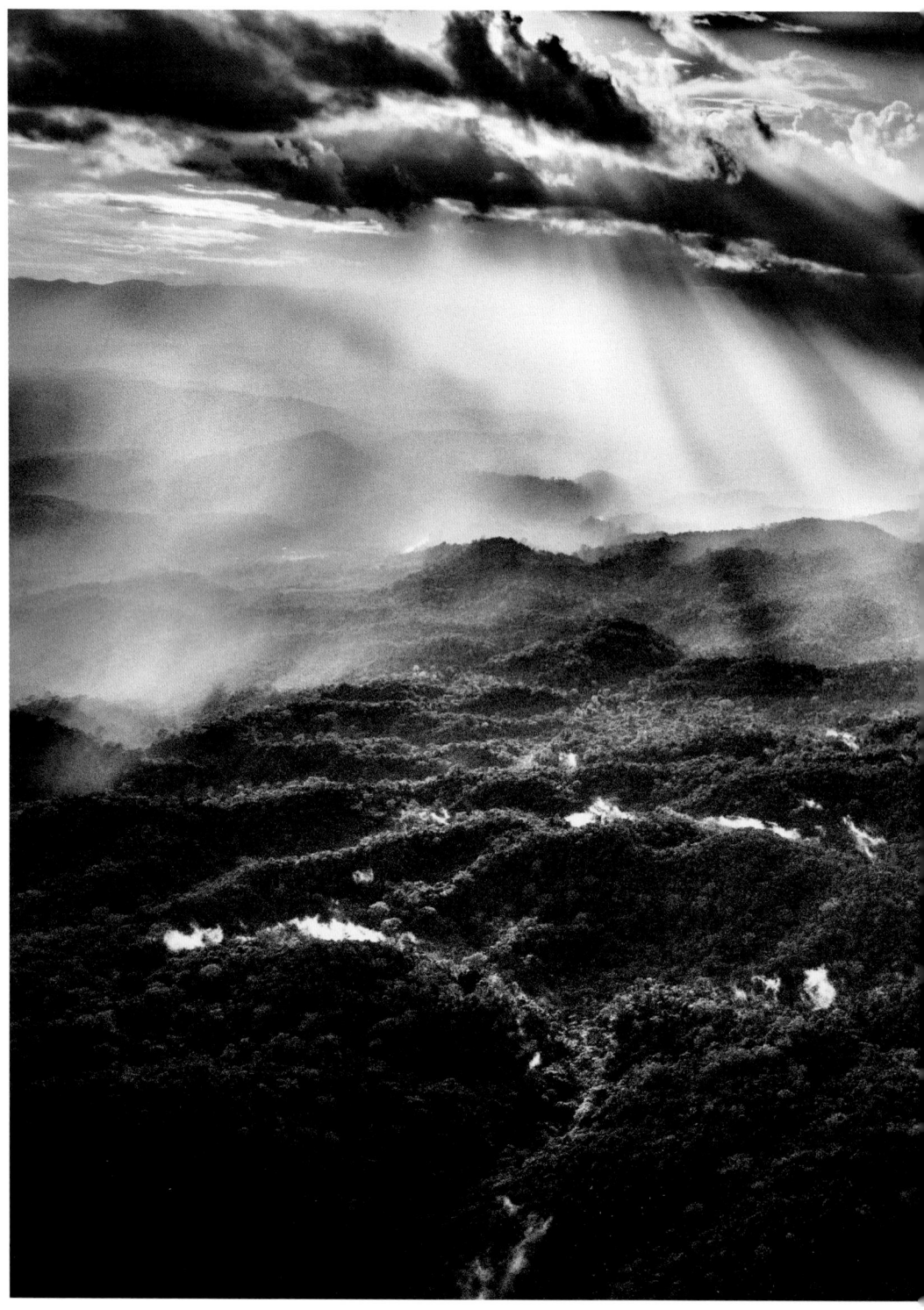

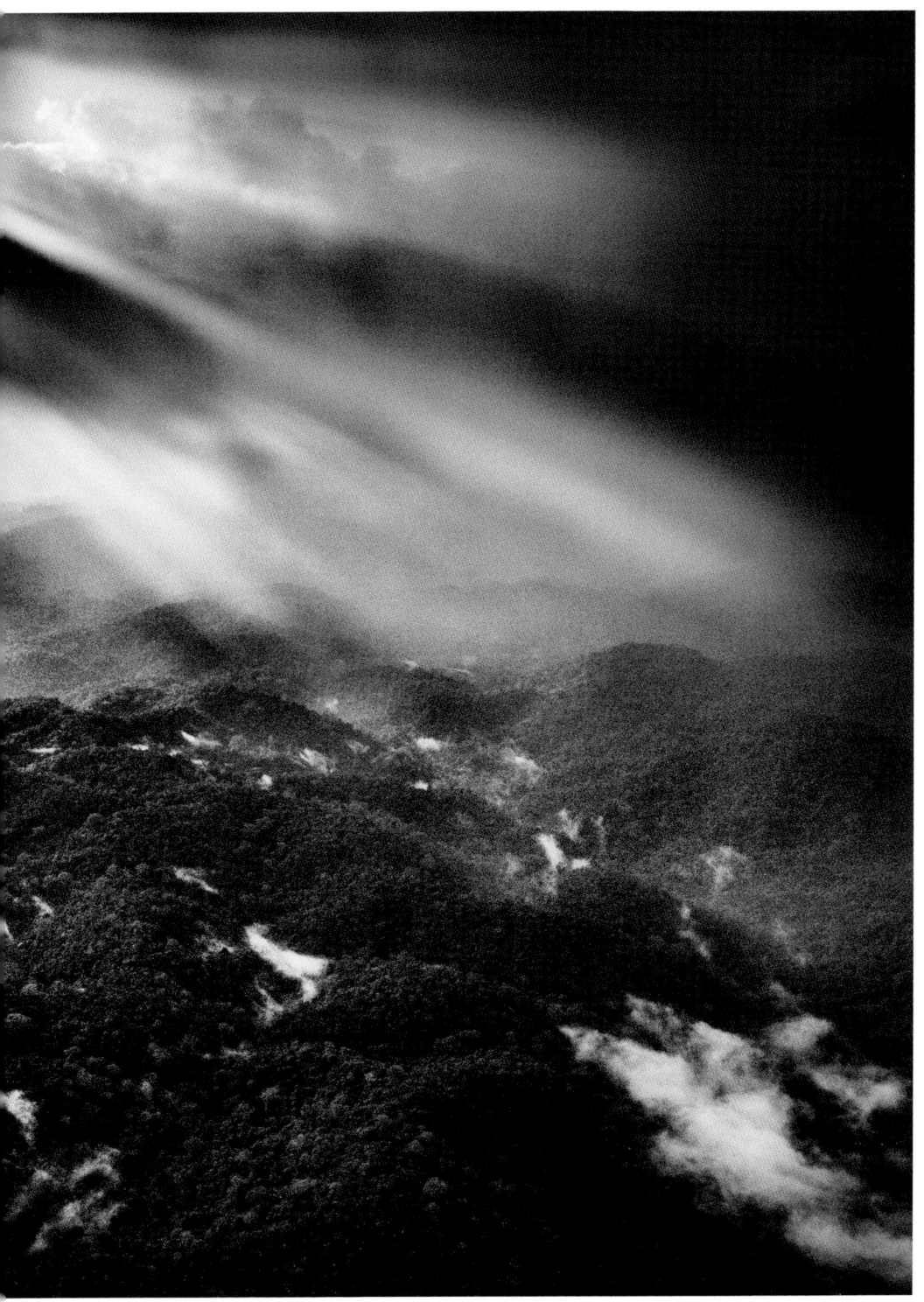

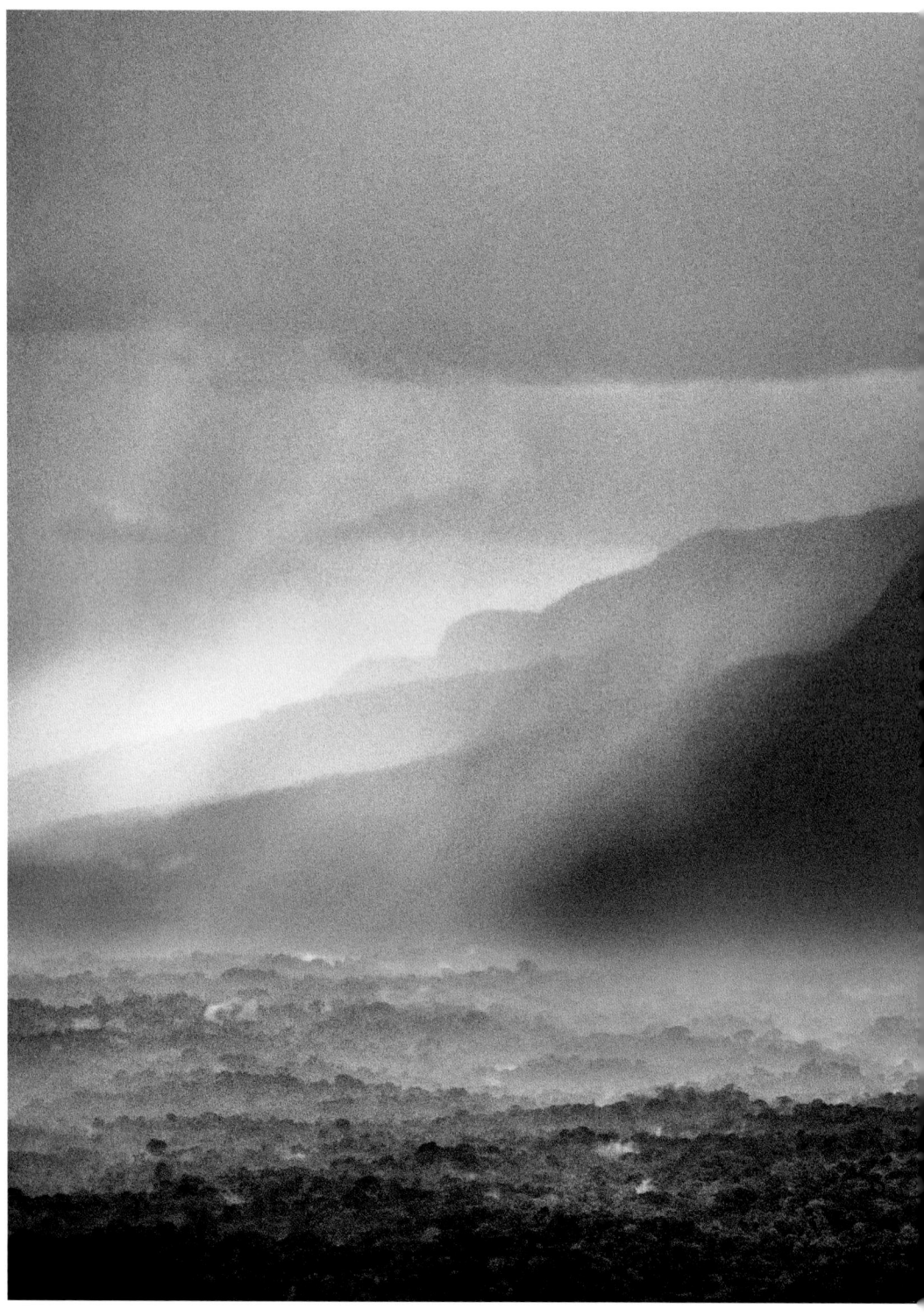

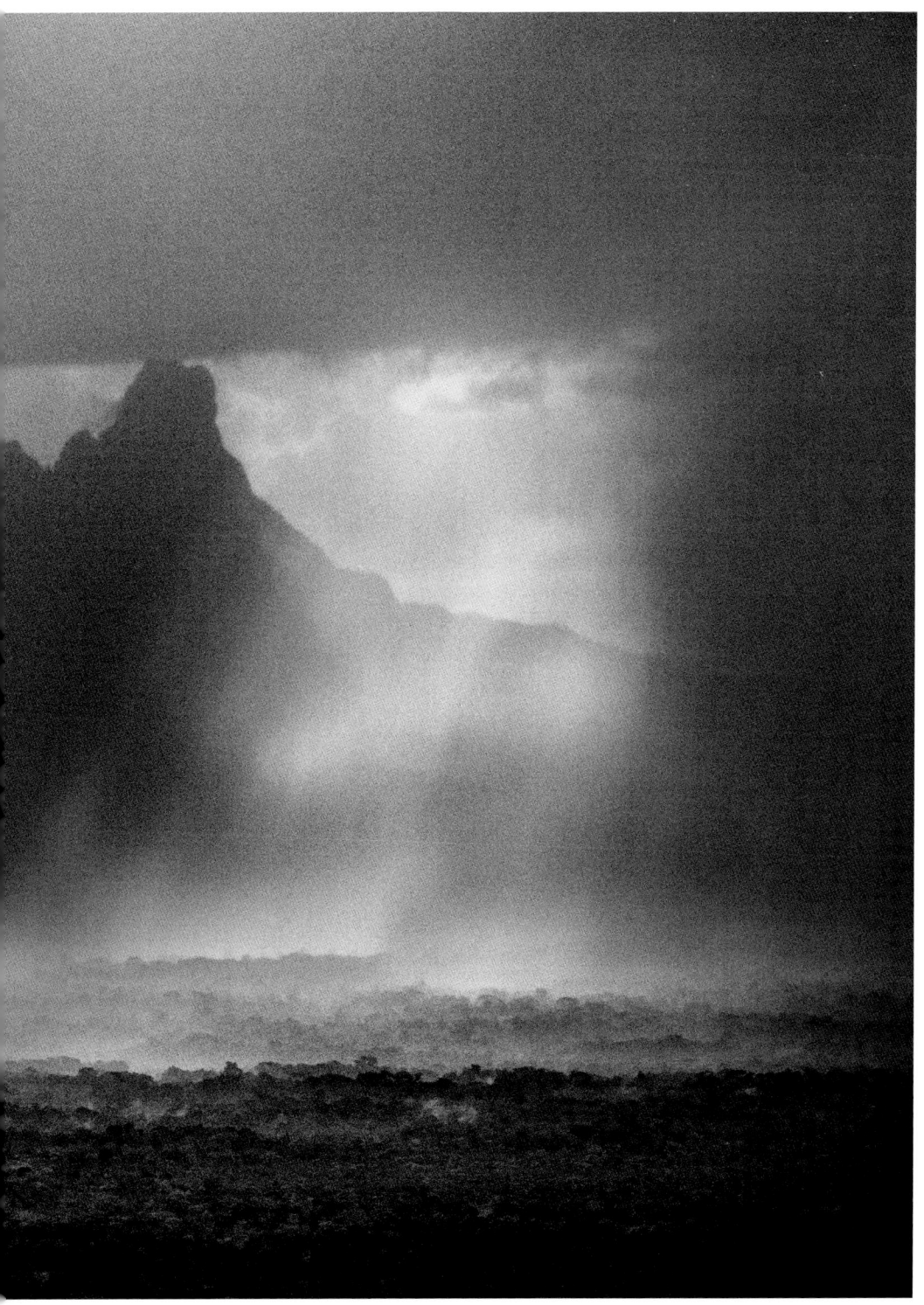

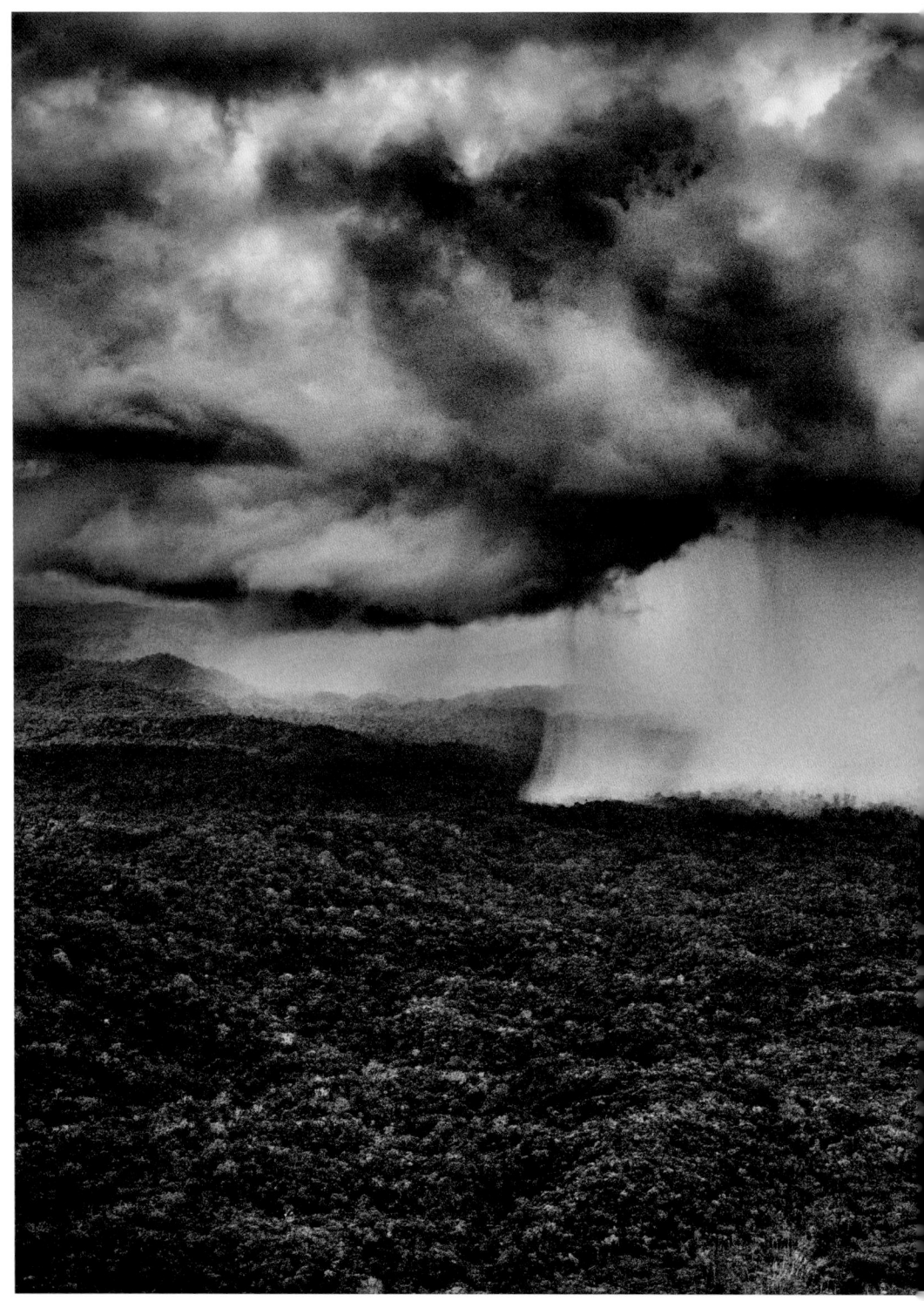

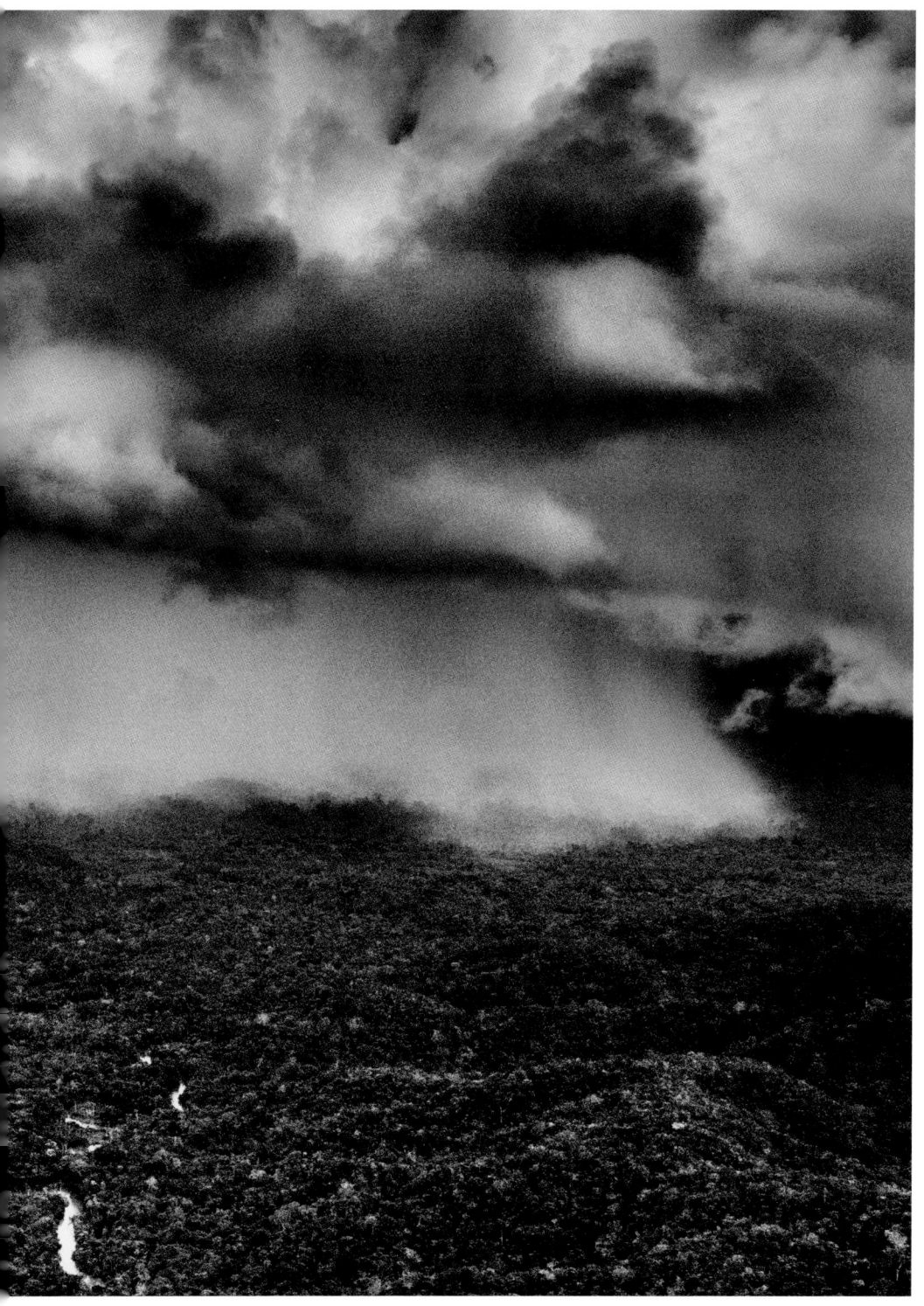

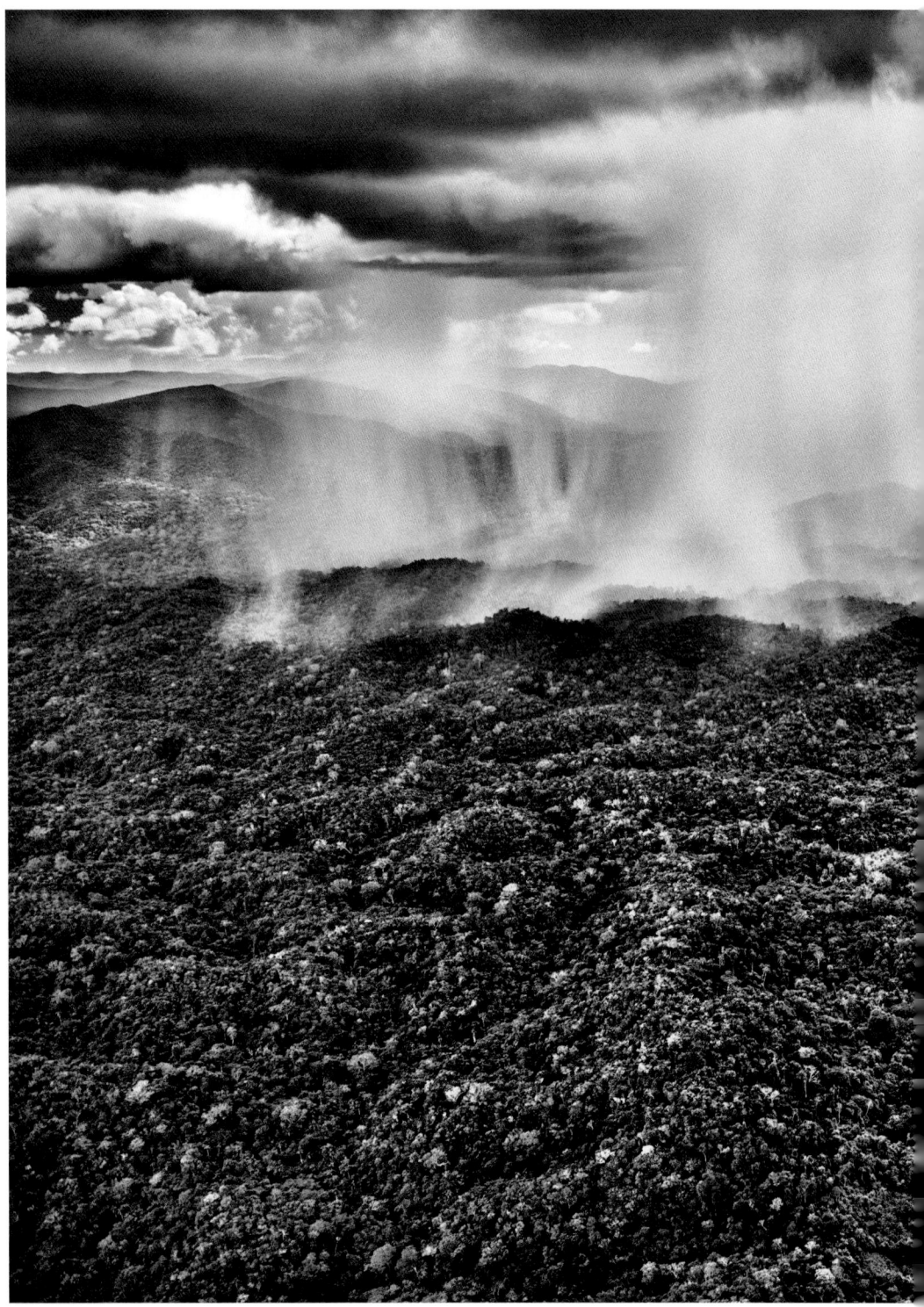

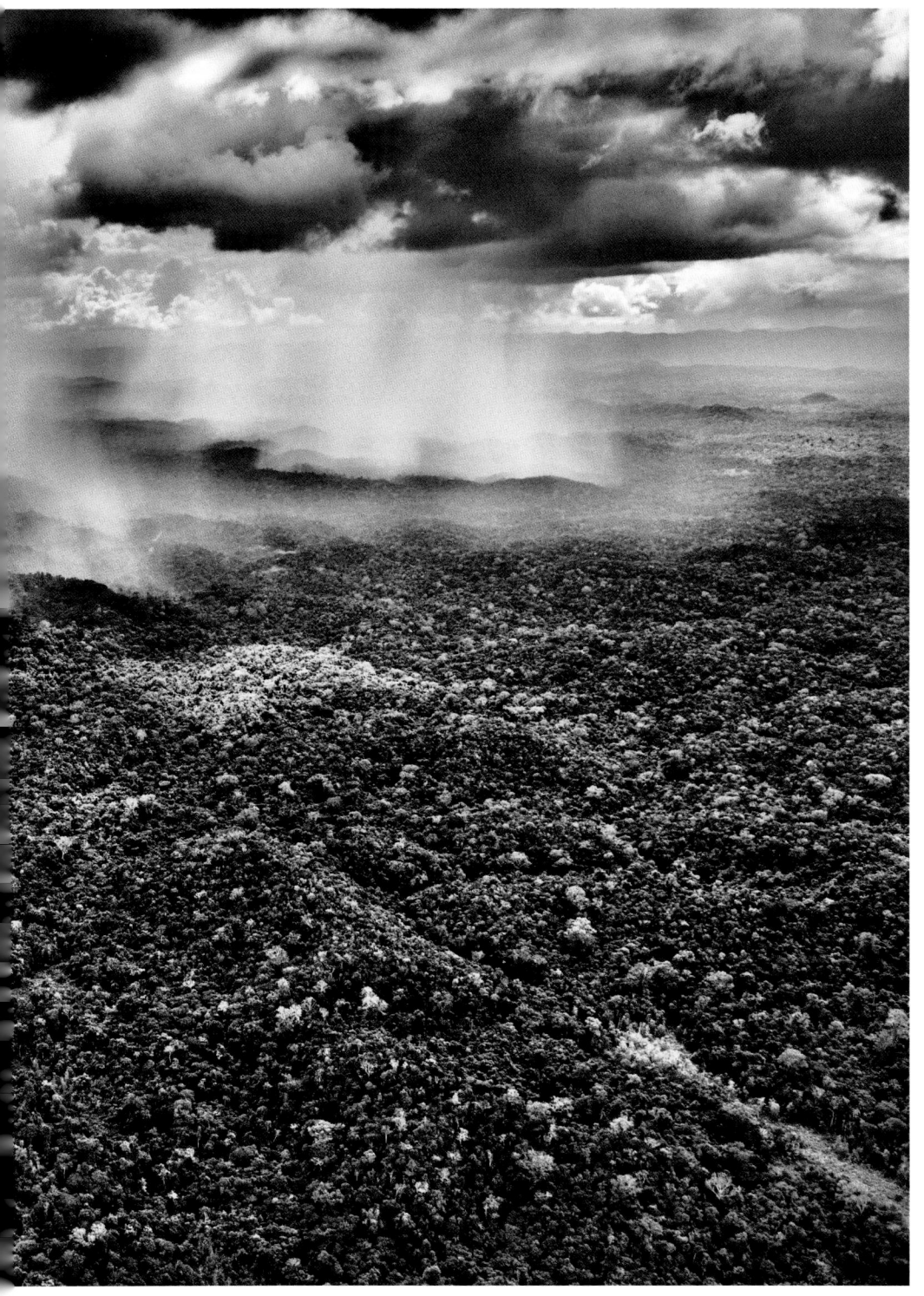

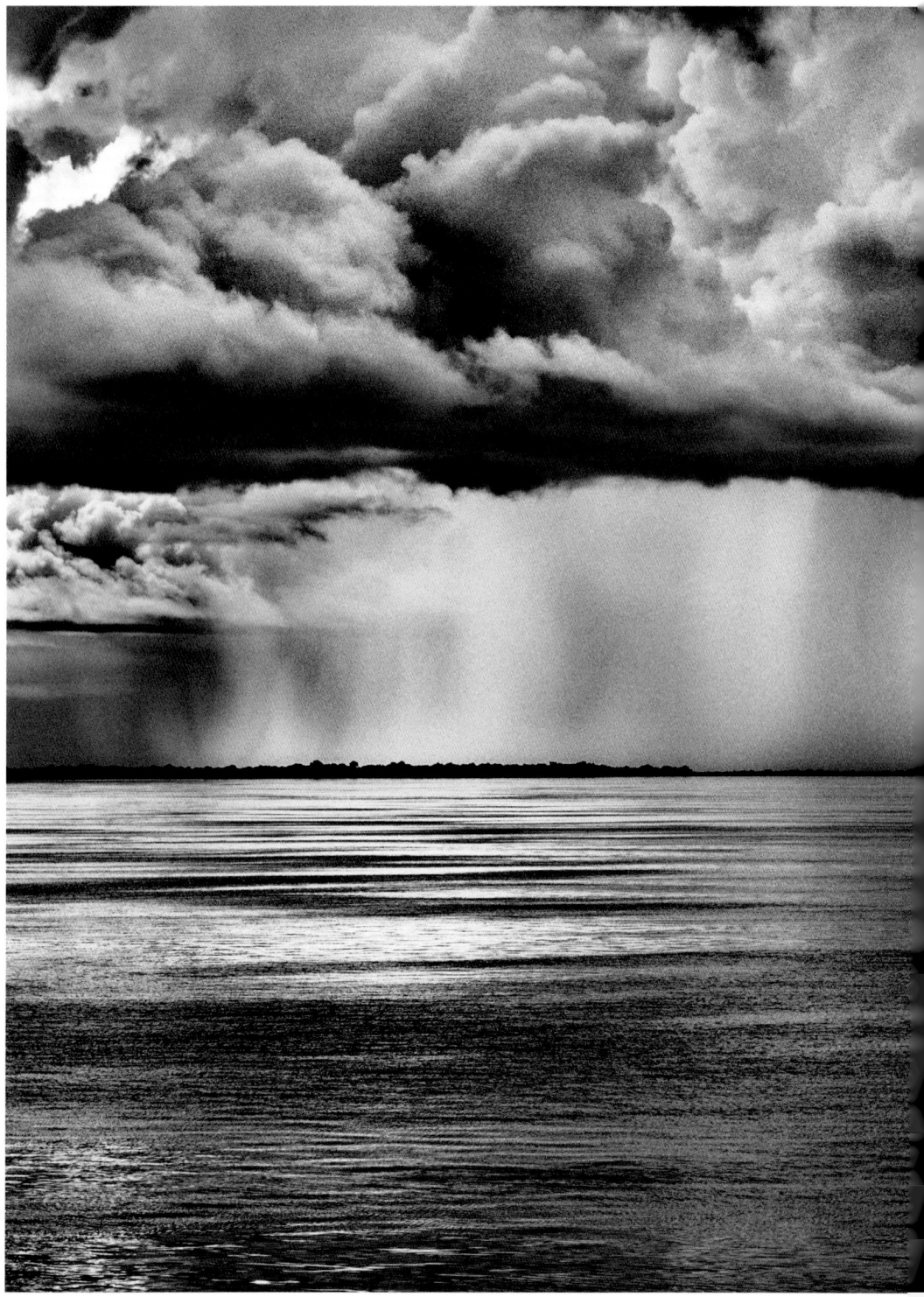

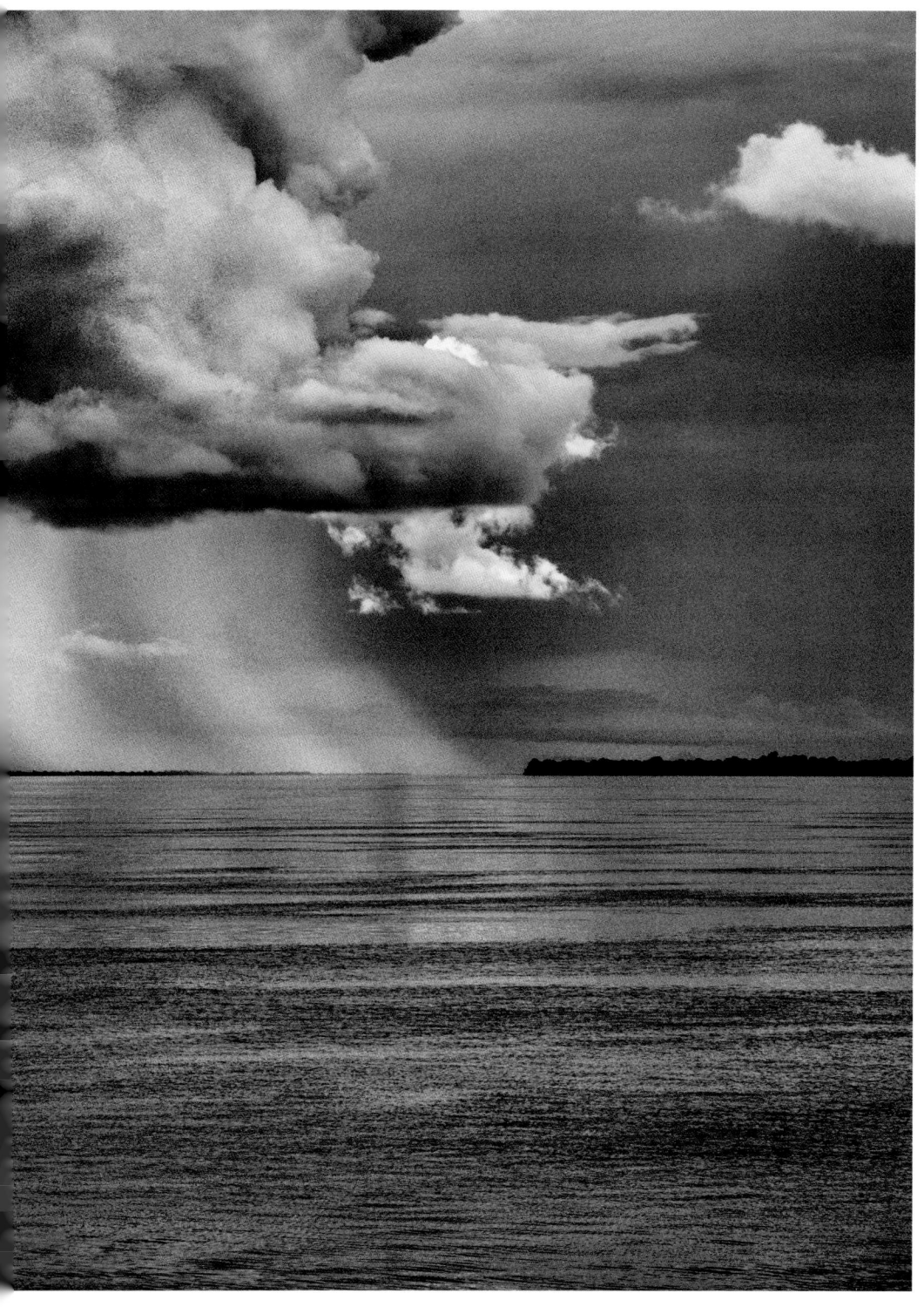

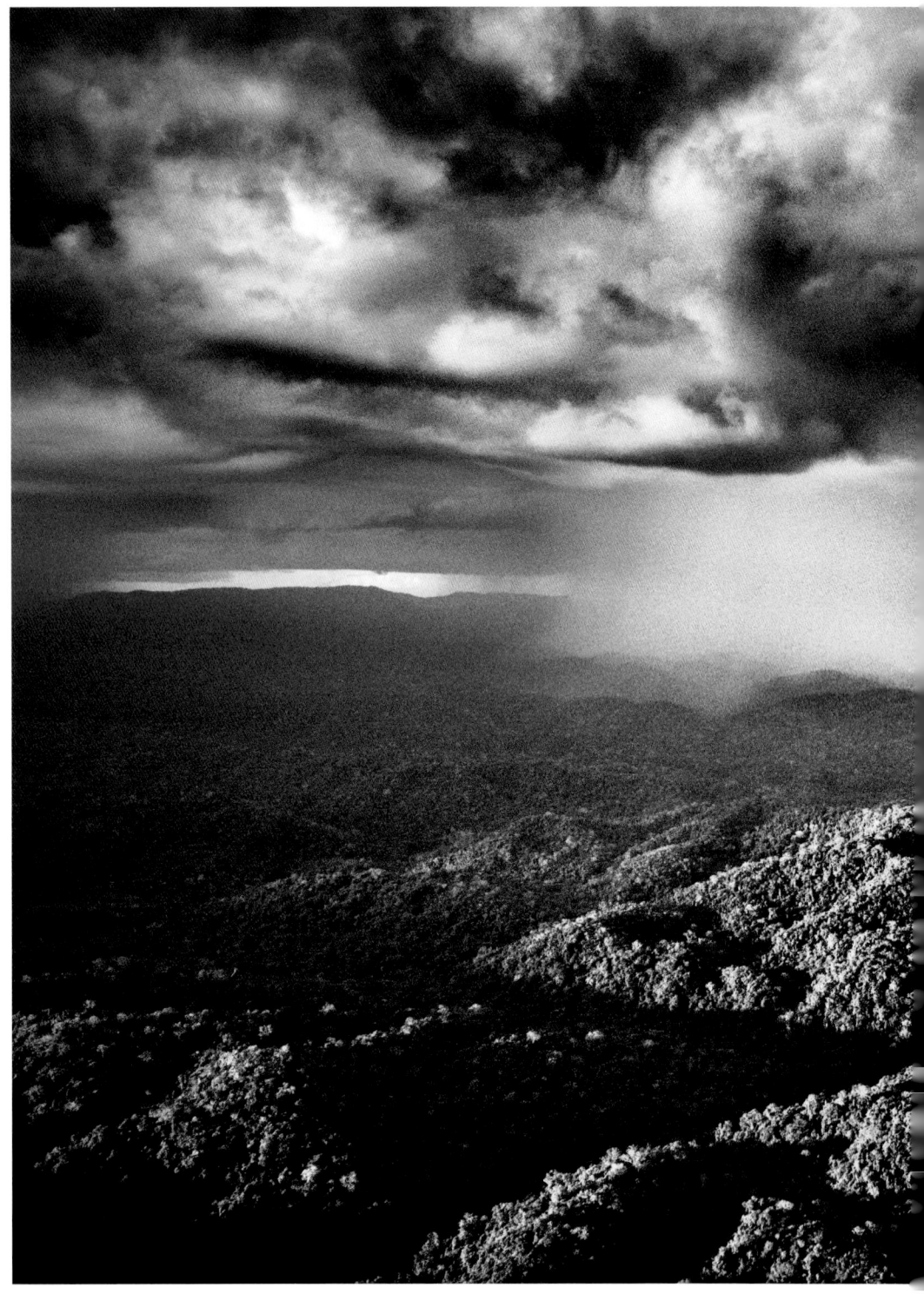

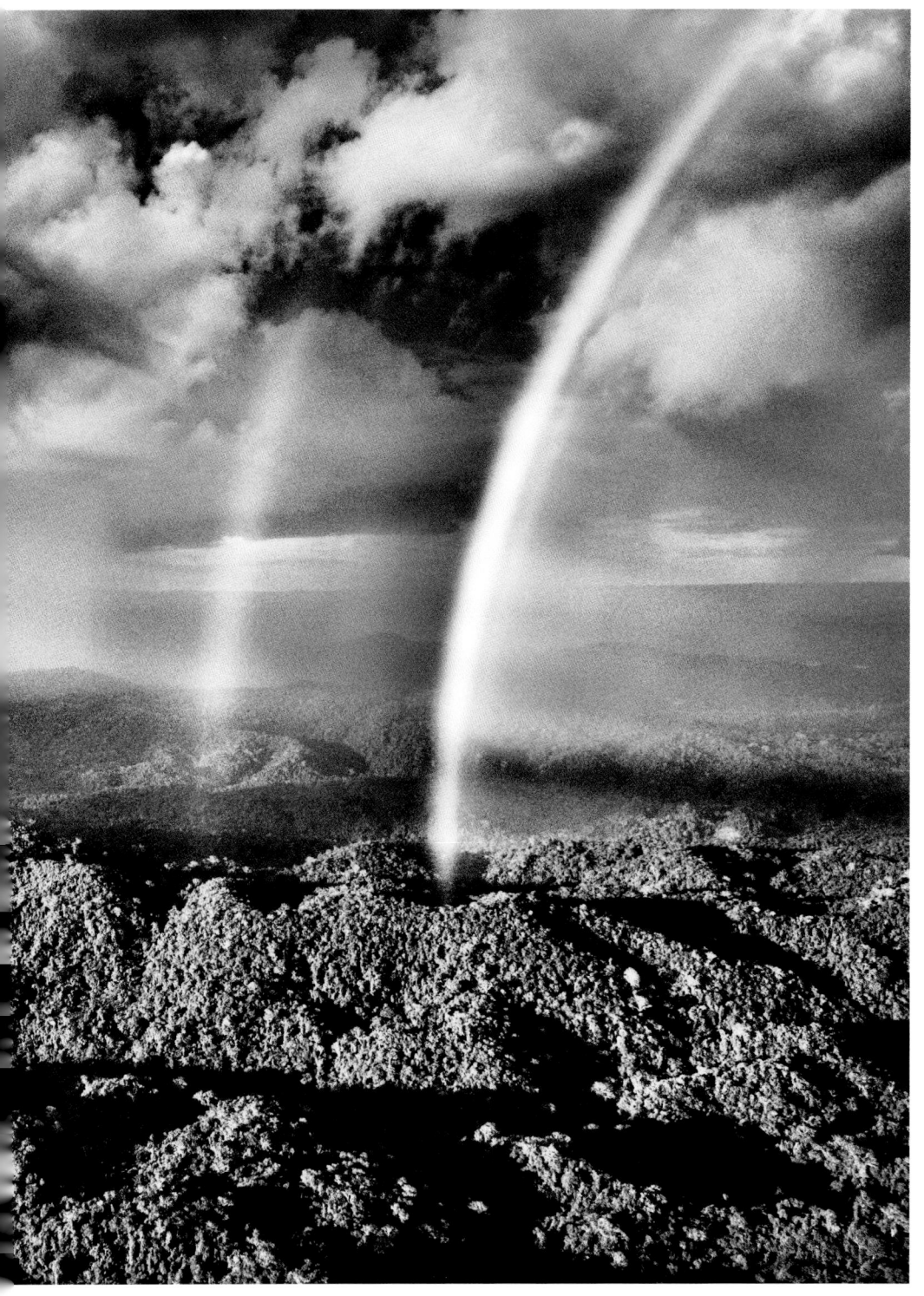

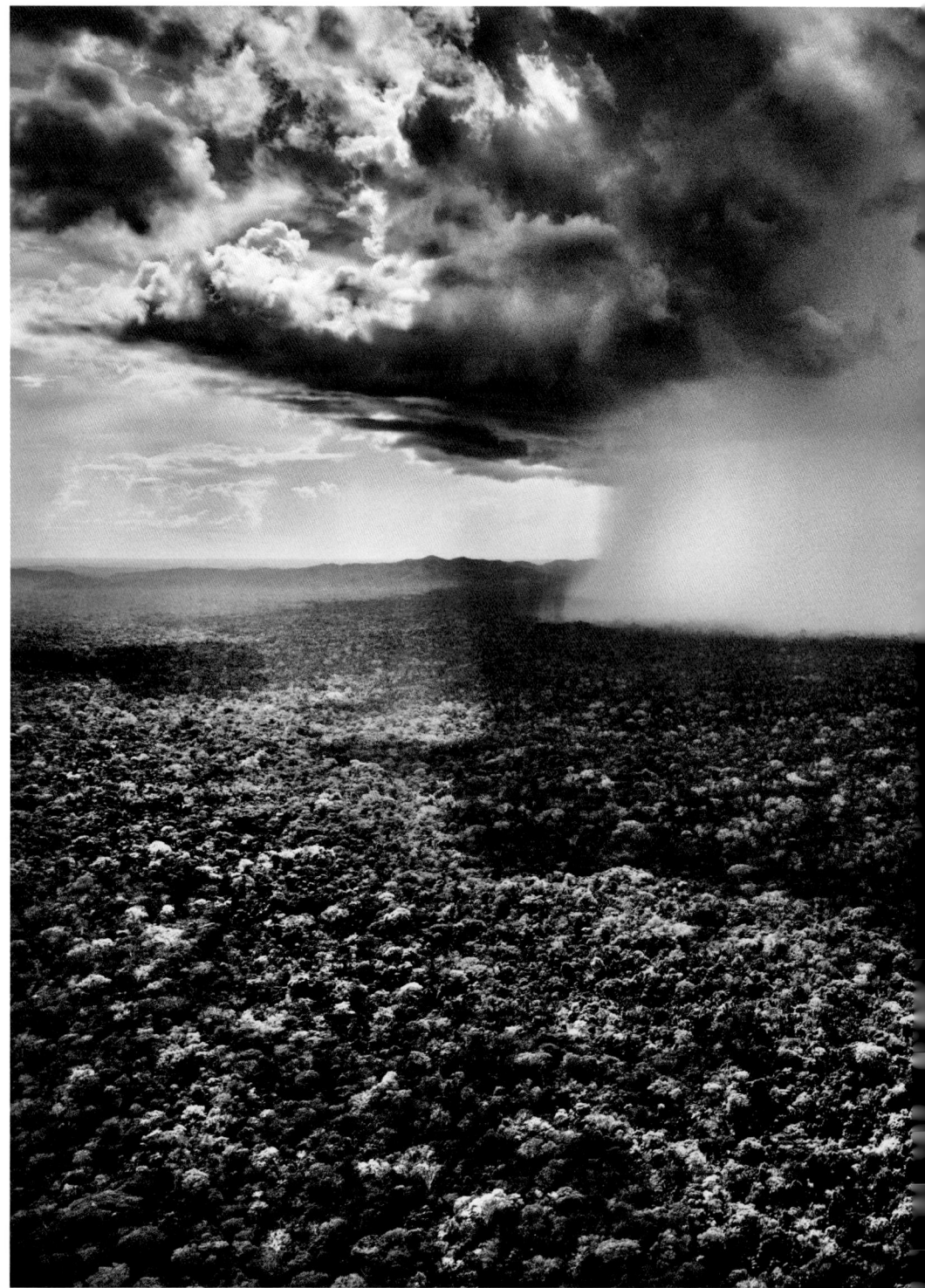

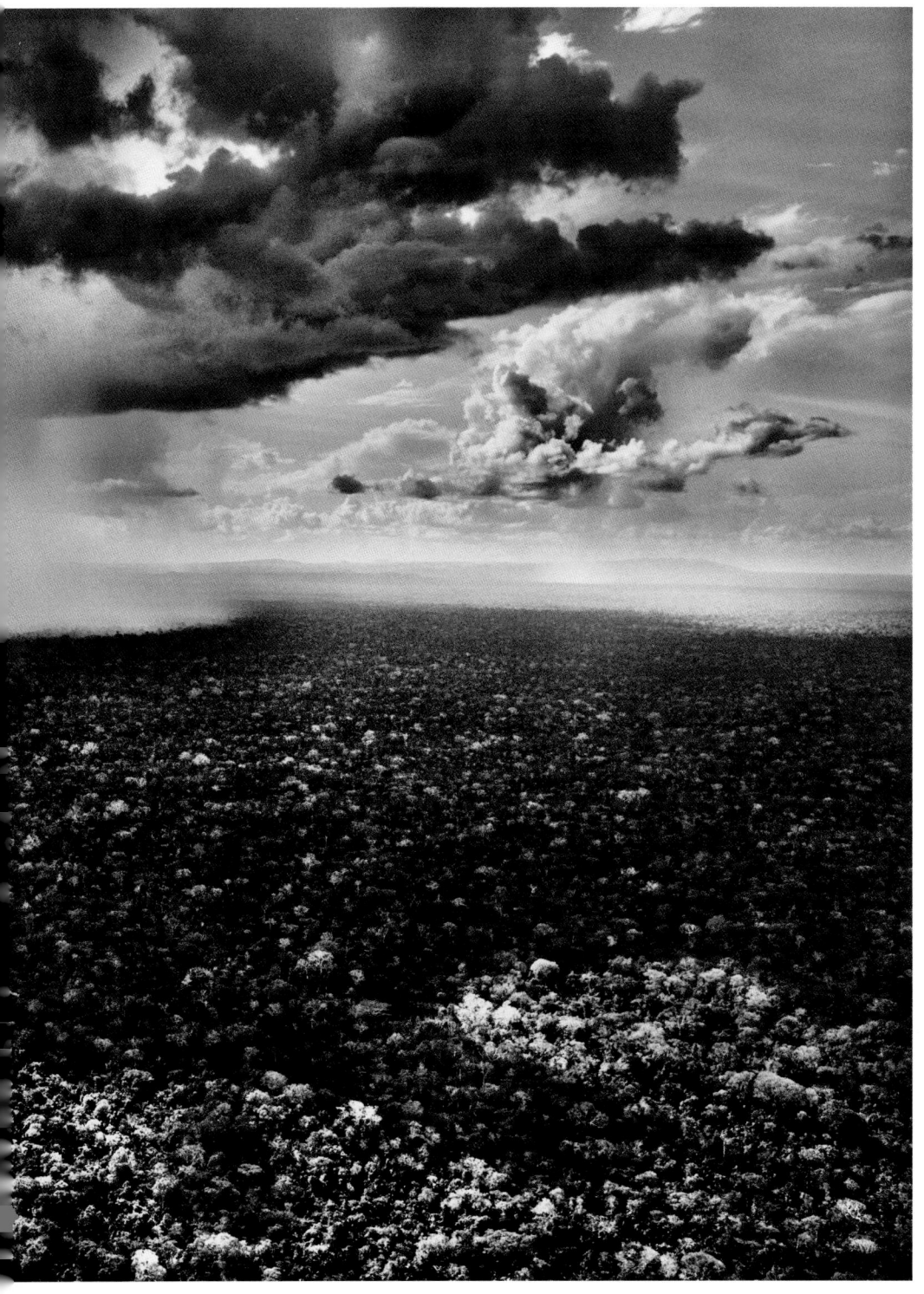

ZO'É

The Zo'é live in the forests of the state of Pará, north of the Amazon River, which are better preserved than those on the south bank, which have suffered rapid devastation. There, practically at Brazil's border with the Guianas, the terrain is steep and hard to reach by river or land. Their territory covers an area measuring 624,000 hectares (1.54 million acres). On December 22, 2009, that land was officially recognized as a protected indigenous reserve. To cover the roughly 300 kilometers (185 miles) from the Amazon River to where the Zo'é live, involves a journey of just over an hour in a single-engine plane, or about 25 days by boat or on foot.

The Zo'é speak a language of the Tupi-Guarani family. They were not called Zo'é when they began their intense interaction with whites in the 1980s. The word "Zo'é", which means "I am me," was used when saying "we are people." However, the expression's repeated use ended up becoming a term of self-definition, the start of understanding the difference between them and the other peoples with whom they would coexist from then on: the non-indigenous people, whom they call *kirahi*.

Their origin myth says that in the remote past the entire world was covered by a flood. However, in their mythology, the great deluge came after a fire had consumed the whole planet. In that destruction by fire and water, all that remained of humanity were a few bones. It was by gathering up the shards that the hero Nipuhan gave new life to the Zo'é. There is a curious aspect to this origin narrative: Nipuhan was a *kirahi*, a white man, who came from the south (as whites generally did when reaching those northern zones of the Brazilian Amazon). In recreating the Zo'é people, the hero did not have to create white people: they had survived the cataclysms because they lived far away. Unlike other Amazonian cultures' stories, in which white outsiders persecute the indigenous people, here they were pioneers.

Like many other original peoples of the Americas, the Zo'é believe that in the beginning, the other animals were people, too, including jaguars. This human element present in animals is why hunters must pay homage to their prey: dead pigs have chestnuts placed in their mouths when they reach the village because they are considered guests of honor at the banquet where they will be eaten.

The women wear thin necklaces of snail shells, and on their heads, like tiaras, beautiful crowns of white feathers taken from the chests of king vultures. Men capture these birds and keep them on a leash as pets. Every time they return from a hunting expedition, the Zo'é feed the vultures first so they will stay healthy and provide the feathers used for the women's crowns.

The Zo'é are the only indigenous people in Brazil who wear the *poturu*, a wooden labret under the lower lip. *Poturu* is the name of the piece of wood worn in that large, distinctive piercing. In an initiation ceremony at the start of puberty, girls and boys have their lip pierced with a bone and then a piece of wood (the *poturu*) is inserted. Each day, the piece of wood is replaced with a thicker one until the right size is achieved. They are polyandrous (women have several husbands) and polygynous (men have several wives). It is their conviction that any given couple is only able to have up to three children together. Therefore, to continue reproducing, they change spouses.

Leadership is exercised subtly, in ways almost imperceptible to an outside observer. Conflicts are resolved in an unusual way, through tickling: adversaries tickle each other to diffuse tensions.

I went on a long expedition with them that felt like a trip to Paradise: I spent two months walking in the jungle with the Zo'é, during which, in 2009, I was able to visit all the villages where the 300 or so inhabitants live. I followed families' day-to-day lives, farming, hunting, and fishing, and saw the two opposite ends of the territory when I camped with fishing journeys on the Cuminapanema and Erepecuru Rivers.

There was an unforgettable moment as I was leaving them. A helicopter came to pick me up. On seeing the aircraft approach, the indigenous guide who accompanied me throughout the journey, Ypó, exclaimed, "It's a tukuruhú, a grasshopper." When asked the reason for the comparison, my host explained, "When airplanes land, they hit the ground and slide. The tukuruhú lands and stays in place." The pilots immediately climbed out of the aircraft with their helmets' dark shields covering their faces. Ypó reacted in fright: "They aren't human, they're flies."

Pages 428/429 Men of Zo'é ethnicity, residents of the village of Towari Ypy, wearing traditional headdresses. Standing, left to right: Biri Zo'é, Xú Zo'é, Sinera'ýt Zo'é, Kurú Zo'é, and Boaté Zo'é. Seated: Kitá Zo'é, Dirik Zo'é, Tuwáj Zo'é, and Toduá Zo'é. In their language, *Zo'é* means "I am me." They probably used the expression during the period of initial contact, as if to say, "We are people." Zo'é Indigenous Territory, state of Pará, 2009.

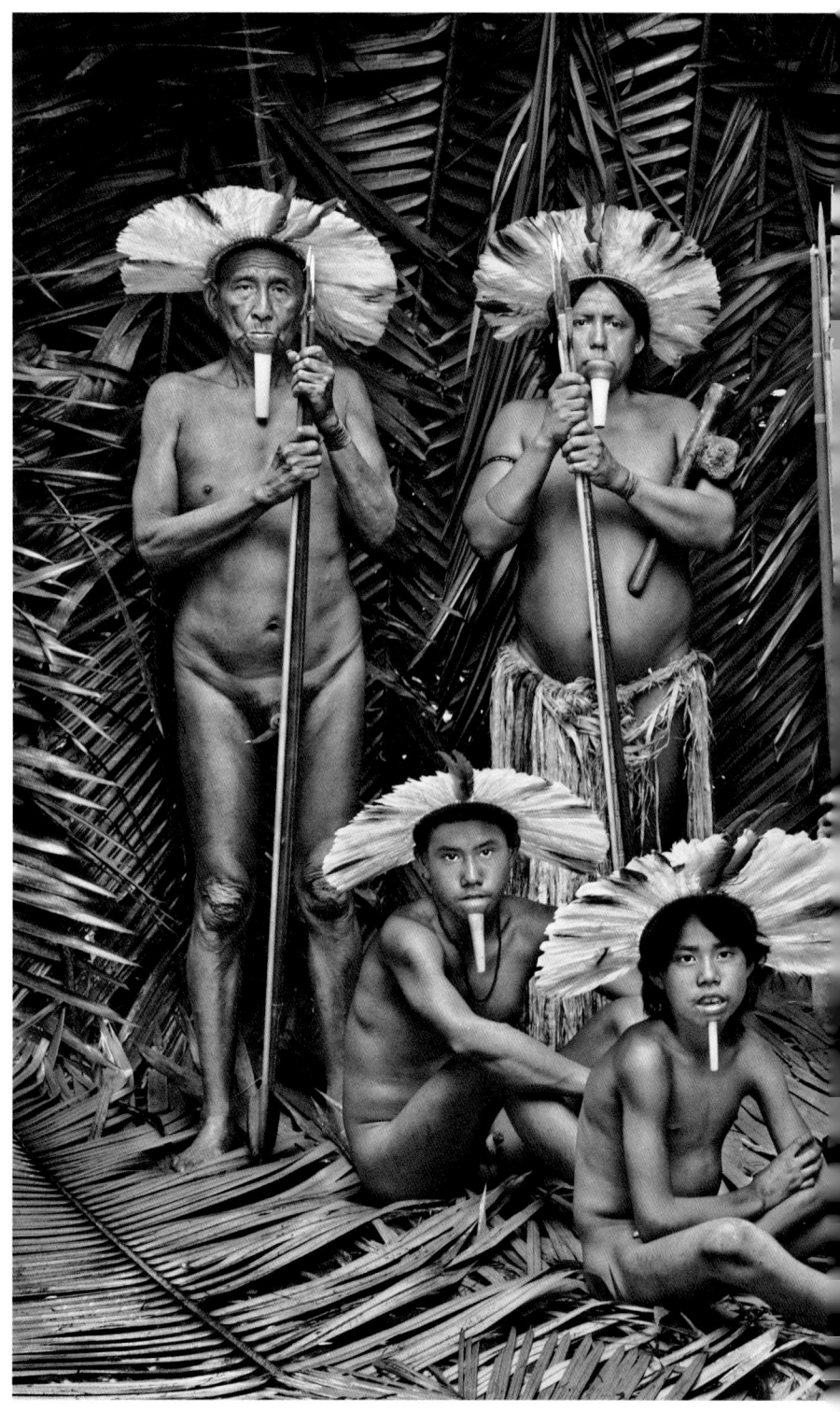

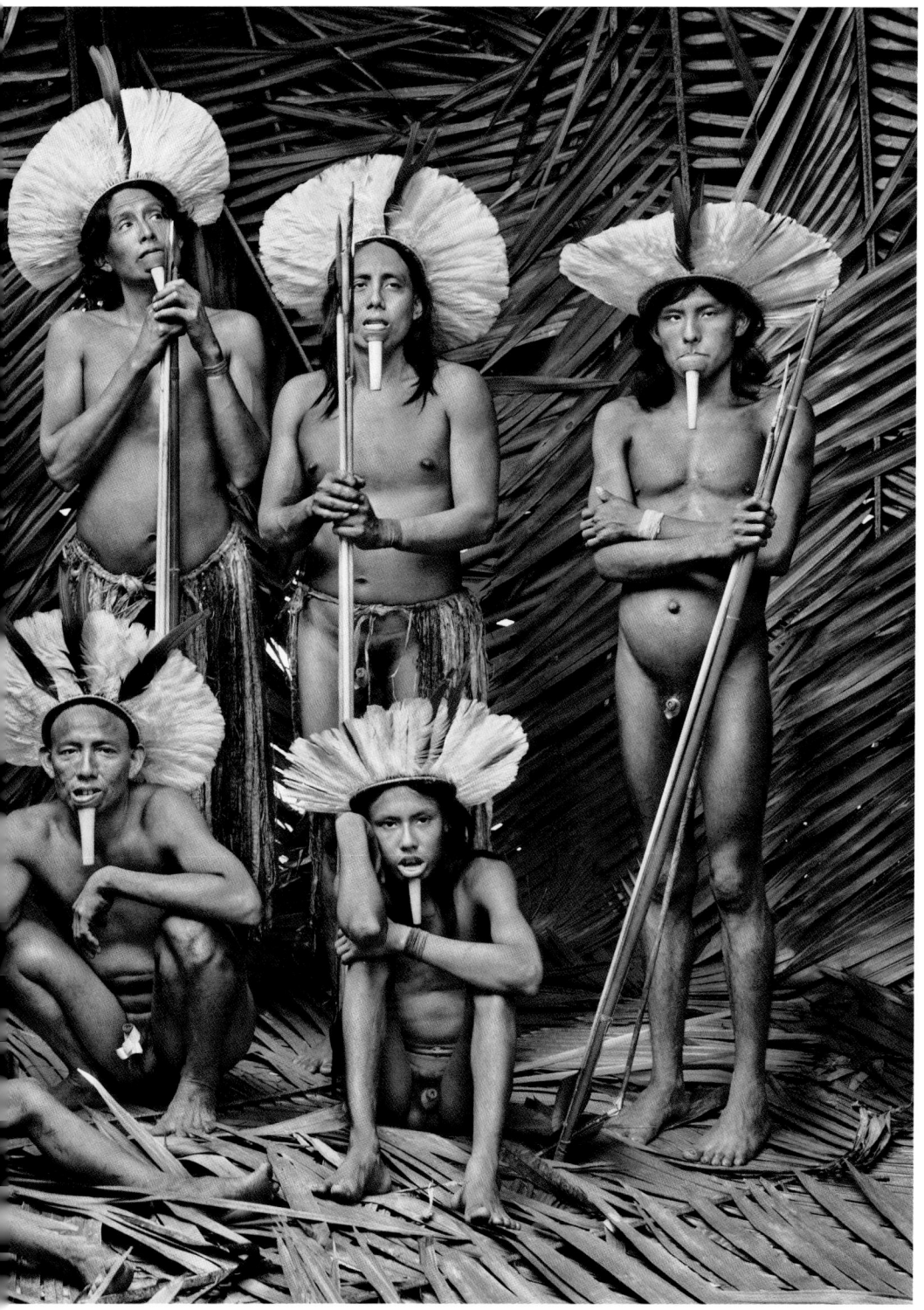

Opposite Aratá Zo'é, Tapesét's husband, a great hunter, hunting monkeys. The Zo'é are polyandrous (women have several husbands) and polygynous (men have several wives). They have a special way of resolving conflicts among themselves, with humor and tickling as a way to defuse tensions. Zo'é Indigenous Territory, state of Pará, 2009.

Pages 432/433 Kujãikwét Zo'é returning from a fishing expedition on the Cuminapanema River. Zo'é Indigenous Territory, state of Pará, 2009.

Pages 434/435 Aratá Zo'é (first at left), Tará Zo'é (center), Kurupáj Zo'é (right), gathering açaí. The men go into the forest to pick the heavy palm bunches that yield a much-desired fruit. Zo'é Indigenous Territory, state of Pará, 2009.

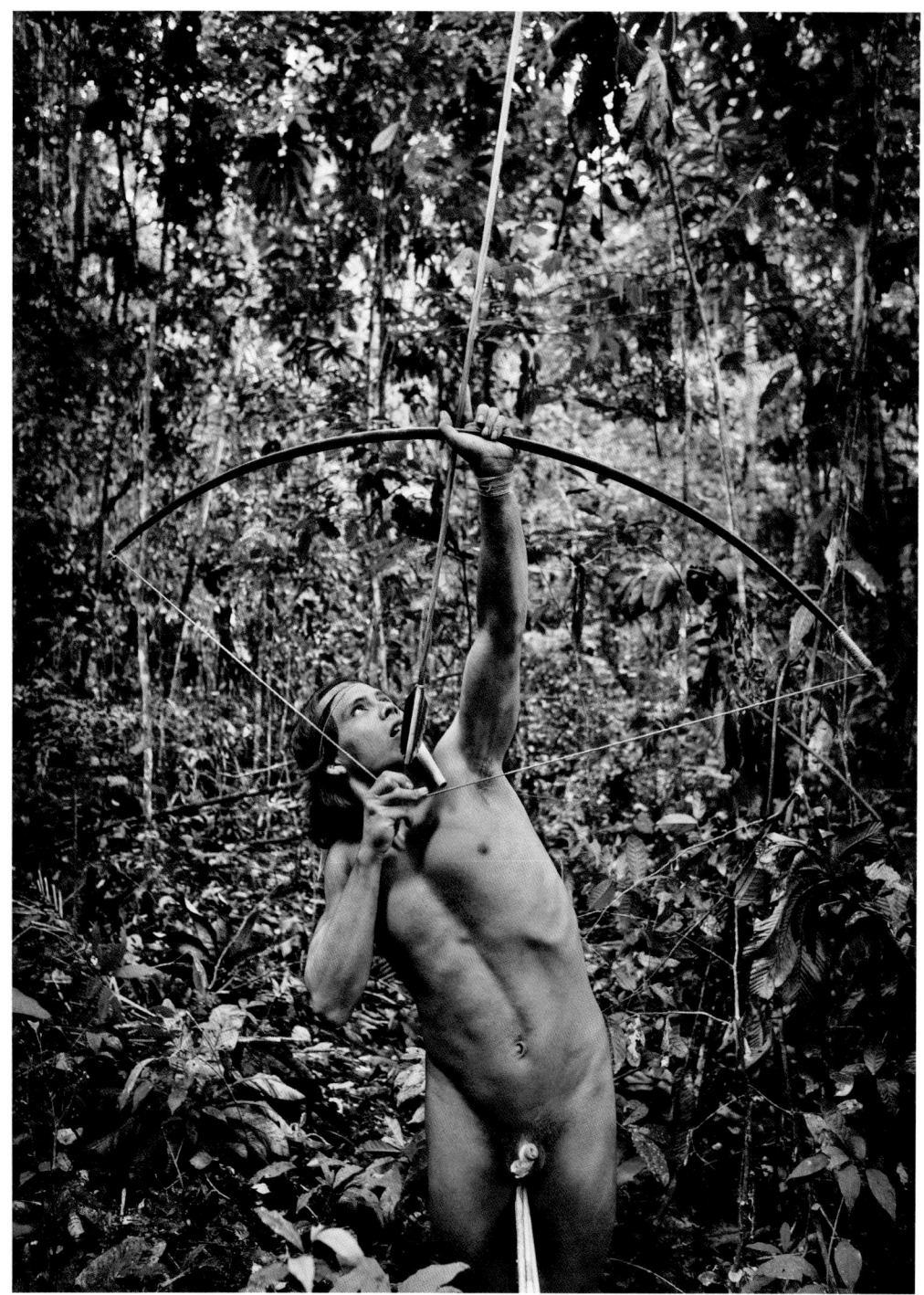

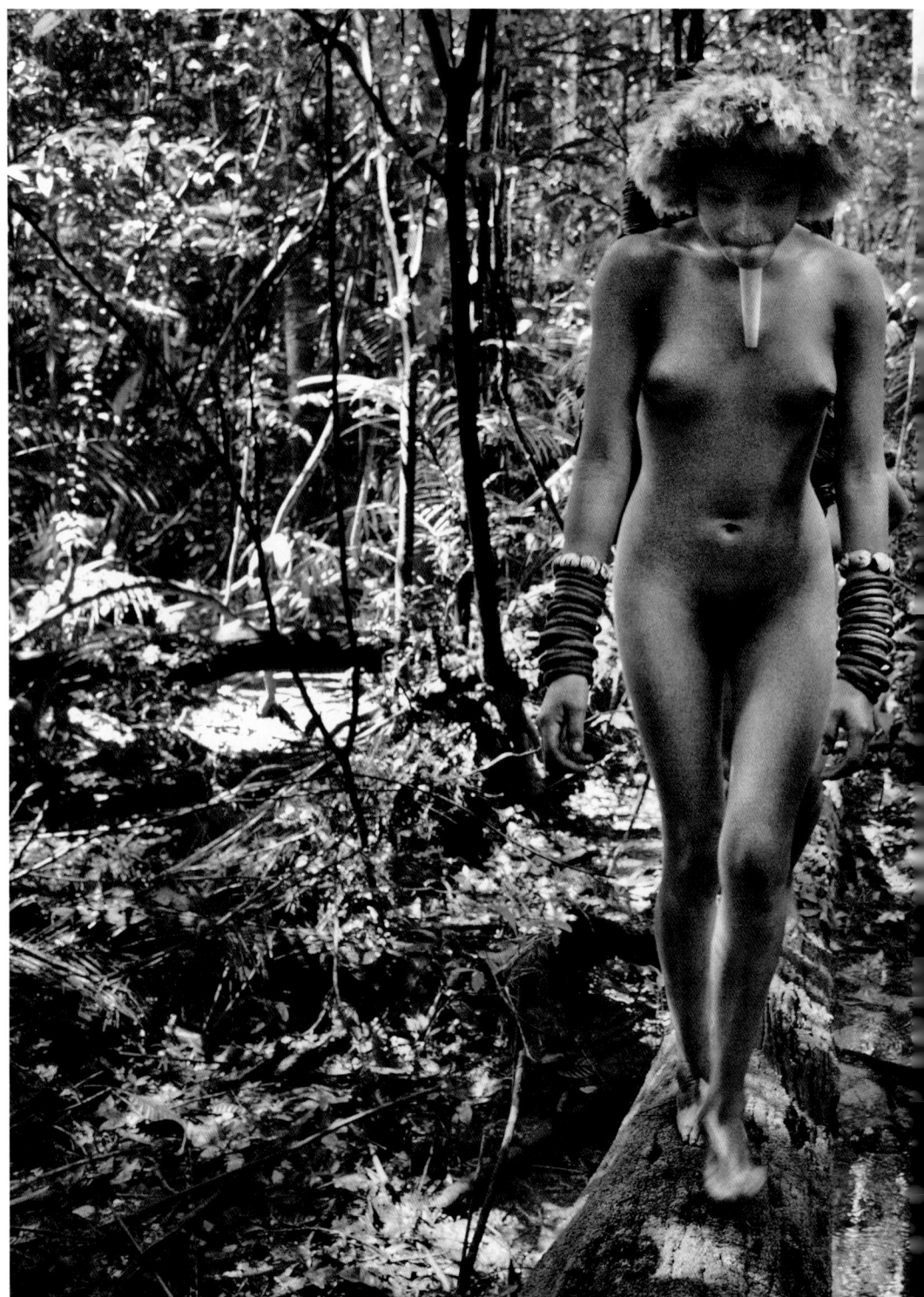

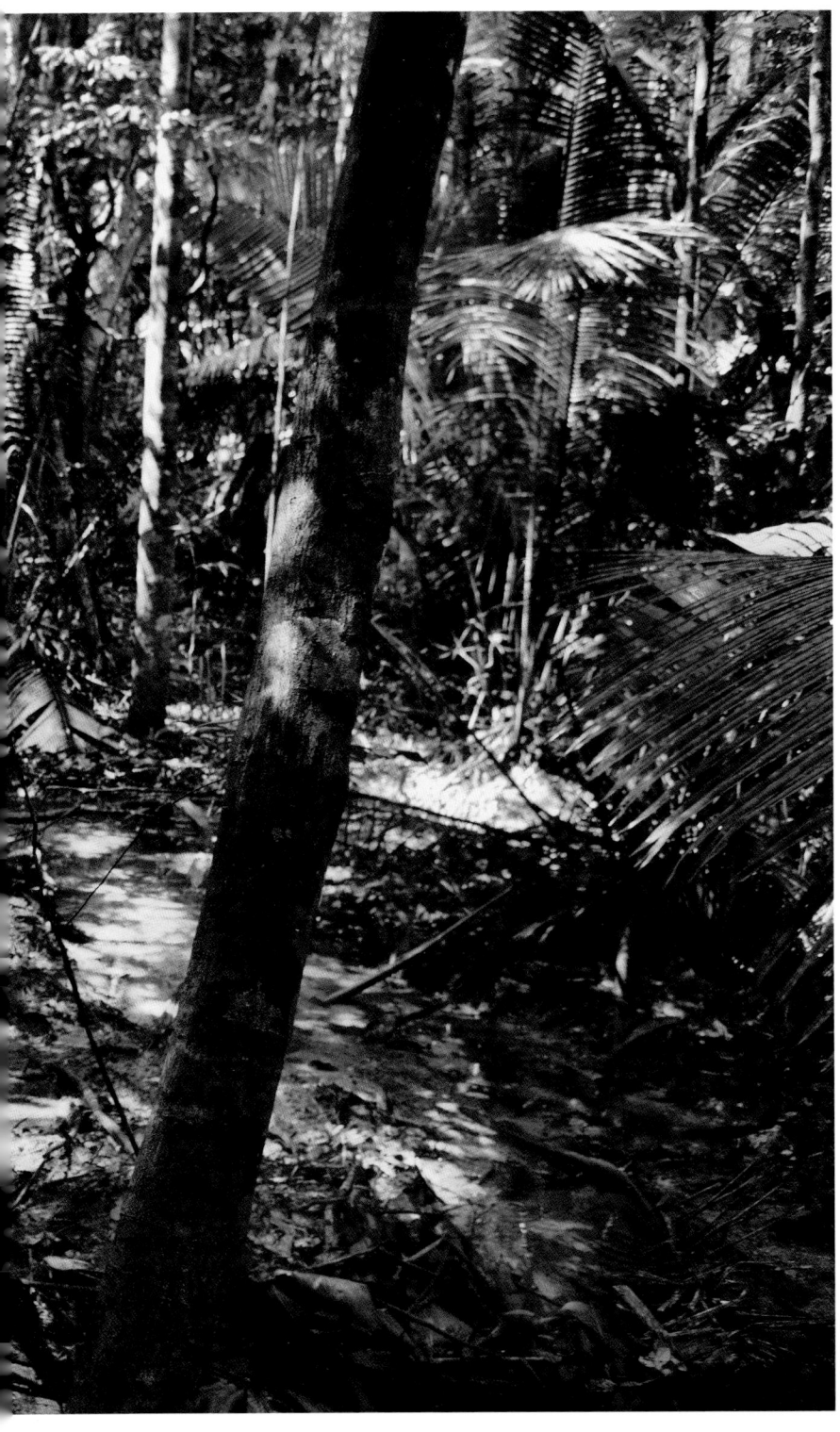

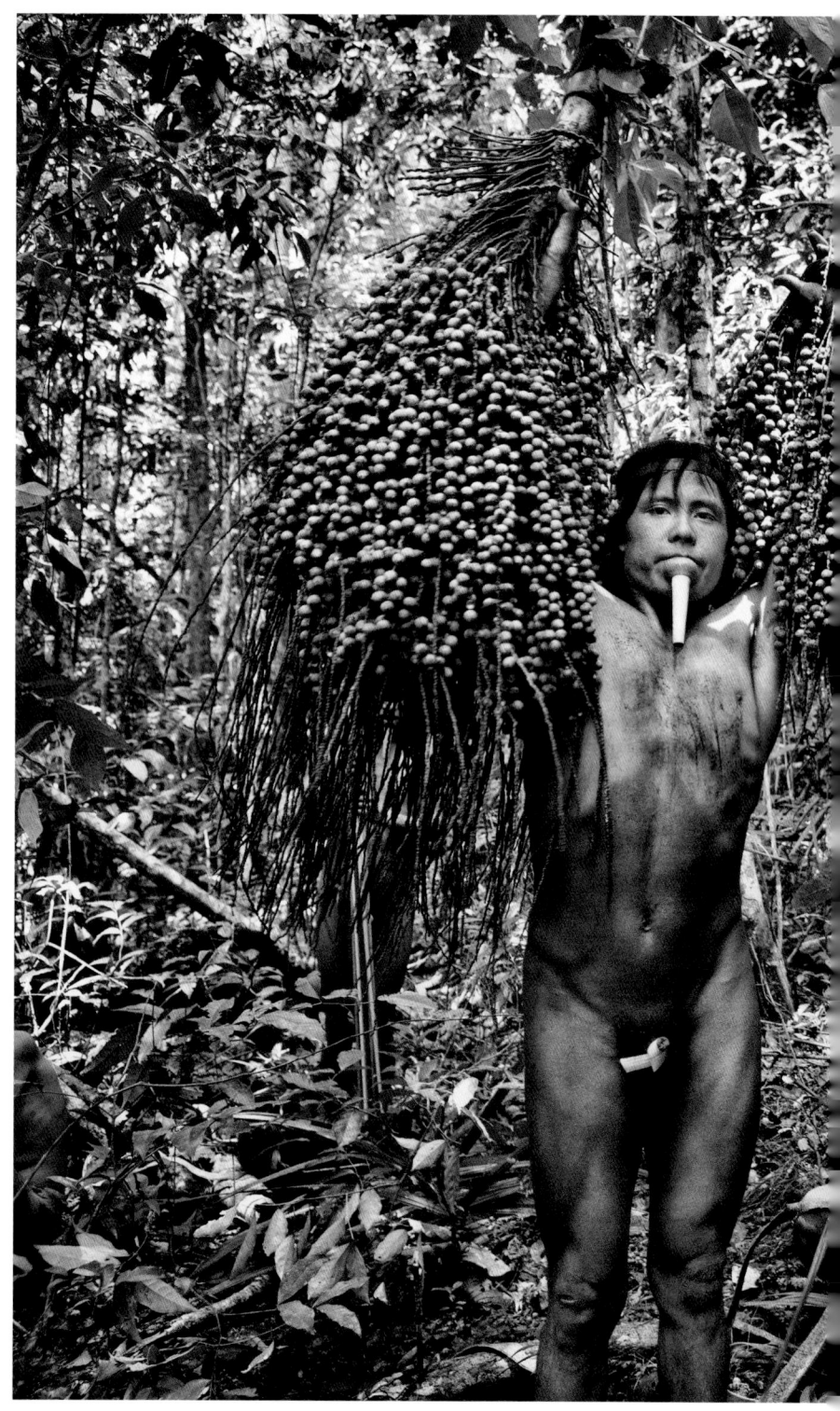

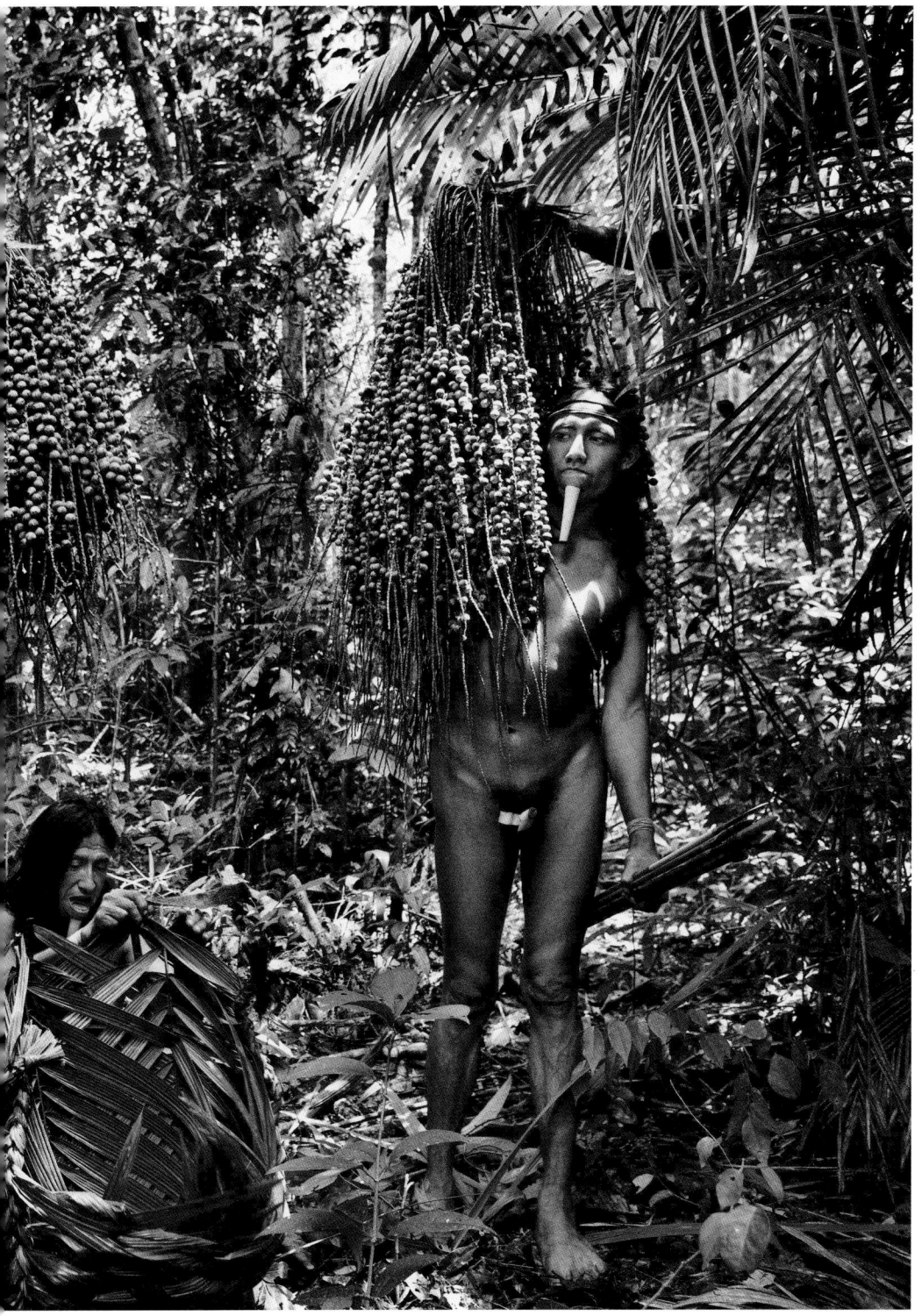

Opposite Sipú Zo'é (on the hammock), preparing açaí. The women separate the açaí fruit from the bunches and prepare a delicious, thick, violet-colored juice, a staple of the Zo'é diet. The fruit is fermented in big clay cauldrons, which is why it is called wine in the Amazon. Açaí is rich in proteins, vegetable fat, vitamins (B1, C, and E), minerals, and fiber. In recent decades, it has become a product coveted around the world for its properties. Zo'é Indigenous Territory, state of Pará, 2009.

Pages 438/439 Háj Zo'é lies in a hammock with his son in his arms. The hammocks are made with plant fibers and cotton yarn. In addition to food crops, the Zo'é grow cotton. They collect fibers in the forest to make hammocks, rope, and other items for daily life. Zo'é Indigenous Territory, state of Pará, 2009.

Pages 440/441 Tamuatá Zo'é and Kujãikwét Zo'é lie in a hammock during the day. Hammocks are used constantly, not only for sleeping but also in daytime as the main piece of furniture, during meals for example. Zo'é Indigenous Territory, state of Pará, 2009.

Pages 442/443 Seated, left to right: Debú Zo'é, Seí Zo'é, Araturú Zo'é, and Seró Zo'é. In back, standing: Husã raijýt Zo'é and Musã raijýt Zo'é painting their bodies with urucum. Zo'é women generally use urucum (*Bixa orellana*), the red fruit of the urucum plant, to color their bodies. They also use it in cooking. Urucum is a shrub native to the tropical zones of the Americas. Indigenous Americans have long used it for body painting, especially for painting the lips, hence its nickname: *árvore-batom* (lipstick tree). Zo'é Indigenous Territory, state of Pará, 2009.

Pages 444/445 Family of Ypó and Tatytú Zo'é, from left to right: Ypó, Tatytú, Abú, Tamuatá, and Urumuru, on a six-day walk from the village of Towari Ypy to the Cuminapanema River, on a fishing expedition. Zo'é Indigenous Territory, state of Pará, 2009.

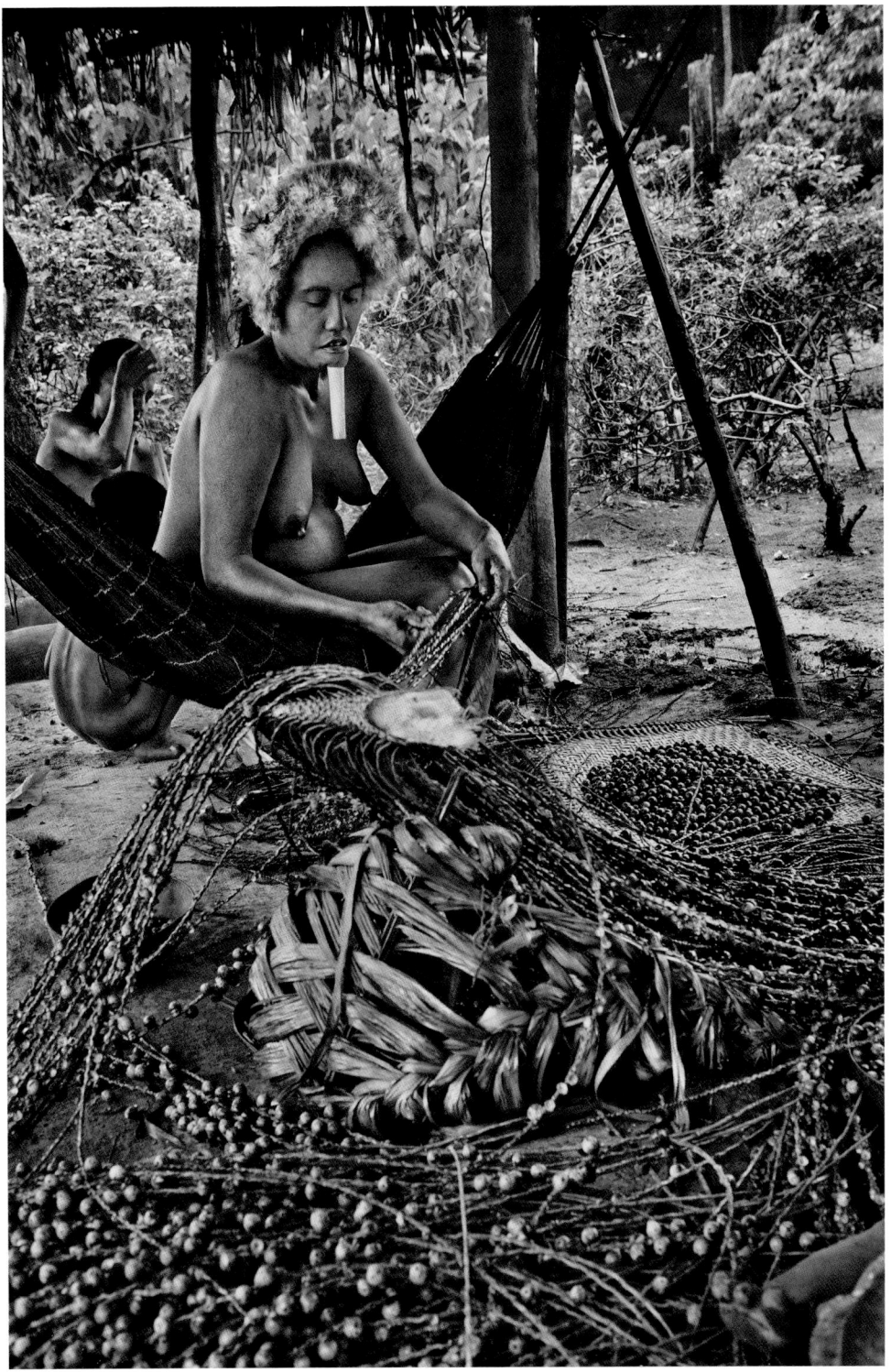

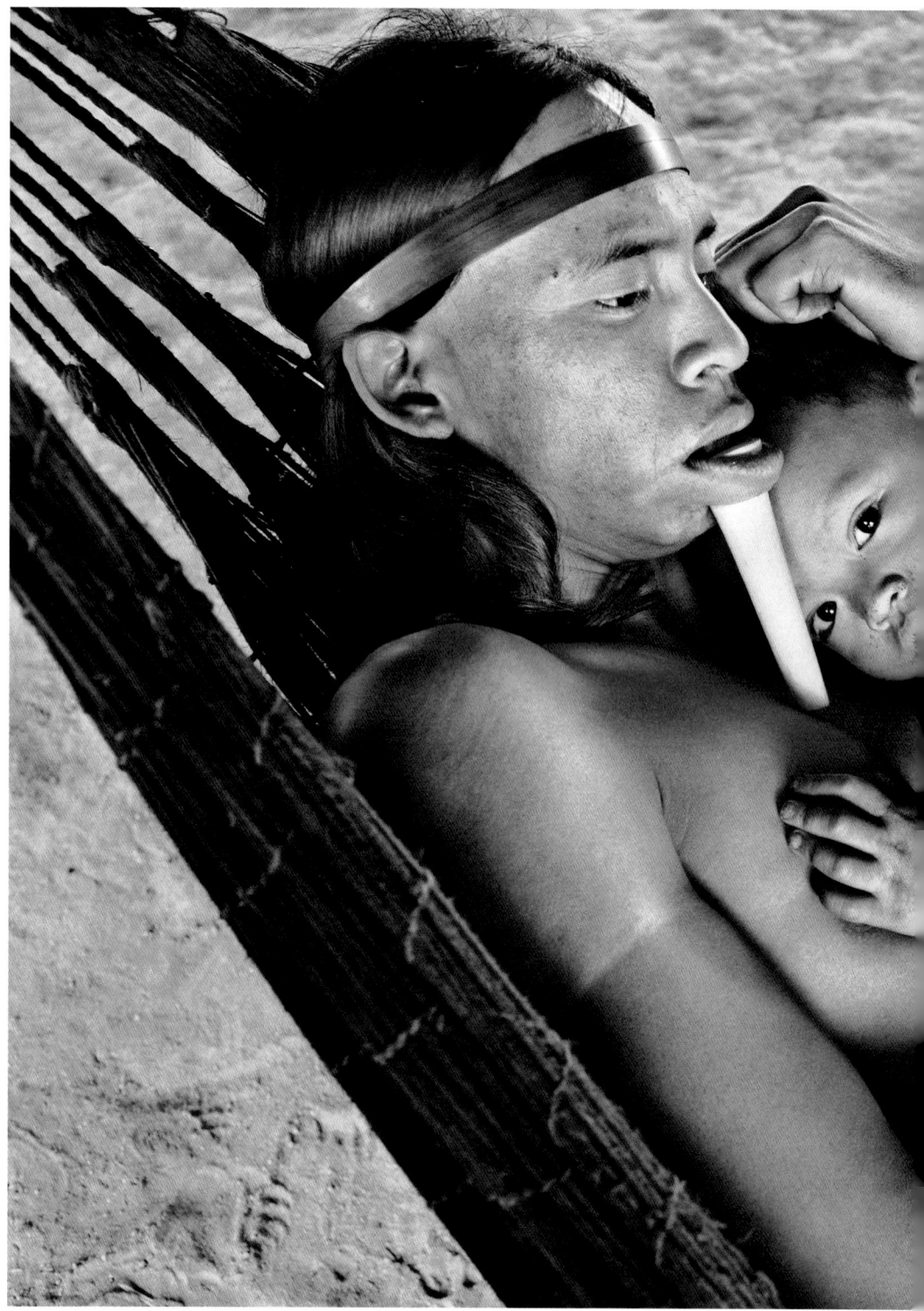

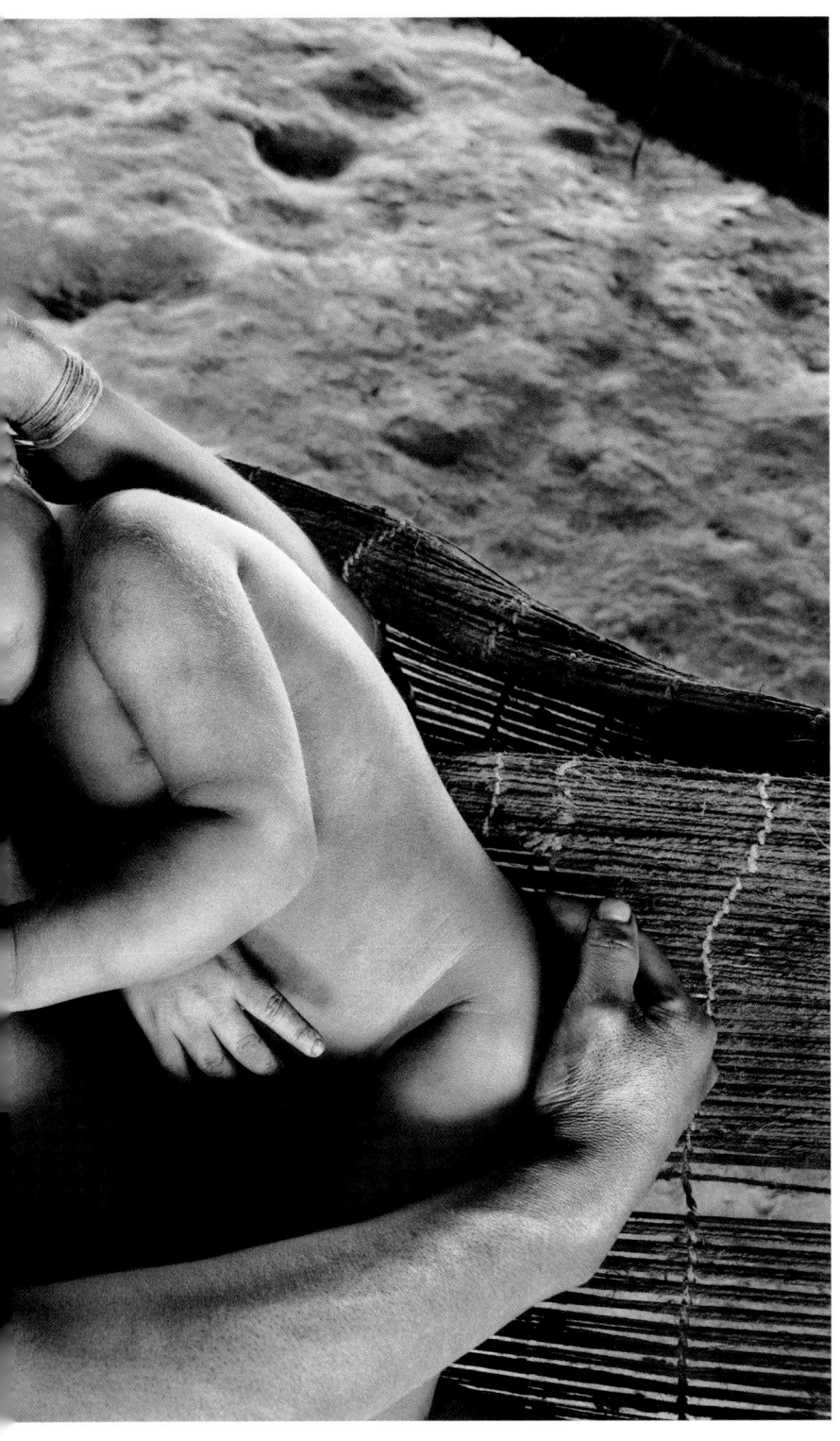

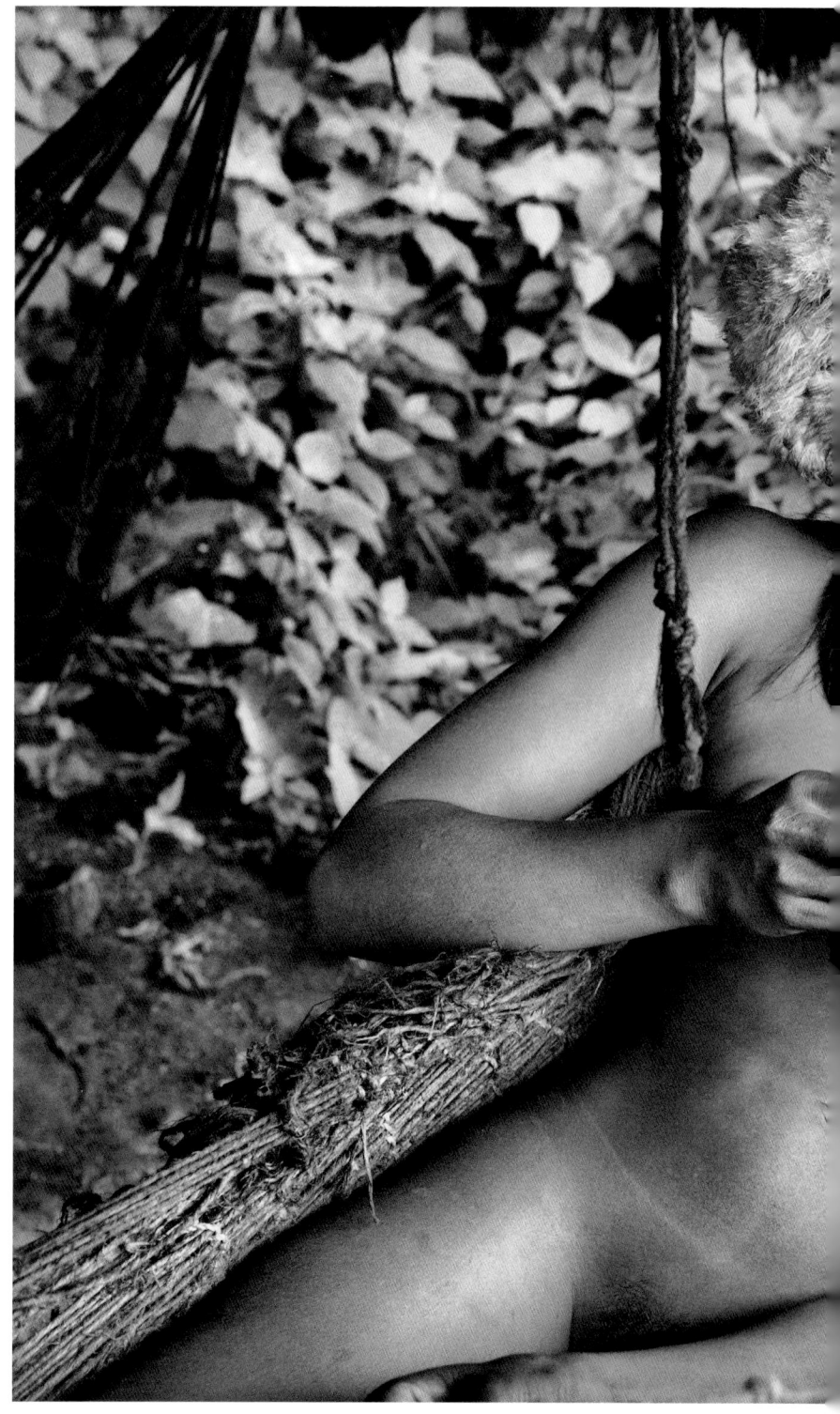

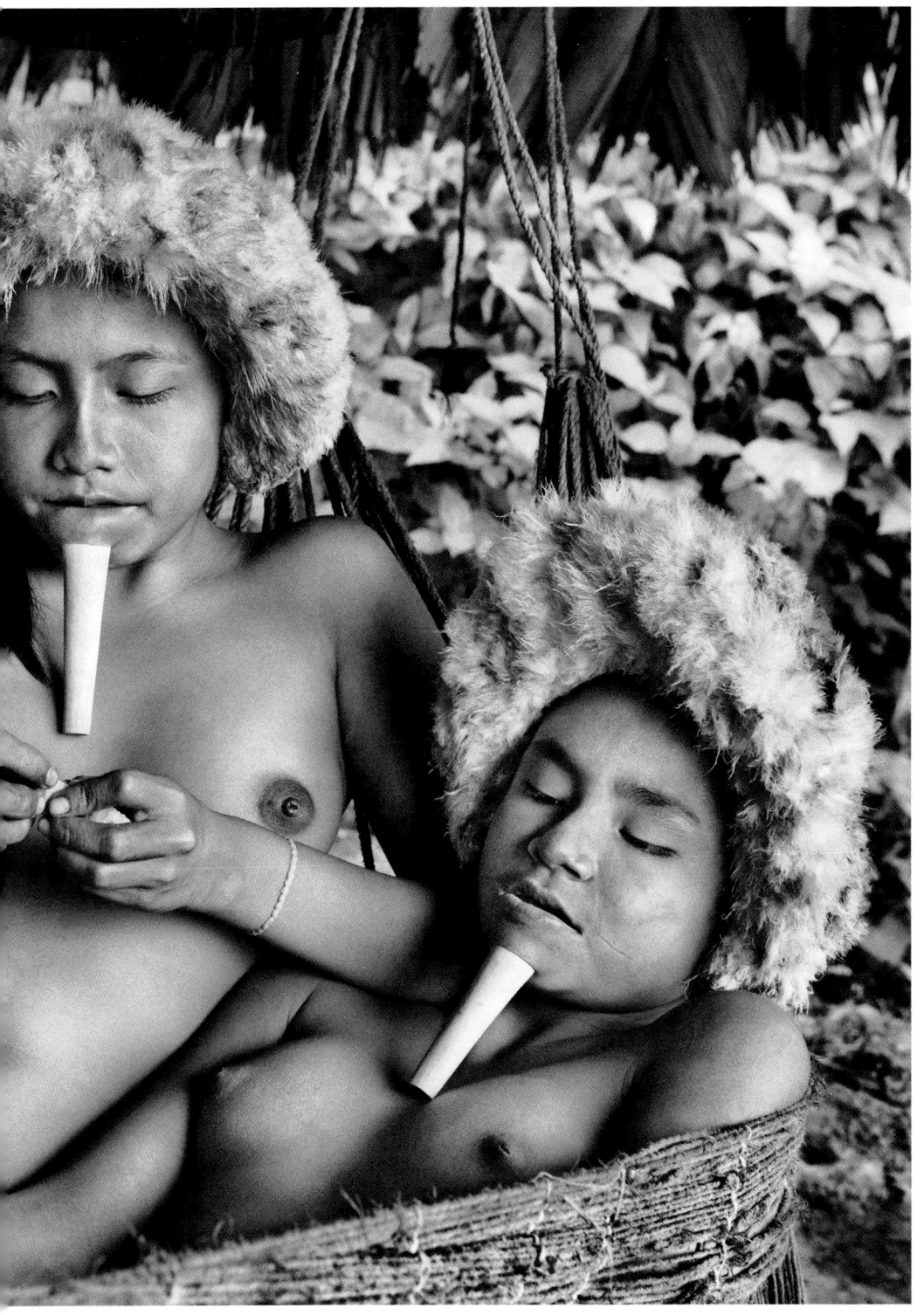

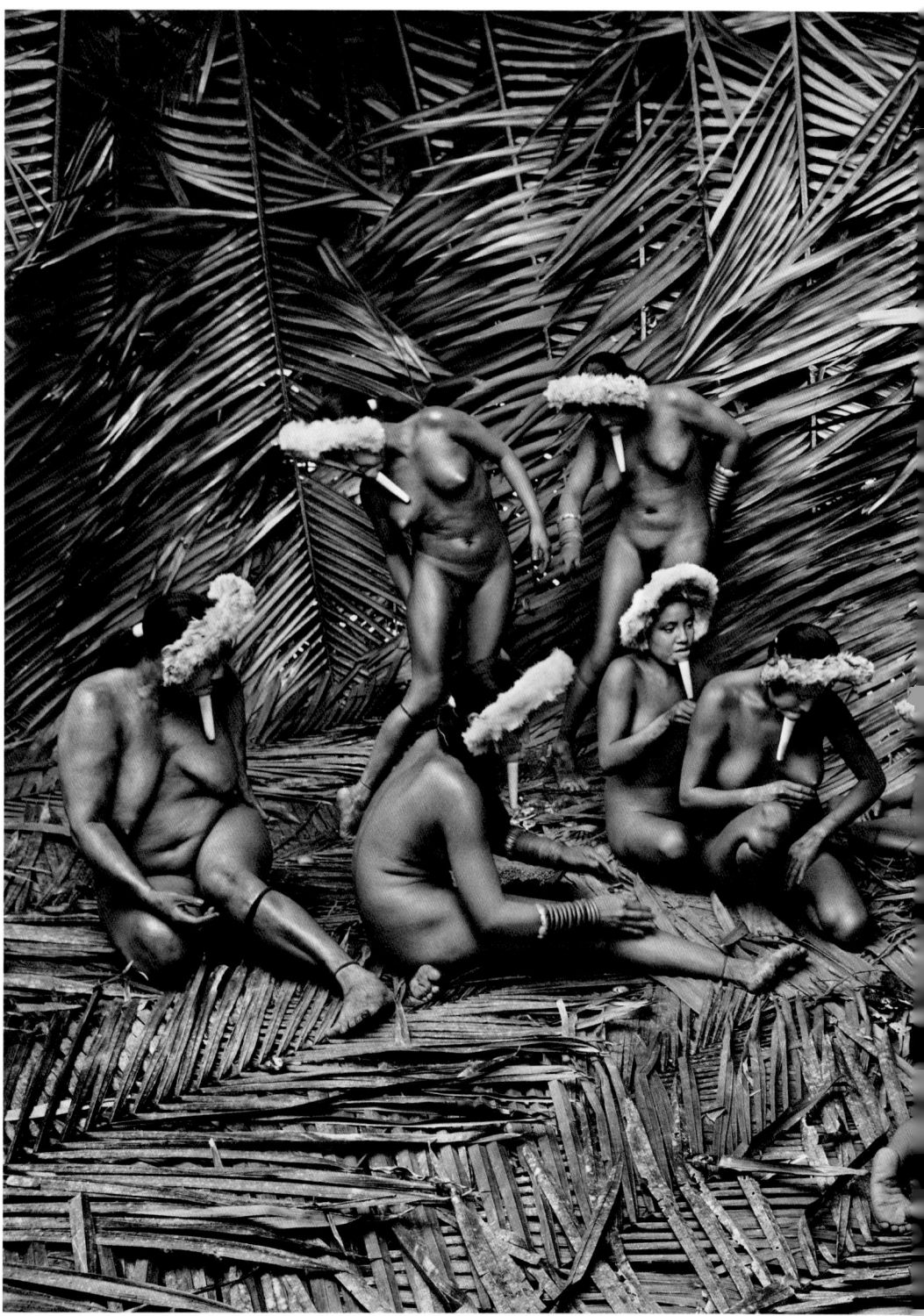

442

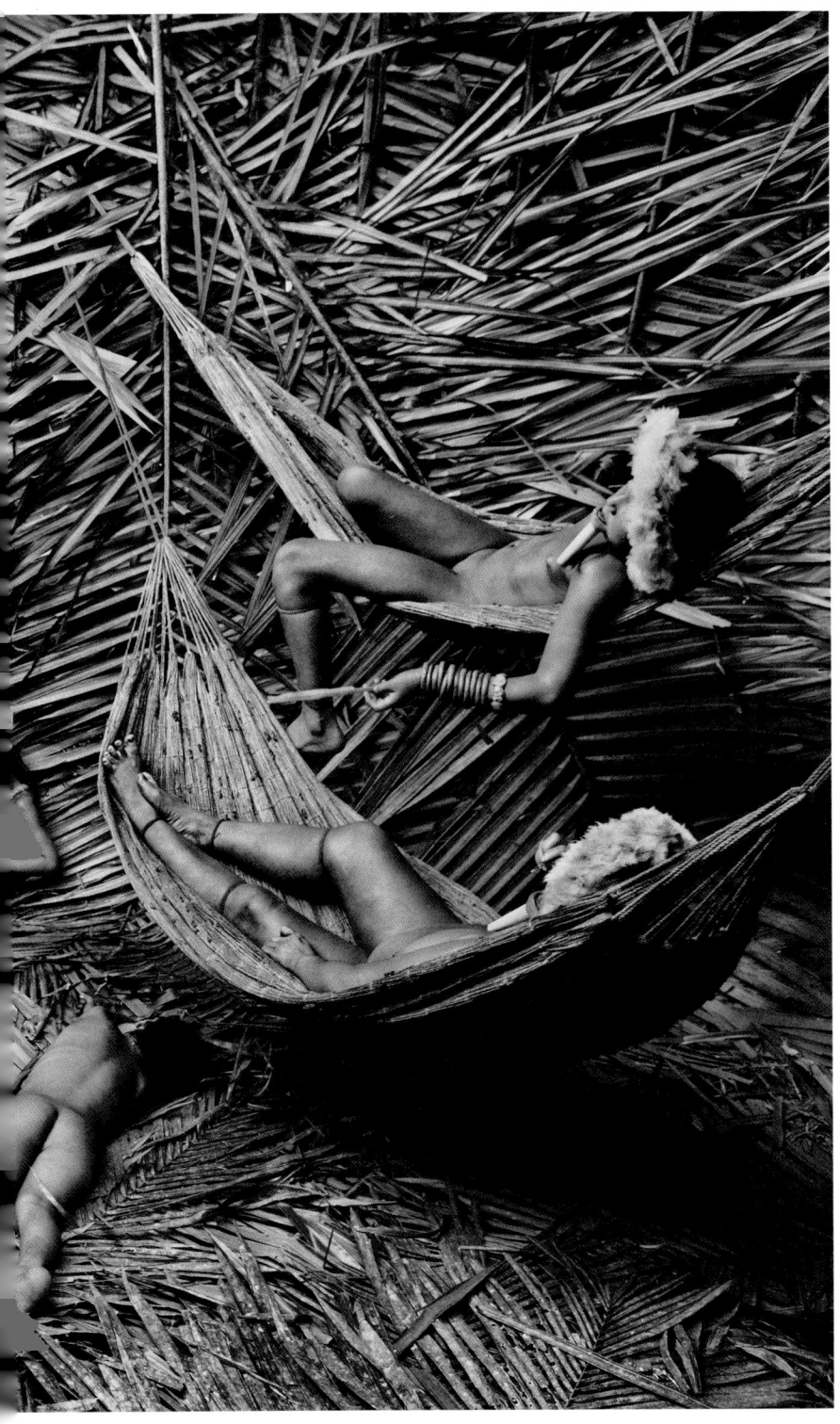

443

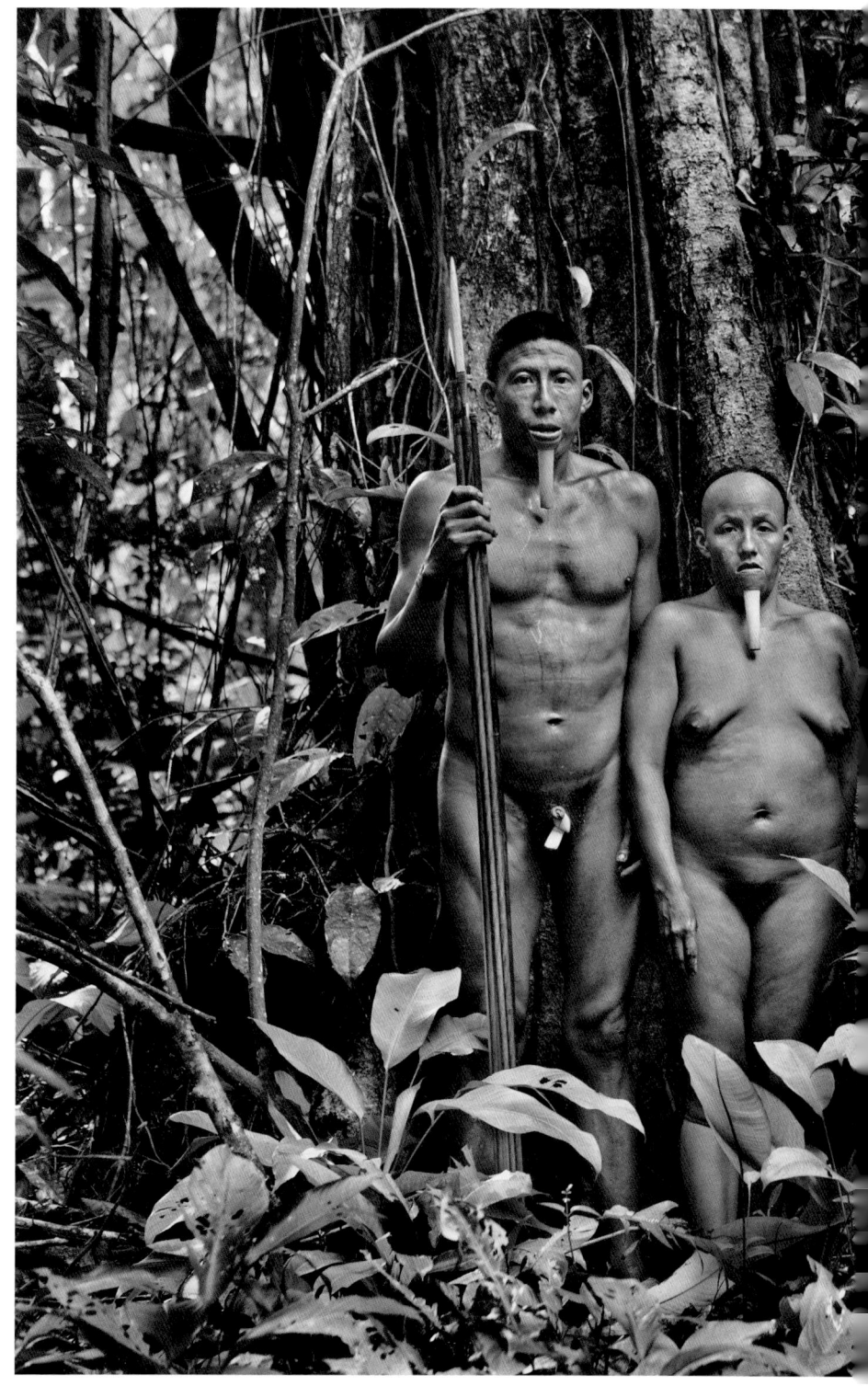

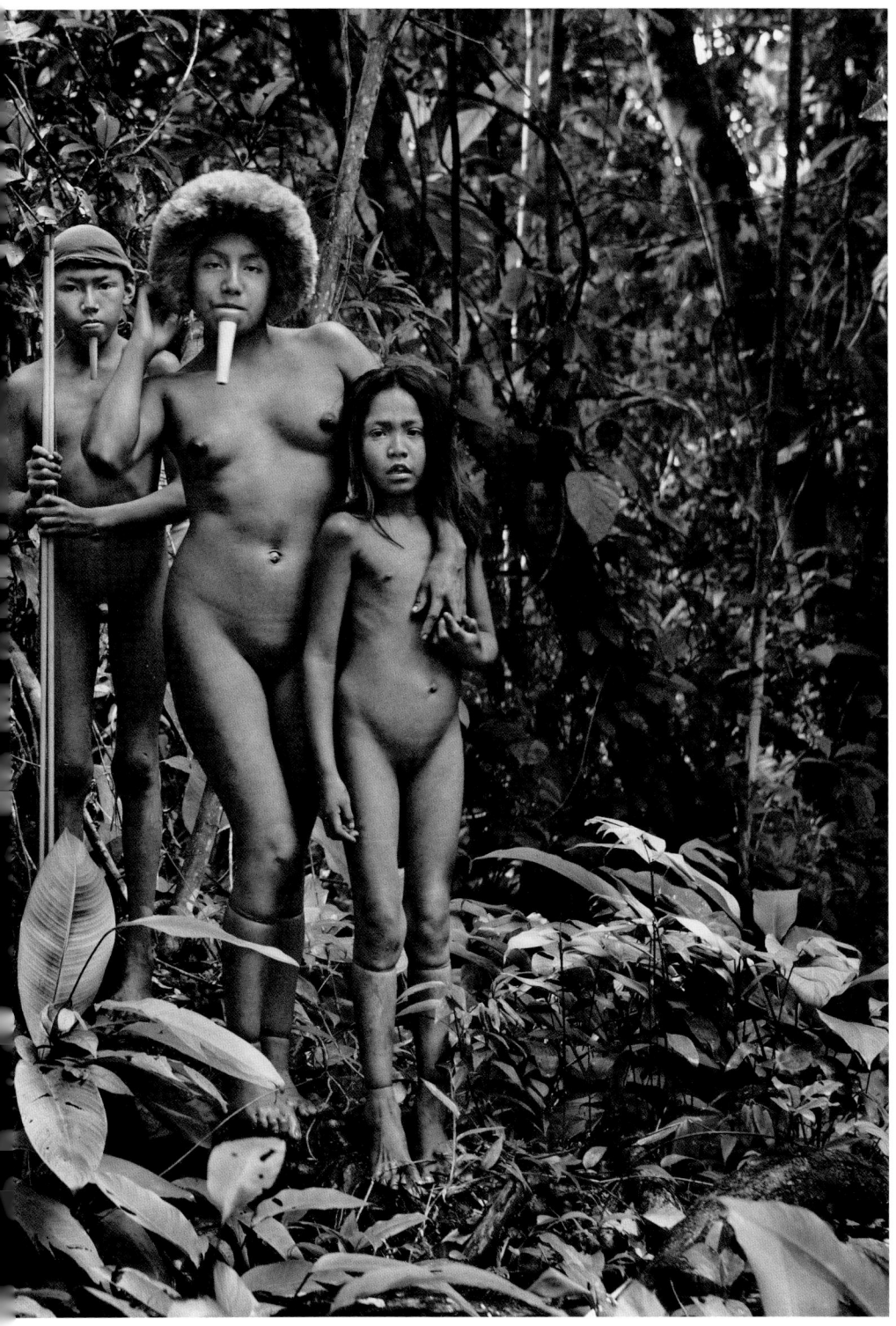

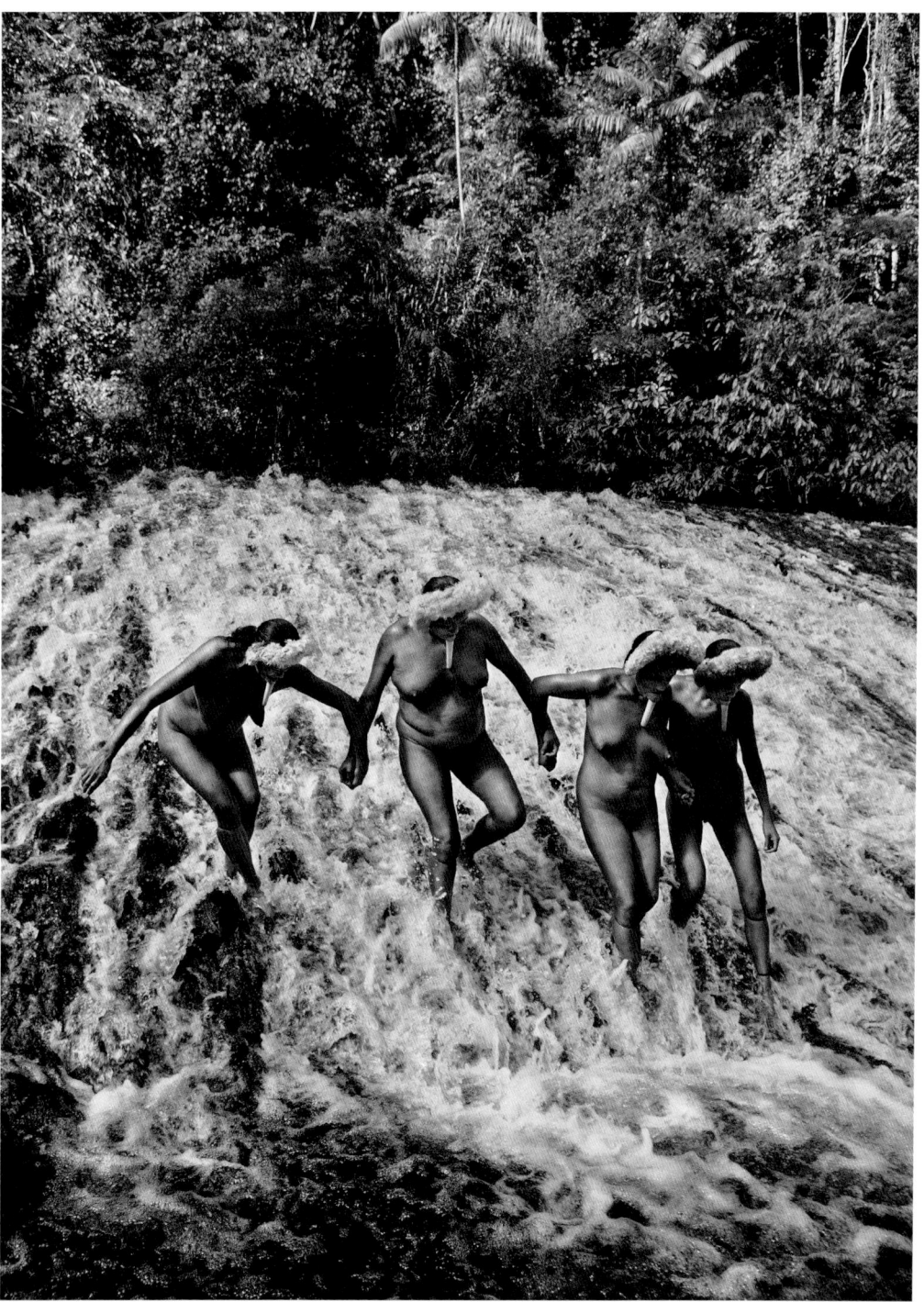

Opposite Four Zo'é women play while bathing in rapids on the Kiaré River near the village of Kejá. From right to left: Kujáikwét, Tatytú, Bohé, and another woman. Zo'é Indigenous Territory, state of Pará, 2009.

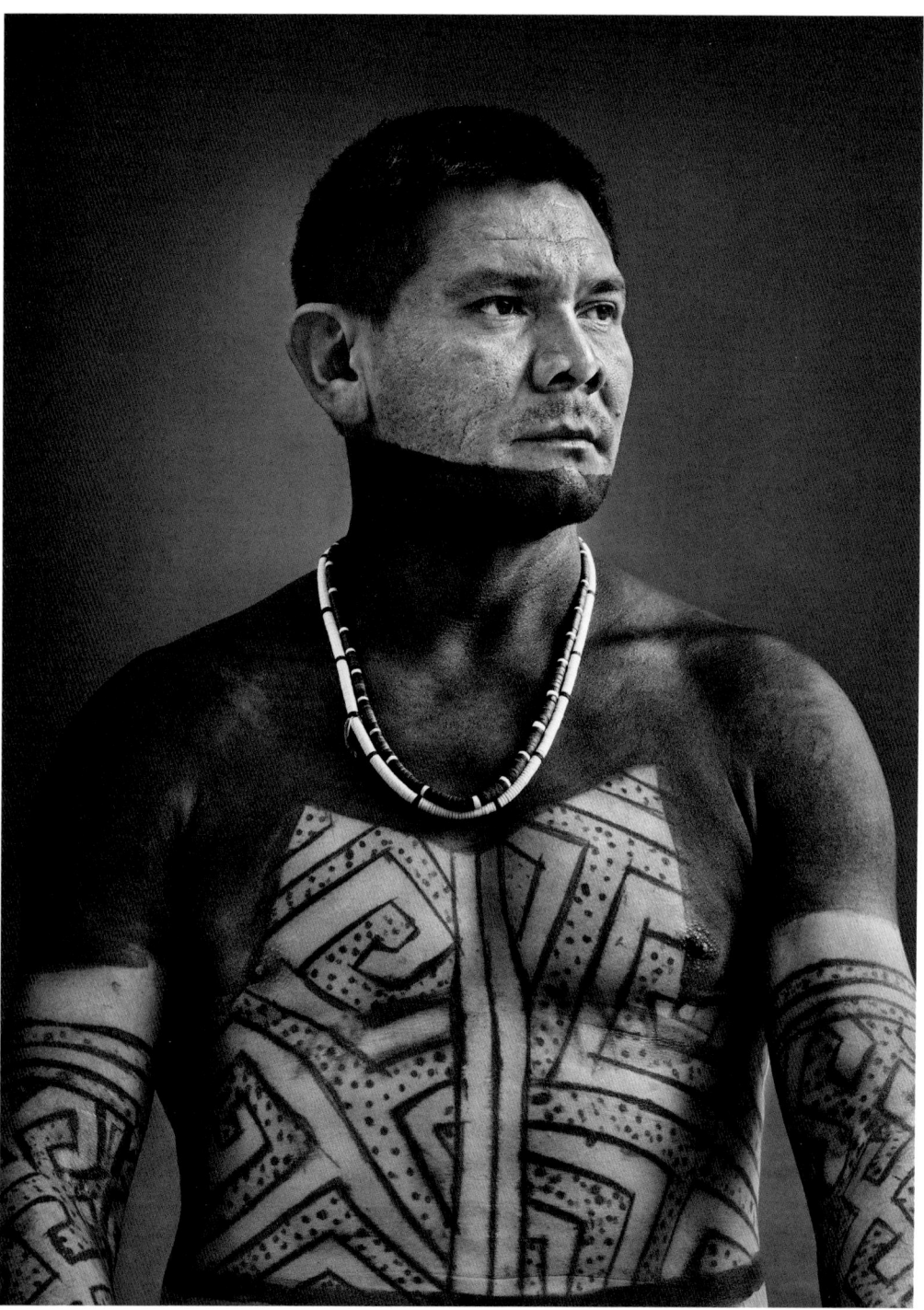

MARUBO

Like other indigenous peoples of the Amazon's far west, the Marubo have myths that reflect a strong memory of their relations with the Inca Empire: several mythical narratives talk of their ancestors' travels to seek goods among the Incas, such as stones, which are so rare where they live in the Javari Valley region, with its sandy soil. Perhaps their name itself comes from their interactions with the Incas: the word "Marubo" means nothing in their own language, part of the Pano language family. One explanation is the name might be a corruption of the Quechua "Mayoruna," people of the river, which also designates the neighboring Matsés.

The Marubo live in communal houses, oblong *malocas* located in the center of the village. They have two entrances: one facing south and another facing north. The southern one is the main entrance, next to which there are two seats where visitors are received and leaders sit to debate public matters or converse at night. Next to it is a *trocano* drum: a hollowed-out tree trunk used in celebrations and to warn nearby communities of an emergency. The opposite entrance is used unceremoniously by the residents to come and go.

Each Marubo house has an "owner," the leader of its community, who also was responsible for building it and who performs its structural maintenance. His family occupies the spaces closest to the main entrance, which makes him a kind of guardian of the house.

The Marubo divide society into 18 sections with names of animals. Marriages must be between people from specific sections, which results in unions between cousins who are children of their parents' opposite-sex siblings (young men marry daughters of their mother's brothers or of their father's sisters; likewise, young women seek to marry sons of their mother's brothers or of their father's sisters). They can be polygamous: when a man gets married, he immediately becomes a candidate to also marry his wife's sisters. If he does not want to, a brother of his may marry them.

The biggest Marubo community, Maronal, consists of six sections like neighboring villages, each with a communal house and many small houses around it. The current Marubo population is just over 2,000 people. The Javari Valley Indigenous Territory that they inhabit is one of the largest in Brazil, measuring 8.5 million hectares (21 million acres) and is home to several other ethnic groups: Korubo, Matis, Matsés, Katukina, and a variety of isolated groups.

Opposite In the Marubo village of Maronal, young leader Wino Këyashëni (Beto Marubo) with body paint made of genipap (the fruit of *Genipa americana*) mixed with ashes to set it, worn during wasp-sting festivals to ward off *panema* (laziness or bad luck). The red urucum paint is worn during corn festivals and in wars. Javari Valley, Marubo Indigenous Territory, state of Amazonas, 2018.

More than a century of coexistence with nonindigenous people is reflected in Marubo children's education, and learning Portuguese well is an important part of growing up there. This is why many of them end up becoming translators and intermediaries in interactions with government employees (such as nurses at indigenous health posts) and to support indigenous organizations' activities, notably through ongoing participation in expeditions to contact other ethnic groups in the region.

Since the 1990s, the region has recorded high rates of hepatitis infection. Documenting the fight against disease was the reason for my first visit to the region in 1998, followed by another visit in 2018.

Opposite A girl, Ino Tamashavo Marubo, holding a parrot. The distinguishing mark of her people is the numerous white necklaces worn through the nose and on the body, made of white shells from river snails. The indigenous people raise baby birds and other young animals as pets. Javari Valley, Marubo Indigenous Territory, state of Amazonas, 1998.

Pages 452/453 Near the Marubo village of Maronal. Foreground: Txomãewa with a hand in the water. In back: Vonchi Peko, Txonani Ewa, Kena, Paichi, and Rao. Javari Valley, Marubo Indigenous Territory, state of Amazonas, 1998.

Pages 454/455 Aerial view of the Marubo community of Maronal: the Marubo live in large communal houses but also have small huts around the main *maloca* in which they keep family belongings that do not fit in each family's area in the main house. These may include the many clay pots they accumulate for personal use or for trade, as well as firearms and ritual masks. Javari Valley, Marubo Indigenous Territory, state of Amazonas, 1998.

Pages 456/457 Heavy rain in the Marubo village of Mati-këyawaiá. Middle ground: Mesempapa's *maloca*. Javari Valley, Marubo Indigenous Territory, state of Amazonas, 2018.

Pages 458/459 Inside the main *maloca* of the Marubo village of Maronal: the *maloca* of Ivinimpa Marubo (chief of the village). The thick cords are used to hang bananas, and at right are bales of corn. The corn can stay there a long time because in that environment, it does not go bad. Javari Valley, Marubo Indigenous Territory, state of Amazonas, 2018.

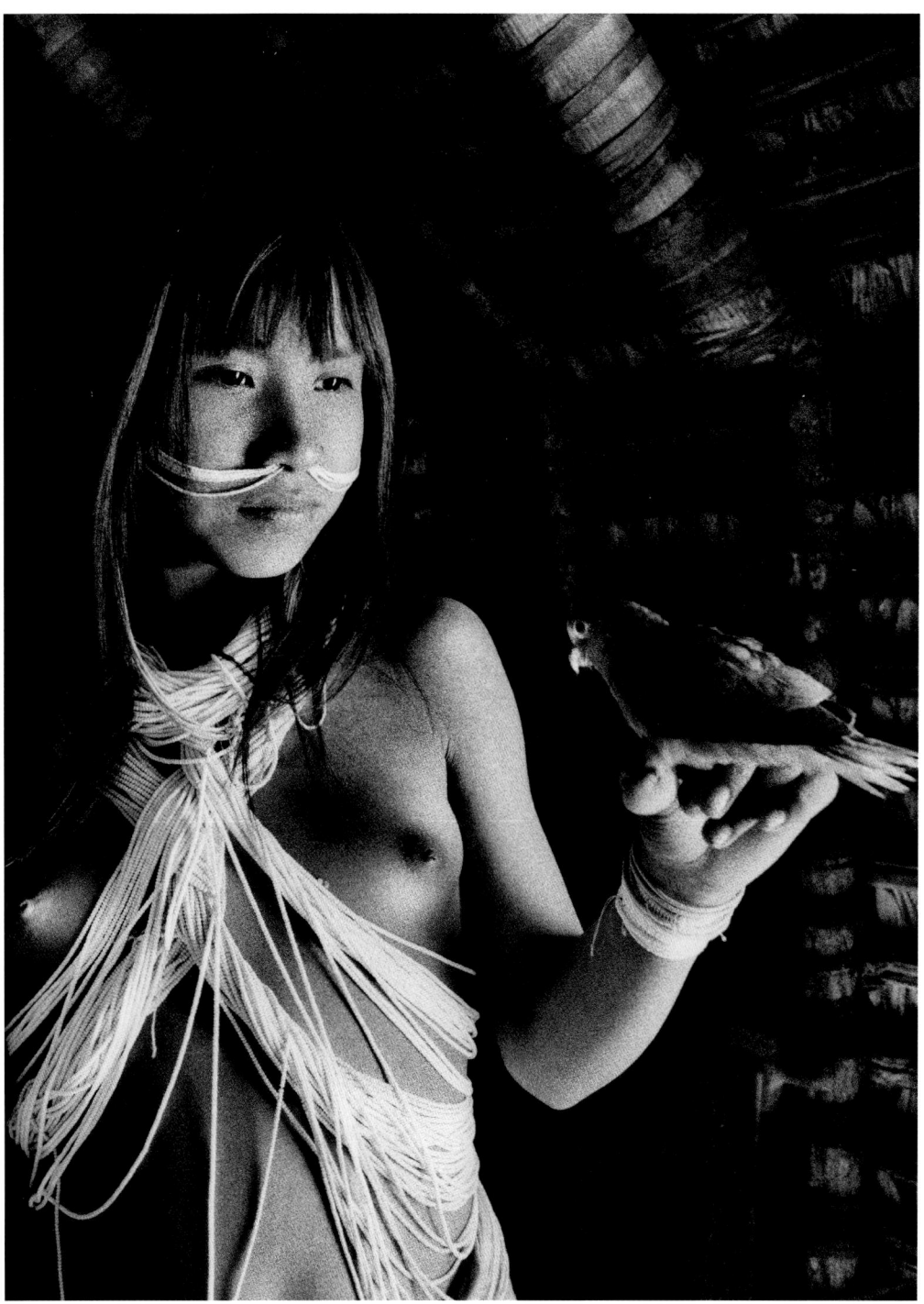

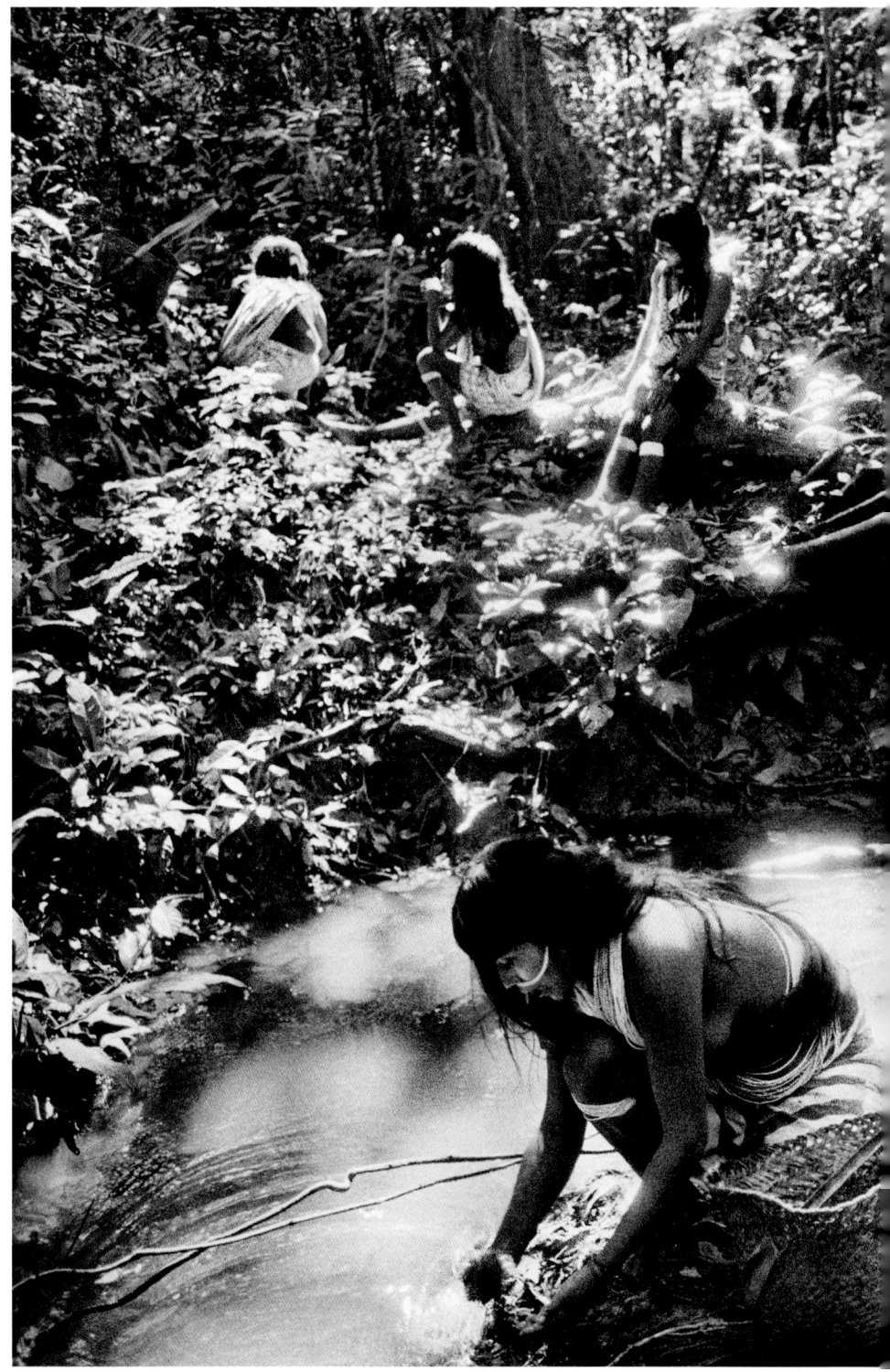

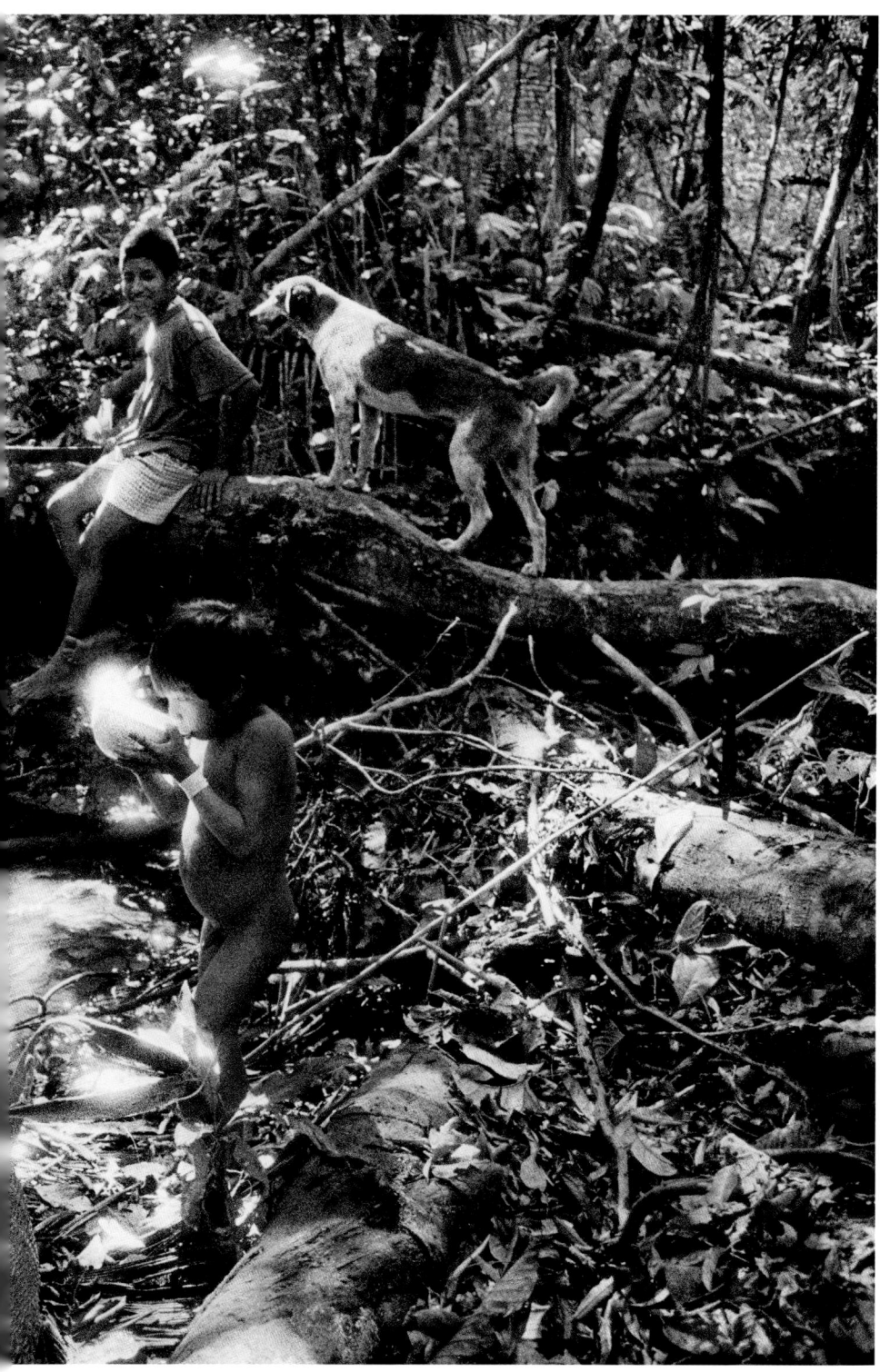

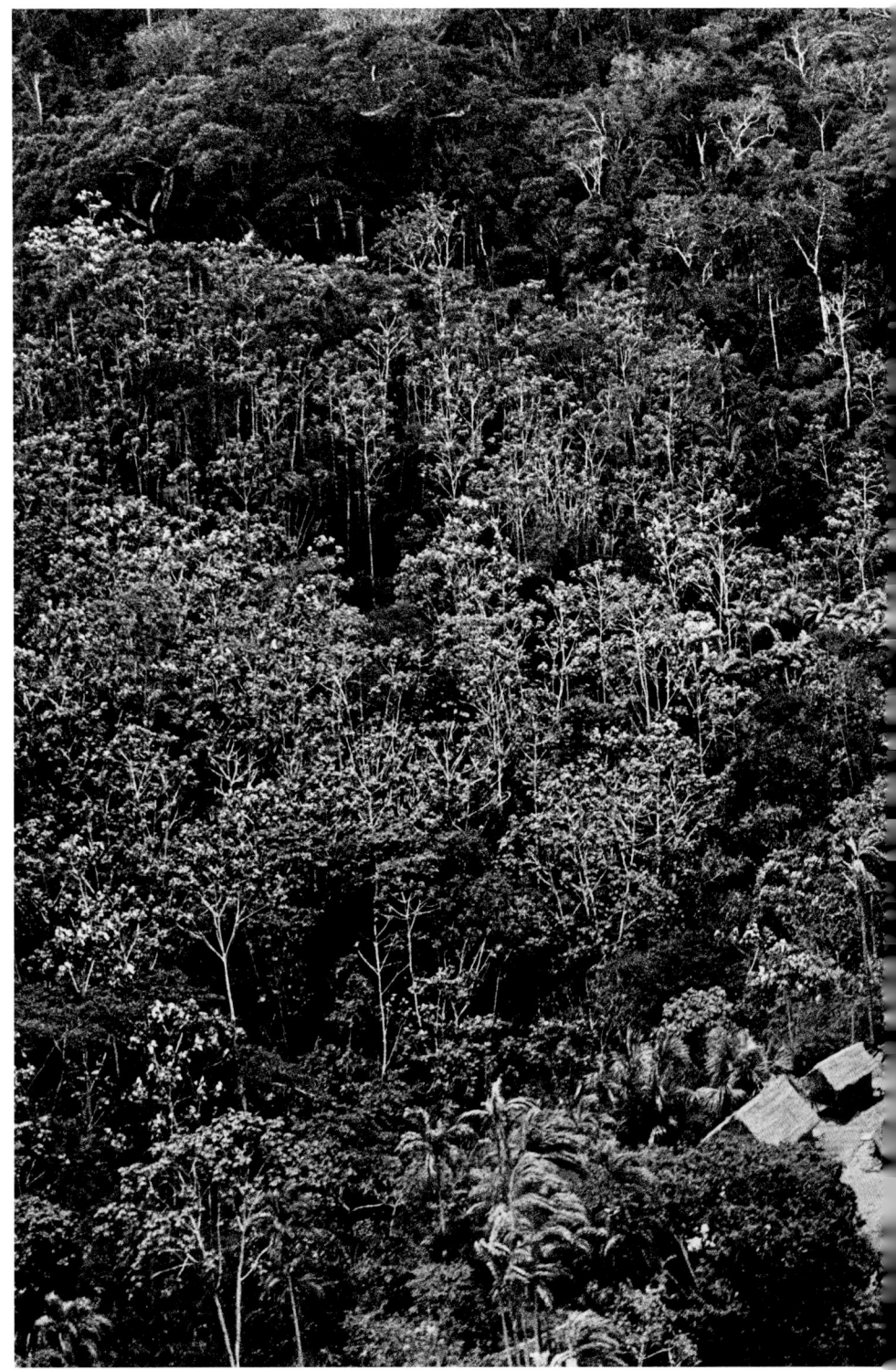

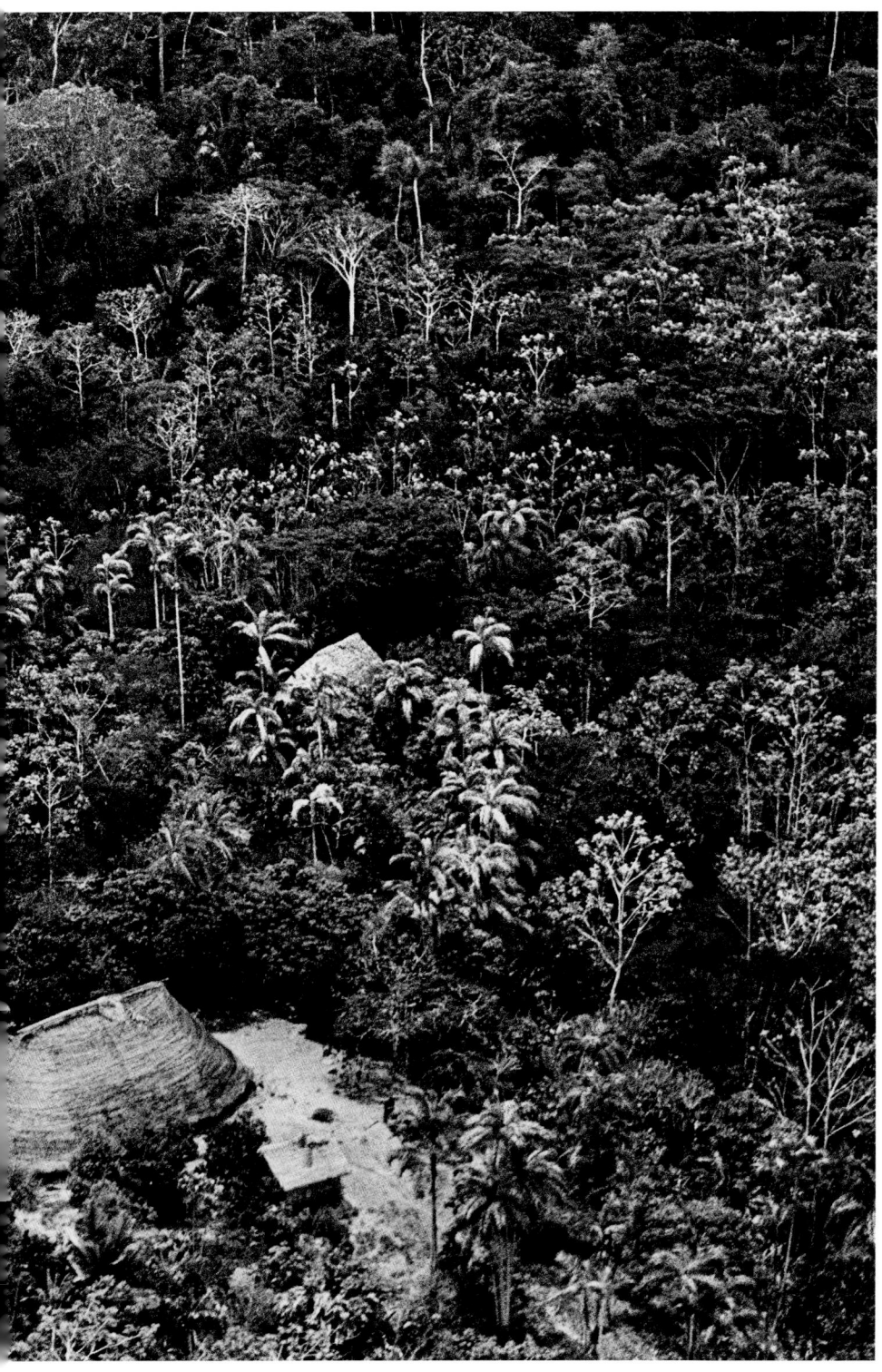

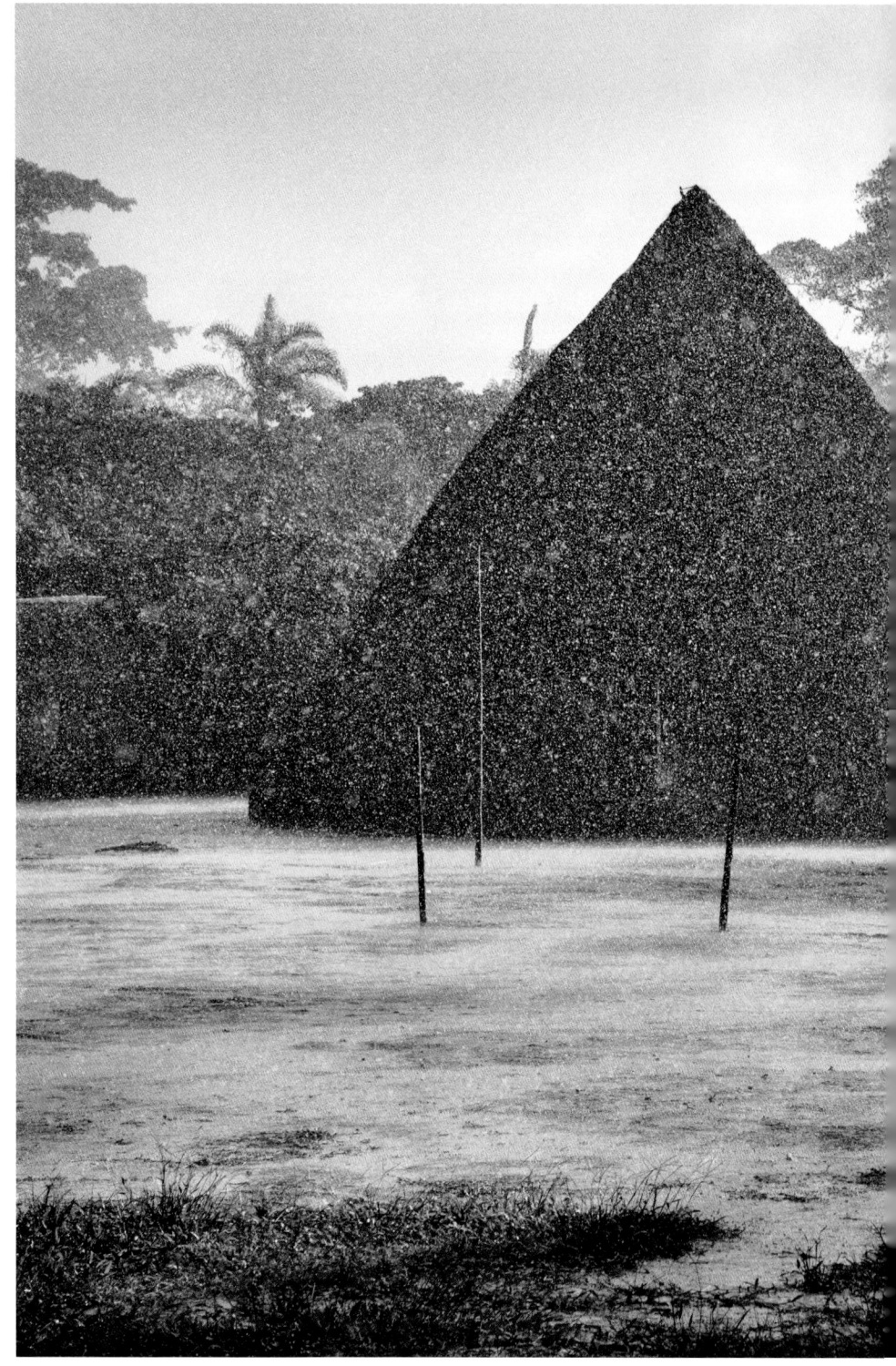

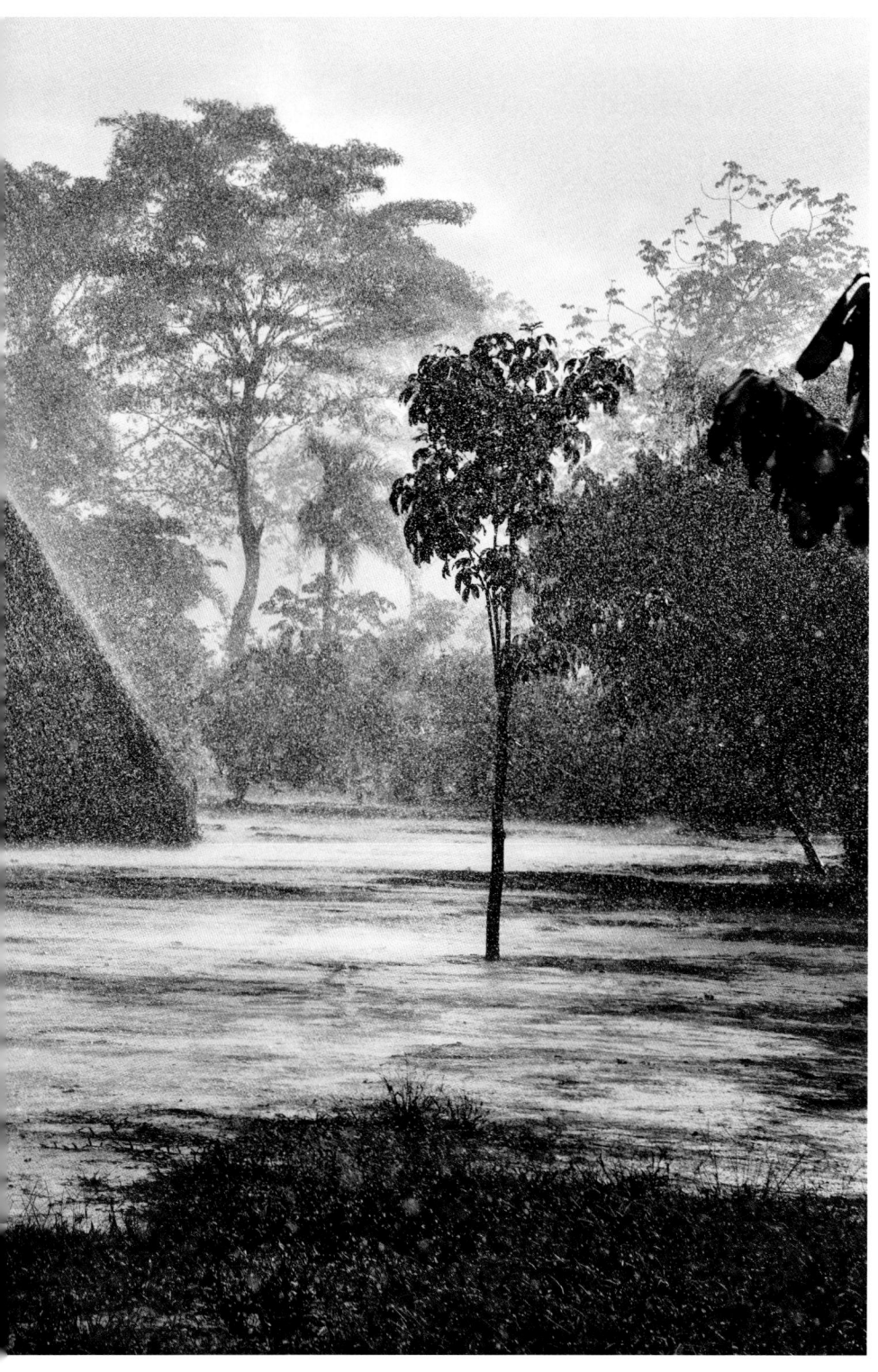

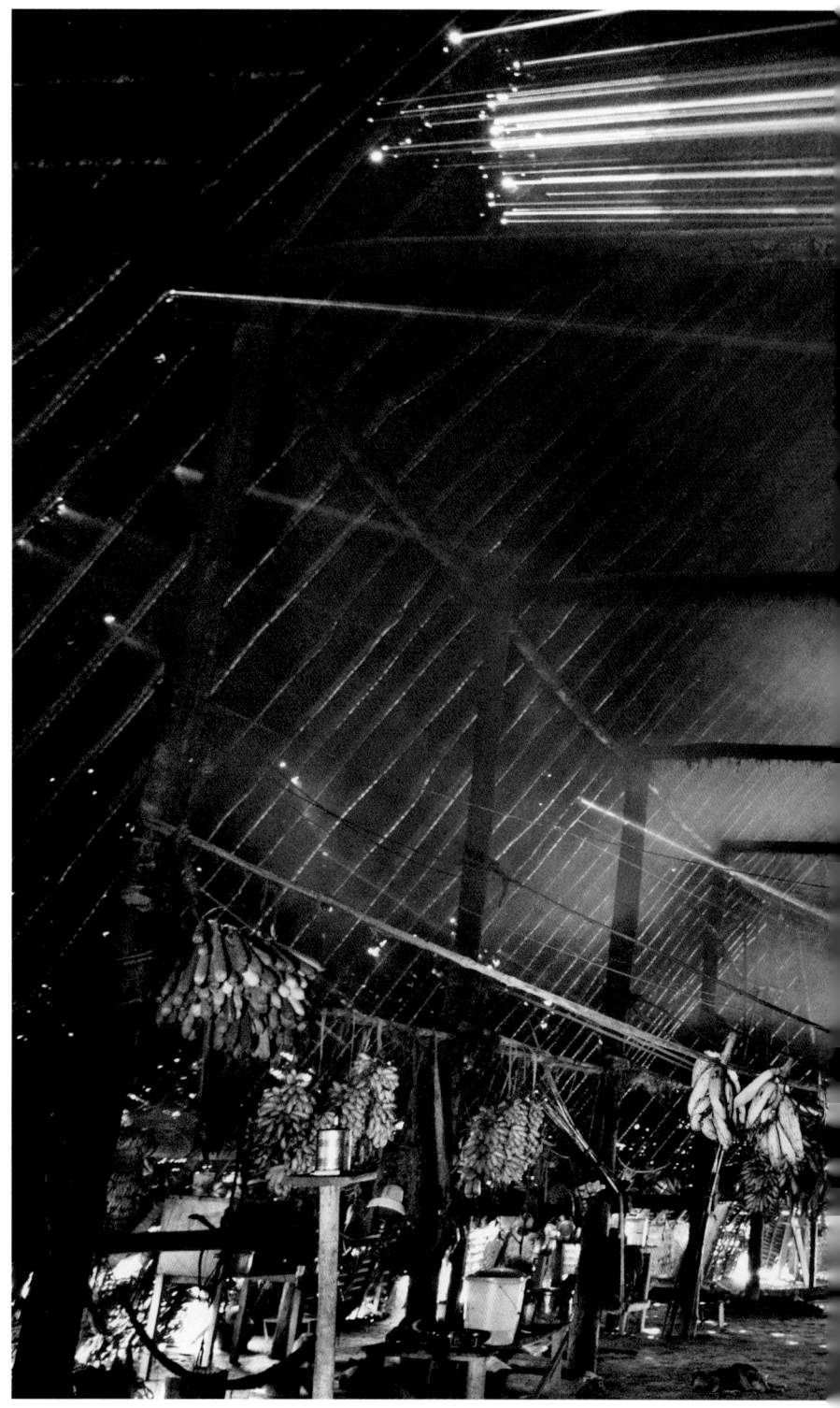

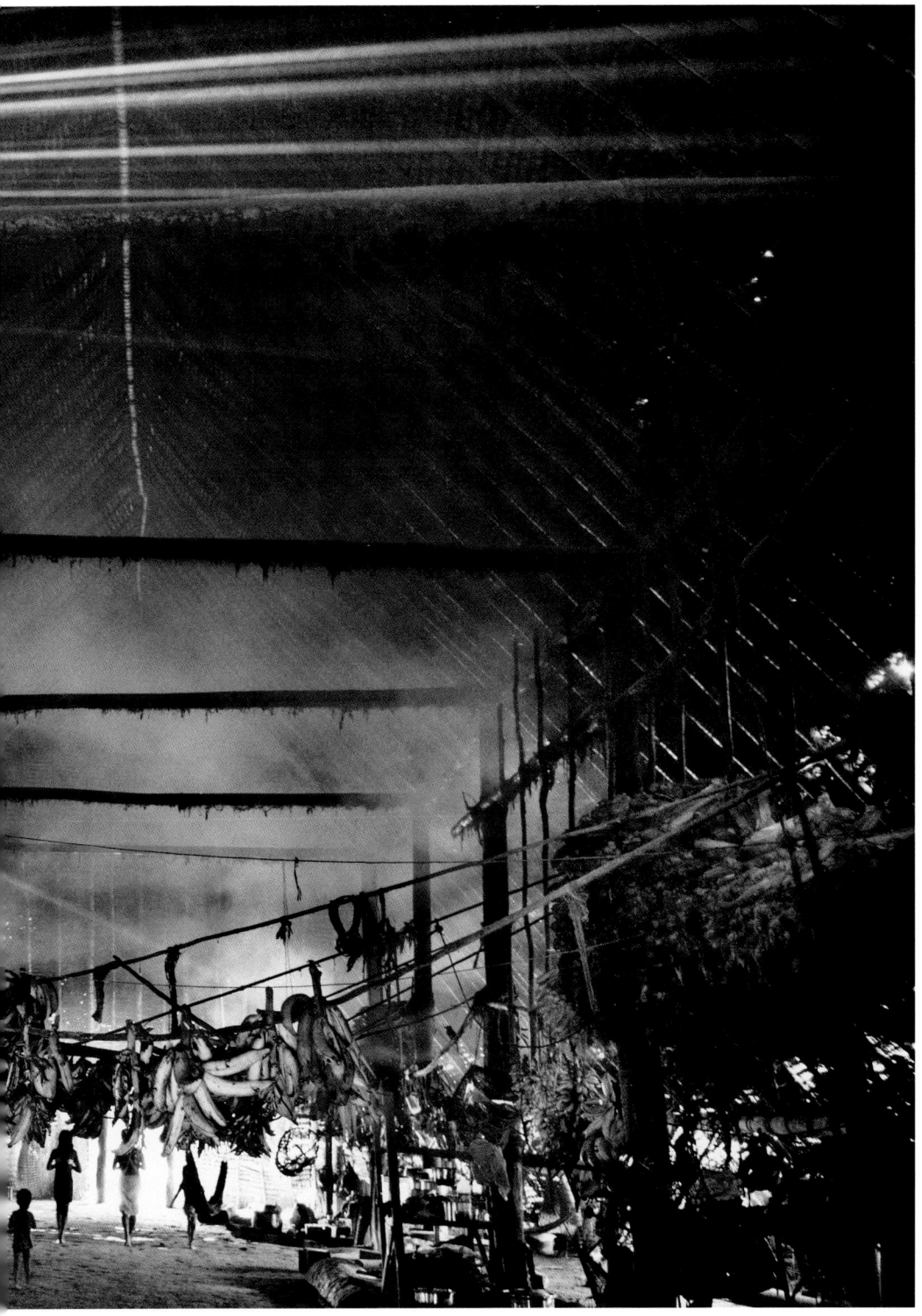

Opposite A girl, Sheta, seated on a traditional Marubo clay pot. Their clay pots are sought after by all the other indigenous peoples of the region. Javari Valley, Marubo Indigenous Territory, state of Amazonas, 2018.

Pages 462/463 Nakua Marubo from the village of Mati-këyawaiá, in the village's main *maloca*, right at the entrance, in the "parlor" where the men sit. Javari Valley, Marubo Indigenous Territory, state of Amazonas, 2018.

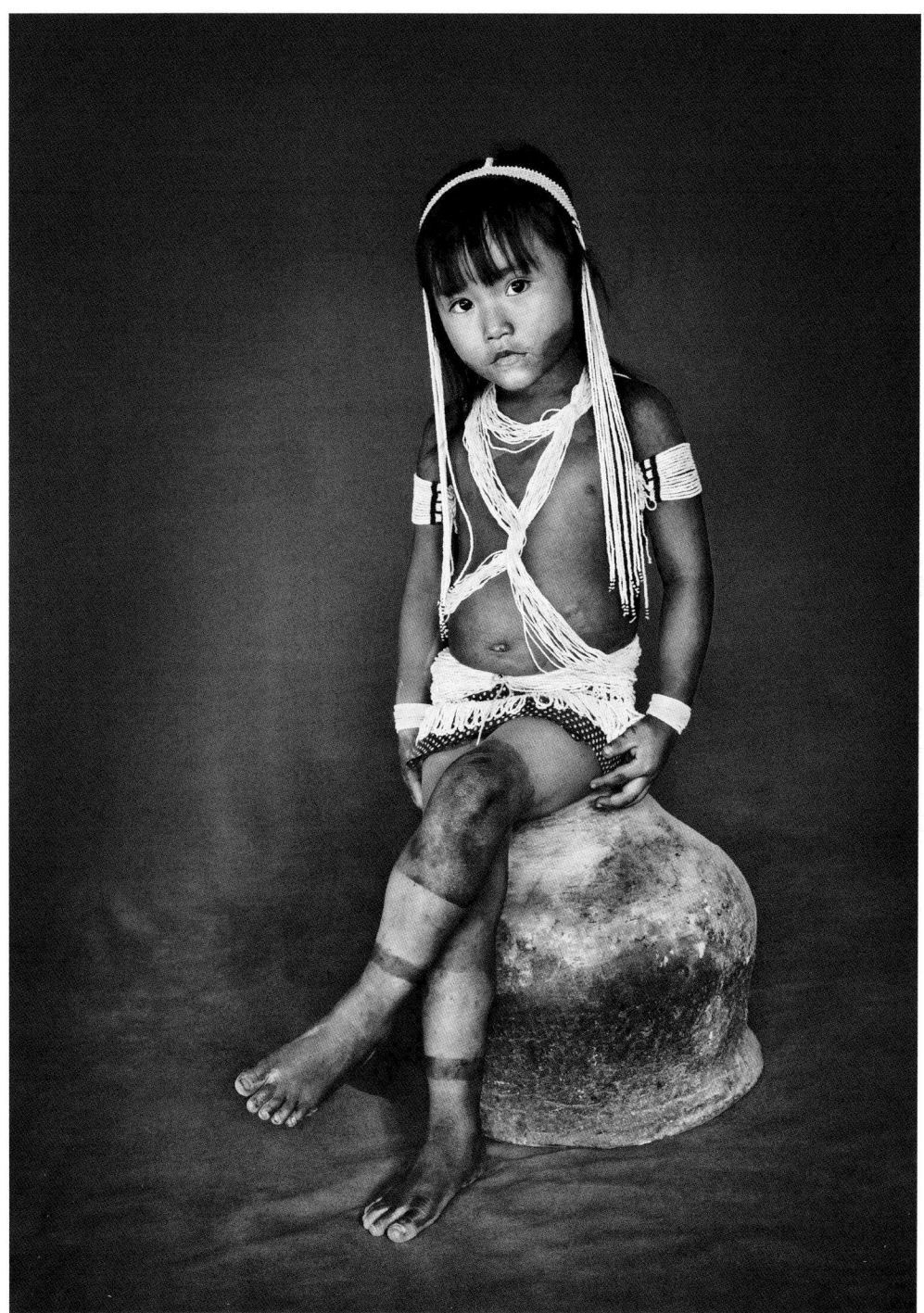

461

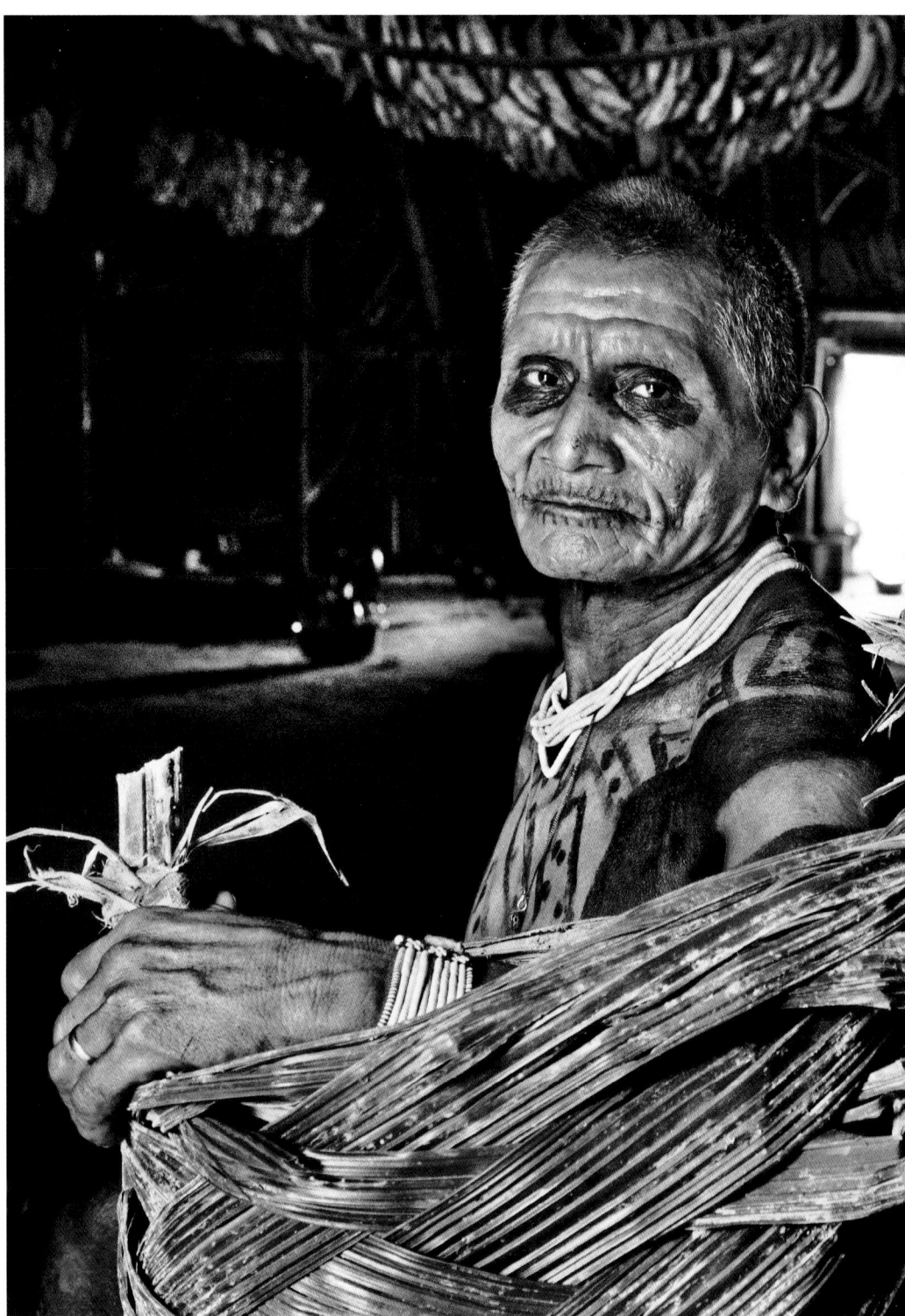

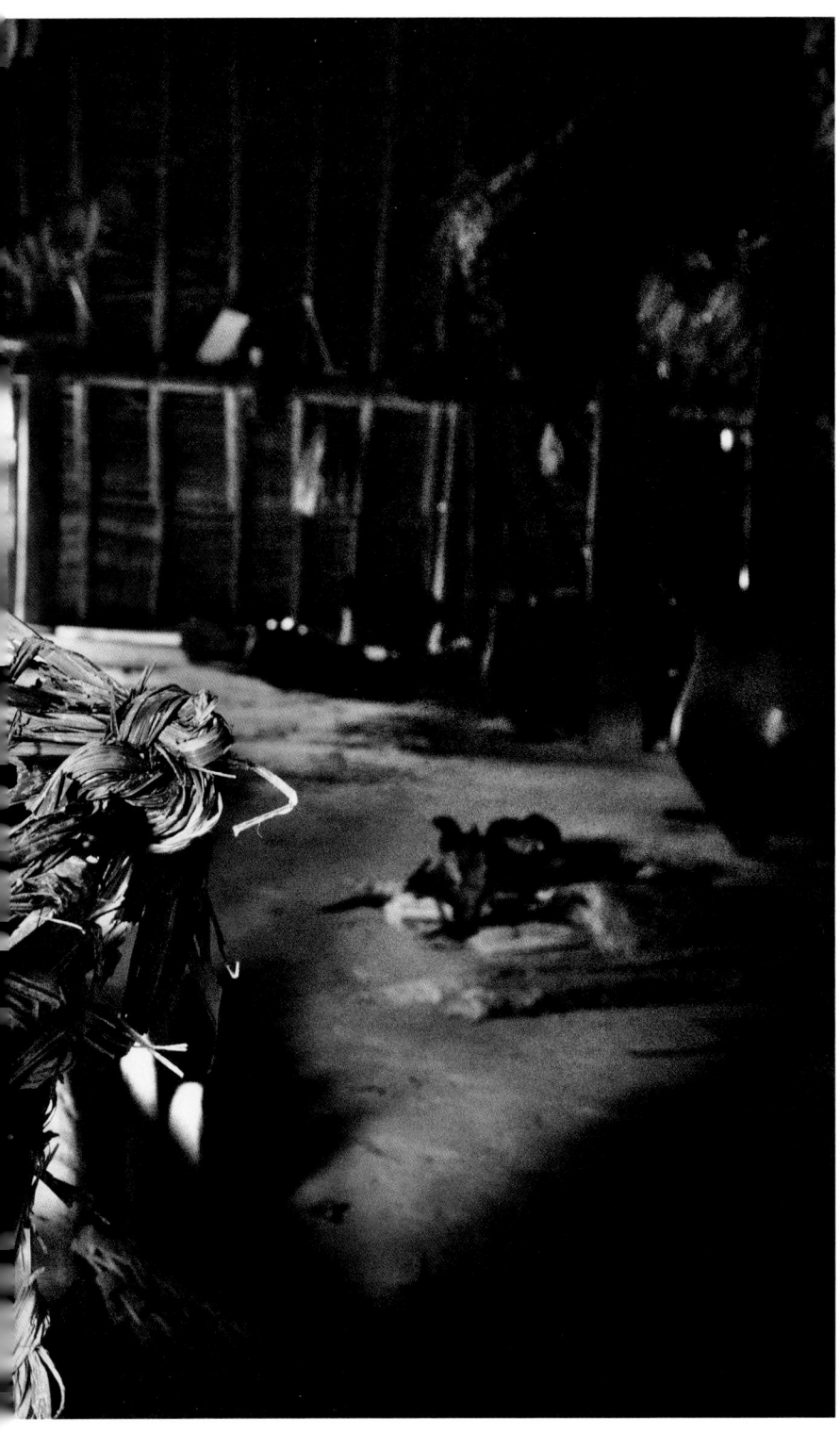

Opposite Maya Marubo, who resides in the community of Kumãya along the upper Kumãya River, holds a small pet parakeet in her hand. Her whole body is adorned with necklaces whose beads are made from river snail shells, common in that area. Javari Valley, Marubo Indigenous Territory, state of Amazonas, 2018.

Pages 466/467 The main *maloca* of the Marubo village of Maronal: Chief Ivinimpa's *maloca*. Shanko Ewa and her son Shanko in the kitchen. Javari Valley, Marubo Indigenous Territory, state of Amazonas, 2018.

Pages 468/469 In the Marubo village of Matikëyawaiá, a girl, Voa. Javari Valley, Marubo Indigenous Territory, state of Amazonas, 2018.

Pages 470/471 Ivinimpa is the main leader of the Marubo people. Javari Valley, Marubo Indigenous Territory, state of Amazonas, 2018.

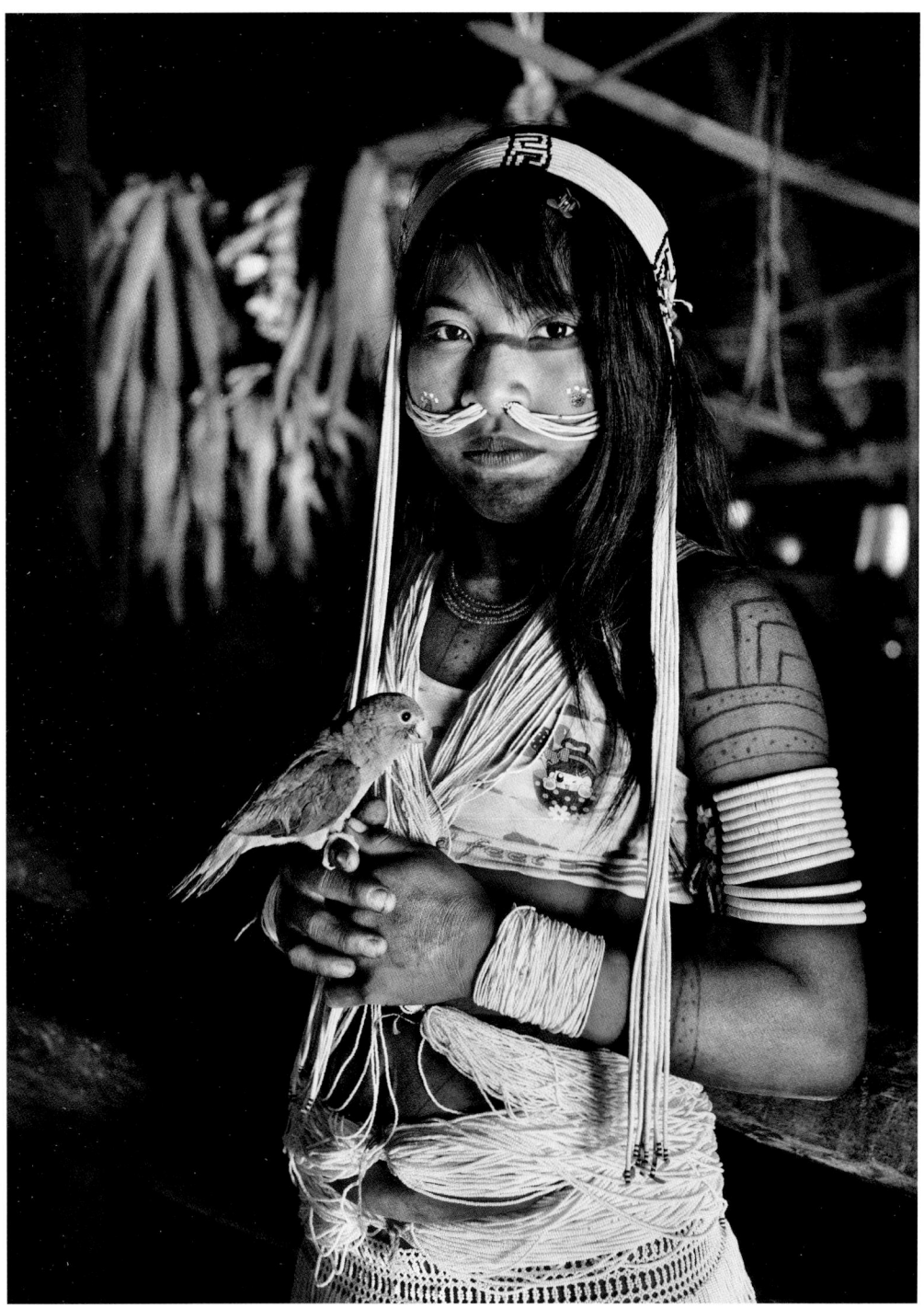

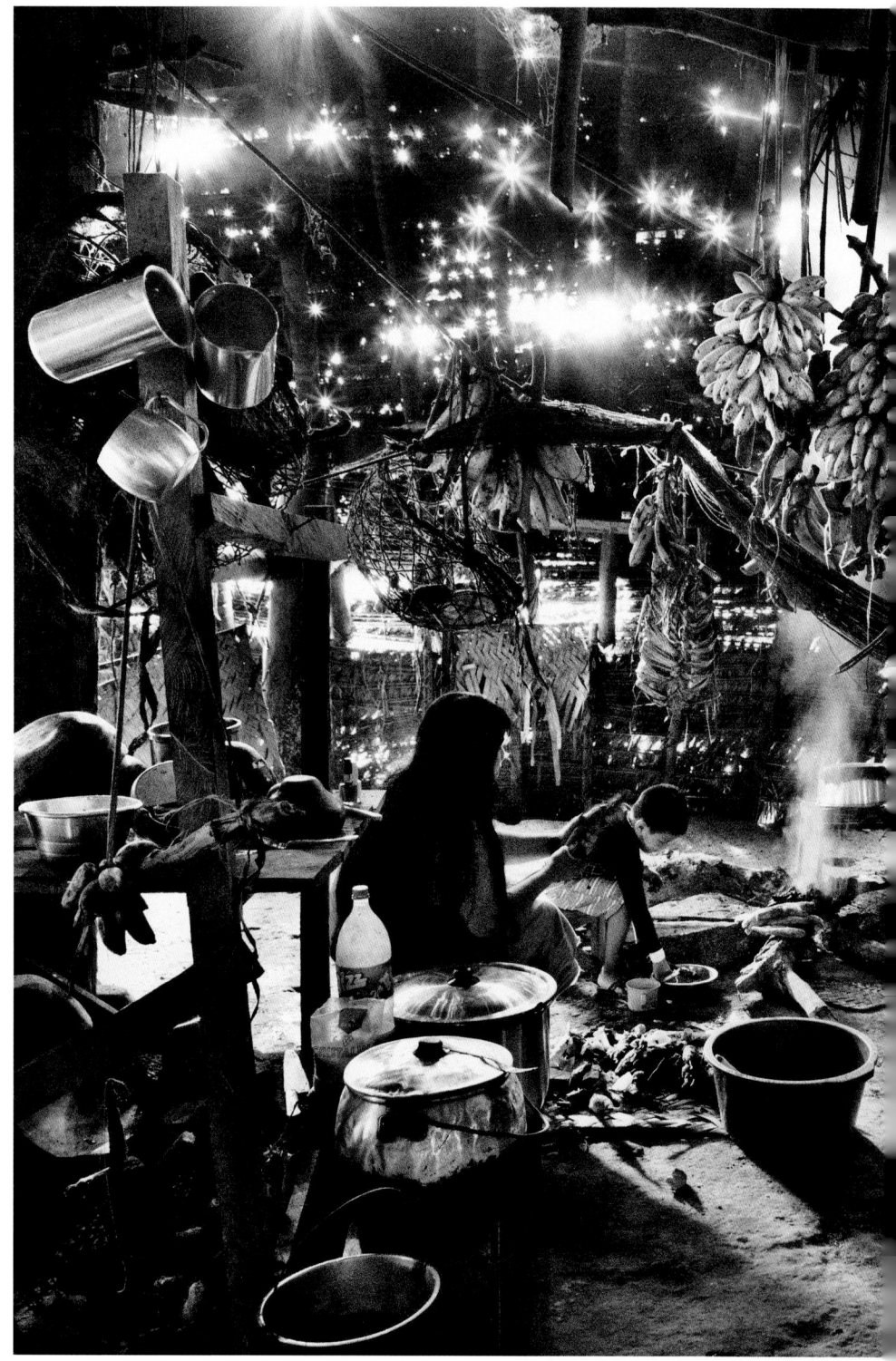

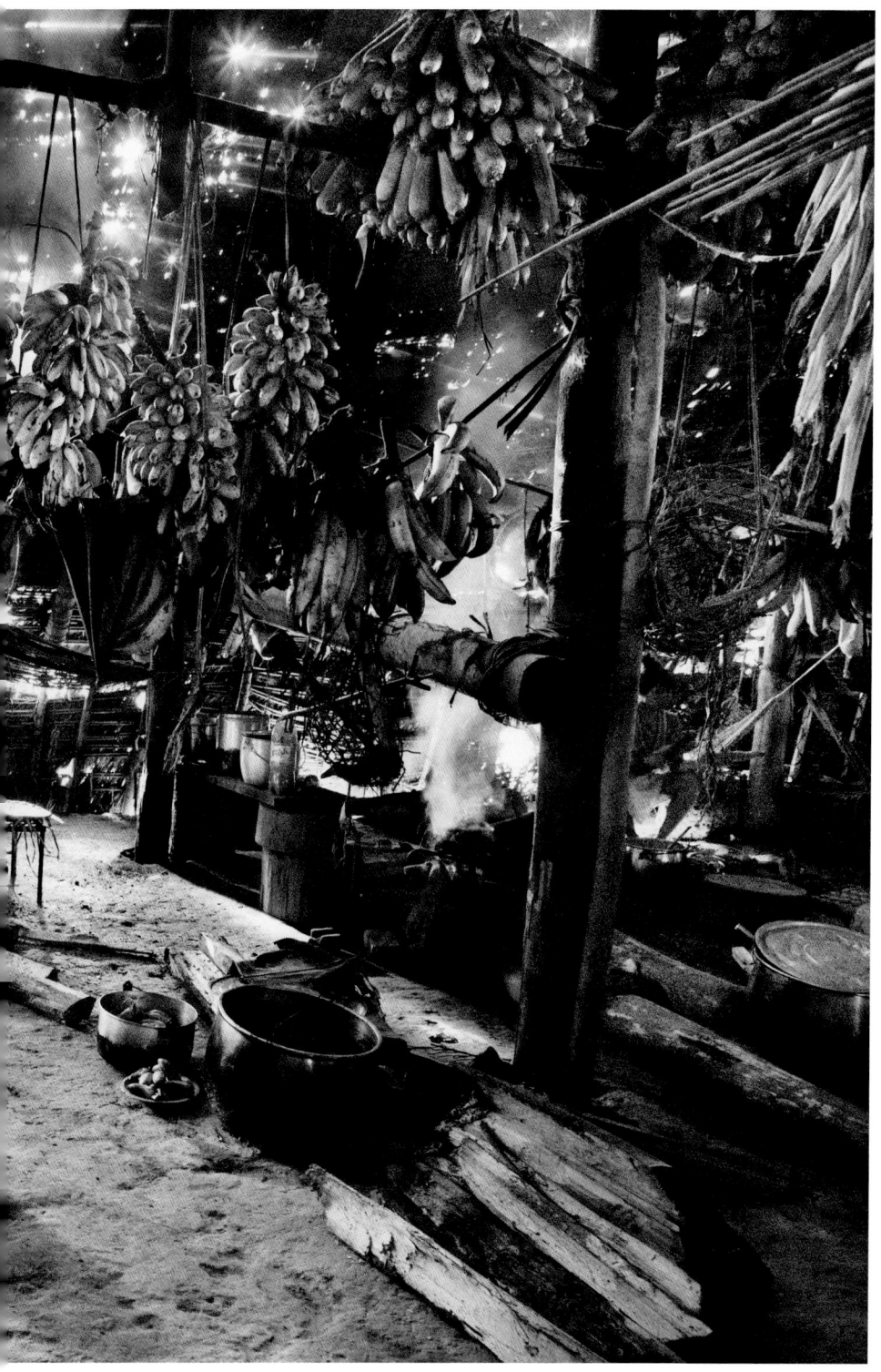

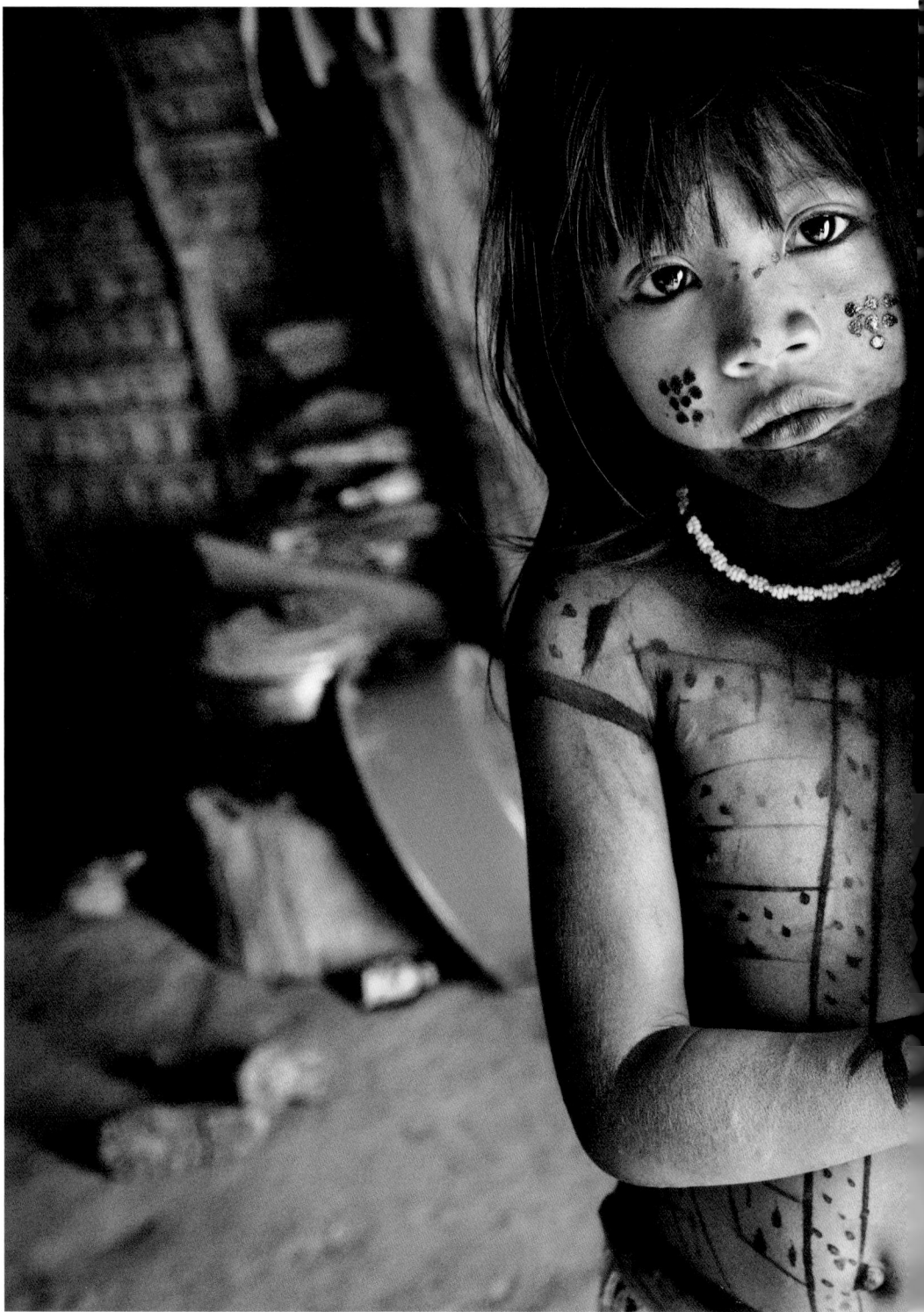

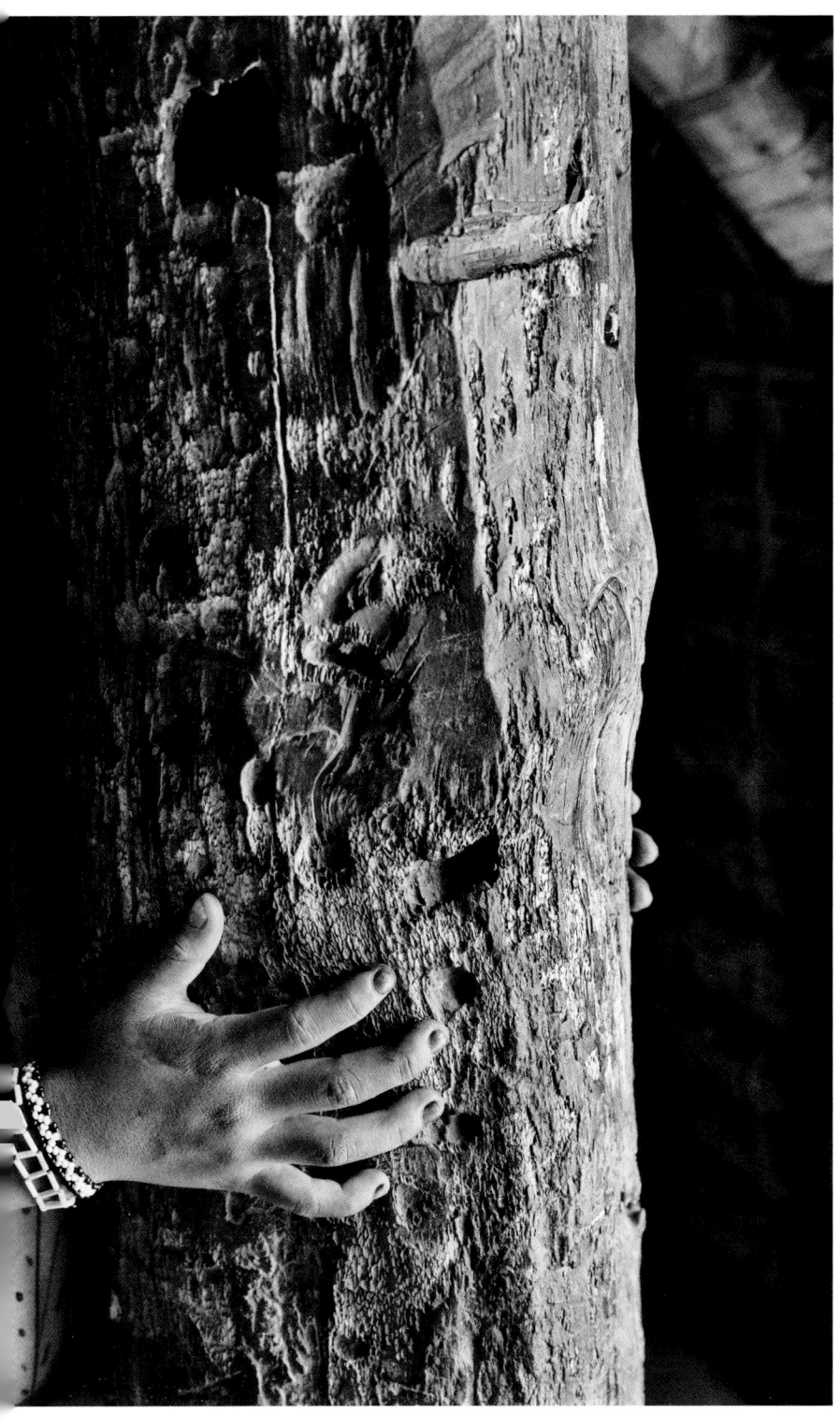

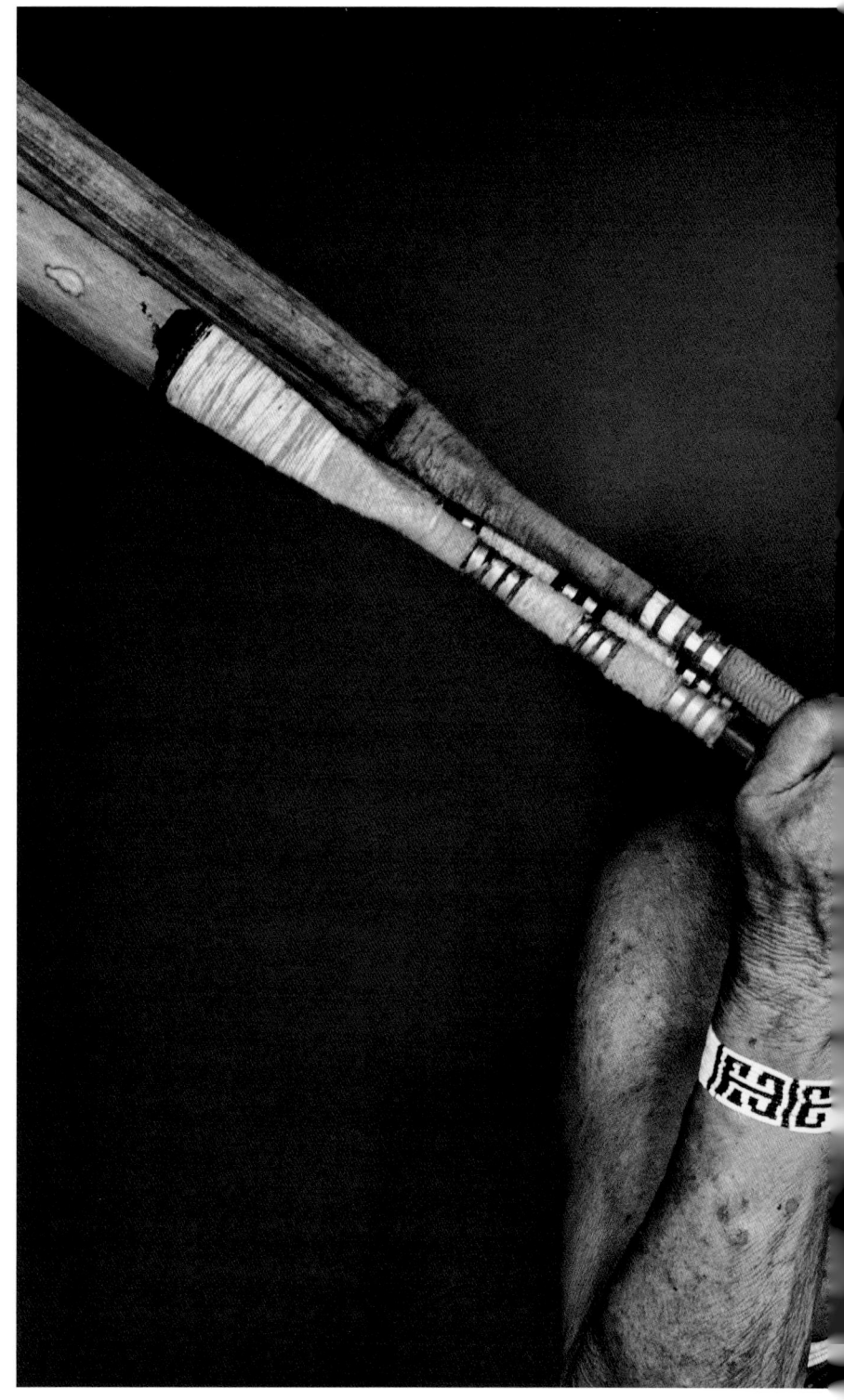

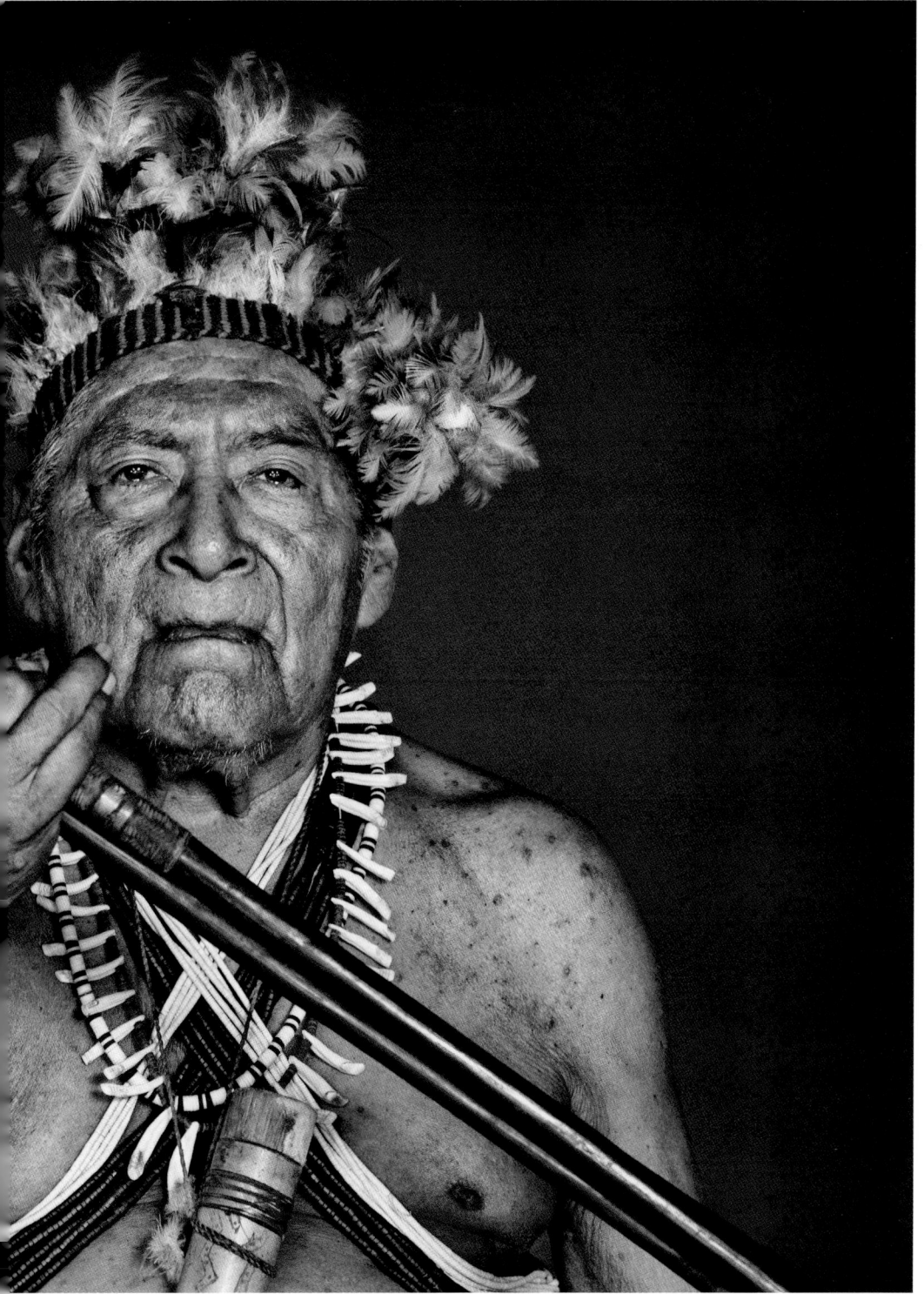

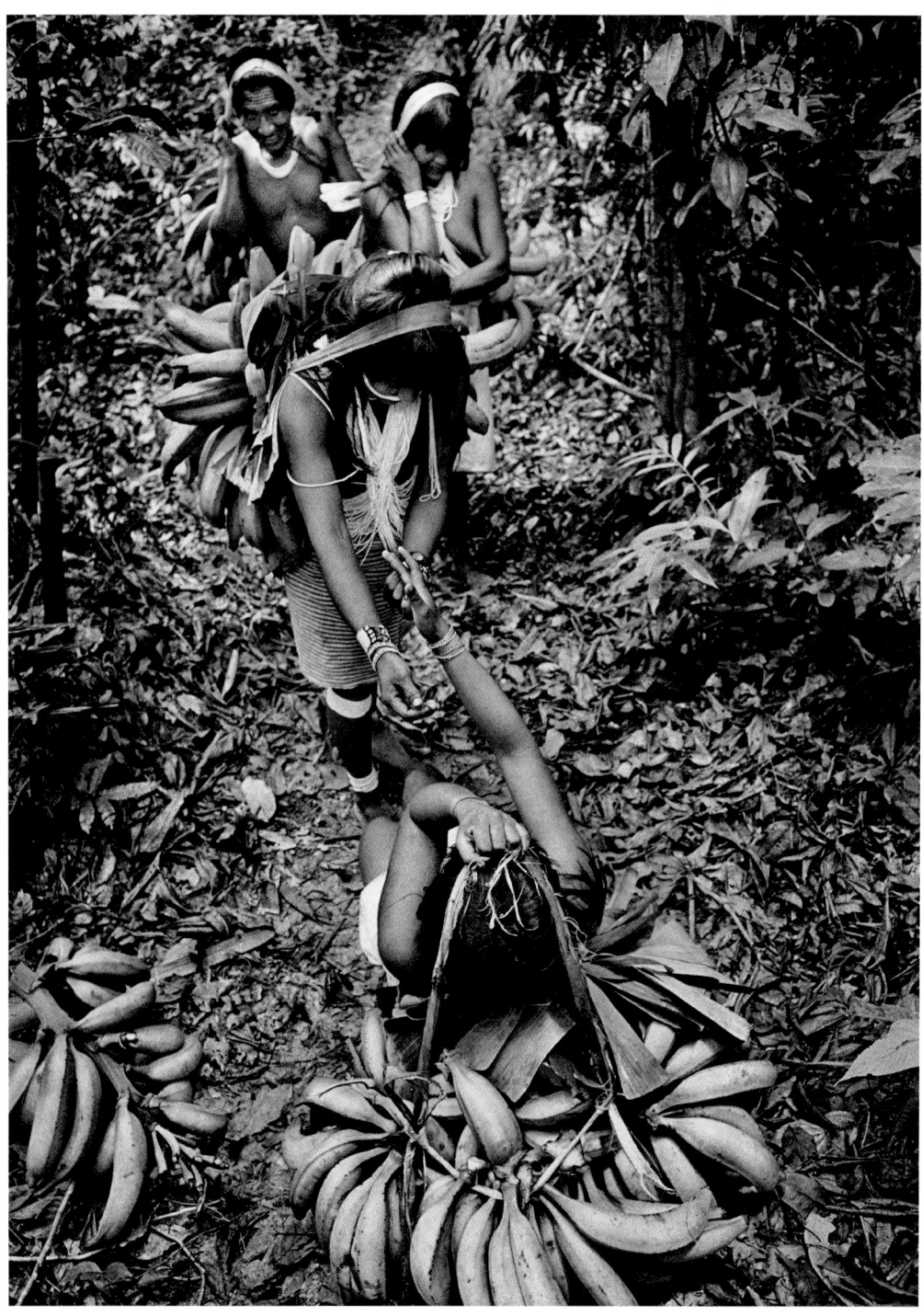

Opposite In the Marubo village of Maronal, Txô-Vanëmpa, in back, accompanies three women: Pei Ewa, Choi Ewa, and Shanka, who are carrying bunches of bananas. Javari Valley, Marubo Indigenous Territory, state of Amazonas, 1998.

Page 474 Vanë from the Marubo village of Matikëyawaiá. Javari Valley, Marubo Indigenous Territory, state of Amazonas, 2018.

Page 475 Sína, from the Marubo village of Maronal, is a teacher. He wears body paint made of genipap (mixed with ashes, to set it), worn during wasp-sting festivals to ward off *panema* (laziness or bad luck). The red urucum paint is worn during corn festivals and in wars. Javari Valley, Marubo Indigenous Territory, state of Amazonas, 2018.

Pages 476/477 Marubo village of Morada Nova: Pakampa, the father, at right; next to him, his wife, Pakã-ewa (which means "mother of Paka"); and their children (Paka and Sheta Konô). Javari Valley, Marubo Indigenous Territory, state of Amazonas, 2018.

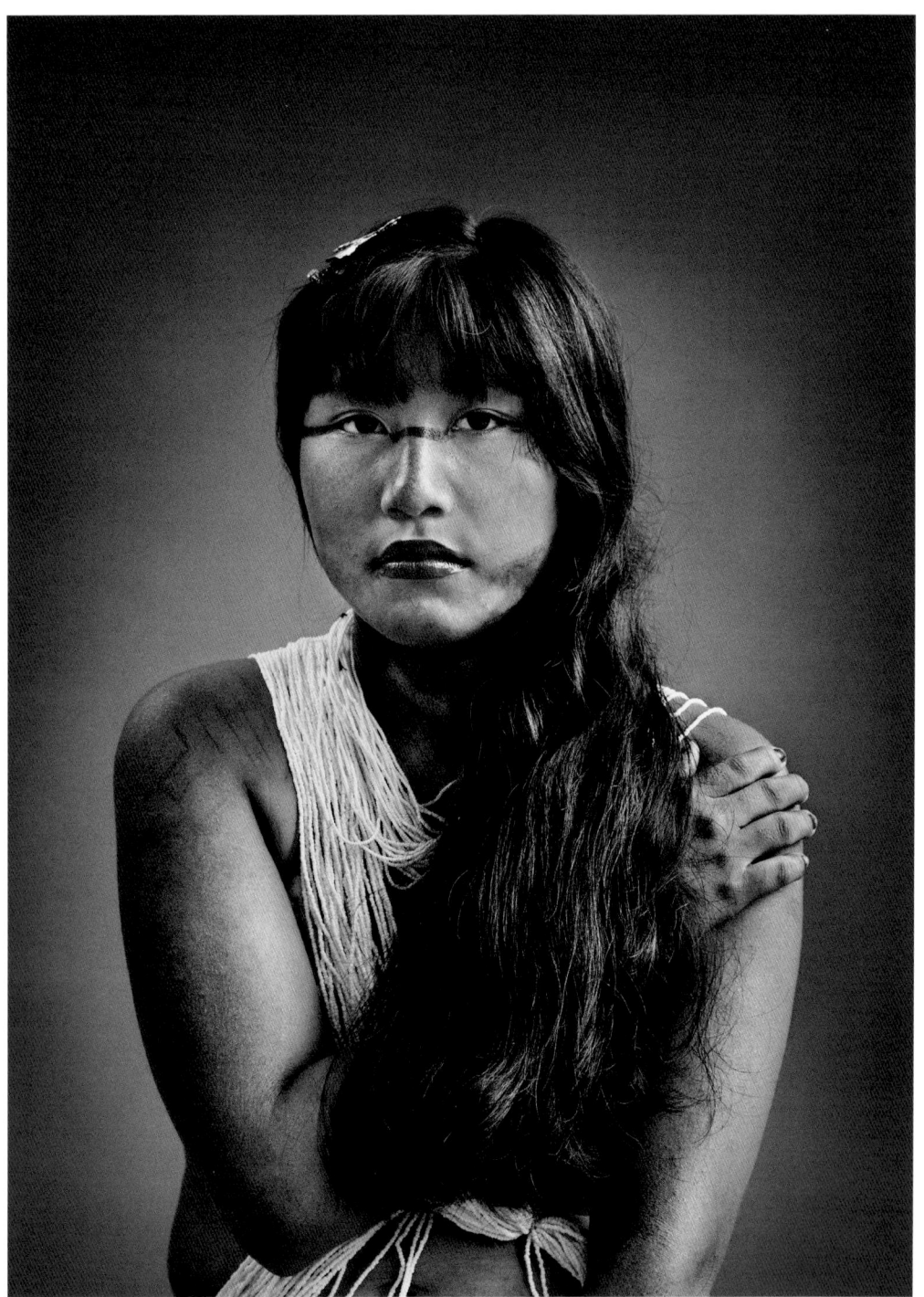

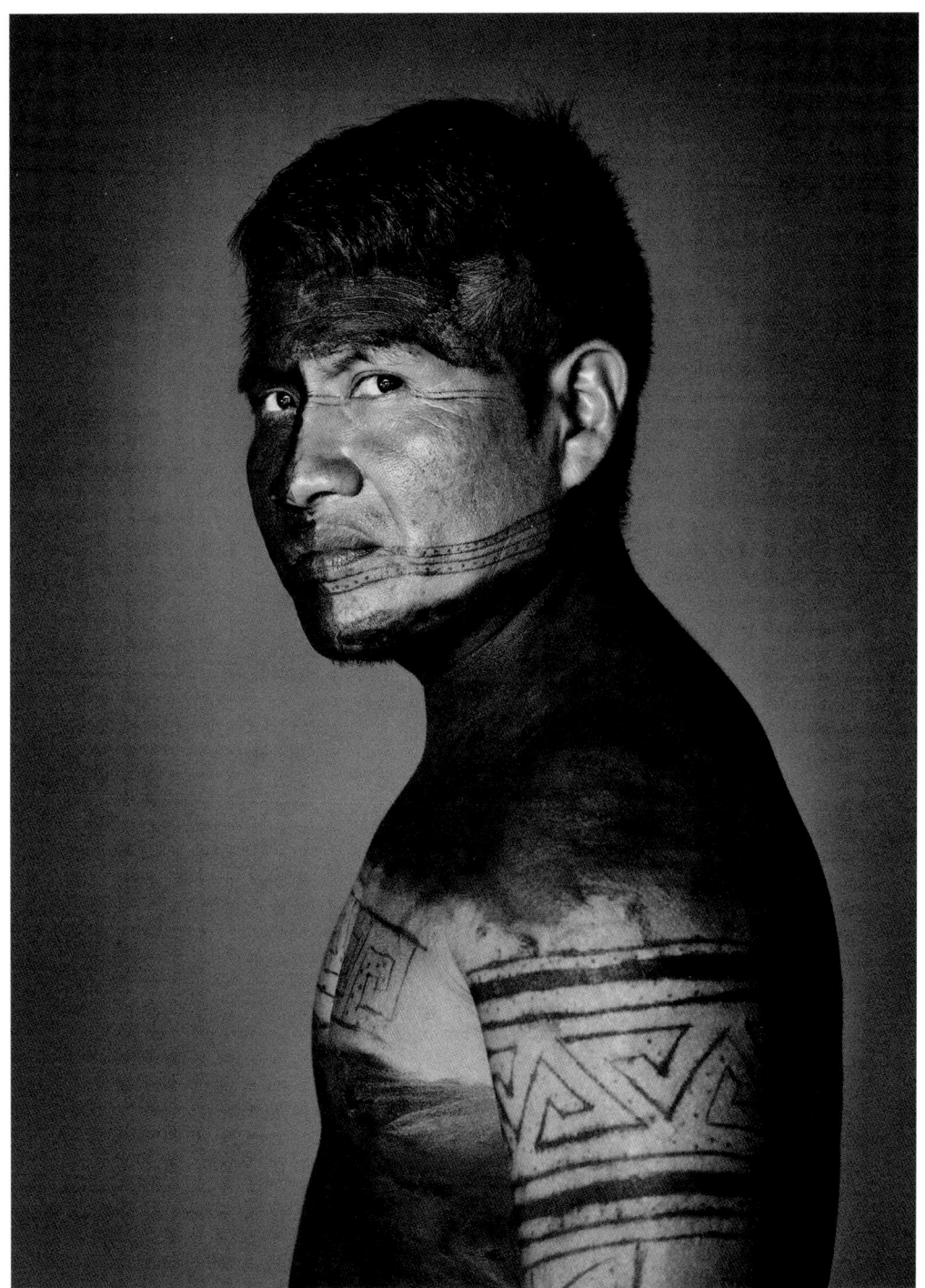

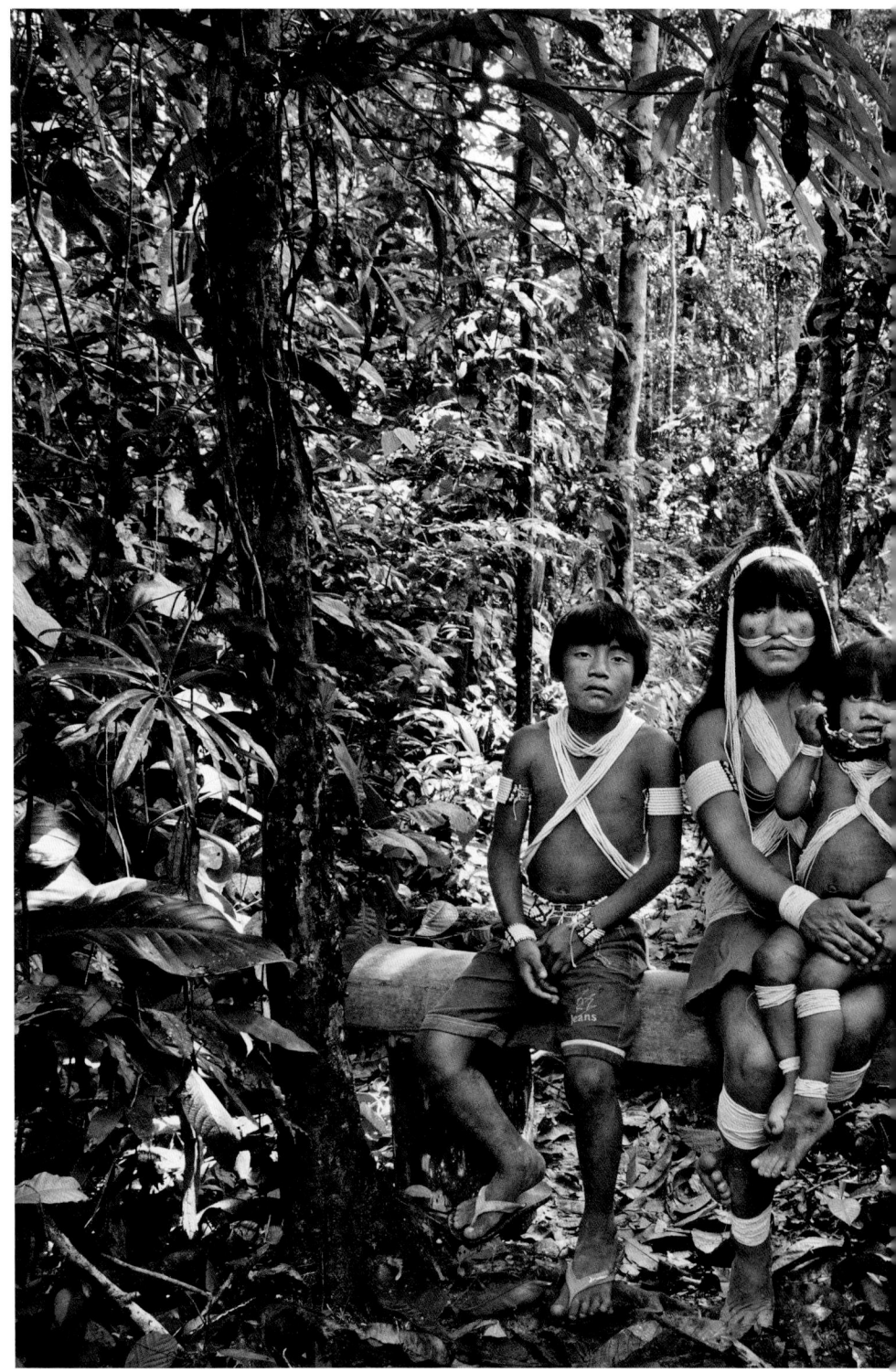

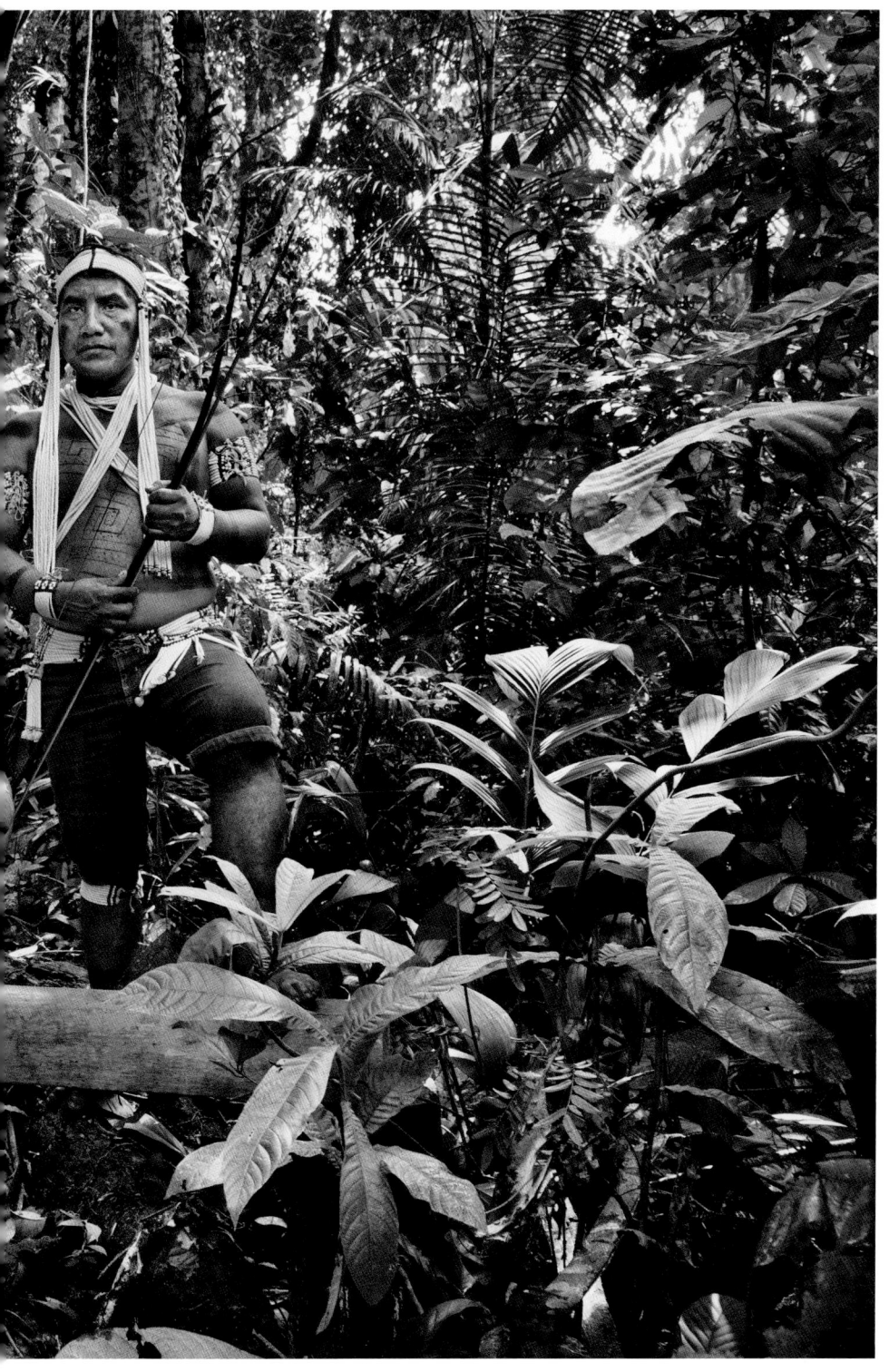

ANAVILHANAS

In the vastness of the Amazon rainforest, the region's age-old battle between land and water has spawned the world's largest freshwater archipelago, known as the Anavilhanas, with islands of every imaginable shape rising out of the dark waters of the Rio Negro. From the air, it is an astonishing sight, stretching as far as the eye can see. From the river, it is an immense puzzle, with only experienced boat pilots able to chart routes that guarantee a safe passage between the myriad natural obstacles.

Most of the larger islands are themselves thick with tropical vegetation, but if estimates of the number of islands range between 350 and 400, it is also because smaller low-lying islands may temporarily or even permanently disappear when the rainy season lifts the river's water level by over 20 meters (65 feet). Thus, from year to year, satellite photographs can record the constantly changing formation of the archipelago.

The Rio Negro, which is fed by rivers with their sources in the mountains of Colombia and Venezuela, is one of two that meet in the Amazonas state capital of Manaus to form the Amazon River. The other, the no-less-massive Solimões River, has its source in the Andes of Peru. Oddly, perhaps, Peruvians already describe this river as the Amazon, but when it reaches Brazil at the border town of Tabatinga, Brazilians rename it the Solimões River. But it is with this river that the Amazon's length is measured at 6,575 kilometers (4,225 miles).

These islands of the Rio Negro first appear about 80 kilometers (50 miles) northwest of Manaus and stretch in two major sections some 400 kilometers (250 miles) upstream as far as Barcelos, the first town founded by Portuguese colonizers traveling in sailboats in the mid-18th century. And it is the first section of some 135 kilometers (85 miles), where the river averages 20 kilometers (12 miles) in width and has islands occupying 60 percent of its surface, that is now protected as the National Park of Anavilhanas. Covering an area of 350,470 hectares (866,000 acres), the park is completely uninhabited except for the small town of Novo Airão on its west bank, 180 kilometers (112 miles) northwest of Manaus.

Beyond its dramatic archipelago, the Rio Negro is no less distinguished by its dark water, as its name suggests. The color is the result of the river's high humic acid content due to the failure of its sandy clearings to breakdown vegetation on its banks. Perhaps surprisingly, despite its high acidity, the Rio Negro is rich in fish species, with over 700 documented by scientists. It also boasts the river dolphin, popularly known as the pink dolphin, otters, and the Amazonian manatee, while jaguars, giant anteaters, and giant armadillos are found on the islands. Interestingly, when the Rio Negro meets the light brown Solimões River, in Manaus, the waters of the two rivers run side-by-side for over 6 kilometers (4 miles) before gradually merging.

Pages 480/481 Rain on the Anavilhanas Archipelago, the largest inland archipelago on the planet, comprising some four hundred islands spread over 400 kilometers (250 miles) of the Rio Negro, from the city of Barcelos to 80 kilometers (50 miles) from the city of Manaus, where the river flows into the Solimões to form the Amazon River. Anavilhanas National Park, state of Amazonas, 2009.

Pages 482/483 The Rio Negro's black water stands out against the green of the forest and the white clouds. The forests on these islands are *igapós*: for much of the year, floodwaters cover the ground and part of the tree trunks. Anavilhanas National Park, state of Amazonas, 2009.

Pages 484/485 Because the water levels can vary by some 20 meters (65 feet) from one season to another, Anavilhanas National Park is ever changing, as canals, sandbanks, and lakes appear in the dry season and some small islands vanish when the waters rise. Many of the larger islands, however, are freestanding stretches of rainforest. Anavilhanas National Park, state of Amazonas, 2009.

Pages 486/487 In the rainy season, the riverbanks on the islands are covered with water that sometimes even covers the treetops, a characteristic feature of *igapó* forests. In the dry season, the islands expand and the shores are covered with the white sand from the sea floor that characterized the region until around ten million years ago. Anavilhanas National Park, state of Amazonas, 2009.

Pages 488/489 The force of the floodwaters is influenced by the thawing of the Andes mountains in Colombia, where one of the sources of the Rio Negro is located. The river's flow shapes the islands into long forms that follow the direction of the water. Anavilhanas National Park, state of Amazonas, 2009.

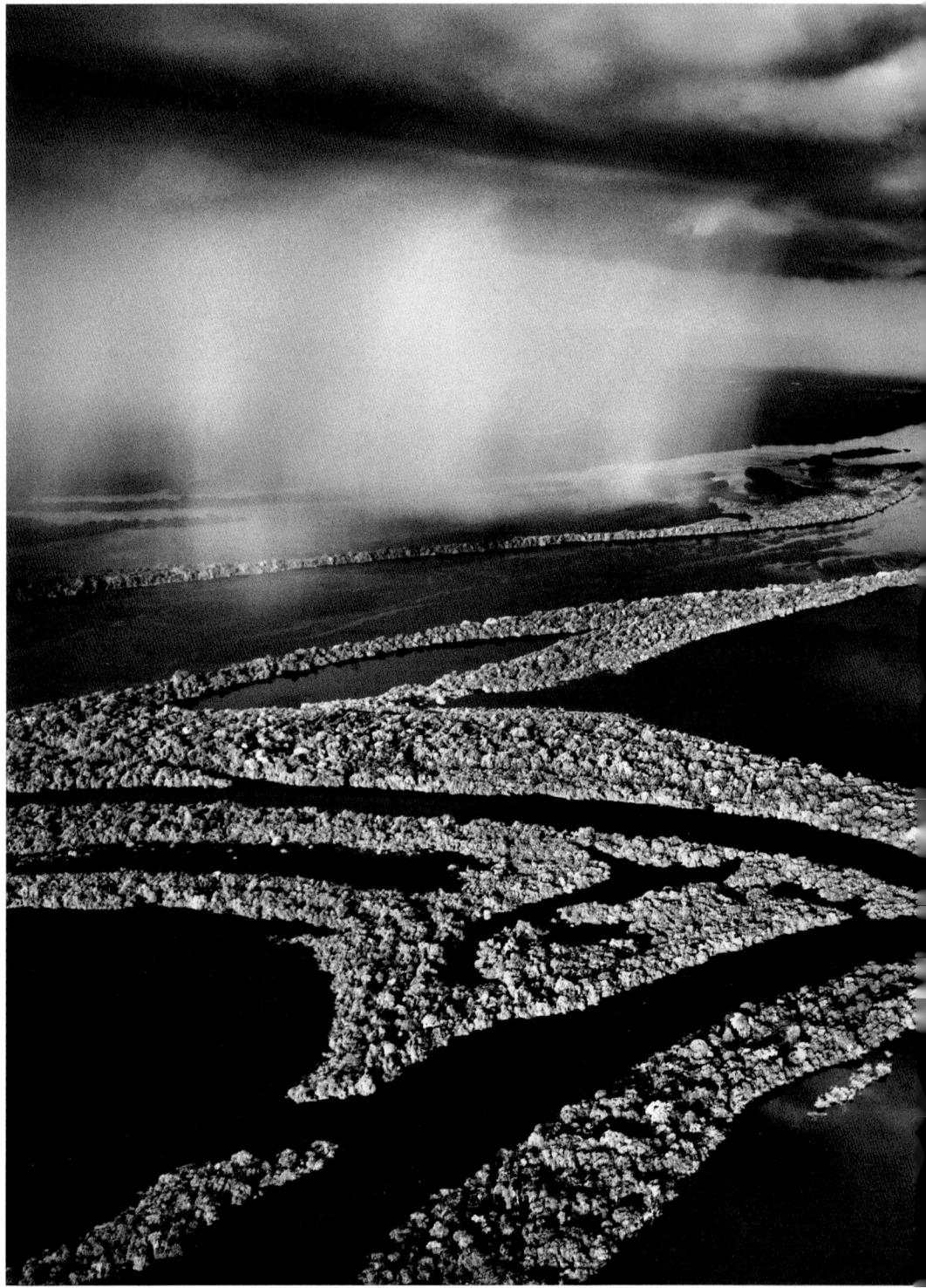

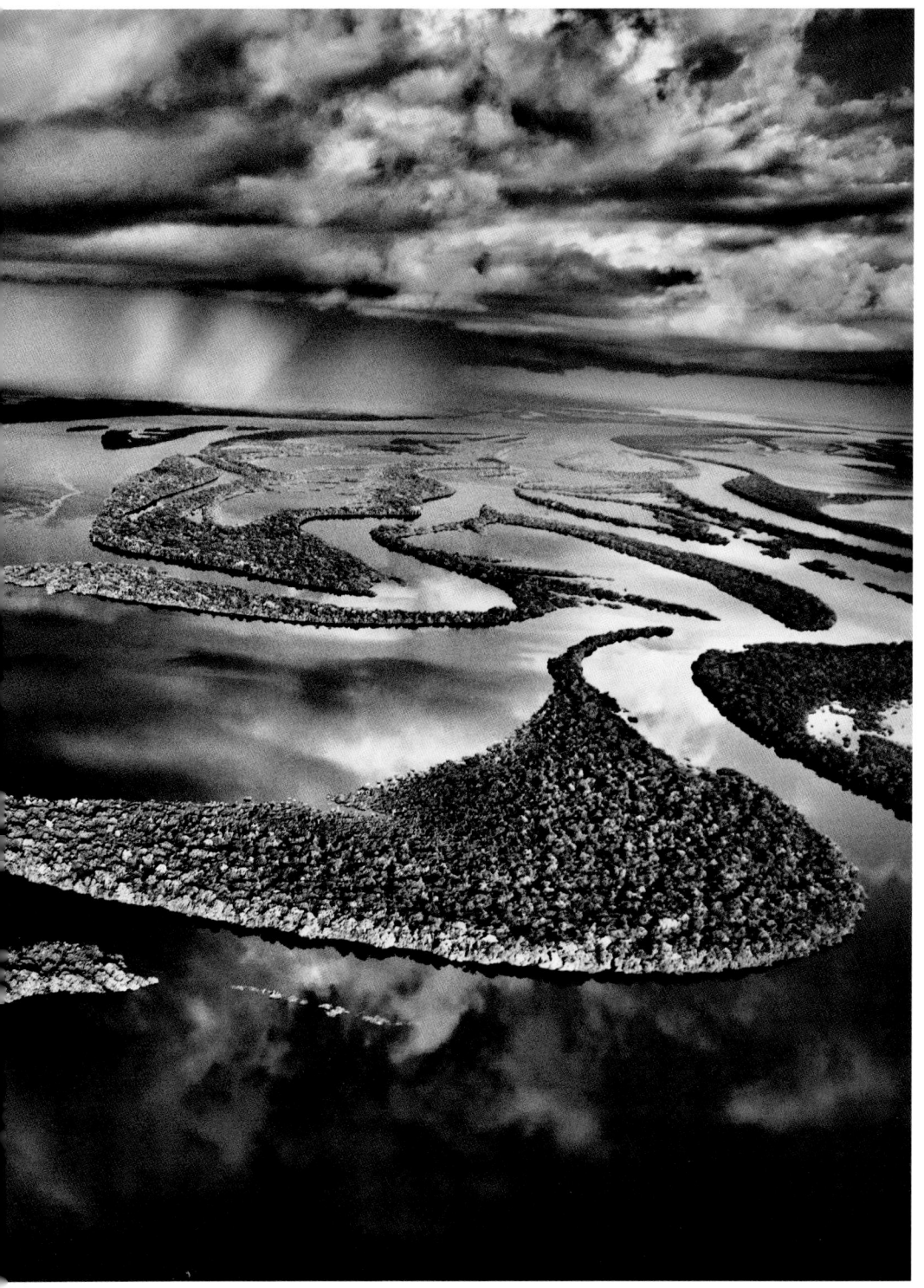

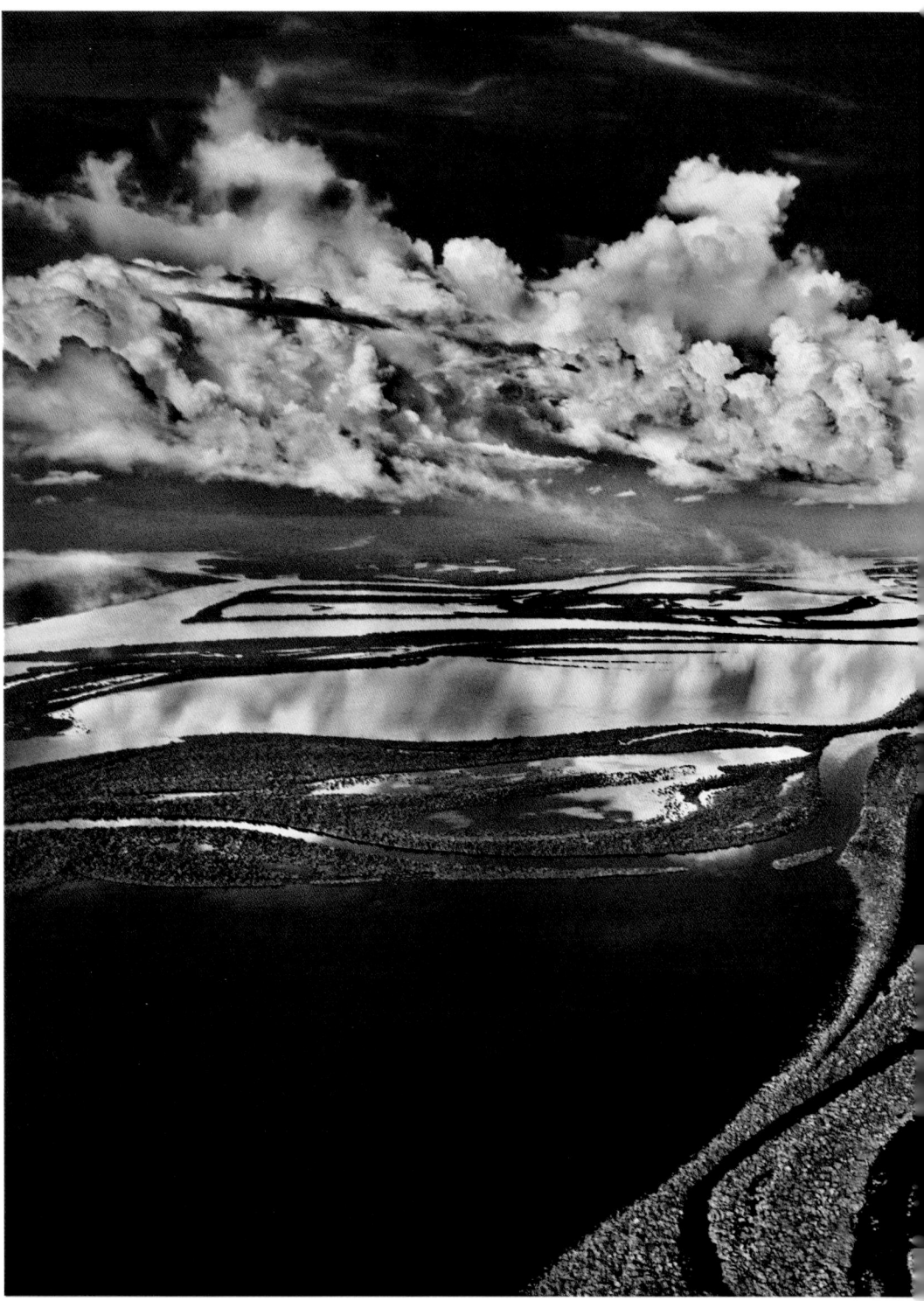

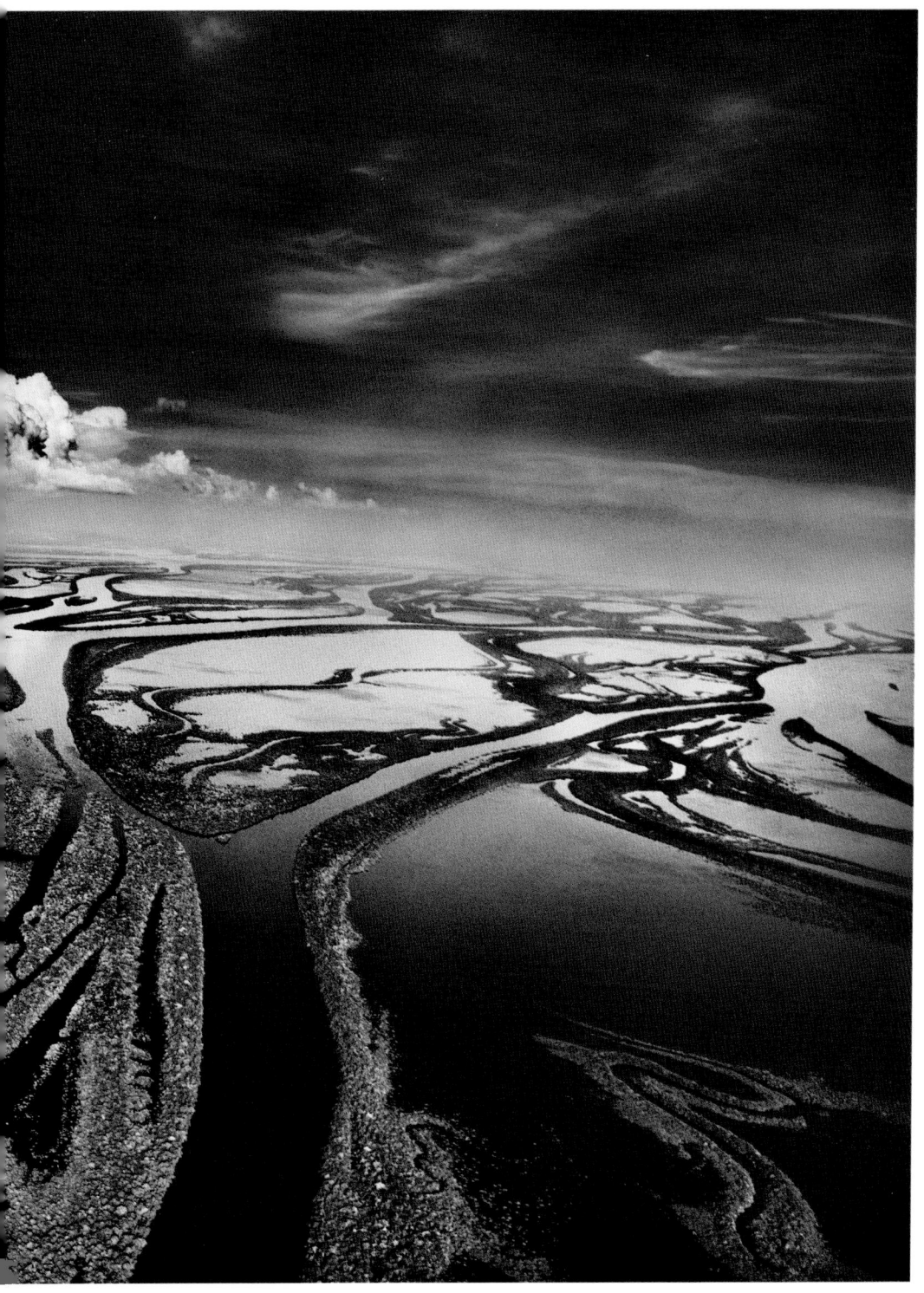

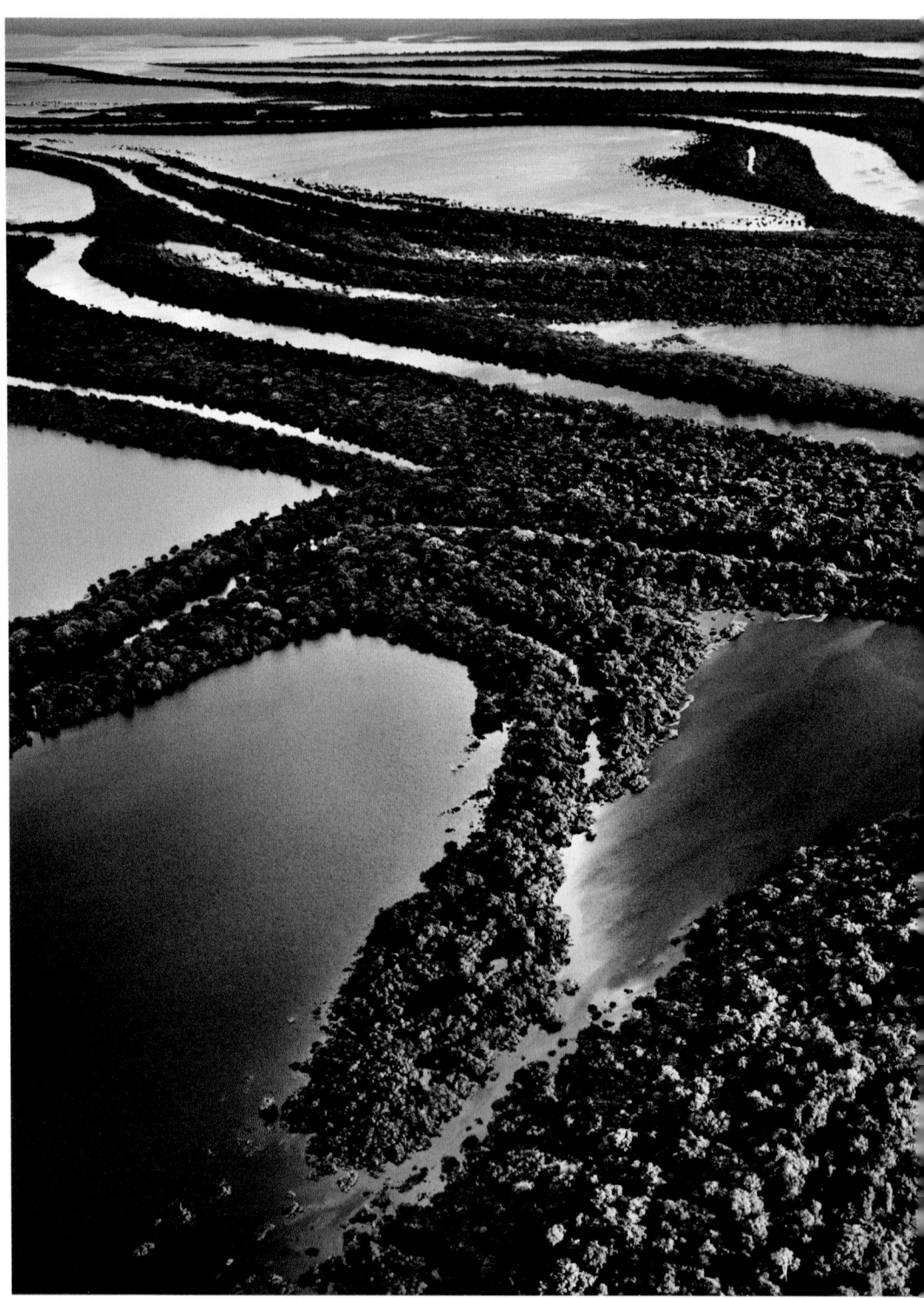

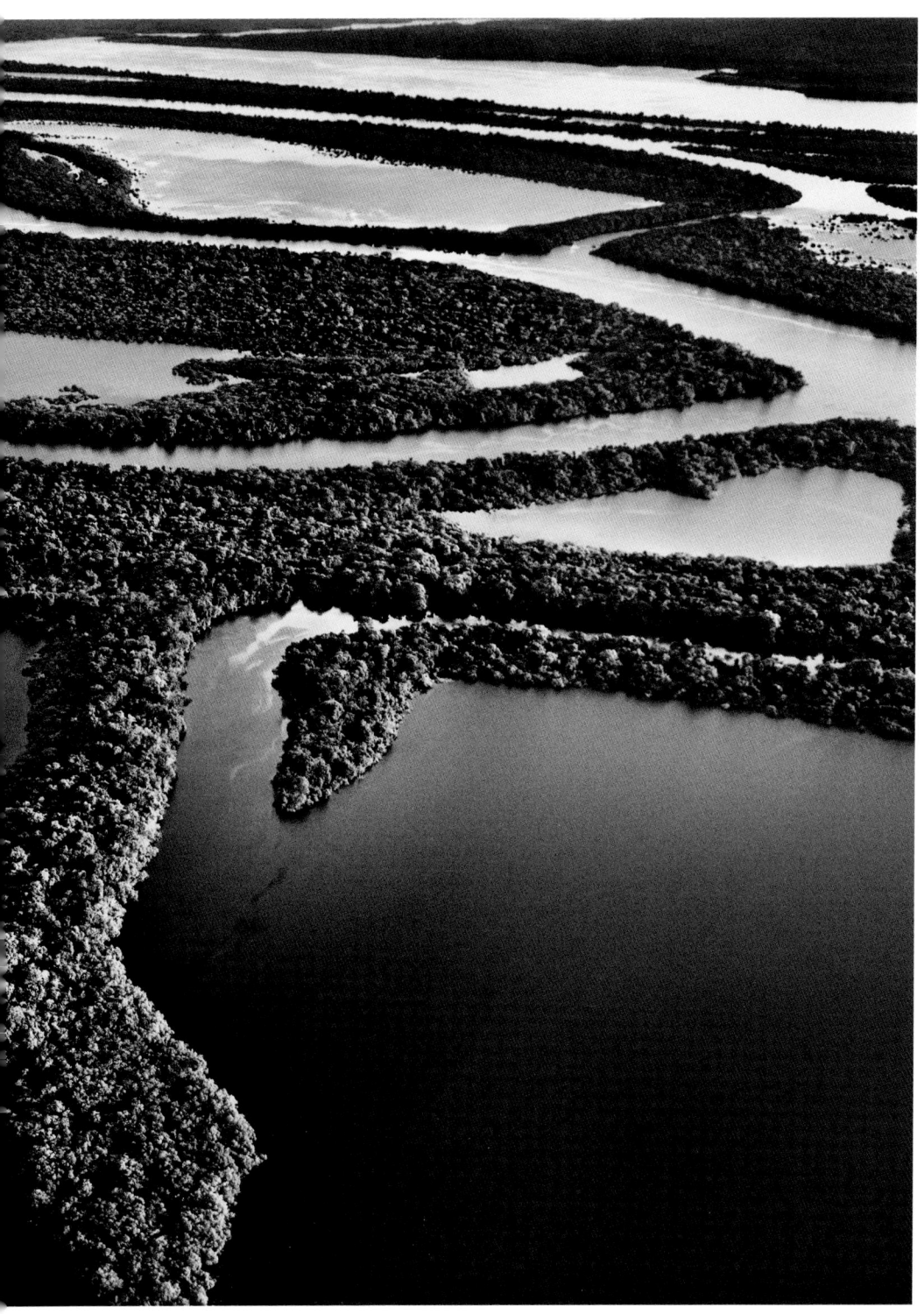

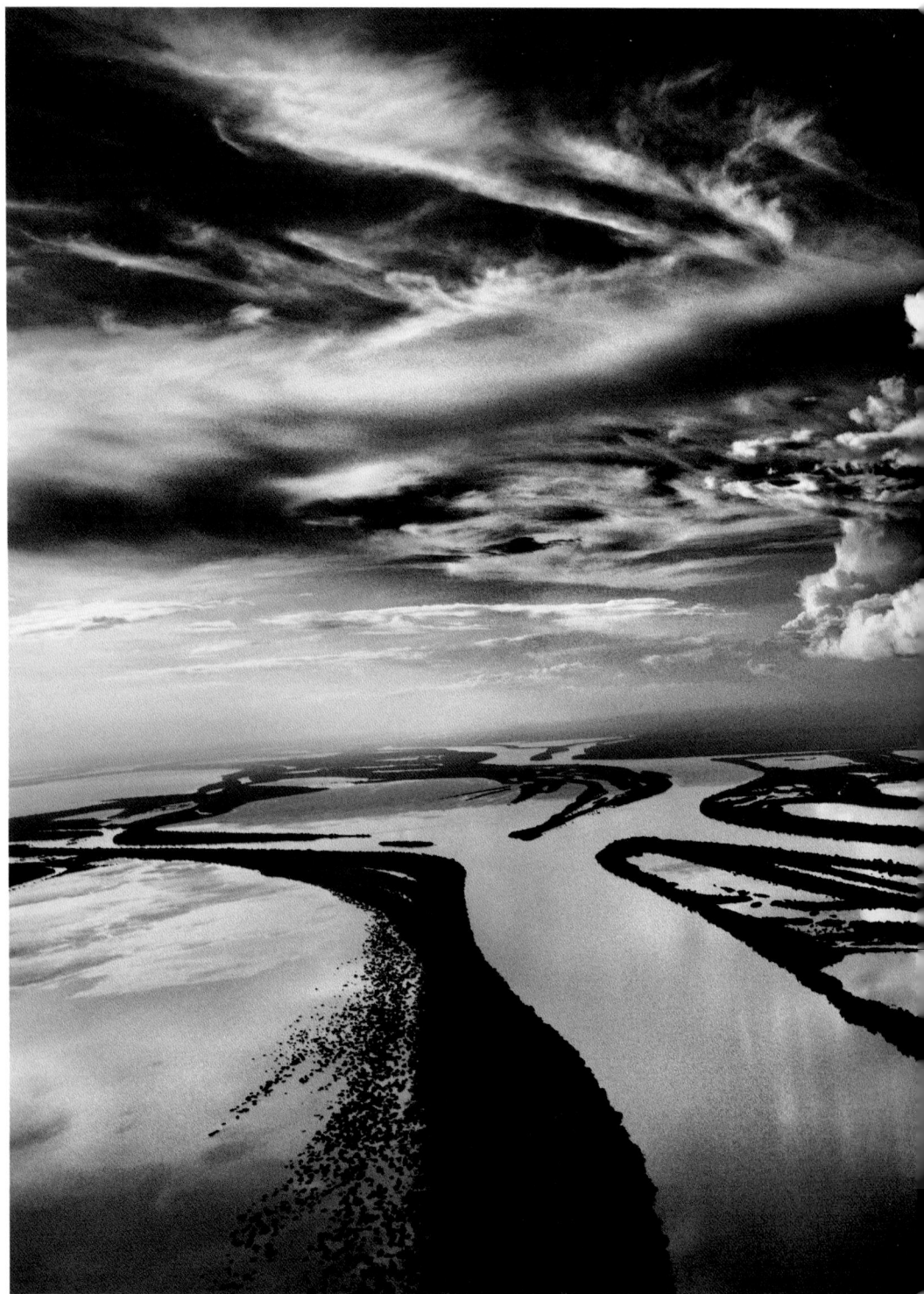

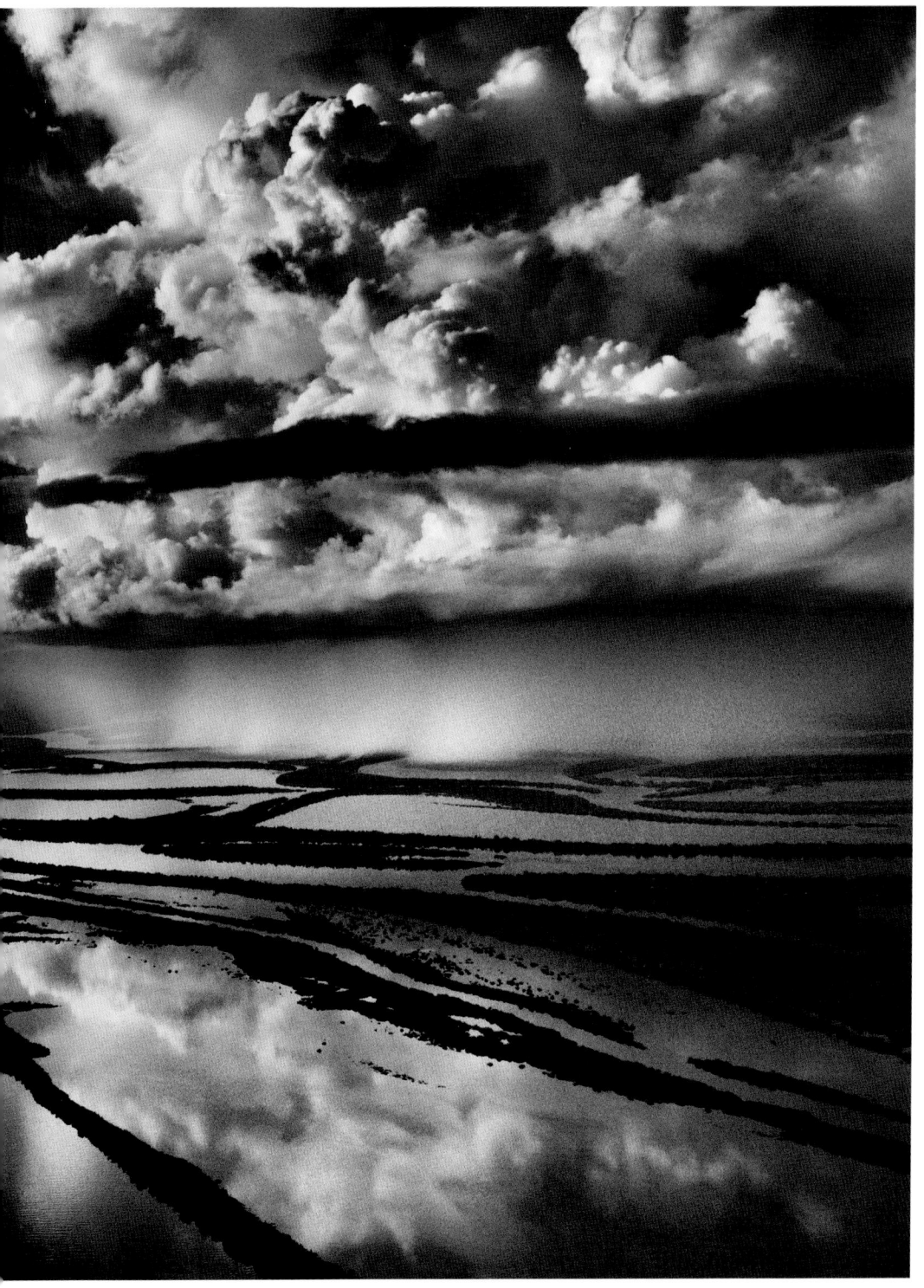

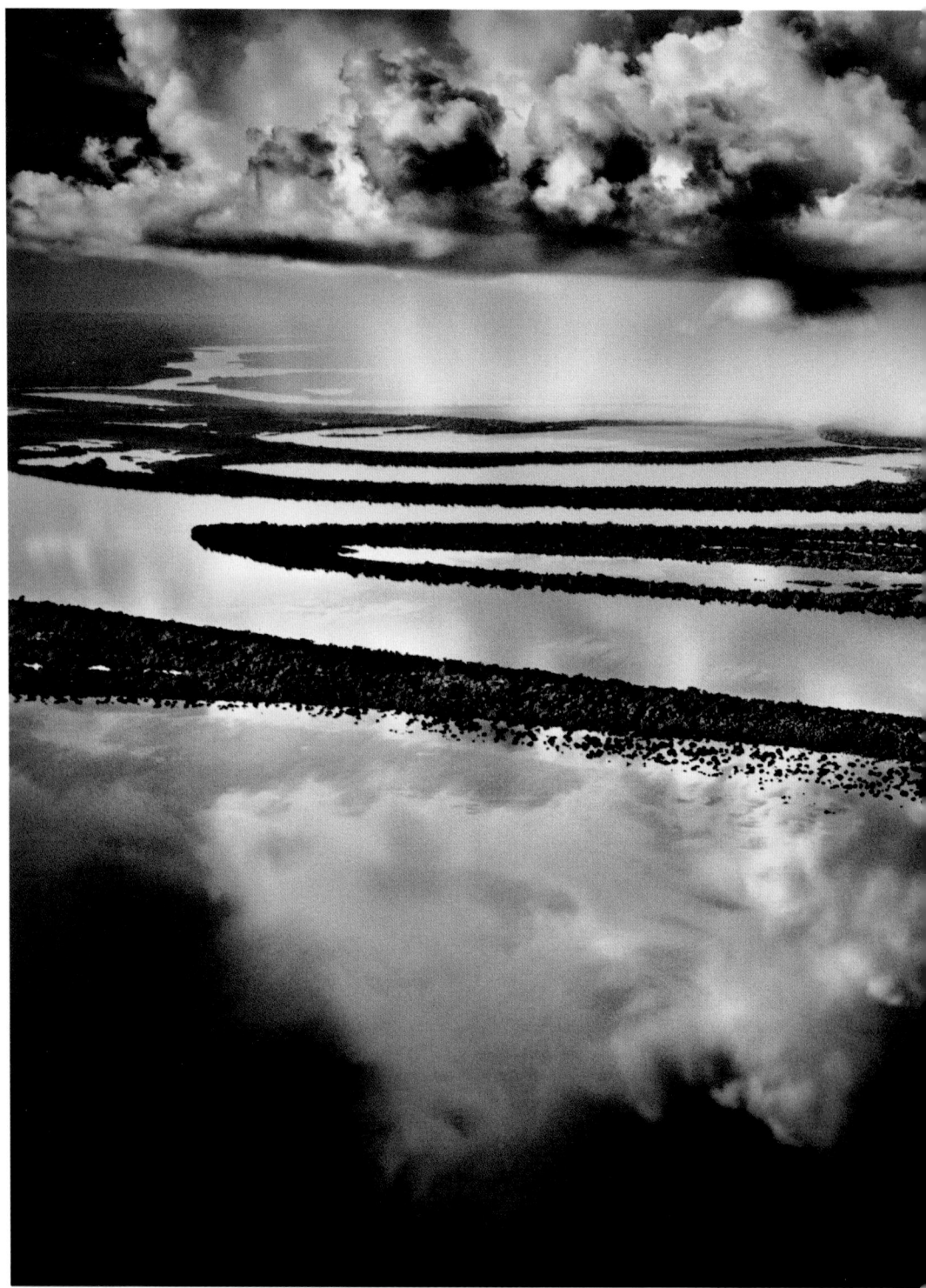

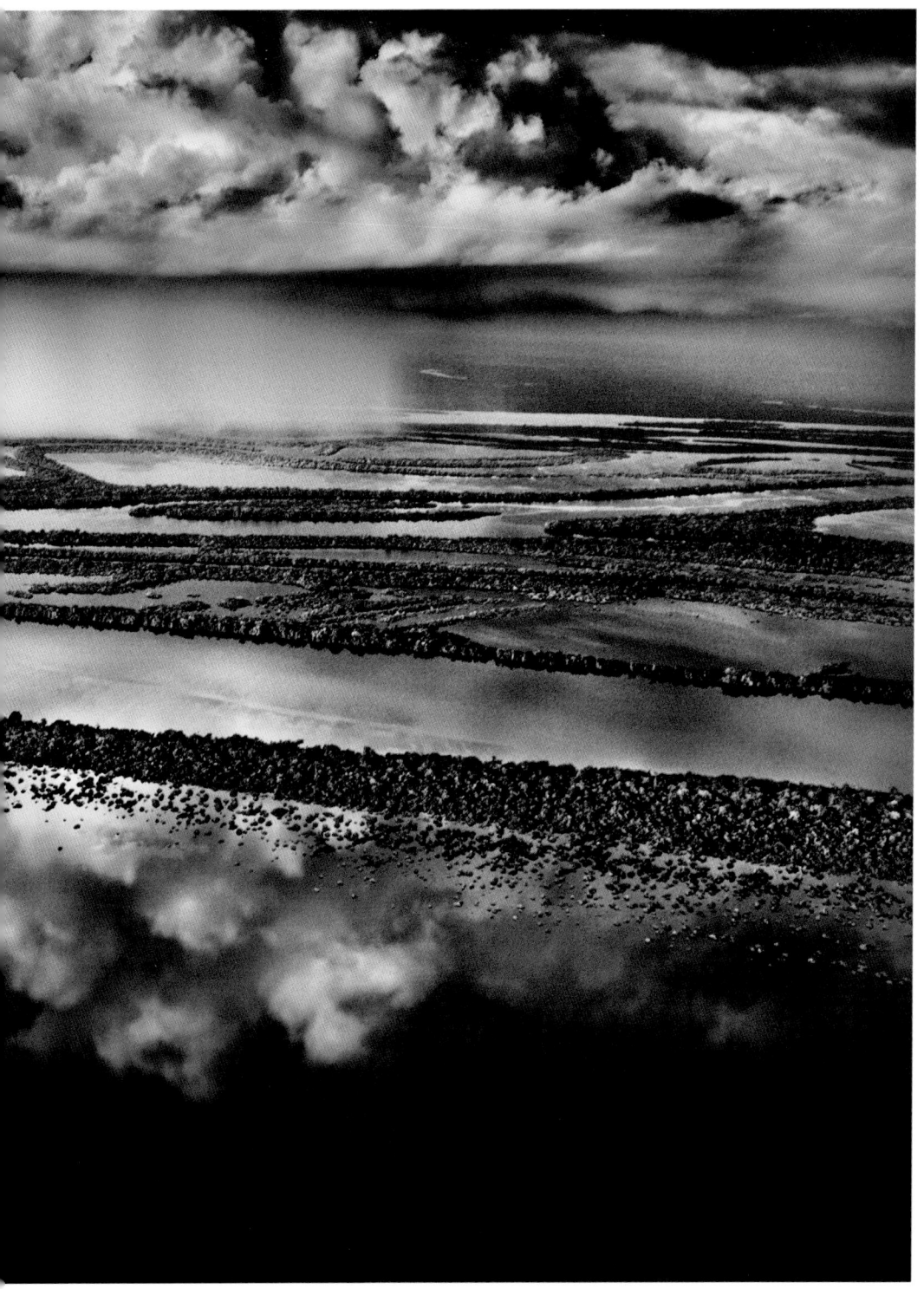

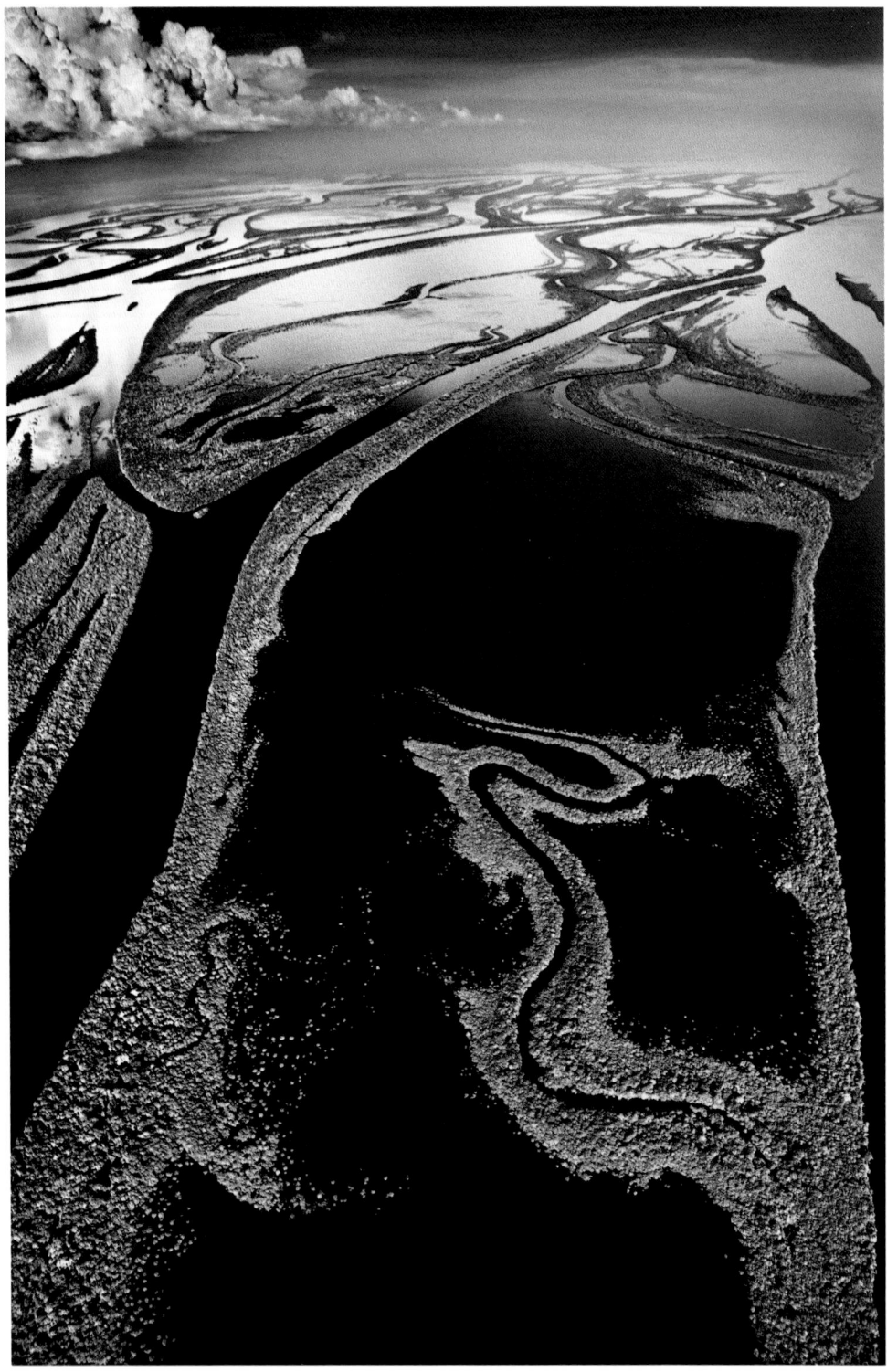

490

Opposite Because its origin and much of its course is in the Northern Hemisphere, the flooding of the Rio Negro follows a different pattern than most of the rivers in the Amazon basin, like all the tributaries on the right bank of the Amazon River. Anavilhanas National Park, state of Amazonas, 2009.

Pages 492/493 and 494/495 The black water of the Rio Negro glints white in sunlight and turns pitch black when not in direct sun. Anavilhanas National Park, state of Amazonas, 2009.

Pages 496/497 The force of the floodwaters is influenced by the thawing of the Andes mountains in Colombia, where one of the sources of the Rio Negro is located. The river's flow shapes the islands into long forms that follow the direction of the water. Anavilhanas National Park, state of Amazonas, 2009.

Pages 498/499 What looks like a lake is just a large backwater surrounded by islands that separate it from the main course of the Rio Negro. As the river's water level varies between winter and summer, whole islands can vanish in the floods and reappear during droughts or may even disappear forever as their sands are carried off to later attach to some other island. The contours of the islands can change frequently. The Anavilhanas are never quite the same in any two moments. Anavilhanas National Park, state of Amazonas, 2009.

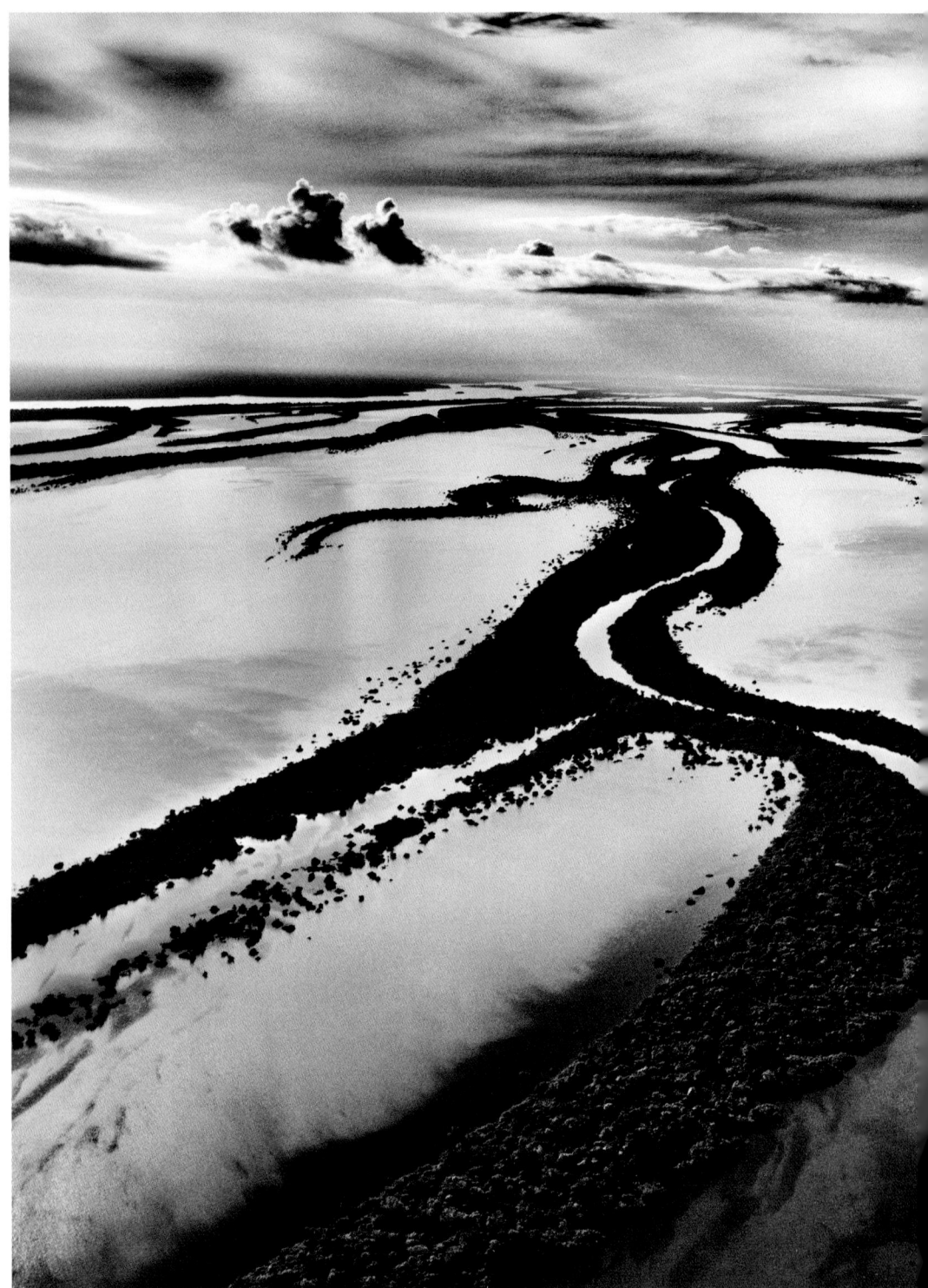

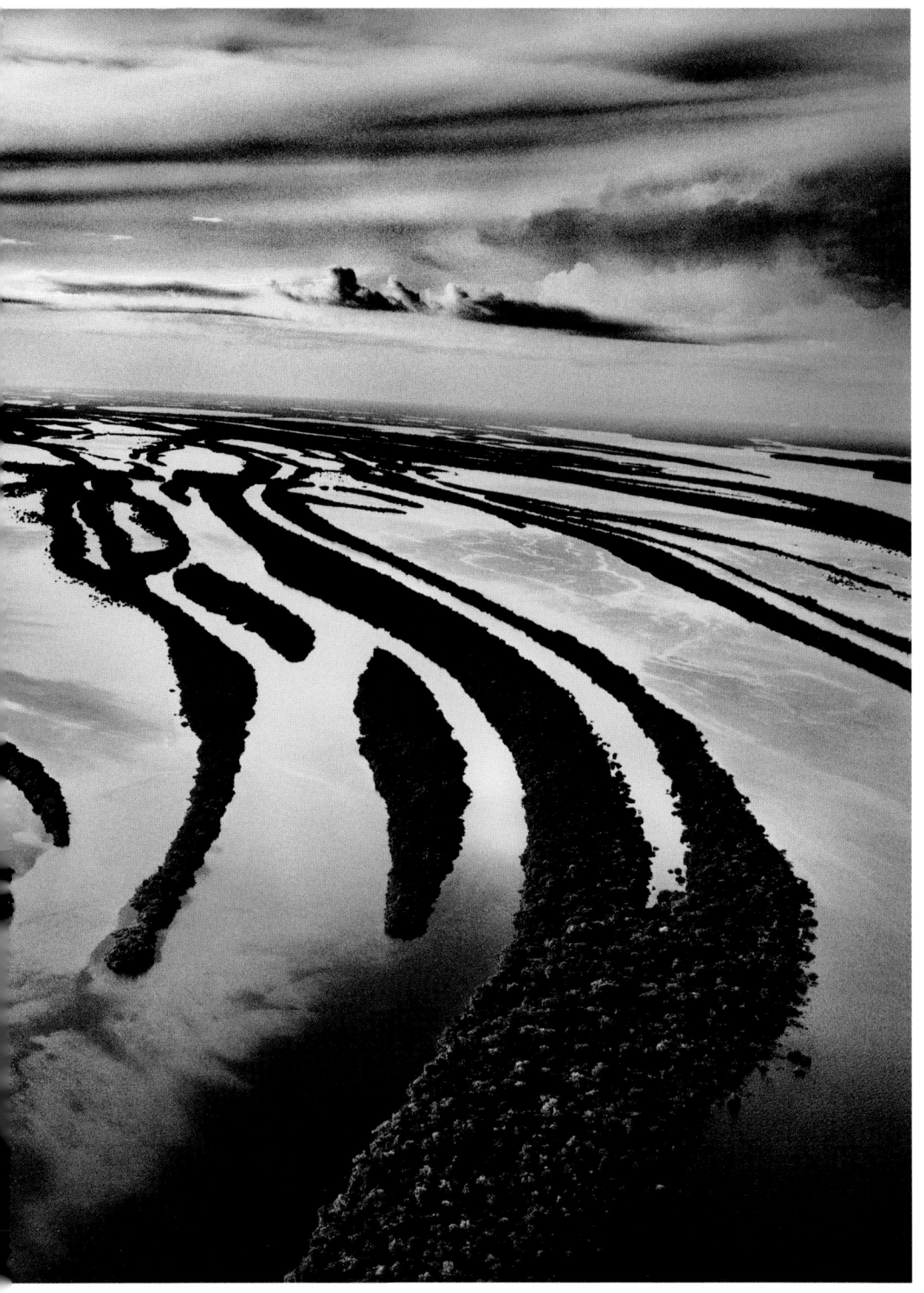

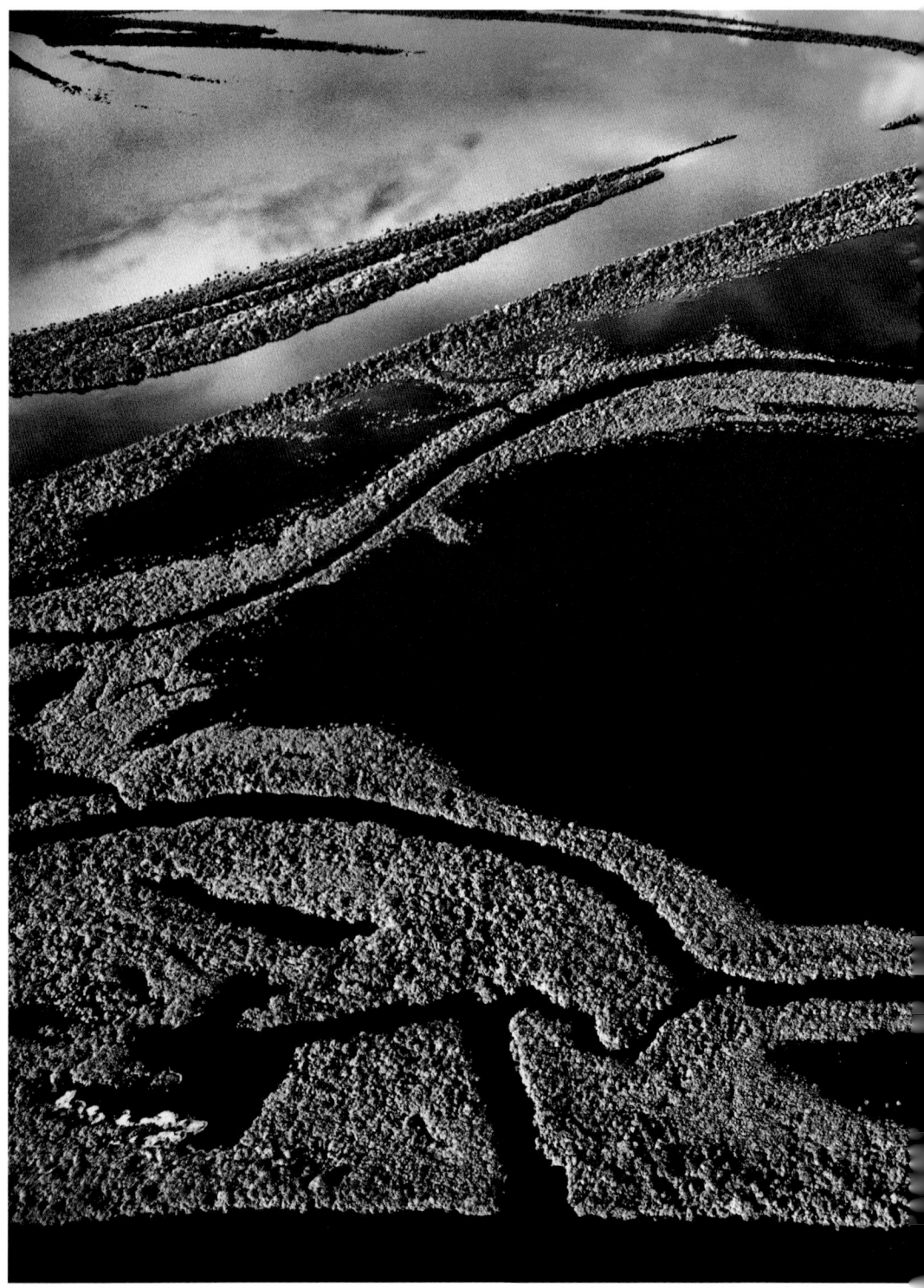

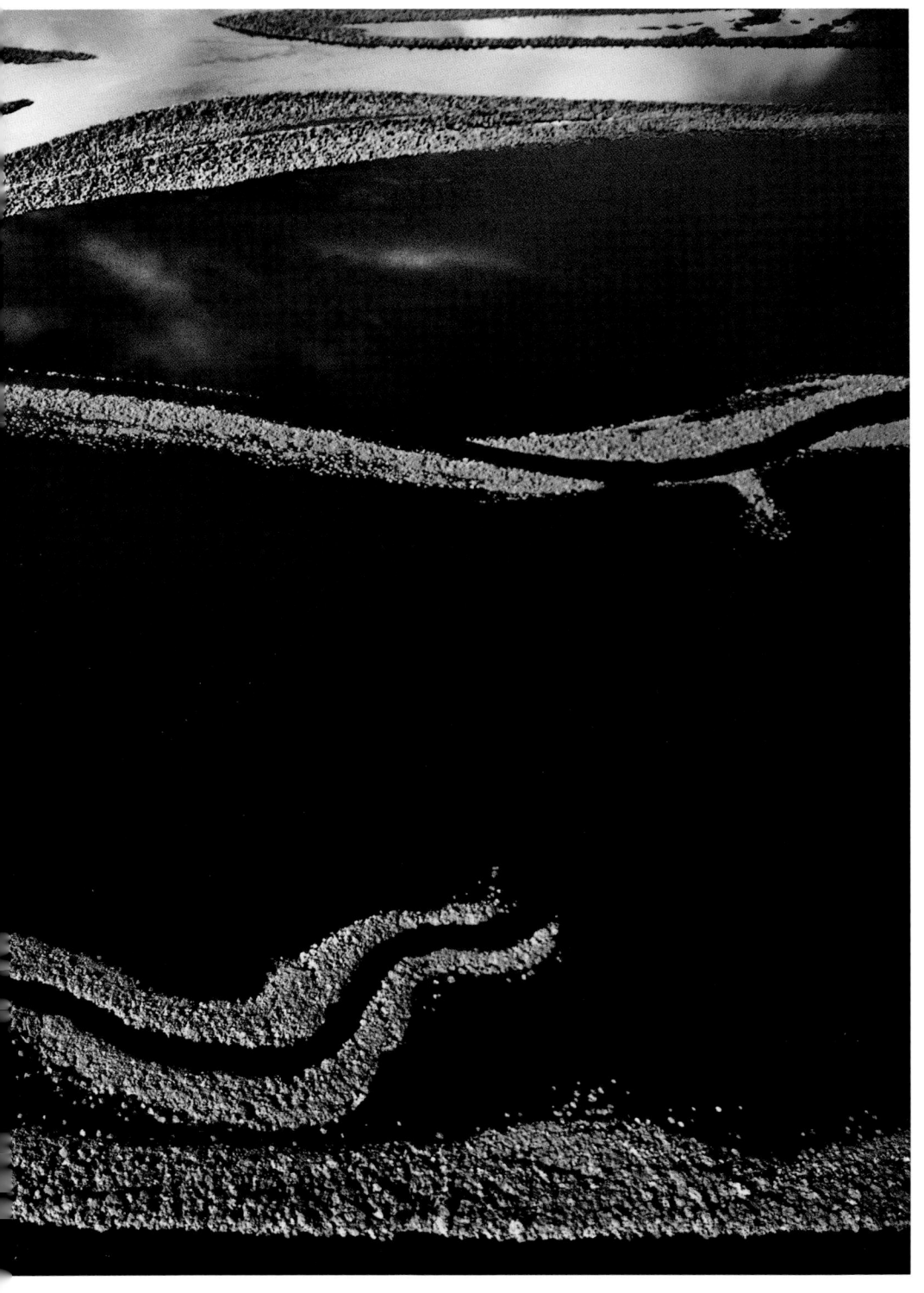

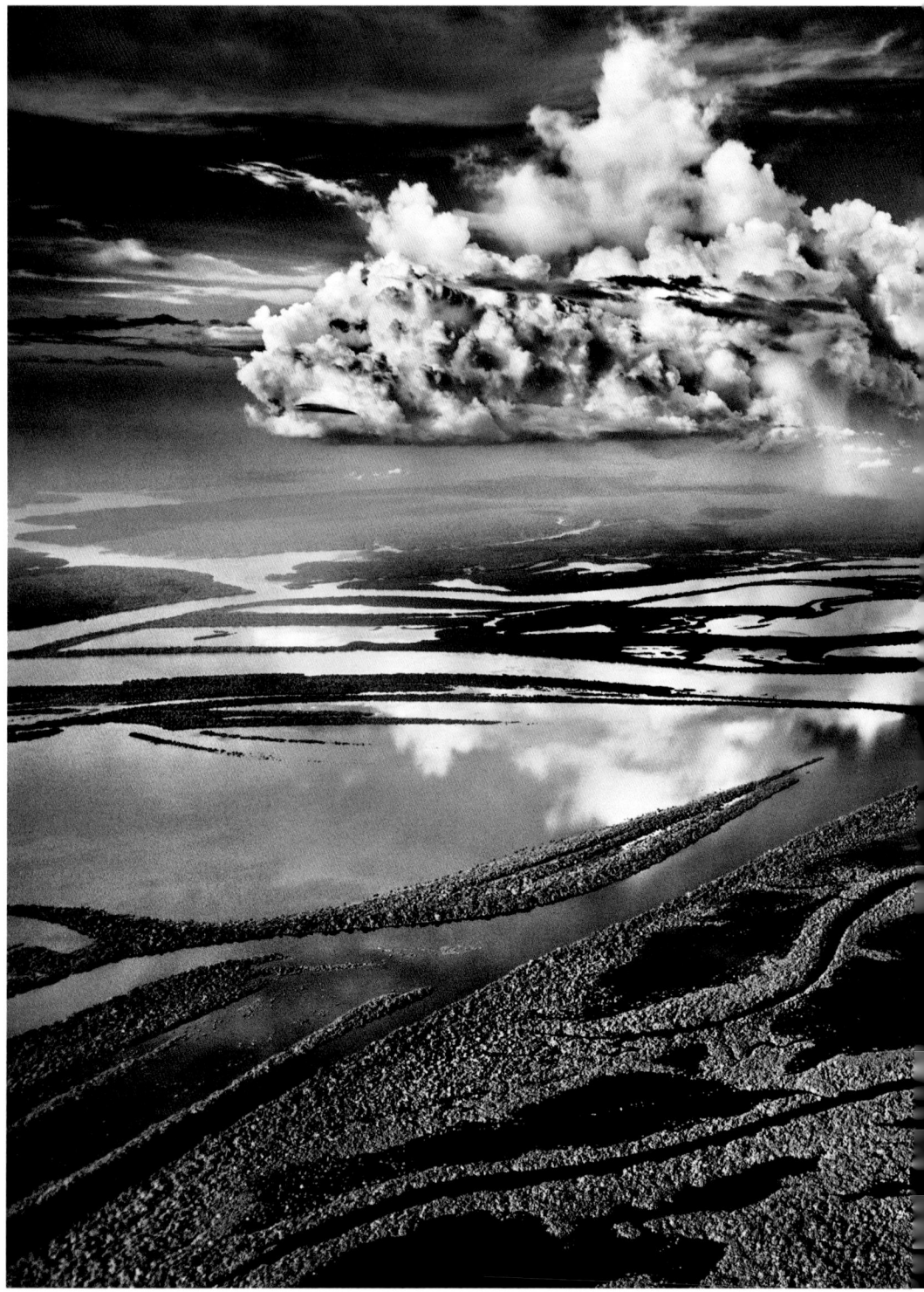

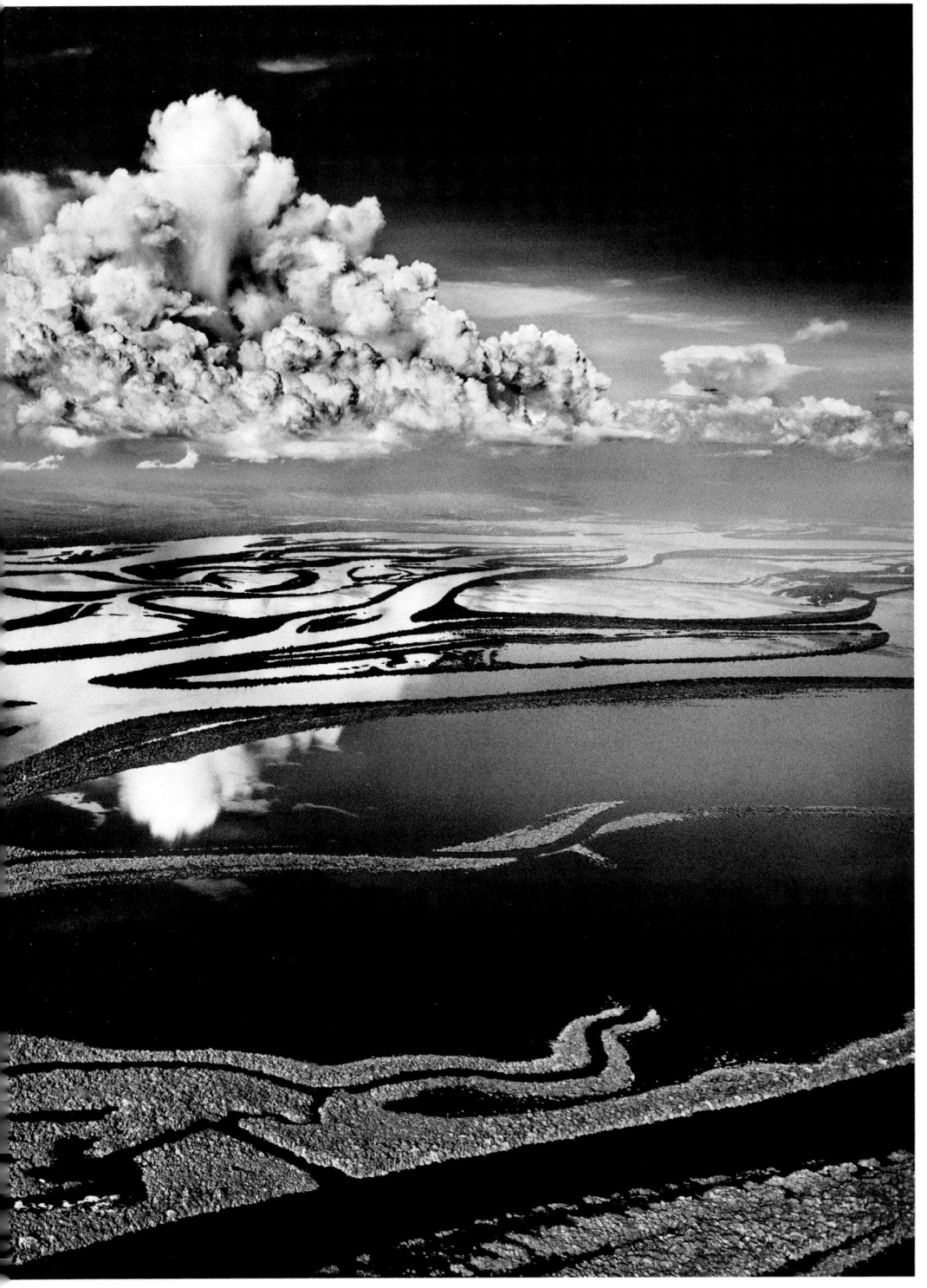

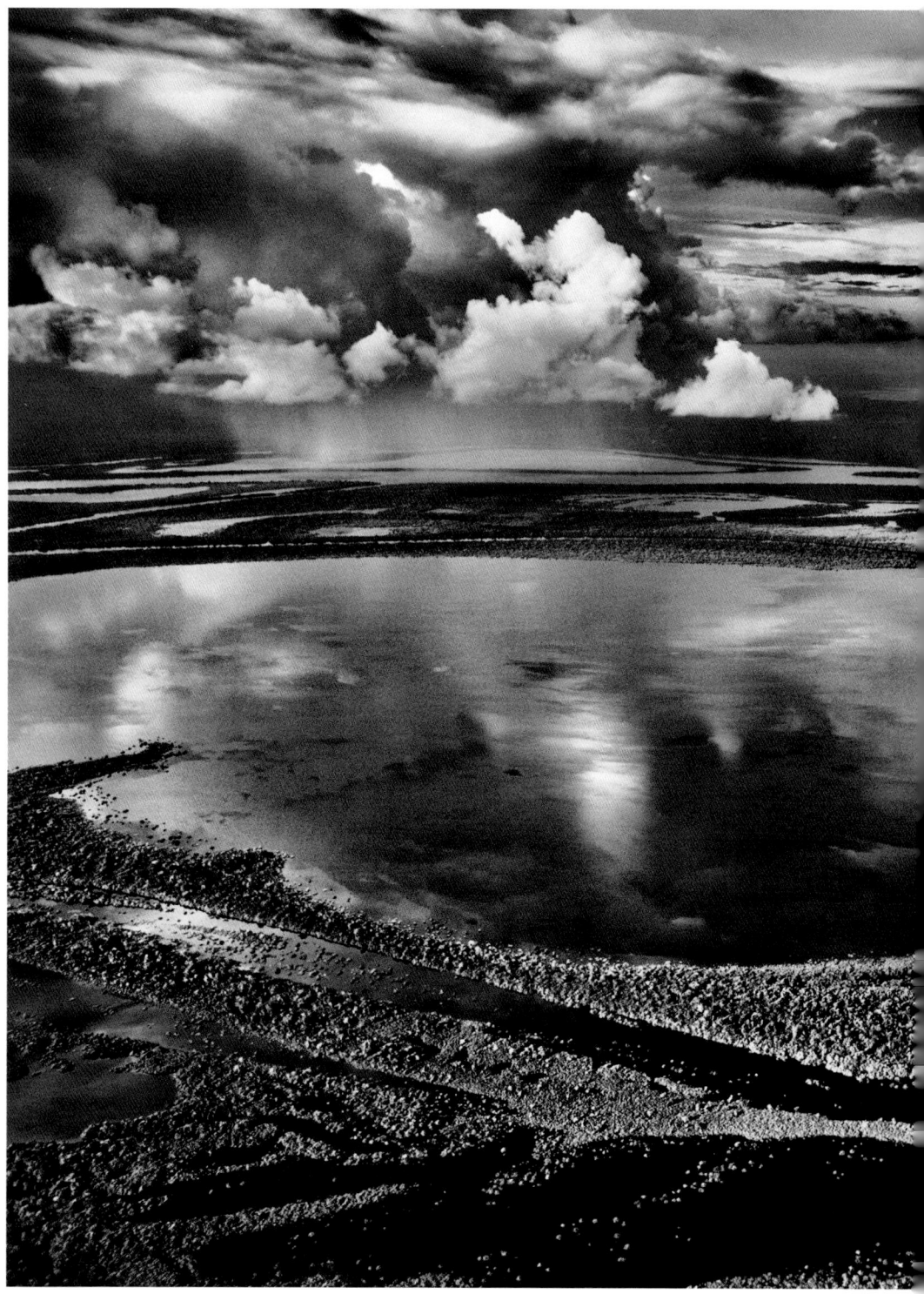

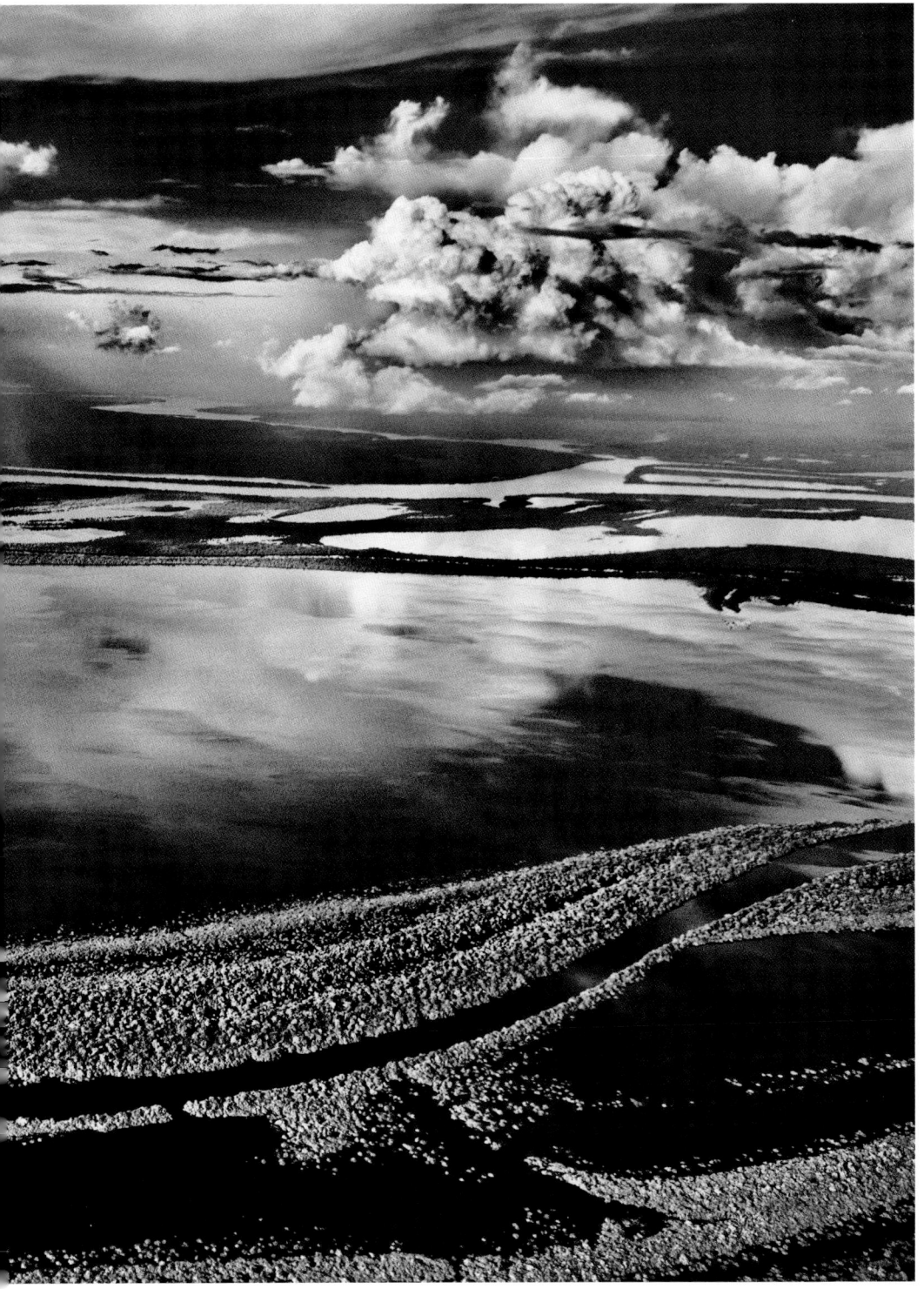

ACKNOWLEDGMENTS

Amazônia is a project that took six years, but in fact began much earlier. It also involved a score of lengthy trips to 12 indigenous tribes, many of them living in remote and hard-to-reach locations in the Amazon region. None of this would have been possible without the help of an extraordinary group of men and women, both in Brazil and in Paris, our home city for the past half century. In thanking them, we want them to know that this book also belongs to them.

For an investigation centered on the Amazon's indigenous peoples, the cooperation of Brazil's National Indian Foundation (FUNAI) was vital and was offered with great generosity at all levels of the institution, from those at its headquarters in Brasília to those researching or protecting native communities in the rainforest. We offer special thanks to successive FUNAI presidents: Márcio Augusto Meira, João Pedro Gonçalves, Marta Maria do Amaral Azevedo, Maria Augusta Assirati, and General Franklimberg Ribeiro de Freitas. Two directors of the institution's indigenous department, Clarisse do Carmo Jabur and Leila Sílvia Burger Sotto-Maior, were particularly helpful. In our contacts with FUNAI in the field, we also counted enormously on the guidance of Daniel Cangussu, Hércules Schiave, João Catalano, João Lobato, Bernardo Natividade Silva, and Leonardo Lenin Covezzi Val dos Santos.

For aerial photography, we were able to ride along with the crews of the helicopters of the Brazilian Army and the Brazilian Air Force as they crisscrossed this immense region. For this privilege we are particularly grateful to General Eduardo Villas-Bôas, former army commander; Army Generals Anísio David de Oliveira Júnior and Omar Zendin; Air Force Brigadiers Maurício Augusto Silveira de Medeiros and Francisco Joseli Parente; Army Colonel André Tavares da Silva; and Army Lieutenant-Colonels Alvaro de Paiva, Marcelo Bailone, and Luiz Claudio Talavera de Azeredo.

The trips also required us to tap the friendship, knowledge, and scientific expertise of a large group of Brazilians, each of whom contributed to the success of the project: Beto and Fany Ricardo of the Instituto Socioambiental, an environmental body, where Alana Almeida and Cícero Cardoso Augusto created important maps of the Amazon region for us; Dr. Ana Suelly Arruda Câmara Cabral, a linguist at the University of Brasília, accompanied us to the Zo'é tribe; Uirá Garcia advised us when we visited the Awá; Betty Mindlin, an anthropologist, and her son, Dr. Manu Mindlin Lafer, provided crucial contacts in the Upper Xingu; former Senator Jorge Viana and his partner, Dolores Nieto, offered us and our team their home and hospitality in Brasília, where his driver João Salustiano de Souza Júnior was always ready to help, and in Rio Branco in the state of Acre, where Jorge's assistant, Gildo César, was generous with his time; and Jorge's brother, Tião Viana, a doctor and former governor of Acre, gave us his unreserved support. Among valued anthropologists with whom we also collaborated were Estevão Senra for the Yanomami and Eliane Fernandes Ferreira for the Asháninka.

Our visits to ethnic communities required complex preparation and execution, and for these we received untiring help from Carlos Lisboa Travassos, former head of FUNAI's Department of Isolated and Recently Contacted Indigenous Tribes, who accompanied us on many trips as an independent consultant and was central to maintaining good relations with native communities; Beto Marubo, a talented young indigenous leader, who smoothed our relations with his own Marubo tribe and with the Korubo, and also set up our contacts along the Valley of Javarí; Agostinho de Carvalho, known in Brazil as a "jungle captain," who went everywhere with us, his talents stretching from hunting and fishing to singing and playing the guitar; and Francisco da Silva Lima, another "jungle captain," better known as Bebé, who must be one of the best fishermen in the Amazon.

Among other Brazilians who generously shared their contacts and knowledge of indigenous peoples were José Carlos Meirelles and Sydney Possuelo, explorers, social activists, and ethnographers, whose careers passed through FUNAI; Izabella Teixeira, a dear friend and former Environment Minister whose advice and support proved invaluable; Carlos Fausto, an anthropologist who was a vital contact with the Kuikuro in the Upper Xingu; Guilherme Quintella, a businessman who was happy to share his address book with us; Cássio Vasconcellos, a fellow photographer who helped to organize our flights over the Amazon; Leão Serva, a fine journalist who accompanied us and reported on many of our trips; Juliano Ribeiro Salgado, who produced eight video interviews with key tribal leaders; Daniel Kfouri, who was the cameraman for several trips; and Paulo Wanick, who was very helpful in the organization of our trips. Other journalists joined us, Arnaldo Bloch to the Yanomami and Miriam Leitão to the Awá, while Francisco de Mello helped to plan the trips to the Asháninka, Yawanawá, and Marubo from his base in Cruzeiro do Sul in Acre.

Our long-term photographic projects have all been made possible by the support of key colleagues in Paris. Jacques Barthélemy, an experienced mountain guide, has accompanied us on difficult expeditions for many years. In our Paris studio, where everyone has multiple roles, Françoise Piffard manages editing and translating texts as well as relations with museums; Márcia Mariano is a whiz with computers, supervises our archives, and oversees all the production processes; and Olivier Jamin is the skilled technician who works on and prepares the files and prints the digital images of photographs. We also count on outside assistance from Gérard Lamarche and Gilles Vaudois, who provide graphic design assistance; Dominique Granier, who produces all silver prints; Eveline Poulain-Waucampt and Yves Waucampt, who helped to create the audiovisual presentation accompanying our exhibition; Marica and Radmilo Ristic, Paris tailors who prepare the cloth used for "studio" backdrops in the forest; Álvaro Razuk for his precious advice, and André Romão, who with unfailing efficiency made all our hotel bookings and organized all our international and domestic flights.

We are grateful to Canon France for lending me cameras and swiftly repairing them when necessary, mainly to Guy Dassonville, Alain Tombois, Eric Deschamps, Raphaël Rimoux, and Jacques Navarre. And also with special recognition to Issei Morimoto, Emmanuel Stock, and Luca Rocco who played a central role in facilitating all our dealings with Canon Europe. Finally, our thanks to two old friends who have supported us in this and earlier ventures, Alain Genestar, former editor-in-chief at *Paris Match* and founder and director of *Polka Magazine*, and Alan Riding, former bureau chief of *The New York Times* in Mexico, Brazil, and France.

Sebastião Salgado and Lélia Wanick Salgado
Paris, 2021

BRAZIL

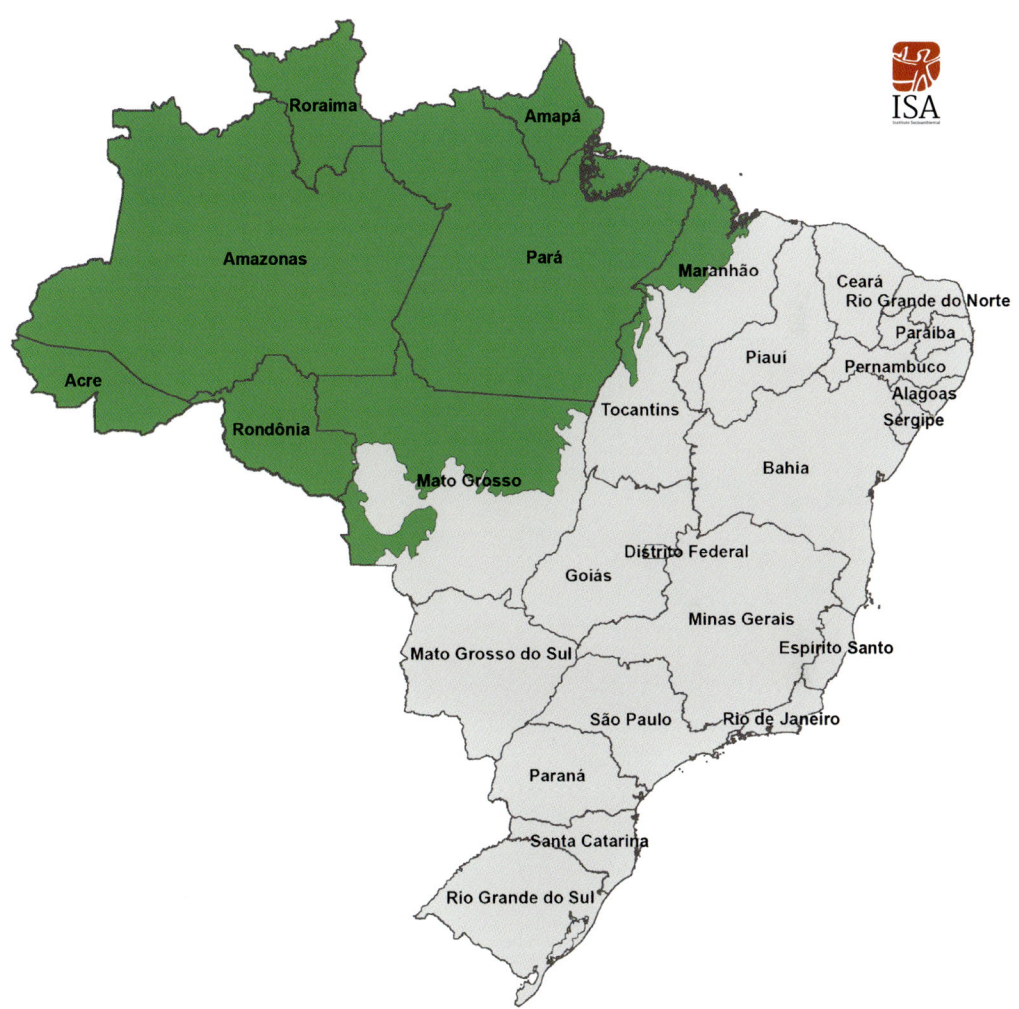

Roraima

Amapá

Amazonas

Pará

Maranhão

Ceará
Rio Grande do Norte

Paraíba

Piauí

Pernambuco

Alagoas

Sergipe

Acre

Tocantins

Rondônia

Bahia

Mato Grosso

Distrito Federal

Goiás

Minas Gerais

Espírito Santo

Mato Grosso do Sul

São Paulo

Rio de Janeiro

Paraná

Santa Catarina

Rio Grande do Sul

THE BRAZILIAN STATES AND THE AMAZONIAN BIOME

Total Surface Area – 8,514,877 km²

Amazonian Biome – 4,196,943 km² – 49.29% of Brazil

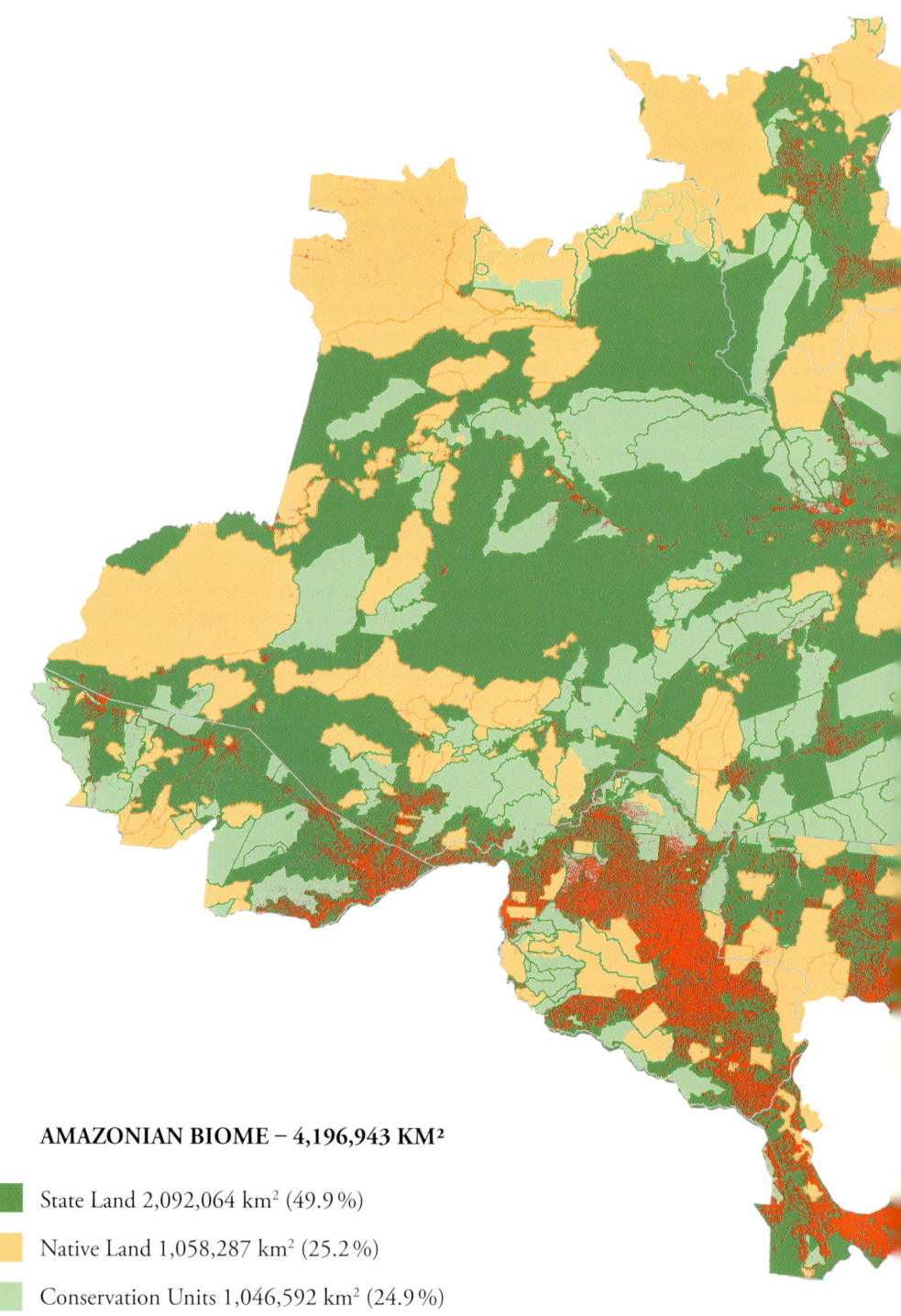

AMAZONIAN BIOME – 4,196,943 KM²

State Land 2,092,064 km² (49.9%)

Native Land 1,058,287 km² (25.2%)

Conservation Units 1,046,592 km² (24.9%)

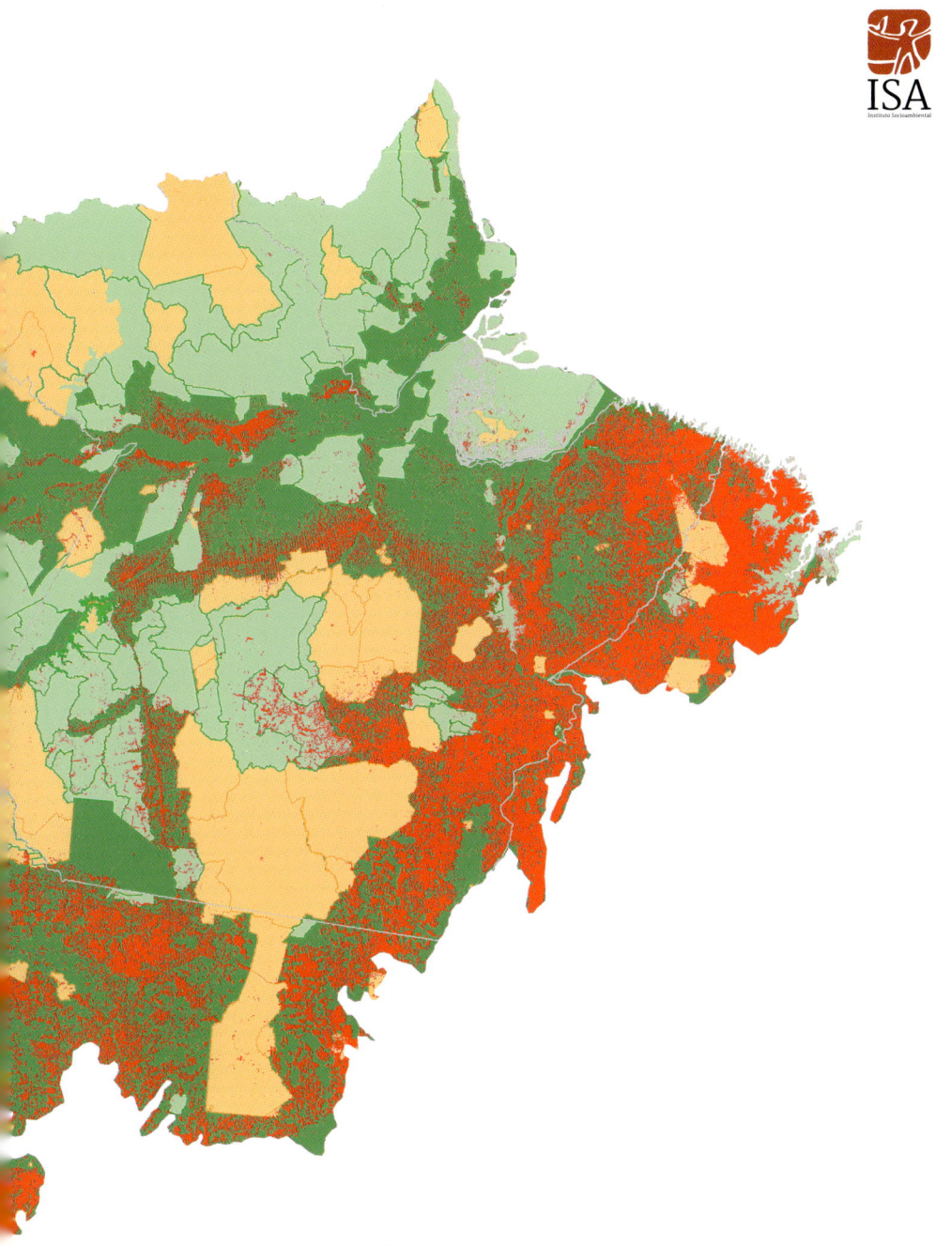

Cumulative deforestation 1988–2019 – 724,104 km²
Approximately 17.25 % of the Amazonian forest is destroyed.

INDIGENOUS TERRITORIES PHOTOGRAPHED

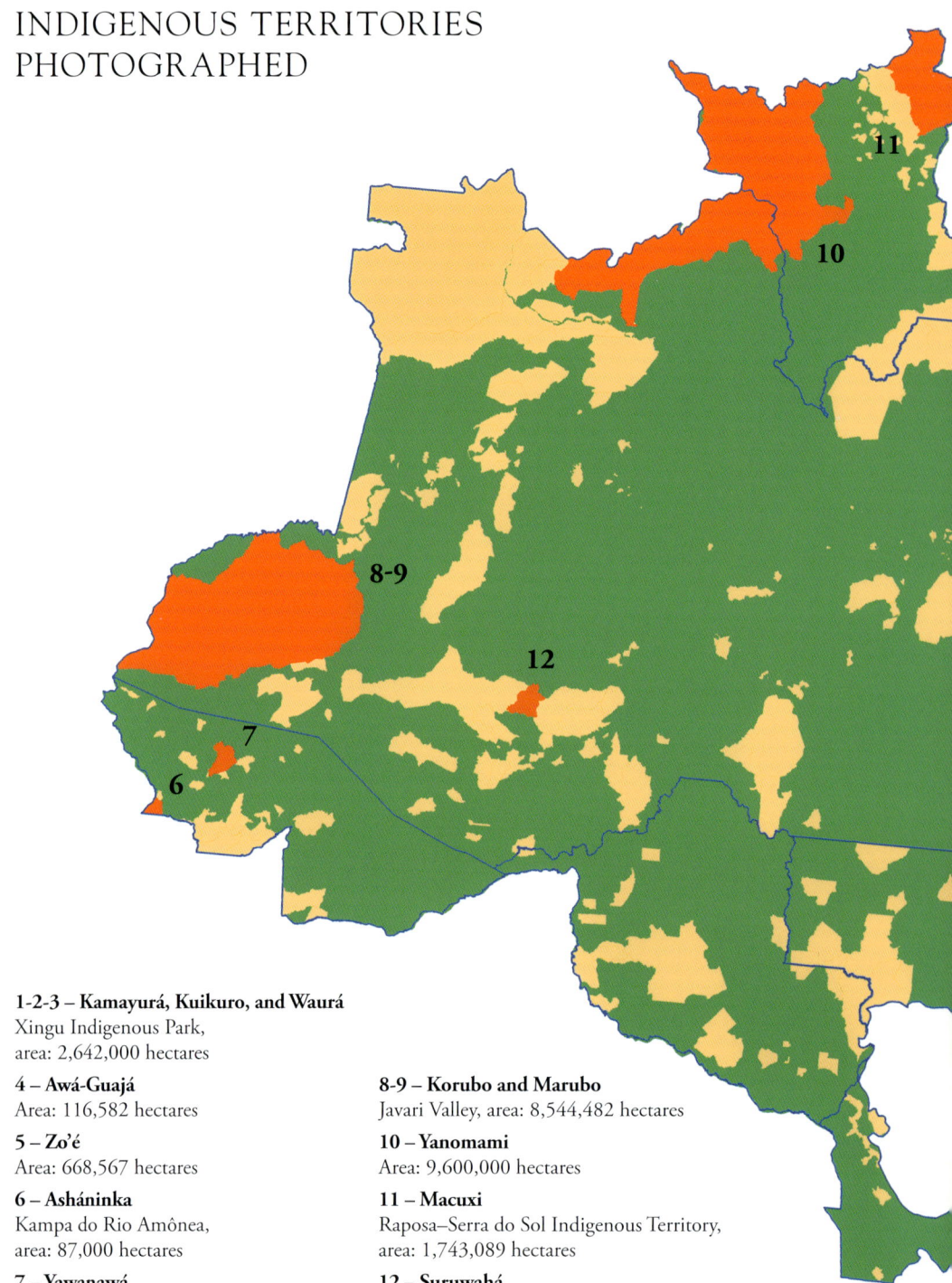

1-2-3 – Kamayurá, Kuikuro, and Waurá
Xingu Indigenous Park,
area: 2,642,000 hectares

4 – Awá-Guajá
Area: 116,582 hectares

5 – Zo'é
Area: 668,567 hectares

6 – Asháninka
Kampa do Rio Amônea,
area: 87,000 hectares

7 – Yawanawá
Rio Gregório, area: 187,000 hectares

8-9 – Korubo and Marubo
Javari Valley, area: 8,544,482 hectares

10 – Yanomami
Area: 9,600,000 hectares

11 – Macuxi
Raposa–Serra do Sol Indigenous Territory,
area: 1,743,089 hectares

12 – Suruwahá
Area: 239,000 hectares

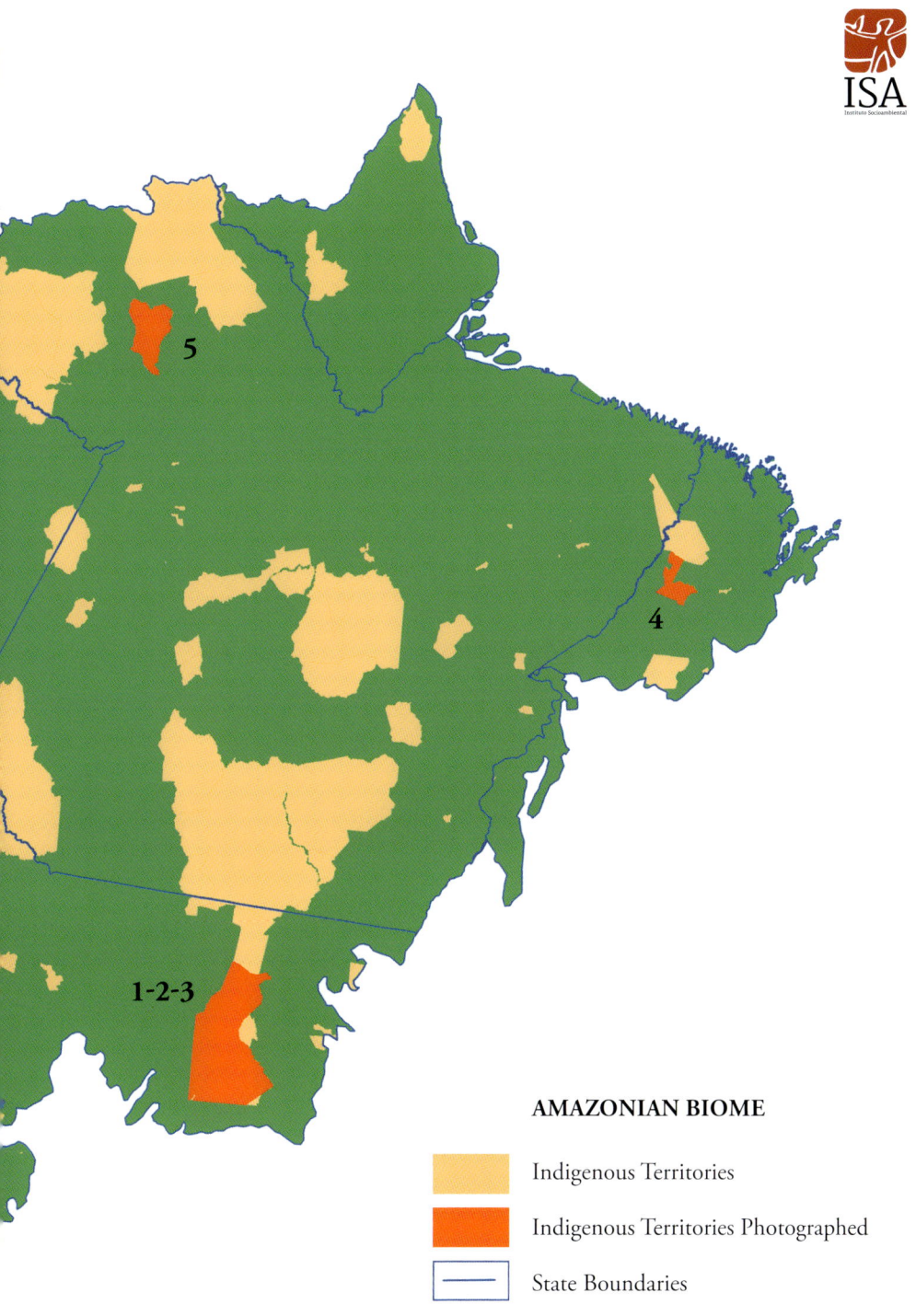

AMAZONIAN BIOME

Indigenous Territories

Indigenous Territories Photographed

State Boundaries

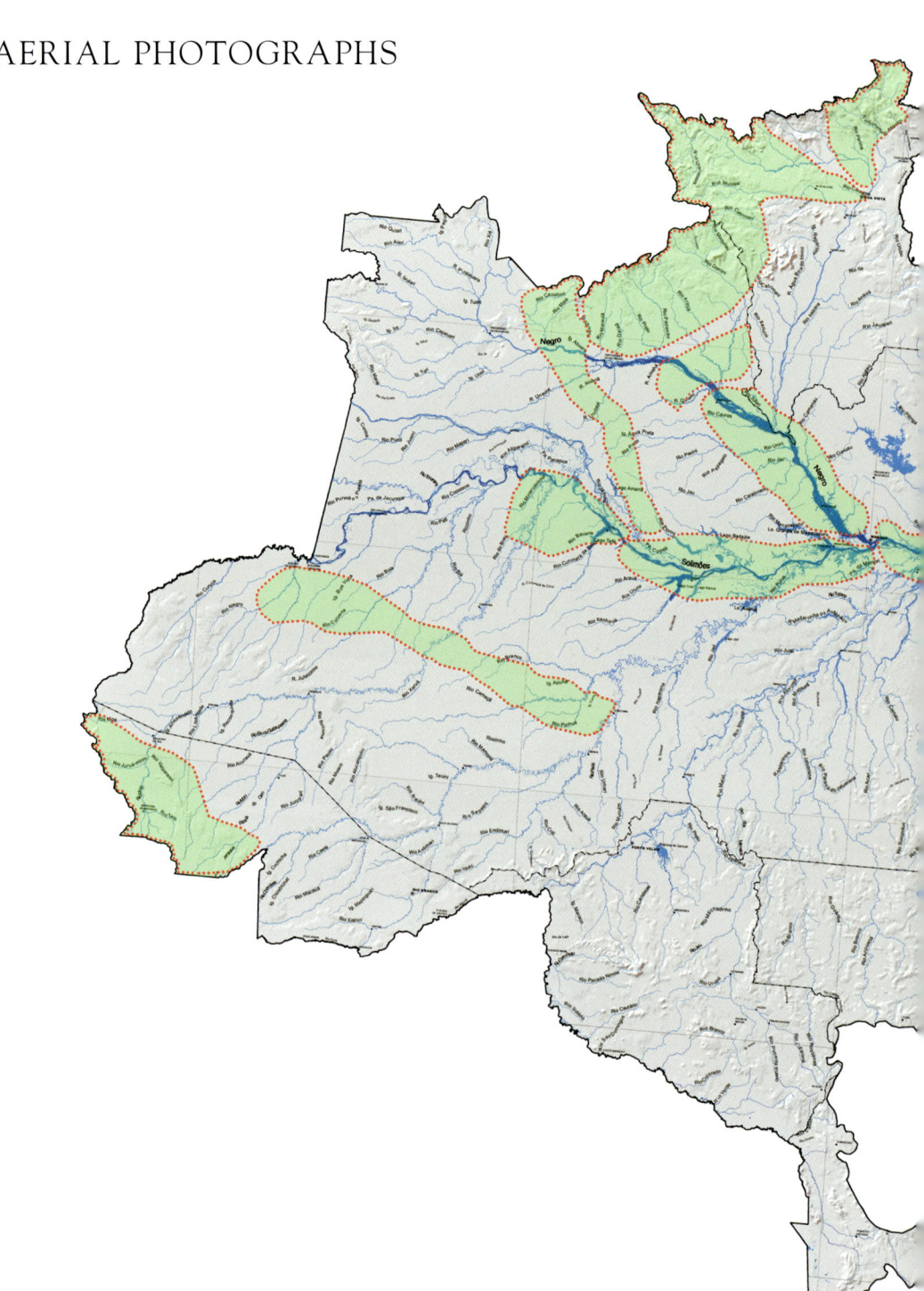

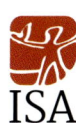

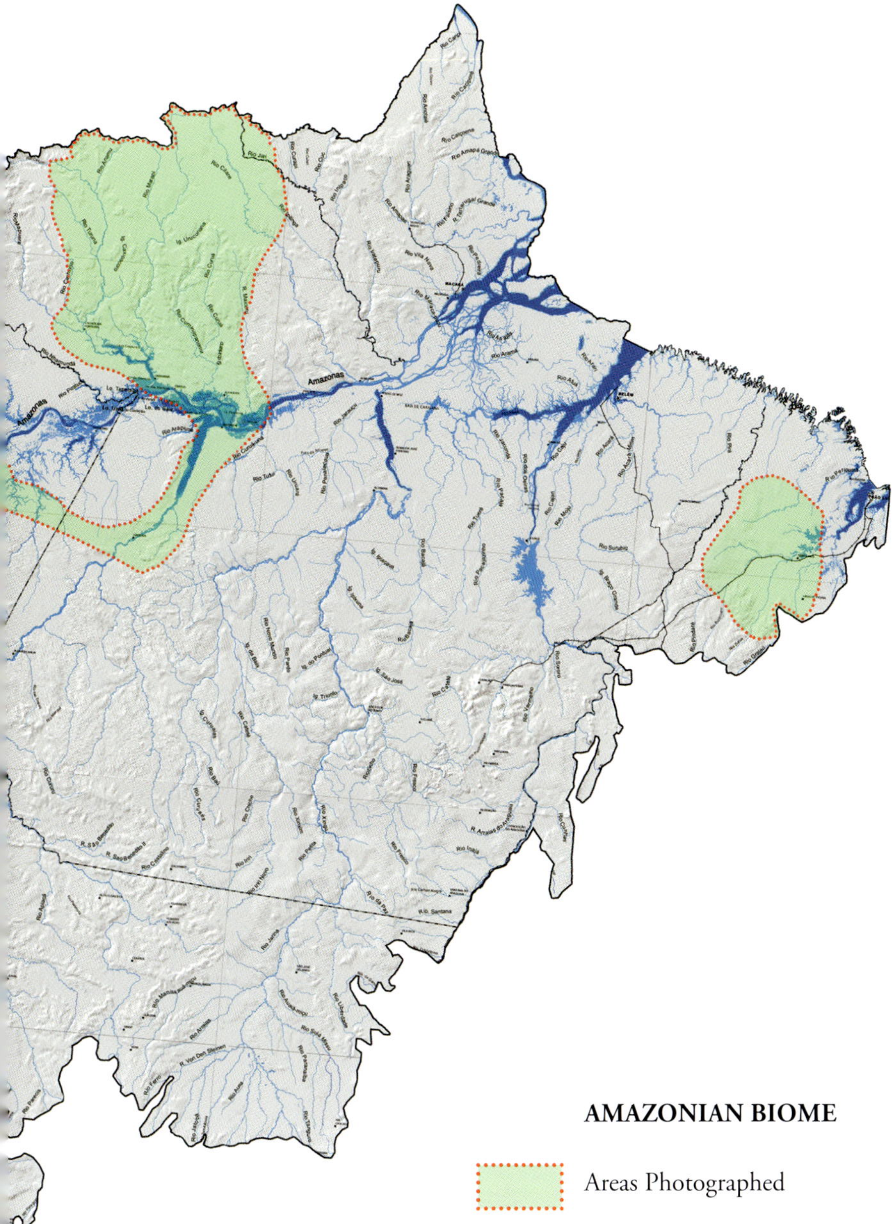

AMAZONIAN BIOME

Areas Photographed

Just being there evokes such an overwhelming sensation that it almost defies description: flying over this planet of infinite horizons, covered with the most beautiful trees in the world, teeming with animal and plant life. On several of my flights over the Amazon rainforest, I was accompanied by my wife, Lélia, and I saw tears stream down her face, tears of happiness and wonder at the sight of the immense paradise below. Trees and foliage in every shade of green, rivers that twist and turn like mad caterpillars, mountains shrouded in mysterious fog, thousands of clouds that are small in the morning but gradually merge to form cumulonimbus clouds so colossal they make you feel tiny, and that then burst into torrential rains which recall atomic explosions. The sensations are almost indescribable. My hope is that my images will at least convey something of Nature's immense generosity here.

Over the past three decades, I have had the privilege of spending extended periods alongside the peoples who have lived in this forest and its mountains, for thousands of years. I have had the good fortune of being able to enter the place that is their universe, this Eden that they have never felt the need to destroy in order to produce and reproduce the goods necessary for their material survival. These human beings live in harmony with the environment, using it with wisdom and with respect in recognition of what they are given. Their astonishing cultural riches are the result of all those lives lived at the heart of a unique natural environment.

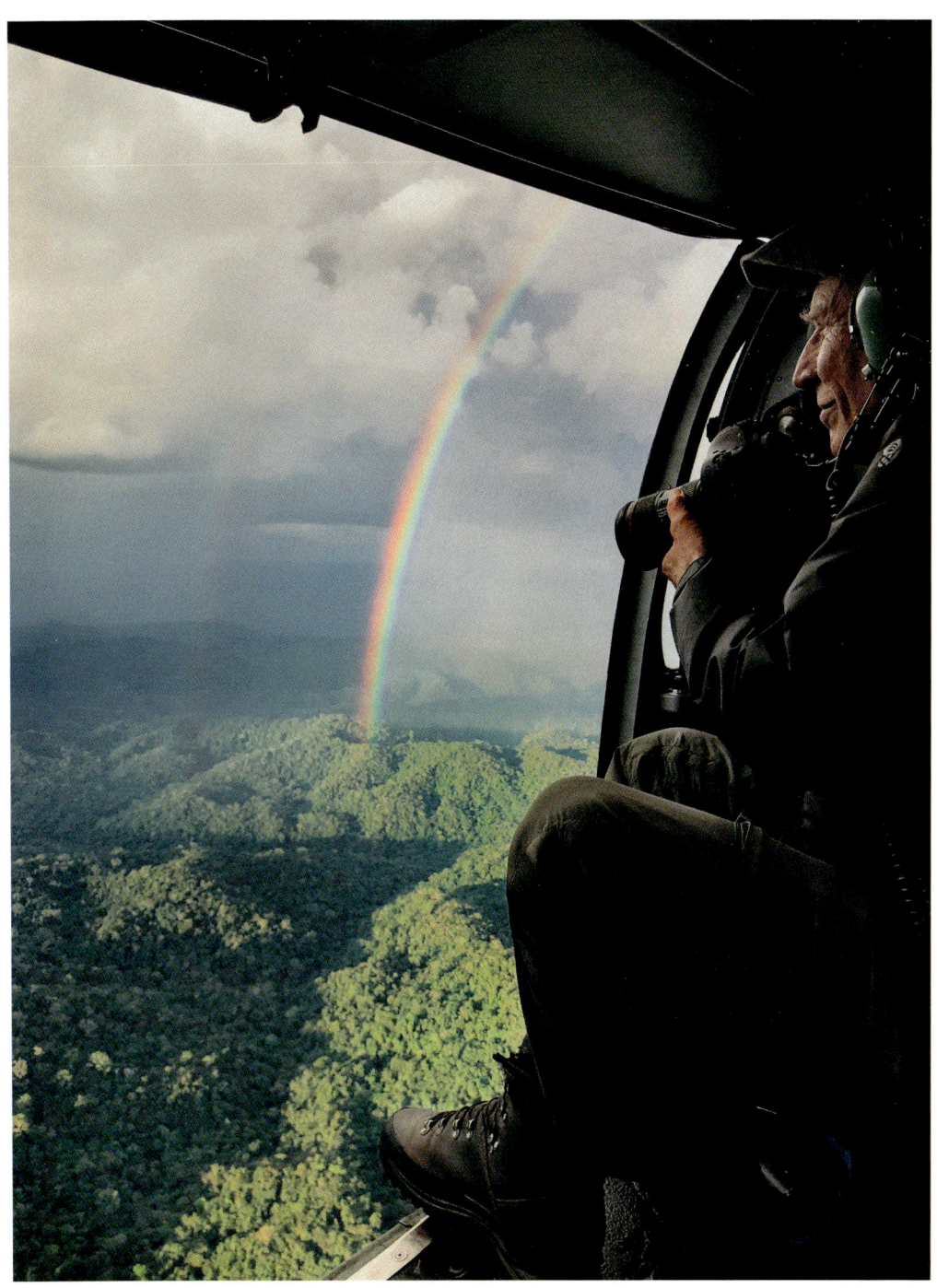

© Captain Felipe Reichert, 2018

EACH AND EVERY TASCHEN BOOK PLANTS A SEED!
Each year, we offset our annual carbon emissions with carbon credits
at the Instituto Terra, a reforestation program in Minas Gerais, Brazil,
founded by Lélia and Sebastião Salgado. To find out more about this
ecological partnership, please check: *www.taschen.com/institutoterra*.
Inspiration: unlimited. Carbon footprint: (almost) zero.

Want to see more? Visit *taschen.com* to view our current publications,
browse our latest magazine, and subscribe to our newsletter.

Photographs
© Sebastião Salgado

Text
© Sebastião Salgado
© Captions: Leão Serva and Alan Riding

Editing, conception, and design
Lélia Wanick Salgado

Staff
Françoise Piffard
Márcia Navarro Mariano
Olivier Jamin, *digital prints*
Jacques Barthélemy, *field assistant*

In collaboration with
Gérard Lamarche, Gilles Vaudois, *graphic designers*
Philippe Bachelier, *consultant*
Dominique Granier, *silver prints*

Editorial coordination
Simone Philippi

English translation
Steven Capsuto for Delivering iBooks & Design

Printed in Bosnia-Herzegovina
ISBN 978–3–7544–0341–9

The majority of the photographs were taken with CANON cameras EOS 1DS
Mark III, EOS 1DX, EOS 1DX Mark II, EOS 5DS, and EOS 5D Mark IV